PARAMAHANSA YOGANANDA

At Self-Realization Fellowship Lake Shrine, 1950

God Talks With Arjuna

THE BHAGAVAD GITA

Royal Science of God-Realization

The immortal dialogue between soul and Spirit
A new translation and commentary

Paramahansa Yogananda

Chapters 6-18

Self-Realization Fellowship
FOUNDED 1920
Paramahansa Yogananda

Second edition, 1999; first paperback printing, 2001

Acknowledgments for quoted material appear on page 1135.

Authorized by the International Publications Council of Self-Realization Fellowship

The Self-Realization Fellowship name and emblem (shown above) appear on all SRF books, recordings, and other publications, assuring the reader that a work originates with the society established by Paramahansa Yogananda and faithfully conveys his teachings.

Library of Congress Catalog Card Number: 95-71657
ISBN 0-87612-031-1 (paperback)
ISBN 0-87612-030-3 (hardcover)
Printed in the United States of America on acid-free paper
13349-54321

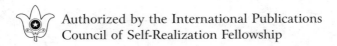

CONTENTS

Volume II

CHAPTER VI

PERMANENT SHELTER IN SPIRIT THROUGH YOGA MEDITATION

True Renunciation and True Yoga Depend on Meditation

Transforming the Little Self (Ego) Into the Divine Self (Soul)

How the Sage of Self-realization Views the World

Krishna's Advice for Successful Practice of Yoga

Attaining Self-mastery and Control of the Mind

Mergence of the Self in Spirit, Pervading All Beings

The Lord's Promise:
The Persevering Yogi Ultimately Is Victorious

ॐ

"The yogi is deemed greater than body-disciplining ascetics, greater even than the followers of the path of wisdom or of the path of action; be thou, O Arjuna, a yogi!"

PERMANENT SHELTER IN SPIRIT THROUGH YOGA MEDITATION

TRUE RENUNCIATION AND TRUE YOGA DEPEND ON MEDITATION

VERSE 1

śrībhagavān uvāca
anāśritaḥ karmaphalaṁ kāryaṁ karma karoti yaḥ
sa saṁnyāsī ca yogī ca na niragnir na cākriyaḥ

The Blessed Lord said:
He is the true renunciant and also the true yogi who performs dutiful and spiritual actions (karyam and karma) without desiring their fruits—not he who performs no fire ceremony (sacrifice) nor he who abandons action.

"HE IS NEITHER A *SANNYASI*-RENUNCIANT nor a yogi who is inactive (*akriya*), performing neither dutiful actions (*karyam*) nor meditative actions (*karma*). He is not a *sannyasi*-renunciant who is *niragni,* i.e., without the fire of renunciation, in whose sacrificial flames the true devotee burns all personal desires, lusts, likes and dislikes, sorrows, and pleasures. Nor is he a yogi who is *niragni,* i.e., without the inner sacrificial fire of meditation-kindled wisdom in which the true yogi burns his desires and unites the fire of his concentration with the flame of God.*

"That devotee is a yogi, one united to God, who merges the soul's spark in the Cosmic Light by the inner fire rite of ecstatic meditation, and who acts his daily part in the divine drama just to please God. That

* See IV:24, page 477, for the symbolic significance of the religious fire ceremony of India: the purification of the ego in the fire of self-discipline, and the ultimate oblation of uniting the purified soul with the eternal flame of Spirit.

same person is also a *sannyasi*-renunciant by relinquishing personal desires while he conscientiously performs dutiful actions."

THE GITA IN THIS VERSE and in its several other references to *sannyas* (*saṁnyasa*), uses this word both in its general sense of "renunciation"—derived from its Sanskrit verb root meaning, literally, "to cast aside"—and, as applicable, in its specialized meaning as designating the monastic life of monks and nuns who have taken final vows of complete renunciation.

Definition of the true renunciant (sannyasi)

The *sannyasi* or man of renunciation emphasizes the external conditions of desirelessness and nonattachment in order to maintain the consciousness of God in his activities; and the yogi emphasizes the inner perception of God in meditation and ecstasy, which he then strives to carry into his daily actions. If a novitiate pursues the spiritual path principally by thinking only of God while performing spiritual activities, he is a *sannyasi*. If a truth-seeker concentrates primarily on seeking God in meditation, he is a yogi. But that devotee who combines the two—thinking of God while working for Him, and also seeking Him in deep meditation—is the one who quickly knows God; he is both a *sannyasi* and a yogi.

Man, made in the divine image, has come on earth to play his role intelligently in the cosmic drama of destiny designed by God. This life is not man's own show; if he becomes personally and emotionally involved in the very complicated cosmic drama, he reaps inevitable suffering for having distorted the divine "plot."

To act with self-interest is to lose sight of the cosmic plan or will of God, thus upsetting the divine arrangements for man's speedy salvation. The egotist and the materialist, busily planning for fulfillment of selfish desires (*sankalpa*), remain entangled in rebirths. The selfishly ambitious man cannot get away from troubles and disillusionment. He is attached to his small family, and excludes the world from his love. He fails to learn the sweet lesson of God, who has inspired us with affection for relatives that we may be able, like the true devotee, to love all men as our brothers. The egotist, thinking himself the doer of all actions, isolates himself from the Divine; he is in fact opposing universal law, pitting his puny strength against Truth. The devotee throws all responsibility for actions on the Lord. For him it is ever "God alone."

This Gita stanza condemns idleness, which is often erroneously equated with desirelessness. Inactivity is a state that proves man to be identified with the lowest (*tamas* or inertia) quality of the ego. The sluggard is worse than the man who is egotistically active. The apathetic individual turns away from God and material activities equally, thus degenerating physically, mentally, and spiritually. He who works with selfish desires is nevertheless developing his mind and body, or one of them, and is far superior to the supine shirker of all duties.

This verse therefore clearly defines the path of yogis and renunciants—not as an escape to the wilderness, but as a life of dutiful and spiritual activity without personal attachment.

THE WORD *KARYAM* IN THIS STANZA signifies all dutiful actions of external value. The instinct for self-preservation, for instance, involves physical activities. That instinct has been implanted in each person by God and Nature. The man who fulfills his duties toward the body with a personal interest ("desire for fruits") remains bound to the wheel of rebirth, i.e., to the operations of karmic law. He escapes it when he performs all actions with the sole purpose of pleasing God, who alone is the true Doer and Bearer of Burdens.

The nature of karyam—actions that are man's duty

Dutiful actions, specifically, are those that are due from each individual—based on his current level of development and karmic involvement—in order for him to strip his consciousness of all evils of delusion to reveal the radiant glories of his soul, and thus to reclaim his lost perfection as a reflection of the image of Spirit.

He who performs those bounden duties assigned to him by God, without harboring selfish desires for the fruits of those actions, is a *sannyasi*-renunciant; conversely, he who renounces dutiful actions simply because he has relinquished the desire to be the beneficiary of the fruits of such actions is not a *sannyasi*.

Good actions (such as an active interest in social service or other humanitarian work) that are performed with any motive in the conscious or subconscious minds other than the desire to please God are considered to be actions done with longing for their fruit. No matter how noble the activity, if it diverts one from the Supreme Goal by its consequent karmic bondage it does not belong to the category of the highest dutiful actions.

The emphasis therefore is on renunciation not necessarily of a life in the world, but of a selfish worldly life. Such renunciation does not involve loss nor the flying away from dutiful activities, but lies in spiritualizing one's life.

Every man should find and fulfill those actions that will harmoniously develop his material life, his body and mind, and, above all, the qualities of his heart and soul. All honest work is good work; it is capable of leading to self-development provided the doer seeks to discover the inherent lessons and makes the most of the potentialities for such growth.

The question arises: How can a person discover his God-ordained duties? Spiritual tradition enjoins that the beginner in the path of yoga should ask his guru to advise him. A guru who knows God is able to determine a man's evolutionary status and rightful duties. If, for reasons of his own, or to respect the divine secrecy pervading the phenomenal world, the guru declines to give specific advice, the student, after deep meditation, should pray: "Lord, I will reason, I will will, I will act; but guide Thou my reason, will, and activity to the right thing I should do." By this method, the devotee, with the guru's inner blessing, is pushed to cultivate his own soul discrimination and thereby hasten his personal attunement with God.

As the devotee progresses in meditation, he will find God directing his activities through his awakening intuition. Naturally, one should also use common sense in deciding the righteous duties connected with the discipline of his own life and the lives of those dependent on him. Blameworthy is the performance of activities not chosen by discrimination. Such actions are like blindfolded horses being led to unknown destinations by the ignorant self, as it asserts its prejudiced, egotistic whims and prepossessed ideas and habits.

Every man should perform the duties involved in finding God and also the worldly duties necessary to maintain himself and to help others. Regardless of heredity, environment, and evolutionary status, the highest and most important duty of every man is to establish his consciousness in unity with God.

Meditation as a form of dutiful action (karma)

THE WORD *KARMA* IN THIS STANZA is used in one of its specialized meanings to denote meditative actions: the use of yoga techniques that scientifically withdraw the attention from the objective world and focus it on the inner being, which alone possesses the ability to experience and commune with God. The yogi is he who practices these techniques to attain union with God.

A devotee in whom the ego is still strong becomes tied to the fruits of his actions and does not attain salvation. If a yoga practitioner's main object in meditating deeply—which should be solely to know God—is compromised by a desire to attain powers or become known as a great yogi, he may attract a host of admirers—but not the Lord.

He also is a sham yogi who sits lazily under a tree, passing his time in careless intellectual perusal of philosophy and in admiring the sense-soothing beauties of nature. Indolent religious mendicants, like those who roam by the thousands in holy cities such as Banaras, are not yogis. Renunciation of dutiful and serviceful actions produces worthlessness, not holiness; it does nothing to root out impure sex thoughts and sensual impulses, and anger and other violent inclinations secreted in the subconscious mind.

The genuine yogi, by contrast, is he who meditates deeply and practices a yoga technique for divine union. His work and efforts in meditation are dutiful and proper actions, God-ordained.

A yogi who performs meditative actions for the attainment of God is not considered to be concentrating on the fruits of that activity. A true devotee does attain the Lord as the Fruit of his actions; nevertheless, because man's efforts for divine union ultimately result in liberation, such actions do not involve him in bondage (even though their Fruit has indeed been desired).

He who devotes himself solely to meditation to find God, and toward that end abandons all other activities, is a true man of renunciation (a *sannyasi*); he has renounced actions not because of idleness but because of divine aspiration. And the same man is a yogi, also, because he works hard to attain ecstasy and soul contact.

But as it is nearly impossible to engage in meditation day and night unless one is already far advanced in ecstatic God-communion, the earnest yogi also engages himself methodically in some kind of work that conduces to the welfare of others.

The yogi may be either a novice striving for God-communion, or an adept who has already attained this blessedness. It is optional whether the yogi follows the path of outer renunciation or carries on a family life with inner nonattachment. But only a yogi who has achieved unbroken God-realization and ultimate freedom—an ideal exemplar of which was the *Yogavatar* Lahiri Mahasaya—can in certainty remain completely detached in a married worldly life. Only a mind firmly established in God is impervious to dilution by a material environment. The spiritual advancement of a yogi without complete God-attainment can hardly remain untainted in the worldly vibrations of a marital relationship. Such an expectation would be both contradictory and unnatural.

But the monk, also, must face his nemesis. Though he remove himself from the environs of many temptations of the senses, his vows of celibacy and renouncement of worldly entanglements do not automatically confer victory over his inner sensory proclivities and inclinations. He may hide himself away from objects of temptation and yet find it very difficult to escape the haunting mental habits of yielding to the seduction of his desires, ever lurking to entrap him.

The yogi who experiences in meditation the enticement of God's charm becomes convinced in his heart that God is far more tempting than material temptations. By such comparison, he spontaneously becomes a man of renunciation. Thus, the path of yoga is superior to the path of renunciation, for the sincere desire and meditative effort to attain God-communion, roused by even a little inner contact with God, are of paramount importance to any attempts at practicing renunciation. The yogi who by meditation becomes also a man of renunciation, supremely engaged in seeking God-contact and at the same time sloughing off sensory attachments, is a true yogi-renunciant.

Monastic ideal of the yogi-swami: complete renunciation

RENUNCIANTS WHO TAKE FORMAL VOWS of *sannyas* by being made a swami by another swami who can trace his spiritual ancestry to the supreme guru of all swamis, Swami Shankara, and who are also yogis striving for God-communion as the foremost object of their spiritual efforts, are yogi-swamis. They are commendable above ordinary swamis who merely don the ocher cloth but lack inner renunciation and a sincere meditative effort.

Yogi-swamis also embrace a higher ideal than aspiring yogi-renunciants: true yogi-swamis are so enwrapped in love for God alone that they are not afraid to take the unconditional vow of complete renunciation to live a life of celibacy and strict self-discipline of the senses and ego—a vow considered by worldly minds to be a grim challenge, if not wholly inconceivable. In commending wholehearted renunciation, Jesus addressed his disciples in these words: "And every one that hath forsaken houses, or brethren, or sisters, or father, or mother, or wife, or children, or lands, for my name's sake, shall receive an hundredfold, and shall inherit everlasting life."*

For myself, such complete renunciation as a monk of the Swami Order was the only possible answer to the ardent desire in my heart to

* Matthew 19:29.

give my life wholly to God, uncompromised by any worldly tie; to me, anything less was to offer the Beloved Lord a second place. When I expressed this resolute intent to my guru, Swami Sri Yukteswar, he adjured me: "Remember that he who rejects the usual worldly duties can justify himself only by assuming some kind of responsibility for a much larger family." His ageless wisdom might indeed have been echoes of Sri Krishna's words in the Gita. As a monk, my life has been offered in unreserved service to God and to the spiritual awakening of hearts with His message. For those on the path I have followed who also feel called to complete renunciation in a life of seeking and serving God through the yoga ideals of meditative and dutiful activities, I have perpetuated in the monastic order of Self-Realization Fellowship/Yogoda Satsanga Society of India the line of *sannyas* in the Shankara Order, which I entered when I received the holy vows of a swami from my Guru. The organizational work that God and my Guru and Paramgurus have started through me is carried on not by worldly hired employees, but by those who have dedicated their lives to the highest objectives of renunciation and love for God.*

FOR THE ASPIRING DEVOTEE in the world and in the ashram, the call of the Bhagavad Gita is to make the heart a hermitage of God wherein, as a renunciant, one strives for inner desirelessness and nonattachment; and, as a yogi, one envelops himself in the meditative bliss of the Divine Presence and then offers his actions in selfless service to share that Presence with other seeking souls.

Gita's advice: make the heart a hermitage of God

All actions of the yogi-*sannyasi,* whether *karyam* or *karma,* should be performed with the loving motive of pleasing God. He who does his duties haphazardly or carelessly, or who meditates without zest, cannot please the Lord nor win liberation. Any action—physical, mental, or spiritual—performed with the desire for divine union as its fruit is not a "selfish" action. Instead, it is a perfect action in the sense that it fulfills the divine motive in creation. The purpose of God is to reveal Himself to His children after they have been victorious in the tests of a dreadful delusion (*maya*) in which He has designedly cast them.

* Single men and women who are free of family obligations, and who have a sincere desire to dedicate themselves singlemindedly to finding God and serving Him as a monk or nun of the Monastic Order of Self-Realization Fellowship, are welcome to contact SRF Headquarters for information about life in a Self-Realization Fellowship ashram. (*Publisher's Note*)

He loves God best who acts rightly. According to the laws of true love (stated succinctly, if crudely, in the adage, "If you love me, love my dog"), the yogi-*sannyasi* in his love for God loves also the action which God has imposed on him. He performs his dutiful and meditative activities joyously, desirelessly, solely to please Him whom he loves. He, indeed, is the true—the ideal—yogi and *sannyasi*.

VERSE 2

yaṁ saṁnyāsam iti prāhur yogaṁ taṁ viddhi pāṇḍava
na hy asaṁnyastasaṁkalpo yogī bhavati kaścana

Understand, O Pandava (Arjuna), that what is spoken of in the scriptures as renunciation is the same as yoga; for he who has not renounced selfish motive (sankalpa) cannot be a yogi.

AS DISCUSSED AT LENGTH in the previous verse, the *sannyasi* or man of renunciation concentrates primarily on removing all material and mental obstructions (worldly ties and selfish desires) in order to realize God, whereas the yogi is primarily concerned with the use of a scientific yoga technique for Self-realization. In a positive way, the yogi, tasting the superior bliss of the Lord, automatically renounces all lesser pleasures to embrace God alone. In a more negative way, the *sannyasi* renounces all material desires and wrong actions by discrimination to prepare himself for union with the Infinite. Both paths lead to the same Goal. But for both the *sannyasi* and the yogi, such achievement requires not only outer mastery of one's actions, but also inner mental victory.

Sankalpa, "selfish motive," referred to in this verse, signifies inner planning for (or expectation of) a desired result formed by the ego-guided mind. Renunciants and yogis are cautioned that though they may remain self-controlled or meditatively quiet outwardly, they may nevertheless be engaged inwardly in egotistical activities inspired by sensations and bodily urges that cause constant fluctuations in the consciousness. The mind ruminates on these impulses, which are either agreeable or disagreeable, and accordingly formulates desired results concerning them. Thus yoga, or perfect evenness of consciousness, is precluded.

Patanjali, in his *Yoga Sutras*, defines yoga as the dissolving of the scintillations or *vrittis* (alternating waves of thoughts, desires, emotions) in the *chitta* or primordial feeling (the totality of individualized consciousness), arising from the likes and dislikes produced from the contact of the mind with the senses.* Yoga has also been defined in the scriptures as the forsaking of all desireful thoughts, and as the attainment of a state of "thoughtlessness." These definitions fit the achievements of both the man of renunciation and the yogi. Real renunciation consists in the ability to dismiss thoughts and desires at will. Supreme yoga ecstasy bestows the "thoughtless" state. It is not a mental coma (in which the mind is unconscious of external sensations and internal perceptions), but is a state of divine equilibrium. Its attainment proves that the yogi has entered the Vibrationless Being—the ever blissful, ever conscious Divine Void beyond phenomenal creation.

No one can be a yogi, maintaining a state of mental equilibrium, free from inner involvement in planned desireful activities, unless he has renounced identification with his ego and its unsatisfiable lust for the fruits of actions. Only he who has reached *samadhi* can be spoken of as no longer working for the ego.

Of course, if a devotee does not plan his activities according to a definite divine purpose, he will be stumbling at every step. The true yogi fills himself with God and intelligently performs all actions inspired by Him. If, for example, he builds a hermitage for his disciples, he is not to be accused of planning with a selfish motive. The aim of all his actions is to please God. He is not inert nor insensitive, but is one who works in the world, doing all activities for God, without personal desires about anything. He sees and appreciates God in all manifestations of goodness and beauty. A true yogi may admire a beautiful horse, for instance; but those who feel a wish to possess the animal become entangled in *sankalpa,* ego-instigated desires. He is a yogi who can remain in any material environment without being involved in likes and dislikes.

When a yogi can remain completely free from personal desires during inner or outer activity, then he is a successful man of renunciation. And when a man of renunciation is able to renounce all outer and inner activities by an act of will and merge his consciousness in the perception of God, he is the same as a yogi who can remain immersed in God by ecstasy, dissolving by yoga all the scintillations of feelings.

A perfected *sannyasi* and an accomplished yogi are thus the same, for by different paths they have attained yoga, God-union.

---

* *Yoga Sutras* I:2. (See page 300.)

VERSES 3–4

āruruksor muner yogaṁ karma kāraṇam ucyate
yogārūḍhasya tasyaiva śamaḥ kāraṇam ucyate (3)

yadā hi nendriyārtheṣu na karmasv anuṣajjate
sarvasaṁkalpasaṁnyāsī yogārūḍhas tadocyate (4)

(3) For the muni desiring ascension, meditative action (karma) for divine union (yoga) is spoken of as "his way"; when he has mastered this yoga, then inaction is said to be "his way."

(4) He who has overcome attachment both to sense objects and to actions, and who is free from all ego-instigated plannings—that man is said to have attained firm union of soul with Spirit.

FOR THE ASPIRING *MUNI* (the spiritual climber) who is advancing toward God-union, his means for attaining the goal is the divine meditative actions of yoga techniques by which he withdraws his mind from the dreams of matter and dissolves it in God. When the yogi has attained this oneness, then the quiescence of unshakable union with God, beyond the dream activities of delusive creation, is thereafter the cause and the instrumentality of all functions of his transformed consciousness. Thus, the devotee climbs by action (*karma,* or scientific yoga). Perfected in yoga, he attains inaction—the state of perfect equilibrium in Spirit, *yogarudha*.

Yogarudha: state of perfect equilibrium in Spirit

When the yogi has freed himself from the dream of matter, by attaining the actionless state in *samadhi* (*yogarudha*), he finds freedom also (1) from all desires for sensory objects, (2) from the selfish plannings (*sankalpas*) that accompany desire, and (3) from the delusion that he, and not God, is the performer of action.

The devotee, desirous of dissolving his mind in God, concentrates his meditative activities on the practice of *pranayama* or life control. The word *karma* in this stanza is used technically to signify the special techniques, such as *Kriya Yoga* and *Kevali Pranayama,** by which the life force can be withdrawn from the senses and concentrated in the seven cerebrospinal centers.

---

* See IV:29, page 504.

The coccygeal center has four rays; the sacral center, six rays; the lumbar center, ten rays; the dorsal center, twelve rays; and the cervical center, sixteen rays.

The medullary center, the "sharp two-edged sword," has two rays of current, positive and negative, that supply the two hands, the two feet, the two lungs, all dual branches of the nervous system, and the dual organs: two eyes, two ears, two nostrils, two tongues (the tongue being forked or bifurcated, i.e., divided into two sections),* and the two hemispheres of the brain.

The brain is a reservoir of cosmic current received through the medulla oblongata (the lowest or posterior part of the brain, tapering off into the spinal cord). The medulla is scripturally referred to as "the mouth of God," "the door," and "the holy opening." Cosmic energy enters the body through the medulla and then passes to the cerebrum, in which it is stored or concentrated. The brain is thus the major reservoir that sends current to the six other minor plexuses. These centers or subdynamos are busily engaged in remitting currents to the different nerve branches and to the various organs and cells of the body.

The medullary center with its two currents, positive and negative, supplies the whole body and creates the dual organs by condensing life force into electrons, protons, and atoms. Thoughtrons are vibrationally condensed into lifetrons; lifetrons into electrons and protons, which in turn condense into atoms. The atoms are transformed into cells, which combine into the different forms of muscular, osseous, and nerve tissues of the various body parts. The two currents in the medulla, therefore, not only supply current to the five senses but condense themselves by grosser vibrations into the actual bodily tissues.

Through pranayama, the astral body and chakras become visible

In the initial state, the yogi is busy withdrawing the life force into the spinal centers. When he succeeds in this work, his astral body with seven astral plexuses becomes visible to him through his spherical astral eye of intuition. The astral body is made of tissues of light condensed from astral rays, even as the physical body is made of fleshly tissues. When the yogi is able to withdraw his life force from the senses, not only does he see his astral body but he can disconnect his mind from the outer world.

* In the human embryo, as the back of the tongue develops (in the throat), it extends forward in the form of a "V" (i.e., "forked"), so as to embrace between its two branches the front of the tongue (in the mouth).

The benefit of seeing the astral body is that the experience helps the yogi to ascend—to lift his soul, as the body-identified ego—from the fleshly prison. Afterward, the devotee learns how to take his ego out of the astral and ideational bodies and commingle it with the pure soul. The yogi is then able to unite his soul with the Omnipresent, Ever Blessed Spirit.

The devotee first learns how to unite his life force, withdrawn from the senses, into the seven cerebrospinal centers; and after that, to unite the lights of these astral plexuses into his astral body. Then he dissolves the astral body into cosmic energy and the ideational body. Finally he learns to dissolve cosmic energy and the ideational body into Cosmic Consciousness.

These are the various complicated processes with which the aspirant busies himself, performing God-uniting yoga activities that enable him to dissolve his body consciousness into the Infinite. His soul becomes expanded in the Omnipresent Lord.

The brain current is spoken of as having a thousand rays; it is these rays that help to sustain the thousands of functions of the body cells.

Cerebrospinal centers described by yogis of India and by Saint John

The original two currents of the medulla are amplified into the thousand currents of the cerebrum, which become specialized as the sixteen, twelve, ten, six, and four currents of the five spinal centers. The different plexuses perform specific functions of the body according to the number and nature of their currents. (See page 131.) The seven physical centers have seven astral counterparts and seven ideational counterparts. These seven plexuses are spoken of by the yogis of India as seven lotuses; and the currents or rays of the centers are described as the petals of the lotuses: four-petaled, six-petaled, ten-petaled, twelve-petaled, sixteen-petaled, two-petaled, and thousand-petaled.

The greatest disciple of Jesus Christ, John, refers to these seven astral centers with different rays as seven golden candlesticks and seven stars.*

The reader of this Gita commentary may wonder why a yogi has to understand the complicated mechanism of the physical, astral, and ideational bodies. A glance at a text like *Gray's Anatomy,* however, will show us the incredibly ramified complications in the organization of

* "The mystery of the seven stars which thou sawest in my right hand, and the seven golden candlesticks. The seven stars are the angels of the seven churches: and the seven candlesticks which thou sawest are the seven churches" (Revelation 1:20).

even the physical body. The astral and ideational bodies, being more subtle, are more highly organized and complicated than is the physical body. Some comprehension of man's threefold anatomy reveals the science underlying yoga techniques and shows why and how they work.

The conception of man's physical, astral, and ideational bodies can be more easily understood by the following explanation. God dreamed the entire creation in terms of ideas. Then He said: "Let there be light: and there was light." He vibrated those ideas into dream lights and out of them created a dream astral cosmos. Then He condensed the dream astral cosmos into a dream physical universe. After the macrocosmic universes were created, God made the microcosmic objects of creation. He created man as a composite of three dreams: a dream ideational body encased in a dream astral body within a dream physical body.

The sages therefore say: The successful yogi has to withdraw his mind from the dream physical body, dream astral body, and dream ideational body, and dissolve those forms into the dream physical cosmos, dream astral cosmos, and dream ideational cosmos. When the yogi can dissolve the dream physical cosmos into the dream astral cosmos and the dream astral cosmos into the dream ideational cosmos, and the multitudinous ideas of the ideational cosmos into the unified perception of Cosmic Consciousness, then he becomes free, like the Spirit.

The Spirit has dreamed Itself into the aspects of God the Father, the Son, and the Holy Ghost (*Sat-Tat-Aum*) and into the dream ideational, astral, and physical universes, and into the dream ideational, astral, and physical bodies. Thus the soul as the image of God has descended from the Omnipresence of Cosmic Consciousness to the limitations of its earthly surroundings and of the three dream bodies. So the aspirant yogi must withdraw his consciousness from all dream illusions, and finally unite his soul with the ever-existent, ever-conscious, ever-new Bliss of Spirit.

In other words, the devotee must rise above all the microcosmic and macrocosmic dreams of God imposed upon him through the hypnosis of *maya* (cosmic delusion), and thus rouse his soul from the experience of delusive dreams into the eternal wakefulness of Spirit. The yogi has then attained "inaction" or freedom from forced phenomenal participation.

A devotee is called an aspirant and a spiritual climber when he tries to dissolve all dreams into the perception of the One Spirit. When he is able completely to dissolve all the "suggestions" or cosmic delusive dreams of *maya*, he becomes anchored in the final Reality. He is then spoken of as having attained *yogarudha* (firm union of soul and Spirit).

TRANSFORMING THE LITTLE SELF (EGO) INTO THE DIVINE SELF (SOUL)

VERSES 5–6

uddhared ātmanātmānaṁ nātmānam avasādayet
ātmaiva hy ātmano bandhur ātmaiva ripur ātmanaḥ (5)

bandhur ātmātmanas tasya yenātmaivātmanā jitaḥ
anātmanas tu śatrutve vartetātmaiva śatruvat (6)

(5) Let man uplift the self (ego) by the self; let the self not be self-degraded (cast down). Indeed, the self is its own friend; and the self is its own enemy.

(6) For him whose self (ego) has been conquered by the Self (soul), the Self is the friend of the self; but verily, the Self behaves inimically, as an enemy, toward the self that is not subdued.

THE PHYSICAL EGO, THE ACTIVE consciousness in man, should uplift its body-identified self into unity with the soul, its true nature; it should not allow itself to remain mired in the lowly delusive strata of the senses and material entanglement. The ego acts as its own best friend when by meditation and the exercise of its innate soul qualities it spiritualizes itself and ultimately restores its own true soul nature. Conversely, the physical ego serves as its own worst enemy when by delusive material behavior it eclipses its true nature as the ever blessed soul.

When the physical ego (the active consciousness) has become spiritualized and united to the soul, it is able to keep the intelligence, mind, and senses under control, guided by the discriminative wisdom of the soul—i.e., the "self (ego) has been conquered by the Self (soul)" —then the soul is the friend, the guide and benefactor, of the active physical consciousness. But if the lower ego-self has not been thus controlled and persists in keeping the consciousness matter-bent, then the soul is the enemy of the ego. This follows the Gita allegory described in chapter one: Krishna (the soul) is the friend and guide of the spiritual endeavors of the devotee Arjuna, along with the Pandava army of divine qualities; Krishna (the soul) is therefore an enemy (an opposer) of Duryodhana's Kaurava army of materialistic inclinations, which is under the guidance of Bhishma (ego).*

The soul, "inimical" to the ego, withholds its blessings of peace and lasting happiness while the ego, behaving ignorantly as its own enemy, sets in motion the misery-making karmic forces of Nature. Without the beneficence of the soul's protection in the world of *maya*, the ego finds to its regret that its own actions against its true soul nature turn back on itself, like boomerangs, destroying each new illusion of happiness and attainment.

In the composition of these two concise verses, the word *atman* ("self") appears twelve times in an ambiguous construction allowing for the interchange of meaning either as "the soul" or "the ego" (the pseudosoul)—a classical example of the dichotomy so characteristic in Indian scripture. As shown in the above commentary, the clever interweavings of the words *soul* and *ego* in this instance consist of a singular thread of truth that runs through the whole fabric of the Gita: Let man be uplifted, not degraded; let him transform his self (ego) into the Self (soul). The Self is the friend of the transformed self, but the enemy of the unregenerate self.

VERSE 7

jitātmanaḥ praśāntasya paramātmā samāhitaḥ
śītoṣṇasukhaduḥkheṣu tathā mānāpamānayoḥ

The tranquil sage, victorious over the self (ego), is ever fully established in the Supreme Self (Spirit), whether he encounter cold or heat, pleasure or pain, praise or blame.

SPIRIT-UNITED AND RETAINING his cosmic consciousness even in the domain of activity, the sage remains unperturbed by the oppositional states of the cosmic dream world.

"If thou canst transcend the body and perceive thyself as Spirit, thou shalt be eternally blissful, free from all pain."†

The persevering yogi succeeds in metamorphosing his physical ego into the true soul. By further spiritual advancement he realizes his soul

* See I:11, page 107, concerning the role of the ego in man's consciousness and how that ego becomes spiritualized.

† *Atmabodha Upanishad* II:21.

as the reflection of omnipresent Spirit. When this state of realization is reached, the soul permanently perceives the Supreme Self or God. The perfected sage works through his transformed ego in the world, never losing sight of the Divine Face behind the Janus-masks of Nature.

HOW THE SAGE OF SELF-REALIZATION VIEWS THE WORLD

VERSE 8

jñānavijñānatṛptātmā kūṭastho vijitendriyaḥ
yukta ity ucyate yogī samaloṣṭāśmakāñcanaḥ

That yogi who is gladly absorbed in truth and Self-realization is said to be indissolubly united to Spirit. Unchangeable, conqueror of his senses, he looks with an equal eye on earth, stone, and gold.

A YOGI WHO HAS REALIZED HIS SOUL by ecstasy and found in it all wisdom is filled with true satisfaction; he rests in bliss. Concentrated on the single Divine Beam, he looks upon a lump of earth, a stone, or gold as dream relativities of that same one Light of God.

The ordinary man considers solids and liquids and the energy manifestations of the material world to be vastly different, but the yogi sees them as various vibrations of the one cosmic light. To him a lump of earth, a stone, and gold are merely substances that vibrate at different rates as atomic forms in a cosmic dream. Always united with the Lord, he realizes the phenomenal world and its various appearances as emanations from the one Divine Consciousness.

VERSE 9

suhṛnmitrāryudāsīnamadhyasthadveṣyabandhuṣu
sādhuṣv api ca pāpeṣu samabuddhir viśiṣyate

He is a supreme yogi who regards with equal-mindedness all men—patrons, friends, enemies, strangers, mediators, hateful beings, relatives, the virtuous and the ungodly.

IN THE PREVIOUS STANZA the perfected yogi is said to perceive all forms of material creation—the props in the dream drama—as dream manifestations of one Cosmic Consciousness. In this stanza, the Bhagavad Gita defines a great yogi as he who similarly regards all human beings—friends and enemies, saints and sinners alike—as dream images made of the one consciousness of God.

The ordinary man, watching the drama of good and bad human beings playing on the space-screen of the world, is affected pleasurably and painfully. But the man who has perceived God looks upon all types of men as dream motion-picture images, made of the relativities of the light of Cosmic Consciousness and the shadows of delusion.

The exalted yogi, however, does not treat gold and earth, saint and sinner, with impartial indifference! He wisely recognizes their dramatic differences on the mundane plane as perceived by other material beings. Even though all beings and objects in the cosmos are made of the divine light and the shadows of delusion, the yogi recognizes relative values. He endorses the activities of the virtuous who serve as harbingers of good to their fellowmen, and he denounces the activities of the evil who harm themselves and others.

KRISHNA'S ADVICE FOR SUCCESSFUL PRACTICE OF YOGA

VERSE 10

yogī yuñjīta satatam ātmānaṁ rahasi sthitaḥ
ekākī yatacittātmā nirāśīr aparigrahaḥ

Free from ever-hoping desires and from cravings for possessions, with the heart (waves of feeling) controlled by the soul* (by yoga concentration), retiring alone to a quiet place, the yogi should constantly try to unite with the soul.

HE WHO KNOWS THAT HIS SOUL is divorced from God—body-bound by the mental waves of feeling—longs to return to Spirit's omnipresence. Stanzas 10–14 give many wonderful pointers to help the devotee attain his goal.

---

* *Yata-citta-ātmā*: See IV:21, page 472 n.

The aspirant who meditates without eliminating desires and hopes (instigators for actions of sensory enjoyment and possession) finds his mind roaming into the realm of materiality, planning for and visualizing various gains. So when the yogi starts to meditate, he must leave behind all sensory thoughts and all longings for possessions by quieting the waves of feeling (*chitta*), and the mental restlessness that arises therefrom, through the application of techniques that reinstate the controlling power of the untrammeled superconsciousness of the soul.

The devotee should choose for his meditation a quiet place. Noise is distracting. Only a yogi who can go into ecstasy at will can meditate in both quiet and noisy places. The devotee should begin his meditation with the practice of the techniques of *Kriya Yoga,* by which he can disconnect his mind from the outer sensory world. Many non-meditating individuals think that it is impossible to do this, not realizing that they accomplish the feat every night in sleep. When the body is relaxed for slumber, the life force begins to withdraw itself from the muscles and motor nerves and then from the sensory nerves. At this juncture the mind is disconnected from all sensations and becomes concentrated in the joy of subconscious rest. (The state of sleep does not involve total unconsciousness, because, on waking, a man realizes the nature of his sleep—whether it was light or deep, unpleasant or pleasant.)

"A quiet place": disconnecting the mind from the sensory world

Kriya Yoga teaches one to go consciously into the state of sense disconnection without entering the eclipsing shadows of sleep. Krishna and Babaji, knowing the science behind the psychological and physiological processes involved in sleep, devised the special form of that science, known as *Kriya Yoga,* by which the spiritual aspirant can pass at will beyond the threshold of the less joyous subliminal state of subconscious slumber into the blissful superconsciousness.

The ordinary devotee tries ineffectually (because unscientifically) to put his mind on God—the mind that is tied to material sensations through the action of the life force flowing in the five sense "telephones." But the *Kriya Yogi* works scientifically to withdraw his mind from the senses by the technique of switching off the life force from the telephonic nerves. Withdrawing both the mind and the life force from the senses, the yogi unites them with the light and bliss of the soul, and eventually with the Cosmic Light and Cosmic Bliss of the Spirit.

In addition to solitary meditation, wherein the devotee cherishes his exclusive communion with God, a restless devotee will find it beneficial to meditate with other sincere souls, and especially with advanced yogis. The invisible vibrations emanating from the soul of a yogi will greatly help the beginner to attain inner tranquility. Jesus said: "For where two or three are gathered together in my name, there am I in the midst of them."*

Conversely, it is spiritually disturbing to a habitually restless devotee when he tries to meditate with someone even more restless than himself. Unless persons meditating together are making a sincere effort to cultivate devotion and meditative self-control of body and mind, a negligent meditator not only makes no progress himself, but is a negative distraction to others who themselves are having difficulty trying to go deep within. Careless indifference and bodily restlessness in meditation cause negative vibrations. Sincere spiritual effort (regardless of inner struggle) sends forth positive spiritual vibrations. The ecstatic meditation of the advanced yogi in deep communion with God radiates supernal blessings of God's presence.

Deeply meditating disciples should concentrate on their guru, or meditate with him if possible. Those who are spiritually advanced do in fact meditate with the guru by visualizing him in the spiritual eye and tuning in with him, whether or not they are in his physical presence. During meditation the spiritual vibration of a great master silently works on lesser yogis who may be meditating with him or who are in tune with him, regardless of distance. It is sufficient for a disciple to think strongly of his guru before meditation. He will then find his meditation on God to be reinforced by the Lord's power flowing through the direct tangible channel of the guru.

Deeper meaning of solitude: absorption in the spiritual eye

THE STUDENT OF METAPHYSICS should understand this stanza in a deeper sense. It is here said that the yogi should remain in solitude and continuously meditate on his soul. The real state of solitude is attained when the yogi can switch off his life force from the senses and keep his mind concentrated, not on the five centers of the spine, but at the single spiritual spherical eye. Through this eye he can perceive Omnipresence and forget the body consciousness (which is produced by the action of the earthly current at the coccygeal center, the water current at the sacral, the fire current at the lumbar, the life force or air current at the dorsal, and the etheric

* Matthew 18:20.

current at the cervical). A yogi attains the perfect state of solitude when he can rest in the superconscious bliss of the soul that exists beyond the subconscious state of sleep. In deep sleep, no disturbance of the senses can easily reach the mind. When the yogi, however, is concentrated at the spiritual eye, in ineffable joy, he is really in the solitude that none of the senses has power to invade.

VERSE 11

śucau deśe pratiṣṭhāpya sthiram āsanam ātmanaḥ
nātyucchritaṁ nātinīcaṁ cailājinakuśottaram

The yogi's seat, in a clean place, should be firm (not wobbly), neither too high nor too low, and covered, first, with kusha grass, then with a deer or tiger skin, then with a cloth.

THE INDIAN YOGI USES *kusha* grass to protect his body against the dampness of the earth. The skin and the cloth placed on top, on which the devotee sits, help to insulate his body against the pull of the earth currents. During meditation the mind tries to withdraw the searchlights of life force from the senses to the soul. During this process, the yogi who meditates with his body insulated avoids the tug-of-war between the upward flow of the life force through the nerves and the downward pull of the earth currents.

In the modern world, in both East and West, neither *kusha* grass nor animal skin is necessary for the meditation seat. (In India it was customary for a forest-dwelling yogi to make his seat on the skin of a tiger or leopard or deer that had died a natural death.) A very satisfactory substitute is a seat made of a folded woolen blanket, with a silk cloth placed over it. Silk repels certain earth currents better than does cotton.

The seat should not be "too low" (too near the earth) nor "too high." The yogi should be careful not to perch on a small high place from which, during ecstasy, he could fall down. Neither should he meditate inside an unventilated cave or closet, where there is insufficient fresh air, or in any place where the air is stale and suffocating. Nor should he place himself on an unstable seat (such as a wobbly old spring mattress) whose unevenness or squeaks might disturb his concentration.

The yogi should meditate on a firm seat, one that is clean—untainted by dirt or unspiritual vibrations of others. The thought or life force emanating from an individual saturates the objects he uses and his dwelling. Sensitive persons can feel the inharmonious vibrations in a house where wickedness has reigned. A saint or other receptive person can feel the spiritual vibrations left by masters in the places where they meditated. A devotee, meditating where a sage has meditated—even if the sage has long since passed away from this earth—by deep mental attunement can feel his vibrations. Devout men who go on a pilgrimage and meditate in a place hallowed by the ecstasy of a master receive definite spiritual benefit.

The *kusha* grass grows abundantly in India. It is rather prickly but has special properties that repel the earth's dampness. Its use was advocated in India because it is easily obtainable. The modern yogi, however, can make a good seat by placing a soft woolen blanket (not scratchy), covered by a silk cloth, on a comfortable cushion or spring pad on the floor, or on a spring mattress (one that doesn't sag) on a firm bed.

If the beginner yogi sits on the hard floor to meditate he will find his legs going to sleep, owing to pressure on his flesh and arteries. If he sits on a blanket over a spring pad or mattress, on the floor, or over a hard bed, he will not experience discomfort in his legs. A Westerner, used to sitting on chairs with his thighs at a right angle to his torso, will find it more comfortable to meditate on a chair with a woolen blanket and silk cloth under him, extending under his feet which rest on the floor. Those Western yogis, especially youths, who can squat on the floor like Orientals, will find their knees pliable, owing to their ability to fold their legs in an acute angle. Such yogis may meditate in the lotus posture, or in the more simple cross-legged position.

No one should try to meditate in the lotus posture unless he is at ease in that position. To meditate in a strained posture keeps the mind on the discomfort of the body. Meditation should ordinarily be practiced in a sitting position. Obviously, in a standing posture (unless one is advanced) he may fall down when the mind becomes interiorized. Neither should the yogi meditate lying down, for he might resort to the "practiced" state of slumber.

The proper bodily posture, one which produces calmness in body and mind, is necessary to help the yogi shift his mind from matter to Spirit. (This point is further detailed in verse 13.)

THERE IS A VERY SUBTLE METAPHYSICAL interpretation about the use of *kusha* grass next to the earth, the animal skin, and the silken cloth on top. The *kusha* grass growing on the earth signifies the earth center or earth current, lodged in the coccygeal center in the spine. The animal skin, which has been made from the nutrients of blood, is the symbol of liquid or the water current in the sacral center. The silken or fire-manufactured cloth represents the fire current in the lumbar center. The successful yogi first takes his ego, mind, and life force through these three lower centers that are connected with material consciousness, and lodges his consciousness in the centrally located ("neither high nor low") heart center.*

Symbolic meaning: ascending earth, water, and fire centers in spine

When the yogi is able to do that, when he finds the mind and life force, ordinarily directed toward the senses and material objects through the three lower centers, turned upward to the heart center, he has reached the threshold of ascension. The best way to accomplish this feat is by *Kriya Yoga.* The uninitiated can begin by sitting in a straight position and drawing in the breath, with deep concentration, imagining it and the life current and mind to be flowing through the three lower centers up into the heart center. The yogi should expel breath and remain breathless as long as comfortably possible when his mind reaches the heart center. By performing this technique with deep concentration, the devotee can feel his breath, life force, and mind flowing into the heart center, and from there on to the higher centers.

VERSE 12

tatraikāgraṁ manaḥ kṛtvā yatacittendriyakriyaḥ
upaviśyāsane yuñjyād yogam ātmaviśuddhaye

Established on that seat, concentrating the mind on one point, and controlling the activities of the fanciful faculty (chitta, feeling—the power that visualizes) and the senses, let him practice yoga for self-purification.

THE ORDINARY PERSON'S MIND is restless and undisciplined. By meditation, once in a while he is able to concentrate on one object at a time, such as the cosmic sound of *Aum,* which can be heard by a special yogic technique.

---

* See I:21, referring to the three "intuitional caravanserai" or "stopping places" in the spine—the dorsal or heart center being the middle one.

Mind passes along with the life current from the brain through the spinal centers and then into the many branches of the nervous system and the innumerable cellular points of perception. The ordinary mind is therefore spoken of as being concentrated on the many points of the flesh; it is entangled principally in sensations in the sensory tracts.

The mind and life force—engaged in looking at duality through the two eyes, listening through the two ears, smelling through the two nostrils, tasting through the forked tongue,* and touching through many points of the skin—are thus dissipated in myriads of perceptions. Man becomes matter-bound, torn by countless distractions.

When the *Kriya Yogi* withdraws his mind and life force and gathers them together to be concentrated at one point, in the single eye, he begins to look into the omnipresent sphere of the Infinite. This is what is meant by making the mind one-pointed, the "single-eyed" vision referred to by Christ. When the yogi meditates more deeply, he finds his mind automatically concentrated at the one point of the spiritual eye, in ecstasy with the Lord.

In the beginning, the devotee by meditation succeeds once in a while in quieting the mind. By deeper progress he finds that half of the time his mind is concentrated on the Divine, and half of the time scattered in bodily and material perceptions. By further spiritual development he remains in a state of continuous and one-pointed concentration, very seldom experiencing restlessness. In the final or *nirudha* state (his consciousness fully liberated from body identification and ascended into Spirit) the yogi becomes permanently one with the Absolute.

In this stanza the Gita points out that, during the effort of being one-pointed, the yogi will be unsuccessful unless he can by concentration withdraw his attention (*manas,* mind) from the activities of the life force in the various senses. Otherwise, he will be constantly distracted by restless thoughts—the mental concepts formed from sensory stimuli by the "fanciful faculty" of feeling (*chitta*). The devotee who sits in a good posture and meditates at the point between the eyebrows learns to practice yoga, the uniting of ego and soul; in deep concentration, he finds his mind and heart (*chitta,* feeling) free from sensory distractions and emotional likes and dislikes. With the mergence of the ego into the taintless soul, he engages in the ultimate "self-purification."

* I.e., bifurcated into two sections—see VI:3, page 595.

VERSE 13

samaṁ kāyaśirogrīvaṁ dhārayann acalaṁ sthiraḥ
saṁprekṣya nāsikāgraṁ svaṁ diśaś cānavalokayan

Firmly holding the spine, neck, and head erect and motionless, let the yogi focus his eyes at the starting place of the nose (the spot between the two eyebrows); let him not gaze around in various directions.

A MAJORITY OF GITA TRANSLATORS and commentators have misinterpreted the word *nasikagram* to mean "tip of the nose." The word literally means "origin of the nose." The origin or starting place of the nose is the spot between the two eyebrows, the seat of spiritual vision. In stanza 13 the yogi is rightly directed to concentrate on this vital spot, *not* on the tip of the nose. My guru Sri Yukteswar, noticing how frequently *nasikagram* is misunderstood, once said drolly:

"The path of a yogi is singular enough as it is. Why counsel him that he must also make himself cross-eyed?"

The Sanskrit word used in this verse in reference to an erect spine is *kaya* (literally, "the body" or "the trunk of a tree"). In XV:1, the body is described as the tree of life with roots above and branches below. The spine is its trunk; the physical nervous system and the channels of astral life force, its branches; the brain and cosmic consciousness (with the cerebral centers of the medulla, spiritual eye, and thousand-petaled lotus) are its roots, its source of life and vitality.

Details of correct meditation posture

Meditation involves the withdrawal, through the spine, of life current from the sensory nerve branches, and the concentration of that accumulation of life force within the spherical spiritual eye. A straight spine and erectness of the neck and head are important in effective meditation. If one adopts an improper posture—his body bent, or his chin tilted up or down—his crooked vertebrae pinch the spinal nerves. This pressure obstructs the reversed flow of mind and life force from the sensory channels to the brain; there is then no reinforcement of the power of the inner telescopic eye to perceive Omnipresence.

One should sit in a comfortable posture with the spine erect. The lumbar region of the spine (opposite the navel) should be gently crooked forward, the chest up and shoulders back (which places the inner edges of the shoulder blades closer together). Each hand, palm upturned, should be put on the corresponding thigh at the juncture of the thigh and abdomen to prevent the body from bending forward. The chin should be parallel to the floor. While maintaining this correct position, undue tension in the muscles should be relaxed. When the yogi holds the spine in the form of a bow by the above-mentioned posture, he is ready successfully to engage his reversed mind and life force in a battle with the outwardly pulling senses. Without any strictures or pinching of the spinal nerves, the mind and life force are easily directed upward by the yogi.

Key to meditation: concentrating at point between the eyebrows

As one switch pours through two channels one electric current into two headlights of an automobile, so the one medullary astral eye of light supplies the two human eyes with two lights—a forked light. This gives the delusive dual and dimensional perception of matter. Thus focused outwardly, the eyes are ordinarily constantly oscillating. The ego directs the two optic searchlights into various angles according to its psychological inclinations. Under the influence of specific stimuli and emotions, the eyes assume different positions and angles. Anger, jealousy, hate, love, determination, all change the angle of vision and the appearance of the eyelids and eyeballs. The thoughts roused by the stimuli keep rotating the searchlight eyes, playing them in various directions to perform a variety of mental and physical activities. In this sense-conscious state, the eyes are rarely still and concentrated. Yet even in the most restless man, when his thoughts are singularly concentrated, his eyes become still and begin to have one angle of vision.

In the concentrated state of superconsciousness, that angle of vision is at the point between the eyebrows (the natural seat of will and concentration, and of divine perception, in the body). The aspirant who wants to produce the superconscious state, characterized by conscious relaxation of life energy from the senses, must learn to fix his eyes and their gaze at this center. When the gaze of the two eyes is concentrated at the point between the eyebrows, the dual currents flowing from the medulla into the two eyes reunite, and the yogi sees at this center the spiritual eye of three colors—a reflection of the actual luminous eye in the medulla oblongata. The illumination of the spiritual eye by this reversal of life force in the two eyes exerts a strong pull on the life force throughout the body. The senses, which were projected outside to cognize matter, are recalled within to concentrate on the source from which all the powers of the senses and mind flow.

This Gita stanza therefore advises the devotee of the necessity of concentrating the light of the two eyes at the point between the two eyebrows, at the origin of the nose, as a prime requisite of yoga meditation.

THE SINGLE EYE OF LIGHT reflected in the forehead from the medulla is the astral eye of intuitive omnipresent perception.* When the light of the two eyes is concentrated between the eyebrows as a single reinforced light, the yogi can see his body as made of the light that emanates from God. The soul uses the spherical astral eye of intuition to perceive Cosmic Light and Cosmic Consciousness.

Concentrating at point between the eyebrows, yogi perceives the spiritual eye

Whereas the characteristic of the physical eyes is to perceive creation or matter by looking at one thing at a time (by shifting the gaze, or by looking at several points at the same time), the nature of the spherical eye is to behold all matter, all energy, and all consciousness simultaneously. Man, made in the image of God, has in his forehead the Lord's all-seeing power. Christ referred as follows to the omniscient eye of God: "Are not two sparrows sold for a farthing? and one of them shall not fall on the ground without (the sight of) your Father."† Jesus, lifting up his eyes and looking through his single omnipresent eye, ever found himself at one with the cosmic consciousness of the Father, the Lord who simultaneously perceives all the material universes, all the astral universes, and all the ideational universes.

The ordinary man, concentrating his vision with half-closed eyes at the point between the eyebrows, feels eyestrain in the beginning, owing to the unfamiliar practice. The yogi, on the other hand, used to concentrating upward on his spiritual eye, finds it distasteful to identify his consciousness with the downward material vision of his two physical eyes. Concentrating on the point between the two eyebrows during meditation helps the devotee to keep his eyes neither fully closed nor fully opened. This practice prevents the onrush of either subconscious slumber or complete conscious wakefulness. Thus the meditating yogi learns to penetrate into the superconscious sphere existing between the subconscious darkness above and the visible light below.

The dividing line between the upper darkness and the lower material light of the half-closed and half-opened eyes is called "the horizon of superconsciousness." A person meditating with closed eyes may

---

* I.e., the astral eye of light and life force, inherent in which is the causal eye of intuition. See IV:1–2, pages 429–30.

† Matthew 10:29.

fall asleep; trying to meditate with open eyes he may be thwarted by the stubborn visions of matter. That is why the yogi is advised to avoid the total darkness of closed eyes and the full light of opened eyes. Instead he concentrates his vision on the superconscious horizon.

If a person deeply concentrates on this horizon at the point between the eyebrows, where darkness and light meet, without straining the eyes, he refocuses the two currents in the two eyes into the original single current, and gradually learns to penetrate through the spiritual eye into the superconscious beatitude. In this way the mortal habit of dual frontal vision or of perceiving dimensional matter is changed into the spherical vision or intuitive perception of the one Omnipresence. In spite of any mild discomfort of the unaccustomed positioning of the eyes, the yogi-beginner should gently and calmly concentrate his vision at the point between the eyebrows, holding the gaze steady—not looking around, or permitting any restless movement of the eyeballs or flickering of the eyelids. In time he will see the spherical spiritual eye.

The presence of a concentration of the light of life force in the eyes is evidenced by the fact that even a gentle pressure on the eyeballs (by the fingers pressing gently and rotating over the eyelids of the closed eyes) will cause the emission of light in the darkness of the closed eyes. Many think that this pressure-induced light is just physical. This is not the case. This light, seen only by the consciousness, is not grossly physical. It is rather a semiphysical and semispiritual manifestation of the life energy that builds, guides, and enlivens all the bodily tissues.

Seeing the inner light by yoga concentration methods of fixing the gaze, attention, and devotion—instead of by physical pressure—refines this semispiritual manifestation, changing it to the finer vibratory rate of its pure spiritual nature. Hence, the quality of the semispiritual light seen by gently pressing the eyes is enhanced with an increase in the depth of the devotee's meditation.

Degrees of perception of the light of the spiritual eye

In deep meditation, when one's eyes and gaze are fixed in between the eyebrows, the life energy pouring from behind the wall of illusive man-made darkness through the sluice gates of the two eyes floods the center of will in the forehead as a mass of brilliant energy—a bubbling lake of white light. This light may change into colors or shapes of infinite variety. The different rates of thought vibrations of the meditating devotee produce the variations. The common first fruit of concentration is white light; expressions of devotion, love, wisdom, all produce different variations. But when the devotee is established in the intensive, desireless, calm intuitive state of meditation, then all variations of the light in the spiritual eye begin to change into the one true spiritual eye.

When the yogi concentrates long enough with half-open eyes at the point between the eyebrows, and when the gaze is without any restless motion, he will be able to see a steady light surrounded by other, but flickering, lights. He should not be diverted by this glimmering halo of the spiritual eye, but should steadfastly look at the center of the eye until he feels his mind completely absorbed within it. In time, he will see the perfect formation of the spiritual eye: a dark opal-blue globe within a quivering ring of flame. Gradually, by deep concentration, an extremely brilliant white star occasionally glimmers in the center of the blue. The star is the gateway through which the consciousness must pass to attain oneness with Spirit.

It requires time and calm practice to steady the light of the intuitive astral eye. It takes deeper and longer practice to see the star. It requires greater realization to hold the perception of the star. And it takes mastery in meditation to march the consciousness, valiantly triumphant, through the starry gate of light.

Penetrating the spiritual eye, yogi reaches progressively higher states

AFTER THE DEVOTEE IS ABLE *at will* to see his astral eye of light and intuition with either closed or open eyes, and to hold it steady indefinitely, he will eventually attain the power to look through it into Eternity; and through the starry gateway he will sail into Omnipresence.

Progression through the spiritual eye, experienced by advancing yogis, unfolds first the wondrous perceptions of superconsciousness, the region of rays of light out of which all matter evolves. The creative cosmic rays hide like veils the presence of the immanent universal Christ or Krishna Consciousness, the Lord omnipresent in creation. By deeper concentration and meditation, the spiritual eye of intuition opens, and through the wisdom star the yogi becomes united to the Christ-Krishna Omnipresence; and thence, in deepest ecstasy, he reaches the Cosmic Consciousness of Spirit.*

Another instruction can be added in this connection: The astral eye of light can most easily be seen at night or in a dark room. The highly developed yogi, however, can see the spiritual eye even in day-

* "I (the universal Christ Consciousness in Jesus) am the way, the truth, and the life: no man cometh unto the Father (mergence in Spirit beyond creation), but by me (ascension through the Christ Consciousness omnipresent in creation)" (John 14:6).

light or in the presence of any strong light. Just as a drowsy man can sleep in the day or night, so the advanced yogi can see the spiritual eye and go into ecstasy at will irrespective of the presence of darkness or of any kind of light. He learns to penetrate his consciousness into the astral eye; and absorbing his whole being therein, he looks into the realm of Spirit, remaining there oblivious of the material world.

Ordinary individuals who yearn to get rid of the obnoxious trials of the conscious life cannot go at will to the subconscious state of restful sleep or to the blissful superconscious state, owing to habits of worry and to lack of control of the life currents in the eyes and the vision, and in the mind behind them. But the yogi learns by closing the eyes, and relaxing the gaze, to sleep at will; by keeping them open, gazing straight ahead, he learns to remain awake indefinitely. Holding his eyes half open and half closed, and concentrating at the spiritual eye, the devotee can at will, and for as long as he chooses, enter and remain in a state of superconscious ecstasy. Thus just by opening or closing his eyes or keeping them half open, the advanced yogi can transfer his concentration at will from the physical world to the subconscious slumberland or to the superconscious state. Summoning or dismissing these states at will, he becomes master of the conscious, subconscious, and superconscious worlds.

As the devotee progresses in meditation from restless consciousness to cosmic consciousness, his conscious and subconscious thoughts may materialize in his inner vision, weaving figures of light, like those seen in movies, both real and unreal—materializations of the will and life energy. Beware, young devotee, of these fairies of the world of life energy. Be not satisfied with anything less than Spirit and the bliss of Spirit. Pay no attention to variations of the inner light, but practice concentration on the light of the spiritual eye. The light of the eye must be used only to look for God, the One whose presence is hidden on the throne of light.

VERSE 14

praśāntātmā vigatabhīr brahmacārivrate sthitaḥ
manaḥ saṁyamya maccitto yukta āsīta matparaḥ

With serenity and fearlessness, with steadfastness in brahmacharya, with the mind controlled, with the thoughts centered on Me, the yogi should sit, meditating on Me as the Final Goal.

HE WHO IS STEADFAST in *brahmacharya* is defined as a celibate student who is faithful in living a holy life, engaging in sacred study and self-discipline. In the prescribed Vedic plan, this was basically the beginning of the spiritual life for all aspirants. *"Brahmachari-vrate"* has also a deeper meaning here: literally, "one whose sphere of action or act of devotion (*vrata*) is practicing (*chāra*) *Aum* (*brahma*: the sacred sound, *shabda-brahman*)." The accomplished *brahmachari,* then, is one who by the practice of meditating on *Aum* roams or progresses in the realm of Brahman manifested as the Creator or Holy Vibration: the *Aum*, Amen, or Holy Ghost.

God manifests in creation as the Cosmic Vibration, which expresses itself as Cosmic Sound and Cosmic Light. The Cosmic Sound or *Aum* is the synthesis of all the sounds of the highly vibrating life forces (lifetrons), electrons, protons, and atoms. By listening to *Aum*, the yogi becomes a true *brahmachari* or one who is attuned to Brahman. By deep concentration the devotee can hear *Aum* at any time and in any place.

Aum spoken of in Bible as "the Word" or Holy Ghost

The Cosmic Sound is spoken of in the Christian Bible as follows: "In the beginning was the Word, and the Word was with God, and the Word was God."* The Word or *Aum* came from God; He manifests as the Cosmic Vibration in creation. The Bible also refers to the Word as the Holy Ghost or intelligent ghostlike unseen vibration that is the creator of all forms of matter. It is called Holy Ghost because this Invisible Force is guided by the Christ Intelligence that exists in creation as the reflection or "sole begotten Son" of the transcendental God the Father. Jesus Christ promised that the Holy Ghost or the great Comforter would come to his disciples after his bodily departure from the earth.† *Kriya Yoga* is a fulfillment of that blessed promise of Christ, as it gives the peoples of the world a scientific technique for contacting the Holy Sound.

St. John spoke of the Cosmic Sound. "I was in the Spirit on the Lord's day, and heard behind me a great voice, as of a trumpet";‡ i.e., "I was in spiritual ecstasy with the Lord and heard behind my conscious, subconscious, and superconscious minds a voice like that of a great trumpet, the great commingled Cosmic Sound coming out of the 'thrum' of lifetrons, protons, electrons, and atoms."

---

* John 1:1. † John 14:26. ‡ Revelation 1:10.

IN THE *YOGA SUTRAS* OF PATANJALI, *Aum* (*Om*) is spoken of as the symbol of Ishvara or God. This great authority on yoga refers to *Aum* as a Cosmic Sound continuously flowing in the ether, unutterable by any human voice, and fully known only to the illuminated. Further, Patanjali says that deep concentration on *Aum* is a means of liberation.

Patanjali's instructions for communion with Aum

Many people who do not understand the inward meaning of the scriptures think that by softly or loudly chanting *Aum* they can reach the superconsciousness. The Hindu scriptures, however, point out that one whose mind is identified with the *kaya* or body cannot possibly perceive the true *Aum* sound. In ancient times only the knowers of Brahman were allowed to utter *Aum* because they were able at will to hear the Cosmic Sound and perceive, behind it, the presence of God. A literal interpretation of this injunction led to the nonsensical belief that only Brahmins (no one of lower castes) or those who take *sannyas* and thereby have renounced all caste, should chant or meditate on *Aum*. In point of fact, none can escape a constant communion with *Aum*, for it pervades the consciousness and every fiber and atom of every being. Those who become *consciously* attuned to the omnipresent Cosmic Vibration receive untold blessings.

The scriptures classify ordinary chanting as (1) repeated loud utterance of the word *Aum*, (2) repetitions of *Aum* in whispers, and (3) continuous chanting of *Aum* in one's mind, listening to it mentally. Superconscious chanting, however, is that in which the mind is deeply directed to the repetition of, and the actual profound listening to, the Cosmic Sound as it vibrates in the ether. This is the true way of contacting God as He is expressed in creation.

The cosmic *Aum* sound is the combined vibration of the three phases of Nature: creation, preservation, and dissolution operative in the physical, astral, and causal universes. The vocal chanting of *Aum* should be intoned first in a high pitch, representing creation; then in a lower pitch, representing preservation; then in a still lower tone that gradually fades away, representing dissolution. The chanting should be first loudly, then softly, and then gently until it is inaudible, or mental only.

The real, or superconscious, chanting of *Aum*, however, consists not in an imitative vocalization of *Aum*, but in actually hearing the Holy Sound. All physical sounds are transmitted through the medium of ether; but although *Aum* vibrates in the ether—which is the background of all manifested activity—the *Aum* sound vibrates independently of the etheric medium. It is thus referred to as *anahata-nada* (a sound produced otherwise than by being beaten or struck—that is, without detonation) because it manifests in the yogi's intuition without striking his eardrum through the medium of ether—as with physical sounds. *Aum,* being a spiritual vibration, is not heard physically, but felt spiritually.

Patanjali meant that only that yogi can attain God whose mind is superconsciously fixed on the Cosmic Sound, the external Divine Manifestation. Such a yogi is an accomplished *brahmachari.* His heart is overflowing with the sacred joy that follows perception of *Aum*. When a devotee experiences the bliss of God (the comfort of the Holy Ghost) behind the Cosmic Sound, his heart becomes serene; he loses all fear of ever being diverted from his exalted state or of becoming entangled in material sensations. A yogi who has united his soul with the Cosmic Sound and thereby experiences its ineffable bliss is spoken of as united to the Lord. His heart, filled with divine joy, is no longer subject to likes and dislikes, as is the ordinary person's heart during the contacts with matter and its essential oppositional states.*

AN AVOWED MAN OF RENUNCIATION, fearlessly, with serene heart and controlled mind, can think of God as his Supreme Goal. But in a higher state the yogi becomes one with God; having found the Lord through *Aum* and Its *pratipadya* (the cosmic bliss that follows after the perception of the Cosmic Sound or Holy Ghost), he achieves complete liberation.

Through Aum, God is accessible to all devotees

The Holy Ghost is spoken of by the Hindus as *Aum,* by the Muslims as *Amin,* and by the Christians as *Amen* or the Word. In Revelation 3:14 we find this definition: "These things saith the Amen, the faithful and true witness, the beginning of the creation of God." This Amen is the Cosmic Sound which, as a divine witness, faithfully accompanies all vibratory creation from its beginning—even as sound accompanies or declares the running of a motor. In other

* "Dive thou into that Ocean of sweetness: thus let all errors of life and of death flee away.

Behold how the thirst of the five senses is quenched there! and the three forms of misery are no more!

Kabir says: 'It is the sport of the Unattainable One: look within, and behold how the moonbeams of that Hidden One shine in you.

There falls the rhythmic beat of life and death:
Rapture wells forth, and all space is radiant with light.
There the Unstruck Music is sounded; it is the music of the love of the three worlds.'"

—*One Hundred Poems of Kabir,* translated by Rabindranath Tagore (London: Macmillan, 1915). (*Publisher's Note*)

words, Amen or *Aum* is an "ear-witness" that declares, as accessible to all devotees, the tangible presence in all creation of the Creator.

The Hindu Bible (Bhagavad Gita), the Christian Bible, and the greatest book on yoga (Patanjali's *Yoga Sutras*) unanimously declare the Cosmic Sound to be the outward manifestation or witness of the Lord in creation. Krishna, Jesus, and Patanjali all taught that man must receive the Holy Ghost (the Comforter) in order to reach the Christ Intelligence within it and God the Father existing beyond it (beyond *Aum* or vibratory creation). All souls have descended into matter from God the Father beyond creation, God the Son or Christ Intelligence, and God the Holy Ghost. Every soul has therefore to ascend to the Spirit (Unmanifested Absolute) through the stages of Its triune manifestation—Holy Ghost, Son, and Father (*Aum-Tat-Sat* of the Hindu scriptures).

VERSE 15

yuñjann evaṁ sadātmānaṁ yogī niyatamānasaḥ
śāntiṁ nirvāṇaparamāṁ matsaṁsthām adhigacchati

The self-governed yogi—he whose mind is fully under control—thus engaging his soul in ceaseless meditative union with Spirit, attains the peace of My being: the final Nirvana (deliverance).

BY PRACTICING THE EIGHTFOLD YOGA, the devotee first experiences ecstasy for a short time; by deeper practice he is able to remain divinely entranced for longer periods. The ecstatic state of perception of God without perception of the universe is called *savikalpa samadhi* or *samprajnata samadhi.** It is seldom, if ever, possible for a yogi to remain during his entire lifetime in the bodily inactive state of *savikalpa samadhi.*

An interesting historical incident, one to which my father was an eyewitness, may be recounted here. Certain Bhukailash princes of Kidderpore (near Calcutta) ordered a pond dug in their property at Sundarban Forest in Bengal. In the course of this operation, the bodies of seven men were unearthed and subsequently taken to the palace compound. Geologists testified that the men must have been interred about two hundred years previously. Thousands of people in Calcutta, my father among them, flocked to see the men, who were engrossed in a state

* See page 117.

of ecstasy, exhibiting no outward signs of life, their bodies in a perfect state of preservation.

It was told that failing to rouse the saints by the application of hot towels on the head, and by other methods of resuscitation commonly known to revive fakirs in demonstrated states of suspended animation, the princes, against the protestations of friends, ordered servants to drive hot pokers into the flesh of the inanimate *sadhus.* This barbaric treatment forced the saints to return to outward consciousness. One of them sternly addressed the Bhukailash princes:

"We had planned to remain for a few more years in this ecstatic state in order to destroy our past karma and attain liberation. Since you have cruelly disturbed us, you must suffer your own karma."

The saints then simultaneously passed away. Their bodies, which soon decayed, were publicly cremated. Some say the Bhukailash princes, soon after, died suddenly; other accounts do not support this contention, but do refer to unusual disasters having caused great sufferings to the family.*

---

* Bhukailash, "abode of the gods on earth," in Kidderpore is regarded by many as a holy and auspicious site, frequented by *sadhus* and holy men. The Bhukailash estate, massive in its day, was built up in 1782 by the pious Maharaja Joy Narayan Ghosal. From his time to the present, religious festivals are celebrated there throughout the year to honor the principal deities.

Remarkable incidents, unless they have been scientifically researched and documented, tend quickly to reach legendary proportions. Though the event of the disinterred Bhukailash *sadhus* (as they came to be known) is lacking in currently available authenticated documentation, fragments of the story have survived and been passed down to succeeding generations of the Ghosal family. Indications are that the event took place sometime between the mid-1850s and early 1860s, and that the princes involved were Sri Satya Charan, Sri Satya Saran, Sri Satya Prasanna, and Sri Satya Bhakta Ghosal. Of the present generation, Sri Satya Harish and Sri Satya Dilip Ghosal (two of the current trustees of the Bhukailash estate) confirm that the incident as recalled by Paramahansaji's father is akin to the bits of information they had heard from their elders. They also conjectured whether it may be significant in relation to the *sadhus* that the present water tank on the estate has seven borings, resembling wells; and that it is a commonly known phenomena that the water level in the tank always remains the same throughout the year, both winter and summer.

Various articles and books, including *The Gospel of Sri Ramakrishna* (by Mahendra Nath Gupta—Master Mahasaya) make reference to an exhumed *sadhu* in *samadhi* who was taken to the Bhukailash estate. It is unclear whether any of these accounts, similar in detail, may have reference to the same incident, or whether they refer to one or more unrelated events. Paramahansaji's father, who would have been a young boy at the time, recalled that the saints were seven in number—other of the accounts refer only to one or two *sadhus,* and also vary in other details, such as the date of the event. The underlying fact of the ability of accomplished yogis to maintain in *samadhi* an indefinite period of suspended animation is averred throughout the varied tellings. *(Publisher's Note)*

The disinterred saints had been experiencing an unusually prolonged state of *savikalpa samadhi.*

Incredible as this story may seem to a skeptic, it is no more so than other, authenticated accounts of varying degrees of life-suspension. Persons have lived for months or years in a comatose state and then returned to normal consciousness. Many cases of complete suspended animation, cessation of all vital signs, with subsequent recovery are accepted fact (e.g., the mother of Robert E. Lee, the famous Civil War general). The ability to enter a trance state of suspended animation *at will* has been demonstrated by yogis and fakirs, renowned among whom was the early nineteenth-century Sadhu Haridas.* If unconscious states

---

* In his book, *Thirty-five Years in the East*, Dr. John Martin Honigberger, physician to the Court of Lahore, India, writes of the feats of Sadhu Haridas, which he gathered from eyewitness accounts. The fakir was buried underground for forty days in a controlled experiment—closely observed and guarded—in 1837 under the auspices of the Maharaja Ranjit Singh of Punjab. His subsequent disinterrment and revival was witnessed by many dignitaries of the court, together with noted Englishmen. (In an earlier test conducted by Raja Dhyan Singh at Jammu, Kashmir, Sadhu Haridas had reportedly remained buried for four months.)

Following his detailed account of the Sadhu Haridas event, Dr. Honigberger adds: "It is related that two hundred and fifty years ago, in the time of Guru Arjun Singh, a yogi fakir was found in his tomb in a sitting posture, at Amritsar, and was restored to life. This fakir is reported to have been below the ground for one hundred years; and when he revived, he related many circumstances connected with the times in which he had lived. Whether this tradition is true or false, it is impossible to say; but I am of the opinion that he who can pass four months below the ground [reference to Sadhu Haridas] without becoming prey to corruption, may also remain there for one year. Granting this, it is impossible to fix a limit to the time during which a suspension of the vital functions may continue, without injury to their subsequent power.

"However paradoxical or absurd this statement may appear, and however persuaded I may be that many a reader, believing himself to be a wise man, will smile at the relation, I cannot, nevertheless, avoid confessing freely that I do not entirely reject all the details given respecting the circumstance, for Haller observes, 'In the interior of nature no mortal can penetrate; happy is he who knows a small part, even of its surface.' We find much credence given to such phenomena in the most ancient traditions. Who will not remember the history of Epimenides of Creta, who after a sleep of forty years in a grotto there is reported to have again reentered the world from which he had so long been separated? Who will not remember also the seven holy sleepers who, according to a Vatican manuscript, were concealed in a grotto near Ephesus in order to escape the persecutions of the Christians during the reign of the Emperor Decius; and who, 155 years subsequently, in the time of Theodosius II, returned to consciousness? But even rejecting these traditions, have we not also similar examples in the animal kingdom? Have not animals, especially toads, been detected in rocks, wherein, according to the calculations made, they had been enclosed for several centuries in a state of sleep or torpor, and which animals, after having been brought into the air, have recovered their vitality."—*Thirty-five Years in the East* (London: H. Bailliere, 1852).

A first-person account of Sadhu Haridas's feat may be found in "On the Voluntary

of suspension be acceptable to the mind of reason, how much more so the ability of advanced yogis to retain conscious activity on a higher plane of perception while the body, a mere physical instrument used on earth, rests in a suspended state. Indeed, mystics and saints of all religious persuasions have been observed in this *savikalpa samadhi* state.

It is good that man is sometimes confronted by the unusual to jar his limitation-drugged mind from its commonplace complacency. The laws of Nature run their fixed course, but they are manipulatable by man, the lords who have been given dominion over the earth. If this were not so, there would be today no travel by airplane, no viewing of images passing through the ether into television sets, no medical wonder drugs—and the "miracles" that are yet to be brought into being in future. Jesus said, "Verily, verily, I say unto you, he that believeth on me, the works that I do shall he do also; and greater works than these shall he do."* While small-minded men cry "Impossible!" the pathfinders of the world calmly pursue their goals and demonstrate that the impossible was, instead, inevitable.

Instances like that of the Bhukailash saints, however, are purposely rare. They are reminders of man's potential for self-mastery, but such extremes are not intended to be a common part of the divine plan. Remaining in the bodily inert state for long periods of time has its dangers. Therefore, the properly instructed yogi learns to enter, and leave, the *savikalpa samadhi* state at will. This achievement enables him to retain his God-communion in the active state of worldly affairs.

The Lord does not wish His children indefinitely to remain inactive in ecstasy. He wants them to work out His drama in a state of divine realization (*nirvikalpa samadhi* or *asamprajnata samadhi*). By entering this highest state the yogi is liberated. He can retain his divine realization during the conscious, subconscious, and superconscious states. The advanced yogi, being united with God, can watch his own body while it is working or while it is inactive in ecstasy, even as God can watch both His immanence and His transcendence. The yogi, one with the Ocean of God, watches It and his little bodily wave as one and the same thing.

Such a yogi is spoken of as having attained the supreme state of *nir-*

Trance of Indian Fakirs," in *The Monist* (1900, Vol. 10, pages 490 ff.). More recently, *The American Heart Journal* (August 1973, Vol. 86, page 282) and *The Indian Journal of Medical Research* (November 1973, Vol. 61, page 1645) reported on a similar demonstration of a yogi's ability to remain in suspended animation for days at a time. (*Publisher's Note*)

* John 14:12.

vana or complete ego extinguishment. The soul does not vanish, but, retaining its individuality, expands into the Spirit. *Nirvana* signifies the final extinction, by destruction of all rebirth-making unfulfilled desires, of the karmic causes that compel a soul to reincarnate.

VERSE 16

nātyaśnatas tu yogo 'sti na caikāntam anaśnataḥ
na cātisvapnaśīlasya jāgrato naiva cārjuna

O Arjuna! The gourmand, the scanty eater, the person who habitually oversleeps, the one who sleeps too little—none of these finds success in yoga.

UNBALANCED STATES ARE OBSTACLES for the yogi. The beginner should fulfill all the normal conditions of healthful bodily existence; otherwise, physical troubles will entangle the mind and preclude the deep meditation upon which spiritual progress is dependent. The *sadhaka* should thus abstain from all excesses, lest his body become an obstruction in the path of divine progress. My guru Swami Sri Yukteswar wisely counseled: "Throw the dog a bone"—give the body its due, neither pampering nor abusing it, and then forget the body. In a natural way, as the inner consciousness becomes spiritualized through success in yoga, the body also becomes spiritualized, and its "normal" demands gradually diminish.

Yoga scriptures enjoin that the aspirant should be a "propereatarian"; that is, he should have a balanced diet, one with sufficient protein, fat, carbohydrates, and vitamins and minerals. But overeating, even of healthful foods, causes disease. Also, when the devotee tries to meditate on a full stomach, he may be conscious of the bodily load and of labored breathing instead of the breathless joyous state of superconsciousness. Eating insufficiently, on the other hand, leads to physical and mental weakness.

Oversleep dulls the nervous system; too little sleep produces a tendency to sleep against one's will.

Yogis point out that oversleep makes the body lazy; the throat and the nasal passages become filled with phlegm. The devotee should always keep his body free from the accumulation of excessive mucus. If a diet of raw food is found helpful in this regard, the yogi should follow it religiously.

Loss of sleep destroys mental freshness. A dull mind cannot concentrate on the joy of the soul within. Some yogis advise sleep in the earlier part of the night; after sleep, performing ablutions, and cleaning the mouth and nostrils, the devotee should practice *Kriya Yoga*. Some yogis advise those who have their time under their control to sleep in the afternoon for five hours, and to practice yoga and ecstasy meditations during the greater part of the night. "Night" consists of the period between sunset and sunrise. But yogis refer to the hours between 9:30 p.m. and 4:30 a.m. as the "great night," particularly suitable for meditation owing to less disturbance from certain magnetic earth currents.

Sleep is spoken of as pseudoecstasy. Compelled by fatigue, the ego is dragged into slumberland to experience subconsciously the state of the peaceful soul. Avoiding all excesses in the enjoyment of the senses of sight, hearing, smell, taste, and touch, the advanced yogi is able to go consciously beyond the state of sleep and thus to enjoy the unending bliss of the superconsciousness.

VERSE 17

yuktāhāravihārasya yuktaceṣṭasya karmasu
yuktasvapnāvabodhasya yogo bhavati duḥkhahā

He who with proper regularity eats, relaxes, works, sleeps, and remains awake will find yoga the destroyer of suffering.

THE YOGI SHOULD BE TEMPERATE in all his habits. This stanza points out that the novice yogi should not try to continue unbrokenly in meditation (with the exception of a few hours of sleep), thus ignoring the performance of good outward actions. It is unnatural—indeed, impossible—for a beginner in the path of yoga to remain in the superconscious state of ecstasy alternated only by sleep and not also by proper activities ordained by God and Nature.

Reference to regularity in eating, relaxing, working, sleeping, and waking admits of a deeper spiritual interpretation. During the practice of yoga, swallowing air (the ingestion of *prana* in oxygen) is called astral eating. Thus, "eating" refers to the breath. The devotee learns to distill life force out of air and thereby to reinforce his supply of *prana;* his body is gradually freed from bondage to solid and liquid foods. The yogi is advised to be regular in the eating of this air food. He should avoid excessive swallowing of air, and also too little breathing of air. Excessive or forceful breathing or willfully holding the breath in the lungs for prolonged periods is harmful. Similarly, the person who unscientifically reduces his breathing takes in insufficient oxygen and thereby poisons his system by too great an accumulation of carbon dioxide in the venous blood.

By regular rhythmic breathing, the yogi learns to distill energy from the proper amount of oxygen present in the naturally inflated lungs during inhalation, and to properly expel poisonous carbon dioxide (accrued from the decarbonization of his blood) during normal exhalation.

"Regularity in relaxation" (recreation) signifies that the yogi should breathe neither too heavily nor too scantily, but evenly—as in *Kriya Yoga* whereby the breath becomes neutralized, i.e., "still" or "relaxed."

By "regularity in work" the yogi is instructed to perform faithfully the divine action of meditation, along with the temperate performance of dutiful actions ordained by God and Nature—those that contribute to his own welfare and salvation; and also those that help to bring other true seekers to the path of God, less by his words than by his example.

Yogic interpretation of "regularity in eating, relaxing, working, sleeping"

The dreamless state of subconscious sleep, the dream subconscious state, and the state of wakefulness have a deep meaning that is explained by yogis in the following way: The ordinary person experiences these three states, which, connected as they are with the body and matter, are collectively called the delusive dream-state. The true wakeful state is perceived when the yogi rises above all his subconscious and conscious dream states and is conscious in the ever-wakefulness of God. The devotee, according to the esoteric interpretation of this stanza, is advised not to indulge excessively in the dream perception of worldly experiences in the sleep of delusion. He is also advised in the initial state not to sleep too little (to remain too little conscious of the material world) by trying to stay in the state of divine ecstasy all the time. The beginner yogi should strike a balance between divine activities and deep meditation. He who, in a balanced way, tries to be both human and divine will automatically find that he experiences equal joy whether he is in the state of human activity or in the state of deep meditation.

When a novice yogi tries continuously to remain in ecstasy and to perform no good outward works, he is unable to do so, and he is also unsuccessful in destroying his mortal karma. The yogi who is not lazy and who performs both divine and worldly duties to please both God and man burns out his seeds of karma. By mastery over outer activities, transforming their material nature by divine thoughts, the yogi attains liberation and the permanent destruction of all causes of suffering.

ATTAINING SELF-MASTERY AND CONTROL OF THE MIND

VERSE 18

yadā viniyataṁ cittam ātmany evāvatiṣṭhate
niḥspṛhaḥ sarvakāmebhyo yukta ity ucyate tadā

When the chitta (feeling) is absolutely subjugated and is calmly established in the Self, the yogi, thus devoid of attachment to all desires, is spoken of as the God-united.

WHEN THE HUMAN HEART is constantly absorbed in divine blessedness, it is automatically disunited from the lesser pleasures of the senses.

If a man sees a beautiful estate, permitting his eyes, mind, and intelligence to enjoy it impersonally (without a desire to possess it), he is not being entangled by his visual perception. But the sense-identified individual, at the very sight of the charming tract, may be seized by lust for its possession. The materialist, therefore, has no control of his *chitta* or feeling; he is ruled by uncontrolled emotions that lead to the miseries born of likes and dislikes.

In this stanza the Gita points out that the yogi should be fully concentrated in enjoying the blessed perception of the soul and thus so absorb his feelings that they are uninfluenced by material longings.

VERSE 19

yathā dīpo nivātastho neṅgate sopamā smṛtā
yogino yatacittasya yuñjato yogam ātmanaḥ

The illustration of an unflickering flame of light in a windless spot may be used in reference to a yogi who has conquered his feeling (chitta) by the practice of meditation on the Self.

"AS A STEADY FLAME OF LIGHT from a candle or oil lamp, sheltered from the wind, reveals the beauty of material objects around it, so the unwavering light of inner concentration, free from gusts of restlessness, reveals the everlasting glory of Spirit."

To keep a candle flame unflickering, it must be sheltered from any breeze. Similarly, the flame of the yogi's meditation-born perception must remain steadily burning, undisturbed and unwavering before the gusts of delusion-impassioned feeling. A yogi who thus guards the flame of peace from the onrush of momentary desires and innate likes and dislikes arising from an uncontrolled restlessness in his faculty of feeling (*chitta*) discovers in that tranquil light the secret presence of God. As a flickering light cannot distinctly reveal the outlines of objects near it, so the spiritual perception of a yogi who is agitated by material desires does not reveal within him the clear presence of the Divine.

VERSES 20–23

yatroparamate cittam niruddham yogasevayā
yatra caivātmanātmānaṁ paśyann ātmani tuśyati (20)

sukham ātyantikaṁ yat tad buddhigrāhyam atīndriyam
vetti yatra na caivāyaṁ sthitaś calati tattvataḥ (21)

yaṁ labdhvā cāparaṁ lābhaṁ manyate nādhikaṁ tataḥ
yasmin sthito na duḥkhena guruṇāpi vicālyate (22)

taṁ vidyād duḥkhasaṁyogaviyogaṁ yogasaṁjñitam
sa niścayena yoktavyo yogo 'nirviṇṇacetasā (23)

(20) The state of complete tranquility of the feeling (chitta), attained by yoga meditation, in which the self (ego) perceives itself as the Self (soul) and is content (fixed) in the Self;
(21) The state in which the sense-transcendent immeasurable bliss becomes known to the awakened intuitive intelligence, and in which the yogi remains enthroned, never again to be removed;
(22) The state that, once found, the yogi considers as the treasure beyond all other treasures—anchored therein, he is immune to even the mightiest grief;

(23) That state is known as yoga—the pain-free state. The practice of yoga is therefore to be observed resolutely and with a stout heart.

WHEN BY THE PRACTICE OF YOGA the feeling no longer flickers with distractions (those gusty conditioned responses to the machinations of Nature), but is immersed in interiorized concentration, the body-identified pseudosoul discovers its true Self and becomes enwrapt in the bliss of the Spirit-identified soul. In the unwavering light of sense-transcendent intuitive perception, the reflected shadowy ego first commingles with the image of its true Self, and then unites with the omnipresent flame of Spirit. The inner blaze of eternal Bliss destroys forever all the dream shadows of suffering.

Stanzas 20 and 21 describe the four states of primary ecstasy attained by the yogi in the advanced stages of yoga (in *samprajnata* or *savikalpa samadhi*), which in turn lead to the highest *samadhi* (*asamprajnata* or *nirvikalpa samadhi*),* the ultimate union referred to in stanza 23 as "the pain-free state."

In the first state of primary ecstasy, the body-identified ego in meditation meets its true Self, the soul; it begins to taste the blessedness of the bliss of the soul and becomes "content" (concentrated, fixed) in the joy of that nature.

As a result of that one-pointed concentration, the yogi attains the second state: "complete tranquility of the feeling." His attention, intellect, and feeling (operative in the *savikalpa* states of *savitarka, savichara,* and *sananda samprajnata samadhi*) have become entirely divorced from their sense-identified gross functions, and in their subtle nature are anchored in the bliss of the soul (in the *sasmita* state of pure individualized being). When the external activities of the faculties of intelligence are arrested and the cognitive instruments turned within, the intelligence then draws its knowing power from the intuition of the soul. In this sense-transcendent state, the inner bliss is thus "known to the awakened *intuitive* intelligence." Discovering the soul, the yogi also begins to perceive within his being the bliss of the Omnipresent God. After the physical ego metamorphoses into its true Self, the soul, then the bliss of the soul expands and merges into the greater bliss of the Spirit.

In the third state, the yogi experiences not only intermittent ecstasy, but finds his cosmic contact existing permanently beneath his con-

* See I:15–18 for definitive references to *samprajnata* and *asamprajnata samadhi*.

sciousness, to be enjoyed anytime he enters the *savikalpa samadhi* state.

The last state of the fourfold primary ecstasy is attained when the yogi becomes absorbed in the Cosmic Bliss not only in the meditative state of *samadhi,* but also when he is able to bring his divine perceptions with him when he returns to the conscious state of bodily activity. He is gradually able to hold on to these aftereffects of *samadhi* for longer and longer periods, during which he is undisturbed by any "pain"—the evil effects of Nature's alternating conditions of duality. When he can remain perpetually in that pain-free state, he is spoken of as having mastered all four states of primary ecstasy.

He then passes on to the state of the secondary or the highest ecstasy (*asamprajnata* or *nirvikalpa samadhi*). He becomes one with Spirit —"enthroned, never again to be removed"—never again to come down to the painful sphere of body identification.

Even in the fourth state of the primary ecstasy, complete liberation from physical and mental pain is not possible, owing to the soul's being conscious of the body and manipulated by its faculties as soon as any diminution occurs in the yogi's perception of divine bliss. The highly advanced yogi may experience brief periods of *nirvikalpa* consciousness (*asamprajnata*) even before becoming permanently established in that state.

Nirvikalpa samadhi: permanent extinguishment of suffering

CLEAR CATEGORICAL DISTINCTIONS are not always possible in defining the yogi's experiences and realizations, for they may be an intermixture of states or a matter of degree, depending on the quality and object of his meditation. For example, a person may point to a leaf in a painting and say, for all practical purposes, it is green; but an artist would more accurately describe it as a mixture of yellow and blue, expressing more or less of either one or the other pigment. Similarly, the term *yoga* or divine union is applicable to various stages of realization, but its ultimate meaning is absolute union with Spirit; *absolute* union is the *permanent* establishment of the consciousness in *nirvikalpa* or *asamprajnata samadhi.* Thus, for purposes of comparison, the true or ultimate *nirvikalpa* state (the state "without difference") is when the yogi is permanently and irrevocably united to God in both the meditative and the physically active spheres of consciousness, as contrasted with intermittent experiences of this state.

When the soul of the yogi is forever united in *nirvikalpa samadhi* to Spirit, it cannot again experience any physical or mental suffering. This state is spoken of in Sankhya philosophy as the "permanent extinguishment" or "uprooting" of all physical, mental, and spiritual causes of suffering.

The true definition of yoga is given in these stanzas. The purpose of yoga is to furnish a practical means for uniting the body-identified ego or pseudosoul with the true Spirit-identified soul. Yoga also means the complete union of the soul with the Spirit—the Source from which it emanated.

IN THE TWENTY-THIRD STANZA, every spiritual seeker is advised to practice yoga, not in a haphazard or depressed state of mind, but with great enthusiasm and perseverance. He should try undauntedly to unite his ego with his soul and his soul with Spirit, until he reaches the final Beatitude in which the soul is never again to be separated from Spirit. The reincarnation-making past seeds of good and bad action are forever roasted in the all-consuming fire of ultimate wisdom.

The Gita points out the impossibility of attaining satisfaction by practicing yoga methods desultorily. Every yogi should joyfully try to make his daily meditation deeper than the previous day's meditation; his yoga practice of tomorrow should always be deeper than the one of today.

Make today's meditation deeper than yesterday's, and tomorrow's deeper than today's

Again, the yogi should not be satisfied by deep meditations for one or two years, but should practice yoga with ever-increasing intensity to the end of his life, and for incarnations if necessary! Better it is to try to be free in one life or in a few lives than to undergo the suffering of thousands of incarnations, owing to lack of continuous efforts for salvation. The yogi who is not determined to meditate until final emancipation is achieved (by the removal of all seeds of karma lodged in the subconsciousness) is apt to be discouraged and to give up his yoga practice because he has not quickly found the ultimate state. He should, however, intensely meditate without concentrating on the fruits of his actions. The following story will encourage laborious disheartened yogis.

A man planted a flower seed in his garden. He looked after it, steadfastly weeding and watering the soil around it. A robust plant appeared—but, for years, no flower. He thought of destroying the plant, but finally decided: "My business is to look after the plant; it is for God to produce the flower. I will keep myself busy in tending the plant and not in concentrating on my flowerless labors." Years passed; he contented himself with the care of the plant and forgot all about the flower. One sunny morning, when a breeze was gently blowing, he smelled a strangely attractive fragrance. He ran to his plant and stood speechless in joy—there in front of him was the gorgeous flower! The aromatic beauty had always been present in the plant, a hidden potential awaiting the right moment of blossoming made possible by his labor of love.

The yogi should similarly keep himself busy nurturing his plant of Self-realization; if he is not impatient, he will find (one day when God in His infinite wisdom deems it proper) the amaranthine flower of eternal freedom.

VERSE 24

saṁkalpaprabhavān kāmāṁs tyaktvā sarvān aśeṣataḥ
manasaivendriyagrāmaṁ viniyamya samantataḥ

Relinquish without exception all longings born of sankalpas (plannings), and completely control, sheerly with the mind, the sensory organs, the sensory powers, and their contact with the ubiquitous sense objects.

TO REACH THE INNER SANCTUM of God, the yogi should race his inwardly marching attention so that it is not seized by the bandits of outer sensations or by the stronger villains of overpowering restless thoughts and desires that lurk in the path of concentration.

The yogi, while meditating upon God, should not distract his attention by allowing himself to ruminate on material objects, mentally planning and replanning material activities for the fulfillment of desired ends. He should renounce without reserve all such desires born of egoistic mental plannings; and he should scoop out from within all desires that are already entrenched in the subconscious. His mind should be withdrawn from those material objects all around him that give rise to sensations of sight, hearing, smell, taste, and touch, and their resultant multifarious thoughts and new longings.

When the mind is singularly concentrated in meditation, all distractions are arrested. But until such interiorization is mastered, the devotee must persistently practice mind control; and he should also take commonsense measures to eliminate, or at least minimize, invasive external stimuli.

All beginner yogis should therefore close their eyes during meditation, shutting off all distracting sights. It is also good for them to meditate in quiet surroundings; in certain techniques, such as meditation on *Aum*, it is advised to practice with ears closed.* These precautions help to eliminate sounds—the most distracting of all sensations. The yogi should be careful, also, to meditate in a place devoid of extreme heat or cold, and of pervasive good or bad odors, lest his senses of touch and smell be stimulated. A place frequented by such tormentors as mosquitoes or ants should be avoided. Nor should the meditator keep in his mouth spices or chewing gum, or other such stimuli that excite gustatory sensations, which in turn might cause mental diversion.

When the senses are quiet, sensations are not aroused; distracted thoughts do not arise. When thoughts do not arise, subconscious thoughts do not spring up. The yogi who is careful to remove all causes of external and inner disturbances can easily concentrate within.

VERSE 25

śanaiḥ śanair uparamed buddhyā dhṛtigṛhītayā
ātmasaṁsthaṁ manaḥ kṛtvā na kiṁcid api cintayet

With the intuitive discrimination saturated in patience, with the mind absorbed in the soul, the yogi, freeing his mind from all thoughts, will by slow degrees attain tranquility.

THE YOGI WHOSE MIND has been freed from external and internal distractions is then advised to guide his intuitive discrimination (*buddhi* in its pure or sense-transcendent state) gradually inward to perceive the soul's bliss, not permitting any form of mental wandering. No matter how often the yogi's mind is distracted during meditation, he should exercise great patience; by continuous daily effort, he will succeed in establishing his mind on the joy of the soul.

The new devotee may be discouraged by receiving only occasional blissful perceptions, interrupted constantly by fierce invasions of restless thoughts. The yogi is therefore exhorted to try patiently again and again until he is able firmly to fix his concentration on his inward Goal.

---

* By pressing the thumbs on the tragi of the ears, the openings are blocked, preventing the entry of sounds.

If a glass vessel is filled with muddy water and is then placed on a table, after a little while the mud particles settle down to the bottom of the glass. Similarly, if a person patiently waits for his mental mud to settle down, and does not nervously stir up the water, the mud will not again rise to the surface.

The particles in a glass of water will be clearly seen to be settling down to the bottom if the glass is not disturbed. The movements of the mud do not indicate agitation, but a mere settling-down process.

The ordinary man's mind, similarly, is muddy with myriads of restless thought-streams running into the river of his consciousness. During ordinary activity the invading thoughts are completely homogenized with his consciousness. This is why the average man does not know how restless he is. He discovers it, to his dismay, when he starts to practice yoga. For the first time in his life, he begins then to stand aside as a conscious witness of the bewildering torrent of his thoughts. He may become erroneously convinced that his mind is made more restless by yoga than by worldly activities!

Such a beginner yogi, watching aghast his unsettled and disobedient thoughts, is cautioned in this stanza not to abandon meditation in despair, thus denying himself all chance of mind control. Rather, he should patiently await the settling-down of his restless thoughts. Their commotion is just a prelude to their dissolution by yoga. The undiscouraged yogi will find his mind finally free from all distractions. Gradually identifying himself with his "witnessing" intuitive discrimination, adroitly bypassing the intruders of restless thoughts, the yogi attains the unshakable divine tranquility.

VERSE 26

yato yato niścarati manaś cañcalam asthiram
tatas tato niyamyaitad ātmany eva vaśaṁ nayet

Whenever the fickle and restless mind wanders away—for whatever reason—let the yogi withdraw it from those distractions and return it to the sole control of the Self.

THIS ADVICE IS FOR THE NEW YOGI on how to cope with the unruly distracting thoughts that arise—for some reason or for no reason!—when he sits to meditate.

When a horse pulling a carriage tugs hard at the reins, through unruliness or fright, and tries to bolt from the path, an experienced driver will be able to subdue the animal. It requires the skill of both firmness and kindly patience. Similarly, as often as the subconsciously excited "stallion" of a restless thought pulls the concentrating mind off on a tangent, the "charioteer" of discrimination should make repeated efforts to establish its authority.

No matter how many times restlessness invades the mind, the yogi should guide his thoughts toward Self-realization. Mental restlessness during meditation causes unhappiness. Inner concentration on the soul produces unending joy.

VERSE 27

praśāntamanasaṁ hy enaṁ yoginaṁ sukham uttamam
upaiti śāntarajasaṁ brahmabhūtam akalmaṣam

The yogi who has completely calmed the mind and controlled the passions and freed them from all impurities,* and who is one with Spirit—verily, he has attained supreme blessedness.

THIS STANZA POINTS OUT that the successful devotee, by repeated mental efforts to destroy restlessness, has overcome all obstacles in the path of yoga. By interiorized concentration, he has stilled the mind, disconnecting it from sensory stimuli, and has also controlled the passions (*rajas*),† the activated and activating emotional responses to sensory stimuli. All activities of nature are a result of *rajas,* the activating quality (*guna*) of material creation. *Rajas* is either good or evil according to which of the other *gunas*—*sattva* or *tamas*—predominates in that activity. The nature-born dualities of good and evil are the "impurities" from which the soul must be freed in order to express its true nature. When the activating power in the mind is stilled by con-

---

* Literally, "*he* is freed from all impurities." The yogi himself is said to be free from all impurities when first the activities of the mind and its passions are stilled by concentration and thereby freed from the taint of dualities.

† Significantly, the Sanskrit word *rajas* used in this stanza to mean "passion" is the same word that is used for the activating aspect of *triguna,* the three qualities operative in nature: *sattva, rajas,* and *tamas.* Whatever is "activating" in nature has as its essence the *guna* of *rajas*.

centration, unruly thoughts wane into nothingness, and all restlessness ceases. The yogi becomes absorbed in the transcendent bliss of the soul, free from all taint of relativities. Owing to the lack of activity (cessation of responses of the mind to external stimuli, and subsequent stilling of inner restlessness), the yogi attains a deep interiorized state of *samadhi* in which his blissful oneness with Spirit is accompanied by bodily fixation.

VERSE 28

yuñjann evaṁ sadātmānaṁ yogī vigatakalmaṣaḥ
sukhena brahmasaṁsparśam atyantaṁ sukham aśnute

The yogi, free from all impurities, ceaselessly engaging the Self thus in the activity of yoga (divine union), readily attains the blessedness of continuous mergence in Spirit.

THE TWENTY-SEVENTH STANZA CITED THE YOGI who becomes free from the dualities of good and evil by forcibly holding the mind in the inactive state of ecstasy; the twenty-eighth stanza now speaks of the yogi who remains free, the enjoyer of cosmic bliss, during the state of activity also—when his mind returns to its normal external functions.

The yogi who at will can perceive the Spirit, in the state of ecstasy without bodily activity, ultimately learns to retain his infinite consciousness during the performance of actions. Every yogi should therefore refuse to succumb to the invasions of restlessness during meditation. When he is able to hold his concentration steady in the state of inner calmness, he perceives the soul. By further perseverance he enters into ecstatic bliss and realizes the Spirit. The fully accomplished yogi can move about in the world of relativity unstained by its dualities, remaining steadfastly in the blessed state of *Brahma-samsparsha,* the bliss of the touch of Spirit.

MERGENCE OF THE SELF IN SPIRIT, PERVADING ALL BEINGS

VERSE 29

sarvabhūtastham ātmānaṁ sarvabhūtāni cātmani
īkṣate yogayuktātmā sarvatra samadarśanaḥ

With the soul united to Spirit by yoga, with a vision of equality for all things, the yogi beholds his Self (Spirit-united) in all creatures and all creatures in the Spirit.

AFTER DESCRIBING IN STANZAS 27–28 how a yogi, in his inactive and active states, can perceive the Divine, the Bhagavad Gita refers in stanza 29 to the God-knowing saint who is free from all karma and material delusions because he realizes "all things" as naught else than Spirit.

The liberated yogi is conscious of the Spirit not only as Cosmic Bliss but also as the Cosmic Light that is the true structure of all beings. Beholding everything as Cosmic Light, the yogi sees his Spirit-united omnipresent Self and all beings as emanations of that Light.*

VERSE 30

yo māṁ paśyati sarvatra sarvaṁ ca mayi paśyati
tasyāhaṁ na praṇaśyāmi sa ca me na praṇaśyati

He who perceives Me everywhere and beholds everything in Me never loses sight of Me, nor do I ever lose sight of him.

THE DIVINE LOVER BEHOLDS GOD through every window of thought and space, and the Cosmic Beloved beholds the devotee through every

* "When there is duality because of ignorance, one sees all things as distinct from the Self. When everything is known as the Self, not even an atom is seen as other than the Self.... As soon as knowledge of Reality has sprung up, there can be no fruits of past actions to be experienced, owing to the unreality of the body, just as there can be no dream after awakening."—*Swami Shankara* (*Publisher's Note*)

window of His omnipresent love. Enlocked in visions of love, God and the devotee enjoy unparted union.

After uniting his soul to God, the yogi may still maintain the dual relation—the liberated devotee, and God as the Object of adoration.

This stanza of the Gita definitely points out that the illumined yogi does not lose the individuality of his soul; instead he finds his being extended into the Being of the Spirit. An ordinary person perceives himself as separate from God. The advanced yogi feels his soul as a wave in the ocean of Cosmic Consciousness. But the completely liberated yogi beholds his soul-wave as a manifestation of the Cosmic Ocean. Such a yogi never says, "I am God," for he knows God can exist without his soul; but, if he wants to, he can say: "God has become myself."

The soul of the emancipated yogi can remain merged, if he wishes, in the Absolute, as the Absolute. Or the liberated yogi, owing to the retention of his God-created individuality (which can never be lost), may remain or reappear in the physical body in which he was liberated, in order to worship God in any personal concept (such as Father–Mother–Friend–Beloved God), or in any desired materialized form (such as one of the deities, or as incarnate in one of the avatars such as Christ or Sri Krishna), or as the All-Pervading Infinite.

This stanza stresses the state of duality that may exist between the devotee and God. The liberated devotee can watch God through every open niche of space, as the Spirit can look at him through every pore of the sky. Such a liberated yogi never loses sight of God nor does God ever lose sight of him. The True Lover is God; we are all His beloveds, mistakenly seeking love in impermanent human beings. The thirst for affection can never be quenched by the imperfect love of mortals. When the devotee, by the practice of loving mortals truly, learns to love all beings, and by meditation learns to love God supremely, then and then only is his longing for love satisfied.

Every man who leaves the earth in an embittered state of unrequited love has to come back here until he finds the perfect love of God. When he recognizes the Lord as the only Perfect Lover, his heart seeks no other affection. After many prodigal wanderings the yogi meets the Cosmic Lover in the bower of eternity. Wherever the yogi turns his attention, he sees his Beloved peeping at him through the windows of stars and flowers, through every opening in the atoms and the pores of the sky. The Cosmic Lover similarly beholds the lost-and-found soul of the yogi steadfastly looking at Him.

To the ordinary person, God seems to be absent or vanished from the universe. But the yogi sees the ever-watching Eye of God gazing at him through all windows of space; the face of his Cosmic Beloved is omnipresent.

VERSE 31

sarvabhūtasthitaṁ yo māṁ bhajaty ekatvam āsthitaḥ
sarvathā vartamāno 'pi sa yogī mayi vartate

That yogi stays forever in Me, who, anchored in divine unity whatever his mode of existence, realizes Me as pervading all beings.

THE YOGI MUST REALIZE THE COSMIC drama as God's dream motion-picture, projected on the screen of space and man's consciousness by the infinite cosmic beam of Spirit. Then he can everywhere behold God's light, no matter what part he plays in this movie of delusive shadows and divine light.

The ordinary individual looks upon the world as made of matter, but the yogi who by ecstasy has united his soul with the Spirit perceives the Absolute Cosmic Consciousness and also Its manifestation as the Cosmic Dream to be made of one Substance. When a dreamer partially wakes up in the middle of his dream, he realizes that his consciousness and the objects in the dream are made of the same substance—his own mind. The yogi awakened in God can similarly perceive all the earthly dream-objects in the so-called material world to be woven of the consciousness of God. It is in this state that the yogi realizes Unity everywhere; he perceives not only that God dwells in all beings, but that all beings are His manifestations. The yogi dissolves all dual perceptions of matter and mind into the sole perception of Cosmic Consciousness.

A yogi who is awake in God is ever united with Him, whether in life or death, whether in this world of activity or in any other mode of existence.

A yogi who has once awakened himself from this cosmic dream can no longer sleep in delusion like the ordinary man. In the subconscious state of slumber or in the conscious state of existence or in the superconsciousness of ecstasy, that yogi remains aware of God as the Creator and Dreamer of all.

VERSE 32

ātmaupamyena sarvatra samaṁ paśyati yo 'rjuna
sukhaṁ vā yadi vā duḥkhaṁ sa yogī paramo mataḥ

O Arjuna, the best type of yogi is he who feels for others, whether in grief or pleasure, even as he feels for himself.

A PERSON IDENTIFIED WITH THE BODY feels its pain and happiness as his own. A yogi who is one with God knows the cosmos to be his own body. Feeling the afflictions and joys of all beings as his own, he tries to decrease their suffering and to increase their true happiness.

God manifesting as cosmic consciousness in the devotee relates through his intuition the following wisdom:

An ordinary man selfishly perceives pleasure and pain only in connection with his own body. But the yogi who is identified with God perceives Him everywhere—in both animate and inanimate worlds. His mind is expanded in Cosmic Consciousness.

As not a sparrow falls outside the sight of God, so the yogi who is one with the Father is conscious simultaneously of the smallest and the greatest happenings in the universe. A devotee who perceives God in all beings feels naturally, as his own, the pleasures and pains of other beings. He wishes evil to none and tries to do good to all. The accomplished yogi is conscious of God alone. When he seemingly identifies himself with his body and outward works he appears like an ordinary mortal, but within himself he always retains the consciousness of the Ever Blessed Lord.

The yogi who is free even while feeling the pleasures and pains of his body is one who can retain God-consciousness. Further, he feels the pleasures and pains of others; yet, beyond all experiences of duality, he realizes the cosmic blessedness of God ever transcendentally existent. Such a yogi tries to help others to realize God and to rise above the alternations of pain and pleasure born of body identification.

THE LORD'S PROMISE: THE PERSEVERING YOGI ULTIMATELY IS VICTORIOUS

VERSE 33

arjuna uvāca
yo 'yaṁ yogastvayā proktaḥ sāmyena madhusūdana
etasyāhaṁ na paśyāmi cañcalatvāt sthitiṁ sthirām

Arjuna said:

O Madhusudana (Krishna), owing to my restlessness, I do not behold the permanent enduring effect of the equalizing yoga that Thou hast related to me.

AT TIMES THE YOGI FEELS HIS invading restlessness to be stronger than the restlessness-dissolving power of yoga; he should then patiently pray to God until that intoxication of delusive habit wears off and he becomes free.

Arjuna, the devotee, prays within: "O God, Thou slayer of Madhu, the demon of ignorance! the yoga that I have been practicing has given me some tranquility; yet I do not see its lasting benefit! Restlessness still invades my mind."

The novice yogi, even after repeatedly experiencing peace during the practice of yoga, may yet be confronted by restless thoughts suddenly springing to the surface of consciousness from long-hidden subconscious sources. This invasion should not influence the yogi to abandon yoga through disbelief in its power to produce a lasting tranquility. He will find that the subconscious habits of restlessness will gradually cease to appear in a mind that becomes strongly fortified by the habit of meditation.

O yogi! if by one or two divings into the ocean of divine perception you do not find the pearls of God-communion, do not blame the ocean as lacking in the Divine Presence! Rather find fault with your skill in diving! Again and again sink into the ocean of meditation and seize there the pearls of blessed communion!

In this stanza we find even an ideal devotee like Arjuna (who has many times experienced the perfect calmness and equilibrium of yoga) to be harboring doubts about the ability of yoga permanently to banish mental disharmony—instead of finding fault with the quality of his own meditations.

VERSE 34

cañcalaṁ hi manaḥ kṛṣṇa pramāthi balavad dṛḍham
tasyāhaṁ nigrahaṁ manye vāyor iva suduṣkaram

Verily, the mind is unsteady, tumultuous, powerful, obstinate! O Krishna, I consider the mind as difficult to master as the wind!

THE DEVOTEE IN DEEP DESPAIR SAYS: "O Krishna, how may one control the mind, which is ever restless like the volatile breath in spite of yoga practice?" When the bad habit of restlessness is conquered by the stronger habit of tranquility that is acquired by patient, enthusiastic, long-continued yoga practice, the devotee finally finds the answer to his question.

The yogi who has often experienced the divine bliss of meditation should remain watchful against the sudden appearance of material desires and worldly moods. Care should be observed lest the devotee stop practicing yoga through the influence of misleading subconscious impulses that mar tranquility and arouse interest in material pleasures. Instead of giving strength to his abnormal nature of restlessness, the yogi should strive to recall his true quiescent nature as manifested during yoga practice, and should strengthen it by deeper meditation.

Arjuna compares the mind to the wind. Here the deeper meaning of "wind" is breath; for the changeableness and waywardness of the human mind is ineluctably bound up with man's breathing patterns. The glory of India's ancient sages is that they discovered the liberating truth: to control the breath is to control the mind.

The ordinary man may try unsuccessfully to restrain his breath by unscientifically holding it in the lungs. The *Kriya Yogi*, on the other hand, is able to oxygenate his blood scientifically and thus to remove from it most of the carbon dioxide; he requires little breath. His is the real way of controlling the breath.

It is impossible to control the breath by the unscientific way of holding it in the lungs. The discomfort of forcibly withholding the breath proves that the act is injurious to health. During the forcible withholding of the breath in the lungs the oxygen is used up, resulting in a greater accumulation of carbon dioxide in the air tubes. This causes pressure, discomfort, and pain in the lungs. No one should hold the breath in the lungs to the point of discomfort.

Similarly, the ordinary man who tries forcibly to control the mind finds himself unsuccessful. But when he practices the scientific method of *Kriya Yoga* and learns to withdraw his life force from the five sense-telephones, his mind is automatically freed from sensations and from the conscious and subconscious thoughts accruing from those sensations.

The aspirant should not be discouraged by initial failure in the most difficult art of mind control. By scientific yoga the beginner finds the right way to free the mind from all conscious and subconscious restlessness. Of course, much depends on one's intensity, zeal, and continuity. These will help the mind to grow into the habit of peace and to rise above the unnatural mortal habit of restlessness that is rooted in the identification of consciousness with the bodily senses.

VERSES 35–36

śrībhagavān uvāca
asaṁśayaṁ mahābāho mano durnigrahaṁ calam
abhyāsena tu kaunteya vairāgyeṇa ca gṛhyate (35)

asaṁyatātmanā yogo duṣprāpa iti me matiḥ
vaśyātmanā tu yatatā śakyo 'vāptum upāyataḥ (36)

The blessed Lord said:
(35) O Mahabaho ("mighty-armed" Arjuna), undoubtedly the mind is fickle and unruly; but by yoga practice and by dispassion, O Son of Kunti (Arjuna), the mind may nevertheless be controlled.

(36) This is My word: Yoga is difficult of attainment by the ungoverned man; but he who is self-controlled will, by striving through proper methods, be able to achieve it.

IT IS NATURAL FOR PEOPLE WHO constantly indulge in restless habits to become more restless; similarly it is natural for calm devotees, those who perseveringly practice the proper methods of yoga, to become more divinely tranquil.

The real nature of the soul as ever new bliss develops, instead, a powerful eclipsing "second nature" of restlessness when identified with the body. In that state it is "natural" for the mind to be boisterous and unruly. Yet, by yoga practice, when the mind contacts the soul's bliss and becomes disengaged from the short-lived sense pleasures, the consciousness of the devotee again displays its true restful divine nature. Man has not to acquire, but to remember, the soul joy within.

In response to the prayer of the ideal devotee Arjuna, his God-incarnate guru, Krishna, revealed to him the following wisdom, applicable to all yogis:

"O mighty-armed devotee, made in the image of Spirit! no doubt the mind is restless and difficult to control! But there are two ways to subdue it. First: By meditation and ecstasy the mind must be taught to regain its natural power of abiding in the soul's tranquil state. Second: At the same time, the mind must be dispassionately disengaged from desires for pleasures of this world and of the hereafter—desires that stimulate the mind to restlessness."

In other words, the yogi should revive by daily deep yoga practice the memory of soul tranquility, and should simultaneously keep the mind away from external and internal temptations. He cannot permanently feel the joy of his soul in meditation if he does not sever his desireful ties with the sensory environment.

The yogi must learn to win the tug-of-war between soul perception and sense perception. In the initial state of yoga practice the devotee is aware of the gripping influence of sense pleasures even though they are short-lasting, but he is little aware of the permanent, unending bliss secreted in his soul. The discriminating yogi will therefore find it natural that the habits of sense pleasures gathered from incarnations will be of stronger influence than his fleeting glimpses of soul bliss perceived during meditation. But he will also realize that even though habits of sense pleasures are very strong, they are not stronger than is the eternal perception of divine bliss present in the soul—the inextinguishable inheritance from Spirit.

The yogi should not stimulate his material habits by remaining, through choice, in unspiritual environments and by merely dreaming of the heavenly joys of sainthood. By staying away from worldly-pleasure-reminding environments and by relinquishing sense attractions, the yogi is better able to concentrate on the divine bliss of the soul. As a naughty boy should be removed from a restless environment and kept, instead, in the company of a calm friend, so the yogi should remove his restless mind from sense entanglements and keep it concentrated on soul perceptions.

The "practice of yoga" (*abhyasa*) is defined as repeated inner and outer efforts to remain in the eternal tranquility of the soul. "Dispassion" (*vairagya*) is the act of disengaging the mind from all forms of sensory pleasures as found in this world or to be found in heaven (the astral realms). Many persons believe paradise (as described in the scriptures) to be a place where they can enjoy unlimited, glorified sensory pleasures. The yogi is warned to keep his mind away from everything that reminds him of impermanent worldly joys and that causes him to forget the everlasting bliss of his soul.

VERSES 37–39

arjuna uvāca
ayatiḥ śraddhayopeto yogāccalitamānasaḥ
aprāpya yogasaṁsiddhiṁ kāṁ gatiṁ kṛṣṇa gacchati (37)

kaccin nobhayavibhraṣṭaś chinnābhram iva naśyati
apratiṣṭho mahābāho vimūḍho brahmaṇaḥ pathi (38)

etan me saṁśayaṁ kṛṣṇa chettum arhasy aśeṣataḥ
tvadanyaḥ saṁśayasyāsya chettā na hy upapadyate (39)

Arjuna said:
(37) O Krishna! what happens to a person unsuccessful in yoga—one who has devotedly tried to meditate but has been unable to control himself because his mind kept running away during yoga practice?

(38) Doesn't the yogi perish like a sundered cloud if he finds not the way to Brahman (Spirit)—being thus unsheltered in Him and steeped in delusion, sidetracked from both paths (the one of God-union and the one of right activities)?*

* Reference to the two paths cited in the first verse of this chapter, in which the yogi was described as he who follows primarily the path of ecstatic meditation for God-union; and the renunciant as he who follows the path of inner renunciation, performing dutiful and meditative actions but without attachment to or desire for their fruits. The meditative yogi who is nonattached and the active devotee of inner renunciation who

(39) Please remove forever all my doubts, O Krishna! for none save Thee may banish my uncertainties.

THE DISCOURAGED DEVOTEE in deepest prayer resorts to God as the mighty Cosmic Physician who alone is able to cure the deep-seated disease of material doubts.

Not all yogis in their present lifetimes realize their Goal just because they practice a yoga technique. There are two kinds of unsuccessful yogis. One type practices yoga with deep enthusiasm in the beginning but afterward relaxes his efforts. His initial enthusiasm carries him along with relative ease for a time; but because he lacks perfect nonattachment, as soon as he allows any slack in his self-discipline he experiences strong resistance from his past bad habits that were only temporarily subdued. The second type of unsuccessful yogi continues to meditate regularly and with devotion almost to the end of his life—even attaining a high degree of advancement. Shortly before death, however, owing to some past bad karma or to present indulgence in bad company or to egotistical spiritual pride, the yogi loses his steady concentration on the soul's bliss, and thus fails to attain the final divine union.

An unsuccessful yogi often feels that he is like a cloud dispersed by the wind, unable to quench the thirst of himself or others by a rainfall of wisdom. He realizes he has strayed away from the path leading to God. He bemoans the fact that he is not established in Him. He feels that he is deluded, unable to ascertain his real duty in life. Such a discouraged devotee allows himself to be diverted from seeking union with God attained by following—with uncompromising determination—the path of right action (both dutiful and meditative actions); or (if he is a more advanced yogi) from becoming permanently established in God-union by securing himself in the highest ecstasy of unceasing contact with Spirit.

VERSE 40

śrībhagavān uvāca
pārtha naiveha nāmutra vināśas tasya vidyate
na hi kalyāṇakṛt kaścid durgatiṁ tāta gacchati

---

meditates are both ideal yogis, pursuing a path to God-union. The present verse addresses the fate of such yogis who have not been wholly successful in their endeavors.

The blessed Lord said:

O Arjuna, My son! a performer of good actions never meets destruction. Whether in this world or in the beyond, he falls not into evil plight!

ARJUNA HERE RECEIVES A WONDERFUL reply from the Divine Preceptor. The words stand as a monument of inspiration to all sincere yogis who have failed to unite their souls with God because of obstructions arising from prenatal and postnatal actions, but who have nevertheless persisted in their spiritual efforts.

A man who does not seek divine union remains steeped in ignorance; his "evil plight" is to be a target for all kinds of physical, mental, and spiritual suffering. A person totally identified with sense pleasures has no chance to get even a glimpse through the gate of eternal freedom.

The fate of a sense addict is comparable, in a way, to that of the musk deer. At a certain age a navel sac of the deer bursts and exudes a fragrant musk substance. Frantically seeking the origin of the perfume, the deer sniffs wildly in every direction; not finding any external source of fragrance, the creature destroys itself by mad dashes among the rocks. Alas! if the deer had only put its nostrils to its navel! The sense addict, similarly, seeking the fragrance of bliss in every place except the soul, perishes in trying to find pleasure. Had he concentrated his attention within, he would have discovered the longed-for happiness.

It would indeed be unnatural for a person to find pleasure in feeding somebody else as often as he himself felt hungry; he would soon starve. The materialist, similarly, caters to the pleasures of his senses while his ego remains starved without divine bliss. His mistaken habit is to feed the senses in the hope of satisfying the inner hunger for happiness.

The yogi sublimates sense cravings into hunger for soul joy

The yogi, on the contrary, devotes himself to those good actions that sublimate the unnatural hunger for sense pleasure into the natural hunger for the soul's joy. The fallen yogi who has occasionally succeeded in experiencing the superior bliss of his soul cannot forget it; he well knows there is no comparison between ever new divine joy and the gross pleasures of the senses. Even a single taste of divine bliss through ecstasy, as attained by *Kriya Yoga* practice, will serve as a high incentive for more earnest spiritual efforts.

God gives encouragement in this stanza to all devotees to seek their natural divine inheritance. Soul joy, no matter how elusive, is every man's forgotten heritage. The sense addict who continues reveling in material pleasures, disregarding the counsel of the prophets, drifts farther and farther away from his true nature. The imperfect yogi, in spite of failures, tries to regain his memory of divinity. Therefore, even a fallen yogi is far superior to the materialist. The former is on the threshold of awakening from sense delusions; the latter is still asleep in ignorance. It is thus far better to be even a brokenhearted fallen yogi than to be a complacent sense addict.

NO MATTER HOW MANY TIMES a sincere yogi falls down in the path of yoga, he struggles again toward his Goal. The devotee who performs meritorious actions develops divine memory and good karma that impel him to seek liberation in this life or in the beyond. The memory of the divine bliss of yoga practice remains lodged in his subconscious mind. If he is not able to find full liberation in one life, in his next incarnation the hidden memory of his past experiences of yoga sprouts forth in spiritual inclinations even in his infancy.

All souls, no matter how many times they fall, will ultimately be rescued

The fallen yogi should never be driven to despair by failures; instead, he should be glad that he possesses sufficient spiritual fortitude to make the yoga effort. All his good inclinations and divine experiences of the past will be causes for further spiritual development in the next life.

The money-mad person, in spite of lifelong failures, continues to seek wealth; the sense addict, heedless of present or future miseries, repeats his indulgences in evils; the "dope fiend" does not give up narcotics even when warned of certain death. The wise man, similarly, is as stubborn in maintaining good habits as the ignorant man is in evil. Right stubbornness is born of divine stability.

It is greater to try unsuccessfully to find God than not to try at all. The trial must come before any possibility of fulfillment. Even if unsuccessful, one should continue endeavoring to the end of his life; in the after-death state he is blessed by the fruits of his efforts, and he will start his next incarnation with divine aspirations instead of with a dull, undisciplined consciousness.

An imperfect yogi should remember that man's relation with God is that of a son who may demand and receive what he asks from his own Father—not that of a beggar who, in response to an appeal, may or may not receive a beggar's pittance.

In this stanza God assures man through His son Arjuna that all His persevering children-devotees, no matter how many times they have stumbled in the path of yoga, shall finally be rescued. The Christian Bible similarly says: "Ask, and it shall be given you; seek, and ye shall find; knock, and it shall be opened unto you."*

VERSE 41

prāpya puṇyakṛtāṁ lokān uṣitvā śāśvatīḥ samāḥ
śucīnāṁ śrīmatāṁ gehe yogabhraṣṭo 'bhijāyate

A fallen yogi, gaining entry to the world of the virtuous, remains there for many years; afterward he is reborn on earth in a good and prosperous home.

ADVANCED YOGIS WHO HAVE not attained the final perfection get an opportunity to live a prolonged afterlife on beautiful astral planets. At the expiration of a certain karmic period, they are reborn on earth in families of righteous and prosperous people in order to enjoy simultaneously both spiritual and material happiness and thus to march toward liberation.

In stanzas 37–39, two kinds of unsuccessful, or "fallen," yogis are described: (1) those who have not found full liberation because of insufficient yoga practice and imperfect nonattachment; such devotees have allowed themselves to become diverted through the slackening of spiritual effort and by yielding to sense temptations; and (2) those accomplished yogis who, owing to the appearance of some hidden bad karma or egoistic tendency just before death, become confused and do not achieve complete liberation. Though highly advanced and on the threshold of liberation, these two kinds of unsuccessful yogis failed to make the final effort in yoga that would have opened the portal to freedom. Thus are they referred to as "fallen," having slipped backward momentarily; thereby removing themselves from the present opportunity for liberation.

In stanza 41, the Lord describes how the first type (the lukewarm yogi-failures) fares in the next world. Such yogis visit other planets inhabited by the virtuous and stay there happily so long as their meritorious karma holds out.

Jesus Christ said: "In my Father's house are many mansions,"† signifying that the universe created by God has many inhabited planets

* Matthew 7:7. † John 14:2.

in the physical, astral, and causal cosmoses. God's cosmic consciousness projected various subdivisional abodes within the three spheres of His universal creation.

Advanced but still imperfect yogis who are disappointed in this world are given a chance to experience the happiness available in the bright astral spheres, or are allowed to reincarnate on other planets of the physical universe that boast better conditions of existence than does our earth.

ASTRONOMERS KNOW THAT THE EARTH belongs to a certain galaxy and that many other island universes float in an infinitude of circular space.* Someday other inhabited physical planets will be discovered; there will be interplanetary communication and travel. The horse-carriage riders of past centuries could not imagine the existence of modern planes that travel in the stratosphere at supersonic speeds. Inventions of atomic-energy-powered planes moving with incredible speed will make obsolete all present-day airplanes. The snail with its slow motion cannot expect to go around the globe during its lifetime; but an airplane can encircle the earth in a few hours. Today we cannot travel even to the comparatively close moon;† but atomic-energy-powered planes will someday enable us quickly to reach distant planets.

---

* See also X:30, page 796. Scientists estimate that there are some 100 billion galaxies in the observable universe. The earth belongs to the Milky Way galaxy, which comprises approximately 300 billion stars, one of which is our own sun. In the entire observable universe there are thought to be a staggering billion trillion (10^{21}) stars.

At this time, scientists can only speculate as to how many of these stars might have planets capable of sustaining life. An interesting discussion on the possibilities, based on logical deductive reasoning, has been put forth by the noted science author Dr. Isaac Asimov in his book *Extraterrestrial Civilizations* (New York: Crown Publishers, 1979): "After all, the existence of intelligence is not a near-zero probability matter since *we* exist. And if it *is* nearly a near-zero probability, considering that near-zero probability for each of a billion trillion stars makes it almost certain that somewhere among them intelligence and even technological civilizations exist. If, for instance, the probability were only one in a billion that near a given star there existed a technological civilization, that would mean that in the universe as a whole, a trillion different such civilizations would exist."

In 1995, observations from the newly launched Hubble Space Telescope provided much new information about the formation of stars and planets. According to Arizona State University astronomer Jeff Hester, quoted in *Time* magazine (June 19, 1995), the new observations "add an important clue to the already strong circumstantial case that planets are the rule rather than the exception in the Milky Way. It doesn't prove that there are extraterrestrials in the cosmos, but it does make their existence more plausible." (*Publisher's Note*)

† In 1969, twenty years after the writing of this passage, man took his first steps on the moon; space-age travel was born. (*Publisher's Note*)

Yogis who can dislodge their astral bodies from their physical casings can travel in the astral world much faster than the speed of light. They can move from planet to planet with incredible swiftness. They realize that the physical, astral, and causal bodies and the physical, astral, and causal universes are all dream condensations of God's thoughts. Such masters are able to resolve everything into divine thought; they can instantaneously traverse eternity with the speed of thought.

Time and space are categories and relativities of God's mind. A master, by his powerful thought, is able to annihilate time and space. Thought is the primary energy and vibration that emanated from God and is thus the creator of life, electrons, atoms, and all forms of energy. Thought itself is the finest vibratory energy, the speediest power among all powers. The vehicle of a great yogi's thought is powerful enough instantaneously to carry and cast a planet into the sun to be dissolved there, even as could God.

The yogi's after-death experiences in the astral world

As worms live in the soil, fish in the water, birds in the air, and man on the surface of this earth, so inhabitants of other physical worlds live under environmental influences far different from those of our planet. Beings who dwell on certain stars, for instance, absorb life energy directly; they do not breathe air like earthly beings. Many people erroneously imagine that no beings could live on a planet lacking in air. (Fish may think that no life is possible without the medium of water!) Just as certain bacteria can live in fiery environments, so there are beings who exist comfortably on planets that exude fiery energies.*

In the astral world, beings live by life force (*prana*) that is finer than electroprotonic or atomic energy. Life force is an intelligent energy, a cross between thought and energy. In the astral world all appearances are energy responses to the thoughts of the inhabitants; the astral scenes change according to the wishes of the astral beings.

The causal world is very fine-textured, superior to all physical and astral universes. Only the most advanced yogis can remain in the causal sphere, perceiving the subtle manifestations of the various

* Many years after Paramahansa Yogananda made this statement, scientists found microorganisms called hyperthermophilic archaebacteria in a variety of high-temperature environments previously thought to be incapable of supporting life—including the active zone of erupting volcanos (*Nature,* May 10, 1990) and in the extreme heat of deep-sea thermal vents. The upper temperature limit at which such organisms can survive has not yet been determined. (*Publisher's Note*)

thought planets in the causal (ideational) universe.

Fallen yogis, those who advanced and then became lukewarm in their spiritual efforts, feel tired of this earth plane because here they have failed to attain supreme realization. If they happen to die in that state of discontentment, they are drawn by their spiritual longings to harmonious astral worlds that offer temporary solace.

After living in such spheres, finding certain satisfactions for their discouraged desires, the imperfect yogis come back to earth, drawn by the force of their past mortal karma. Such confused yogi-failures are reborn in prosperous, pure families with whom they live in comfort and at the same time have the opportunity to seek and attain further spiritual progress. In this way they satisfy simultaneously their innate desires for sense pleasures and for salvation. This opportunity is justly afforded them because of good karma earned by their past-life yoga efforts.

VERSES 42–43

athavā yoginām eva kule bhavati dhīmatām
etad dhi durlabhataraṁ loke janma yad īdṛśam (42)

tatra taṁ buddhisaṁyogaṁ labhate paurvadehikam
yatate ca tato bhūyaḥ saṁsiddhau kurunandana (43)

(42) Or he may reincarnate in a family of enlightened yogis; verily, a birth like that is much harder to gain on this earth!

(43) There, O Arjuna, he recovers the yoga discrimination attained in his former existence, and tries more strenuously for spiritual success.

THE LORD HERE RELATES WHAT HAPPENS to the second kind of imperfect yogi, he who is closest to liberation (described in VI:37–39 commentary, page 643). When an advanced devotee is true to God to the end of his life and yet does not receive complete emancipation owing to the obstruction of some buried past karma, he receives a fresh, providential opportunity. He is not to be diverted and longer detained by astral splendors or by the luxuries of a carefree earthly environment like the first kind of fallen yogi. Rather, he is suitably rewarded by rebirth in the home of a great yogi who is also a family man. There in the company of his exalted parents he finds no incentive to seek sense pleasures but tries from his very infancy to achieve the final spiritual glory.

This kind of rebirth is very rare because few yogis marry after receiving divine illumination. Some perfected yogis enter the householder's life at God's command in order to supply worldly people with an example of a perfect marriage. Weak yogis who have lust in their hearts and who marry to satisfy secret desires for sense enjoyment are not great masters. Because the Lord seldom asks devotees to marry after they have found salvation, birth in a family of emancipated yogis is naturally a rare occurrence.

Shukadeva, the son of Vyasa, achieved birth in such a rare family. At the age of seven Shukadeva left his relatives to find a guru. His father followed him to ask him to return home; he felt he could give his son liberation. But the great son of the great father said, "Are you suffering from the delusion that I am your son? Though I know you could give me God-realization, still I prefer to seek it from a disinterested guru."

Vyasa smilingly admitted the truth in his son's surmise, and then directed Shukadeva to King Janaka of India, who was not only a monarch but a great yogi.

When the better type of fallen yogi is born amongst liberated saints, he finds his aspirations reinforced by the spirituality and example of his parents. They can transfer their God-consciousness to their child at will. He therefore quickly attains the final freedom.

The divine attainments of a yogi's past lives are everlastingly retained. All seeds of good karma are lodged in the cerebrum of the astral body; when they are watered by remembrances and by vibrations of a good environment in a new life, they sprout forth and grow into the infinite tree of liberation.

Stored-up good desires and experiences tending toward liberation are the great forces that impel a yogi to make supreme efforts to reach his Final Goal.

VERSE 44

pūrvābhyāsena tenaiva hriyate hy avaśo 'pi saḥ
jijñāsur api yogasya śabdabrahmātivartate

The power of former yoga practice is sufficient to force, as it were, the yogi on his onward path. An eager student of even theoretical yoga is farther advanced than is a follower of the outward scriptural rites.

AN ALTERNATIVE TRANSLATION of the second sentence of this verse uncovers its esoteric meaning in reference to the practice of yoga:

He who is eagerly desirous of realizing yoga-union with Spirit transcends the mere recitation of the word of Brahman—the sacred sound of Aum.

As past evil karma powerfully stimulates a man to indulge in sense pleasures, so strong past habits of God-communion compel a reincarnated yogi to seek divine union. Like a shooting star, that yogi crosses the skies of delusion and reaches his spiritual destination.

The spiritually inquisitive person who with sincere eagerness takes up the study of yoga, the science of sciences, receives more benefit than does the devotee who mechanically practices the exoteric ceremonies enjoined by the four Vedas (Rik, Yajur, Sama, and Atharva). The words of the Vedas or wisdom books are considered to be emanations of the omniscient sound of *Aum* (*shabda-brahman*). The great sages (*rishis*) heard the sounds and memorized them; later, the holy instructions were committed to paper.

A deep seeker knows that a mechanical performance of sacred ceremonies and religious rites, or the mere chanting of the word *Aum,* does not bring liberation; it is the person that communes with the *Aum* sound who is the real knower of the Vedas—and of all truth to be known. In fact, a body-identified person, one unable to commune with the Cosmic Sound, was not allowed in ancient times to read the Vedic scriptures. The Gita therefore points out here that the yogi who is spiritually inquiring will not be satisfied with outward rituals, but will seek a knowledge of yoga, first in theory and then in practice. By yoga techniques he will learn to contact the presence of God in creation through communion with His holy Word, or creative vibration; and merging with its omnipresence, he will find the Blessed Absolute existing beyond the curtains of vibratory phenomena.

VERSE 45

prayatnād yatamānas tu yogī saṁśuddhakilbiṣaḥ
anekajanmasaṁsiddhas tato yāti parāṁ gatim

By diligently following his path, the yogi, perfected by the efforts of many births, is purged of sin (karmic taint) and finally enters the Supreme Beatitude.

A GOOD YOGI IS HE WHO FOLLOWS the spiritual meditative path with gradually increasing speed and with nonattachment; with steady thoroughness he renounces material attachments; and with intense mental alacrity he seeks God-communion.

As the yogi proceeds in the path, he finds his mind passing through the various stages of concentration—of being once in a while calm and most of the time restless; of being half the time calm and half the time restless; of being nearly all the time calm and once in a while restless; of being all the time calm without ever being restless. When the yogi reaches the fourth or unchanging state, he finds his feeling free from dislikes and likes; the limiting effects of all his past actions have been removed by yoga practice.

A yogi cannot be sure of finding complete liberation just by acquiring the calm state. He must establish on that altar of ineffable peace the blissful Cosmic Presence.

If the yogi is not able to stabilize his communion with the Absolute on the altar of everlasting calmness, he may have to undergo a few or many incarnations of divine contact, in a state of unshakable calmness and self-control, before he attains final emancipation.

LAHIRI MAHASAYA, THE FIRST MODERN exponent of the deepest spiritual interpretations of the Bhagavad Gita, gives an esoteric meaning to the words "many births" in this stanza. His explanation is as follows:

When a man breathes out and cannot breathe in, he experiences the state of great dissolution or death. Later, when the soul enters into another physical body, that transition is called rebirth. Similarly, when a man exhales and does not breathe in, that state is said to be one of partial dissolution. When he breathes again, after perceiving the breathless state of partial dissolution, he is spoken of as being born again. As a yogi finds liberation after many great dissolutions (many deaths and rebirths), so he may also attain freedom by the practice of *Kriya Yoga*—by consciously experiencing death during breathlessness, and rebirth during inhalation, in the superconscious state. If the accomplished yogi can keep concentrated on the Absolute Bliss without attachment to material pleasures during a certain number of births and deaths (inhalations and exhalations, in one or more incarnations, in the natural course of evolution), he becomes emancipated. But the *Kriya Yogi* may hasten his evolution by the esoteric births and deaths (breathing and breathless states) of *Kriya Yoga.* By the repeated superconscious experience of these esoteric births and deaths, the *Kriya Yogi* becomes purged of sin, the karmic taint of material attachments, and is freed.

Esoteric explanation of "many births" in light of yoga science

In the science of *Kriya Yoga,* Lahiri Mahasaya has thus given to the world a short route to liberation. When the yogi in the highest ecstasy perceives his soul united to Spirit, and no longer identifies himself with the ever-changing dream inhalations and exhalations of the dream body, that devotee has received salvation.

The consciousness of breath or inhalation and exhalation gives rise to the consciousness of the body. Thus, the soul during the wakeful state is identified with the body and breath; it thereby becomes entangled in matter. During the state of deep slumber, for a while the soul remains oblivious of the body and the breath; thus it subconsciously perceives its joyous state.

When the yogi learns superconsciously to contact his soul and to transcend his breath and body, he finds the Infinite reflected in his being. All finer subconscious or superconscious experiences take place without the consciousness of breath. Therefore, when in ecstatic meditation the yogi learns to remain in his soul without the mortal breath that causes rebirths, and when he can retain the unity with his breathless, God-united soul when his consciousness reenters the physically active breathing state, he is spoken of as one who has liberated himself.

The consciousness of breath in the wakeful state makes people daily aware of a "new birth"; in sleep, in the breath-forgetting state, one experiences a counterfeit "death." Hence, a man who regularly wakes up and sleeps experiences 365 rebirths and deaths in one year. In a lifetime of a hundred years he experiences 36,500 births and deaths. If a yogi, from his infancy to the fullness of his life—during his many births in wakefulness and his many deaths in slumber—can equally retain his unity with Cosmic Blessedness, remaining free from all attachment, then in that one lifetime of many short "births" and "deaths" he may achieve complete liberation.

In a case where there is a great amount of stored-up bad karma, such a yogi may require several lives for full emancipation.

Patanjali says, "The yogi who makes keen efforts without being impatient—he who possesses devotion, vital energy, recollection of his true self, discrimination, and calm persistence in deep meditation—achieves emancipation in a short time."* Pedestrians in the path of yoga may take many lives to reach the goal, whilst fast spiritual travelers may arrive in one life.

VERSE 46

tapasvibhyo 'dhiko yogī jñānibhyo 'pi mato 'dhikaḥ
karmibhyaś cādhiko yogī tasmād yogī bhavārjuna

The yogi is deemed greater than body-disciplining ascetics, greater even than the followers of the path of wisdom or of the path of action; be thou, O Arjuna, a yogi!

ASCETICISM IS A BYPATH BECAUSE it teaches man to reach God indirectly by outer renunciation and physical discipline. The path of theoretical wisdom is also a bypath, because it teaches the confusing way of academically reasoning about Him. The path of action is also a bypath, because it teaches the circuitous way of reaching God through external good actions.

The Lord Himself here extols the royal path of yoga as the highest of all spiritual paths, and the scientific yogi as greater than a follower of any other path.

The real *Kriya Yoga* way (life-force control) is not a bypath. It is the direct highway, the shortest route, to divine realization. It teaches man to ascend heavenward by leading the ego, mind, and life force through the same spinal channel that was used when the soul originally descended into the body.

---

* *Yoga Sutras* I:20–21. See detailed commentary in Gita I:4–6, page 70 ff.

THE SPIRIT AS SOUL HAS DESCENDED through the subtle astral cerebrospinal centers into the brain and the spinal plexuses, and into the nervous system, the senses, and the rest of the body, and becomes entangled there as the pseudosoul or ego. In the body-identified state, the ego engages in further involvements in and with the objective world. The ego has to be made to ascend through the same spinal path until it realizes its true Self as the soul, and the soul reunites with the Spirit.

Spinal route of ascension is universal highway to be traveled by all souls

Yoga points out that this spinal route is the one straight highway that all earth-descended mortal beings must follow in the final ascension to liberation. All other paths—those that emphasize performance of *tapasya* (bodily and mental self-discipline), or theoretical knowledge of the scriptures (the gaining of wisdom by discrimination), or the performance of all good actions—are auxiliary paths that somewhere join the highway of practical yoga that leads straight to liberation.

The ascetic who is busy with disciplining the body, putting it through rigorous austerities, may attain a degree of control over the physical instrumentality; but merely practicing postures, enduring cold and heat, and not giving in to sorrow and pleasure—without simultaneously concentrating on Cosmic Consciousness—is only a roundabout pathway to gaining the mental control necessary for God-communion. The yogi attains communion with the Lord directly, by withdrawing his consciousness from the senses and nervous system, the spine, and the brain, and uniting it with his God-knowing soul. Many devotees are so engrossed in following the precepts of external asceticism and renunciation that they forget that ecstasy with the Infinite is the purpose of such self-discipline.

When the scriptural philosopher dissects words and thoughts with the scalpel of his reason, he may grow so fond of theoretical knowledge and of mentally separating wisdom into various segments that he may "dry up" through lack of the experience of truth in divine ecstasy.* If a person spent his lifetime in analyzing the properties of water and in examining water from different sources all over the world, he would not thereby quench his thirst. A thirsty man, without fussing over the atomic constituencies, selects some good water; drinking it, he becomes satisfied. An exoteric *jnana yogi*—a follower of the path of discriminative reason—may read and analyze all the scriptures and still not slake his soul thirst.

* "Philosophy will clip an angel's wings."—Keats: *Lamia.*

A theoretical knowledge of scriptures often produces a conviction that one knows the truth when he actually does not know it. Only by communing with God, the "Library of All Knowledge," may one know all truths in their exactitude, without wasting time in the theoretical understanding and misunderstanding of scriptures. That is why a wide gulf may exist between scripture readers and men of realization who are themselves embodiments of scriptural truths.

The Pharisees were willing to crucify Christ because they surmised fearfully that he was a threat to their authority, having actually perceived the truths that they knew only in theory.

Lastly, the yogi is also deemed greater than the man of action. The missionary, the social worker, the man of goodwill who practices the "golden rule" toward others, the teacher who tries to instruct others in the technique of God-communion—all no doubt perform good actions. But unless they also devote themselves to the inner science by which they can know God through their own direct experience, they will remain without divine realization. That is why the yogi meditates and concentrates on the attainment of ecstasy. Until he achieves that state of inner attunement with God, he performs his duties but does not divert himself with many outward activities at the cost of forgetting the Lord.

The yogi teaches and serves others in the highest way—by his inspiring life; example ever speaks louder than words. Reform thyself and thou wilt reform thousands. Forgetting God is the greatest sin. Communion with God is the highest virtue.

A little study of scriptures with the continuous desire to practice the truths enjoined in them is desirable in the path of yoga. Renunciation of all entanglements in order to commune with God is also helpful. Performance of dutiful actions that satisfy one's own needs and that are serviceful and uplifting to others provides a beneficial balance in the life of the yogi.

THE PATHS OF RENUNCIATION AND WISDOM and action may be followed in two ways: externally and internally. The man who concentrates on external renunciation is an outer renunciant. But the *tapasvin** who destroys all internal desires and attachments, and who keeps his mind away from sense temptations, is a man of esoteric renunciation.

---

* An ascetic; one who practices religious austerities (such as physical and mental discipline, or renunciation of possessions).

Similarly, the external follower of the wisdom path (*Jnana Yoga*) is busy in solving scriptural problems and in analyzing word structures. The esoteric *jnanin,** according to Vedanta philosophy, is he who not only listens to the scriptural truths and perceives their meaning in his mind but becomes one with them by complete assimilation. Therefore the Vedantic way of spiritual realization is to listen to the scriptural truth (*shravanam*), then to perceive it (*mananam*), then to be one with it (*nididhyasanam*).

External and internal paths of renunciation, action, and wisdom

The man who performs good actions is the external *karma yogi*. He who practices yoga meditation performs the highest action; he is the esoteric *karmin*.† But he who performs or practices *Kriya Yoga,* the highest technique of contacting God, is the *raja yogi* or the royal *Kriya Yogi*. He attains ascension and is thus among the highest yogis.

ANOTHER INTERPRETATION OF THIS STANZA has been given by Lahiri Mahasaya: When a yogi practices *Kriya Yoga,* withdrawing his mind from the senses by disconnecting the life force from the five sense-telephones, he is spoken of as following the path of *karma yoga;* he is a true *karmin*. During this earlier state of attempts at God-union, the yogi has to perform various spiritual actions of proper breathing, life-force control, and fighting distractions with concentration. Therefore he is spoken of as following the path of esoteric *karma yoga*. At this state the yogi is identified with actions; he is a *karmin*.

Esoteric meaning of Karma Yoga, Jnana Yoga, and tapasya

When the yogi is able to see the spiritual light at the *Kutastha* or Christ center between the eyebrows and to withdraw his life force from the nervous system of the five sense-telephones, he enters the state of esoteric *tapasya* (ascetical renunciation). His mind, being disconnected from the senses, then exists in a state of esoteric renunciation; he is a *tapasvin*.

When the yogi is further able to unite his mind with the wisdom and bliss of his soul, he is a follower of esoteric *Jnana Yoga*. This is called the *jnanin* state of the yogi.

In the last high state when the soul, free from all bodily and worldly consciousness, is united with the blessed Cosmic Spirit, the devotee is called the esoteric *raja yogi*. This state of final yoga or union of soul and

* A *jnana yogi,* or follower of the path of wisdom.

† A *karma yogi,* or follower of the path of action.

Spirit is the loftiest; he who attains it is the true yogi. He has reached higher spiritual planes than the one who has achieved only the state of a *tapasvin, karmin,* or *jnanin*. The real yogi knows God as the ever-existing, ever-conscious, ever-new Bliss; he perceives all creation as God's dreams.

The path of *Kriya Yoga* is distinctive and scientific because it teaches the exact method of withdrawing the mind from the senses by switching off the life force from the five sense-telephones. Only when this interiorization is accomplished can the meditator enter the inner temple of God-communion. In other words, the *Kriya Yogi* follows a sure, definite method of leading not only his mind but his life force through the spinal channel to unite them with the soul. In the highest ecstasy he then unites his soul with Spirit.

Kriya Yoga, or the indirect reference to it in the scriptures as *Kevali Pranayama,** is the true *pranayama,* in which the inhaling and exhaling breath has been transmuted into interiorized life force under the full control of the mind. By distilling *prana* from the breath, and by neutralizing the life currents that control the breath, all the cells of the body are vitally recharged by the reinforced bodily life force and the Cosmic Life; the physical cells neither change nor decay. *Kriya Yoga* is a suitable practice for any sincere seeker of God who is free from serious acute illness, and who observes in his daily life the cardinal moral precepts.

Yoga: the scientific highway to the Infinite

THE THEOLOGIES OF ALL GREAT RELIGIONS have one common foundation—the finding of God. But religious truth without practical realization is necessarily limited in its value. How can the blind lead the blind? Few men understand the Bhagavad Gita as its writer, Vyasa, understood its truths! Few men understand the words of Christ as he understood them!

Vyasa, Christ, Babaji, and all other perfected masters perceived the same truth. They described it variously, in different languages. In the study of the Bhagavad Gita and the New Testament I have perceived their meanings as one. I have therefore been quoting the words of Christ to show their unity with the truths of the Gita.

In order to understand fully the Bhagavad Gita and the Bible, the spiritual aspirant must learn to go into the state of ecstasy and commune with Vyasa and Christ through Cosmic Consciousness.

As all colleges in the world teach the same principles of science,

---

* See IV:29, page 504.

which can be proven by application, so all true religious schools, if they followed yoga, would be aware that it is the one scientific highway to the Infinite. That is why each man should become a God-united yogi. In this stanza of the Bhagavad Gita, the voice of God sounds a trumpet call to all spiritual aspirants: Become yogis!

VERSE 47

yoginām api sarveṣāṁ madgatenāntarātmanā
śraddhāvān bhajate yo māṁ sa me yuktatamo mataḥ

He who with devotion absorbs himself in Me, with his soul immersed in Me, him I regard, among all classes of yogis, as the most equilibrated.

VARIOUS METHODS AND BYPATHS are termed yoga: *Karma Yoga* (the path of good actions); *Jnana Yoga* (the path of discrimination); *Bhakti Yoga* (the path of prayer and devotion); *Mantra Yoga* (the path of God-union by chanting and incantations of seed sounds); *Laya Yoga* (the path that teaches how to dissolve the ego in the Infinite); and *Hatha Yoga* (the path of bodily discipline). *Raja Yoga,* specifically *Kriya Yoga*, is the quintessence of all yoga paths, the path especially favored by royal sages and great yogis in ancient India.

Here the Lord is emphasizing that the *raja yogi* or *Kriya Yogi* who with devotion withdraws his life force and mind from the body, and who unites his ego with his soul and his soul with the ever blessed Spirit, and who can maintain constant ecstasy with the Infinite equally during action and during meditation, is the highest of all yogis. Such great devotees do not remain "locked up" always in ecstasy, refusing to take part in the drama of life created by the Lord; they perform their duties and their God-reminding actions with blissful consciousness, under divine direction. Being supremely united to God, such a yogi maintains the poise or equilibrium of yoga (divine union) equally in ecstatic meditation and in dutiful activity.

The devotee who performs actions in a state of ecstasy (maintaining unbroken inner union with Spirit both in meditation and in external activities) is the greatest of all yogis; he has attained an even higher state than the yogi who remains one with the Lord for years in *savikalpa samadhi* without performing any bodily actions.

Kriya Yoga teaches the householder, as well as the man of renunciation, to commune with God as his first duty; and then to perform all proper physical, mental, moral, and spiritual duties with divine consciousness, directed by Him alone.

om tat sat iti śrīmadbhagavadgītāsu upaniṣatsu
brahmavidyāyām yogaśāstre śrīkṛṣṇārjunasaṁvāde
dhyānayogo nāma ṣaṣṭho 'dhyāyaḥ

Aum, Tat, Sat.
In the Upanishad of the holy Bhagavad Gita—the discourse of Lord Krishna to Arjuna, which is the scripture of yoga and the science of God-realization—this is the sixth chapter, called "Dhyana Yoga (Union Through Meditation)."*

* Some commentators entitle this chapter "Atmasamyamayoga"—"Union Through Self-Mastery." (*Publisher's Note*)

CHAPTER VII

THE NATURE OF SPIRIT AND THE SPIRIT OF NATURE

❖

"Hear How Thou Shalt Realize Me"

❖

Prakriti: The Dual Nature of Spirit in Creation

❖

How the Creator Sustains the Manifested Creation

❖

Cosmic Hypnosis (Maya) and the Way to Transcend It

❖

Which "God" Should Be Worshiped?

❖

Perceiving the Spirit Behind the Dream-Shadows of Nature

ॐ

"Man, made in the image of God, must learn to be transcendent like his Maker. The triple qualities of cosmic delusion, and the cosmic dream tinged with those entangling attributes, all proceed from God; but as He remains unaffected by them, so man may learn, through constant yoga communion with God, how to remain uninvolved in maya and how to view the panorama of life's experiences as sheer entertainment."

THE NATURE OF SPIRIT AND THE SPIRIT OF NATURE

"HEAR HOW THOU SHALT REALIZE ME"

VERSE 1

śrībhagavān uvāca
mayy āsaktamanāḥ pārtha yogaṁ yuñjan madāśrayaḥ
asaṁśayaṁ samagraṁ māṁ yathā jñāsyasi tac chṛṇu

The Blessed Lord said:
O Partha (Arjuna), absorbing thy mind in Me, taking shelter in Me, and following the path of yoga—hear how thou shalt realize Me beyond all doubts, in full completion (knowing Me with all My attributes and powers).

WHEN A YOGI MECHANICALLY PRACTICES yoga methods, without focusing his attention with devotion on the omnipresent God, his mind becomes concentrated on the path rather than on the Goal.

The path of yoga is only a means to reach the Divine Destination. When one communes with the Lord, the technique of yoga has fulfilled its purpose. I knew a devotee in India who for years so enjoyed the practice of yoga techniques that he forgot to love God. He was a spiritual robot—accomplished in the mechanics of yoga but lacking its heart and spirit, which is God-communion.

The blossom precedes the fruit; when the fruit appears the flower falls. The flower of deep yoga practice similarly precedes the fruit of divine realization. When the fruit of final freedom arrives, only then are yoga techniques no longer necessary. Presumptuous devotees often make the spiritually dangerous mistake of imagining that they have attained God-realization; they prematurely give up the practice of yoga. Many truly liberated men, however, just to set a good example to other devotees, practice yoga even after achieving complete union with God.

Emancipation is a sum total composed of the yogi's wholehearted effort, the guru-preceptor's guidance and blessing, and the grace of God.* The Lord is the Maker of the laws of salvation. It is necessary to follow the yoga technique with both devotion and divine grace in order to reach the all-knowing Father who yearns for the love of His children even more than they want His affection. Yoga should therefore be practiced by the devotee with deepest love and spiritual thirst for the Father of all.

The way to acknowledge and know Him, as taught in the highest Yoga philosophy, is by constantly keeping the attention absorbed in His holy vibration, *Aum*. If the yogi hears that vibration—through the medium of intuition—and merges his attention in it, and worships it continuously, then he will see beyond doubt that there is a God—a God who responds to his prayers, a Spirit to whom he can appeal with childlike trust, no matter what his frailties and weaknesses. Such a Spirit is; such a Spirit ever has been and ever will be, unto eternity. All may know Him through the right method of meditation on *Aum*. Through *Aum* only can the manifested Spirit be realized.†

When the yogi in meditation expands his consciousness with the cosmic *Aum* sound emanating from the cosmic vibration, he feels himself expanding with it. He clearly perceives the ever-existent, ever-conscious, ever-blessed God who is present behind *Aum*. It is then that the yogi realizes the immeasurable stores of energy, power, joy, wisdom, and grace that are manifested in the cosmic sound *Aum*—the first expression of God in the universe; he begins to glimpse the full vastness of God.‡

---

* See XVIII:56, page 1074.

† See commentary on VI:14, pages 614 ff.

‡ They have sung of Him as infinite and unattainable: but I in my meditations have seen Him without sight....

This is the Ultimate Word: but can any express its marvelous savor? He who has savored it once, he knows what joy it can give.

Kabir says: "Knowing it, the ignorant man becomes wise, and the wise man becomes speechless and silent,

The worshipper is utterly inebriated,
His wisdom and his detachment are made perfect;
He drinks from the cup of the inbreathings and the outbreathings of love."

—*One Hundred Poems of Kabir,* translated by Rabindranath Tagore (London: Macmillan, 1915)

Verse 2

jñānaṁ te 'haṁ savijñānam idaṁ vakṣyāmy aśeṣataḥ
yaj jñātvā neha bhūyo 'nyaj jñātavyam avaśiṣyate

I shall relate to thee without omission both theoretical wisdom and that wisdom which can be known only by intuitive realization—knowing which, naught in this world will remain unknown to thee.

Here Krishna prefaces his forthcoming discourse with the promise to reveal to the questioning Arjuna all the mysteries of the universe—everything that can be known through theoretical knowledge, together with the ultimate wisdom that can be fully perceived only by Self-realization. After realizing every phase of cosmic wisdom, the devotee will be omniscient.

Verse 3

manuṣyāṇāṁ sahasreṣu kaścid yatati siddhaye
yatatām api siddhānāṁ kaścin māṁ vetti tattvataḥ

Among thousands of men, perhaps one strives for spiritual attainment; and, among the blessed true seekers that assiduously try to reach Me, perhaps one perceives Me as I am.

The precious state of God-realization is very difficult to attain, because in the average man the searchlights of his five senses are turned toward the perception of material objects and not inward toward God. Animals are instinct-guided; unlike men, animals have no power of free will by which they may reverse their sensory searchlights from matter to God. But even with free will, most men are habit-bound. They do not try to change their material habits into spiritual habits. Through the influence of cosmic delusion man is outwardly attracted to the spurious luster of matter and not inwardly attracted by the eternal effulgence of God.

It is an undeniable truth that man's life-wave, no matter how far projected away, still exists as a part of the Cosmic Sea. Sooner or later it must yield to the divine pull and go back to the Cosmic Ocean Home from which it sprang forth.

However, when the soul-wave of man becomes accustomed, through bad habits, to staying away from the calm depths of the Cosmic Ocean, it is reluctant to return there. It is true also that God, as the Cosmic Ocean with Its storms of delusion, wishes to enact a play with the soul-waves; hence they are not easily allowed to return to His bosom! But when the soul-waves are fiercely battered by the raging tumults of cosmic delusion, they send an inner call for help and try to respond to the underlying unceasing pull of God.

Owing to the influence of the storms of delusion, and to Spirit's desire to play with Its individualized soul-waves, and to the evil desire and habits of the soul-waves not to return to the depths of the Sea of Cosmic Consciousness, few human waves make an effort to seek their original Home. If all delusion-buffeted souls would raise a hue and cry, God would certainly create a lull in His cosmic storm and help the soul-waves to return to Him! And whenever a determined soul-wave tries assiduously to attain the deeps of the Divine Ocean, it may do so by special divine grace.

God's grace, and man's adamant demand for release, conquer delusion

When the vast majority of incarnate souls tire of clashing with cosmic delusion, they crave for release. This accumulated desire of great souls, good souls, and the masses of suffering souls, and also the strong urge of single souls adamantly demanding release, stirs God to cause a lull in the storm of His delusion. When this interlude comes through God's grace and man's united desire for liberation, or through the strong urge of single souls seeking salvation, then many of those souls together, or a few souls singly, dive deep into His blessed oceanic bosom, never to return to play again. They have had enough. Only those who cling to unfinished mortal desires have to reincarnate again to play with Cosmic Nature on the storm-buffeted surface of life.

This stanza of the Bhagavad Gita points out that most men use their free will to choose to ride on ceaselessly with the storm of delusion. Out of many thousands of human beings, perhaps only one desires to reenter the Divine Ocean. Even that one, desirous of returning to the Cosmic Bosom but tested by cosmic delusion and obstructed by past evil karma, cannot easily merge in the freedom of the Blissful Sea. Nevertheless, out of these many good seekers, one or two of them, here and there, will succeed in overcoming the outward thrust of delusion and evil karma and be able to plunge headlong with forceful faith into the ever-pulling power of the Divine Deeps.

God, in His oceanic cosmic consciousness, is fully aware of having caused so much trouble by having sent away His individualized soul-children, without their permission, to be buffeted and tested by the storm of delusion. The cosmic plan, therefore, is to help all souls to return Home, sooner or later. The same oceanic Spirit that cast forth all the soul-waves from Its bosom will in time dismiss delusion and bring them all back to their Home of freedom.

What a paradox that in spite of so much suffering and misery only one among thousands of men is shrewd enough to seek God; and that among such true seekers, perhaps only one will cultivate the unceasing spiritual tenacity to neutralize the effects of bad karma and of cosmic delusion and thus attain the Reality—God.

Liberating power of Kriya Yoga and undiscourageable perseverance

MANY SINCERE DEVOTEES of the Lord do not force themselves to seek Him with ever-increasing intensity in meditation, nor are they persistent in their search for Him. That is why they have only meager or fleeting inspirations and do not realize Him continuously. But a persevering devotee, in spite of much bad karma and the temptations of cosmic delusion, will certainly reach God in the end.

Elsewhere the Bhagavad Gita says: "Even a devotee who realizes only shortly before death that God is real and all else unreal will be able to commune with Him in the after-death state" (II:72). Some great saints tell us that God has relaxed certain spiritual regulations for the benefit of devotees who must live in this modern age of confusion. A present-day devotee, they say, who will *continuously* pray for God-communion for three days and nights, or even for twenty-four hours, will realize his Goal.

Yogavatar Lahiri Mahasaya, emphasizing the potential power of *Kriya Yoga*, said that a person with much liberating karma from past-life spiritual endeavors who gives three years to deep practice of *Kriya Yoga* according to the guru's instructions may achieve not only God-communion but may become forever united to Him. Failing in that, a devotee with considerable past liberating karma, by deep practice of *Kriya Yoga* under a guru may in six years attain complete liberation. Others, with some liberating karma, can find liberation in twelve years, by the deep practice of *Kriya Yoga* and by the guru's guidance and blessings. And all deep seekers, even those with very little past liberating karma, may find liberation in a period of twenty-four years.

Others, with no previous liberating karma but possessing now supreme determination and the guidance of a true *Kriya Yoga* guru, by deep and steady practice of *Kriya Yoga* may be able to find realization in forty-eight years. If a devotee is unable to find realization in forty-eight years, he will certainly be attracted in his next life to *Kriya Yoga* and will practice it deeply until final salvation is achieved.

The successful *Kriya Yogi* is that rare blessed one among thousands of seekers who, as the Lord says in this Gita verse, strives undauntedly until he "perceives Me as I am."

Anyone who makes a tenacious effort will find God

MY BELOVED STUDENT, SAINT LYNN,* once observed: "Out of each thousand greedy men, one adamantly seeks money; and out of those determined seekers, one becomes rich!" He also told me: "When a dollar bill drops within sight, twelve wolves of businessmen jump to get it! The one who most quickly grabs it and with tenacity hangs on to it while being pounded by other greedy businessmen, may, half alive, get away with that dollar!" Just as no one may amass wealth without resourcefulness and determination, so the infinite wealth is not to be attained without courage and tenacity. Man, however, as the divine image, should understand that God has not to be earned but realized. A determined devotee by steady efforts recovers this eternal divine forgotten heritage, ever existing within the soul.

God-realization is not reserved for the specially privileged, nor for one son of God only, nor for a few sons of God. God is ready to take back all prodigal sons—anyone who makes the supreme effort to return to Him. Only the wanderer who has traveled far away from his cosmic heritage, through a tortuous evil way, will find difficulty and delay in returning Home.

I often say that if a hundred persons in various circumstances of life prayed deeply and made supreme efforts to become millionaires, all of them could not, in one lifetime, succeed. Most of them would have to wait several lives to get into the proper environment that would

---

* Mr. James J. Lynn, a self-made business magnate to whom Paramahansa Yogananda referred as a saint in recognition of his great spiritual advancement. In 1951, Paramahansaji conferred on him the monastic title and name of Rajarsi Janakananda (after the illustrious *rishi* King Janaka of India). Rajarsi was the first successor to Paramahansa Yogananda, serving from 1952–1955 as the president and representative spiritual head of Self-Realization Fellowship/Yogoda Satsanga Society of India. Rajarsi was succeeded by Sri Daya Mata. (*Publisher's Note*)

make them eligible, by the acquirement of proper human karma, to become millionaires. But I also point out that all men, being already made in the image of God, can attain Him in one lifetime by making the proper spiritual effort under the guidance of a true guru.

God has not to be earned like money. By His grace He is already earned and deposited in every soul. But owing to human forgetfulness He has to be rediscovered. The poet rightly sang:

'Tis heaven alone that is given away.
*'Tis only God may be had for the asking.**

PRAKRITI: THE DUAL NATURE OF SPIRIT IN CREATION

VERSE 4

bhūmir āpo 'nalo vāyuḥ khaṁ mano buddhir eva ca
ahaṁkāra itīyaṁ me bhinnā prakṛtir aṣṭadhā

My manifested nature (Prakriti) has an eightfold differentiation: earth, water, fire, air, ether, sensory mind (manas), intelligence (buddhi), and egoism (ahamkara).

SHADOWS OF FILMS AND THE BEAM of light in a cinema booth combine to manifest motion pictures of subjective beings acting with their egos, sense minds, and discriminative intelligences on an objective earthly stage.

The eight elements of cosmic material nature

God similarly uses the delusive films of relativity offered by Cosmic Nature to produce His dream motion-pictures of intelligently active sentient human individualities playing on a stage of matter: manifestations of the elements of earth, water, fire, air, and the invisible all-pervasive ether—vibrant dynamic beings, and beautiful continents surrounded by oceans, illuminated by the sun and moon, and abounding in vital air.

This stanza of the Bhagavad Gita gives a summary of the eight el-

* James Russell Lowell, "The Vision of Sir Launfal."

ements or forces of cosmic material nature. The ancient scientists spoke loosely of nature as matter. The modern scientists think of matter as coordinated forces. They describe all mineral, plant, and animal substances as made of ninety-two elements,* which are further explained as nothing more than permutations and combinations of different atoms or wave-energies.

Matter, according to Hindu philosophy, is made of the intelligent thoughtrons of God, which materialize into grosser forces of intelligent lifetrons (*prana*), electrons and protons, atoms, molecules, cells, tissues, and organic matter. Both inorganic and organic matter are composed of *anu* (atoms), *paramanu* (subatomic particles and energies), *prana* (lifetrons), and *chaitanya* ("consciousness," thoughtrons) of God. This is the constitution of physical cosmic nature or matter from the metaphysical standpoint.

The yogis maintain that matter—physical cosmic nature or Jada-Prakriti (gross nature) or Apara-Prakriti (the gross expression of God)—may be spoken of as the physical dream-body of the Lord. This cosmic physical dream-body is made of five objective elements (subtle vibratory forces) of earth, water, fire, air (life force), and ether; two perceptive cognitive processes, sensory mind and intelligence; and one perceiving entity, the *ahamkara* or egoistic consciousness of cosmic nature. The little body-dream of man, the copy of cosmic physical nature, is included in the latter's larger dream. Even as cosmic nature is the physical dream-body of God and is made of eight elementary forces, so the human body is also made of eight elementary forces and is the dream body of the human soul—the perfect image of God.

As a dreamer in sleep becomes the cognitive entity or ego and uses his sensory dream-mind and dream-intelligence to perceive his dream-objectified body (made of earth, water, fire, air, and ether), so God in His cosmic dream becomes the cognitive physical dream-entity, the cognitive dream-processes, the dream-mind, and the dream-intelligence, in order to perceive His objective physical body of Nature, made of eight cosmic-dream physical elements.

Two aspects of Holy Ghost/Cosmic Nature: Para-Prakriti and Apara-Prakriti

As a man's homogeneous consciousness during the perception of a dream divides itself by the law of relativity to become the subjective dreamer, the process of dreaming, and the objective dream, so God through His cosmic delusory force (*maya*) cre-

* Science has now named and defined over a hundred such elements. (*Publisher's Note*)

ates the egoistical dream-entity of cosmic physical Nature with its manifold perceptions of mind and intelligence and its cosmic dream-body of five gross dream-elements. In the impure state, this cosmic physical Nature, the physical dream-body of God, is called Apara-Prakriti. Hidden behind Apara-Prakriti is the Para-Prakriti (pure nature of God) constituting the finer cosmic astral universe and the cosmic causal universe guided by the superior intelligent entity of cosmic nature, *Aum* or the Holy Ghost.

In the human body, the pure soul is the neutral witness of all its operations. The physical ego—the pseudo reflection of the soul—acts in conjunction with cosmic nature, Prakriti, to operate the workings of the physical body. The finer discriminative astral ego and causal ego* (in attunement with the soul in advanced devotees) act, respectively, as the representatives of the finer cosmic astral and cosmic causal Nature to operate the workings of man's astral and causal bodies.

Similarly, God's *Kutastha* Intelligence (the Krishna or Christ Consciousness) is the neutral witness of cosmic creation. The *Kutastha* Intelligence manifests itself through the Holy Ghost or *Aum* Intelligence as Apara-Prakriti, the cosmic-dream physical entity, directing the cosmic-dream physical universe. The same *Kutastha* Intelligence, through the Holy Ghost or *Aum* as Para-Prakriti in the finer state, directs the subtler cosmic astral and cosmic causal universes. The two aspects of the Holy Ghost vibrations are thus the Apara-Prakriti (Impure Nature) and the Para-Prakriti (Pure Nature).

Dream nature of the universe and the human body

A dream has a threefold aspect: the dreamer, his perception, and the dream objects made of the five dream elements of earth, water, fire, air, and ether. The complex cosmic triple dream universes are run by the intelligent Cosmic Mother Nature or intelligent Cosmic Holy Ghost in a finer and in a grosser way. The physical universe is guided by the external vibrations of the Holy Ghost—the impure Apara-Prakriti. The astral and causal universes are guided by the pure Holy Ghost—pure Nature, or Para-Prakriti.

The whole physical universe is a true-to-sight, true-to-hearing, true-to-smell, true-to-taste, and true-to-touch "technicolored" cosmic-dream motion picture, created and sustained by the physical, mental, and intelligent beam of the Cosmic Dream Entity—Nature, or intelligent Holy Ghost. The latter is a reflection of the *Kutastha* Christ Intelligence *in cre-*

* See reference to astral and causal ego in relation to the soul, I:8 pages 6–7.

ation, which in turn is the reflection of God the Father *beyond creation.*

As a man's one basic consciousness may create in dreamland another dream entity and bestow on it egoism, mind, and intelligence to carry on, for example, the building of a mansion, so the Spirit dreams Itself to be the triune entity: God the Father beyond creation, God the Christ or *Kutastha* Intelligence of creation, and the intelligent Cosmic Nature or Holy Ghost with its eight potential differentiations through which it creates and sustains the three objective mansions of creation—causal, astral, and physical.

After understanding the dream nature of the universe, the devotee should learn the dream nature of the human body, made of the five dream elements. The body exists in a sphere of dream ether; it inbreathes vital dream air; its chemical processes are carried on by the heat of fiery energies; it is composed of dream "water" or blood (which constitutes the greater part of the dream body) and of dream "earth" or so-called solid flesh. This dream body is perceived by the dream sense-mind and dream discriminative intelligence, and is guided by the dream entity of the little nature, ego. As the Spirit dreamed Itself into God beyond creation, God in creation, and God as the Cosmic Nature with a cosmic body, so God as the transcendental soul and the discriminating intelligence and the physical ego sustains the physical dream-body.

The five dream elements commingled together constitute the physical dream-body. The sense-identified physical ego and the mind (the coordinator of the ten senses) are centered outside of the spiritual eye; the intelligence works through the inside of the spiritual eye; the seat of man's soul consciousness extends from the point between the eyebrows to the central top of the head, in the subtle spiritual centers of the *Kutastha* and thousand-petaled lotus. The advanced yogi, half awake in this cosmic dream, beholds this cosmic technicolored dream motion-picture of five dream elements, the human body, and observes its operations as directed by the triune divine entities. He is able to see the little body as it is operated by the soul, by the discriminative ego or intelligence, and by the physical ego.

VERSE 5

apareyam itas tv anyāṁ prakṛtiṁ viddhi me parām
jīvabhūtāṁ mahābāho yayedaṁ dhāryate jagat

Thus My lower nature (Apara-Prakriti). But understand, O Mighty-armed (Arjuna)! that My different and higher nature (Para-Prakriti) is the jiva, the self-consciousness and life-principle, that sustains the cosmos.

THE *JIVA* IS THE CONSCIOUSNESS of the soul identified with its manifested or incarnate state, the self-consciousness or individualized existence of the soul.

On the macrocosmic scale, *Kutastha Chaitanya* (the Krishna or Christ Consciousness) is the intelligence of God immanent in all creation as the unchanged and unchanging pure reflection of God—the "Soul" of the universe; and Para-Prakriti is that same consciousness, but containing within it and expressing itself through the creative elements of individuality and diversity—the *"jiva"* of the cosmos.

On the microcosmic scale, the soul in man is the ever unchanged and unchanging image of God; the *jiva* is that same divine consciousness which recognizes its essential oneness with God, but operates as an individualized entity—the discriminative ego that is identified with the soul.

The creative intelligence and life principle in man and cosmos

The *"jiva"*—as Para-Prakriti attuned to the *Kutastha* Krishna-Christ Intelligence in the universe, and as the discriminative ego attuned to the soul in man—is the creative intelligence and life principle in all individualized forms, the active divine intelligence of God the Creator and of His individualized image, the soul. Without this superior nature behind the gross manifestation, the physical universe and body of man would not exist.

The cosmic-dream physical nature of eight aspects or forces was explained in the last stanza as being operated by the gross nature of the cosmic physical Holy Ghost (Apara-Prakriti). In this fifth stanza Krishna is revealing to Arjuna how the finer, superior, astral and causal universes and bodies of man are vivified and sustained, respectively, by the God-identified nature of the cosmic intelligent Holy Ghost (Para-Prakriti), and by the soul-identified intelligent discriminative ego.

As the physical ego is responsible for the sustenance of the physical body, so the physical impure cosmic nature (Apara-Prakriti) is responsible for the creation and sustenance of the cosmic-dream physical universe. As the discriminative ego identified with the soul is the sustainer of the astral and causal bodies of man, so the Holy Ghost (Para-Prakriti), purely identified with *Kutastha* Intelligence and with

God, is the sustainer of the finer astral and causal universes.

As the physical ego makes the body appear as a mass of flesh, weighing so many pounds, so the cosmic physical Holy Ghost (Apara-Prakriti) makes the cosmic universe look like a mass of gross matter. When the discriminative ego becomes one with the soul it perceives through its intuitional vision that the body is made of intelligence and finer dream lifetrons with an electroprotonic-atomic aura. Similarly, the yogi identified with the finer intelligent Cosmic Holy Ghost (Para-Prakriti) beholds the cosmos not as matter but as a structure of intelligence and cosmic life-energy with an electroprotonic-atomic cosmic radiation. This finer Holy Ghost, Cosmic Nature, endows the external universe with an appearance, not of gross matter, but of cosmic vitality (*prana*) and the cosmic light of intelligence.

VERSE 6

etadyonīni bhūtāni sarvāṇīty upadhāraya
ahaṁ kṛtsnasya jagataḥ prabhavaḥ pralayas tathā

Understand that these dual Natures of Mine, the pure and the impure Prakriti, are the womb of all beings. I am the Progenitor and also the Dissolver of the entire cosmos.

GOD, BY HIS INNER SPIRITUAL Cosmic Nature, creates causal and astral universes and their beings; by His outer physical Cosmic Nature, He creates the physical cosmos and its material beings.

Thus the one consciousness of God, through the finer and grosser natures of His Prakriti, is the creator of the dream physical universe with all the objects and varieties of human beings and animals contained within it. Out of the intelligent womb of Cosmic Nature and Her dual manifestation emerge all kinds of good and evil beings—all life of minerals, plants, animals, human beings, and angels. Minerals, plants, and animals are helpless products of Prakriti; but man, endowed with intelligence, begins to give resistance to the delusive influence of Cosmic Nature. He tries by goodness and spirituality to become a superman and to escape from the mayic net of cosmic dreams back into the blessed region of Supreme Spirit.

It is God's one consciousness that is responsible for the creation of the two-natured, intelligent Cosmic Being (Mother Nature, Maya,

Shakti, or Prakriti) and of the objective dream-universe. Therefore, whenever God withdraws the cosmic delusion of relativity and dissolves Cosmic Nature within Himself, all its dreamings and creations of objective dream-universes then retire as invisible thoughts of the Great Dreamer, God.

The Lord dreams Cosmic Nature; He instills into it the individuality and power to dream the universe. Thus it is solely God who is the originator of Cosmic Nature and of the cosmic-dream universe. And by dissolving Cosmic Nature in Himself, He can thus dissolve the cosmic-dream universe.

HOW THE CREATOR SUSTAINS THE MANIFESTED CREATION

VERSE 7

mattaḥ parataraṁ nānyat kiṁcid asti dhanaṁjaya
mayi sarvam idaṁ protaṁ sūtre maṇigaṇā iva

O Arjuna! There is nothing higher than Me, or beyond Me. All things (creatures and objects) are bound to Me like a row of gems on a thread.

ALL OF NATURE'S MANIFESTATIONS can be ascribed to the Sole Origin, Spirit. But no cause of Spirit can be traced; It is self-evolved and causeless.

The Infinite contains all finite objects and also exists beyond them. There is naught beyond Infinity. God's consciousness threads through creation's shining garland of dream appearances.

Spirit, the Supreme Unity, is the sole Cause of the triune dream creation. It is the one cosmic string of Spirit's consciousness that holds together God beyond creation, God in creation, and God the Intelligent Cosmic Nature with its dream jewels of human beings, animals, vegetation, blossoms, and sparkling minerals that compose the garland of creation. The Cosmic Dreamer's consciousness keeps all dream images and objects strung together as a lei of decorative dreams. God playfully wears His dream wreath of creation to entertain Himself and His children. When the string of the Divine Dreamer's consciousness is withdrawn, the garland of dream persons and objects falls apart and vanishes into the Being of Spirit.

As infinite space contains all finite manifestations of planets, stars, and universes, so the infinite sky of Spirit contains within it all the finite manifestations of creation. It is natural but erroneous to think that because all finite things are contained in the Infinite, therefore the Infinite must be contained in something else! All finite things are caused by the Infinite, but the Infinite Being—the Supreme Cause, the Thing-in-Itself—is not the effect of any cause. The Infinite Being, the container of all finite objects, is not contained by anything else existing beyond it. The Measureless Spirit cannot be measured by a finite category. Finite things are caused; but the Infinite evolves Itself, exists by Itself, and causes Itself by Itself. Otherwise It would be not infinite but finite.

An Arabian dependent on dates as a mainstay of his diet asked a Bengali visiting him in Arabia: "Do edible dates grow in Bengal?" "No," replied the Bengali. "How then do the Hindus live?" inquired the Arabian.

Finite beings, living by finite causes, think that the Infinite cannot exist without a cause. Because a person asks: "Who made me and my brother man?" he also wonders: "Who made God?"

EXPERIMENT: Close your eyes and picture the sun as a small saucer in the sky. Then by visualization make the sun as big as the whole sky. Then make that expanded mental image of the sun as big as eternity—far, far beyond the most distant planets; still you will see space and eternity ever extending beyond that mentally enlarged spherical finite image of the sun. It will become evident to you that the biggest finite sphere that can be imagined is not as big as an eternity that has no end. All finite things have limits; but eternity, the home of God, has no boundary.

Krishna is saying in this stanza that there is nothing beyond God. All finite things live in eternity, but eternity lives in nothing else. All finite beings live in God, but the Infinite God lives in nothing else beyond Him. All dreams exist in the consciousness of the dreamer, but his consciousness exists beyond all his dreams. Consciousness can exist by itself without dreams. All finite dreams of creation exist in the formless consciousness of the ever-existent, ever-conscious, ever-new God of Bliss; but His cosmic consciousness can exist by itself, without the dream forms of creation.

The nature of Infinity

All finite objects produce the illusion of something beyond them. Therefore mortals ask: "What is beyond the Infinite?" The answer is: Nothing. Naught could be bigger than the Infinite that is the container of all else.

"Look unto Me, and be ye saved, all the ends of the earth: for I am God, and there is none else."*

As the thread is hidden behind the beads of a necklace, and as the dreamer's consciousness is secreted behind the garlands of dream images, so the Divine Coordinator remains unseen behind the dream lei of creation.

As the thread is the support of a row of beads, and as the dreamer's mind upholds his dream images, so it is God's consciousness alone that sustains all the dream appearances of creation.

VERSE 8

raso 'ham apsu kaunteya prabhā 'smi śaśisūryayoḥ
praṇavaḥ sarvavedeṣu śabdaḥ khe pauruṣaṁ nṛṣu

O Son of Kunti (Arjuna), I am the fluidity in waters; I am the radiation in the moon and the sun; I am the Aum (pranava) in all the Vedas; the sound in the ether; and the manliness in men.

FLOWING WATERS, THE SHINING MOON and sun, the truths of the scriptures as expounded by wise men, the roaring sounds in the ether, and the deeds of valiant men—all can be presented by the shadows, lights, and sounds of a motion picture. God similarly creates, on the screen of human consciousness, all the "real" motion pictures of the world.

The eighth to the twelfth stanzas of this chapter describe how the Cosmic Dreamer, God, sustains all the manifestations of His cosmic dream.

Man lives in a very small dream world; he cannot conceive of the vast dream of God. Man's little consciousness cannot picture the measureless power of the Lord's cosmic consciousness. In the daytime a man looking at the sun sees only a portion of the sky. All objects on earth are invisible to him except those few that lie within the small range of his vision. By the aid of a telescope man can view the stars,

* Isaiah 45:22.

the bands around Saturn, the many moons of Jupiter, and other objects invisible to the naked eye. With the aid of a microscope, man can also see the millions of crawling microscopic germs in a drop of water. In the dreamland man can transform his mind into a microscope to see germs, or can create a giant mental telescope to see into the farthest astral or physical worlds. The ordinary man during the day sees a shining portion of the earth. At night in the light of the moon he sees another, a very different, dream picture of this earth. At night he can create a small dream of his own in the world of his subconscious mind.

Attaining the vision of the vastness of the Lord's creation

During conscious calmness with closed eyes and during deep sleep, man feels only his existence, without perception of restless thoughts or sensations or sense objects. Man in that state of stillness is confined in a little space; during his perception of the waking dreamworld or of the dream world in slumber, he remains confined in dreams. The ordinary man therefore has no adequate vision of the vastness of the physical universe nor of the astral and causal cosmoses.

The yogi with closed eyes dismisses his thoughts and sensations through the proper technique of meditation. When he is able to do that, he finds within himself the knowing, knower, known—all converted into the one perception of ecstasy. Experiencing soul bliss, the devotee feels his consciousness circling into space. Then he feels the cosmic vibration manifesting as the audible cosmic sound and the visible cosmic light. It is at this time that the yogi's intuitive spherical awareness begins to spread with the ever-expanding cosmic sound, cosmic light, and cosmic consciousness.

Then the yogi learns to expand his being into Spirit and Its cosmic consciousness, and to project his sphere of audition into the realm of the cosmic sound, and to enlarge his visible inner life force into the cosmic life force. It is then that he finds his soul no longer confined in the little dream of sleep or in the dream of the world. Instead the yogi's soul not only feels the cosmic consciousness in all creation, but beyond it, to the farthest reaches of the vibrationless sphere. The yogi, at one with both the Infinite and Its finite creation, perceives the cosmic dream and his own body as projections of his infinite consciousness.

The yogi, being one with God, beholds His consciousness appearing as the sapidity in waters, the luminescence of the moon and the sun, the cosmic sound and light roaming in the universes and the eternal ether, the perceptions of all sentient beings and saintly souls, and the *Aum* or Truth-vibrations of the Vedic scriptures and of all other books of deep wisdom. The yogi perceives the cosmic energy, emanating from God's consciousness, to be sustaining the vitality of all dream human bodies. As the motion-picture beam supports all the images and objects in a motion picture, and as the dreamer's consciousness upholds his dream images and objects, so the consciousness of God converts itself into the Cosmic Beam that maintains all the images and objects of the universal dreamland.

The yogi perceives how God sustains all cosmic manifestations

The meditating yogi also understands the words of Krishna in this stanza as follows: "Fluidity of waters": the creative vibratory motion of the five elements (earth, water, fire, air, and ether) in the spinal centers. "Sun and moon": the positive and negative forces in creation and in man's body (duality), whose property of cosmic light is the building block of all objects and beings in God's dream cosmos. "*Aum* in the Vedas": the variations of the *Aum* vibration manifesting in the spinal centers (see II:45, page 279). "The sound in the ether": the cosmic *Aum* with its creative power immanent in the ubiquitous ether. "Manliness in men": the soul and its attributes (see II:3, page 177).

VERSE 9

puṇyo gandhaḥ pṛthivyāṁ ca tejaś cāsmi vibhāvasau
jīvanaṁ sarvabhūteṣu tapaś cāsmi tapasviṣu

I am the wholesome fragrance exuding from the earth; the luminescence in the fire am I; the life in all creatures, and the self-discipline in anchorites.

THE YOGI PERCEIVES THE BODY and its vibrating elements as a miniature dream of God's consciousness, even as he perceives all matter, all lights, the subtlest cosmic energy in beings, and the high consciousness of ascetics to be dream manifestations of the Divine Mind.

Krishna reveals to Arjuna that it is God's consciousness which vibrates as the sacred fragrance in the dream vibration of the earth. God's consciousness also appears as the dream luminescence of the fire element. It is His consciousness that vibrates as cosmic energy in the astral bodies of all beings. And it is His consciousness that manifests as the cosmic perceptions of purified ascetics.

In this stanza, as in the previous one, is reference not only to the omnipresence of God in nature, but also to His immanent manifestation in the cerebrospinal centers. The yogi feels God's consciousness vibrating in the coccygeal center with its sacred fragrance of the earth element. He feels in the lumbar center the presence of God's vibratory fire element. He feels God's cosmic vitality that vibrates in the dorsal center of all beings. He feels His cosmic consciousness in the cerebral center as experienced by self-disciplinarians.

A spiritual magnetic polarity exists between the coccygeal (earth) center and the dorsal (life force) center that aids in the upliftment of the yogi's life force and consciousness through the spine.* The meditating yogi, through the fire of self-control ("self-discipline") manifested in the lumbar center, lifts his life force and consciousness from the three lower centers associated with the senses; and through the same fire of self-control ascends to the dorsal life-force center, and thence upward to the higher cerebral centers of superconsciousness, *Kutastha* Christ consciousness, and cosmic consciousness.†

VERSE 10

bījaṁ māṁ sarvabhūtānāṁ viddhi pārtha sanātanam
buddhir buddhimatām asmi tejas tejasvinām aham

Know Me to be the eternal seed of all creatures, O Son of Pritha (Arjuna)! I am the understanding of the keen, the radiance of vital beings.

AS COUNTLESS SEEDS CAN PRODUCE innumerable trees, and as the one dream consciousness of man can produce many dream objects and images, so the consciousness of God is the eternal seed-cause for the continuous creation of the images of dream beings and dream worlds.

As a sleeping man through his dream consciousness bestows intelligence and radiant vitality on his dream images, so the Cosmic Dreamer instills intelligence in men and radiance in angelic souls.

---

* See I:21–22, page 130. † See II:3, page 177.

VERSE 11

balaṁ balavatāṁ cāhaṁ kāmarāgavivarjitam
dharmāviruddho bhūteṣu kāmo 'smi bharatarṣabha

Among the powerful, O Best of the Bharatas (Arjuna), I am the power that is free from longings and attachment. I am that desire in men which is in keeping with dharma (righteousness).

IT IS GOD'S CONSCIOUSNESS THAT INSTILLS the desire for liberation in wise men and the desire for good results in righteous worldly people. It is the Lord who moves the springs of actions in human beings and urges them to perform proper actions according to the scriptural injunctions of the sages.

God's power sustains the desireless renunciant. And it is His same power that creates good desires in worldly men who long for the fruits of good actions. Desire for the result of good actions neutralizes the desire for the fruits of evil actions. But superior to action inspired by good desires is nonattached, desireless, self-controlled action. The former brings only temporary merit; the latter brings liberation.

VERSE 12

ye caiva sāttvikā bhāvā rājasās tāmasāś ca ye
matta eveti tān viddhi na tv ahaṁ teṣu te mayi

Know thou that all manifestations of sattva (good), rajas (activity), and tamas (evil) emanate from Me. Though they are in Me, I am not in them.

ALL GOOD AND EVIL DREAM-PICTURES are projected by the cosmic motion-picture beam. Yet these illusory dream-pictures, made manifest by God's light, do not reveal His essentiality. They cannot exist without the underlying beam of Cosmic Consciousness, but Spirit remains ever changeless beyond the flux of phenomena.

A man may dream good, worldly, and evil dreams, yet discover on waking that his consciousness is unaffected by them. Similarly, a yogi on waking in cosmic consciousness finds that God's dream of creation, through the action of the Lord's own power of cosmic delusion (*maya*), produces myriads of good, worldly, and evil men without any involvement of Himself in the triple attributes of Nature.

Though the cosmic dream does not condition the transcendental consciousness of the Lord, the divine Dreamer, yet what of man? The cosmic display of the triple qualities undeniably affects him on whom this dream is imposed. Why does the Lord thus test man? The answer is: God knows how to remain unaffected while participating in this cosmic dream that is tainted with the binding attributes; and because He made man in His image, He expects him to use his discrimination and to play his part in this cosmic dream of good and evil without being inwardly affected by it.

Why are evil and suffering part of God's creation?

When God created the mayic dream of entangling attributes, He hoped that man would use his divine free choice to resist the insidious evil influences. Through the storm of cosmic delusion, the Lord created soul-waves in order that He might play with them. Indeed, the little good soul-waves soon return to the safety of the Spirit's vast bosom. Even the world-entangled soul-waves and the evil-enshackled soul-waves, keeping far away from Spirit by buffeting one another in the storm of delusion, pounded by misery, eventually abandon their evil inclinations and respond to the cosmic pull of the Divine Ocean that is ever summoning them to return to Its deeps.

Therefore, God may not be blamed *wholly* for the suffering that comes to those who obdurately desire to remain a part of the ever-tempting cosmic delusion. Knowing that He is responsible for having sent man out into the hazards of Nature, the Lord ever keeps His Spirit attached to human souls, constantly pulling them toward Him, lest unrestrained they persist in hurting themselves by playing too long and too violently.

The question, "What about helpless animals that have been cast into the delusions of Nature?" is answered by the fact that animals, having no free choice, cannot long keep themselves enmeshed. Whether good or evil or active, like the sweet-voiced canary, venomous snake, and useful horse, the subhuman orders are not karmically entangled by the triple modes of Nature that definitely affect man.

Instinct-bound, the canary chirps and trills. The snake through fear may injure a man who accidentally steps on it or who tries deliberately to hurt it. After causing a man's death, a snake is not punished by evil karma, for it was unaware of the consequences of its action: it did not know that poison was introduced into its fangs by Nature.

But a human murderer who, influenced by wrath, stabs his enemy to death, incurs evil karma because of his improper use of the gift of divine free choice.

A workhorse, performing its duties pleasurably or grudgingly, is not subject to the law of karma because it has no free choice and is instinct-bound. But a businessman, toiling to make money willingly or unwillingly, is harnessed to the karmic effects of his actions because he has free choice either to work for God and the welfare of others and become emancipated, or to work for the satisfaction of his ego and selfishness and thus to remain in bondage to the thousand inexorable laws of Nature.

A snake is impervious to its own poison, but the venom is harmful to a person who is bitten; therefore one's only sensible course is to not go near snakes, or to exterminate them, or to find an antidote for snakebites. Similarly, the poison of *maya* or dream delusion does not affect God though it is in His manifested form, Prakriti; it does, however, affect all the unenlightened creatures that throng the worlds of His creation. To remedy the situation, the intelligent man should remain in good company; or, at least, should remove himself from evil company. Poisoned from birth by *maya*, he should strive to meet good persons, follow virtuous ways and the guidance of a true guru, and, most importantly, practice yoga. Through the cumulative effects of meditation, he should remain ever calm and spiritually watchful. Those are practical methods to neutralize the effects of delusion.

If God had not created the triple qualities that pleasurably and excitingly and painfully affect man, His cosmic-dream play would be meaningless. By these triune influences He tests His children; and by such tests guides them in the right use of their free choice that, after manfully and successfully playing in the dream-drama, they might find their way back to Him. He created this cosmic-dream play to entertain Himself and His children. He never meant for it to hurt His offspring. They injure themselves by not properly playing their parts. If they enact their roles intelligently, they will find happiness in this life and eternal bliss in the great hereafter.

The ultimate message of this stanza of the Bhagavad Gita is that man, made in the image of God, must learn to be transcendent like his Maker. The triple qualities of cosmic delusion, and the cosmic dream tinged with those entangling attributes, all proceed from God; but as He remains unaffected by them, so man may learn, through constant yoga communion with God, how to remain uninvolved in *maya* and how to view the panorama of life's experiences as sheer entertainment.

COSMIC HYPNOSIS (MAYA) AND THE WAY TO TRANSCEND IT

VERSE 13

tribhir guṇamayair bhāvair ebhiḥ sarvam idaṁ jagat
mohitaṁ nābhijānāti mām ebhyaḥ param avyayam

This world of mortal beings does not perceive Me, unchangeable and beyond all qualities, because they are deluded by the triple modes of Nature.

EMOTIONAL MOVIEGOERS ARE TOO INTENT on beholding motion pictures to notice overhead the picture-causing beam. Similarly, worldly men are too deeply engrossed in God's dream pictures of life to perceive His taintless omnipresent Beam that is the sole Creator, the only Doer.

As a dreamer engaged in viewing his dream of good and evil experiences cannot capture the consciousness of his wakeful state, free from the excitation of dreams, so the people of the world are so much engrossed in viewing and participating in the triply affecting cosmic dream that they fail to observe it, with unattachment, as a divine spectacle.

But leave the Wise to wrangle, and with me
The Quarrel of the Universe let be:
And, in some corner of the Hubbub coucht,
*Make Game of that which makes as much of Thee.**

The cosmic-dream delusion is imposed like a hypnotic spell on men from their birth; they remain unaware of its insidiousness. If God made His supreme blessedness evident to all men (as He does to the tested and victorious supermen), they would not be influenced by the lesser lures of the senses. God, the perfect ever-new unending Bliss, is the greatest temptation to the soul of man. Therefore He tests His children first with inferior temptations of the senses; when man has rejected those in a proper spirit of wisdom, the superior divine treasures are revealed to him.

* *The Rubaiyat of Omar Khayyam,* quatrain XLV, translated by Edward FitzGerald. Paramahansa Yogananda's spiritual interpretation of this poetic classic, *Wine of the Mystic,* is published by Self-Realization Fellowship, Los Angeles.

The secret of the cosmic game is that God hides His surprise, His bliss, behind the temptations of the world. He knows that man—made in His image, with supreme joy hidden within him—will not forever wallow in the mud of the senses. Disillusioned by unsatisfying sense pleasures, man is haunted by the memory of his lost soul peace. Harmed by the poisoned honey of pleasures, he ultimately seeks the pure divine nectar. God's game of hide-and-seek with His sons in this cosmic dream would be pointless if He had not made it hazardous with pain and pleasure. He blindfolded men with ignorance and hid His perfect Face. The surprise goal to be achieved by His children, one by one, is consciousness of identity with Him.

The secret of the cosmic game of hide-and-seek

Supermen have not received the realization of God as an unearned gift. Those who attain divine communion in infancy had entered that state in a previous life by a deep practice of yoga and meditation. No one should helplessly envy the God-realization of saints nor be discouraged by his own self-created ill luck and ignorance of God. Like the supermen, he too has been in the heart of God throughout eternity; even when he started on his round of human incarnations he came as one made in His image.* Thus remembering his divine heritage, he should not wait for good karma to arrive by sheer luck. He should put forth right effort and fan the desire to recover his forgotten bliss by accumulating good karma through meditation. Man already possesses God within himself; and, as soon as he takes the proper steps, may regain consciousness of Him.

VERSE 14

daivī hy eṣā guṇamayī mama māyā duratyayā
mām eva ye prapadyante māyām etāṁ taranti te

It is difficult indeed to go beyond the influence of My divine cosmic hypnosis, imbued with the triple qualities. Only those who take shelter in Me (the Cosmic Hypnotizer) become free from this power of illusion.

* "The Lord possessed me in the beginning of His way, before His works of old. I was set up from everlasting, from the beginning, or ever the earth was" (Proverbs 8:22–23).

IT IS HARD TO BANISH COSMIC HYPNOSIS and its entrancing phenomena, even after its influence has been detected, without constant prayer to its Maker: God. A hypnotized person is unable to escape from the potent spell until he has obtained the help of the mesmerist. When a subject learns, through the comments of others, that he is acting like an automaton, he should himself try to overcome the irrational influence. If he finds himself powerless, he must implore the aid of the hypnotist in dissolving the spell.

Ordinary people are unable to escape from the triply delusive realm of *maya*, and their only hope for freedom is in beseeching the aid of the Cosmic Magician: God.

Freeing oneself from the spell of cosmic hypnosis (maya)

Experiments of psychologists prove that a hypnotized person may be made to experience any bodily sensation even though no sensory stimulus is present; and may be made to think, feel, will, and act according to the directions of the hypnotist.

A hypnotized man may pleasurably swallow salt or quinine with the firm conviction that it is sugar; and may make the motions of swimming while on a dry floor, believing that he is surrounded by the coolness and splash of the water. By suggestion he feels chilled during warm weather; and, during a simple walk, thinks that he is riding on a train or flying in an airplane. He may be made to hear music in a silent place, to see colors and scenes and persons without their objective presence, and to smell a roselike fragrance around a skunk! He may be directed successfully to read the thoughts of others; to review forgotten scenes in the earlier parts of his life; and, while blindfolded, to read the pages of a book. In other words, a hypnotized person is partially or totally amenable to the suggestions of the mesmerist; the individuality of the subject becomes submerged in his subconscious mind and does not appear so long as he is responsive to the hypnotist.

It does not befit man, the image of God endowed with free choice, to act mechanically under the influence of the cosmic dream and to behave like an automaton under the spell of cosmic hypnosis.

LEGENDS AND TALES, COUCHING in illustrative narratives probably every conceivable quandary that has played on the human mind, abound in the ancient spiritual lore of India. "Has the Lord, who is untouched by the effects of His cosmic *maya*, ever subjected Himself to the overpowering delusion He inflicts on those He has created?" Certainly the Lord incarnate in a fully liberated being takes on something of the cosmic hypnosis in order to interrelate with His mortal contemporaries. When Jesus was tempted by Satan, his feelings were not a feigned struggle; they were a real test.

To underscore the power of delusion, a tale is told of an experiment agreed to by Lord Vishnu:

Narada, one of the immortal *rishis*—and sometimes referred to as a divine trickster for the discomfiting situations he often engendered in order to test the gods—suggested to Vishnu an unusual demonstration: "Lord, do You realize how potent the delusion is that You inflict on mortals? Would You not know better about its force if You applied it on Yourself?"

A legend of Vishnu and Narada: The power of delusion

Ever ready to satisfy the questing heart of the devotee, Vishnu responded: "Narada, what do you want Me to do?"

"Attachment is not easily renounced when one is enveloped in delusive feelings," Narada said. "Why don't You go into the body of a mother sow and see what it is like to care for a family of piglets."

Vishnu lightly accepted the proposal, but prudently added: "If you find Me staying in the sow's body longer than six months, it will be for you to release Me. After chanting an invocation, pierce the body of the sow and I will come out." Vishnu thereupon disappeared from Narada's sight into the body of a wild mother pig.

Six months passed—eight months, ten months, twelve months! In vain Narada awaited Vishnu's return by His own accord. Finally, armed with a javelin, Narada approached a rock cave where the sow lived with her young ones. When the mother sow observed Narada approaching with a spear, she bolted inside the cave with her family. Standing in the entranceway, Narada pleaded: "Please, Lord, come out." To which the sow replied, "Go away, Narada, don't bother Me."

As prearranged, Narada then chanted. At the end of the invocation, the mother sow reluctantly emerged from the cave. A voice from within her said: "Throw the javelin at Me, Narada!"

Narada complied, and Vishnu laughingly sprang out of the dead sow's body. "Oh, Narada, it felt awfully nice feeding those little piggies! How potent, indeed, is My delusion! I promise you, even the greatest among sinners who, counseled by a noble guru, unceasingly seeks Me as the Immutable Spirit, will soon have a purified soul and be liberated."

VERSE 15

na māṁ duṣkṛtino mūḍhāḥ prapadyante narādhamāḥ
māyayāpahṛtajñānā āsuraṁ bhāvam āśritāḥ

The lowest of men, perpetrators of evil and misguided fools, whose discrimination has been stolen by maya (delusion), follow the path of demoniac beings, failing to take shelter in Me.

LORD KRISHNA IS REVEALING TO ARJUNA: "Men who willingly respond to the evil quality in My cosmic delusion and who continue to indulge in promiscuous sex relations, cruelty, drinking, getting money by dishonest means, and so on, are manifesting the nature of demons that live in dark worlds. Such men do not become interested in the superior activating and good qualities of Nature and hence do not find the divine bliss trickling down from My Spirit into their souls."

Those who develop a taste for eating rotten cheeses and extremely hot spices do not enjoy mild milk cheese and delicately flavored food. Similarly, evil men who overindulge in gross pleasures become sense slaves, repeatedly acting under wrong influences, without the desire to taste the subtle happiness of the soul.

Though cosmic delusion has the strongest influence on evil men, even they can escape it by using discrimination, which can be rescued from *maya* by meditating upon God. But if evildoers persist in their wrong habits, they are reborn after death in a demoniac world.*

The Gita has emphasized again and again, however, that between all beings and their Creator is an immortal bond—indulgently elastic but breakable never. None can stray so far as to withstand forever the pulling power of God's saving grace.

Therefore, forsaking pride and obstinacy, for his own sake the evil man should cooperate with the Lord's redeeming power; he should seek good company and should learn to meditate on God.

VERSE 16

caturvidhā bhajante māṁ janāḥ sukṛtino 'rjuna
ārto jijñāsur arthārthī jñānī ca bharatarṣabha

---

* See pages 975–76.

The afflicted, the questers for wisdom, the cravers for power here and in the hereafter,* and the wise—these, O Arjuna, are the four kinds of righteous men who pursue Me.

HERE THE GITA ENUMERATES the four kinds of virtuous actors in the earthly dream drama who, to a lesser or greater degree, follow the wishes of the Cosmic Dreamer. All performers of good actions, whether their motives are selfish or unselfish, are traveling slowly or swiftly on the path of liberation. They are unlike the persons who by evil actions walk the tortuous path of bondage.

The four kinds of God-seeking souls

Most people in distress seek God, though with the selfish desire of banishing physical or mental ills. They pray to God for money or the healing of sickness for themselves or dear ones, or for some personal advantage such as avoiding a business failure or winning a lawsuit. Finding temporary relief by the grace of God and by good karma or by the power of prayer, they then easily forget Him. But other persons, undergoing even slight suffering in this life, receive superconscious intimations or memories of all the sufferings of past lives. Knowing themselves capable of violent moods and foolish actions, and fearing the consequent pain and misfortune, such men make up their minds to find God as the permanent relief from all grief. These devotees, heeding the spiritual injunctions of a God-realized guru, embark on the path of yoga (divine union) through which they can learn to commune with God.

Men of inconstant wisdom again and again seek divine aid during affliction, then revert to their interest in material solaces. Yet, even though their prayers are for selfish benefit, such men are performers of spasmodic good actions that remind them of God. They are on the right path.

The second class of people are those who unconditionally seek wisdom in order to realize their divinity and to solve the mystery of life. They use their innate endowment of free choice to good purpose and are therefore better men than the previously mentioned selfish seekers of God. It is natural that the Lord responds more eagerly to unconditional suppliants for His love than to favor-seekers!

The third class of people are those who seek complete fulfillment,

---

* *Artharthi,* lit., "he who has a strong desire to attain his aim or object"; that is, he who craves the power of fulfillment in the present and in the hereafter.

which must, necessarily, include the Giver along with His gifts. Such seekers look for God's help in attaining wealth, friends, health, power; they also practice yoga to attain bliss and all-fulfilling spiritual power in this life and in the beyond after death. In a balanced way they are trying to find a good life as well as divine realization.

The fourth class of men are the sages, defined in the next verse as the greatest of all. Their goal is not the acquisition of knowledge, nor do they seek the Lord for any ulterior purpose; they have already attained steady wisdom and divine communion. Such souls, liberated from the temptations and attachments of delusion, perpetually united to God within their hearts, unconditionally love Him. They live for Him, act for Him, and commune with Him, just to respond to His love and to revere Him willingly as a son naturally loves his father.

VERSES 17–18

teṣāṁ jñānī nityayukta ekabhaktir viśiṣyate
priyo hi jñānino 'tyartham ahaṁ sa ca mama priyaḥ (17)

udārāḥ sarva evaite jñānī tv ātmaiva me matam
āsthitaḥ sa hi yuktātmā mām evānuttamāṁ gatim (18)

(17) Chief among them is the sage, ever constant and one-pointed in devotion. For I am exceedingly dear to the sage, and he is exceedingly dear to Me.

(18) All these (four kinds of men) are noble, but the sage I consider indeed as My own Self. Unwaveringly is he settled in Me alone as his utmost goal.

INWARDLY FIXED IN GOD, devoted only to Him, the sage is ever constant (*nityayukta*), always tranquil, unchanged and unaffected by the oscillating waves of Nature's delusive forces that play over the surface of his being. Naught can turn his attention from God as his supreme goal.

He is the wisest who wholeheartedly and one-pointedly seeks God, for he is the dearest to Him. When a devotee's yearning is deep enough, it brings the rare loving response from God. Such a man fulfills God's desire for a unique romance with each of His creatures.

Therefore, among the four kinds of devotees, the sage who acts in this cosmic dream with God-consciousness only, and with supreme one-minded devotion, is closest to Him. That devotee has an unconditional love. He loves God without a selfish motive, without a businesslike arrangement: "I'll pray to Thee, O Lord, provided Thou dost give me health, money, and grace." Between the wise devotee and God there is a deeper exchange, that of fathomless love and affection. The sage's devotion is spontaneously actuated, without reservation, because it is offered in full faith that the loving, omniscient Creator—the sole Giver of all things—knows every necessity of every being. The sage is content with whatever the Lord deems best to give—or withhold.

In one's conditional seeking of the Lord, He is conscious that the suppliant is more anxious for His inferior or superior gifts than for the Giver Himself.

It is not wrong to pray to God for necessities. But when the devotee prays for divine communion he should not be hoping in the background of his mind for the bestowal of a favor. His mind should not be concentrated on gifts but solely on the Giver. When the devotee can do that in reality, all the Giver's gifts also, as the Bible says, are added unto him: "But seek ye first the kingdom of God, and His righteousness; and all these things shall be added unto you."*

VERSE 19

bahūnāṁ janmanām ante jñānavān māṁ prapadyate
vāsudevaḥ sarvam iti sa mahātmā sudurlabhaḥ

After many incarnations, the sage attains Me, realizing, "The Lord is all-pervading!" A man so illumined is hard to find.

A RARE DEVOTEE IS HE WHO DISCERNS only the Omnipresent Beam of Spirit that creates the many dreams of births and deaths, including his own. Such a man, concentrating on the Cosmic Beam alone, becomes liberated from the witnessing of the many dreams of births and deaths, forced upon mortals who are infested with lusts and pursued by karma. He can quicken his evolution by living many lives materialized in daily visions.

A person who emotionally identifies himself with the daily dream,

* Matthew 6:33.

the motion pictures of his life, does not find liberation because he becomes entangled in the web of births and deaths. He does not realize that in an average life span of sixty years a man is "born" or reawakened 21,900 times; and "dies" or enters the sleep or "little death" state 21,900 times.

Certain yoga treatises explain that with every exhalation a person dies, and with every inhalation is reborn. (On the average, man breathes eighteen times a minute.)

Some yogis say that with every "lub" sound of the heart, there is a birth; and with every "dub" sound of the heart, there is a death. According to that theory, a man lives and dies perhaps seventy times a minute—according to the normal beat per minute of his heart; in a lifetime, a person would have many more experiences of heartbeat births and deaths than those involved in inhalations and exhalations.

Medical science claims that a normal person's brain is substantially changed every eight years. According to that theory, a man is reborn eight times in a lifetime of sixty-four years.

Some sages say that evil men who die without the desire for liberation may experience bodily births and deaths during many million-year cycles.

Kriya Yoga reduces the "many incarnations" required for realization

However, Lahiri Mahasaya, Sri Yukteswar, and their advanced disciples have testified from their own realization that people with past good karma can quicken their evolution by *Kriya Yoga* practice and find liberation in three or six or twelve or twenty-four or forty-eight years in one lifetime—a liberation that ordinarily comes to a righteous person, without conscious effort, only in a million years of births and deaths, by natural evolution. A "righteous person" in this sense is one who lives in harmony with his soul and offends not the laws of Nature.

By bullock cart and boat, and by a circuitous way, it would take many years for a man to go around the earth. But by the fastest airplane and the shortest route, a person may traverse the earth in a few days and possibly in a few hours. The time will come when this distance will be covered in a matter of minutes. Similarly, the individual who makes no conscious effort may take countless lives to become liberated; but a wise man, through his knowledge of quickening evolution by *Kriya Yoga,* may find emancipation in one life.

A wisdom expert, an accomplished *Kriya Yogi,* may banish the karma of his past unfinished actions by living many births and deaths enacted in daily visions during *samadhi.* In this way, within three years he may work out all his past desires of many, many lives, by materializing them in visions through the power of *samadhi.* A sage understands that a human incarnation is a motion picture of many dreams. Such an illumined devotee does not have to go through many mortal births and deaths; on the superconscious level he can condense the requisite karmic experiences of many lives into the dreams of the present.

Fulfillment of reincarnation-making desires through superconscious visions

An advanced yogi living in the bleak Himalayas need not go to a city nor be reborn in a new body in order to work out some lingering desire. If he has a hankering for curries, for example, he can create a "technicolored," true-to-all-the-senses motion picture of tasty curries and enjoy them in this novel way, until by wisdom his karmic desires for food are dissipated forever.

On a grand scale, Mahavatar Babaji created a golden palace to fulfill a long-forgotten desire of Lahiri Mahasaya—an event I have recorded in *Autobiography of a Yogi*. The "miracle" was explained thus: "There is nothing inexplicable about this materialization. The whole cosmos is a projected thought of the Creator. The heavy clod of the earth, floating in space, is a dream of God's. He made all things out of His mind, even as man in his dream consciousness reproduces and vivifies a creation with its creatures.... In tune with the infinite all-accomplishing Will, Babaji is able to command the elemental atoms to combine and manifest themselves in any form. This golden palace, instantaneously brought into being, is real—in the same sense that the earth is real. Babaji created this beautiful mansion out of his mind and is holding its atoms together by the power of his will, even as God's thoughts created the earth and His will maintains it."

It was by means of a vision that God fulfilled to my great satisfaction a desire to be a world philanthropist. By this experience He showed me the freeing power of visions.

In my travels, visiting many countries of the world, I could not help feeling sickened at the sight of the slums throughout Europe and Asia. A desire to relieve the world of its physical poverty lodged itself in my consciousness. The desire grew and kept corroding my mind. Subconsciously I wished to be a multibillionaire so that I would have the means to alleviate this human suffering. But I realized the mortal limitations of material life and the improbability of gathering that sum for human good. To carry on such a program might indeed take not one but many incarnations! It was an irrational and presumptuous desire of which I decided I must rid myself. It was my spiritual duty to perform in this life only those actions that God so ordained and pointed out to me in my periods of silence. Nevertheless, the pain of suffering humanity would not release its grip on my heart.

One night, as I meditated, a vision stole over me. I found myself a multibillionaire businessman. In my vision I traveled with engineers, scientists, artisans, architects, industrial and agricultural experts, through every slum in the world, building modern houses, opening cooperative industries and farms and medical centers, and feeding and giving gainful employment to all needy people.

When every one of the fifteen hundred million members of the global family had a job and was well-fed, I was supremely happy. Then my vision vanished, leaving me completely contented. God had satisfied in a few minutes a desire unlikely to be fulfilled even by several incarnations of hard earthly working and planning.

Alas, the captive world, prisoner of its own karmic bonds, could not avail itself of the freeing influence of my cosmic vision. Each being dreams its own environment and ultimately its own divine awakening according to God's orderly evolutionary plan and compassionate grace.

Therefore, God would not like everyone to avoid work, service, mental effort, and perseverance, nor to try to perform philanthropic actions, by satisfying themselves only in dreams and visions. The average person, in fact, cannot produce true visions—only hallucinatory imaginings, at best—so he is unable thereby to free himself from duties through this method. But the liberated or nearly liberated yogi who can create visions at will can in this manner destroy all karmic effects of his actions and prevent new desire-seeds from taking root. Visions may include the detailed happenings of many years, yet since they are seen through the spiritual eye on the superconscious plane, not on the material plane of relativity, they occupy an incredibly short span of time. Many incarnations are thereby accelerated by condensation into one or a few lifetimes.

The yogi thus rejects the slow-paced formula of "many incarnations" as a necessary prelude to his final entry into the kingdom of God. By *Kriya Yoga* he hastens his evolution multifold; and by employing visions he dismisses reincarnation-making lingering desires. Above all, by divine communion in *samadhi* meditation he realizes the Supreme Lord as the All-in-All, the singular all-pervading Reality.

Krishna says in this stanza, "Even a wise man attains Me only after many births—because a yogi aware of My omnipresence is rare." These words have a wonderfully cryptic meaning: "Wise men attain Me only after many births, because it is so seldom that even a sage understands that I—as the Indweller in the tiniest atom and in the soul of man—am the Nearest of the near, attainable instantly!"

Which "God" Should Be Worshiped?

Verse 20

kāmais tais tair hṛtajñānāḥ prapadyante 'nyadevatāḥ
taṁ taṁ niyamam āsthāya prakṛtyā niyatāḥ svayā

Led by their own inclinations, their discrimination stolen by this or that craving, pursuing this or that cultic injunction, men seek lesser gods.

A butterfly mind willy-nilly sails on with the breeze of its innate moods acquired in past lives. Indiscriminately it dwells on various blossoms of desires, or is fitfully engaged in superficial religious worship, drinking the honey of their meager pleasures or temporary inspirations. Such a restless, shallow mind is for a time engrossed in any dear object or action, deifying it, and thus forgetting to seek the supreme nectar of bliss and God-realization.

Many people in this world become engaged without discrimination in the performance of various material and religious actions. According to their innate natures, inclinations, and habits of past lives and of this life, they devote themselves to worship of money, fame, power, and so on. They deify the object of their desires and the lesser gifts of God. They thus forget to worship the God of gods, the Giver of all gifts. The choice of most people concerning religious practices and beliefs is similarly indiscriminate and whim-led; ritualism or dogmatism is their "lesser god."

Every person, by self-analysis, should detect his injurious mental and material habits. He should cease to identify himself with his "second nature," and rather assist his true nature of the soul, loving the divine bliss of Spirit, to emerge from behind the clouds of indiscretion, ignorantly formed useless habits, and spiritual indifference.

VERSES 21–22

yo yo yāṁ yāṁ tanuṁ bhaktaḥ śraddhayārcitum icchati
tasya tasyācalāṁ śraddhāṁ tām eva vidadhāmy aham (21)

sa tayā śraddhayā yuktas tasyārādhanam īhate
labhate ca tataḥ kāmān mayaiva vihitān hi tān (22)

(21) Whatever embodiment (a God-incarnate, a saint, or a deity) a devotee strives faithfully to worship, it is I who make his devotion unflinching.

(22) Absorbed in that devotion, intent on the worship of that embodiment, the devotee thus gains the fruits of his longings. Yet those fulfillments are verily granted by Me alone.

A TRUE DEVOTEE EXPRESSING DEVOTION to God through any lesser or higher mode of worship will find response to his desire from the Supreme Being. He who worships representative forms of the Godhead—because for him the Absolute is unfathomable—will receive the grace of God that blesses his devotional endeavor.

Formless Spirit manifests in whatever form is dear to the devotee

Therefore, even the worshiper of lesser gods, personifications of the Supreme Deity, does not go divinely unrecognized or unrewarded. If a person of deep devotion offers homage to the form of any deity symbolically representing God, He silently responds by materializing that form in visions before the devotee. God is secreted in that manifestation, although the form itself reveals only a modicum of Spirit.

In India, Cosmic Nature and the Infinite—in one common depiction—are symbolized in the form of Kali, the Mother of the Universe, standing on the breast of her husband Shiva, or God. This symbolism (unraveled!) signifies that Cosmic Nature does not test or tempt the devotee with delusion if he is consciously united to the Infinite (the breast of Shiva). Many pious Hindus worship God and His immanence in the cosmos in the forms of Shiva and Kali.

No matter what mode of worship the devotee adopts to find God, the Lord accepts it, if the devotion be genuine. This divine acceptance enables the mind of the devotee to concentrate on the Spirit behind the specific symbol. When a great devotee worships a symbolical deity as God, He manifests His unseen omnipresence by a visible display of that symbolical form. He appears before, talks with, and blesses the earnest devotee through the form that is beloved by him.

The symbolical form of God appearing to a Hindu devotee as Kali, Durga, Vishnu, Shiva, or Krishna, for example, becomes a permanent blueprint in the ether. If any other devotee concentrates very deeply on that deity, which has actually been seen and worshiped by a great saint, that same manifestation appears in living form to satisfy the devotee's true heart-call. Similarly, any devotee fervently worshiping God in the form of Jesus Christ, the Holy Mother, Saint Francis, Babaji, Lahiri Mahasaya, or any saint or true guru (either mentally, or before an image or a picture) may see that form first in vision, and then, by deeper spiritual advancement, as a materialized being, living and talking.

Any devotee who ardently meditates on the picture or form of a true guru or any other master becomes attuned to him, imbibing his qualities, and ultimately feels in that saint the presence of God. As people can talk back and forth over the radio by tuning in, so a devotee may tune in with a saint and may see him televised in the crystal sphere of the spiritual eye. That is what is implied in this stanza of the Bhagavad Gita. Elsewhere it says: "In whatever way people are devoted to Me, in that measure (according to their desire, understanding, and mode of worship) I manifest Myself to them."*

After all, the Omnipresent God knows all His true devotees, no matter in what form they love Him. Christ said, "Are not two sparrows sold for a farthing? and one of them shall not fall on the ground without your Father."† If God's omniscience is aware of a small sparrow, how much more deeply is He cognizant of His true lovers!

The Omniscient alone, who knows the hearts of His children, answers their prayers in many ways. Devotion shown to God always evokes some form of plain or mysterious response. No true devotee is ignored by God.

However, shallow seekers who worship astral deities for the fulfillment of desires do not realize that it is God who will fulfill their wishes through the instrumentality of the divine beings. The Lord is consciously present in all higher beings and in their devotees. It is He who is *Chintamani,* "the jewel that grants all desires."

---

* IV:11. † Matthew 10:29.

VERSE 23

antavat tu phalaṁ teṣāṁ tad bhavaty alpamedhasām
devān devayajo yānti madbhaktā yānti mām api

But men of scant knowledge (worshiping lesser gods) receive limited results. The devotees of the deities go unto them; My devotees come unto Me.

"THOSE WHO ADORE THE STARRY dream beings, shining by a little borrowed light of My omniscience, fail to perceive My subtle luminescence spread everywhere, sustaining the manifestations of all entities. Worshipers of little gods—lesser aspects of My omnipresent Being—go unto them and then must be reborn on earth. Devotees who everywhere perceive My Cosmic Light commingle with It and do not have to experience further dream motion pictures of births and deaths."

Men of small understanding, worshiping lesser deities for the boons they are known to grant, receive those favors and after death attain the beautiful astral spheres; but, at the expiration of good karma, they have to return again to the earth. By the same amount of spiritual labor, these shortsighted worshipers could have gained, by adoring the Supreme Being and dissolving all the darkness of human karma in the quenchless light of ecstasy, the eternal blessed spheres from which there is no return.

It would be foolish for a person to work as an employee eighteen hours a day for his lifetime to earn only one hundred twenty thousand dollars, if, in the same number of years, by the same amount of intelligent labor invested in running a business of his own, he could earn a million dollars. Similarly, man is shortsighted to worship lesser astral gods (who, too, must expire at the end of their long life span) just to gain favors and a temporary stay in the beautiful astral worlds.

Why not determinedly seek the Supreme God, the Lord of all other gods, and attain for all time endless blessedness and freedom? Devotees who commune with the Supreme Spirit in this life dissolve all their rebirth-making karma in the fire of highest ecstasy and thus reach the Eternal Abode, never again to return to the troublesome earth. What could be greater than getting in touch with the Life of life, the Maker of the law of karma, the "Boss" of the universe? What use in bothering with His lesser manifestations—His humble employees?

Krishna's words to Arjuna (words of promise from Spirit to the devotee) are sweetly reassuring to all of us: "My devotee comes unto Me."

VERSE 24

avyaktaṁ vyaktim āpannaṁ manyante mām abuddhayaḥ
paraṁ bhāvam ajānanto mamāvyayam anuttamam

Men without wisdom consider Me, the Unmanifest, as assuming embodiment (like a mortal being taking a form)—not understanding My unsurpassable state, My unchangeable unutterable nature.

IGNORANT DEVOTEES WHO HAVE VISIONS of lesser deities in meditation do not know that all those forms are merely temporary, meager manifestations of the essentially unmanifested Spirit. They concentrate on the finite forms of the Infinite God and thus, in their minds, limit Him.

As unseen vapor can be condensed into water and frozen into an iceberg, so the invisible impersonal God can be projected into a form by devotion's frost, and worshiped as a personality. However, a devotee is foolish if he limits God to that form and forgets His omnipresence. A great master, Sri Ramakrishna Paramahansa, who saw God constantly as Mother Kali, conversing often with Her, later said: "I had to destroy that finite form of my Mother with the sword of wisdom, to behold Her as the formless Infinite."

Many devotees in India, for instance, limit their conceptions of Godhead to images of Krishna. They put an idol to sleep under sheets on the altar at night; and "awaken" it by singing chants before it in the morning, placing the image in a standing position on the altar. They lay food and fruits in front of the idol each morning and evening, a symbolic act of feeding it. If a devotee performs such worship with sincere devotion, of course God receives the spirit of love behind the offering. But a devotee who makes his worship too personal obliterates the thought of God's impersonal all-pervading nature. He who worships God merely as a finite form will not attain the transcendental divine union with His infinite nature.

PERCEIVING THE SPIRIT BEHIND THE DREAM-SHADOWS OF NATURE

VERSE 25

nāhaṁ prakāśaḥ sarvasya yogamāyāsamāvṛtaḥ
mūḍho 'yaṁ nābhijānāti loko mām ajam avyayam

Seemingly eclipsed by My own Yoga-Maya (the delusion born of the triple qualities in Nature), I am unseen by men. The bewildered world knows not Me, the Unborn, the Deathless.

THE UNCHANGEABLE, CAUSELESS, invisible light of Cosmic Consciousness remains hidden behind the dream shadows of creation, unperceived by its countless dream entities.

Only a few wise men, detached in their outlook by a practice of yoga ecstasy, look up into the spiritual eye and through its omniscient vision see the pure spherical cosmic beam—the manifested power of the Unmanifested Spirit—that produces within its heart the technicolored motion pictures of life. Just as the shadows of motion pictures hide the beam that produces them, so God's Light is hidden in the delusive scenes of life, all shadowed by the triple qualities. Except to the uplifted, awakened spiritual gaze of the sage, the cosmic beam and the Spirit within it are invisible, unnoticeable.

VERSE 26

vedāhaṁ samatītāni vartamānāni cārjuna
bhaviṣyāṇi ca bhūtāni māṁ tu veda na kaścana

O Arjuna, I am aware of the creatures of the past, the present, and the future; but Me no one knows.

IF YOU ARE A DREAMER with a good memory, you can relive in your mind a past dream. It might have been one in which you had a heated argument with your brothers. You would be aware of all the details of your dream, but your dream brothers would possess no such memories.

The Cosmic Dreamer, on the other hand, possessing omniscient memory and omnipresence, is aware not only of His present cosmic dreams, but of all that went on within Him in the past, and of all that is going to happen within Him in the future—appearing and disappearing in His spaceless, timeless consciousness of an eternal present. But, alas, none of the transient, living, sentient human beings in this cosmic dream (except those who are liberated saints) are aware of the unchangeable light of Cosmic Consciousness that creates, within its omniscience, the cosmic dream pictures of all time.

Human consciousness is limited by the threefold relativity of time—past, present, and future. Man usually forgets past happenings, has consciousness of the present incidents in his life, and is unaware of the future. But God's consciousness is ever aware throughout eternity.

Divine consciousness has no past, no future, because it is never interrupted, like man's, by death or limitation. Eternal consciousness has one time—the ever present. God looks through the window of infinite consciousness on the films of finite happenings of the past, present, and future shown on the screen of time and space, continuously moving backward and forward in an eternal now.

Mortals are not aware of God because of their identification with His cosmic dream. Only liberated yogis, united with the Lord, are aware of Him and know all the past, present, and future happenings that are going on within Him in an ever-now.*

God's presence is veiled in His cosmic dream and in its sentient creatures. Behind the Yoga-Maya, the magical dream pictures of Cosmic Nature, stained with triple qualities, God's Beam is adroitly hidden.

Human beings can behold one another on the screen of cosmic delusion, but they cannot perceive the cause, the unseen Cosmic Light.

Within this magical shadow of Yoga-Maya, God is secreted, beyond even the most subtle understanding of man. Yet the Lord, unaffected by delusion, is ever aware that He veils Himself by His self-created Maya. The liberated beings tear off this shroud and gaze on the Eternal Beauty.

* "People like us, who believe in physics," said Einstein, "know that the distinction between past, present, and future is only a stubbornly persistent illusion." (*Publisher's Note*)

VERSE 27

icchādveṣasamutthena dvandvamohena bhārata
sarvabhūtāni saṁmohaṁ sarge yānti paraṁtapa

O Descendant of Bharata, Scorcher of Foes (Arjuna)! at birth all creatures are immersed in delusive ignorance (moha) by the delusion of the pairs of opposites springing from longing and aversion.

A MAN WITNESSING A DREAM is affected from the very start by its pleasant or unpleasant nature. Similarly, as soon as a human being is born in a particular part of this cosmic dream, he begins to respond emotionally. He views the pairs of opposites as either pleasurable or disagreeable according to his individual liking or disliking. Thus, beholding the drama of contrary elements, he knows desire and aversion. Succumbing to the impulses of likes and dislikes, the discrimination and free choice of his soul are overwhelmed and he is plunged into delusive ignorance, *moha,* the ego's indivisible cohesion to delusion.* The subjection from birth to the oppositional states of delusion, good and evil, is man's state of "original sin."

A person who looks out of a clean window and who then gazes through a dirty window will first see the objects outside clearly and in their natural colors, and then obscurely, as though dimmed by darkness. Similarly, according to the good or evil character of his own dream drama, a man is happily or adversely affected.

To be born in a physical body—to breathe at all—is to be subject to maya

To be born in a physical body at all is a clue that man is in soul ignorance and has not realized his identity as formless Spirit. (The exceptions are masters who return here at God's command to guide their stumbling brothers.) To breathe at all is to breathe in *maya*. Thus from their very birth children are exposed to cosmic delusion and grow up helplessly under it. God gives them delusion first, and not Himself, in order to carry on His dramatic scheme of creation. If He did not cover Himself with the veils of *maya,* there could be no Cosmic Game of creation, in which men play hide-and-seek with Him and try to find Him as the Grand Prize.

When man is disillusioned by the lesser temptations of sense pleasures, he seeks the supreme temptation of life, God's bliss. In this way

---

* See reference to *moha,* I:9, page 93.

man learns to use His divine gifts of discrimination and free choice to find the Reality behind the appearances of life. At birth human beings fall into delusion, that they be disposed to play at least a little while with God. Then, motivated by discrimination or by suffering for misbehaving, they make the effort to return forever to His Eternal Blessed Home. Knowing this truth, no devotee should be despondent about finding ultimate liberation.

When the water in a pot is agitated, the moving water disturbs any reflected object. Similarly, when the calm waters of a man's heart are stirred by likes and dislikes, he is unable to solve his problems and to make wise decisions. Nor can a restless heart reflect the inward presence of the blissful soul.

Owing to prenatal habits of desires and aversions, a human being is agitated from birth by the triple qualities of cosmic *maya*. Except the wise, all men are born with delusion (*moha*), attachment to body consciousness. When an individual from early childhood shows signs of soul qualities, that person has been born with inherent superconsciousness earned by good karma in the past.

VERSE 28

yeṣāṁ tv antagataṁ pāpaṁ janānāṁ puṇyakarmaṇām
te dvandvamohanirmuktā bhajante māṁ dṛḍhavratāḥ

But righteous men, their sins obliterated, and subject no longer to the oppositional delusions, worship Me steadfastly.

ADVANCED YOGIS DO NOT automatically come under the sway of delusion when they are reborn. Having performed good actions in past lives, they have quelled the agitating effects of past karma by self-discipline. Thus the calm waters of their hearts are free from the ripples of likes and dislikes; they devotedly concentrate on the Spirit reflected within the human soul.

Men of good actions, without sinful, misery-making attachments and repulsions to sense objects, find their hearts free from the battle of opposite qualities. Wholeheartedly and with purified minds they worship God firmly as the Abode of All Goodness.

VERSE 29

jarāmaraṇamokṣāya mām āśritya yatanti ye
te brahma tad viduḥ kṛtsnam adhyātmaṁ karma cākhilam

Those who seek deliverance from decay and death by clinging to Me know Brahman (the Absolute), the all-inclusiveness of Adhyatma (the soul as the repository of Spirit), and all secrets of karma.

THE DEVOTEE, ON WAKING IN GOD, realizes that he has been dreaming through *maya* about dual experiences of life governed by the law of karma, actions and their fruits.

Wise men do not rely on imperfect material methods of medicine, diet, or magic in seeking freedom from the ultimate mortal limitations of disease, old age, and death. Instead, they find shelter in God, the only permanent protection against the devastations of misery. Identified with Him, yogis know all secrets of the law of karma, which binds human lives to the wheel of births and rebirths; they also know the way of escape from the wheel, and all other deep mysteries and realities hidden in the soul—the omniscient, individualized image of Spirit.

VERSE 30

sādhibhūtādhidaivaṁ māṁ sādhiyajñaṁ ca ye viduḥ
prayāṇakāle 'pi ca māṁ te vidur yuktacetasaḥ

Those who perceive Me in the Adhibhuta (the physical), the Adhidaiva (the astral), and the Adhiyajna (the spiritual), with heart united to the soul, continue to perceive Me even at the time of death.

BY PRACTICING YOGA THE DEVOTEE learns to perceive the presence of God in his physical, astral, and causal bodies, and learns to unite his heart*

* *Chetas,* the feeling or awareness that is the sum of the consciousness existent and operative in man. The meaning of the terms *Adhibhuta, Adhidaiva,* and *Adhiyajna* (and *Adhyatma* from VII:29) are elaborated in VIII:1–4.

with the bliss of the soul. Such a God-conscious yogi retains his divine consciousness even at the time of the colossal earthquake of death.

In order to keep the continuity of God-awareness at the time of the most important event—earthly transition—the yogi must be highly advanced. When the "canary" (an ordinary devotee) is caught by the "cat" (approaching death), it forgets its divine warblings and starts screeching in terror. It is therefore necessary to establish the ecstatic divine union so deeply that severe trials of disease or the approach of death will not cause the devotee to scream in dread and to forget the holy presence of God. A great master, even during the state of a painful death, can commune with his Maker.

Why the ordinary man is terrified at the onset of physical death

The Lord's tests are sometimes very subtle. Jesus, during his agony on the cross, for a minute felt God slipping away from Him. So he cried, "My God, my God, why hast Thou forsaken me?" Other fully illumined masters have similarly known a moment or two of trial at the time of death; yet, like Christ, they emerged triumphant.

The ordinary man's center of consciousness is the body; he is constantly troubled by its changes. He should practice meditation until he feels his consciousness centered on God. In that state the devotee has no more concern about his body; he feels Divinity within and without. When his body, mind, and soul are saturated with the Lord, he can rise above all tests of dire sufferings and the approach of death. Experiencing the unparalleled joy of God, the devotee forgets all pain.

An ordinary man usually leads a reckless life, little understanding its purpose. He does not realize that his whole life is a spiritual military training school in which he should discipline his body, mind, and emotions to achieve victory at the final battle of death on the last day of his earthly sojourn.

Lacking this realization, the mortal man finds himself unprepared for death. At that time the soul, with its ego-consciousness, gradually retires to the astral and causal bodies. Man's dimming mind is then disturbed by the awakened memory of all kinds of battling good and evil karma of this life and of past lives. Then he finds death inexorably separating his soul (encased in the astral and causal bodies) from his physical body. The ego is aghast to discover that the long-familiar bodily instrument is becoming inert and insensible at the approach of death. Accustomed to think and feel with the body, the ego is bewildered and senseless when deprived of the brain and the sense organs.

The ego enters a tug-of-war with death. So long as desire for physical life remains, the ego lodges adamantly in the brain and spine, even while a state of apparent death is manifesting in the physical form. When the ego utterly fails to arouse the paralyzed body, it reluctantly makes its exit in the astral body into the astral world. Then the ego sleeps for a while in the astral body, or is conscious of life in an astral world.

After a while the ego begins to be disturbed by its innate subconscious material desires and by the muffled longing to express itself through a physical vehicle. At this time the cosmic law of karma, acting according to the desires and nature of the physically disembodied ego, sends it to be reborn on earth to parents similar in certain karmic respects to this wandering soul.

The parents-to-be unknowingly generate, during coition, an astral light of united positive-negative currents in their coccygeal regions, which is referred to the sperm and ovum. When the sperm and its genetic and karmic potential from the father unites with the ovum and its pattern from the mother, there is a flash of astral light from this fertilized cell that attracts and guides the physically disembodied ego with its compatible karmic blueprint into the haven of its new primal cell of life.

How the yogi prepares himself during life to be victorious at death

A yogi thoroughly trains himself throughout his life, practicing nonattachment to the objects of sense, and harmoniously uniting his ego with his soul by disconnecting life force and mind from the senses. Thus he can withdraw his ego at will from the material world. Then, by sensory-motor relaxation, he learns to withdraw his ego, life force, and mind from the physical body into the inner organs and spine. By voluntary relaxation he withdraws his ego, life force, and mind upward through the seven cerebrospinal centers and unites them with the bliss of the soul. Finally he withdraws his soul (detached from its ego nature, his bodily operative consciousness, his life force, and his astral and causal bodies) and unites it with Spirit. Thus an expert yogi who can merge his soul at will in God and who is free from all material desires does not ordinarily feel, at the approach of death, any physical or mental agony, or the tug-of-war between death and the physical desires. Finding his karmic term in the bodily prison over, he gladly makes a "grand exit." He does not again return to this world, unless he is so commanded by God, for he has learned all the lessons that this earth was created to teach.

om tat sat iti śrīmadbhagavadgītāsu upaniṣatsu
brahmavidyāyām yogaśāstre śrīkṛṣṇārjunasaṁvāde
jñānavijñānayogo nāma saptamo 'dhyāyaḥ

Aum, Tat, Sat.
In the Upanishad of the holy Bhagavad Gita—the discourse of Lord Krishna to Arjuna, which is the scripture of yoga and the science of God-realization—this is the seventh chapter, called "The Yoga of Knowledge and Discriminative Wisdom."

CHAPTER VIII

The Imperishable Absolute: Beyond the Cycles of Creation and Dissolution

The Manifestations of Spirit in the Macrocosm and Microcosm

The Yogi's Experience at the Time of Death

The Method of Attaining the Supreme

The Cycles of Cosmic Creation

The Way of Release From the Cycles of Rebirth

"A part of God's consciousness (Tat)—undifferentiated, and Itself unmanifested—is reflected in Nature, the worlds of becoming, in which He dreams eternally the cycles of evolution and involution. But in His essential nature He is the Unmanifested One, beyond all vibratory realms of cosmic dreams, Sat or Eternal Being, Existence Itself."

THE IMPERISHABLE ABSOLUTE: BEYOND THE CYCLES OF CREATION AND DISSOLUTION

THE MANIFESTATIONS OF SPIRIT IN THE MACROCOSM AND MICROCOSM

VERSES 1–2

arjuna uvāca
kiṁ tad brahma kim adhyātmam kiṁ karma puruṣottama
adhibhūtaṁ ca kiṁ proktam adhidaivaṁ kim ucyate (1)

adhiyajñaḥ kathaṁ ko 'tra dehe 'smin madhusūdana
prayāṇakāle ca kathaṁ jñeyo 'si niyatātmabhiḥ (2)

Arjuna said:
(1) O Best of the Purushas (Krishna)! Please tell me, what is Brahman (Spirit)? What is Adhyatma (the Kutastha Consciousness underlying all manifestations and existing as the souls of all beings in the cosmos)? And what is Karma (cosmic and meditative actions born of Aum)? What is Adhibhuta (the consciousness immanent in phys [redacted] ***creatures and the physical cosmos)? And what is*** [redacted] ***nsciousness manifest in astral bodies and th*** [redacted]

(2) O Slayer [redacted] ***dhu (Krishna)! What is Adhiyajna (the Supreme Cre*** [redacted] ***and Cognizing Spirit), and in what manner is Adhiyajna present (as the soul) in this body? And how, at the time of death, art Thou to be known by the self-disciplined?***

THE TERMS USED BY KRISHNA (in the last two stanzas of Chapter VII) have bewildered Arjuna. He beseeches the Lord to enlighten him about the cosmic mysteries.

VERSE 3

śrībhagavān uvāca
akṣaraṁ brahma paramaṁ svabhāvo 'dhyātmam ucyate
bhūtabhāvodbhavakaro visargaḥ karmasaṁjñitaḥ

The Blessed Lord replied:
The Indestructible and Supreme Spirit is Brahman. Its undifferentiated manifestation (as Kutastha Chaitanya and as the individual soul) is called Adhyatma. The Aum (Cosmic Vibration or the Visarga) that causes the birth and sustenance and dissolution of beings and their various natures is termed Karma (cosmic action).

THE COSMIC DREAMER FROM HIS divine consciousness creates by *Aum* vibration the dreams of the physical cosmos and of human bodies. He reflects Himself therein as the omnipresent *Kutastha* Consciousness and expresses facets of His individuality as dream souls. The Cosmic Dreamer, in order to carry on continuously His objective cosmic vibratory dream drama of Nature and the actings of all dream beings on the stage of life, governs them all by the disciplining rhythmic law of karma.

The Spirit is imperishable, ever existent in the changeless nonvibratory sphere. As the moon is able to reflect itself on objects as a shining light, so the nature of Spirit enables It to reflect Itself as Cosmic Intelligence (*Kutastha Chaitanya*) and as individual souls shining through physical bodies.

The cosmic vibration (*Aum*) with its law of duality and relativity emanates from Spirit and causes the birth, sustenance, and dissolution of all matter and beings through the law of karma. This law of action holds sway over all activities of man and Nature.

Arjuna asked seven questions in stanzas one and two: (1) about Spirit; (2) about *Adhyatma* (Spirit's pure reflection as Cosmic Intelligence and as the individual soul); (3) about karma (cosmic and meditative actions born of *Aum*); (4) about *Adhibhuta* (the physical body and the physical universe); (5) about *Adhidaiva* (the astral body and astral cosmos); (6) about *Adhiyajna* (the supreme creative-cognizing Spirit, and how It is present in the body as soul); and (7) about the yogi's perceptions of God at the time of death.

In this third stanza the first three questions are answered. In the fourth stanza the fourth, fifth, and sixth questions are answered. The seventh question is answered in the fifth and sixth stanzas.

The three questions explained in this section are about the Spirit, the soul, and karma (the cosmic *Aum* vibration that manifests itself internally as meditative and spiritual actions and externally as bodily and cosmic activities).

THE TRANSCENDENTAL SUPREME SPIRIT exists in relation to the vibratory cosmos but is also beyond it. *Sat* or Being; God the Father, of the Christian Bible; Para-Brahman of the Bhagavad Gita and the Vedanta philosophy; Paramatman of the yogis; and Para-Purusha, Transcendental Spirit, are various names of this unchangeable supreme Spirit existing beyond the dream-structures of vibratory creation.

1. Para-Brahman, the absolute and all-inclusive Spirit

A man in a half-sleep state can remain conscious of himself and of his restfulness without thoughts or dreams. Similarly, the unmanifested Spirit can remain as ever-existing, ever-conscious, ever-new joy, without the dreams of creation. In this state, Spirit is without thoughts, or vibrations—Its existence, consciousness, and bliss merged as one single perception. As the undifferentiated Absolute, Spirit keeps Its existence, Its consciousness, and Its dream creations dissolved in one joyous perception of Itself.

As a man half-consciously can perceive a dream, so the unmanifested Spirit, after creating Its cosmic dream, keeps Its consciousness divided (into three parts).

In the first state the transcendental dreamless Spirit (or Supreme Brahman) exists beyond Its vibratory dream creations, beyond the cosmic *Aum*.

In the second state Spirit materializes Its consciousness into a vibratory dream universe. This objective cosmic dream structure is variously spoken of as the Cosmic *Aum,* the *Abhasa Chaitanya* or reflected light of *Kutastha* Intelligence; as the reflected creative consciousness of God, or the Word, the intelligent Holy Ghost vibration, which is the same as the intelligent Cosmic Prakriti, the Cosmic Sound, or the Cosmic Light. Still other terms for this objective dream universe are the *Mahatattva* or the great Vibratory Elements; and Mother Nature, or the Cosmic Virgin Mary, the Cosmic Intelligent Consort of God. This cosmic vibratory force derives its power from *Kutastha Chaitanya,* the pure reflection of God's intelligence in creation, and is the mother of all spiritual (elevating), material (activating), and evil (obstructing) activities (the three *gunas*) in the world.

This Cosmic *Aum* is also called *visarga* or "the two dots of duality," because by the dual law of relativity and by the triple qualities of the *gunas* it produces the cosmic film of delusion.* God's beam of consciousness passing through this cosmic film of relativity produces the cosmic dream pictures. When these two dots of duality become one with God, the Cosmic *Aum* manifests Him. A yogi listening to the cosmic sound of *Aum* can see, on the external side, the dream of creation and all the activities issuing out of it; on the inner side he hears the cosmic sound that melts into the absolute bliss of Brahman.

The unmanifested Spirit uses the third part of Its consciousness to reflect Itself as the undifferentiated intelligence of creation (which becomes differentiated and active in the reflected creative *Aum* vibration —as previously noted). This Intelligence shining on creation is called the *Kutastha* or Christ Intelligence, "the only begotten Son of God," the sole undistorted pure reflected intelligence of the transcendental God in creation, or (in Sanskrit) the *Tat*. In the unmanifested state the Spirit is ever-existing, ever-conscious, ever-new Bliss. When It dreams creation, It becomes a Trinity. The transcendental God, dreaming through the *Kutastha* Intelligence and the Cosmic Vibratory Intelligence, becomes the objective dreams of causal, astral, and physical universes. The unmanifested Spirit thus in the creative state becomes the three: *Aum-Tat-Sat;* Holy Ghost, Son, and Father; or the objective Cosmic Dream.

This answers Arjuna's first question as to who is Para-Brahman or the transcendental God.

❖
2. Adhyatma (soul)
❖

KRISHNA REVEALS TO ARJUNA that an aspect of the nature of the transcendental God is to dream the cosmic universe and the creatures in it. His pure unchanging consciousness within the dream, providing the underlying intelligence, is the *Kutastha Chaitanya,* individually expressed as the soul.

---

* The *visarga* is a symbol in Sanskrit grammar consisting of two perpendicular dots (:) and is expressed by a strong audible "h" aspiration. The various grammatical symbols (such as the *visarga*), as well as each of the letters in the Sanskrit alphabet, represent by their sounds a specific vibratory force. (See I:21–22, pages 130–31.) The vibratory powers of the alphabetical sounds are integral with the activities of the rays of life and consciousness of the "petals" of the thousand-petaled lotus (*sahasrara*); the *visarga* vibration is said to be at the top of the Brahmarandhra, doorway to Spirit—and conversely, the doorway through which Spirit descends into the body. The word *visarga* derives from *vi,* "division, dividing into two parts," and *sarga,* "primary creation; the creation of the world." The *visarga* grammatical symbol with its two dots of duality, and the word itself, thus refer to the *Aum* vibration, which through duality and the law of karma or action creates a multitude of forms from the One Spirit, and resolves again the many into the One.

As a dreamer in dreamland creates various images having life or soul, so the Divine Dreamer, God, becomes the various dream bodies of human beings and manifests in them as their dream souls. Each soul subjectively dreamed by God as an individuality in a specific body makes a composite dream man in the cosmos. *Adhyatma* signifies the underlying soul, *adhy* meaning "underlying" and *atma* meaning "soul." Therefore, Arjuna's question about *Adhyatma* is answered: *Adhyatma* is the underlying "universal soul" or *Kutastha Chaitanya,* and the individual dream soul encased in a body dreamed by God. It is said that He loves to dream Himself as separate souls. This gives the Lord an opportunity to play with the conscious dream-souls in His cosmic drama.

3. Cosmic Karma or meditative actions born of Aum vibration

KARMA SIGNIFIES ALL COSMIC divine and material activities as well as the spiritual and worldly activities of human beings. These activities emanate from the two cosmic dots of duality of the *visarga,* the cosmic *Aum* vibration. The intelligent cosmic vibration, the Nature aspect of God, externally emanates all material cosmic activities and spiritual and worldly activities of human beings. Internally it makes manifest all divine activities emanating from God in the macrocosm of Nature; and it helps man to adopt those good karmic activities that assist him in understanding his own soul and the Supreme Spirit.

In the vibrationless perfect God there is no action. Action or karma denotes the intelligent vibrations of a Self-conscious being. The *Aum* or cosmic intelligent vibration is the first manifestation of God in creation. Therefore all the cosmic activities emanating from the intelligent cosmic Vibratory Being—the *Aum*—are termed Supreme Cosmic Karma. Man is a miniature or microcosmic manifestation of the macrocosmic Vibratory Being (the invisible intelligent Holy Ghost, or *Aum,* or the Word).

Man's spiritual, worldly, and evil activities are termed human karma. God, manifested as the cosmic Vibratory Being or *Aum,* is the direct Originator of all cosmic and human activities, governed by the law of karma, or cause and effect. The whole cosmos and all its sentient beings are subject to this law. The cosmic Vibratory Being, as God's representative, is not only the maker of this law of karma but the giver of its fruits. According to this divine decree, when man properly uses the gift of free choice he receives good results. Similarly, when man performs material or evil activities he reaps material or evil effects. Animals, not subject to individual karma, are under the sway of group or mass karma.

The word *karma* signifies any intelligent activity issuing out of the cosmic Vibratory Being or of any intelligent creature in the cosmos.

Definition of individual karma and mass karma

Each cosmic or human activity according to its specific nature produces good, worldly, or evil results. For example, the planetary positions devised by the cosmic Vibratory Being reflect the planetary karma that affects man's life and actions in the world in a good or an evil way. Similarly, when man initiates a good, worldly, or evil activity, that action produces its suitable result.

Therefore, just as a middle-aged man can say: "My life and habits are the results of my activities since childhood," so each human life is the effect of the activities of past lives. And the sum total of the activities of a man's entire life will determine the specific nature of one or more of his future incarnations.

An animal's life is predestined; man's is not. The tiger is ferocious and bloodthirsty by instinct. The lamb is characteristically meek and gentle. Since animals have no free choice, their traits are not the results of past actions, but are forced upon them according to the good, active, or evil qualities in intelligent Nature. But man's early good and evil traits are not thus forced upon him. They are the result of the good and bad actions of his past life or lives. Therefore, even though each man may be influenced by the triple qualities of cosmic delusion (*maya*), he still has the divine gift of free choice, which he can use properly or improperly, to his benefit or harm.

A person may say of an event in his life: "This is my karma; that is why it happened." He refers to past good or bad karma resulting in a specific happening in this life. Good, worldly, or evil actions performed with independent free will, or through the influence of past actions, are all called karma. Actions of individuals are called individual karma, and the collective actions of large segments of human beings are called mass karma. For example, if people in a community live in unsanitary conditions, the result may be the mass karma of an epidemic affecting that whole populace, the collective consequence of transgressions against the health laws of Nature.

Actions performed by free will are called *purushakara*. Stored-up impressions of past-life actions that compel present actions are called *prarabdha* karma. Therefore, in using the word *karma*, a person should specify whether it is good, worldly, or evil karma; and whether it is present or past karma (karma that is the result of the present use of free will, or karmic actions influenced by the past).

Man, endowed with the gift of free choice, is influenced by the cosmic storm of delusion in a triple way. When he misuses his free will under the influence of the evil quality (*tamas*) in Nature, he becomes evil. But when man uses his free will under the influence of the good quality (*sattva*), thus resisting the evil influence in Nature, he manifests goodness. By the misuse of the divine gift of free choice under the influence of the activating quality (*rajas*), man becomes enmeshed in the worldly activities and eventually the evil activities of the *gunas*. After trials and tribulations a man wants to become better; God, ever aware through His intelligent cosmic vibratory omnipresence, then sends the seeker a guru—a divine saint, or the teaching of such a one, thus trying to bring the devotee back to His divine kingdom.

The factors that influence man's free will

A worldly man is influenced chiefly by the external vibrations of activity that emanate from the cosmic Vibratory Being, *Aum;* he thus becomes entangled in matter. On the other hand, a yogi who follows the highway of yoga reverses his consciousness into the inner activity of the cosmic Vibratory Being, *Aum*. In other words, the yogi learns by the meditative activity of yoga to listen to the cosmic sound of *Aum* and expands his consciousness with it into the cosmos. Thus the yogi's soul, being one with the cosmic vibration of *Aum,* the symbol of omnipresent God, becomes one with God in the vibrationless region.

This elaborate explanation answers the questions of Arjuna and all true devotees as to what the transcendental supreme Spirit is; and what the underlying soul (*Adhyatma*) is; and what karma is. Yoga activities are necessary to unite the matter-dreaming soul with the dreamless transcendental God (Para-Brahman).

VERSE 4

adhibhūtaṁ kṣaro bhāvaḥ puruṣaś cādhidaivatam
adhiyajño 'ham evātra dehe dehabhṛtāṁ vara

O Supreme Among the Embodied (Arjuna)! Adhibhuta is the basis of physical existence; Adhidaiva is the basis of astral existence; and I the Spirit within the body and the cosmos am Adhiyajna (the Causal Origin, the Great Sacrificer, the Maker and Cognizer of all).

ADHIBHUTA REPRESENTS THE MACROCOSMIC objective material universe and also the microcosmic physical body of man. *Adhibhuta* means "that which becomes," the never-fixed, the ephemeral—hence, the material world of transitoriness. Spirit manifesting Its creative consciousness in the physical macrocosm and microcosm is designated as Virata and Vishva, the governing angels of the material creation.*

Answers to Arjuna's questions about the physical, astral, and causal universes

Adhidaiva signifies the macrocosmic objective astral universe that is hidden behind the gross vibration of the physical cosmos, as well as the microcosmic astral body of man that is concealed by his physical form. *Adhidaiva* refers to the *daivas* or *devas,* literally, "the shining ones," or astral angels—God's consciousness governing the astral macrocosm and microcosm as Hiranyagarbha and Taijas.†

Adhiyajna designates the objective macrocosmic causal universe and the microcosmic causal body of man. Spirit differentiates Its consciousness into the subjective specialized Intelligence of Ishvara and Prajna‡ to create and govern the causal macrocosm and microcosm. These primal manifestations emanating from Spirit are the ideational origin of all existences. Thus *Adhiyajna* means, ultimately, God as the Originating Dreamer whose pristine dreaming is a causal manifestation consisting of the thoughts or ideas of Spirit that are the cause of the astral and physical dream condensations.

Yajna means "performance of a holy rite or sacrifice." God is thus the *Adhiyajna* who performs all the dream ceremonies necessary for the creation of His universes. Through these "ceremonies" He causes the *maya* magic that transforms the Absolute, the Sole Substance, into the active Creator, the *Aum* Vibration or Prakriti; the inactively active underlying Observer and Intelligence, *Kutastha Chaitanya* and the soul; and the six subdivisions of Prakriti (which along with Prakriti or Holy Ghost constitute the "seven angels before the throne of God") that create and govern the causal, astral, and physical macrocosms and microcosms.

Spirit as *Adhiyajna*—existing in the cosmos as the originating and governing Intelligences, and in the body of man as the soul—is therefore the all-creative underlying Substance of the physical, astral, and causal universes with their various kinds of beings. It is God as both the Originating Dreamer and the Supreme Cognizer of all creation.

---

* See IV:25, page 480. † Ibid. ‡ Ibid.

In the universe of physical matter, the One Spirit is thought of as a Presence that has given to the complexity of the cosmos a coordinated unity and harmony. That same Spirit is conceived in a brighter, more powerful way in the intelligent energy present in all the atoms of the universe, and in the conscious life present in all living creatures—empowerment derived from the underlying astral universe, the universe possessing the powers of life. The deeper conception of the universe as an idea in the mind of God envisions the living Spirit—with personality, individuality, and conscious power of evolution: Ishvara, God the Father—expressing Itself in the grand causal creation, the consummate primal rudiments of all becomings.

In the macrocosms and microcosms the Lord is truly the *Adhiyajna* or the One Indweller. In the gross material universe, the manifestation of Spirit has to be inferred. In the astral universe of vibratory life, the manifestation of Spirit has to be felt. In the causal universe of ideational consciousness, the manifestation of Spirit is known through intuitive perception.

THE YOGI'S EXPERIENCE AT THE TIME OF DEATH

VERSE 5

antakāle ca mām eva smaran muktvā kalevaram
yaḥ prayāti sa madbhāvaṁ yāti nāsty atra saṁśayaḥ

Lastly, he enters my Being who thinks only of Me at the hour of his passing, when the body is abandoned. This is truth beyond doubt.

KRISHNA NOW BEGINS HIS ANSWER to the final question posed by Arjuna in verse two: "How, at the time of death, art Thou (the Lord) to be known by the self-disciplined?"

A yogi who practices meditation throughout life is able to commune with God at any time, especially the crucial time of death. A man's thoughts at the last moments of life determine his status in the hereafter.

A true yogi finishes the dream actings of his role in life and makes his final exit from the earthly stage, his mind fixed only on the bliss of Spirit, his heart untainted by any mundane longings.

After death a devotee is not required by karmic law to return to earth if, during his lifetime, he had been able through yoga practice to disconnect his life force and consciousness from the body; and if he had been successful, at will, in entering the conscious breathless state, maintaining life in the body by drawing a supply of cosmic energy from God; and if he had been nonattached to the body and to sense objects; and if he had had no personal desires but had remained undisturbed by egoistic wishes for any person or object or sense enjoyment, thus knowing only the joy and love of his Creator.

Such a devotee without doubt attains freedom and merges with the Divine Being. He needs no further incarnations on earth for the satisfaction of unfulfilled desires, for he has rendered them all nonexistent. A self-disciplined yogi who has trained his mind to be detached at will from the sensory world and to unite that emancipated mind with the Lord thinks of nothing but Him at the time of death. According to the law of karma, that man has automatically created the cause that must manifest as the effect of God-attainment. He who in life avoided all inharmony and who was accustomed to being absorbed in yoga ecstasy remains after death in the same state of divine union.

Such a yogi throughout life sees his physical form as a dream of God; when the atoms of that body dream are dispersed by death, he wakes up in the Dreamless Bliss.

VERSE 6

yaṁ yaṁ vāpi smaran bhāvaṁ tyajaty ante kalevaram
taṁ tam evaiti kaunteya sadā tadbhāvabhāvitaḥ

O Son of Kunti (Arjuna), that thought with which a dying man leaves the body determines—through his long persistence in it—his next state of being.

THE ENTIRETY OF A HUMAN LIFE is a preparation for the final examination at death. A man, suddenly finding himself at death's door, reviews in a flash the thoughts and desires and habits of his entire life. He is quickly invaded by one overwhelming feeling or desire, whose nature will be in accordance with the character of his life. He may feel predominantly guilty, for his evil actions; or predominantly happy, because of his good deeds; or predominantly worldly, because of his material activities. Whatever his feeling, it is the determining cause that will lead him to a particular part of the astral worlds and then to another suitable incarnation on earth. "For as he thinketh in his heart, so is he."*

THE PARAMOUNT HABIT OF THOUGHT and feeling during a man's years on earth is thus the most important factor on "the day of judgment." The final thought, inexorably produced by the tenor of a lifetime, is indeed the karmic judge that at the sound of "Gabriel's trumpet" announces a man's next destination.

Gabriel's trumpet is the sound of the Cosmic *Aum* that ushers man from the physical body at death. The *Aum* vibration, being the repository of all creative blueprints, presents to each man at the time of death the self-created pattern of his next existence. A human being leading a meaningless, mechanical existence, or an evil life, little realizes that on the last day he will bring judgment upon himself, with a Gabriel's trumpet of karma proclaiming his "fate." If a person is tired of material life or evil habits, why should he continue in that way to the end, only to be required to go on with the same kind of obnoxious living after death? Each man should endeavor to lead a righteous life, that at its termination he will not have a guilty conscience and be reborn among evildoers.

Meaning of "Gabriel's trumpet"

By practice of nonattachment the yogi dissolves all the inclinations and desires of his heart and remains in continuous ecstasy with the *Aum* vibration, the expression of God in creation. When death arrives, the yogi finds Gabriel's trumpet, issuing from the Cosmic *Aum,* ushering him into the transcendental spheres of God. Lahiri Mahasaya went through this *Aum* into the Infinite and resurrected himself in a physical body one day after that of his "death."†

Those devotees are liberated who can manifest the Christ or *Kutastha* consciousness by emerging, through the Cosmic *Aum,* from all three useless dead bodies (the physical, astral, and causal). The Christ or *Kutastha* consciousness is "the first begotten of the dead,"‡ the first experience of omnipresence of the liberated being through which he "cometh unto the Father (Cosmic Consciousness)."§ In this state the emancipated being knows divine thought to be the matrix of creation; he too is now able to materialize thought into the shape of his former

* Proverbs 23:7.

† See *Autobiography of a Yogi,* end of Chapter 36.

‡ Revelation 1:5.

§ John 14:6.

body or into the shape of any other body in which he may wish to appear. Or, by choice, he may remain merged in the Formless Absolute, in the bliss of the Transcendental Spirit.

VERSE 7

tasmāt sarveṣu kāleṣu mām anusmara yudhya ca
mayy arpitamanobuddhir mām evaiṣyasy asaṁśayam

Therefore, remember Me always, and engage thyself in the battle of activity! Surrender to Me thy mind and thine understanding! Thus without doubt shalt thou come unto Me.

KRISHNA ADVISES: "O DEVOTEE, I am the Dreamer of the whole panorama of existence. Behold your body and the battle of daily activity as dreams emanating from My cosmic consciousness. If you prevent your mind with its sensory impressions, and your discriminative intellect that is often influenced by the heart, or feeling, from being emotionally agitated by the dream drama on earth, and keep them beholding My Blessed Beam that projects these pictures, you will experience no terror. Without doubt you shall enter My transcendental dreamless state."

The wise devotee so deeply meditates in the bliss of *Kriya Yoga* that he does not forget that blessed consciousness during the daily battle of activity in which his sensory mind and discriminative intellect are perforce engaged. When he is able always to act with his whole consciousness absorbed in God, at death he becomes fully one with Him.

VERSE 8

abhyāsayogayuktena cetasā nānyagāminā
paramaṁ puruṣaṁ divyaṁ yāti pārthānucintayan

He attains the Supreme Effulgent Lord, O Partha (Arjuna), whose mind, stabilized by yoga, is immovably fixed on the thought of Him.

KRISHNA TELLS ARJUNA TO PREPARE himself spiritually throughout life, that at death, in the manner of a great yogi, he may carry his divine consciousness into the ineffable presence of God. Krishna advises his disciple to practice *pranayama* life-control technique, or *Kriya Yoga,* and to learn to switch off the life current from the five senses in order to still restless fluctuations of the mind; and then to unite his mind and life with the soul, and the soul with the Shining Light of Spirit.

It is necessary for man to practice a scientific technique such as *Kriya Yoga* to prevent his mind during meditation from wandering away (*na-anya-gamina*) from divine ecstasy into the domain of thoughts and material sensations. As a *Kriya Yogi* relaxes his life force from the five sense-telephones, he automatically finds that sensations and thoughts have vanished from his consciousness. Thus freed, his mind becomes magnetized toward the blissful soul and its everlasting communion with Spirit.

VERSES 9–10

kaviṁ purāṇam anuśāsitāram aṇor aṇīyāṁsam anusmared yaḥ
sarvasya dhātāram acintyarūpam ādityavarṇaṁ tamasaḥ parastāt (9)

prayāṇakāle manasācalena bhaktyā yukto yogabalena caiva
bhruvor madhye prāṇam āveśya samyak sa taṁ paraṁ puruṣam
upaiti divyam (10)

At the time of death a yogi reaches the Supreme Effulgent Lord if, with love and by the power of yoga, he fully penetrates his life force between the eyebrows (the seat of the spiritual eye), and if he fixes his mind unwaveringly on the Being who, beyond all delusions of darkness, shines like the sun—the One whose form is unimaginable, subtler than the finest atom, the Supporter of all, the Great Ruler, eternal and omniscient.

POINTED OUT IN THESE VERSES are the three qualifications by which a great yogi passes from his physical body into the Divine Essence. First, love of God. Second, mastery of that kingly science, *Kriya Yoga*, by which he can usher his consciousness into the Infinite through the agency of the "single eye" in the forehead. Third, perfect control of the mind, made possible through constancy in yoga, that enables him to place his thought undeviatingly on the Lord at the time of death—an hour whose finality is always known in advance by a true yogi.

These stanzas, making two references to God as Light ("the Supreme Effulgent Lord" and "the Being who shines like the sun"), also mention a specific yoga technique. (See VIII:12–13.) The point Krishna wished to make by such a juxtaposition is that a man who devotes himself to yoga beholds the Lord as Light.

God as Light

In meditation a great yogi takes his ego, life force (*prana*), and consciousness beyond his physical body to a vast realm ablaze with soothing light. This radiancy as from a thousand suns dissolves into an ever new display of multicolored rays issuing from an endlessly enlarging spherical fountain.

The single eye in the forehead of man possesses spherical vision. In meditation that vision gradually expands for the yogi into an ineffable sphere of constantly changing luminosity, blissful and omnipresent.

After experiencing this vibratory vision of *Aum* as the Cosmic Light, the emancipated yogi goes beyond all delusive relativities of vibrations. He then feels and realizes the Transcendental Lord—He who exists behind the transitory dreams of cosmic matter and its myriad components of cells, molecules, atoms, electrons and protons, "lifetrons" (*prana* or energy), and "thoughtrons" (the ultimate basis of matter).

IN THE TRANSCENDENTAL STATE God spins out His dreams of ideational (causal), astral, and physical universes. The physical cosmos, with its many "island universes" floating in the eternal void, is encircled by a nimbus of radiant energy that melts away into the larger astral world. The astral cosmos is a grander manifestation of creation than the physical, and runs through and beyond the latter. In the astral cosmos many luminous galaxies of various densities, with their astral solar and stellar systems, are roving in a vaster sphere of eternity.

Astral and causal worlds described

The largest or causal cosmos contains countless causal galactic systems with their suns and planets, roaming all through the physical and astral cosmoses and far beyond their boundaries to the outermost sphere of vibratory space. The causal universe is the womb of creation. In the causal universe, God's finest creative forces of consciousness, and highly evolved beings with their intuitive processes, objectify universes from subtle divine thought forces.

Through pure soul intuition, an accomplished yogi can behold the physical cosmos and its beings as the cosmic dream of God. Or he can project his consciousness into the astral world and perceive its panorama of indescribably beautiful island universes and beings made of ethereal blendings of various colored lights. Or he can lift his consciousness into the sublime causal sphere, with its galaxies upon galaxies of dazzling wisdom-objects and beings and their interactions—a glorious diadem in the eternally still, endless skies of Spirit.

The yogi who has attained complete control over his consciousness can behold the physical, astral, or causal worlds, or go beyond to the transcendent vibrationless region of God. He is able to perceive one portion of the Lord's consciousness as the transcendental eternal peace, and another portion as the ripple of cosmic dreams—the worlds of creation. It is the vibrationless, blessed consciousness of God that in the last analysis is the causative and omniscient Supporter of the dream cosmos and all its forces, subtle and gross. The manifestations of the Divine are in evidence in the cosmic dream, but He—the Ruler—remains hidden.

The process of death: exit through the spiritual eye

TO ATTAIN THE CREATOR, Krishna tells us in this passage, the yogi must completely penetrate his life force through the single or spiritual eye. This seat of omniscience in man is referred to in the Bible:* "And he that overcometh, and keepeth my works unto the end, to him will I give power over the nations.... And I will give him the morning star." Christ thus assured Saint John of the divine reward for those who are faithful to God "unto the end." The "morning star" or the "star of the East" is the spiritual single eye in the Christ or *Kutastha* center of the forehead (east), a microcosm of the creative vibratory light and consciousness of God. Through the spiritual eye the adept yogi attains mastery over the forces ("nations") in his physical, astral, and causal bodies, and gains entry into the realm of Spirit.

It is through the opening in the spiritual eye that the astral vehicle of man emerges from the physical body at death. Deprived of their astral counterparts, the sense organs and the myriad cells of the human form are left powerless. They then decay and return to their native state of "dust." The astral-body forces can be seen by the yogi as they pass up through the spinal tunnel and the brain (the seven "trap doors" of the plexuses) and enter an astral form.

The spiritual eye in the average man is not awakened during his lifetime. Therefore he is not aware at death of the passage of the astral body through the plexuses. An unconscious person who is carried from one

* Revelation 2:26,28.

place to another does not notice the stages of his journey. Similarly, the ordinary individual does not see his life energy being freed from the physical vehicle at death and manifesting itself as an astral form.

At death man is overcome by fear at his strange experience—that of gradually finding himself unable to feel, or express his will, through a physical body. Then drowsiness overtakes him and for some time he remains in a state of peaceful slumber. Awakening from this sleep of death—much needed after the hard trials of life—he becomes aware of his encasement in an astral body, one whose tissues are made of light. Amid the new beauties of the astral world, he forgets the whole of his past physical existence.

But a great yogi consciously observes through his spherical spiritual eye the various phenomena of death. Even a person whose soul is only partially awakened by good karma may at the advent of death have glimpses of the glory and joy of the mortal transition from the physical body to the astral heaven.* The advanced yogi sees his life

---

* A medical view of death parallel to that long known to yogis is emerging as a result of scientific research. Among the most comprehensive of these studies are those by Raymond Moody, M.D.; Karlis Osis, Ph.D., and Erlendur Haraldsson, Ph.D.; and Kenneth Ring, Ph.D. By comparing thousands of descriptions given by dying patients in the moments just before passing, and by people who were revived after a state of temporary clinical death, these and other doctors at major universities and medical research centers have identified a consistent pattern in these so-called "near-death experiences."

"Despite the wide variation in the circumstances surrounding close calls with death and in the types of persons undergoing them," writes Dr. Moody in his book *Life After Life* (New York: Bantam Books, 1975), "it remains true that there is a striking similarity among the accounts of the experiences themselves. In fact, the similarities among various reports are so great that one can easily pick out about fifteen separate elements which recur again and again in the mass of narrations that I have collected."

A composite scenario includes the gradual departure of feeling from all parts of the body; a sensation of moving swiftly through a long, dark, tunnel-like passageway toward a light at the end; the separation of consciousness from the body (patients frequently mention hovering above the inert physical form); beholding and being engulfed in a light of supernatural brilliance, which evokes a sense of transcendent peace, joy, and love; encountering the spirits of friends and relatives who have previously passed on; meeting a benevolent being of light, sometimes described as a "guide," who appears along with an instantaneous panoramic review of the events of one's life; a feeling of not wanting to return to the physical body.

Dr. Moody further writes: "[The person undergoing this experience] notices that he still has a 'body,' but one of a very different nature and with very different powers from the physical body he has left behind....Later he tries to tell others, but he has trouble doing so. In the first place, he can find no human words adequate to describe these unearthly episodes....Still, the experience affects his life profoundly, especially his views about death and its relationship to life."

In their book *At the Hour of Death* (New York: Avon Books, 1977), Dr. Osis and Dr.

forces move backward like a mass of rolling light from the cells, nerves, organs, and spine, and then enter an astral body, which hovers over the inert physical form.

The yogi who in life or at death withdraws his life force from the senses and focuses it in the single eye finds himself in a joyful state of breathlessness. He thrills to see streams of *prana* rolling backward from the countless cells and ascending the spinal tunnel through the coiled stairway (*kundalini*), out from the single-eye passage in the forehead into a subtle astral body.

A yogi who has arrived at this state—a midway perception of the physical plane and the astral plane—is overwhelmed with joy. He sees a double splendor, that of two worlds. As a person standing on a narrow strip of land may simultaneously view two lakes that lie on either side, so the yogi is simultaneously aware of the physical sphere and the astral sphere. His range of perception increases, through meditation on his intuitive spherical eye, until he can behold the omnipresence of God in all creation and beyond it.

When the yogi has freed himself from the physical body, he is still encased in an astral and a causal body. By further yoga meditation on the spiritual eye, he ascends from the astral body by withdrawing his astral life force and consciousness upward through the triune tunnels of the astral spine, through the spiritual eye, into the causal body.

The ideational or causal body contains the seed thoughts of man's physical and astral bodies. When by deeper ecstasy the yogi dissolves his chronic thoughts or delusions that have caused him to be encased in physical and astral bodies, his soul then moves through the seven idea-knots or plexuses of his causal body out into the vibrationless Transcendental,

---

Haraldsson write: "Although most patients apparently drift into oblivion without awareness of it, there are some, clearly conscious to the end, who say they 'see' into the beyond and who are able to report their experiences before expiring....These experiences are transformative. They bring with them serenity, peace, elation, and religious emotions. The patients die a 'good death' in strange contrast to the usual gloom and misery commonly expected before expiration." (*Publisher's Note*)

THE METHOD OF ATTAINING THE SUPREME

VERSE 11

yad akṣaraṁ vedavido vadanti viśanti yad yatayo vītarāgāḥ
yad icchanto brahmacaryaṁ caranti tat te padaṁ saṁgraheṇa pravakṣye

That which the Vedic seers declare as the Immutable, That which is gained by renunciants of vanished attachments, desiring which they lead a life of self-discipline—the method for attaining That I will relate to thee in brief.

THE DIVINE GOAL IS ATTAINABLE, Krishna assures Arjuna, through certain definite methods (described in the following stanzas).

VERSES 12–13

sarvadvārāṇi saṁyamya mano hṛdi nirudhya ca
mūrdhny ādhāyātmanaḥ prāṇam āsthito yogadhāraṇām (12)

om ity ekākṣaraṁ brahma vyāharan mām anusmaran
yaḥ prayāti tyajan dehaṁ sa yāti paramāṁ gatim (13)

He who closes the nine gates of the body,* who cloisters the mind in the heart center, who fixes the full life force in the cerebrum—he who thus engages in the steady practice of yoga, establishing himself in Aum, the Holy Word of Brahman, and remembering Me (Spirit) at the time of his final exit from the body, reaches the Highest Goal.

A *JYOTI MUDRA* TECHNIQUE THAT IS TAUGHT to *Kriya Yogis* has for its purpose the making manifest the light (*jyoti*) of the spiritual eye by "closing of the nine gates of the body," which Lord Krishna here advocates as a means for man's illumination.

---

* *Sarvadvārāṇi deham,* "all gates of the body." These were identified in verse V:13 as nine in number: "the bodily city of nine gates." They consist of the two eyes, two ears, two nostrils, the two organs of excretion and of procreation, and the mouth.

The advanced *Kriya Yogi* by this technique is able to control the life current that is ordinarily diffused throughout the body, and to withhold its usual copious flow outward through the nine gates or openings of the body. The mind (*manas,* or sense consciousness) is withdrawn from the three lower spinal centers associated with the physical senses, uplifted to the heart center (the second "stopping place" in the ascension to the highest spiritual centers in the brain).* With the attention focused at the point between the eyebrows, the withheld life force becomes concentrated there and in the cerebrum, illumining the omniscient spiritual eye, the divine gateway to the Infinite. The yogi hears the Cosmic Sound of *Aum,* the Holy Word of Brahman. Merging in the *Aum* vibration, the yogi enters the spiritual eye and releases his soul from the three bodies (as aforementioned). Experiencing the omnipresence of *Aum,* he merges in *Kutastha* or Christ Consciousness inherent therein, and then ascends through Cosmic Consciousness to the transcendental Absolute beyond vibratory manifestation.

The yogi who steadfastly and successfully practices this method of realization attains consciously at the time of death complete liberation in Spirit.

VERSE 14

ananyacetāḥ satataṁ yo māṁ smarati nityaśaḥ
tasyāhaṁ sulabhaḥ pārtha nityayuktasya yoginaḥ

O Partha (Arjuna)! I am easily reached by that yogi who is single-hearted, who remembers Me daily, continually, his mind intensely focused only on Me.

SUCCESS IN SELF-REALIZATION depends on whole-souled effort. The true devotee knows the value of constant and regular meditation, by which his life becomes an uninterrupted prayer. Yoga should not be practiced mechanically or from an oppressive sense of duty, but with joy and perpetual zeal, thus causing each day's meditation to yield a deeper bliss than that of the previous day.

---

* See I:21 and VI:11.

VERSE 15

mām upetya punarjanma duḥkhālayam aśāśvatam
nāpnuvanti mahātmānaḥ saṁsiddhiṁ paramāṁ gatāḥ

My noble devotees, having obtained Me (Spirit), have reached supreme success; they incur no further rebirths in this abode of grief and transitoriness.

SUPREMELY SUCCESSFUL YOGIS are the high-souled perfected beings who in ecstasy or the after-death state have achieved the ultimate union with the transcendental Spirit. Their souls escape the karmic bonds of all three bodies and no longer dream the dreams of desires and attachments of mortal existence. Rebirths in the temporal, sorrow-fraught realms are no longer imposed upon them. They are awake in the cosmic dream of God and in the dreamless blessedness of Spirit.

Striving yogis should pragmatically view this world as a school. The highest lesson set for each man is the realization that he is not a mortal, beset by pain and mutability, but a free son of God. The good student who is successful in the tests of earthly life and who passes the "final examination" has no need to return for further instruction. He has earned the divine Ph.D.

THE CYCLES OF COSMIC CREATION

VERSE 16

ā brahmabhuvanāl lokāḥ punarāvartino 'rjuna
mām upetya tu kaunteya punarjanma na vidyate

Yogis not yet free from the world* revolve back again (to the world) even from the high sphere of Brahma (union with God in samadhi). But on entering into Me (the transcendental Spirit) there is no rebirth, O son of Kunti (Arjuna)!

---

* *Lokas* may be translated either as "worlds" (see page 731) or as "human beings," as in the above verse (i.e., those who yet possess mortal consciousness).

ELABORATING ON THE PREVIOUS VERSE, Krishna points out that merely reaching the abode of Brahman, Spirit, may not in itself assure complete liberation. Even though the yogi may attain in ecstatic meditation high states of God-union—merging the consciousness in *Aum* in the vibratory dominion of Brahma, experiencing His omniscience in omnipresent *Kutastha* or Christ Consciousness, and even reaching the highest Brahma sphere of Cosmic Consciousness—he cannot remain in those states but must revolve again to bodily consciousness if there persists within him any mortal desires or karmic bonds. If death occurs in this imperfect state, he will be reborn on earth or in some high astral realm with a new opportunity and the spiritual potential to free himself.

In meditation, the yogi gradually ascends his consciousness and life force upward through the spinal centers of divine awakening, experiencing expanded Self-realization with each higher step. He who attains union with the triune manifestation of Brahma as the Cosmic *Aum* vibration or Holy Ghost in the medulla, as the Krishna or Christ Consciousness in the *Kutastha* center, and as Cosmic Consciousness in the thousand-petaled lotus in the cerebrum, still will have to return to limited mortal consciousness if he has not broken all karmic bonds, desires, and attachments and consciously ascended from all three bodily encasements—physical, astral, and causal. The more the yogi is able at will to gain the elevated states of consciousness, and the longer he is able to hold on to them in meditation and after meditation, the more he diminishes his binding karmic reflexes and dream delusions. When these are vanquished, the yogi dissolves the body-conscious ego into the soul and takes his soul, with its astral and causal bodies, out of the physical body; he then takes his soul and causal body out of the astral body; and, finally, his soul ascends from the causal form and merges into the transcendental Spirit, from which there is no compulsory return to the vale of distressing dualities.

THE SANSKRIT WORD *LOKAS* IN THIS VERSE may also be rendered as "worlds." With that interpretation, the verse translates as follows, and leads into the succeeding verses:

> *All worlds, from the high sphere of Brahma (to the gross earth), are subject to (the finite law of) recurrence. But those devotees, O Arjuna! who become merged in Me are freed from rebirth.*

The law of recurrence is inexorably operative not only for all mortal beings, but also for all finite worlds including the sphere of Brahma

—that portion of Spirit that is immanent in creation as the Dreaming Creator-Preserver-Destroyer during each cycle of cosmic manifestation. Man escapes from that law when he "comes to Himself" or remembers his essential divinity and becomes irrevocably united to the transcendental Absolute.

VERSES 17–19

sahasrayugaparyantam ahar yad brahmaṇo viduḥ
rātriṁ yugasahasrāntāṁ te 'horātravido janāḥ (17)

avyaktād vyaktayaḥ sarvāḥ prabhavanty aharāgame
rātryāgame pralīyante tatraivāvyaktasaṁjñake (18)

bhūtagrāmaḥ sa evāyaṁ bhūtvā bhūtvā pralīyate
rātryāgame 'vaśaḥ pārtha prabhavaty aharāgame (19)

(17) They are true knowers of "day" and "night" who understand the Day of Brahma, which endures for a thousand cycles (yugas), and the Night of Brahma, which also endures for a thousand cycles.

(18) At the dawn of Brahma's Day all creation, reborn, emerges from the state of nonmanifestation; at the dusk of Brahma's Night all creation sinks into the sleep of nonmanifestation.

(19) Again and again, O son of Pritha (Arjuna), the same throng of men helplessly take rebirth. Their series of incarnations ceases at the coming of Night, and then reappears at the dawn of Day.

BRAHMA THE CREATOR IS THAT ASPECT of Divinity which is active in creation, the Lord of Time. (Brahman or Para-Brahman signifies God as the Absolute, the Transcendental.)

"For a thousand years in Thy sight are but as yesterday when it is past, and as a watch in the night.

"Thou carriest them away as with a flood; they are as a sleep: in the morning they are like grass which groweth up.

"In the morning it flourisheth, and groweth up; in the evening it is cut down, and withereth."*

* Psalms 90:4–6.

THE YUGAS, COSMIC CYCLES OF EVOLUTION AND DECAY

KRISHNA REFERS TO THESE vast cycles or *yugas** to impress on Arjuna's mind the folly of man in allowing himself to remain a part of phenomenal existence, mechanically revolving from cycle to cycle.

The Christian Bible makes the following mention of the cycles, the Night of nonmanifestation and the Day of manifestation:

"And the earth was without form, and void; and darkness was upon the face of the deep. And the Spirit of God moved upon the face of the waters [vibrations].

"And God said, Let there be light: and there was light.

"And God saw the light, that it was good: and God divided the light from the darkness.

"And God called the light Day, and the darkness He called Night. And the evening and the morning were the first day."†

Many complex formulas exist in the *shastras,* in astronomical treatises known as *Siddhantas,* for measuring time and space—from the infinitesimal atom to the cyclic ages of the cosmos. Any unprepared student who has challenged himself to this study will appreciate the wry comment of the renowned Sanskrit scholar Monier-Williams in his treatise *Indian Wisdom:* "An astronomical Hindu ventures on arithmetical conceptions quite beyond the mental dimensions of anyone who feels himself incompetent to attempt the task of measuring infinity."

The word *yuga* is a general term for designating an age, or particular span of time. Depending on the formula, and the interpretation and application thereof, various figures are arrived at in the determination of the length of *yugas* (see reference to cosmic cycles, page 734).

My gurudeva Swami Sri Yukteswar, in *The Holy Science,* deplored the error made by Hindu almanac-makers during the last Kali Yuga. By misunderstanding, they abandoned all reference to the 24,000-year Equinoctial Cycle by translating it into *daiva* years of a vast universal cycle (each *daiva* or divine year being equal to 360 solar years). The Jnanavatar, a venerable authority in the science and art of spiritual astronomy and astrology, urged the reintroduction and adoption of the 24,000-year cycle by which man is directly affected in his allotted space in this current solar system. Measurements of the human creature's place in a vast universal scheme are notably irrelevant to the divine purpose that has placed the body-circumscribed mortal in his pres-

* See also IV:1–2 and 7–8.

† Genesis 1:2–5.

ent position. He is already well-taxed merely to keep pace with the minutes and hours of his earthly years, fraught with intrusions from the natural and subtle events and influences of his immediate worldly and celestial environment.

EXOTERICALLY, THE COSMIC CYCLES cited in these three verses refer to the various phases of creation: a "Day of Brahma" being a time of manifested creation; a "Night of Brahma" being a time of equal length wherein creation is dissolved, its "seeds" held unmanifest in Mula-Prakriti. Recurrent cycles of manifestation and dissolution are applicable to the life spans of solar systems, galaxies, or a specific spectrum of the objects and life-forms within them; and, ultimately, of the universe as a whole. Dissolutions may be partial—as the removal of vast segments of objects or beings from the cosmic dream movie as a result of cataclysmic events; or total—the resolution of matter into ethereal energy, or its complete withdrawal into Spirit.*

Exoteric and esoteric meaning of yugas

* Astronomer Carl Sagan of Cornell University has written in *Cosmos* (New York: Random House, 1980): "The Hindu religion is the only one of the world's great faiths dedicated to the idea that the cosmos itself undergoes an immense, indeed an infinite, number of deaths and rebirths. It is the only religion in which the time scales correspond...to those of modern scientific cosmology. Its cycles run from our ordinary day and night to a day and night of Brahma, 8.64 billion years long, longer than the age of the Earth or the Sun and about half the time since the Big Bang. And there are much longer time scales still.... A millennium before Europeans were willing to divest themselves of the Biblical idea that the world was a few thousand years old, the Mayans were thinking of millions, and the Indians of billions....

"In India there are many gods, and each god has many manifestations. The Chola bronzes, cast in the eleventh century, included several different incarnations of the god Shiva. The most elegant and sublime of these is a representation of the creation of the universe at the beginning of each cosmic cycle, a motif known as the cosmic dance of Shiva. The god, called in this manifestation Nataraja, the Dance King, has four hands. In the upper right hand is a drum whose sound is the sound of creation. In the upper left hand is a tongue of flame, a reminder that the universe, now newly created, will billions of years from now be utterly destroyed.

"These profound and lovely images are, I like to imagine, a kind of premonition of modern astronomical ideas. Very likely, the universe has been expanding since the Big Bang, but it is by no means clear that it will continue to expand forever. The expansion may gradually slow, stop, and reverse itself. If there is less than a certain amount of matter in the universe, the gravitation of the receding galaxies will be insufficient to stop the expansion, and the universe will run away forever. But if there is more matter than we can see—hidden away in black holes, say, or in hot but invisible gas between the galaxies—then the universe will hold together gravitationally and partake of a very Indian succession of cycles, expansion followed by contraction, universe upon universe, Cosmos without end." (*Publisher's Note*)

Esoterically, and more importantly as they directly affect man's scheme of existence, the cosmic cycles refer to the inner microcosmic solar universe of man's astral body, which governs his individual evolution. The spiritual eye, which receives its light and energy from its connection with the divine center of consciousness in the thousand-petaled lotus (*sahasrara*) in the brain, is the sun of the microcosm; and the six subtle plexuses or *chakras* of the astral spine (twelve by polarity) are the twelve astral signs of the zodiac. The cosmic sun of our solar system moves through the signs of the celestial zodiac in one-year cycles, and this whole system moves around a dual star or magnetic center in the cosmos in a 24,000-year cycle, referred to as the Equinoctial Cycle, consisting of four *yugas* or ages (Kali, Dwapara, Treta, and Satya), in a 12,000-year ascending arc of these four *yugas* and a corresponding 12,000-year descending arc. Similarly, the individual evolution of man is marked by the cycles of his miniature solar cosmos—the energizing effect of the sun of the spiritual eye on the zodiacal astral centers of the spine. In twelve-year cycles man is slowly advanced in his spiritual evolution. These twelve solar years are for man a *yuga,* or cyclic time span. It is said by the ancients that if the human being could remain "awake"—anchored in spiritual consciousness uninterrupted by lapses caused by death or disease or mental impairment—for a period of 1,000 *yugas,* or the equivalent of 12,000 years of one cosmic cycle of the four cosmic *yugas,* he would evolve through all stages of these four ages from the material Kali Yuga to the sublime Satya Yuga, manifesting the full realization thereof.

TO APPRECIATE THIS PROGRESSION, it is necessary to comprehend the nature of the ideal being of each age—one who manifests the full potential thereof—as each of the four *yugas* contains also a relative proportion of all four *yugas.*

Characteristics of each yuga correspond to caste

In Kali Yuga, the intellect and capacity of man are characteristically confined to gross matter and concerns of materiality. His natural caste is Sudra; he is wholly servile to the circumscriptions of nature. In Dwapara Yuga, he gains comprehension and use of the electrical and atomic constituents of matter, realizing the nature of matter to be energy. He is said to be *dvija,* or of the "twice-born" class. In Treta Yuga, the mental age, man acquires knowledge and mastery of the attributes of universal magnetism with its polarized subtle electricities from which his astral and physical instrumentalities evolve. He is able to discard many of the "mechanisms" that enhance his sensory faculties, as his natural powers of telepathy, clairaudience, and clairvoyance (clear vision) develop. He is then said to be of the *vipra,* or nearly perfect class of being. And in Satya Yuga, the spiritual age, the ideal man has the capacity to comprehend the source of universal magnetism with its duality (the primal movement or expression of the consciousness of God from which evolve the twenty-four principles of Nature that inform all of creation).* He will have the power of continuous contact with God, becoming a Brahmin, or knower of God. His perception will be through intuition; interplanetary and interastral travel will be accomplished not by airplanes or atomic airships, but by instantaneous astral projection. He will have mastered the full spectrum of *aishvaryas,* or divine powers.†

Alas, the attainment of the ultimate man through 12,000 years of unimpeded evolution is beyond the instrumentality of the ordinary mortal, who is constrained to pace himself with nature's forward and backward movements—progress along with retreats occasioned by the onslaughts of delusion and its interruptions of death and rebirth. But to assure man's ultimate return to his true Self, the Lord has built into man's being and his cosmic environment the evolutionary cycles that by divine decree push him forward toward the fulfillment of his sublime destiny. Without error against the natural laws that govern body and mind, it is said that about a million solar years of evolution are necessary for a human to attain Self-realization. Mortal man, inevitably error-prone, must face a multiple of these evolutionary years. The lackadaisical being who dallies in his physical or astral evolution, or who perhaps desires to remain for aeons in the nearly perfect causal world, enjoying in blissful perception and participation the awesome magnitude of the wonders of the Lord's creation, will at the approach of the "Night of Brahma" enter a state of partial, or temporary, dissolution—a cosmic nighttime of rest in Spirit.

---

* See page 267 n.

† The eight principal divine powers, referred to as *aishvaryas,* which can be manifested by the incarnate being who has attained mastery over the forces of creation, are as follows: the power to make one's body or any object (1) as small as desired (*anima*), (2) as large as desired (*mahima*), (3) as light in weight as desired (*laghima*), and (4) as heavy as desired (*garima*); the power (5) to obtain anything desired (*prapti*), (6) to bring anything under his control (*vashitva*), (7) to satisfy all desires by the force of his will (*prakamya*), and (8) to become *Isha,* Lord, over everything. In the *Yoga Sutras* of the sage Patanjali, other powers (*siddhis*) are also discussed. The attainment of mastery over phenomenal creation is not a goal of the enlightened man, but is a natural endowment of the omnipotent, omniscient soul—the immortal Self, which becomes manifest as it gradually sheds its coverings of delusion.

Except for a few liberated men, the same multitude of beings are reborn many times during a Day of Brahma. They rest (without further incarnations) during the Night of cosmic dissolution. But with the coming of the Day or cycle of cosmic creative manifestation, again they start a round of karmically compulsory journeys in physical, astral, and causal encasements.

Kriya Yoga: The way to early liberation

FOR THOSE WHO REJECT the indignity of mortal encumbrances on their immortality, and who seek early liberation with the free choice to select their dwelling in physical, astral, or causal form or in formless Blissful Infinity, the Lord sends His avatars to show the way to hasten salvation. By *Kriya Yoga,* in which consciousness and life energy (*prana*) are circulated up and down the spine (around the spinal centers), equaling the effect of the sun's passage through the signs of the zodiac, one such revolution in a period of one-half to one minute produces one year of evolution. The adept *Kriya Yogi* in deep states of meditation and *samadhi* can increasingly multiply this evolutionary effect of each *Kriya*. The sincere *Kriya Yogi,* according to the degree of his past-life spiritual attainments and present merit, may achieve liberation in three, six, twelve, twenty-four, or forty-eight years, or in only one or a few additional incarnations.

Through the Lord's outwardly expressive principle, vibratory *Aum,* God is perpetually floating dream beings on waves of creation, preservation, and dissolution. Though the cosmic dreams of the Divine are eternal processes, man is not eternally bound to them. By *Kriya Yoga* meditation and divine grace, God-communion and its concomitant spiritual awakening can be immutably established in daily life. The advanced *Kriya Yogi* learns by ecstasy to shut off the delusion-imposed dream of this world and of his body and to substitute a Self-created dream world and dream existence in which he can interact with the Lord's cosmic dream, playing any part, without the fearsome coercions and entanglements of delusion. By the power of concentration, the *Kriya Yogi* dismisses from his consciousness the cosmic dream world, and his dream body and its subconscious dreams, and reaches the awakened, dreamless state of ecstasy. In the blessedness of divine communion between soul and Spirit, he realizes his causal body as a concentrated matrix of God's thoughts, and that his astral and physical bodies are the subtle and gross dream manifestations of these ideations. By continuous ecstasy throughout life, he transcends the circumscriptions of a body-bound ego and lives solely as the immaculate Self, the pure image of God incarnate, able to perceive and express through his astral or physical body-dreams or to dissolve them at will.

In the early stages of Self-mastery, the yogi is able to dissolve the perception of his dream body in the realization of his oneness with God, but the dream body itself does not dematerialize. After he loses the wakefulness of his ecstasy, he again perceives as a definite reality—too hard to forget—his physical dream body and the astral dream body encased within it. Only by deeper ecstasies, when the yogi secures unbrokenly his soul union with the transcendental Spirit, can he consciously dissolve the cosmic dream of his physical, astral, and causal bodies and then recreate them at will, forever realizing them to be naught but dreams of God, with whom his soul and its conscious dreaming are one. Whether awake in Blissful Transcendence or consciously dreaming with God the cosmic fantasy of being, the liberated soul suffers no more the ignoble confinement that binds the majority to the ceaseless cycles of Brahma's Days and Nights. The Wheel rotates forever, but, one by one, wise men slip away from it.

"Give glory to the Lord your God, before He cause darkness, and before your feet stumble upon the dark mountains, and, while ye look for light, He turn it into the shadow of death, and make it gross darkness."*

VERSE 20

paras tasmāt tu bhāvo 'nyo 'vyakto 'vyaktāt sanātanaḥ
yaḥ sa sarveṣu bhūteṣu naśyatsu na vinaśyati

But transcending the unmanifested (states of phenomenal being) there exists the true Unmanifested, the Immutable, the Absolute, which remains untouched by the cycles of cosmic dissolution.

A PART OF GOD'S CONSCIOUSNESS (*Tat*)—undifferentiated, and Itself unmanifested—is reflected in Nature, the worlds of becoming, in which He dreams eternally the cycles of evolution and involution. But in His essential nature He is the Unmanifested One, beyond all vibratory realms of cosmic dreams, *Sat* or Eternal Being, Existence Itself.

In this stanza Krishna explains that the unmanifested state (*avyakta*) of cosmic dissolution is not one of final freedom, but merely a temporary

* Jeremiah 13:16.

resting place for unenlightened beings who are again to emerge as actors in the cosmic dream. Beyond, and dissimilar to, that periodically unmanifested state of cosmic vibration remains the ever-existent vibrationless state (*avyakta avyaktat para sanatana*), the Eternal Unmanifested.

Thus it is said that even the pure, undifferentiated aspect of Spirit in creation (*Tat*) has an impermanency, punctuated by comings and goings, in that this Heart of the Universe at the time of cosmic dissolution, for want of a form in which to beat, is resolved again into Spirit. This is symbolized in the Hindu scriptures as Vishnu, the Preserver of the Worlds, asleep on Shesha, the thousand-headed serpent, awaiting the dawn of the next cycle of manifestation when He will send forth again those worlds and nonliberated beings He has preserved in an unmanifested state during the long night of cosmic dissolution.

VERSES 21–22

avyakto 'kṣara ity uktas tam āhuḥ paramāṁ gatim
yaṁ prāpya na nivartante tad dhāma paramaṁ mama (21)

puruṣaḥ sa paraḥ pārtha bhaktyā labhyas tv ananyayā
yasyāntaḥsthāni bhūtāni yena sarvam idaṁ tatam (22)

(21) The aforesaid Unmanifested, the Immutable Absolute, is thus called the Supreme Goal. Those who attain it, My highest state, undergo no more rebirth.

(22) By singlehearted devotion, O son of Pritha (Arjuna), that Supreme Unmanifested is reached. He alone, the Omnipresent, is the Abode of all creatures.

THE SOLE GIFT A HUMAN BEING may present to the Infinite Giver is love. To bestow that gift on God, or miserly to withhold it, is man's only private power. All else already belongs to the Maker of heaven and earth. By pure humble *bhakti* man becomes fit to enter even the ultimate haven, the Immutable and Unmanifested.

THE WAY OF RELEASE FROM THE CYCLES OF REBIRTH

VERSES 23–26

yatra kāle tv anāvṛttim āvṛttiṁ caiva yoginaḥ
prayātā yānti taṁ kālaṁ vakṣyāmi bharatarṣabha (23)

agnir jyotir ahaḥ śuklaḥ ṣaṇmāsā uttarāyaṇam
tatra prayātā gacchanti brahma brahmavido janāḥ (24)

dhūmo rātris tathā kṛṣṇaḥ ṣaṇmāsā dakṣiṇāyanam
tatra cāndramasaṁ jyotir yogī prāpya nivartate (25)

śuklakṛṣṇe gatī hy ete jagataḥ śāśvate mate
ekayā yāty anāvṛttim anyayāvartate punaḥ (26)

(23) I shall now declare unto thee, O Best of the Bharatas (Arjuna), the path, traversing which at the time of death, yogis attain freedom; and also the path wherein there is rebirth.

(24) Fire, light, daytime, the bright half of the lunar month, the six months of the northern course of the sun—pursuing this path at the time of departure, the knowers of God go to God.

(25) Smoke, nighttime, the dark half of the lunar month, the six months of the southern course of the sun—he who follows this path obtains only the lunar light and then returns to earth.

(26) These two paths for exiting from the world are reckoned eternal. The way of light leads to release, the way of darkness leads to rebirth.

THESE MYSTERIOUS STANZAS, woefully misinterpreted by nearly all commentators, in reality contain symbolic references to the science of yoga. They describe the opening of the spiritual eye, the awakening of the cerebrospinal centers, and the ascension of life force and consciousness through them to Cosmic Consciousness and liberation in Spirit of the yogi who follows the "way of light." And, on the contrary, they describe also the descension or return to body consciousness or rebirth of those yet unable to open fully all the cerebrospinal doors that lead ultimately to Spirit. Liberation, freeing the soul from the physical, astral, and causal bodies, is the purport of these verses. The ponderous scriptures of the *rishis* have defined in veiled terms the labyrinth of the soul's descension and ascension. Krishna has here stated this portion of the yoga science succinctly for the comprehending Arjuna—the advanced yogi-devotee. The rudiments are as follows:

THE ESOTERIC PATH OF FIRE AND LIGHT FOLLOWED BY THE YOGI TO LIBERATION

STANZA 24 STATES that the yogi who attains liberation must follow the path of "fire." Here "fire" means the life energy, the *kundalini* power. The devotee's first scientific step toward emancipation is to gain control of his life force. In ordinary men the course of *prana* is downward, "the way of darkness," flowing from the brain to the sensory nerves and the countless cells of the body. This dispersion and diffusion of life energy reveal to human consciousness the material world.

In the successful yogi, on the other hand, the course of *prana* is upward, "the way of light." By yoga he reverses the direction of the flow and is able to concentrate the whole of his life force within the brain, in the "sun" of Cosmic Consciousness. In this way God is revealed.

The "sun" of Cosmic Consciousness is the Supreme Source of life and intelligence in the body, with Its abode in the seventh or highest spiritual center, in the cerebrum, in the thousand-petaled lotus—a sunburst as of a thousand suns. All life and faculties in the body evolve from this powerhouse of luminosity through its projected rays of the spiritual eye.*

"Light" in stanza 24 refers to the divine eye in the forehead, whose awakening enables the yogi to say with Christ: "I am the light of the world: he that followeth me shall not walk in darkness, but shall have the light of life."†

* "I entered and beheld with the eye of my soul, above the same eye of my soul and above my mind, the Light Unchangeable—not this common light, which shines for all flesh; nor as it were a greater of the same kind, as though the brightness of this should shine out more and more brightly and with its greatness take up all space. Not such was this light, but different, yea, far different from all these. Nor was it above my soul as oil is above water, nor yet as the sky is above the earth; but it was above me because it made me, and I was below it because I was made by it. He that knoweth the Truth, knoweth that Light; and he that knoweth it, knoweth Eternity."—St. Augustine's *Confessions*

† John 8:12.

The light of the spiritual eye is a projection of the "sun" of Cosmic Consciousness. Through the light of the spiritual eye, the yogi moves along the path to Spirit.

"Daytime" is the manifestation of the spiritual eye during the *samadhi* state of meditation. This is the yogi's "daytime," for he has awakened from the sleep of delusion.

"The bright half of the lunar month" is that half of the advanced yogi's consciousness that remains "awake" and attuned to Cosmic Consciousness even when the other half of his consciousness is "asleep," or active, in the material world of delusion. A similar reference is made in II:69: "That which is night to all creatures is wakefulness to the man of self-mastery. And what is wakefulness to ordinary men, that is night to the divinely perceptive sage." (See commentary, page 317 ff.)

The moon, whose light is a reflection of the sun, has a bright fortnight (waxing period) and a dark fortnight (waning period) in its monthly cycle. The sun of Cosmic Consciousness shining on matter (the light of the astral world and body that upholds and enlivens the material world and body) is here referred to as reflected or lunar light. In man, a miniature universe, its bright side is when it is spiritualized and turned toward Cosmic Consciousness; and its dark side is when it is turned toward delusion. In the advanced yogi, the cerebrospinal centers, though performing their activities that externally enliven the body (necessitating their working through the instruments of Nature, or delusion, the outward-flowing or "dark side"), remain nevertheless inwardly in a spiritualized or illumined state. When the yogi withdraws from external activities and enters *samadhi* through the light of the spiritual eye, this is the true "bright fortnight," that period of the day when his whole being is inwardly ablaze, turned toward Spirit, basking in the "sun" of Cosmic Consciousness.

The "six months" are the six spinal centers, the coccygeal to the spiritual eye. Thus, the "six months of the northern course of the sun" refers to the six periods of spiritual perceptions in these centers as consciousness and life (descended from the "sun" of Cosmic Consciousness into the body) are reversed to flow upward, "north,"* to their Supreme Source in the cerebrum.

What transpires as the yogi moves along this "way of light" is a veritably intricate transition of his life and consciousness through the

---

* "North" is the upper part of man's body, specifically the brain with its spiritual center of Cosmic Consciousness. See similar reference in I:11, page 110, in relation to the death of Bhishma, who would not leave his body "until the sun moves north in the heavens."

spiritual eye: First, life and consciousness move upward through the physical spine and brain, freeing the yogi from the physical body; then transition through the three astral spines of light (*sushumna, vajra, chitra*), freeing the yogi from the astral body; and, lastly, ascension through the causal "spine" of consciousness (*brahmanadi*), whereby the soul is liberated in Spirit. At death, the soul of the successful yogi, following this path, rises majestically, unencumbered, from the revolving cycles of obligatory rebirths.

THE WAY OF DARKNESS AND MORTAL BONDAGE

NOW IS DESCRIBED, in verse 25, by contrast, the "way of darkness" that leads to continued mortal bondage.

"Smoke" means ignorance, or delusion, that obscures divine perception of reality, and that holds man, even the still-aspiring yogi, in body consciousness.

"Nighttime" is the state of darkness caused by ignorance. Jesus said: "The light of the body is the eye (the omniscient single or spiritual eye): if therefore thine eye be single, thy whole body shall be full of light. But if thine eye be evil (obscured by delusion), thy whole body shall be full of darkness. If therefore the light that is in thee be darkness, how great is that darkness!"*

"The dark half of the lunar month" is the outflowing life and consciousness from the cerebrospinal centers in the spiritually unawakened man that causes him to dream the dreams of delusive material activity in his nighttime of ignorance.

"The six months of the southern course of the sun" refers to the descent of the delusion-clouded "sun" of Cosmic Consciousness through the six spinal centers to the lower or "southern" part of the body, specifically the three lower spinal centers associated with material consciousness.

These references in this context are specifically in relation to the time of death or departure from the physical body. Those whose inner divine sight is clouded by the "smoke" of delusion leave the body in the "nighttime," or darkness of ignorance—unconscious, or at least not fully conscious, of the transition from the physical to the astral body and world. Departing in the "dark lunar fortnight," with his unawakened consciousness in the spinal centers still attracted to delusive material activities, his exiting consciousness and life force retire from the physical body and flow downward, "the southern course." In this way, uncon-

* Matthew 6:22–23.

sciously moving through the "dark side" or outflowing energy, of the six spinal centers, he descends into the astral body. His state of advancement and good karma determine whether his exit from the physical body and subsequent stay in the astral are passed through in oblivious darkness, like a deep sleep, with perhaps occasional dreams or glimpses of the astral world (only evil persons experience astral nightmares, or "hell"), or whether he is fully awake in the glory of the heavenly realms. In any case, not having attained freedom in Spirit, but only the "lunar light," or astral encasement of his soul, he remains in the astral world for a karmically predetermined time; and then his physical desires and karma cause him to take rebirth. In the "darkness" or sleep of astral death, he passes into the sperm-and-ovum-united cell and begins his rebirth in the dark womb of his new mother.

❖
Death-experience of the unenlightened man
❖

Even the accomplished yogi who in *samadhi* meditation attains high states of divine communion but has not opened all doors to liberation from the physical, astral, and causal soul-encasements, has to return from *samadhi* to body consciousness. At death, his astral sojourn is a glorious one. But having attained only the "lunar light" of the astral heaven, and harboring unfinished material desires and karma, he revolves back to rebirth on earth, but with divine aspiration that predisposes him to a spiritual life.

A literal interpretation of these verses, that the yogi must die in the daytime as well as in a luminous fortnight occurring within the six-month period of the northern passage of the sun, is senseless. An illumined yogi leaves his body instantaneously at any time he chooses during the day or night, the bright or dark lunar fortnight, the northern or southern course of the sun! He does not have to consult the brainless stars for an auspicious hour. Since time began, never has there been an "inauspicious" hour for man to awake from delusion!

VERSES 27–28

naite sṛtī pārtha jānan yogī muhyati kaścana
tasmāt sarveṣu kāleṣu yogayukto bhavārjuna (27)

vedeṣū yajñeṣu tapaḥsu caiva dāneṣu yat puṇyaphalaṁ pradiṣṭam
atyeti tat sarvam idaṁ viditvā yogī paraṁ sthānam upaiti cādyam (28)

(27) No yogi who understands these two paths is ever deluded (into following the way of darkness). Therefore, O Arjuna! at all times maintain thyself firmly in yoga.

(28) He who knows the truth about the two paths gains merit far beyond any implicit in the study of the scriptures, or in sacrifices, or in penances, or in gift-giving. That yogi reaches his Supreme Origin.

To know that he lives in a state of cosmic delusion is man's first precious glimpse of truth. To learn and practice yoga—the method of deliverance from delusion—is to possess an incomparable treasure. So, O devotee! "at all times maintain thyself firmly in yoga."

om tat sat iti śrīmadbhagavadgītāsu upaniṣatsu
brahmavidyāyām yogaśāstre śrīkṛṣṇārjunasaṁvāde
akṣarabrahmayogo nāmāṣṭamo 'dhyāyaḥ

Aum, Tat, Sat.
In the Upanishad of the holy Bhagavad Gita—the discourse of Lord Krishna to Arjuna, which is the scripture of yoga and the science of God-realization—this is the eighth chapter, called "Union With the Absolute Spirit."

CHAPTER IX

THE ROYAL KNOWLEDGE, THE ROYAL MYSTERY

❖

Direct Perception of God, Through Methods of Yoga "Easy to Perform"

❖

How the Lord Pervades All Creation, Yet Remains Transcendent

❖

The Right Method of Worshiping God

"Thus does Bhagavan Krishna summarize the discourse in this chapter on resolving by Self-realization through yoga the mystery of the simultaneous immanence and transcendence of Spirit. Through the divine science of yoga, or union, with God, the yogi unites himself with the transcendent Spirit, beyond the dreams of manifestation, while also remaining immanent and active, with Spirit, in the cosmic dream drama."

THE ROYAL KNOWLEDGE, THE ROYAL MYSTERY

DIRECT PERCEPTION OF GOD, THROUGH METHODS OF YOGA "EASY TO PERFORM"

VERSES 1–3

śrībhagavān uvāca
idaṁ tu te guhyatamaṁ pravakṣyāmy anasūyave
jñānaṁ vijñānasahitaṁ yaj jñātvā mokṣyase 'śubhāt (1)

rājavidyā rājaguhyaṁ pavitram idam uttamam
pratyakṣāvagamaṁ dharmyaṁ susukhaṁ kartum avyayam (2)

aśraddadhānāḥ puruṣā dharmasyāsya paraṁtapa
aprāpya māṁ nivartante mṛtyusaṁsāravartmani (3)

The Blessed Lord said:
(1) To thee, the uncarping one, I shall now reveal the sublime mystery (the immanent-transcendent nature of Spirit). Possessing intuitive realization of this wisdom, thou shalt escape from evil.

(2) This intuitive realization is the king of sciences, the royal secret, the peerless purifier, the essence of dharma (man's righteous duty); it is the direct perception of truth—the imperishable enlightenment—attained through ways (of yoga) very easy to perform.

(3) Men without faith in this dharma (without devotion to the practices that bestow realization) attain Me not, O Scorcher of Foes (Arjuna)! Again and again they tread the death-darkened path of samsara (the rounds of rebirth).

LORD KRISHNA HERE PROCLAIMS Self-realization, true wisdom, as the highest branch of all human knowledge—the king of all sciences, the very essence of *dharma* ("religion")—for it alone permanently uproots the cause of man's threefold suffering and reveals to him his true nature of Bliss.* Self-realization is yoga or "oneness" with truth—the direct perception or experience of truth by the all-knowing intuitive faculty of the soul. This intuitive realization is the basis of all valid religious experience, the very essence of *dharma* (religion or righteousness), as here stated in the Gita.

The devotee who, through ways of yoga, becomes established in Self-realization possesses the all-knowing intuitive wisdom of direct perception that penetrates to the core of the mystery of how the Lord is at once both immanent and transcendent. Realizing his own oneness with God, the yogi knows that he himself is a microcosm of immanence and transcendence; he remains working in the world without losing awareness of his sublime soul nature, and thus escapes the "evil" of delusive entanglements.

Many philosophers, particularly in the West, take the defeatist attitude that God is unknowable. The opposite view is expounded in the Gita—and nowhere more clearly than in these verses: The highest Truth is knowable by direct experience.

Our present Atomic Age was inaugurated by scientists who had faith in the possibility of a vast expanse of human knowledge. By courageous vision and laborious experiment they accomplished a task that men of previous centuries considered vain and chimerical—the splitting of the atom and the release of its hidden energies. Men of goodwill who carry on that work will be divinely guided to use the new knowledge for constructive purposes and the betterment of human life.†

---

* *Dharma,* from the Sanskrit root *dhri,* "to uphold or support"—often translated simply as religion or righteousness—is a comprehensive term for the natural laws and eternal verities that uphold the divine order of the universe and of man, a miniature universe. Sankhya philosophy thus defines true religion as "those immutable principles that protect man permanently from the threefold suffering of disease, unhappiness, and ignorance." India's vast body of Vedic teachings are amassed under the umbrella-term *Sanatana Dharma,* "Eternal Religion."

† Reflecting on the course of world affairs that began with the discovery of atomic energy, one of the most renowned historians of modern civilization, Dr. Arnold Toynbee, observed: "It is already becoming clear that a chapter which had a Western beginning will have to have an Indian ending if it is not to end in the self-destruction of the human race.... At this supremely dangerous moment in human history, the only way of salvation for mankind is the Indian way—Emperor Asoka's and Mahatma Gandhi's principle of nonviolence and Sri Ramakrishna's testimony to the harmony of religions. Here we have

The science of yoga was similarly developed by men of high aspiration. They hungered for Eternal Truth and perfected a science of inwardly applied techniques that succeeded in bridging the otherwise impassable gulf between man and his Maker. The Indescribable Unique is indeed not to be won lightly, but won It has been, by many royal sages; and won It will be, whenever there arises a devotee of sufficient yearning and determination. But "the way" has to be known. That secret path is yoga, "easy to practice" and conferring "imperishable enlightenment."

HOW THE LORD PERVADES ALL CREATION, YET REMAINS TRANSCENDENT

VERSES 4–6

mayā tatam idaṁ sarvaṁ jagad avyaktamūrtinā
matsthāni sarvabhūtāni na cāhaṁ teṣv avasthitaḥ (4)

na ca matsthāni bhūtāni paśya me yogam aiśvaram
bhūtabhṛn na ca bhūtastho mamātmā bhūtabhāvanaḥ (5)

yathākāśasthito nityaṁ vāyuḥ sarvatrago mahān
tathā sarvāṇi bhūtāni matsthānīty upadhāraya (6)

(4) I, the Unmanifested, pervade the whole universe. All creatures abide in Me, but I do not abide in them.

(5) Behold My Divine Mystery! in which all beings are apparently not in Me, nor does My Self dwell in them; yet I alone am their Creator and Preserver!

(6) Understand it thus: Just as air moves freely in the infinitudes of space (akasha), and has its being in space (yet air is different from space), just so do all creatures have their being in Me (but they are not I).

---

an attitude and spirit that can make it possible for the human race to grow together into a single family—and, in the Atomic Age this is the only alternative to destroying ourselves." (*Publisher's Note*)

THESE WORDS EMBODY A PORTION of the highest wisdom, "the sublime mystery" Krishna promised to reveal to Arjuna (IX:1). The thought, "Creation, although permeated with God, yet does not comprise Him nor reveal His essence," is liberating to the true devotee—he who does not cling to any state of phenomenal being but finds his own Reality only in the Unnameable Originless.

All this cosmic dream and its creatures are produced by the pure undistortable beam of God's consciousness. But His formless infinite consciousness is ever transcendent, not limited to or by the finite dream manifestations.*

A man looking at the sky and the mountains and the ocean does not detect in them the Divine Presence. The subtle beam of the Creator is imperceptible to the human gaze. Because He is everywhere, it is as if He were nowhere.

Though all creatures are formed of God-texture, He is not contained nor exhausted by them. This interpretation explains the seeming contradiction in these verses—that, although the Lord pervades the world, yet He does not dwell in it.

By God's mysterious power (*Yogam Aishvaram* or Divine Yoga), His vibrationless unmanifested cosmic consciousness underlies all vibratory beings, who nevertheless cannot be observed to exist in Him, nor do they affect Him. Even though a beam of light conveys and sustains motion picture scenes, with all their varieties and contrasts, the beam itself undergoes no transformations. Similarly, the motion pictures of creation do not disturb the Lord's originating beam.

---

* "Today modern science is venturing into realms that for more than four millennia have been the fiefdoms of religion and philosophy," wrote Professor Amit Goswami, Ph.D., in *The Self-Aware Universe: How Consciousness Creates the Material World* (Los Angeles: Tarcher, 1993). "Until the present interpretation of the new physics, the word *transcendence* was seldom mentioned in the vocabulary of physics. The term was even considered heretical." However, he states, a 1982 experiment by a team of physicists in France has confirmed the idea of transcendence in quantum physics. The experiment, conducted by Alain Aspect and collaborators, proved that two quantum particles emitted from the same source remain inextricably correlated: When a change is made to one particle, instantaneously the other particle is affected similarly—even when separated by vast distances. Says Goswami: "When there is no signal in space-time to mediate their connection...where, then, exists the instantaneous connection between correlated quantum objects that is responsible for their signal-less action at a distance? The succinct answer is: in the transcendent domain of reality.

"The technical name for signal-less, instantaneous action at a distance is nonlocality.... According to physicist Henry Stapp, the message of quantum nonlocality is that 'the fundamental process of Nature lies outside space-time but generates events that can be located in space-time.'" (*Publisher's Note*)

As the wind, wandering in all directions over the infinite sky, is yet unable to affect the sky, so the colossal panorama of creation uninfluentially abides in God's eternal consciousness.

As the changing images of a dream do not alter the essential nature of a dreamer's consciousness, so the evanescent scenes of the cosmic dream, with its hordes of tumultuous emotional beings that work and play within it, do not involve the Divine Unchangeable Dreamer.

Such is the paradox of creation, that God exists as the Soul of all men, creating and supporting them, yet does not Himself become entangled with them. And human beings, although saturated with God, are overcome by cosmic delusion and made subject to birth and death. A mystery indeed!

In the end all speculations about the ultimate secrets of God and creation are profitless. The stark fact is always with us: man is here and now undergoing the painful tests of human incarnation. Just as prisoners plot ceaselessly to regain their freedom, so the wise among men endeavor to escape the confinement of mortality. In His own good time, from His own ineffable lips, the Lord will reveal to His devotee all mysteries of heaven and earth.

VERSES 7–8

sarvabhūtāni kaunteya prakṛtiṁ yānti māmikām
kalpakṣaye punas tāni kalpādau visṛjāmy aham (7)

prakṛtiṁ svām avaṣṭabhya visṛjāmi punaḥ punaḥ
bhūtagrāmam imaṁ kṛtsnam avaśaṁ prakṛter vaśāt (8)

(7) At the end of a cycle (kalpa), O Son of Kunti (Arjuna), all beings return to the unmanifested state of My Cosmic Nature (Prakriti). At the beginning of the next cycle, again I cast them forth.

(8) By revivifying Prakriti, Mine own emanation, again and again I produce this host of creatures, all subject to the finite laws of Nature.

IF THE MOTION-PICTURE FILM on an unwinding reel is suddenly destroyed, the images on the screen at once disappear. Similarly, when the

God-illumined film of Nature or Prakriti is dissolved at the end of a *kalpa,* all cosmic-dream pictures of creation vanish. Again, at the start of another *kalpa,* the Lord awakens Mother Nature and causes her to resume the objective display—that of materialized beings acting their parts on the "screen" of time and space.

These cycles of evolution and involution are eternal. "The show must go on," though one by one the actors become liberated and are replaced by a new cast. A portion of God's consciousness will always be engaged in the exhibition of phenomenal worlds—the stage whereon a multitude of His children must perform their roles until through true Self-realization they earn an "honorable dismissal."

In the time span of infinity, beginning and end provide only an inscrutable concept that turns in on itself to come out again where it went in.

Verse 9

na ca māṁ tāni karmāṇi nibadhnanti dhanaṁjaya
udāsīnavad āsīnam asaktaṁ teṣu karmasu

But these activities entrammel Me not, O Winner of Wealth (Arjuna), for I remain above them, aloof and unattached.

Just as a person whose business it is to operate a Ferris wheel in an amusement park feels no identity with the personal emotional involvement of the riders, even so the Master of this rotating Ferris wheel of creation—which is alternately started and stopped by His will—remains an Onlooker, an Impartial Witness.

So long as men enjoy riding the wheel of cosmic entertainment, so long must they be bound to it, helplessly experiencing the scenes of birth and death, of pleasure and pain. But the Lord here tells us the secret by which He participates without involvement in creation: nonattachment. Although the sole Doer, He has no egoism and so remains free. Man, realizing that "all this is God, not I and mine," becomes a disinterested spectator, free from selfish motives and inflammatory emotions, whether viewing his own life or the lives of others.

In placing His children on this mechanical marvel, the rotating earth, God wishes them to manage the cosmic show, but with His guidance, not in the chaotic ways of deluded men.

To exist without peace of mind in this world is to dwell in a kind of Hades. But the man of divine perceptions finds the earth a blissful abode. A dreamer experiencing a nightmare is tortured; but as soon as he realizes it to be a subconscious prank of consciousness, he laughs about it.

The average man attaches great importance to the worldly spectacle. But a yogi takes the dream show lightly, and only God seriously.

VERSE 10

mayādhyakṣeṇa prakṛtiḥ sūyate sacarācaram
hetunānena kaunteya jagad viparivartate

O Son of Kunti (Arjuna), it is solely My impregnating presence that causes Mother Nature to give birth to the animate and the inanimate. Because of Me (through Prakriti) the worlds revolve in alternating cycles (of creation and dissolution).

EVEN THOUGH GOD AS THE Divine Cosmic Light is the Creator-Director of the delusive films of Nature and her happy and hurtful dream-picture productions, still He is not the direct Doer. Prakriti, animated by His light, does all the mischief and all the good in creation.

Yet the Cosmic Mother could not exist nor operate without the power and guidance of the unmanifested Divine. God and Nature are thus indivisible though diverse, like two sides of a coin. The Hindu scriptures tell us that even Prakriti, so close to the transcendental Lord, finds it hard to grasp the way in which He mysteriously manifests through her, making her feel that she is the creator, while in reality He is the unseen Origin of all.

VERSES 11–12

avajānanti māṁ mūḍhā mānuṣīṁ tanum āśritam
paraṁ bhāvam ajānanto mama bhūtamaheśvaram (11)

moghāśā moghakarmāṇo moghajñānā vicetasaḥ
rākṣasīm āsurīṁ caiva prakṛtiṁ mohinīṁ śritāḥ (12)

(11) The ignorant, oblivious of My transcendental nature as the Maker of all creatures, discount also My presence within the human form.

(12) Lacking in insight, their desires and thoughts and actions all vain, such men possess the deluded nature of fiends and demons.

PRAKRITI HAS THREE *gunas* or manifesting qualities. These two stanzas refer to men with a predominance of *tamas* or ignorance (the nature of demons) and those with an overabundance of *rajas* or activity for selfish goals (the nature of fiends).

The following stanza (13) mentions men filled with the third *guna, sattva* or wisdom.

VERSES 13–15

mahātmānas tu māṁ pārtha daivīṁ prakṛtim āśritāḥ
bhajanty ananyamanaso jñātvā bhūtādim avyayam (13)

satataṁ kīrtayanto māṁ yatantaś ca dṛḍhavratāḥ
namasyantaś ca māṁ bhaktyā nityayuktā upāsate (14)

jñānayajñena cāpy anye yajanto mām upāsate
ekatvena pṛthaktvena bahudhā viśvatomukham (15)

(13) But mahatmas ("great souls"), O Son of Pritha (Arjuna), expressing in their nature divine qualities, offer the homage of their undeviating minds to Me, knowing Me as the imperishable Source of all life.

(14) Constantly absorbed in Me, bowing low with adoration, fixed and resolute in their high aspiration, they worship Me and ever praise My name.

(15) Others, also, performing the yajna of knowledge, worship Me, the Cosmic-Bodied Lord, in various ways—first as the Many, and then as the One.

SATTVIC BEINGS, FREE FROM THE BLINDING delusions of the *rajas* and *tamas* qualities, see God within and without, in all things, and thus remain always in His proximity. Their uncompromising goodness and undistracted devotion offer no resistance to the natural pull of the soul toward Spirit—the pull of the Lord's love that pursues every soul, even unto the farthest reaches of delusion.

Stanza 14 refers to the devotional path (*bhakti*). The mind and heart of the *bhakta,* immersed in God's love, are always intent on Him. Every thought and action is grasped as a new opportunity to love and worship Him. Through their love-emanating eyes and actions, and the magnetic bliss of their silent devotion, they draw other souls unto God. The Lord is glorified by the eloquence of such an exemplary life. There is no other way to praise Him.

Stanza 15 refers to the way of wisdom (*jnana*). As the yogi progresses spiritually he offers his manifold states of knowledge as oblations in an ever-increasing fire of wisdom. In this way he worships the Infinite as the myriad manifestations of his divine perceptions; finally all are commingled in One Blessed Blaze. Through many perceptions the devotee learns to worship the Lord with a sole perception—the knowing of Him as the Absolute. First the yogi sees, "God is All," then grasps the ultimate simplicity, "God."

VERSE 16

ahaṁ kratur ahaṁ yajñaḥ svadhāhaṁ aham auṣadham
mantro 'ham aham evājyam aham agnir ahaṁ hutam

I am the rite, the sacrifice, the oblation to ancestors, the medicinal herb, the holy chant, the melted butter, the sacred fire, and the offering.

THE VEDIC SACRIFICIAL CEREMONIES, in which clarified butter is poured on fire, symbolize the surrender of the self to the Self. All the gifts that God has bestowed on man are offered in turn to Him by the devotee.

The sattvic devotee considers all his actions—whether secular, spiritual, or ritualistic—as holy rites and oblations offered in the purifying fire of God-awareness. As dream objects and beings cannot be separated from their dreamer, similarly, the oblating devotee honors the Lord as the Giver, the Offering, and the Receiver.

VERSE 17

pitāham asya jagato mātā dhātā pitāmahaḥ
vedyaṁ pavitram oṁkāra ṛk sāma yajur eva ca

Of this world I am the Father, the Mother, the Ancestor, the Preserver, the Sanctifier, the all-inclusive Object of Knowledge, the Cosmic Aum, and also the Vedic lore.

THE UNMANIFESTED SPIRIT IS the Supreme Cause, the Ancestor of God the Father of Creation (*Sat,* or Cosmic Consciousness); God the Son, His reflection in creation as the Preserver (*Tat,* the Krishna or Christ Consciousness); and God the Holy Ghost (*Aum,* the Mother or Cosmic Nature, bringing forth the worlds through Her creative vibration).

Spirit as the Sole Reality is the One Object of Knowledge, comprehending which man will simultaneously understand all other knowledge. Spirit is the Sanctifier that purifies man of sin and delusion; and It, too, is the Source of Vedic or eternal wisdom.

VERSE 18

gatir bhartā prabhuḥ sākṣī nivāsaḥ śaraṇaṁ suhṛt
prabhavaḥ pralayaḥ sthānaṁ nidhānaṁ bījam avyayam

I am the Ultimate Goal, the Upholder, the Master, the Witness, the Shelter, the Refuge, and the One Friend. I am the Origin, the Dissolution, the Foundation, the Cosmic Storehouse, and the Seed Indestructible.

GOD IS THE ONE FRIEND OF MAN, He who eventually restores to His bosom all His dream children. He is the One Consciousness that creates, preserves, dissolves, and witnesses all creation; the One Storehouse wherein all cosmic-dream blueprints are kept during the *kalpas* of dissolution. And at the beginning of the great *kalpas* of manifestation it is He as the Imperishable Seed that fertilizes Prakriti and vivifies her protean forms.

VERSE 19

tapāmy aham ahaṁ varṣaṁ nigṛhṇāmy utsṛjāmi ca
amṛtaṁ caiva mṛtyuś ca sad asac cāham arjuna

I bestow solar heat, O Arjuna, and give or withhold the rain. Immortality am I, and also Death; I am Being (Sat) and Non-Being (Asat).

THE LORD HERE PRESENTS HIMSELF as the Great Paradox. As the Creator of Maya, the Cosmic Magician, He is responsible for the "pairs of opposites," the contrasting suggestions accepted by all creatures under *maya's* hypnotic sway—heat and cold, life and death, truth and falsehood (reality and illusion).

THE RIGHT METHOD OF WORSHIPING GOD

VERSES 20–21

traividyā māṁ somapāḥ pūtapāpā yajñair iṣṭvā svargatiṁ
prārthayante
te puṇyam āsādya surendralokam aśnanti divyān divi
devabhogān (20)

te taṁ bhuktvā svargalokaṁ viśālaṁ kṣīṇe puṇye martyalokaṁ
viśanti
evaṁ trayīdharmam anuprapannā gatāgataṁ kāmakāmā
labhante (21)

(20) The Veda-ritualists, cleansing themselves of sin by the soma rite, worship Me by yajna (sacrifice), and thus win their desire of entry into heaven. There, in the sacred kingdom of the astral deities, devotees enjoy the subtle celestial pleasures.

(21) But after delighting in the glorious higher regions, such beings, at the expiration of their good karma, return to earth. Thus abiding by the scriptural regulations, desiring the enjoyments (the promised celestial rewards thereof), they travel the cyclic path (between heaven and earth).

THOSE WHO DESIRE CELESTIAL FRUITS of actions and who therefore purify themselves by Vedic rites (or any other scriptural rituals or injunctions), and by right living, receive the satisfaction of their hearts' aspiration: entrance into the holy astral abodes. But that "entrance" leads inevitably to an "exit," because such devotees did not desire God but only His gifts.

For such aspirants, good karma produces only a period of astral enjoyments. Whether long or short, that period will end. But those who single-heartedly love the Lord and who work for Him without desire for the fruits of action—those who perform the true *yajna* of yoga, offering the self into the Self, and who by guru-given yoga techniques purify their bodies and consciousness with the *soma* nectar of divine life energy*—win the eternal liberation.

Good dreams—those of the high astral spheres—are still dreams, and keep the soul deluded. A wise yogi does not wish to spend incarnations traveling from one good dream to another. Confinement in beautiful dream-prisons has no lure for him. Oneness with the Ultimate Reality is his sole goal.

VERSE 22

ananyāś cintayanto māṁ ye janāḥ paryupāsate
teṣāṁ nityābhiyuktānāṁ yogakṣemaṁ vahāmy aham

To men who meditate on Me as their Very Own, ever united to Me by incessant worship, I supply their deficiencies and make permanent their gains.

DEVOTEES WHO ARE FAITHFUL to their Creator, perceiving Him in all the diverse phases of life, discover that He has taken charge of their lives, even in the smallest detail, and makes smooth their paths by bestowal of divine foresight. Thus saith the wise King Solomon: "Trust in the Lord with all thine heart....In all thy ways acknowledge Him, and He shall direct thy paths."†

---

* The juice extracted from the *soma* plant is used to prepare a purifying ritualistic libation offered during ceremonial worship. The true *Soma,* however, is known to advanced yogis as a nectar-like secretion of divine life energy produced in the throat by the perfected practice of such techniques as *Kriya Yoga* and *Khechari Mudra* (see X:28, page 792).

† Proverbs 3:5–6.

He who preserves the colossal cosmic dream upholds lovingly the wisdom of yogis, once they have found it. And the Inexhaustible Lord finds no difficulty in supplying His devotees with food and shelter for the body as well as all other needful accessories of dream life.

This stanza of the Gita reminds us of Christ's words: "But seek ye first the kingdom of God, and His righteousness; and all these things shall be added unto you."*

Most men foolishly spend their valuable lives in seeking material riches, which must be forsaken at death. Yogis use their efforts to find imperishable wisdom. Their spiritual wealth is deposited for them by God in the bank of eternity, to be used by them forever.

VERSES 23–24

ye 'py anyadevatābhaktā yajante śraddhayānvitāḥ
te 'pi mām eva kaunteya yajanty avidhipūrvakam (23)

ahaṁ hi sarvayajñānāṁ bhoktā ca prabhur eva ca
na tu mām abhijānanti tattvenātaś cyavanti te (24)

(23) O Son of Kunti (Arjuna), even devotees of other gods, who sacrifice to them with faith, worship Me alone, though not in the right way.

(24) I am indeed the only Enjoyer and Lord of all sacrifices. But they (the worshipers of My lesser forms) do not perceive Me in My true nature; hence, they fall.

A DEVOTEE WHO OFFERS HIS ALLEGIANCE to other gods, even the highest astral deities, does not worship God as the Infinite but only as one or more of His finite manifestations. These, like the rest of creation, are mere appearances and not Reality.

A devotee can rise only as high as the object and the objective of his worship. If a virtuous man propitiates lesser gods, or worships with the goal of attaining the glorified pleasures of a life in heaven, the Supreme Being is indeed touched by the seeker's devotion to Him in whatever form, and in the afterdeath state in the celestial regions

* Matthew 6:33.

grants him the fulfillment of his expectations. But after a time, being still in the realms of return, he falls again to mortal birth and must work anew to gain divine merit. Thus does he dream the dreams of coming and going so long as he remains asleep in delusive separation from the Indivisible Spirit who is at once the dream, the Dreamer, and the ever awake Dreamless One.

The "right way" of worship, which leads to liberation, is through yoga meditation that bestows the *samadhi* of divine union with Spirit.

VERSE 25

yānti devavratā devān pitṝn yānti pitṛvratāḥ
bhūtāni yānti bhūtejyā yānti madyājino 'pi mām

Devotees of the astral deities go to them; ancestor worshipers go to the manes; to the nature spirits go those who seek them; but My devotees come to Me.

THE GITA (VIII:6) STATES that the predominant feeling at the time of death determines one's future residence. It is in accordance with their devotional trends that men go to the high astral worlds of the deities, or to the regions of the ancestral heroes, or to the abode of elemental spirits, or to eternal freedom—the supreme vibrationless sphere of God.

Those who commune throughout their lives with the Lord are at death not cast by the Karmic Judge into any cosmic-dream prison, but go unto their Father to become pillars in His mansion (unmanifested cosmos). Having no attachment to this or any other world or form of existence, they need "go no more out."*

VERSE 26

patraṁ puṣpaṁ phalaṁ toyaṁ yo me bhaktyā prayacchati
tad ahaṁ bhaktyupahṛtam aśnāmi prayatātmanaḥ

---

* Revelation 3:12.

The reverent presentation to Me of a leaf, a flower, a fruit, or water, given with pure intention, is a devotional offering acceptable in My sight.

JESUS SAID THAT THE SMALL GIFT of two mites, presented with devotion by a poor widow, was more pleasing to God than the wealth that was ostentatiously proffered by irreligious men.* The outpouring of heartfelt love is the only "sacrifice" the Lord desires from His creatures.

God says: "Great yogis are rare, so I seldom receive from earth-dwellers the most precious gift—complete soul surrender to Me. Therefore I accept happily even a little flower, tear-sprinkled and devotionally fragrant, from those who have little time for Me, though I give My time and gifts to them."

This stanza also means that man's most fleeting thought and most trifling action may be used as stepping-stones toward His presence. True devotees devoutly offer to Him the living leaves of their proliferating spiritual understanding and perceptions, the choicest blossoms of love from the secret garden of their hearts, the fruits of their selfless actions, and the sanctifying sacred waters of intuitive inner divine communion gathered reverently from the river of meditation.

Indeed, how compassionately indulgent and impartial the Lord is that He so readily recognizes not only the mighty ecstasy of lordly yogis, but also the "widow's mite" of those who can give little to Him, but do give all they have. Yogis perceive God's response in glorious, even spectacular, ways; striving devotees are blessed with divine thoughts and aspirations, God's loving silent voice encouraging and coaxing them forward to His waiting presence.

VERSES 27–32

yat karoṣi yad aśnāsi yaj juhoṣi dadāsi yat
yat tapasyasi kaunteya tat kuruṣva madarpaṇam (27)

śubhāśubhaphalair evaṁ mokṣyase karmabandhanaiḥ
saṁnyāsayogayuktātmā vimukto mām upaiṣyasi (28)

* Mark 12:38–44.

samo 'haṁ sarvabhūteṣu na me dveṣyo 'sti na priyaḥ
ye bhajanti tu māṁ bhaktyā mayi te teṣu cāpy aham (29)

api cet sudurācāro bhajate mām ananyabhāk
sādhur eva sa mantavyaḥ samyag vyavasito hi saḥ (30)

kṣipraṁ bhavati dharmātmā śaśvacchāntiṁ nigacchati
kaunteya pratijānīhi na me bhaktaḥ praṇaśyati (31)

māṁ hi pārtha vyapāśritya ye 'pi syuḥ pāpayonayaḥ
striyo vaiśyās tathā śūdrās te 'pi yānti parāṁ gatim (32)

(27) Whatever actions thou dost perform, O Son of Kunti (Arjuna), whether in eating, or in observing spiritual rites, or in gift bestowing, or in self-disciplining—dedicate them all as offerings to Me.

(28) Thus no action of thine can enchain thee with good or evil karma. With thy Self steadfastly anchored in Me by Yoga and renunciation, thou shalt win freedom and come unto Me.

(29) I am impartial toward all beings. To Me none is hateful, none is dear. But those who give Me their heart's love are in Me, as I am in them.

(30) Even a consummate evildoer who turns away from all else to worship Me exclusively may be counted among the good, because of his righteous resolve.

(31) He will fast become a virtuous man and obtain unending peace. Tell all assuredly, O Arjuna, that My devotee never perishes!

(32) Taking shelter in Me all beings can achieve the Supreme Fulfillment—be they those of sinful birth, or women, or Vaishyas, or Sudras.

IN THESE STANZAS THE LORD OFFERS the sweetest solace and the highest hope to all of His children, even the erring and bewildered. Through steadfast practice of yoga meditation, renunciation of desires and attachments by loving dedication of all actions to God, repentance, and right resolution, not only can the righteous attain liberation, but even the wickedest of men may speedily emerge from sin into sanctity, from ignorance into the healing light of wisdom.

No man may be said to be so depraved that he is outside the pale of Divine Mercy. And such are the potency and mysterious workings of the soul that sometimes even the most evil of men have changed into saints.

Vicious persons, convicting themselves by their own consciences, often judge their souls to be lost forever. But the Gita gives assurance that they too may recover their long-forgotten spiritual heritage. No sin is unforgivable, no evil insuperable, for the world of relativity contains no absolutes.

Stanza 32 does not cast a slur against women and those of low birth and worldly businessmen (Vaishyas) and body-identified laborers (Sudras). No scripture suggests that these are the "worst among sinners"! The meaning is: For a true devotee all social inequalities are negated.

Unlike society, God never disqualifies anyone because of occupation, sex, or birth. In reality the "family tree" of all beings is divinely impressive. Are they not children of the Most High, and coheirs to an eternal kingdom?

VERSE 33

kiṁ punar brāhmaṇāḥ puṇyā bhaktā rājarṣayas tathā
anityam asukhaṁ lokam imaṁ prāpya bhajasva mām

How easily, then, may I be attained by sainted Brahmins (knowers of God or Brahman) and pious royal sages (Rajarishis)! Thou who hast entered this impermanent and unhappy world, adore only Me (Spirit).

IF EVEN SINFUL MEN AND WOMEN may retrace their footsteps to the Hallowed Home, how unhampered is the journey, then, for spiritually inclined people!

VERSE 34

manmanā bhava madbhakto madyājī māṁ namaskuru
mām evaiṣyasi yuktvaivam ātmānaṁ matparāyaṇaḥ

On Me fix thy mind, be thou My devotee, with ceaseless worship bow reverently before Me. Having thus united thyself to Me as thy Highest Goal, thou shalt be Mine own.

THUS DOES BHAGAVAN KRISHNA summarize the discourse in this chapter on resolving by Self-realization through yoga the mystery of the simultaneous immanence and transcendence of Spirit. Through the divine science of yoga, or union, with God, the yogi unites himself with the transcendent Spirit, beyond the dreams of manifestation, while also remaining immanent and active, with Spirit, in the cosmic dream drama.

In yoga meditation, O devotee, fix thy mind unwaveringly on God; with devotion, surrender to Him the ego consciousness and all its dream delusions. In the inner rite of true worship, oblate the little self into the Self in the sacred fire of divine communion with Spirit. Look solely to Him who is the Lord of All, for He is the consummation of the rainbow-chases of incarnations. In Him, all motley-hued desires merge in the one splendor of Bliss in which the soul is forever diademed with Spirit.

The Self-realized yogi is a prince of peace sitting on the throne of poise directing his kingdom of activity, wholly devoted to God in heart and mind, sacrificing to Him the fruits of all his actions. "That devotee," saith the Lord, "having obtained Me and remaining continually united to Me, shall truly be Mine own!"

om tat sat iti śrīmadbhagavadgītāsu upaniṣatsu
brahmavidyāyām yogaśāstre śrīkṛṣṇārjunasaṁvāde
rājavidyārājaguhyayogo nāma navamo 'dhyāyaḥ

Aum, Tat, Sat.
In the Upanishad of the holy Bhagavad Gita—the discourse of Lord Krishna to Arjuna, which is the scripture of yoga and the science of God-realization—this is the ninth chapter, called "Union Through the Royal Knowledge and the Royal Mystery."

CHAPTER X

The Infinite Manifestations of the Unmanifest Spirit

❖

The Unborn and Beginningless, Beyond Form and Conception

❖

The Diverse Modifications of God's Nature

❖

In Joy and Devotion, the Wise Adore Him

❖

The Devotee Prays to Hear From the Lips of the Lord Himself: "What Are Thy Many Aspects and Forms?"

❖

"I Will Tell Thee of My Phenomenal Expressions"

ॐ

"O Scorcher of Foes (Arjuna), limitless are the manifestations of My divine attributes; My concise declaration is a mere intimation of My proliferating glorious powers.... But what need hast thou, O Arjuna, for the manifold details of this wisdom? Understand simply: I, the Unchanging and Everlasting, sustain and permeate the entire cosmos with but one fragment of My Being!"

THE INFINITE MANIFESTATIONS OF THE UNMANIFEST SPIRIT

THE UNBORN AND BEGINNINGLESS, BEYOND FORM AND CONCEPTION

VERSES 1–3

śrībhagavān uvāca
bhūya eva mahābāho śṛṇu me paramaṁ vacaḥ
yat te 'haṁ prīyamāṇāya vakṣyāmi hitakāmyayā (1)

na me viduḥ suragaṇāḥ prabhavaṁ na maharṣayaḥ
aham ādir hi devānāṁ maharṣīṇāṁ ca sarvaśaḥ (2)

yo mām ajam anādiṁ ca vetti lokamaheśvaram
asaṁmūḍhaḥ sa martyeṣu sarvapāpaiḥ pramucyate (3)

The Blessed Lord said:
(1) O Mighty-Armed (Arjuna), hear thou more of My supreme utterance. For thy highest good I will speak further to thee, who listeneth joyfully.

(2) Neither the multitude of angels nor the great sages know My Uncreated Nature, for even the devas and rishis (are created beings, and hence) have an origin in Me.

(3) But whoever realizes Me to be the Unborn and Beginningless as well as the Sovereign Lord of Creation—that man has conquered delusion and attained the sinless state even while wearing a mortal body.

STANZA 2 DOES NOT MEAN that liberated angels and *rishis* do not understand the Self-evolved nature of Deity, for stanza 3 expressly states that even a mortal may become a *jivanmukta* ("freed while living") by that very realization—God as both beyond creation (*Sat*) and in creation (*Tat*).

These stanzas signify, however, that full mergence in the Divine Transcendence is not attainable by any created being; he who has origin cannot be the Originless. God's essential nature is Spirit, not form; Infinity, not finiteness.

Disembodiment—the state of unimaginable freedom achieved by the devotee after he has dissolved by wisdom his three imprisoning vehicles, physical and astral and causal—is necessary before the soul of man can rejoin Spirit per se.

Stanza 2 affirms the metaphysical truth that all emancipated beings who accept reembodiment (at God's command) are required to work in harmony with the Cosmic Mother or Lawful Nature, to whom the Lord has given full power over the phenomenal worlds. To a certain extent even such exalted beings have to place themselves nominally under Nature's cosmic delusion and thus forgo full realization of Spirit—immutable, unborn, and unmanifested. They are obliged to accept *maya* or delusion as the only means by which their bodies assume visibility at all. The beam of light from a motion-picture projector produces no images on the screen unless it passes through shadow-forms on a film. Similarly, the Sole Reality has no form without the presence of the variegated vibratory film of *maya*, the principle of duality that divides the Indivisible and through cosmic vibration projects forms on the screen of time and space. Manifestation of any form testifies to the operation of Nature's mayic cosmic vibration, and thus pertains to creation, not to the Uncreated and Vibrationless.

Even liberated saints are required to accept some delusion when they incarnate

This stanza therefore gives us an explanation for the sometimes puzzling conduct of fully illumined masters. During his crucifixion Jesus became temporarily conscious of cosmic delusion; perceiving his dream body and feeling its agonies, he cried: "My God, my God, why hast Thou forsaken me?"* Other liberated saints, also, have appeared to undergo physical sufferings, or to display sympathetic identifications with other people in their troubles and joys. Jesus and other masters wept and behaved in various other ways like mortal beings.

But no one should wrongly think that the great sages and prophets are not aware of God's true nature. Those perfect devotees who, even af-

* Matthew 27:46.

ter liberation, wear an earthly body in order to carry on certain activities in the world of phenomena are simply watchful about the ever present power of cosmic delusion. However, such exalted ones are able to dismiss their body dream at will and thus to perceive the transcendental Spirit.

THE DIVERSE MODIFICATIONS OF GOD'S NATURE

VERSES 4–5

buddhir jñānam asaṁmohaḥ kṣamā satyaṁ damaḥ śamaḥ
sukhaṁ duḥkhaṁ bhavo 'bhāvo bhayaṁ cābhayaṁ eva ca (4)

ahiṁsā samatā tuṣṭis tapo dānaṁ yaśo 'yaśaḥ
bhavanti bhāvā bhūtānāṁ matta eva pṛthagvidhāḥ (5)

Discrimination, wisdom, lack of delusion, forgiveness, truth, control of the senses, peace of mind, joy, sorrow, birth, death, fear, courage, harmlessness, equanimity, serenity, self-discipline, charity, fame, and infamy—these diverse states of beings spring from Me alone as modifications of My nature.

AS EVERYTHING IN A MAN'S DREAM is made of his consciousness, so everything in the cosmic dream proceeds from the Mind of God. Because He is the Creator of Cosmic Nature—with her dualistic principle of delusion (*maya* or the law of opposites) and her triple qualities of *sattva, rajas,* and *tamas*—the Lord is responsible for all good and evil, for all contrasts and contradictions and relativities in the unfoldments of the human mind and the human destiny.

This is not to say that a person is good or evil, joyous or sorrowful, because God has so ordered it. Rather, all contrasting potentials are God's doing through the laws of Nature; but how they manifest in or through the individual depends on that person's karmic pattern created by his own use and misuse of free will, which sets into operation in his life the *sattva, rajas,* or *tamas* qualities of Nature.

All mental states and all inner and outer conditionings of mankind subserve a divine purpose. By discrimination, wisdom, self-control, and other righteous means, and by experience in many incarnations of oppositional states—birth and death, courage and fear, fame and infamy, joy and sorrow—the human being seeks at last the Secondless, the true Unique.

VERSE 6

maharṣayaḥ sapta pūrve catvāro manavas tathā
madbhāvā mānasā jātā yeṣāṁ loka imāḥ prajāḥ

The seven Great Rishis, the Primeval Four, and the (fourteen) Manus are also modifications of My nature, born of My thought, and endowed with (creative) powers like Mine. From these progenitors come all living creatures on earth.

AS CITED IN GITA IV:25 and VIII:4, the universe is created through the differentiation of Spirit. The Absolute becomes God the Father (transcendental beyond creation), the Christ or *Kutastha* Intelligence (His pure reflection omnipresent in creation), and Maha-Prakriti or Holy Ghost with its six other intelligences or deities (the Lord's active creative consciousness).

This present stanza refers to further modifications of God's variant presence in cosmic activity. Like an infinite kaleidoscope, the individualized multidivisions of His ubiquitous intelligence, "by hundreds and by thousands" as declared in Chapter XI, unite and divide, combine and recombine, within the mayic cylinder of time and space to produce the myriad patterns of creation that delight and awe both gods and men. Each new modulation, according to its unique purpose, is assigned in Hindu scriptures a characteristic personality and name.*

The Bible refers to the symbolic Adam and Eve and their descendants as the origin of the human race. The Hindu scriptures describe the becomings of all creatures from the Prajapatis, the divine "lords of the universe" born from the mind of God.

The Primeval Four mind-born sons of Brahma the Creator are Sanaka, Sanandana, Sanatana, and Sanat-kumara. Symbolically, they are the firstborn differentiation of Spirit from which creation evolves. They

* "The apparent multiplication of gods is bewildering at first glance. But soon you discover that they are all the same God in different aspects and functions. There is always one uttermost God who defies personification. This makes Hinduism the most tolerant religion in the world, because its one transcendent God includes all possible gods."—*George Bernard Shaw*

are the pure creative Nature of God, Maha-Prakriti or Holy Ghost. As their very names imply, they are the Lord's eternal (Sanatana, "everlasting") consciousness of bliss (Sanandana, "having joy"), that exists from the beginning (Sanaka, "former, ancient"), and is ever new (Sanat-kumara, "ever a youth"). These sons of Brahma remained ever pure, innocent youths, declining to create progeny. Yet all things evolve from this Bliss (Ananda); for inherent in Maha-Prakriti, along with the Lord's eternal joy, are the three *gunas* or attributes of creation—*sattva, rajas,* and *tamas.* These qualities are equilibrated in a quiescent state in Maha-Prakriti. But when *rajas,* the activating attribute as Brahma the Creator, is roused, it enlivens also *sattva,* the nourishing quality (Vishnu the Preserver), and *tamas,* the degenerative quality (Shiva the Destroyer; dissolution, the inevitability of all things in the realm of change and illusion). The will of God to enjoy His bliss through many forms sends forth His Ananda as four fundamental creative ideas impinged in these three *gunas:* vibration (*Aum*); time (*kala*), the idea of change; space (*desha*), the idea of division of the One Eternal Being; and atom (*anu*), the idea of particles for the manifestation of form.*

❖
Everlasting, ever-conscious, ever-new Bliss from which creation evolves
❖

The Sapta-Maharishis are the seven original *rishis* to whom the Vedas were revealed—divine beings said to have been liberated in Spirit in the Solar Age: Marichi, Atri, Angiras, Pulaha, Kratu, Pulastya, and Vasishtha. These represent seven principal powers of life and consciousness proceeding from the macrocosmic "sun," or vibratory light, of the creative Cosmic Energy (*Aum*) and the microcosmic "sun," or light, of the spiritual eye in man.

From the lineage of the fourteen Manus, fathers of mankind, all beings descend. They are Svayambhuva, Svarochisha, Auttami, Tamasa, Raivata, Chakshusha, Vaivasvata, Savarni, Daksha-savarni, Brahma-savarni, Dharma-savarni, Rudra-savarni, Rauchya or Deva-savarni, and Bhautya or Indra-savarni. Each successive Manu is associated with a particular cycle of creative manifestation and dissolution. The seventh Manu, Vaivasvata ("Sun-born" from Vivasvat, the Deity of the Sun) is defined as the progenitor of the present race of beings. See IV:1–2 (page 423) concerning the symbology of Vivasvat and Manu as representing the descension of consciousness from Vivasvat, the "sun" or light of creative Cosmic Energy, to Manu, the mind (*manas*), the instrument from which sentient human consciousness derives—hence, the "origin" of man.

---

* See XIII:1, pp. 867 ff. concerning the evolution of matter from the action of the *gunas.*

IN JOY AND DEVOTION, THE WISE ADORE HIM

VERSES 7–8

etāṁ vibhūtiṁ yogaṁ ca mama yo vetti tattvataḥ
so 'vikampena yogena yujyate nātra saṁśayaḥ (7)

ahaṁ sarvasya prabhavo mattaḥ sarvaṁ pravartate
iti matvā bhajante māṁ budhā bhāvasamanvitāḥ (8)

(7) He who realizes by yoga the truth of My prolific manifestations and the creative and dissolving power of My Divine Yoga is unshakably united to Me. This is beyond doubt.

(8) I am the Source of everything; from Me all creation emerges. With this realization the wise, awestricken, adore Me.

THE LIBERATED MAN, BEHOLDING Spirit as the Creator of countless universes; of the endless procession of angels, Manus, *rishis,* human beings, and the lower forms of life; and of the innumerable processes of their perceptions and the modes of their becomings, is filled with awe at the hitherto unknown oceanic vastness spread out behind the little wave of his consciousness.

Ekam sat—only One exists. In the Vedas the cosmos is said to evolve like a spider's web out of God's being. The Lord is the Divine Thread (Sutra) or unifying essence running through all experiences and all expressions of life and matter.*

---

* "Experiment and theory alike indicate that the universe began in a state of perfect simplicity, evidence of which was burned into the heart of every atom in the heat of the Big Bang at the beginning of time," says Timothy Ferris, a science writer for *The New York Times.* "The search for simplicity is bringing science face-to-face with the ancient enigma of creation."

"We don't really see the Creator twiddling twenty knobs to set twenty parameters to create the universe as we know it. That's too many," says physicist Leon Lederman, author of *The God Particle.* "There is something simple underneath all this. Six quarks, and six leptons, and their antiparticles, and their coming in different colors and different charges, is too complicated."

Physicist John Wheeler agrees: "To my mind, there must be at the bottom of it all, not an utterly simple equation but an utterly simple idea. When we finally discover it, it will be so compelling, so beautiful, that we will all say to each other, 'Oh, how could it have been otherwise?'" (*Publisher's Note*)

"The universe is represented in every one of its particles. Everything is made of one hidden stuff. The world globes itself in a drop of dew....The true doctrine of omnipresence is that God appears with all His parts in every moss and cobweb."*

VERSE 9

maccittā madgataprāṇā bodhayantaḥ parasparam
kathayantaś ca māṁ nityaṁ tuṣyanti ca ramanti ca

Their thoughts fully on Me, their beings surrendered to Me, enlightening one another, proclaiming Me always, My devotees are contented and joyful.

GOD-UNITED YOGIS, THEIR CONSCIOUSNESS and life merged in Him, perceive the immense panorama of creation through the Lord's omnipresent life and consciousness. Such great devotees are aware through intuitional power of one another's presence. They commune together to give expression to their overflowing love for God. Such men alone know joy and the contentment of spirit that causes them to cry: "I am full, O Lord! In Thyself I have found all treasure." What wonder then that the yogi urges the worldly man to forsake the momentary pleasures of the earth and to embrace the Giver of Everlasting Bliss!

As a drunken man feels throughout his body the injurious thrill of alcohol, so a God-intoxicated devotee, conscious of his augmented being in the vast cosmic body of Nature, feels an ever-rejuvenating exaltation at the contact of the omnipresent joyful *Aum*. It was this bliss-wine, the cosmical vibration of *Aum*, the Holy Ghost, that filled Christ's disciples on the day of Pentecost.†

A desireless yogi, withdrawing his mind from the excitements and bewilderments of the cosmic dream, experiences an endless satisfaction that is unknown to seekers of sense pleasures. As a prisoner regaining his liberty after many years is suffused with happiness, so the

---

* Emerson, in *Compensation*. This great American writer was a deep student of Vedic thought.

† "And when the day of Pentecost was fully come, they were all with one accord in one place. And suddenly there came a sound from heaven as of a rushing mighty wind, and it filled all the house where they were sitting. And there appeared unto them cloven tongues like as of fire, and it sat upon each of them. And they were all filled with the Holy Ghost, and began to speak with other tongues, as the Spirit gave them utterance" (Acts 2:1–4).

yogi who emerges from the confinement of numerous incarnations into the freedom of Spiritual Identity is overwhelmed by inexhaustible joy.

VERSES 10–11

teṣāṁ satatayuktānāṁ bhajatāṁ prītipūrvakam
dadāmi buddhiyogaṁ taṁ yena mām upayānti te (10)

teṣām evānukampārtham aham ajñānajaṁ tamaḥ
nāśayāmy ātmabhāvastho jñānadīpena bhāsvatā (11)

(10) To those thus ever attached to Me, and who worship Me with love, I impart that discriminative wisdom (buddhi yoga) by which they attain Me utterly.

(11) From sheer compassion I, the Divine Indweller, set alight in them the radiant lamp of wisdom which banishes the darkness that is born of ignorance.

THE REALIZED YOGI, THROUGH the intuitive discriminative wisdom he receives from attunement with God, knows both the immanent and the transcendent states of Spirit. He can merge in divine unity with the Absolute in *samadhi;* and he can also delight in a dualistic relationship with his Creator, as a devotee beholding and worshiping in the temple of reverential love the all-pervasive connate Spirit, the Cosmic Dream Idol whose form is the phenomenal universe.

As it is the Lord who has caused man to dream this dream of delusion, it is He alone who can bestow awakening. When a mortal being tires of groping through the darkness of unknowing, and uses his God-given intelligence to ask the right questions, follow the right actions, and demand enlightenment, God in His infinite compassion responds to that sincere entreaty. His grace lights the inner wisdom-lamp in that devotee, dispelling dark shadows of delusive dreamings. With the banishment of ignorance, the awakened devotee "attains Him utterly."*

---

* In my house, with Thine own hands, light the lamp of Thy love!
Thy transmuting lamp entrancing, wondrous are its rays.
Change my darkness to Thy light, Lord,
And my evil into good.
Touch me but once and I will change,

THE DEVOTEE PRAYS TO HEAR FROM THE LIPS OF THE LORD HIMSELF: "WHAT ARE THY MANY ASPECTS AND FORMS?"

VERSES 12–13

arjuna uvāca
paraṁ brahma paraṁ dhāma pavitraṁ paramaṁ bhavān
puruṣaṁ śāśvataṁ divyam ādidevam ajaṁ vibhum (12)

āhus tvām ṛṣayaḥ sarve devarṣir nāradas tathā
asito devalo vyāsaḥ svayaṁ caiva bravīṣi me (13)

Arjuna said:
The Supreme Spirit, the Supreme Shelter, the Supreme Purity art Thou! All the great sages, the divine seer Narada, as well as Asita, Devala, and Vyasa, have thus described Thee as the Self-Evolved Eternal Being, the Original Deity, uncaused and omnipresent. And now Thou Thyself tellest me!

IN AWE ARJUNA ACCLAIMS the Lord for having made known to him His Transcendental Being. The Uncreated is indeed the very One to whose reality the illumined sages of all lands and all epochs have testified.

VERSE 14

sarvam etad ṛtaṁ manye yan māṁ vadasi keśava
na hi te bhagavan vyaktiṁ vidur devā na dānavāḥ

All my clay into Thy gold.
All the sense lamps that I did light, sooted into worries.
Sitting at the door of my soul,
Light Thy resurrecting lamp!

This poem by Rabindranath Tagore, India's Nobel-winning poet, was set to music by Paramahansa Yogananda, and included in his *Cosmic Chants* (published by Self-Realization Fellowship). (*Publisher's Note*)

O Keshava (Krishna)! I consider as eternal truth all Thou hast revealed to me. Indeed, O my Lord! neither the Devas (gods) nor the Danavas (Titans) know the infinite modes of Thine appearances.

THE ASTRAL FORCES OF CREATIVE INTELLIGENCE, the powerful personifications of good and evil (the gods, or divine forces, and the anti-gods, or delusive forces), are nevertheless only partial expressions of Deity. So even they, the agents of creation—owing to their innate limitations and to their degree of identification with their divinely ordained roles in the phenomenal worlds—cannot know the whole of the Infinite and Transcendent Lord. How much less, then, may be grasped by the mortal being, howsoever divinely endowed, who is circumscribed by embodiment and demonic ignorance.

VERSES 15–16

svayam evātmanātmānaṁ vettha tvaṁ puruṣottama
bhūtabhāvana bhūteśa devadeva jagatpate (15)

vaktum arhasy aśeṣeṇa divyā hy ātmavibhūtayaḥ
yābhir vibhūtibhir lokān imāṁs tvaṁ vyāpya tiṣṭhasi (16)

(15) O Divine Purusha, O Origin of beings, O Lord of all creatures, O God of gods, O Sustainer of the world! verily Thou alone knowest Thyself by Thyself.

(16) Therefore, please tell me exhaustively of Thy divine powers and qualities by which Thine Omnipresence sustaineth the cosmos.

THE UNENLIGHTENED MAN SPINS a thousand speculative webs, hoping to seize the elusive Truth. But what theory has captured It?

The yogi, however, seeks the solutions to the cosmic mysteries from the lips of the omniscient Mystifier. "He alone knoweth Himself by Himself." Arjuna therefore sought the answers to the final enigmas from the "Lord of all creatures"—He who abides in each heart as the Divine Teacher.*

* "Who can tell how powerful and fruitful will be the science of the future when men and women of science return in humility to that first great quest, to think God's thoughts

VERSE 17

kathaṁ vidyām ahaṁ yogiṁs tvāṁ sadā paricintayan
keṣu keṣu ca bhāveṣu cintyo 'si bhagavan mayā

O Great Yogi (Krishna)! how shall I always meditate in order to know Thee truly? In what aspects and forms, O Blessed Lord, art Thou to be conceived by me?

ARJUNA SALUTES THE LORD as the "Great Yogi" or Uniter—He who joins triple factors (the Cosmic Dreamer, the process of dreaming, and the objective cosmic dream) in one single and simultaneous perception of His inimitable Mind.

As God is both the Absolute and the Manifest, the query of the devotee is, "Shall I meditate on Thee as Cosmic Consciousness, the

---

after Him?" wrote Sir John Marks Templeton and Robert Hermann, in *Is God the Only Reality?* (New York: Continuum, 1994). "We see the future open to the scientific exploration of spiritual subjects such as love, prayer, meditation, thanksgiving, giving, forgiving, and surrender to the divine will. It may be that we shall see the beginning of a new age of 'experimental theology,' which may reveal that there are spiritual laws, universal principles that operate in the spiritual domain, just as natural laws operate in the physical realm."

Nobel physicist Brian Josephson of Cambridge University agrees. In *Nobel Prize Conversations With Sir John Eccles, Roger Sperry, Ilya Prigogine, and Brian Josephson* (Dallas: Saybrook Publishing Co., 1985) he said: "What one finds if one studies the various forms of mysticism is that the doctrines of the mystics are much less diverse than are religious doctrines. My interpretation of this is that mysticism is concerned with very fundamental laws.... I consider mysticism to be something universal like science [and that] religions are based on the facts of this science. Thus mysticism is a kind of universal foundation for the diverse and different religions. I should mention here that I'm not talking entirely about Eastern mysticism, because there is Western mysticism as well: e.g., Christian mysticism, Islamic mysticism (Sufism), and Jewish mysticism. These all say rather similar things.

"...Mystical experience by self-development through meditation, etc., is not only the key to one's own development but also the key...to putting this attempt to synthesize science and religion on a solid foundation.... If we follow this path of a synthesis of science with religion (using meditation as an observational tool), what we are doing is using our own nervous systems as instruments to observe the domains in which God works. Ordinary scientific instruments like telescopes, galvanometers, and particle detectors are not going to be good in this context because they are designed to function in the material domain. Our nervous systems, on the other hand, are designed to allow us to interact not only with the material level of existence but also with the spiritual levels. ...All the different levels are open to exploration if we develop our nervous systems so that they tune in. One can imagine that this would be a part of the scientific training of the future." (*Publisher's Note*)

Dreamless Spirit? or on one of Thy various dream aspects? If I worship Thee as having attributes, what are Thy many aspects and forms, O Lord, knowing which I shall know how to focus my mind on Thee in meditation? In which of Thy manifestations may I best recognize Thee?"

"I WILL TELL THEE OF MY PHENOMENAL EXPRESSIONS"

VERSES 18–20

vistareṇātmano yogaṁ vibhūtiṁ ca janārdana
bhūyaḥ kathaya tṛptir hi śṛṇvato nāsti me 'mṛtam (18)

śrībhagavān uvāca
hanta te kathayiṣyāmi divyā hy ātmavibhūtayaḥ
prādhānyataḥ kuruśreṣṭha nāsty anto vistarasya me (19)

aham ātmā guḍākeśa sarvabhūtāśayasthitaḥ
aham ādiś ca madhyaṁ ca bhūtānām anta eva ca (20)

(18) O Janardana (Krishna)! tell me more, at great length, of Thy yoga powers and Self-manifestations; for never can I hear enough of Thy nectared speech!

The Blessed Lord said:
(19) Very well, O Best of the Princes (Arjuna), I will indeed tell thee of My phenomenal expressions—but only the most outstanding ones, for there is no end to My variety.

(20) O Conqueror of Sleep (Arjuna)! I am the Self in the heart of all creatures: I am their Origin, Existence, and Finality.

IN ADDRESSING ARJUNA AS *Gudakesha,* "Conqueror of Sleep," the Lord implies that divine truths are known only by the man who has awakened from the *maya*-trance of delusion.

God here assumes total responsibility for all living things. He dreams the procession of created beings, He preserves them in their existences, and He merges them in the state of cosmic dissolution. A liberated man attains the true Finality by realizing that his only Life has been ever present within him as the Immutable Self.

VERSE 21

ādityānām ahaṁ viṣṇur jyotiṣāṁ ravir aṁśumān
marīcir marutām asmi nakṣatrāṇām ahaṁ śaśī

Among the Adityas (twelve effulgent beings), I am Vishnu; among luminaries, I am the radiating sun; among the Maruts (forty-nine wind gods), I am Marichi; among heavenly bodies, I am the moon.

IN THE PREVIOUS STANZA, God was described as the origin, existence, and finality of all beings. From stanzas 21 through 41, the Lord elaborates on His prominent manifestations among the beings, forces, and objects that are the causes and the results of His creative, preservative, and terminative activities in the cosmos. The light of God equally pervades all beings and all objects. But those of superior qualities reflect His manifestation to a greater degree; just as a diamond, by its transparency, reflects more light than a piece of charcoal, though both are made of carbon.

Government of the universe assisted by many minor manifestations of the Creator Lord

As noted in X:6, in addition to the primary powers of creation (transcendental God, His reflection as the *Kutastha* Intelligence immanent in creation, and Cosmic Nature with its six other intelligences, "angels"), the government of the universe is assisted by many minor manifestations of the Creator Lord. This chapter of the Gita is designated *The Discourse on Vibhuti Yoga,* depicting the attributes of God that declare His all-pervading manifestation in the universe. The differentiation of His consciousness—of which there is no limit (X:40)—is God's Divine Yoga by which substantial worlds and beings are spun of ethereal threads of consciousness. Much of the contents in this chapter, especially in these latter verses, has an esoteric relevance to the intricate science of yoga that defines the subtle powers behind the gross becomings. To interpret these fully would proliferate this text unduly. Intimation of the symbology will suffice, for as Sri Krishna says in verse 42: "What need hast thou for the manifold details of this wisdom?" Toward this end, the seers developed simple yoga techniques of meditation, such as *Kriya Yoga*, that set into motion the forces that purify and uplift the consciousness to divine realization of the Transcendent Lord, the Ultimate Simplicity who is the repository of all complexities. To touch the Infinite is to know in an instant all knowledge that could scarce be contained in ponderous volumes!

Cosmic Nature, Mother of all vibrations, has three phases, as previously noted: the creative, preservative, and dissolving states, governed respectively by Brahma, Vishnu, and Shiva. These deities are indigenous in the Cosmic Mother Vibration. They work through the six angels and the twelve celestial Adityas (referred to in the literal translation of this stanza), and through many other "beings," or intelligent creative powers, to carry on the creation, preservation, and dissolution of the vast universe and its government.

"In the beginning...God said: Let there be light"; God vibrated His wish to create, and light became manifest: He brought forth the intelligent Holy Ghost *Aum* vibration, which became manifest as objective light and sound. These two properties of *Aum,* in various combinations, constitute all objective creation. The twelve effulgent deities mentioned in this stanza derive their immutable light and power from *Aum,* the Holy Ghost or Maha-Prakriti. They are variously referred to in the scriptures as eternal sustainers of the celestial light that is the source of all luminosities. In the Upanishads,* they are described as the twelve months of the year. In the microcosm of man, their powers are manifested as the instigators of the activities of the six spinal centers, from the coccyx to the medulla. See Gita VIII:23–26 wherein the twelve months of the year are explained as the six months of the northern course of the sun, the way of light (ascension through the six centers to cosmic consciousness); and the six months of the southern course of the sun, the way of darkness (descension of the consciousness through the spinal centers into body consciousness).

Vishnu is hailed as chief among these primal luminous Intelligences, for He is the maintainer of the constructive-preservative state of creation. There can be no manifestation of Spirit without this power of preservation. Creation in the formative state is incomplete, therefore imperfect; it decays and disappears during the state of dissolution. But the preservative or Vishnu state is stupendous, spectacular—an awesome display of the Lord's attributes made manifest.

Among objective manifestations in the solar system, God prominently displays His cosmic light in the positive sun and the negative

---

* *Brihadaranyaka Upanishad* III:9.5.

moon. The sun represents the fatherhood of God, and the moon the motherhood of Cosmic Nature, the consort of God. This positive-negative principle repeats itself throughout nature, "parenting" all objectified matter. The sun-moon analogy is recurrent throughout yoga treatises, representing positive and negative, Spirit and Nature.

Marichi is proclaimed as chief of the Maruts, or forty-nine wind gods. According to the ancients, various air currents blow around the earth, and the one referred to as Marichi is the most beneficial. The esoteric implication is evident in the fact that Marichi is also designated as one of the seven *maharishis* (see X:6). In the body of man, there are seven principal life currents that are amplified into forty-nine specialized life forces.

VERSE 22

vedānāṁ sāmavedo 'smi devānām asmi vāsavaḥ
indriyāṇāṁ manaś cāsmi bhūtānām asmi cetanā

Among the Vedas, I am the Sama Veda; among the gods, I am Vasava (Indra); among the senses, I am mind (manas); in creatures, I am the intelligence.

SOME PEDANTS DO NOT CONCUR with the Gita's commendation of the Sama Veda, as it is generally considered a derivation in the form of metric hymns from the verses in the more honored Rig Veda. A deeper significance is here implied. *Sāma* means "calm" or "tranquil" (from the word *sāman:* "calming, tranquilizing," from *sā,* "meditation"). The acquisition of true knowledge (*veda*), truth realization, comes not from scriptural tenets or outward rituals, but from inner intuitive perception. When by meditation, interiorization, the mind is tranquil (*sāmana*), the attention of the yogi focuses at the *Kutastha* center of universal consciousness in the forehead; and through the omniscient intuitive vision of the spiritual eye, the devotee becomes a seer of *veda,* truth. In the Vedas, and particularly in the rhythmic meter of the Sama Veda, there is a strictly regulated order (*anupurvi*) of the words, and phonological rules for combinations of sounds (*sandhi*) and for the recitation of letters (*sanatana*), which conduce to such interiorization. Each syllable (*akshara*) is endowed with significance and a spiritualizing vibration.

This Gita verse goes on to hail Indra as Vasava, chief of the astral gods. A yogi who has controlled the oscillating emotions of the heart, which arise from likes and dislikes, attraction and repulsion—the causes of pleasures and pain—is spoken of as having attained a spiritual state akin to that of the all-conquering Indra.

Manas, the sense mind, is the coordinator of the ten senses (five of perception and five of action) and the cause of their externalization in the sensory organs. Mind is thus superior to its sensory instruments. Without mind, no sensations could be received, nor could activities be performed in response to sensations or to thoughts of the ego. Mind exists even without the physical senses. In the dreamland the mind can see, hear, smell, taste, and touch; and can perform all actions without the instruments of the sensory organs.

God manifests externally through the senses to enable man to perceive the physical cosmic dream of matter, a replica of which can be created by the mind within in the dreamland. But an even greater manifestation of God is the intelligence in creatures, that which interprets sensory impressions and discriminates. It is intelligence that gives man the power to choose the good dreams of life in preference to nightmares of evil. The discriminative faculty persuades the mind to turn away from the spurious pleasures of the senses and helps it to concentrate on soul blessedness so that liberation can be achieved.

The senses reveal the fluctuating dream world of matter; the mind reveals the changeable inner world in man; and intelligence converted into intuitive wisdom reveals the immutability of God.

VERSE 23

rudrāṇāṁ śaṁkaraś cāsmi vitteśo yakṣarakṣasām
vasūnāṁ pāvakaś cāsmi meruḥ śikhariṇām aham

Of the Rudras (eleven radiant beings) I am (their leader) Shankara ("the well-wisher"); of the Yakshas and Rakshasas (astral demi-goblins), I am Kubera (lord of riches); of the Vasus (eight vitalizing beings), I am Pavaka (the god of fire, the purifying power); and of mountain peaks I am Meru.

THE RUDRAS ARE TEN *PRANAS* or intelligent life forces, plus their empowering supreme intelligence, Shankara, "the well-wisher," which sustains their existence.

Like Croesus of old who ruled in fabulous wealth in ancient Lydia,

Kubera is considered "the lord of riches" in the astral world. This intelligence is the supreme power among the Yakshas and Rakshasas (demigoblins noted for their avaricious behavior), the negative forces that counter the good works and benefactions of the gods, or divine forces—fulfilling the duality essential to the cosmic drama. When human beings succumb to delusive evils such as selfishness, greed, possessiveness, they take on the nature of Yakshas, the generally inoffensive but sometimes dishonest and traitorous spirit-forces that serve Kubera, the god of wealth. Carried to the extreme of evil inclinations, human beings take on the demonic personality of Rakshasas, the most infamous of which was Ravana (a younger brother of Kubera) who plays the villainous role in the exalted epic *The Ramayana*.

The Vasus (gods) referred to in this context are eight vitalizing deities or intelligent forces, among whom, the purifying, radiant energy, Pavaka (Agni, god of fire), is supreme.

Among mountain peaks, God manifests Himself most majestically as the sacred Mt. Meru. Allegorically, Meru is the highest place of divine consciousness in the body, the top part of the cerebrum where God dwells as the soul. The spine with its spiritual centers of divine consciousness is often referred to as *meru-danda,* the staff or rod whose crest is Meru. It is the scepter of the soul's sovereign power over the kingdom of the body.

Verse 24

purodhasāṁ ca mukhyaṁ māṁ viddhi pārtha bṛhaspatim
senānīnām ahaṁ skandaḥ sarasām asmi sāgaraḥ

And, O son of Pritha (Arjuna), understand Me to be the chief among priests, Brihaspati; among generals, I am Skanda; among expanses of water, I am the ocean.

Brihaspati, preceptor of the astral deities, is the prototype of the priestly order. In his position as chief priest of the gods, he intercedes with the gods on behalf of men; and is a protector of men against evil. In the Vedas, Brihaspati is also called Brahmanaspati, lord of the evolution or expansion of creation through the great power of cosmic delusion. In the golden ages, wise priests were the spiritual protectors and advisers of the royal sages, *rajarishis* such as King Janaka. In this Gita verse, God declares His manifestation in all true gurus as well as in the chief preceptor, Brihaspati.

Skanda (another name for Karttikeya, god of war, son of Shiva) is the supreme warrior-general among the armies of the gods. Allegorically, Skanda, "Attacker," represents self-control, the leading warrior of the discriminative faculties in their fight with the sense-bound mental faculties. It is the spiritual quality of self-control that drives Ego and its armies of sense desires from the bodily kingdom and establishes therein the reign of King Soul.

Water, because of its fluidity, which spreads out in all directions, is a symbol of the omnipresence of God in creation. Vishnu, the all-pervasive preserver of the universe, is depicted as Narayana, "He who moves in the waters" (from *nara,* "water," and *ayana,* "moving"). He rests on the great serpent Shesha (creative power) floating on the eternal waters (creative elements), which are in motion during the cycles of creation and are quiescent in Spirit during periods of dissolution. A similar metaphor is found in Genesis 1:2 in the Bible: "And the Spirit of God moved upon the face of the waters (creative elements)."

The vastness of the ocean and the sky have always captivated the human attention, stirring forgotten soul memories of the everlasting infinity of God. When one contemplates the expanse of ocean and sky, he escapes momentarily the confinements of finite matter and glimpses the Infinite. The horizon where the azure sky and the blue brine meet I call the "altar of God." Meditating before that most splendid altar of nature, I perceive the enthronement thereon of the majestic Divine Presence.

VERSE 25

maharṣīṇāṁ bhṛgur ahaṁ girām asmy ekam akṣaram
yajñānāṁ japayajño 'smi sthāvarāṇāṁ himālayaḥ

Of the Maharishis (mighty sages), I am Bhrigu; among words, I am the one syllable Aum; among yajnas (holy ceremonies), I am japa-yajna (silent, superconscious chanting); among stationary objects, I am the Himalaya.

A *MAHARISHI* IS A COMPLETELY LIBERATED soul. He can remain in ecstatic union with the Absolute in the meditative state or carry on material activities with no loss of his divine perception. Wisdom is extolled as superior to action; the former denotes intuitive perception of the Infinite, the latter is a means for that divine realization. Most *maharishis* remain in the inactive wisdom state, but Bhrigu was a master of both wisdom and activity. Hence, God cites him as the exemplar of liberated sages. Wisdom with divine action is the balanced ideal most pleasing to God, for that is also His nature.

As the roar of the ocean is the composite sound of all its waves, so the cosmic sound of *Aum* is the essence of all differentiated creative vibrations. *Aum* is the symbol of God. "In the beginning was the Word, and the Word was with God, and the Word was God."* His first manifestation in creation is the cosmic intelligent vibration, the intelligent Holy Ghost vibration, whose sound is *Aum* or the Word. The spoken word and all languages, the astral lore of the gods, every natural and mechanical sound—all owe their origin to the cosmic sound of *Aum.* Yogis tune in with this cosmic sound to expand their consciousness into the omnipresent perception of God.

Yajna signifies a sacrificial rite for uniting the oblation, or what it symbolizes, with the object of worship—such as offering human desires into the purifying flame of Spirit, or casting the sense mind into the fire of cosmic consciousness. The ultimate purpose is yoga, the union of soul and Spirit.

Japa: Chanting God's name to neutralize material consciousness

Japa, in general, is devotional repetition, aloud or mentally, of sacred prayers, words, or names of God. Chanting of any word creates a certain vibration; practice of *japa* fills the mind with holy vibrations that neutralize vibrations of material consciousness. There are special incantations used in India, called *mantras,* which have great vibratory force.† Repeating them aloud or mentally—with sincere feeling, intelligent understanding, and intense concentration and determination to persevere until divine contact is actually felt—produces distinct results; body and mind are charged with power as their vibratory rate is heightened.

Though any kind of *japa* offered sincerely as *yajna* is advantageous, chanting or praying aloud has the defect of diluting the attention—

---

* John 1:1.

† The *Tantras,* one of the main categories of *shastras* or scriptures of Hinduism, deal extensively with the science of vibratory incantation. As pointed out in IV:25, the high spiritual purpose of such practices is often misunderstood and misapplied. The proper use of specific mantras that elevate the consciousness Godward—as meditation on *Aum,* for example—is a sacred part of the science of *Kriya Yoga* (see I:21–22).

diffusing the energy in the outer action of vocalizing. (Overemphasis on devotional paraphernalia or on the external arrangements of the place of worship also tends to divert the soul outward.) Silent worship has greater power; one's mental energy goes more quickly and directly to the indwelling Spirit.

The supreme form of *japa-yajna* is superconscious chanting, divine union through the actual perception of the purifying vibration of holy sound. It does not involve any physical or mental repetition of a word or words. The yogi's attention is concentrated on listening to the actual cosmic sound of *Aum,* the Word of God, vibrating within him. Through this superior *japa,* the yogi expands his life into cosmic energy, his joy into divine ecstasy, his soul consciousness into cosmic consciousness, as he floats in the sphere of the ever-expanding cosmic sound of *Aum.*

Among immobile creations in God's dream world—those manifestations in which animate life, mind, and intellect have not unfolded—His divine loftiness is most prominently displayed in the massive Himalaya, snow-crowned pinnacle of the earth, abode and guardian of saints.

VERSE 26

aśvatthaḥ sarvavṛkṣāṇāṁ devarṣīṇāṁ ca nāradaḥ
gandharvāṇāṁ citrarathaḥ siddhānāṁ kapilo muniḥ

Among all trees, I am the Ashvattha (the holy fig tree); among the devarishis (divine sages), I am Narada; among the Gandharvas (demigods), I am Chitraratha; among the siddhas (successful liberated beings), I am the muni (saint) Kapila.

"TREES" SYMBOLIZE THE BODIES of all living things—plants, animals, man—possessing their own distinct type of roots, trunks, and branches with their life-sustaining circulatory and nervous systems. Of all living forms, only man's body with its unique cerebrospinal centers has the potential of expressing fully God's cosmic consciousness. The sacred Ashvattha tree (the pipal or holy fig tree associated with worship of the Divine) therefore symbolizes the human body, supreme among all other forms of life. (See also XV:1–4.)

Man's physical-astral-causal body is like an upturned tree, with roots in the hair and brain, and in astral rays from the thousand-petaled lotus, and in causal thought emanations which are nourished by cosmic consciousness. The trunk of the tree of life in man is the physical-astral-causal spine. The branches of this tree are the physical nervous system, the astral *nadis* (channels or rays of life force), and thought emanations of the magnetic causal body. The hair, cranial nerves, medulla, cerebral-astral rays, and causal thought emanations are antennae that draw from the ether life force and cosmic consciousness. Thus is man nourished not only by physical food, but by God's cosmic energy and His underlying cosmic consciousness.

Narada is a preceptor of the deities of the astral world, and he also has taken part in many dramas and affairs of men on earth. As a *rishi,* he is one who is "a seer of mantra," the way in which creation evolves from the vibration of *Aum,* and the methods by which the mind may be saved from the influence of the enslaving vibratory delusions of the cosmic dream. These yoga techniques unite the body dream with the dreamless blessedness of Spirit. Hence, the *devarishi* Narada, who has helped many earthly and astral souls to God-realization, is a glorious divine manifestation of the Creator Lord.

The name Chitraratha means, literally, "having a bright chariot," for which reason it is sometimes used in reference to the sun. The significance of Chitraratha the demigod* is he whose heart is concentrated on the chariot of infinite perception, the sun of the spiritual eye. Such a one earns the acclamation of the Lord.

Among *siddhas,* perfected beings, the divine Spirit declares Itself as manifested in the life of Kapila-Muni. A *muni* in the highest tradition, "united with the One" by withdrawal of the mind at will from objects of the senses and from attraction to them, Kapila is also the inspired author of the Sankhya philosophy.

VERSE 27

uccaiḥśravasam aśvānāṁ viddhi māṁ amṛtodbhavam
airāvataṁ gajendrāṇāṁ narāṇāṁ ca narādhipam

Among stallions, know Me to be the nectar-born Uchchaihshravas; among elephants, Indra's white elephant, Airavata; and among men, the emperor.

---

* *Chit-ra,* from *chit,* "to fix the heart (the pure feeling or consciousness) on"; and *ratha,* "vehicle or carrier."

TRADITIONALLY, UCHCHAIHSHRAVAS is the wondrous king of horses that arose out of the legendary churning of the ocean by the gods and demons who were seeking to recover the lost nectar of immortality. It is also a name given to one of the horses of the god of the sun.

Allegorically in the Hindu scriptures, the symbol of the horse is often used to represent a force that carries with it another force, as the horse supports its rider. The life current flowing downward from the brain carries the mind to the senses and to identity with the physical body and the domain of entangling matter. By a technique such as *Kriya Yoga,* the life current is reversed to flow upward to the centers of spiritual perception in the brain, carrying the mind from the senses to the soul and Spirit. In this Gita verse, this uplifting life current is called Uchchaihshravas (from *uchchais,* "upwards; from high above," and *shravas,* "a rushing stream"; also, "sounding"—the currents of life force being differentiated vibrations of the creative vibratory light and sound of *Aum*).

Allegory of horse: carrying mind to Spirit on the current of life force

This uplifting current is spoken of as being born of nectar because its source is in the bliss of Spirit (the divine nectar of immortality, *amrita*) in the cerebral thousand-petaled lotus. This reservoir of life and consciousness with its thousand petals or rays of currents enliven the whole body through the subdynamos of the cerebrospinal centers: through the two-edged positive-negative current in the medulla, the sixteen-petaled current in the cervical center, the twelve-petaled current in the dorsal center, the ten-petaled current in the lumbar center, the six-petaled current in the sacral center, and the four-petaled current in the coccygeal center. When the yogi withdraws the life force from material objects, sensory organs, and sensory-motor nerves and takes the concentrated life upward through the spiral passageway of *kundalini* (coiled energy) in the coccyx, he perceives, as he ascends, the various spinal centers with their petaled light-rays and sounds of life energy. When the yogi's consciousness reaches the medulla and the spiritual eye at the point between the eyebrows, he finds the doorway into the star-lotus of "a thousand" (innumerable) rays. He perceives the omnipresent light of God spreading over the sphere of eternity, and his body as a minuscule emanation of this light.

In deepest ecstasy, the yogi perceives the cosmic light change into the vibrationless, ever-existing, ever-conscious, ever-new bliss of Spirit. It is this vibrationless Cosmic Consciousness that has become the one vibrating cosmic light. This light, projecting away from God, becomes shadowed with delusion, producing the cosmic motion picture of dream images, including the body of man.

God thus manifests in all currents in the body, which emanate from the cerebral sun, or star-lotus of light. But His supreme manifestation among all these bodily forces is the redeeming uplifting current, or Uchchaihshravas—the upward soaring "stallion of the sun" of the spiritual eye and cosmic consciousness that carries the yogi to Spirit.

The elephant is a symbol of wisdom. Significantly, Airavata is referred to as the guardian or supporter "of the east quarter" (in man's body, the "east" or center of wisdom in the forehead).

The word *Indra* implies one who is a conqueror of the senses (*indriya*). Wisdom is the vehicle of the yogi who has conquered his senses. God is indeed prominently manifested in the colossal wisdom of the sense conqueror.

God's almightiness is obviously more reflected in powerful leaders than in weak men. But there is further significance in the Lord's declaring Himself in emperors among men. When a man's ego is identified with his senses, he is spoken of as a slave. But when through yoga he ascends the throne of superconscious soul bliss, he is a supreme ruler of his bodily kingdom. In the kingly yogi God is more manifest than in a sense slave.

VERSE 28

āyudhānām ahaṁ vajraṁ dhenūnām asmi kāmadhuk
prajanaś cāsmi kandarpaḥ sarpāṇām asmi vāsukiḥ

Among weapons, I am the thunderbolt; of bovines, I am Kamadhuk (the celestial cow that fulfills all desires). I am Kandarpa (the personified creative consciousness), the cause of childbirths; and I am Vasuki among serpents.

SYMBOLICALLY IN THIS VERSE, the tremendously powerful "thunderbolt" with its display of light and sound is the cosmic creative vibration. God is often mentioned in the scriptures as speaking through thunder.* The

* In the words of the Psalmist: "The voice of the Lord is upon the waters: the God of glory thundereth....The voice of the Lord is powerful, the voice of the Lord is full of majesty" (Psalms 29:3–4).

Lord's first expression in matter is this "Word," or cosmic vibration. It is this cosmic thunder that is both the creator and destroyer ("weapon") of delusive matter—as cosmic energy in the macrocosm of the universe and as *prana* in the microcosm of the human body. Mastery of this formidable power is the yogi's best weapon against delusion.

Kamadhuk, the desire-fulfilling celestial milch cow, was cited in III:10 as symbolic of divine wisdom, the nourishment of which satisfies all hungers of physical, mental, and spiritual longings. Christ spoke similarly of this principle when he said, "Whosoever drinketh of the water that I shall give him shall never thirst...[it] shall be in him a well of water springing up into everlasting life."*

Yogic significance of "cow of plenty"

The "cow of plenty" has also another significance in yoga. When a yogi in the exalted states of meditation disconnects his life force from the senses and unites his mind to the soul, he perceives a corresponding reaction in his physical body as a thrill of ecstasy. The advanced yogis know how by a certain technique called Khechari Mudra†—which should be practiced only according to the instructions of one's guru—to unite the masculine positive current in the tongue with the feminine negative current in the uvula. In *samadhi* meditation, the conjunction of these currents produces a thrill of divine joy, and also a secretion of nectar into the mouth. Nourished by this nectar, the yogi can keep his body immobile indefinitely in the state of ecstasy. Many yogis, including the twentieth-century Giri Bala,‡ have remained for long periods, even years, without food. This highly charged nectar is the "milk" from the fabulous "cow of plenty," Kamadhuk—one of the treasures that came out of the "churning of the ocean" of cosmic consciousness in the highest spiritual center in the cerebrum.

Kandarpa is another name of Kamadeva, "Desire; the god of love." He is popularly compared to the Greek god Eros and the Roman Cupid. In the original Vedic concept of Kama, however, he represents the first awakening desire of the One Spirit to become many. Kandarpa is God's all-creative cosmic consciousness, the Creator-Dreamer of all cosmic dreams and their objects and beings. Through this consciousness,

---

* John 4:14.

† Mudras are specific positions or gestures of the hands or other parts of the body by which these externalized physical channels of energy are used to create a beneficial effect on the flow of the inner life force.

‡ See *Autobiography of a Yogi,* Chapter 46.

God created the symbolic "Adam and Eve" by an act of special creation, individualizations of His dream consciousness. Then, through His law of evolution, He empowered these beings to procreate their own species. It is God's Kandarpa, or all-creative consciousness, manifesting through parents that is responsible for the begetting of children.

The coiled creative life force at the base of the astral spine, *kundalini,* has always been symbolized as a serpent. When this creative force is "asleep" in delusion, it flows down and outward and feeds all the senses; uncontrolled, its stinging venom causes insatiable lusts. But when the pure *kundalini* force is "awakened" by the yogi, it rises to the brain and is transformed into the bliss of Spirit. This uplifting serpentine current is Vasuki, the supreme force for human liberation.

The analogy can be made that God is manifested in the downwardly flowing creative power, Kandarpa, which through sex is responsible for the creation of children; and He is also in the uplifting current, Vasuki, which begets the offspring of divine realization.

VERSE 29

anantaś cāsmi nāgānāṁ varuṇo yādasām aham
pitṝṇām aryamā cāsmi yamaḥ saṁyamatām aham

I am Ananta ("the eternal" one) among the Naga serpents; I am Varuna (god of the ocean) among water creatures; I am Aryama among Pitris (ancestral parents); I am Yama (god of death) among all controllers.

ANANTA, THE ETERNAL KING OF SERPENTS, is symbolic of cosmic delusion, the lord of all delusive forces that bemuse creation. In this and the previous verse, two supreme "serpents" are mentioned, thus implying a categorical distinction between Vasuki and Ananta. Vasuki is referred to in stanza 28 as *sarpa*, having a serpentine crawling motion—that is, the coiled or circular motion of the *kundalini* force in the microcosm of the human being. Ananta, "eternal or infinite," is a macrocosmic or universal principle. It is another name of Shesha, the thousand-headed serpent that couches and canopies the sleeping Preserver, Vishnu, during the states of dissolution (*pralaya*) between cycles (*kalpas*) of creation. Thus the name Shesha, "that which remains"—the preserved potentialities of creation that in a suspended state await new expression in the next creative cycle. During active creation, Shesha or Ananta is represented as supporting all spheres of manifestation. This is none else than cosmic delusion, Maha-Prakriti, the sole power by which universes and beings are formed from the one consciousness of Spirit. Prakriti is eternal, *ananta,* in active and quiescent states, throughout the endlessly revolving *kalpas* of creation, preservation, and dissolution.

Varuna, "all-encompassing," is the "deity of the ocean"—the oceanic cosmic consciousness of God. In the Vedas, Varuna is extolled as excellent and preeminent above all other deities, the primal maker and upholder of the universe; therefore, he is the lord of all other "water creatures," all primal creative forces or elements arising out of the ocean of cosmic consciousness. Even as an ocean is the force and essence of all its waves, so all manifested things issue from the enveloping cosmic consciousness.

Aryama, an Aditya and chief of the Pitris, ancestors, is the supreme creative light of the astral world—the parent of all parents. As the head of a dynasty is the source of his clan, so God and His consort Cosmic Nature are the real parents of all beings. In the world of matter, Adam and Eve are the atomic-bodied ancestors of humanity. In the astral world, God and His consort Maha-Prakriti produce Aryama light, the supreme cosmic beam that is the primal parent of astral forms. An advanced yogi sees the physical universe and its original human parents as a material atomic dream of God, behind which is the astral lifetronic dream universe with God's finer Aryama light as the creator, "ancestral parent," of all astral forms and beings.

Yama, "the god of death," is represented as a deity who leads the astrally embodied souls of men after death into one of the darker or brighter regions of the astral world, according to each individual's karmic merit. The word *yama* means "control," and specifically, self-control—the power to guide, restrain, and govern one's self. Among all forms of self-control (the "controllers"), the paramount force is that associated with control over the life principle. Through Yama, the god of death, there is enforced control or restraint of life as it is forcibly withdrawn from the body at death. The yogi who attains full self-mastery, however, has conscious control over life and death. He can take his consciousness and life force at will in and out of these mystery portals, as a free traveler in Yama's after-death regions, and also in the boundless domain of Spirit beyond vibratory taint where no specters of death and compromising change may enter.

VERSE 30

prahlādaś cāsmi daityānāṁ kālaḥ kalayatām aham
mṛgāṇāṁ ca mṛgendro 'haṁ vainateyaś ca pakṣiṇām

Among the Daityas (demons and giants), I am Prahlada; among measurers, I am time; among the animals, I am the king of beasts (the lion); and among birds, I am Garuda ("lord of the skies," vehicle of Vishnu).

THE DAITYAS ARE MYTHOLOGICALLY a class of demons and giants who warred against the gods. They are the offspring of Diti, the antithesis or polar opposite of Aditi, mother of the Adityas, the shining gods (see X:21). As the Adityas are the divine uplifting creative forces, the Daityas are the dual or opposing matter-bent forces. The Daitya, Prahlada, however, from early childhood shunned all evil ways and became God-minded. His name signifies one who is full of the divine blessedness, one who "rejoices" in divine joy. Prahlada is revered as the exemplary devotee; he endured the wrath and persecution of his father and remained unflinching in his devotion. In India, children are exhorted by their parents to become saintly like Prahlada. When the yogi reverses the delusion-bound forces in his body, turning them Godward, he becomes "Prahlada"; and like that holy one, attains union with God.

Time and its corollary, space, as observed in the world of relativity are "man-made" categories, suggested by Nature's power of illusion and applied to a series of changes happening in God.

In the tides of Life, in Action's storm,
A fluctuant wave,
A shuttle free,
Birth and the Grave,
An eternal sea,
A weaving, flowing
Life, all-glowing,
Thus at Time's humming loom 'tis my hand prepares
*The garment of Life which the Deity wears!**

* *Faust I*, "The Song of the Earth Spirit" by Goethe. (Translation by Bayard Taylor, 1878–1925.)

God is the Eternal Consciousness, unchanging and indivisible, in which the illusions of time (change) and space (division) present an infinite variety of forms interacting in a progressive mode of past, present, and future. When a dreamer travels around the world in his dream, he does so, not in space and time, but in his consciousness only. Similarly, the cosmic dream is occurring neither in vast space nor in a series of past, present, and future time, but in the Eternal Now of God's dream consciousness. Because Jesus was attuned to this eternal consciousness, he could say: "Before Abraham was, I am."* He knew his everlastingness was in no manner interrupted by the illusory changes called birth, existence, and death.

God has no respect for "history," man's limited and erroneous measuring conceptions of time and space, for He can produce any past being, object, or event instantaneously in His ever present dream consciousness. Likewise, in a second, He can dissolve this world and its beings—or the entire cosmos—and then bring them back at will, just as they were. All He has to do is to stop dreaming this world and it ceases to be; or He can dream it back again by materializing it in His consciousness. These capricious categories of time and space are offshoots of the Cosmic Dreamer's fancy. By Divine Imaginings, dream pictures of universes can be made to appear and disappear in the tiniest space and minutest moment in a single frozen thought of the Cosmic Dreamer.†

Devotees who realize the dream nature of this cosmos and the

---

* John 8:58.

† "...the cosmic sphere of light, of joy, of love, in which worlds and universes are floating like bubbles." Thus did Paramahansa Yogananda describe one of his experiences of God as the Infinite Lord of creation.

An article in the *Los Angeles Times* (October 21, 1991), called "Other Universes?" stated: "Contemplating one universe is hard enough. Thinking about several at once is new ground even for scientists, who are tiptoeing through brave new theoretical worlds of 'space-time foam,' 'false vacuums,' and 'baby universes.'...

"Two of the leaders in these efforts are Stephen Hawking of Cambridge University and Alexander Vilenkin of Tufts University in Medford, Massachusetts. They begin by proposing, in effect, that space itself...continually produces tiny entities that Hawking calls 'baby universes.'

"As Vilenkin describes it, space as we see it is like an apparently smooth ocean seen from an ocean liner. Up close, however, the surface of the sea is full of waves and foam. Similarly, at sufficient magnification we would see the baby universes forming and dissolving in space like tiny bubbles, forming what he calls 'space-time foam.' 'The universe comes out of this,' he declares.

"Under this theory, a baby universe usually flashes momentarily into existence and then winks away. But sometimes it acts as a seed, capable of growing into a full-fledged universe. This can happen because a baby universe can consist of a most unusual form

dreaming power of God no longer rely on the misleading illusions of Nature's measurers, the conclusions from which make creation seem often harsh and unjust. They look to the Eternal Consciousness, the Sole Time, that knows no distress of change—Immutable Time, referred to in X:33.

The proverbial king of beasts is the powerful lion; here symbolizing that omnipotent God is the Lord of all "beasts," or material-bodied beings—both animals and man. The human being, which alone in the animal kingdom possesses the full potential of Divinity, has been commissioned by God to be the supreme ruler over all other forms of matter.

Garuda, the lustrous king of birds, is the divine mythological vehicle of Vishnu, famed as an "enemy and destroyer of serpents" (delusion). Partially developed devotees, like birds, can fly into the free skies of *samadhi,* but must return again to the bodily nest that is vulnerable to serpentine predators, the forces of delusion. But a liberated soul soars away from delusion forever and becomes one with God; He is compared in this stanza to the lustrous golden-bodied Garuda, "the lord of the skies," the "devourer" of delusion.

Verse 31

pavanaḥ pavatām asmi rāmaḥ śastrabhṛtām aham
jhaṣāṇāṁ makaraś cāsmi srotasām asmi jāhnavī

---

of space: 'false vacuum.' It has bizarre properties because it contains, for a very brief instant, a great deal of energy within a very small volume....

"It balloons from microscopic size to the dimensions of a cantaloupe. As it inflates in this fashion it cools....and releases an enormous burst of energy. This energy takes the form of very hot particles, which are produced in vast quantities. There are enough of them, in fact, to form all the stars and galaxies in the new universe, once these particles have the chance to cool. The rapid inflation of the false vacuum, followed by this release of energy, constitutes the Big Bang. The newly born universe, formed in this fashion, will then settle into a long era of expansion. Our own universe has been expanding in this manner for about 15 billion years....

"As the false vacuum inflates, it can readily produce new baby universes that act as seeds for the formation of other universes....'Once the process has begun, it seems like it goes on forever, continually spinning off new universes as pieces of the false vacuum,' says Alan Guth, Ph.D., of Massachusetts Institute of Technology....Other seeds might be sprouting this very minute, anywhere, perhaps within your own living room."

"According to Hawking, there may be an infinite number of alternative universes coexisting with ours," writes Michio Kaku in *Hyperspace* (New York: Oxford University Press, 1994). "These universes might be compared to a vast collection of soap bubbles suspended in air." (*Publisher's Note*)

Among purifiers, I am the breeze; among wielders of weapons, I am Rama; among aquatic creatures, I am Makara (vehicle of the god of the ocean); among streams, I am Jahnavi (the Ganges).

THE WIND OR AIR (*PAVANA*) IS THE BREATH of life through which God sustains vegetation, animals, and man. His purifying, cleansing, purging power is manifested in all wind currents active throughout the universe, but is preeminent in the subtle vital air (the "breeze" or gentle wind) that is life-giving—*prana.* When by *Kriya Yoga pranayama* the accomplished yogi distills the life current out of the oxygen in the human breath and uses this pure *prana* to recharge his body, he unites his life with cosmic life. Breath mastery through *pranayama,* or life-force control, is not only the best means of drawing on cosmic energy to sustain life in the physical body, but also the highest method for attaining liberation. Life control produces control of the breath, the cord that ties the soul to the body; and breathlessness in the *samadhi* state produces God-consciousness.

Rama, revered as an avatar (an incarnation of Vishnu), was a great and noble king of ancient India. It is said that throughout his reign no death or disease touched his kingdom. Of great righteousness, he possessed divine weapons by which he was conqueror of all evil enemies. Among wielders of weapons, the greatest—as was Rama—is the vanquisher of one's inner enemies of delusion, using the bow of calmness with its taut bowstring of a straight spine in meditation, fitted with unerring arrows of self-control and concentration.

Makara is a mythical sea creature, the vehicle of Varuna, "god of the ocean" (see X:29). Makara is sometimes referred to as a shark, the undisputed mightiest of fishes. This mythical creature is the emblem on the standard of Kamadeva, "desire," showing desire's deference to this higher power. The spiritual significance is that the presence of God, inherent in man's consciousness, becomes active in the ocean of *samadhi* consciousness as a divine predator devouring all little "fishes" of the devotee's earthly desires.

The Ganges is revered as the holiest of rivers, blessed by God through the vibrations of the many liberated saints who have bathed in her waters and meditated on her banks. Symbolically, the Ganges represents the ever-flowing intuitive wisdom in the liberated yogi. It also represents the taintless *sushumna* life-current, which flows through the astral spine from the coccyx to the thousand-petaled lotus in the brain. The life force and soul perception of the yogi is carried on this river of life away from bodily material entanglements to the shores of blessedness in Spirit.

VERSE 32

sargāṇām ādir antaś ca madhyaṁ caivāham arjuna
adhyātmavidyā vidyānāṁ vādaḥ pravadatām aham

Of all manifestations, O Arjuna, I am the beginning, middle, and end. Among all branches of knowledge, I am the wisdom of the Self; for debaters, I am discriminative logic (vada).

EVEN AS THE LORD IS THE ETERNAL SELF in the transitory mortal forms of beings, bearing sole responsibility for their comings and goings (see X:20), so does He create, uphold, and call back to Himself all objectified dream images of His consciousness.

Human knowledge, no matter how proliferate, will always be limited without the wisdom (intuitive perception) of the soul, the singular revealer of the Creator.

Without the inherent presence of God, there would be no powers of cognition, reason, and disputation. In logic and dialectics He has given the potentiality to conceive the fickleness and unreality of the cosmic dream, and to infer the reality of the Cosmic Dreamer. On man alone, in all creation, has God bestowed the power of abstract reasoning. Except by the right exercise of reason, no man under Cosmic Delusion would ever have come out from it, for he would not have known he was in it!

VERSE 33

akṣarāṇāṁ akāro 'smi dvandvaḥ sāmāsikasya ca
aham evākṣayaḥ kālo dhātāhaṁ viśvatomukhaḥ

Among all letters, I am the letter A; of all compounds, I am the dvandva (connective element). I am Immutable Time; and I am the Omnipresent Creator (the all-pervading Dispenser of Destiny) whose face is turned on all sides.

LETTERS ARE DIVIDED INTO VOWELS and consonants; no consonant can be pronounced without the aid of a vowel. The letter *A*, in nearly all languages, is the first among vowels; in Sanskrit it is also the component of every consonant, which allows for the intonation of that letter: *ka, ta, ba,* and so forth. *A* is the first letter of the primordial syllable *Aum,* whose cosmic sound is the mother of all sounds, and therefore of all languages. *Aum* is the conglomerate sound of the creative, preservative, and dissolving vibrations of Nature, represented, respectively, by its letters *a* (*akara*), *u* (*ukara*), *m* (*makara*). It is thus the Word of God that was with Him from the beginning,* His symbol in creation. The Lord in this Gita verse declares Himself preeminently in the letter *A* (creation), for He is the origin, the infinite source of being, the power that sends forth the modes of Nature. "I am Alpha and Omega, the beginning and the ending, saith the Lord, which is, and which was, and which is to come, the Almighty."† The Hindu scriptures deal at length with the importance of chanting this sacred Word, *Aum,* and of listening in deep meditation to the actual sound of this holy vibration declaring God's presence in creation.

In Sanskrit grammar, *dvandva* refers to compounds of words (aggregate compounds) in which the words, though conjoined, do not change their character in construction or meaning. The concomitant analogy of God's manifestation as the *dvandva* is that His consciousness is the copulative element that holds together in intelligent play and interplay all beings and objects. Cosmic delusion in the ordinary man suppresses his perception of the ubiquitous Infinite; he sees only the cosmic dream without the presence of the Cosmic Dreamer. The yogi, however, beholds the Cosmic Dreamer and His cosmic dream as one. By rising above the mortal state, he sees God as the conjoining power (*dvandva*) among all compounds (*samasa*) in the cosmic dream. He perceives God's subjective consciousness and His objective dreams as held together by His conjoining cognitive dream-consciousness. As a man requires self-awareness to be conscious of himself and of his dreams, so God cognizes His cosmic dreams through His ever conscious Self-awareness—the essential faculty by which His Dreamless Being and His cosmic dreams exist together, in complete harmony. As one twig may support two flowers, so the stem of Self-awareness—the unifying *dvandva,* or God's cognitive power—holds together the blossom of His Absolute nature and the blossom of His diversified cosmic dream.

God is Immutable Time, the Eternal Consciousness. In the Atharva Veda, God is personified as Time and hailed as the "father" (creator) of all the worlds, and also as their "son" (their existence). Time (*kala*) is the idea of change in the Eternal Immutable, a gossamer illusion in which all illusions dance. Stanza 30 of this chapter referred to man's concep-

---

* John 1:1–2. † Revelation 1:8.

tion of time, imposed on him by Nature as one of its illusory "measurers." This present verse refers to God's everlasting consciousness, the Sole Time, which is the eternal receptacle of all His ever-changing illusory dreams of creation.

A subtle principle is cited in the esoteric description of God as the Omnipresent Creator, the Dispenser (or Bestower) of Destiny (*dhata*) who faces in all directions (*visvato-mukha*). A dreamer is the creator and sustainer of the destiny—both good and bad—of the images in his dream. Similarly, in the cosmic dream, the Divine Dreamer is the Creator and Sustainer of all beings, and the Dispenser of their destiny through their good and bad karma. In this sense, God predetermines to a great extent the happenings in His cosmic dream and the parts to be played therein by His dream actors. This doesn't mean, however, that man's fate is wholly predestined by an authoritarian Deity. God is the Maker of destiny, but He has given man the power to react upon destiny. Each human being receives from God the gift of free choice by which he can make changes in himself and his world environment. This very power of free will is an expression of the image of God in man, the image in which man is made—the soul or individualized consciousness of God. Therefore, all happenings are determined by a conjunctive effort between God the macrocosmic Creator, and God the microcosmic creator through individualized expression in man. No individual is spared his share of the responsibility for any evils or seeming injustices. If one disdains his lot, he may exercise the God-power within him to operate those laws of Nature that can change those circumstances. If he tires of the alternating entertainments and harassments of dualities, he can exert his God-power to awaken himself from this cosmic dreaming. The nonuse or misuse of free will is man's own choice to remain in the dream and be subjected to the laws that rule the realm of manifestation.

Predestination and man's free will

Visvato-mukha, "omnipresent, facing all sides," has also a further meaning: "an omnipresent aperture or opening." God's eternal presence, His all-encompassing consciousness, is the "doorway" through which His created beings go back and forth between the physical plane and the astral world as His consciousness enacts on them the illusory changes called birth and death. Through good and bad karma (the fruits of man's actions dispensed by God according to His just law of compensation), the recurrent cycles of birth, existence, and death of all beings are continuously occurring in the consciousness of God. Thus is He the Sustainer and Bestower of all happenings.

VERSE 34

mṛtyuḥ sarvaharaś cāham udbhavaś ca bhaviṣyatām
kīrtiḥ śrīr vāk ca nārīṇāṁ smṛtir medhā dhṛtiḥ kṣamā

I am all-dissolving Death; and I am Birth, the origin of all that will be. Among feminine manifestations (qualities of Prakriti), I am fame, success, the illumining power of speech, memory, discriminative intelligence, the grasping faculty of intuition, and the steadfastness of divine forbearance.

THIS VERSE REFERS TO GOD'S CONSCIOUSNESS active in the three *gunas* of Nature: *tamas,* dissolution; *rajas,* creation; and *sattva,* preservation, the nurturing motherly or feminine quality.

The *rajas* and *sattva* manifestations both undergo continuous changes as a result of *tamas.* Death, or dissolution, necessitates the creation and preservation of new forms for the continuity of Cosmic Nature with her many beings and objects. God's consciousness as transforming death, the Dissolver, changes the forms and states of all subjective and objective creations and transfers them from one place to another in His physical-astral-causal cosmos. God, who is unsubject to the illusory change of death that infects all the appearances in His cosmic dream, expresses His transforming power of death through the tamasic quality of His cosmic delusion, Nature.

As whatever exists in the realm of Nature is subject to dissolution in God's consciousness, so everything yet to come into manifestation will have birth from its origin in God's consciousness. His all-creative power is carried on by the rajasic activating quality in Nature.

The preservative aspect of God, the activities of which are carried on by the sattvic quality of delusive Nature, is referred to in this verse as having seven "feminine" attributes—Nature being God's consort, the Cosmic Mother, the Shakti or vibratory power of Spirit. These seven "daughters" of God and Cosmic Nature bestow their qualities on all objects and beings. Man has the ability to negate or enhance their beneficial effects in his life.

1. Fame or glory (*kirti*) is the subtle power of expression, the declaration that makes something known—such as the glory in a flower; or the subtle character of man's desires that nurtures either his good or ill repute.

2. Success or prosperity (*sri*) is the auspicious power that promotes and sustains well-being and all forms of success.

3. Speech (*vach*) is a cardinal attribute in Nature's realm of cosmic delusion, deriving from the sound of the Cosmic Vibration with its *gunas* of creation, preservation, and destruction. All nature possesses this attribute of vibratory expression, evidenced in everything from the hum of atoms to the songs of birds and utterances of beasts—and, above all, in the articulation of man. Through vibratory sound, all nature communes. In its highest expression, *vach* is the repository of all knowledge, that vibratory intelligence through which the Vedas were divinely revealed to the *rishis,* who in turn through their own voice conveyed this illumination to others. It is incumbent on man, similarly, to use his God-given powerful instrument of speech to do only good and to spread enlightenment.

4. Memory (*smriti*) is the power of continuity of consciousness, Nature's way of connecting the past with the present. The vibratory consciousness in a seed (though not self-conscious) "remembers" how to grow a plant or a mighty tree from its evolutionary record or "memory." Man is able to recall past experiences—all of which are recorded in his brain—and thereby proliferate his growth and capabilities. The divine man can recall not only the accumulated experiences of his present life, but of his past incarnations as well—the legacy of the continuity of his consciousness—and thereby draw upon a vast storehouse of knowledge and achievements.

5. Intelligence (*medha*) as an attribute of Nature is the discriminative or manifested intelligence of the Supreme Intelligence, Spirit. It is what maintains order and harmony in the universe and in man. Through the use of his mental power of discriminative intelligence, the deluded, ignorant man attains wisdom.

6. The grasping power of intuition is the fixity of the mind (*dhriti*) in soul perception—the soul's direct realization of or connection with truth or Reality.* Even the sleeping consciousness in the stone and the semi-awake consciousness in the animal never loses its connection with its true nature. Man, the being in whom discrimination awakens, begins in lesser and greater degree to draw on his innate intuition, the underlying source of all his mental powers. The fully awakened divine man, anchored in his true Self, becomes all-knowing through the omniscience of pure soul intuition.

7. Forbearance (*kshama*) is the calm, patient stability in nature and man, the power that resists the disturbing fluctuations of Nature's

* See also commentary on *sattvic-dhriti,* XVIII:33.

dualities. It is the harbor of peace, and the anchor of steadfastness sought by all beings. This attribute in cosmic delusion is a reflection of the Eternal Calm, the Everlasting Patience—the Uncreate Spirit.

There is also a deeper significance in this verse, understood by the yogi. These glorious attributes of the Cosmic Mother displayed throughout the universe may be consciously tapped in deep meditation. As the yogi's life and consciousness ascend through the subtle cerebrospinal centers, awakening or unlocking their mysteries, the effulgence of these attributes illumine his whole being and bestow on him their grandest treasures according to his heart's desire.

VERSE 35

bṛhatsāma tathā sāmnāṁ gāyatrī chandasām aham
māsānāṁ mārgaśīrṣo 'ham ṛtūnāṁ kusumākaraḥ

Among Samas (hymns), I am Brihat-Saman; among poetic meters, I am Gayatri; among the months, I am Margasirsha (an auspicious winter month); among seasons, I am Kusumakara, the flower-bearer (Spring).

THE SACRED VEDIC HYMNS OF SPECIAL FORMULAS of meter and syllabication are cited for their potent vibratory power (see page 783)—the Saman promotes wisdom, and the Gayatri deals with the salvation of man. Brihat-Saman and Gayatri, respectively, refer to two classes of sacred verses, each with its own distinct formula; and they are also the names of two chief hymns representative of these categories.

In India, the month of Margasirsha (spanning a portion of November and December) is considered the most auspicious and healthiest period of the year. The coolness of this winter month destroys or inactivates many germs and bacteria that flourished in the preceding heat of summer and humidity of monsoon. In the blossoming spring, God decorates His consort, Nature, with matchless ornaments of many-hued blossoms as she busily tends to the rebirth and nurturing of her vast progeny.

Metaphorically, *Kusumakara* ("abounding with flowers") refers to the time of spiritual fulfillment. The novitiate yogi struggles with prenatal instincts and mental restlessness throughout years of vigorous meditation. As a result of devoted persistence, he finally beholds wondrous flowers of wisdom; and the astral lotuses blooming in the finer regions of the subtle centers in his spine and brain open before him, bathing him in their fragrance of many realizations. Within this blossoming garden, the yogi's meditative efforts confront and in time remove all vestiges of prenatal and postnatal karma, and of the ego and its forces of delusion. He ascends the divine pathway that opens through the spinal centers to the summit of cosmic consciousness, in the uppermost part of the brain, and thence to liberation in Spirit. This is symbolically represented in the reference to the auspicious month Margasirsha: *marga,* "the divine path to" *sirsha,* literally, "the head or topmost part"—the supreme center of cosmic consciousness in the brain, the gateway to liberation, the "crowning pinnacle" of the yogi's strivings.

VERSE 36

dyūtaṁ chalayatām asmi tejas tejasvinām aham
jayo 'smi vyavasāyo 'smi sattvaṁ sattvavatām aham

I am the gambling of the practicers of fraud; I am the radiance of the radiant; I am victory and the striving power; I am the quality of sattva among the good.

AS GOD PASSES THROUGH HIS consciousness His film of cosmic delusion, shadowed with the triple qualities—*tamas, rajas,* and *sattva*—evil, activating, and good pictures are produced from His one Being. He cannot, therefore, wholly disassociate Himself even from the evil or dark concepts of the drama. Indeed, it is His cosmic *maya,* the ultimate deceiver, that deranges reason in those who court the dark tamasic quality. They ignorantly gamble their happiness and well-being on chances of quick and easy self-gratification.

The Divine Trickster, however, also teaches His acolytes how to turn the tables on His cosmic delusion—by nonattachment, right activity, practice of yoga, and ecstatic union with Him, the Undeluded Reality. Thus, through God's activating quality, *rajas,* radiant pictures of life are produced, depicting vitally energetic beings valiantly and nobly struggling and winning victories.

At last, in the conqueror, God displays Himself as Sattva—Goodness and Purity.

In the devotee, the triple nature of God's cosmic delusion similarly enacts its drama. In the beginning, with no evident certainty of gain—

except the conviction of faith and devotion—the seeker boldly gambles his efforts against the deceptive obstacles of delusion. With the fiery energy and self-control of *rajas,* he practices penance, renunciation, strict discipline, and subjugation of restless thoughts by meditation on God. In time, he is gratifyingly astonished at occasional glimpses of God playing hide-and-seek with him. When the yogi can hold the full realization of God in his concentration for even a little while, his mind and body become thrilled with a radiating energy that may even cause the hairs of his body to stand on end.

With persistence and unabated zeal, and with the activating inner Divine Grace, the yogi's body consciousness, breath, and mind dissolve into one perception of divine love, the partial union of his soul with God. The inner Divine Radiance imbues his whole body, mind, and soul with unexcelled bliss; even the gross body becomes subtly aglow with a divine astral halo; the still eyes glisten with unseen tears of blessedness. He worships the Cosmic Beloved Spirit with the all-embracing adoration of his soul, until his soul becomes the blessedness of Spirit. In the ultimate *samadhi* state, the yogi's consciousness, without losing its Self-awareness, expands into the omnipresent consciousness of God. The devotee realizes that throughout all of these states God was the ever present Reality within the delusive forces, the valiant efforts to conquer them, and the temporary and ultimate victories—the Supreme Good, the Ultimate Radiance within all delusive dream enactments.

VERSE 37

vṛṣṇīnāṁ vāsudevo 'smi pāṇḍavānām dhanaṁjayaḥ
munīnām apy ahaṁ vyāsaḥ kavīnām uśanā kaviḥ

Among the Vrishnis, I am Vasudeva (Krishna); among the Pandavas, I am Dhananjaya (Arjuna); among the munis (saints), I am Vyasa; among the sages, I am the savant Ushanas.

FROM HIS STATE OF GOD-UNION, Bhagavan Krishna could proclaim in an impersonal way that Spirit, whom he realized as the whole of his being, was incarnated in the Vrishni dynasty as Krishna, known as Vasudeva, the Lord as Creator, Preserver, and Destroyer.

Similarly, among those in the wise Pandava dynasty, the Lord is eminent in the ideal disciple Arjuna, Dhananjaya, "winner of wealth"

—he who attains the Divine Treasure by conquering desires and appetites, pain and pleasure, birth and death.

Still impersonally, Krishna as Spirit declares Himself in His ideal devotee Vyasa, the writer of the Bhagavad Gita, who received this revelation humbly and impersonally and then recorded it in the form of this divine discourse. Vyasa is proclaimed foremost among the *munis*—saints enlocked in ecstatic communion with God—when he is in the *samadhi,* actionless state. In tune with Cosmic Consciousness, Vyasa perceived what Bhagavan Krishna revealed to Arjuna. When Vyasa was in the divinely active state, as during the writing of the Bhagavad Gita, he was referred to as a *rishi,* one who performs spiritual activities with no loss of the supreme divine contact.

God extols also the ancient poet and sage, Ushanas, who had great powers, including that of resurrecting the dead.

VERSE 38

daṇḍo damayatām asmi nītir asmi jigīṣatām
maunaṁ caivāsmi guhyānāṁ jñānaṁ jñānavatām aham

I am the rod of the discipliners; I am the art of those who seek victory; I am also the silence of all hidden things, and the wisdom of all knowers.

THE ROD IS GOD'S LAW OF CAUSE and effect, karma, the ultimate discipliner. The errant man may escape the punishment of man-made laws, but karmic justice is inexorable, appeasable only by right actions which earn rewards of merit and ultimate pardon. The Bible also refers to the law of karma as "the rod": "Thy rod and Thy staff they comfort me."* The karmic principle is a source of comfort to those who understand its discipline and rewards as pointing the way to true happiness and liberation. Job referred to the "rod of God" when he lamented that oftentimes the righteous suffer while the wicked have great material gain and pleasure. "Their houses are safe from fear, neither is the rod of God upon them." But then he knowingly concludes: "How oft is the candle of the wicked put out! and how oft cometh their destruction upon them! God distributeth sorrows in His anger."† The karmic law

* Psalms 23:4. † Job 21:9,17.

dispenses justice; the wicked for a time may enjoy rewards of past good karma, but present evil will as surely exact its toll.

God's all-conquering power is manifested in right actions and in noble motives and goals. These are the divine science and art through which His rewarding karmic law grants victory to the valiant.

God is the Uncreate Silence, hidden in all forces and objects of cosmic nature. The creatures of nature see only the gross expressions that *maya* displays, not the hidden Mystery that makes them seem so real and vital. God's silent Presence within all phenomena of the cosmic dream is His best-kept secret, discoverable by no limited human mind.

It is written, "He who knows, he knows; naught else knows." Only through divine realization does one know God and truth, and *knows* that he knows. God is the wisdom, the perceiving and the perception, of that knower.

As applied to yoga, *danda,* "a rod, staff, trunk" (of the tree of life), represents the spine in which the yogi performs self-discipline to spiritualize his consciousness. This verse, therefore, commends *pranayama* (the *Kriya Yoga* technique of life control) as the most effective mode of disciplining the wayward senses, the restless mind, and the misguided will, that they be turned toward God. Through this "art," or practice, of scientific yoga, the yogi becomes victorious. When his body consciousness and thoughts are stilled, he finds within him in that "silence" the unimaginable bliss of God. He becomes a true knower, one with the Eternal Wisdom.

VERSE 39

yac cāpi sarvabhūtānāṁ bījaṁ tad aham arjuna
na tad asti vinā yat syān mayā bhūtaṁ carācaram

I am, furthermore, whatsoever constitutes the reproductive seed of all beings. There is nothing, O Arjuna, moving or motionless, that can abide without Me.

THE LORD BEGAN THE CATEGORICAL enumeration of His manifestations in X:20 with the declaration that He is the origin, existence, and finality of all creatures. He now concludes His recounting with the statement that it is He also who is the seed within all beings by which He perpetuates His creation through Nature's power of reproduction in all of its various forms.

Everything that moves (that is, expresses the *sattva*-perceptive and/or the *rajas*-active attributes of God—from animate creatures to the motion of wind, fire, planets, all forces in cosmic nature) and all that is stationary (inert gross matter, the product of the *tamas*-obstructive quality) owe their being solely to the omnipresent consciousness of God and the omnipotence of His divine will.

All are but parts of one stupendous whole,
*Whose body Nature is, and God the soul.**

VERSE 40

nānto 'sti mama divyānāṁ vibhūtīnāṁ paraṁtapa
eṣa tūddeśataḥ prokto vibhūter vistaro mayā

O Scorcher of Foes (Arjuna), limitless are the manifestations of My divine attributes; My concise declaration is a mere intimation of My proliferating glorious powers.

COUNTLESS ARE THE DREAM DRAMAS enacted in the creation, preservation, and dissolution of the causal, astral, and physical universes, and in the experiences of their dream actors—all of which are manifestations of God's powers. Ever-changing endlessness; how may the Infinite be fully defined?

* Alexander Pope: "An Essay on Man," Part I.

VERSE 41

yad yad vibhūtimat sattvaṁ śrīmad ūrjitam eva vā
tat tad evāvagaccha tvaṁ mama tejoṁśasaṁbhavam

Any being that is a worker of miracles, that is a possessor of true prosperity, that is endowed with great prowess, know all such to be manifested sparks of My radiance.

"ALL INDIVIDUALIZED COSMIC EXISTENCES (man, angels, *devas,* intelligent forces) that wield the laws of Nature, that are possessed of the auspicious power of prosperity which bestows all forms of success and well-being, that exhibit mighty prowess against dark or negative powers of delusion—understand these to be divine circumscribed expressions of My Illimitable Being, scintillating sparks of My Infinite Effulgence."

VERSE 42

athavā bahunaitena kiṁ jñātena tavārjuna
viṣṭabhyāham idaṁ kṛtsnam ekāṁśena sthito jagat

But what need hast thou, O Arjuna, for the manifold details of this wisdom? (Understand simply:) I, the Unchanging and Everlasting, sustain and permeate the entire cosmos with but one fragment of My Being!

THE BEWILDERING COMPLEXITIES of man and creation are finally resolvable in the Divine Simplicity.*

* "The cosmic order is underpinned by definite mathematical laws that interweave each other to form a subtle and harmonious unity," wrote physicist Paul Davies, Ph.D., in *The Mind of God: The Scientific Basis for a Rational World* (New York: Simon and Schuster, 1992). "The laws are possessed of an elegant simplicity, and have often commended themselves to scientists on grounds of beauty alone. Yet these same simple laws permit matter and energy to self-organize into an enormous variety of complex states, including those that have the quality of consciousness, and can in turn reflect upon the very cosmic order that has produced them."

"Perhaps the most profound discovery of the past century in physics," said Michio Kaku in *Hyperspace* (New York: Oxford University Press, 1994), "has been the realization that nature, at its most fundamental level, is simpler than anyone thought." (*Publisher's Note*)

With human understanding, only vague glimpses of God are possible. But every query of a devotee's heart will be answered when in cosmic consciousness he attains realization of the Lord's transcendental omnipresence—in and beyond creation. All the magnificence in the cosmos, evident and hidden, will be seen as but a glimmer resting on an infinitesimal thought in the eternally blissful consciousness of Spirit.

O Thou Self-manifested cause and substance of creation, O Thou indwelling Self of all, Thou source of Illumination, guide me beyond Thy rays of creation, transport me beyond Thine objective form that, by Thy grace, I may behold Thy glorious Self. That absolute Self abiding in the transcendental effulgence, verily, I am He.

—Isha Upanishad

om tat sat iti śrīmadbhagavadgītāsu upaniṣatsu
brahmavidyāyām yogaśāstre śrīkṛṣṇārjunasaṁvāde
vibhūtiyogo nāma daśamo 'dhyāyaḥ

Aum, Tat, Sat.
In the Upanishad of the holy Bhagavad Gita—the discourse of Lord Krishna to Arjuna, which is the scripture of yoga and the science of God-realization—this is the tenth chapter, called "Vibhuti Yoga (Divine Manifestations)."

CHAPTER XI

Vision of Visions: The Lord Reveals His Cosmic Form

Up to this point Arjuna had accepted by faith the sacred revelations, but now he has attained the yogi's goal—direct experience of Deity....

These verses from the Bhagavad Gita are an unparalleled ode to the Universal Form of Spirit, a paean to the glory of the Cosmic-Bodied Dream Idol enshrined in the wall-less Temple of Infinity. Massive universes and their tiniest particles, majestic gods of Nature and the most insignificant of creatures, the shadow-plays of good and evil—all hold their special place in the conformation of the Cosmic Image.

Often are these verses sung in worship in India. When properly intoned in the original Sanskrit, the vibratory blessing awakens a thrill of knowing in the receptive devotee, stirring sleeping memories of truth-realization held sacredly safe in the inner sanctum of the soul.

VISION OF VISIONS: THE LORD REVEALS HIS COSMIC FORM

VERSES 1–4

arjuna uvāca
madanugrahāya paramaṁ guhyam adhyātmasaṁjñitam
yat tvayoktaṁ vacas tena moho 'yaṁ vigato mama (1)

bhavāpyayau hi bhūtānāṁ śrutau vistaraśo mayā
tvattaḥ kamalapatrākṣa māhātmyam api cāvyayam (2)

evam etad yathāttha tvam ātmānaṁ parameśvara
draṣṭum icchāmi te rūpam aiśvaraṁ puruṣottama (3)

manyase yadi tac chakyaṁ mayā draṣṭum iti prabho
yogeśvara tato me tvaṁ darśayātmānam avyayam (4)

Arjuna said:
(1) Thou hast compassionately revealed to me the secret wisdom of the true Self, thus banishing my delusion.

(2) O Lotus-Eyed (Krishna)! Thou hast told me extensively of the beginning and end of all beings, and of Thine eternal sovereignty.

(3) O Great One! truly hast Thou thus declared Thyself. Yet, O Purushottama! I long to see Thee in Divine Embodiment (Thine Ishvara-Form).

(4) O Master, O Lord of Yogis! if Thou deemest me able to see It, show to me Thine Infinite Self!

HINDU SCRIPTURES CONTAIN A THOUSAND names for God, each one conveying a different shade of philosophical meaning. Purushottama (XI:3) or "Supreme Spirit" is an appellation for Deity in His highest aspect—the Unmanifested Lord beyond creation. Ishvara (XI:3) is God in His aspect of Cosmic Ruler (from the verb root *īś,* to rule). Ishvara is He by whose will all universes, in orderly cycles, are created, maintained, and dissolved.

Although Arjuna fully accepts the truth of the Lord as Purushottama, his human heart yearns to see Him as Ishvara, the Divine Ruler whose body is the universe.

VERSES 5–7

śrībhagavān uvāca
paśya me pārtha rūpāṇi śataśo 'tha sahasraśaḥ
nānāvidhāni divyāni nānāvarṇākṛtīni ca (5)

paśyādityān vasūn rudrān aśvinau marutas tathā
bahūny adṛṣṭapūrvāṇi paśyāścaryāṇi bhārata (6)

ihaikasthaṁ jagat kṛtsnaṁ paśyādya sacarācaram
mama dehe guḍākeśa yac cānyad draṣṭum icchasi (7)

The Blessed Lord said:
(5) Behold, O son of Pritha (Arjuna)! by hundreds and by thousands My divine forms—multicolored, omnifarious!

(6) Behold the Adityas, the Vasus, the Rudras, the twin Ashvins, the Maruts, and many wonders hitherto unknown!

(7) Here and now, O Conqueror of Sleep (Arjuna)! behold as unified in My Cosmic Body all worlds, all that moves or is motionless, and whatever else thou desirest to see.

THE LORD SAID: "BEHOLD ME EMBODIED as the Cosmic Idol in the Temple of Omnipresence—the whole cosmos of gods, men, and Nature!"

And, because for the devotee God is the inexhaustible Wish-Fulfiller, He added: "Ask of Me anything! Whatever thou desirest to see—whether of the past, the present, or the future—shall appear before thee!"

Mindful of His promise, He grants (XI:32–34) Arjuna's unspoken request to know the outcome of the impending battle on the field of

Kurukshetra. That knowledge He had previously withheld (see II:37). Now Arjuna, purified by humility and devotion, has become a fit receptacle for truth.

VERSE 8

na tu māṁ śakyase draṣṭum anenaiva svacakṣuṣā
divyaṁ dadāmi te cakṣuḥ paśya me yogam aiśvaram

But thou canst not see Me with mortal eyes. Therefore I give thee sight divine. Behold My supreme power of yoga!

THE DUAL EYES OF MAN'S physical body are adapted to visions of *maya,* the world of duality—day and night, birth and death, and so on. The single eye in the forehead* is the "divine gaze" by which alone the yogi may perceive the Unity in variety. The Lord now awakens that eye in His devotee. Up to this point Arjuna had accepted by *faith* the sacred revelations, but now he has attained the yogi's goal—direct *experience* of Deity.

VERSE 9

saṁjaya uvāca
evaṃ uktvā tato rājan mahāyogeśvaro hariḥ
darśayām āsa pārthāya paramaṁ rūpam aiśvaram

Sanjaya said to King Dhritarashtra:
With these words Hari (Krishna), the exalted Lord of Yoga, revealed to Arjuna the Consummate Embodiment, the Cosmic-Bodied Ishvara-Form.

THE LORD HAS NO FORM, but in His aspect as Ishvara He assumes every form. By virtue of His supreme Yoga Power, the Unmanifested becomes the visible miracle of the universe.

Hari, "the Stealer" of hearts, is a name given to Sri Krishna as an incarnation of Vishnu. In this role as an avatar, he takes away the evil

* See VI:13, page 608.

of *maya* from the hearts of receptive devotees so that their purified devotion flows unceasingly in worshipful adoration of the Lord.

VERSES 10–14

anekavaktranayanam anekādbhutadarśanam
anekadivyābharaṇaṁ divyānekodyatāyudham (10)

divyamālyāmbaradharaṁ divyagandhānulepanam
sarvāścaryamayaṁ devam anantaṁ viśvatomukham (11)

divi sūryasahasrasya bhaved yugapad utthitā
yadi bhāḥ sadṛśī sā syād bhāsas tasya mahātmanaḥ (12)

tatraikasthaṁ jagat kṛtsnaṁ pravibhaktam anekadhā
apaśyad devadevasya śarīre pāṇḍavas tadā (13)

tataḥ sa vismayāviṣṭo hṛṣṭaromā dhanaṁjayaḥ
praṇamya śirasā devaṁ kṛtāñjalir abhāṣata (14)

(10–11) Arjuna saw the multifarious marvelous Presence of the Deity—infinite in forms, shining in every direction of space, omnipotence all-pervading, adorned with countless celestial robes and garlands and ornaments, upraising heavenly weapons, fragrant with every lovely essence, His mouths and eyes everywhere!

(12) If a thousand suns appeared simultaneously in the sky, their light might dimly resemble the splendor of that Omnific Being!

(13) There, resting within the infinite Form of the God of gods, Arjuna beheld the entire universe with all its diversified manifestations.

(14) Then the Winner of Wealth (Arjuna), wonder-struck, his hair standing on end, his palms together in a prayerful gesture, bowing his head in awe before the Lord, addressed Him:

The Vision of Visions

Verses 15–34

arjuna uvāca
paśyāmi devāṁs tava deva dehe sarvāṁs tathā bhūtaviśeṣasaṁghān
brahmāṇam īśaṁ kamalāsanastham ṛṣīṁś ca sarvān uragāṁś ca divyān (15)

anekabāhūdaravaktranetraṁ paśyāmi tvāṁ sarvato 'nantarūpam
nāntaṁ na madhyaṁ na punas tavādiṁ paśyāmi viśveśvara viśvarūpa (16)

kirīṭinaṁ gadinaṁ cakriṇaṁ ca tejorāśiṁ sarvato dīptimantam
paśyāmi tvāṁ durnirīkṣyaṁ samantād dīptānalārkadyutim aprameyam (17)

tvam akṣaraṁ paramaṁ veditavyaṁ tvam asya viśvasya paraṁ nidhānam
tvam avyayaḥ śāśvatadharmagoptā sanātanas tvaṁ puruṣo mato me (18)

anādimadhyāntam anantavīryam anantabāhuṁ śaśisūryanetram
paśyāmi tvāṁ dīptahutāśavaktraṁ svatejasā viśvam idaṁ tapantam (19)

dyāvāpṛthivyor idam antaraṁ hi vyāptaṁ tvayaikena diśaś ca sarvāḥ
dṛṣṭvā 'dbhutaṁ rūpam ugraṁ tavedaṁ lokatrayaṁ pravyathitaṁ mahātman (20)

amī hi tvāṁ surasaṁghā viśanti kecid bhītāḥ prāñjalayo gṛṇanti
svastīty uktvā maharṣisiddhasaṁghāḥ stuvanti tvāṁ stutibhiḥ puṣkalābhiḥ (21)

rudrādityā vasavo ye ca sādhyā viśve 'śvinau marutaś coṣmapāś ca
gandharvayakṣāsurasiddhasaṁghā vīkṣante tvāṁ vismitāś caiva sarve (22)

rūpaṁ mahat te bahuvaktranetraṁ mahābāho bahubāhūrupādam
bahūdaraṁ bahudaṁṣṭrākarālaṁ dṛṣṭvā lokāḥ pravyathitās
tathāham (23)

nabhaḥspṛśaṁ dīptam anekavarṇaṁ vyāttānanaṁ
dīptaviśālanetram
dṛṣṭvā hi tvāṁ pravyathitāntarātmā dhṛtiṁ na vindāmi śamaṁ ca
viṣṇo (24)

daṁṣṭrākarālāni ca te mukhāni dṛṣṭvaiva kālānalasaṁnibhāni
diśo na jāne na labhe ca śarma prasīda deveśa jagannivāsa (25)

amī ca tvāṁ dhṛtarāṣṭrasya putrāḥ sarve sahaivāvanipālasaṁghaiḥ
bhīṣmo droṇaḥ sūtaputras tathāsau sahāsmadīyair api
yodhamukhyaiḥ (26)

vaktrāṇi te tvaramāṇā viśanti daṁṣṭrākarālāni bhayānakāni
kecid vilagnā daśanāntareṣu saṁdṛśyante cūrṇitair
uttamāṅgaiḥ (27)

yathā nadīnāṁ bahavo 'mbuvegāḥ samudram evābhimukhā
dravanti
tathā tavāmī naralokavīrā viśanti vaktrāṇy abhivijvalanti (28)

yathā pradīptaṁ jvalanaṁ pataṅgā viśanti nāśāya samṛddhavegāḥ
tathaiva nāśāya viśanti lokās tavāpi vaktrāṇi samṛddhavegāḥ (29)

lelihyase grasamānaḥ samantāl lokān samagrān vadanair
jvaladbhiḥ
tejobhir āpūrya jagat samagraṁ bhāsas tavogrāḥ pratapanti
viṣṇo (30)

ākhyāhi me ko bhavān ugrarūpo namo 'stu te devavara prasīda
vijñātum icchāmi bhavantam ādyaṁ na hi prajānāmi tava
pravṛttim (31)

śrībhagavān uvāca
kālo 'smi lokakṣayakṛt pravṛddho lokān samāhartum iha pravṛttaḥ
ṛte 'pi tvāṁ na bhaviṣyanti sarve ye 'vasthitāḥ pratyanīkeṣu
yodhāḥ (32)

tasmāt tvam uttiṣṭha yaśo labhasva jitvā śatrūn bhuṅkṣva rājyaṁ samṛddham
mayaivaite nihatāḥ pūrvam eva nimittamātraṁ bhava savyasācin (33)

droṇaṁ ca bhīṣmaṁ ca jayadrathaṁ ca karṇaṁ tathānyān api yodhavīrān
mayā hatāṁs tvaṁ jahi mā vyathiṣṭhā yudhyasva jetāsi raṇe sapatnān (34)

Arjuna said:
Beloved Lord,
Adored of gods!
Behold,
Thy body holds
All fleshly tenants, seers fine,
And diverse angel-gods divine.
Dwelling deep in mystery cave,
The Serpent Nature's forceful crave,*
Though fierce and subtle, now is tame,
Forgetful of her deadly game;
And Sovran Brahma, God of gods,
On lotus seat is snug secured.

Great Cosmic-Bodied Lord of worlds,
Oh, I behold, again behold
Thee all and everywhere,
Thy countless arms, trunks, mouths, and eyes!
Yet drooping, dark, my knowledge lies
About Thy birth and reign and ending here.

This day,
O Blazing, Furious Flame,
O Blinding Ray,
Thy focused power's aglow: Thy Name†

* *Uragan divyan:* "celestial serpents"; reference to the creative forces that have their origin in the *kundalini,* the coiled life energy in the base center of the spine that enlivens the sense faculties when it flows down and outward into the body, but which bestows enlightenment when "tamed" and uplifted to the higher centers of spiritual perception.

† The cosmic vibratory light of *Aum,* the holy "Name" of God.

Spreads everywhere
To dark'st abysmal lair.
Gilded with a crown of stars
And wielding mace of sovereign power,
Thou whirlest forth, O Burning Phoebus,
Thine evolution's circling discus.

Immortal Brahma, all Supreme,
Thou Cosmic Shelter, Wisdom's Theme,
Eternal Dharma's Guardian true,
Thou diest not I ever knew!

O Birthless, Fleshless, Deathless One,
I see Thine endless, working arms,
Thine ever-watching eyes
Of suns and moons, the staring skies;
And from Thy mouth spumes throbbing flame,
*As utterest Thou the Aum, Thy Cosmic Name.**
Thy Self-born luster shields from harm,
And all creation, distance-flung, doth warm.

O Sovereign Soul! 'twixt earth and home of gods,
Directions all, and earthly sods,
All high abodes and all encircling spheres,
By Thee pervaded, far and near.
The worlds-triune awestruck by fear,
Thy dreadful wondrous form adore.

In Thee the gods their entry make;
With folded hands, afraid, some pray to shelter take
In Thee. The seers great, and heaven's-path successful ones,
With superb chants of "Peace!" do worship Thee and Thee alone.

Th' eleven lamps of heaven;
The twelve bright suns;
The grizzly eight,
The starry lusters great;

---

* *Hutasha*, "fire" and *vaktra*, "mouth or organs of speech" from *vach*, "voice, utterance."

Aspiring hermits; patron gods,
The agents of the cosmic lords;
The twin-born princes strong,
Of valor known so long;
Two-score and nine noil breezes' force,
That binds the atom close;
The long-passed guardian spirits all;
The demigoblins, demigods, and demons tall;
And mighty ones in Spirit's path,*
In wonder gaze upon Thy blazoned worth.

I Thee behold, Colossal-Armed!
With starry eyes and countless cheeks,
With endless hands, and legs adorned with lotus feet.
Thy chasmed mouth with doomsday's teeth
Doth yawn to swallow swooning worlds above, beneath,
And leaves a distilled joyous awe in me:
Thy grandeur I and all are wonder-struck to see!

To view the bowels of the void deep all filled with Thee—
Thy gaping mouth and diverse hues of fiery lustrous body—
O Vishnu of the flaming sight,
Thou quite o'erpowerest me, my peace dost fright.

Ferocious teeth and deadly fires do howl
In mouths of Thine that at me scowl.
Directions four are lost and gone;
Compassion show! I find no peace alone;
O Cosmic Guardian, Lord of gods,
Be pleased t'accept my humble pleading words.

---

* "*Eleven lamps*": the Rudras. "*Twelve suns*": the Adityas. "*Grizzly eight*": the Vasus. "*Aspiring hermits*": Vishvedevas (godly beings honored for their austerities in the Himalayas). "*Patron gods*": Sadhyas (a class of lesser deities). "*Twin-born princes*": the Ashvins ("physicians of heaven," the gods of morning twilight heralding the dawn—thus representing the mixture of light and darkness or duality; as such, they were mythically the fathers of the Pandu princes Sahadeva and Nakula). "*Two-score and nine breezes*": the Maruts. "*Long-passed guardian spirits*": the Manes (Ushmapas). "*Demigoblins, demigods, demons tall*": Yakshas, Gandharvas, Asuras, respectively. "*Mighty ones in Spirit's path*": Siddhas ("perfected ones").

The sons of senses swayed with kingly pride,
With ego, karmic habit, worldly lure, abide
*And wait to leap upon our wisdom's chiefs;**
And yet they all do ride
The race of death, to fall and hide
Fore'er in Thy devouring mouth,
Adorned with crushing cruel teeth uncouth.
The victor and the vanquished must
(Thine offspring both, the righteous and ungodly ones)
Thy love still claim; yet all some day shall kiss the dust,
And sleep on common floor of earth.
The shattered skulls of some are seen,
As caught Thy greedy teeth between.

As diverse, restless, watery waves
Of river branches all do crave
To force through crowded wavelets' way
And meet where Neptune's home long lay,
E'en so, heroic streams of life
Do plunge to meet in maddest strife
Within Thy foaming mouth of flaming sea,
Where sparks of lives all dance in Thee.

As insects lost in beauty's game
All swiftly, thoughtless, rush to flame,
So fog-born passion's fires pretend
To glow like heavenly light of Thine,
And draw on mortals to attend
The trumpet call to deathly line.

Thy mouth ablaze
Doth bring to gaze
Its leaping tongues to lick
The angry blood of strong and weak;

* "*Sons of senses*": Offspring of the Kuru King Dhritarashtra (symbolically, the blind sense-mind with its one-hundred sense proclivities led by material desire); "*Ego*": Bhishma; "*Karmic habit*": Drona; "*Worldly lure*": Karna (material attraction and attachment). "*Wisdom's chiefs*": the Pandavas (symbolically, the divine discriminative forces). See analysis of Kuru-Pandu allegory in Chapter I.

Thou, Gourmand God, dost eat
With hunger infinite.
O Vishnu, Thou dost scorch
The worlds with all-pervading fiery torch.

Be pleased, O First of gods;
I ache to know, Primeval Lord,
True who Thou art—O Fiery Mood,
Yet so benign and good.
Oh, tell to me Thy Royal Will;
For it I know not still.

The Blessed Lord then said:
In guise of Endless Doom
I come as avaricious Time to seize and room
In burning maw
Of Mine the weaklings' awe,
And all the mortal meat
Of weary worlds of deathly change, and treat
Them with My nectar-life
To new and fearless, better strife.
E'en if thou dost forbear to slay
Thy wicked foes, still they—and warriors all in brave array—
Will sure and certain timely have to fall,
Ah, in My righteous teeth-of-law, withal.

Arise, awake! Arise, awake!
*Dash thou upon the foe, the flesh a captive make;**
And win the victor's fame
With battle-hunted game;
Wealth of the King
Of Peace, and heaven's kingdom, bring!
I know right now the happenings all
That mystic future forth doth call;
And thus thy foes and warriors true,
Long, long ago I slew,
Ere shalt thine agent-hand

* Reference to the battle of Kurukshetra as an allegory of the war between the forces of good and evil, not only in the macrocosm, but within the body and consciousness of man.

(That I would wield to land
Thy foes on death's dim shore). Now understand!

My agent thou;
Oh, this is how
I work My plans—the universe—
Through instruments diverse;
'Tis I who slew and yet will slay the senses' train*
Through thee, as through both past and future ones,
My soldiers sane!

THESE VERSES FROM THE BHAGAVAD GITA are an unparalleled ode to the Universal Form of Spirit, a paean to the glory of the Cosmic-Bodied Dream Idol enshrined in the wall-less Temple of Infinity. Massive universes and their tiniest particles, majestic gods of Nature and the most insignificant of creatures, the shadow-plays of good and evil—all hold their special place in the conformation of the Cosmic Image. Often are these verses sung in worship in India. When properly intoned in the original Sanskrit, the vibratory blessing awakens a thrill of knowing in the receptive devotee, stirring sleeping memories of truth-realization held sacredly safe in the inner sanctum of the soul.

Through the portals of this song of praise, oft have I entered the Cosmic Temple to worship at the altar of the Manifested Lord. Many years ago, after one such experience in cosmic consciousness, I wrote the "Vision of Visions," a lyrical rendition of these verses interwoven with an interpretation of their significance. I have offered this rendering herewith, rather than a more constrained verse-by-verse literal translation, in the conviction that the unique animation of feelings characteristic of poesy is a proper medium for the eloquence of this Sanskrit scriptural canticle.

Spirit, the blissful consciousness of the Unmanifested Absolute, inconceivable to circumscribed minds, spins within an infinitesimal part of Its Cosmic Consciousness a universal form, a dream of Being. Each component of universal creation is individualized Cosmic Consciousness, unified with all other manifestations by the bonds of Nature and Cosmic Law. God as the Supreme Dreamer of Nature and God as individualized delimited intelligences subject to Nature—from gods to

* "*The senses' train*": Reference to "Drona, Bhishma, Jayadratha (attachment to mortal existence), Karna, and others." See allegory in Chapter I.

men—together create all happenings in the universal drama through the operation of Cosmic Law.

The human consciousness is perplexed and unable to reconcile the benign and destructive aspects of the Lord—bestowing good and beauty to man and the world on the one hand, and bringing death and destruction on the other. But if Spirit be omnipresent and the Essence of all being, naught can be outside of Him. Thus does God declare in the Bible also: "I am the Lord, and there is none else, there is no God beside Me: I girded thee (invested thee with thy powers and attributes), though thou hast not known Me....I form the light, and create darkness: I make peace, and create evil: I the Lord do all these things."*

The dualities of good and evil, joy and sorrow, life and death, are meant neither to hurt nor to please anybody, but to afford infinite opportunities to the Lord's children to experience the cosmic drama, and by right participation to evolve to higher and higher states of wisdom and freedom.

The Lord is the sole Reality; the cosmic drama is His dream. The value of all dualities is relative to their end result. The hue and cry of mortals is because their consciousness is shortsighted, forgetful of causes and ignorant of the ultimate consummation. Arjuna's vision represents the operation of the great Cosmic Law as seen, not from the point of view of creatures, but from that of the Lord Himself. His design is beyond finite questioning and justification. To the Lord, the destruction of life is not an absence of benignity, nor the giving of life a presence of it. The reality is that life and death, and all experiences enveloped therein, are mere forms of change, varying according to His Cosmic Law and leading the cosmos with all its individuals to progressively loftier stages of unfoldment. Every human being is expected to do his duty with nonattachment and with the consciousness that he is not a hapless victim but an intelligent agent of the One Infinite Being.

Man begins to reestablish his innate divine nature first by perceiving and honoring the Creator in the goodness, beauty, and harmony in his environs. As his understanding penetrates deeper into the core of all manifestations, he recognizes an inexplicable Something as their Source and Essence. Having glimpsed the Heart of Reality, he intuits the summum bonum of truth, that God is All, even the contrasts that seemingly do not declare Him—just as no image in a dream, neither the beautiful nor the nightmarish, may be dissociated from the dreamer. Still,

* Isaiah 45:5,7.

such an inclusive concept defies even the expanded scope of the devotee's understanding. Like Arjuna, he hears the words that portray the Omnific One, but without the experience of Cosmic Consciousness to which he may relate them, they lack reality.

Bhagavan Krishna says to Arjuna (XII:5), "Arduous is the path to the Absolute for embodied beings." What mortal faculty may know the Unknowable, or perceive the Imperceptible? It is less difficult for man to conceive of a personal, immanent God who has dreamed Himself into this universe of definite forms. The worship of God as personal (in one of His many aspects, or as represented by His divine emissaries such as Krishna or Christ who instruct and intercede on behalf of erring humanity) is easy and beneficial, and even necessary, for the beginner. The Lord is interested in the devotee's genuine devotion to Him, no matter what true concept formulates the worship. The devotee who realizes the personal God in a form will eventually realize Him also as the Omnipresent Formless Infinite.

Arjuna, with the frontal vision of his two physical eyes, saw his divine guru Krishna standing before him on the field of Kurukshetra. Sri Krishna then opened the all-seeing spiritual eye of Arjuna. Being at one with the cosmic consciousness of Spirit, Krishna transferred his omnipresent vision to Arjuna, whose spiritual advancement had now prepared him to receive the awakening touch of the Guru's bestowal of God-realization. It was then that Arjuna beheld the very form of Krishna metamorphose into an omnipotent image of the oneness of Krishna's consciousness with the Infinite. Arjuna saw the entire astral and physical universes in the shape of a Cosmic-Bodied Idol, having evolved from the causal universal dreamings of God as Ishvara, the Supreme Being, the Absolute become God the Father of Creation. The vision was at once both wondrously sublime and fearfully dreadful—creation, preservation, and dissolution continuously and successively roiling in the omnipresent blessed light of Spirit. The benign, attractive forms within the Cosmic Idol represent the creative and preservative forces of Nature. The gruesome aspects (the devouring of worlds and beings) are expressions of the dissolving power in creation whereby all dualities, ugly in contrast to the Singular Infinite Purity, are consumed and spumed forth again and again, to be transformed ultimately into the Divine Essence of their origin.

Urging Arjuna, the representative devotee, to take up unreservedly his divine duty in the supernal cosmic workings, the Universal Lord exhorts him: "Arise, awake…My agent thou; Oh, this is how I work My plans—the universe—through instruments diverse!" The awakened man no longer feels himself in competition with God, but in partnership with Him.

Verses 35–42

saṁjaya uvāca
etac chrutvā vacanaṁ keśavasya kṛtāñjalir vepamānaḥ kirīṭī
namaskṛtvā bhūya evāha kṛṣṇaṁ sagadgadaṁ bhītabhītaḥ
praṇamya (35)

arjuna uvāca
sthāne hṛṣīkeśa tava prakīrtyā jagat prahṛṣyaty anurajyate ca
rakṣāṁsi bhītāni diśo dravanti sarve namasyanti ca
siddhasaṁghāḥ (36)

kasmāc ca te na nameran mahātman garīyase brahmaṇo 'py
ādikartre
ananta deveśa jagannivāsa tvam akṣaraṁ sad asat tatparaṁ
yat (37)

tvam ādidevaḥ puruṣaḥ purāṇas tvam asya viśvasya paraṁ
nidhānam
vettāsi vedyaṁ ca paraṁ ca dhāma tvayā tataṁ viśvam
anantarūpa (38)

vāyur yamo 'gnir varuṇaḥ śaśāṅkaḥ prajāpatis tvaṁ
prapitāmahaś ca
namo namas te 'stu sahasrakṛtvaḥ punaś ca bhūyo 'pi namo
namas te (39)

namaḥ purastād atha pṛṣṭhatas te namo 'stu te sarvata eva sarva
anantavīryāmitavikramas tvaṁ sarvaṁ samāpnoṣi tato 'si
sarvaḥ (40)

sakhe 'ti matvā prasabhaṁ yad uktaṁ he kṛṣṇa he yādava he sakheti
ajānatā mahimānaṁ tavedaṁ mayā pramādāt praṇayena vāpi (41)

yac cāvahāsārtham asatkṛto 'si vihāraśayyāsanabhojaneṣu
eko 'thavāpy acyuta tatsamakṣaṁ tat kṣāmaye tvām aham
aprameyam (42)

Sanjaya said to King Dhritarashtra:
(35) After hearing the words of Keshava (the maya-transcendent Krishna), the diademed one (Arjuna, haloed with cosmic vision), trembling and awestricken, joining his palms in worshipful supplication, again made humble obeisance and addressed Krishna in a quavering voice.

Arjuna said:
(36) O Hrishikesha (Krishna)! Rightly are the worlds proud and gladdened to exude Thy glory! The demons, terrified, seek safety in distance; while the multitudes of siddhas (perfected beings) bow down to worship Thee.

(37) And why should they not pay Thee homage, O Vast Spirit? For greater art Thou than Brahma the Creator, who issued from Thee. O Infinite One, O God of gods, O Shelter of the Universe, Thou art the Imperishable—the Manifested, the Unmanifested, and That beyond (the Ultimate Mystery).

(38) The Primal God art Thou! the Pristine Spirit, the Final Refuge of the Worlds, the Knower and the Known, the Supreme Fulfillment! Thine Omnipresence shines in the universe, O Thou of Inexhaustible Form!

(39) O Flowing Life of Cosmic Currents (Vayu), O King of Death (Yama), O God of Flames (Agni), O Sovereign of Sea and Sky (Varuna), O Lord of Night (the Moon), O Divine Father of Countless Offspring (Prajapati), O Ancestor of All! To Thee praise, praise without end! To Thee my salutations thousandfold!

(40) O Endless Might, O Invincible Omniscient Omnipresence, O All-in-All! I bow to Thee in front and behind, I bow to Thee on the left and the right, I bow to Thee above and beneath, I bow to Thee enclosing me everywhere!

(41) Unaware of this, Thy Cosmic Glory, and thinking of Thee as a familiar companion, often have I audaciously hailed Thee as "Friend" and "Krishna" and "Yadava."* For all such words, whether spoken carelessly or with affection;

(42) And for any irreverence I have displayed toward Thee, O Unshakable Lord! in lighthearted mood at mealtimes or while walking or sitting or resting, alone with Thee or in others' company—for all such unintentional slights, O Thou Illimitable! I beg forgiveness.

STANZAS 41–42 SYMBOLICALLY PORTRAY a devotee's state of mind after the first experience of cosmic consciousness through the awakening of his "divine eye." He then reproaches himself for his previous blindness to God's omnipresence.

"With what readiness I took the world for granted, thoughtless of its Source!" he mourns. "I was sensible of creation, but of its Creator how insensible! knowing not that only by His power did I eat and walk and talk and observe and reason and pray. Of itself what atom could exist at all? Forgive my past heedlessness and ungrateful indifference to Thee, O Silent Witness of every thought and action, O Unshakable Supporter of all!"

VERSE 43

pitāsi lokasya carācarasya tvam asya pūjyaś ca gurur garīyān
na tvatsamo 'sty abhyadhikaḥ kuto 'nyo lokatraye 'py
apratimaprabhāva

Father of All art Thou! of animate and inanimate alike. None but Thee is worthy of worship, O Guru Sublime! Unparalleled by any other in the three worlds, who may surpass Thee, O Lord of Power Incomparable?

THE BIBLE PUTS THE SAME THOUGHT thus: "I am the Lord thy God,

* *Yadava:* "A descendant of Yadu," the patriarch of the Yadava race of eminent Kshatriyas. Krishna's father, Vasudeva, was a Yadava and a brother of the mother of the three elder Pandava princes. Therefore, Krishna was a cousin to Arjuna.

which have brought thee out of the land of Egypt, out of the house of bondage. Thou shalt have no other gods before Me. Thou shalt not make unto thee any graven image, or any likeness of any thing that is in heaven above, or that is in the earth beneath, or that is in the water under the earth: thou shalt not bow down thyself to them, nor serve them: for I the Lord thy God am a jealous God."*

Man is essentially Spirit; he misunderstands his real Being if he seeks fulfillment by embodiment in any of the three worlds (physical, "the earth"; astral, "the water under the earth," the vast enveloping astral sheath of light waves around the material cosmos; and causal, the "heaven above"). So long as he "bows down" before the attractions of the created or phenomenal universe, so long is he an idolater of "graven images," a follower of false doctrines, a heathen unaware of the One True God.

Only by identifying his soul with the Uncreated, the Pure and Ever-Undefiled Spirit, may man be delivered from the flux of creation—"Egypt," darkness, delusion, "the house of bondage."

From those who do not seek the Lord for Himself, the Ultimate Truth, but remain satisfied with His "untruth" (the "unreal" because transitory worlds), He turns away, "jealously" brooking no flaw in the devotee's right perception of Him.

The man who knows that God is without peer will worship none but Him. No secondary objective will serve; his goal is the Primal Unique.

Verses 44–55

tasmāt praṇamya prāṇidhāya kāyaṁ prasādaye tvām aham īśam īḍyam
piteva putrasya sakheva sakhyuḥ priyaḥ priyāyārhasi deva soḍhum (44)

adṛṣṭapūrvaṁ hṛṣito 'smi dṛṣṭvā bhayena ca pravyathitaṁ mano me
tad eva me darśaya deva rūpaṁ prasīda deveśa jagannivāsa (45)

kirīṭinaṁ gadinaṁ cakrahastam icchāmi tvāṁ draṣṭum ahaṁ tathaiva
tenaiva rūpeṇa caturbhujena sahasrabāho bhava viśvamūrte (46)

* Exodus 20:2–5.

śrībhagavān uvāca
mayā prasannena tavārjunedaṁ rūpaṁ paraṁ darśitam ātmayogāt
tejomayaṁ viśvam anantam ādyaṁ yan me tvadanyena na
dṛṣṭapūrvam (47)

na vedayajñādhyayanair na dānair na ca kriyābhir na tapobhir
ugraiḥ
evaṁrūpaḥ śakya ahaṁ nṛloke draṣṭuṁ tvadanyena
kurupravīra (48)

mā te vyathā mā ca vimūḍhabhāvo dṛṣṭvā rūpaṁ ghoram īdṛṅ
mamedam
vyapetabhīḥ prītamanāḥ punas tvaṁ tad eva me rūpam idaṁ
prapaśya (49)

saṁjaya uvāca
ity arjunaṁ vāsudevas tathoktvā svakaṁ rūpaṁ darśayām āsa
bhūyaḥ
āśvāsayām āsa ca bhītam enaṁ bhūtvā punaḥ saumyavapur
mahātmā (50)

arjuna uvāca
dṛṣṭvedaṁ mānuṣaṁ rūpaṁ tava saumyaṁ janārdana idānīm asmi
saṁvṛttaḥ sacetāḥ prakṛtiṁ gataḥ (51)

śrībhagavān uvāca
sudurdarśam idaṁ rūpaṁ dṛṣṭavān asi yan mama
devā apy asya rūpasya nityaṁ darśanakāṅkṣiṇaḥ (52)

nāhaṁ vedair na tapasā na dānena na cejyayā
śakya evaṁvidho draṣṭuṁ dṛṣṭavān asi māṁ yathā (53)

bhaktyā tvananyayā śakya aham evaṁvidho 'rjuna
jñātuṁ draṣṭuṁ ca tattvena praveṣṭuṁ ca paraṁtapa (54)

matkarmakṛn matparamo madbhaktaḥ saṅgavarjitaḥ
nirvairaḥ sarvabhūteṣu yaḥ sa mām eti pāṇḍava (55)

(44) Therefore, O Adorable One, I cast myself in obeisance at Thy feet to implore Thy pardon. As a father to his son, as a friend to a close friend, as a lover to his beloved, do Thou, O Lord, forgive me!

(45) Overjoyed am I at having gazed upon a vision never seen before, yet my mind is not free from terror. Be merciful to me, O Lord of gods, O Shelter of the Worlds! Show to me only Thy Deva-form (as the benign Vishnu).

(46) I long to see Thee as before, as the Four-Armed Vishnu, diademed and holding Thy mace and discus. Reappear in that same form, O Thou who art Thousand-Armed and Universe-Bodied!

The Blessed Lord said:
(47) I have graciously exercised Mine own Yoga Power to reveal to thee, O Arjuna, and to none other! this Supreme Primeval Form of Mine, the Radiant and Infinite Cosmos!

(48) No mortal man, save only thyself, O Great Hero of the Kurus! is able to look upon My Universal Shape—not by sacrifices or charity or works or rigorous austerity or study of the Vedas is that vision attainable.

(49) Be not affrighted or stupefied at seeing My Terrible Aspect. With dreads removed and heart rejoicing, behold once more My familiar form!

Sanjaya said to King Dhritarashtra:
(50) After speaking thus, Vasudeva, "the Lord of the World," resumed his own shape as Krishna. He, the Great-Souled One, appearing to Arjuna in the form of grace, consoled His fear-stricken devotee.

Arjuna said:
(51) O Granter of All Wishes (Krishna)! As I gaze on Thee again in gentle human shape, my mind is quieted and I feel more like my natural self.

The Blessed Lord said:
(52) Very difficult it is to behold, as thou hast done, the Vision Universal! Even the gods ever yearn to see it.

(53–54) But it is not unveiled through one's penance or scriptural lore or gift-giving or formal worship. O Scorcher of the Sense-Foes (Arjuna)! only by undivided devotion (commingling by yoga all thoughts in One Divine Perception) may I be seen as thou hast beheld Me in My Cosmic Form and recognized in reality and finally embraced in Oneness!

(55) He who works for Me alone, who makes Me his goal, who lovingly surrenders himself to Me, who is nonattached (to My delusive cosmic-dream worlds), who bears ill will toward none (beholding Me in all)—he enters My being, O Arjuna!

om tat sat iti śrīmadbhagavadgītāsu upaniṣatsu
brahmavidyāyām yogaśāstre śrīkṛṣṇārjunasaṁvāde
viśvarūpadarśanayogo nāmaikādaśo 'dhyāyaḥ

Aum, Tat, Sat.
In the Upanishad of the holy Bhagavad Gita—the discourse of Lord Krishna to Arjuna, which is the scripture of yoga and the science of God-realization—this is the eleventh chapter, called "The Vision of the Cosmic Form."

CHAPTER XII

BHAKTI YOGA: UNION THROUGH DEVOTION

❖

Should the Yogi Worship the Unmanifest, or a Personal God?

❖

The Levels of Spiritual Practice and the Stages of Realization

❖

Qualities of the Devotee, Endearing to God

ॐ

"Dearest to God, inseparable from Him, are those yogis who with total devoted concentration keep their souls united to the all-sheltering, undying Spirit beyond creation—the Immutable Absolute, devoid of all delusive imaging—while worshipfully engaged in living and manifesting the eternal, immortalizing principles of God-union. Such yogis remain as one with Him, embraced in His bosom of transcendent bliss."

BHAKTI YOGA: UNION THROUGH DEVOTION

SHOULD THE YOGI WORSHIP THE UNMANIFEST, OR A PERSONAL GOD?

VERSE 1

arjuna uvāca
evaṁ satatayuktā ye bhaktās tvāṁ paryupāsate
ye cāpy akṣaram avyaktaṁ teṣāṁ ke yogavittamāḥ

Arjuna said:
Those devotees who, ever steadfast, thus worship Thee; and those who adore the Indestructible, the Unmanifested—which of these is better versed in yoga?

HERE ARJUNA REFERS TO THE DEVOTEE described in the last stanza of the eleventh chapter (he who thinks of God as the Cosmic-Bodied Lord, immanent in all manifestations and who therefore works for Him without personal attachment to anything, without feeling enmity to anyone, enshrining God as his supreme Goal); and to the devotee who worships God as formless or unmanifested Spirit (considering God and Nature as two separate entities). Which devotee is better acquainted with the technique of uniting soul and Spirit?

VERSE 2

śrībhagavān uvāca
mayy āveśya mano ye māṁ nityayuktā upāsate
śraddhayā parayopetās te me yuktatamā matāḥ

The Blessed Lord said:

Those who, fixing their minds on Me, adore Me, ever united to Me with supreme devotion, are in My eyes the perfect knowers of yoga.

THE YOGI DESCRIBED IN THE LAST stanza of the eleventh chapter, and again in this stanza, is better versed in the processes and yoga techniques that lead to God-union than is the devotee described in the third and fourth verses of this chapter—he who concentrates on the realization of imperishable, unmanifested Spirit. But, ultimately, both kinds of devotees attain the Cosmic Spirit.

All manifestations and activities in creation are the Lord's Cosmic Yoga. He is the Singularity that evolves as these multi-expressions and that unifies them in the one cosmic consciousness of His Eternal Being. The devotee who recognizes this immanence of God, and who follows the prescribed yogic steps to attain full realization of Divinity, understands how the One became individualized and active in the many; and how, in a scientific way, that descension from cosmic consciousness may be reversed in oneself into ascension or reunion with Spirit.

The devotee who advances by means of step-by-step methods of yoga is therefore acknowledged by the Lord to be the better versed in the science of the union of soul and Spirit. Concentrating on the immanence of God in His primal manifestation as the Cosmic *Aum* Vibration (Holy Ghost) and its creative differentiations in the cosmos and in the microcosm of his own being, the yogi experiences the primary *savikalpa samadhi.* While in a transcendent ecstatic state, oblivious of external creation, he perceives God in one of His divine qualities or aspects—in form or formless. Ultimately, he attains the highest *nirvikalpa samadhi* in which he experiences—with no loss of sensory awareness of his body and surroundings—both the Form and Formless Lord immanent in creation and also the Absolute beyond creation.

Step-by-step methods of yoga lead to realization of God in and beyond creation

Such a yogi ever devotedly realizes God in duality as well as in unity. Thus, by following the scientific steps of yoga, he attains fixity of the mind on God and remains ever united to Him. Rising above all material attachments as he acquires progressively elevated states of consciousness, he works for God through love and service to all beings, knowing that in them the Lord is manifested. He worships the Lord with supreme single-hearted devotion, realizing that God is the

Sole Object and Goal of life. He is an example of scientific yoga that all divine seekers can follow to reascend to God.

Verses 3–4

ye tvakṣaram anirdeśyam avyaktaṁ paryupāsate
sarvatragam acintyaṁ ca kūṭastham acalaṁ dhruvam (3)

saṁniyamyendriyagrāmaṁ sarvatra samabuddhayaḥ
te prāpnuvanti mām eva sarvabhūtahite ratāḥ (4)

But those who adore the Indestructible, the Indescribable, the Unmanifested, the All-Pervading, the Incomprehensible, the Immutable, the Unmoving, the Ever-Constant; who have subjugated all of the senses, possess evenmindedness in every circumstance, and devote themselves to the good of all beings—verily, they too attain Me.

In these two stanzas, Lord Krishna speaks to Arjuna about the type of worshiper who is devoted to the concept of God as the transcendent Supreme Being who is the Creator and Ruler of the universe. In deference to the Supernal Spirit, such a devotee leads a disciplined life of self-control, maintains evenmindedness by faith in God, and behaves in a righteous, serviceful manner; but he follows no formal course of scientific yoga.

Attaining the Absolute through intense, worshipful devotion

Such devotees, purified by a holy life, during periods of intense worshipful devotion subdue their senses and attain a state of perfect mental calm by simple but wholehearted concentration on the Lord. Mentally they plunge into the darkless dark, the lightless light, in which the indestructible Spirit, the indescribable, unthinkable One, exists as the *Kutastha* Intelligence (the Krishna or Christ Consciousness) in creation—omnipresent, immovable, and unchangeable, the pure formless reflection (or Son) of the transcendental Lord. Christian mystics, such as St. John of the Cross, St. Thomas Aquinas, and St. Teresa of Avila, experienced this Transcendental Consciousness. Of this divine communion, St. Teresa declared, "I have seen the Formless Christ." Gradually increasing their perceptions of the reflected Eternal Intelligence in creation, such devotees ultimately realize the cosmic consciousness of God existing in the vibrationless realm beyond the phenomenal worlds. This type of devotee (in effect, a yogi or one who has attained yoga or union with God) reaches the Absolute, but is not necessarily conscious of the intermediate scientific stages that have transpired within him to lead his consciousness to emancipation.

The life of a scientific yogi, as noted in the preceding verse, is therefore more balanced. He understands and follows those laws and principles of Nature by which he sees God as the All in all, and thereby consciously releases himself from the limitations of personal attachments to property and relatives and friends, serving the Lord in all human beings irrespective of their creed, race, or condition. By various methods of concentration, he gradually detaches his ego from the senses and attaches his life force, mind, and ego to the superconscious soul. Then by primary ecstasy he experiences the *Kutastha* Intelligence in all creation, and by *nirvikalpa* ecstasy he attains the Spirit beyond phenomena.

The two types of "yogis" may be compared to two stenographers, one of whom develops speed on the typewriter by the unscientific "hunt and peck" method, and the other who develops speed by the scientific "touch" system. As the latter typist may be considered to be better versed in the art of typewriting, so the scientific yogi may be said to be more knowledgeable as to the whys and hows of seeking God.

VERSE 5

kleśo 'dhikataras teṣām avyaktāsaktacetasām
avyaktā hi gatir duḥkhaṁ dehavadbhir avāpyate

Those whose goal is the Unmanifested increase the difficulties; arduous is the path to the Absolute for embodied beings.

THE PATH OF THE WORSHIPER of the Unmanifested Infinite is very difficult, because the devotee has no support from the imaging power of his mind. Worship implies an Object of veneration that holds the attention and inspires reverent devotion, a God of manifested qualities. The Formless Unknown does not well serve this purpose for most mortal minds. He who is born in a world of forms can scarcely attain a true formless conception of Spirit. Worship of the Indescribable therefore automatically presupposes the actual experience of the Infinite. Only those who are already spiritually advanced enough to intuit the "Formless Christ," as did Teresa of Avila, find joy in this relationship with the Divine.

The systematic yogi progresses through various stages of divine perception, which coax and strengthen his efforts and devotion; but the fruits of worship of the Unmanifested are forthcoming only in the consummate union of the devotee's consciousness with God. Worshipers of the Absolute must therefore be so intent on Spirit that all their perceptions transcend inner and outer limitations and commingle as the singular intuitive realization of the Infinite Spirit. Such transcendent self-mastery requires from the very beginning the practice of stringent renunciation and relinquishment of all bodily attachment. Total relinquishment of earthly identifications is hard indeed for a human being. The endeavor to do so has given rise to the practice of severe austerities for the purpose of subduing the rebellious human nature.

The yogi who worships a personal God, on the other hand, utilizes step-by-step methods of realization by which he progresses gradually and naturally toward his goal. The natural method for renunciation of lesser pleasures and attachments is to taste the superior joys of the Spirit. The worshiper of a personal God finds all around him and within the inner temple of his consciousness constant reminders of the immanence of God, which fill his heart with divine love and joy, without courting the hardships of a renunciant's life of rigorous asceticism. The yogi loves God so deeply that gradually all lesser desires leave him.

God likes the personal relationship with the devotee

It would seem, therefore, that God likes the personal relationship with the devotee, for He makes it easier for the seeker who sees the Divine Immanence in creation and concentrates on God as the Heavenly Father or the Cosmic Mother or Divine Friend possessing "human" qualities. Or, just as in slumber the unseen formless human consciousness can shape itself into dream images, so the Formless Spirit as the Creator God can inform His consciousness into any manifestation dear to the devotee's heart. If the devotee's *ishta* (object of worship) is Krishna or Christ, for example, the Lord will assume that concept. All such aspects are in no manner a limitation of God to that form, but are rather like windows opening to the Infinite Spirit.

VERSES 6–7

ye tu sarvāṇi karmāṇi mayi saṁnyasya matparāḥ
ananyenaiva yogena māṁ dhyāyanta upāsate (6)

teṣām ahaṁ samuddhartā mṛtyusaṁsārasāgarāt
bhavāmi na cirāt pārtha mayy āveśitacetasām (7)

But those who venerate Me, giving over all activities to Me (thinking of Me as the Sole Doer), contemplating Me by single-minded yoga—remaining thus absorbed in Me—indeed, O offspring of Pritha (Arjuna), for these whose consciousness is fixed in Me, I become before long their Redeemer to bring them out of the sea of mortal births.

AGAIN SRI KRISHNA REFERS to the devotee who through scientific yoga worships the Manifested God. In deep, devoted meditation, concentrating on God as the Sole Doer of all life-giving actions, the yogi suspends outer and inner sensory-motor activities of body and mind, dissolving their outgoing vibratory force into the pure consciousness of Spirit whence they came.

By quieting the heart through practice of *Kriya Yoga pranayama,* life-force control, the yogi disconnects his mind not only from the senses, but also from the disturbing activities of breath, with its 21,000 daily inhalations and exhalations—each one, considered by yogis, to be a birth and death. With freedom from the bondage of breath and sensory perceptions, which tie the consciousness to the body, the yogi dissolves his ego in the blessed soul, his true Spirit-nature. Having attained soul perception, the yogi continuously realizes the Omnipresent Spirit behind all individualized souls—and all manifestations in Nature. He ever remains absorbed in God by this single-minded union.

The devotee may also become united with the divine bliss of the immanent-transcendent Spirit by the yogic method of listening to the cosmic sound of *Aum,* the Holy Ghost—the divine voice of God, the abode of all truth—and by meditating upon this holy vibration and becoming one with it.

Yogis who attain the perception of the Infinite find that this realization leads to final emancipation. Once the devotee becomes fixed in the changeless Spirit, he is subject no longer to the permutations of births and deaths, or of good and evil karma. Thus does the Lord exhort the devotee, "Get away from My ocean of suffering and misery! Give thyself single-heartedly to Me and I will lift thee out of the sea of delusion."

THE LEVELS OF SPIRITUAL PRACTICE AND THE STAGES OF REALIZATION

VERSE 8

mayy eva mana ādhatsva mayi buddhiṁ niveśaya
nivasiṣyasi mayy eva ata ūrdhvaṁ na saṁśayaḥ

Immerse thy mind in Me alone; concentrate on Me thy discriminative perception; and beyond doubt thou shalt dwell immortally in Me.

THE BODY-IDENTIFIED BEING keeps his mind and powers of discrimination busy with sensory and material objects. Thus he undergoes untold dissatisfaction and trouble.

All yogis who disconnect their minds and discrimination from the senses and place them on inner perceptions attain the state of changeless soul consciousness.

The practice of yoga frees the mind (*manas*) and the discrimination (*buddhi*) from slavery to the senses, and concentrates these faculties of perception on the all-knowing intuitive wisdom of the soul—the microcosmic image of Spirit manifested in the body. In realizing the oneness of soul and Spirit, the yogi is then able to feel the blessedness of the Infinite Being existing not only in the material world, but also in endlessness beyond vibratory creation.

VERSE 9

atha cittaṁ samādhātuṁ na śaknoṣi mayi sthiram
abhyāsayogena tato mām icchāptuṁ dhanaṁjaya

O Dhananjaya (Arjuna), if thou art not able to keep thy mind wholly on Me, then seek to attain Me by repeated yoga practice.

FROM THE EIGHTH TO THE ELEVENTH STANZAS of this chapter, Krishna reveals various methods of attaining liberation—each path suitable to devotees who have attained a certain grade of spirituality. My guru Sri Yukteswarji often remarked that the various modes of liberation mentioned in the Bhagavad Gita make its precepts so sweet, sympathetic, and useful in healing the manifold sicknesses of suffering humanity.

Thus Krishna says: "O Arjuna, if a devotee, through prenatal bad karma, cannot disconnect mind and discrimination naturally and easily from the senses and remain unbrokenly in that God-knowing state of soul-realization, he should faithfully engage himself in practicing repeatedly the scientific step-by-step methods of yoga for soul union." When the fruit appears on the tree, the precedent flower falls away. The devotee who has permanently established his consciousness in God no longer requires the "flower" of yoga practice; but for the aspiring devotee, regularity and continuity in yoga (*abhyasa-yoga**) is essential. Those who persist in meditation will ultimately succeed.

When a yogi again and again fights his restlessness and distractions, and with ever-increasing intensity tries to feel divine communion in meditation, he will form a good habit of calm interiorization. In time this habit will displace the mortal habit of restive sensory bondage and will lead ultimately to realization of Divinity.

Though I was born with the blessed perception of Spirit, once in a while during my youth, my mind became very restless when I was engaged in the practice of yoga meditation. During some of these periodic attacks, I would visualize myself as playing football—a game I very much enjoyed, and at which I was adept. At first it seemed that my habit of mentally playing football could not be erased. Nevertheless, I tried persistently to make my meditations longer and more intense, endeavoring to make each day's realizations deeper than the spiritual perceptions of the previous day. In this way I became accustomed to remaining continuously in soul joy. The formation of this habit led to the experience of ecstatic bliss in omnipresent Spirit.

VERSE 10

abhyāse 'pyasamartho 'si matkarmaparamo bhava
madartham api karmāṇi kurvan siddhim avāpsyasi

If, again, thou art not able to practice continuous yoga, be thou diligent in performing actions in the thought of Me. Even by engaging in activities on My behalf thou shalt attain supreme divine success.

---

* Repetitive effort to hold the mind continuously in its pure state of divine attunement.

IF A DEVOTEE FALTERS IN YOGA PRACTICE, being habitually restless and materially active, then with devotion and faith in God, he should support his meditations by increasing efforts to perform in God's name all physical, mental, and spiritual actions. His meditative activities and the outer work of physically, mentally, and spiritually helping others should be motivated by the sole desire to please God. In time he will feel the presence of Him who is ever conscious of the struggling devotee's efforts.

The Bible tells us: "Faith is the substance of things hoped for, the evidence of things not seen."* By performance of right actions with faith in the Lord, a devotee will ultimately find, through perceptible response from Him, proof of His unseen presence.

Even if the seeker is discouraged by lack of tangible results, with blind conviction he should keep on with his meditations and serviceful actions, out of awe and love for God. One who slackens or discontinues his efforts will find that his mind returns quickly to the sphere of matter, its habitual resting place. But the devotee who perseveres with unabated zeal, desiring to please God, will ultimately find Him.

Counsel for the restless devotee on the path of meditation

The cure for restlessness is continuous effort to be peaceful regardless of success or failure. Strong, die-hard restive habits at last are destroyed by the gradual strengthening of the good habit of practicing interiorized calmness in meditation.

I knew two extremely ignorant students, in my high school days in Calcutta. Owing to their inability to grasp the class lessons, they were subjected to daily chastisement from the teachers. One of the students "couldn't take it": he quit school and remained uneducated. The other boy, no matter what insults he suffered, kept on trying. Everybody was astounded when at the end of the year he passed creditably his final examinations.

Similarly, the Bhagavad Gita here advises even the most restless devotee—one who lacks a karmic predisposition that facilitates yoga practice—to meditate persistently anyway, out of love for God and a desire to please Him, for by that continuous spiritual activity he will ultimately succeed in God-realization.

* Hebrews 11:1.

VERSE 11

athaitad apy aśakto 'si kartuṁ madyogam āśritaḥ
sarvakarmaphalatyāgaṁ tataḥ kuru yatātmavān

If thou art not able to do even this, then, remaining attached to Me as thy Shelter, relinquish the fruits of all actions while continuing to strive for Self-mastery.*

IF A DEVOTEE, OWING TO MATERIALISTIC tendencies and mental perversity, is unable to perform material and meditative actions in the thought of God just to please Him, he should cling to the Lord with faith, seeking refuge in His unconditional love, and perform all actions without concentrating on their fruits. Such relinquishment means renouncing preconceived expectations and trusting in the Lord's compassion and grace to so order the outcome of one's endeavors that they will conduce to the devotee's ultimate highest good.

Just by cultivating a simple faith in God—even a blind faith in the beginning will do—and by trying unselfishly to perform good deeds and meditative actions without focusing on their results, that devotee in time will grow in spirituality; his mind and heart will become purified. A mind freed from the likes and dislikes that are born of the results of selfish activities is able to manifest soul qualities.

Right attitude toward experiences in meditation

When a restless person, for example, assiduously performs scientific meditation techniques without a preconditioned expectation of results, he meditates better; he will not be disturbed and distracted by any frustrated craving for rewards. The spiritual novice, used to the entertainment of the senses, often expects similar experiences from his meditative efforts. His mind is long conditioned to considering as stupendous and desirable anything dazzling to sight, sound, or sensory feeling. But in the highest thought-realms of divine consciousness, spiritual experiences are very subtle—and therefore sometimes pass unrecognized by the devotee expecting dramatic manifestations. The greater the subtlety of one's spiritual experience, the greater its relative physical and spiritual effect. Phenomena are the manifestations of the Noumenon, or God. The former are cognized by the sensory fac-

* *Yata-atma-van:* lit., "like a mastered self"; that is, emulate those who have attained Self-mastery; keep endeavoring to reach that goal.

ulties (physical or astral) and the latter by soul intuition. In the words of my guru, Sri Yukteswarji: "To know God, don't expect anything. Just launch yourself with faith into His blissful Presence within."

Thus, even without the singularity of desire to please God, the devotee will ultimately find Him if he remains sheltered in the Lord by thinking about Him during all good activities, and by fully surrendering to Him the outcome of all actions and all happenings in his life. Here the devotee might wonder: "How can I think of God and surrender to Him without knowing Him?" That is the value of scientific yogic techniques of meditation. The devotee has a specific concept on which to concentrate that leads to the experience of God, and a proven method for making that concentration effective. For example, if the seeker, in spite of extreme restlessness, continues to practice the Self-Realization Fellowship technique of meditation on God as *Aum,* he will eventually hear the cosmic sound, the Word or Amen, the vibratory presence of God as the Holy Ghost. As he keeps on listening to the cosmic sound with devotion, and without restless eagerness for results, in time he will feel a blissful expansion of consciousness in the omnipresence of *Aum;* and behind the sacred vibration he will come to know the blessed Spirit.

Just as a person who uses the right methods to squeeze olives or grind mustard seeds will be able to extract the hidden oil, so the devotee to whom God is not perceptible in the beginning will find Him by the "pressure" of loyal devotion and the unselfish performance of good actions, material and meditative. Some day the merciful Omniscience, feeling the constancy of the devotee's goodness, will flow into and permeate every fiber of his being.

VERSE 12

śreyo hi jñānam abhyāsāj jñānād dhyānaṁ viśiṣyate
dhyānāt karmaphalatyāgas tyāgāc chāntir anantaram

Verily, wisdom (born from yoga practice) is superior to (mechanical) yoga practice; meditation is more desirable than the possession of (theoretical) wisdom; the relinquishment of the fruits of actions is better than (the initial states of) meditation. Renunciation of the fruits of actions is followed immediately by peace.

THE LITERAL READING OF THIS VERSE is commonly taken as extolling the virtue of the so-called "easiest" path to the Divine embraced by the *bhakta,* the devotee who takes shelter in God and relinquishes to Him the outcome, or fruits, of all actions—as described in verse 11. Such renunciation, total nonattachment, is emphasized throughout the Gita as the very foundation of spiritual progress; for it provides the altar of inner tranquility before which the devotee can wholeheartedly worship God—whether in wisdom, action, or yoga meditation.

The deeper meaning of this verse cites the subtle differentiation of the states experienced by the yogi as he attains realization of God by any of the modes of worship defined in the preceding verses.

The perception of wisdom—intuitive realization attained by the eager and proper practice of yoga—is superior to any intermediate results precipitated during the mechanical physical and mental efforts of repeated practice of yoga techniques. During the mere practice of yoga, the mind is a battleground of distractions and warring states of consciousness, with intermittent lulls of transcendent peace and inner experiences of astral or cosmic forces, such as divine light or the sound of *Aum.* In the perception of pure wisdom, there is an absence of all inner tumult, a stilling of all oscillating waves of the mind. Perception is solely through the all-knowing intuition of the soul.

Progressively higher states experienced by the yogi in meditation

The true state of meditation is oneness of the meditator with the object of meditation, God. It is superior to the preliminary meditative state of theoretical wisdom—knowledge attained through divine perceptions in meditation by the devotee who is an observer apart from his experience—the knower who is knowing the thing to be known. Thus this state is tinged with the relative consciousness that the triune knower, knowing, and known exist separately. When the yogi is aware that he is the knower separate from his perception of divine wisdom, he is experiencing the relativity of consciousness involved in the triple factors of knowledge. In the supreme state of meditation, the devotee is no longer conscious of the triple factors, but only of oneness with Spirit.

Greater than the initial experience of the state of meditative oneness with God is constant establishment in that state, which leads to freedom from all bondage to karmic fruits of actions. The initial experience of divine oneness is temporary, allowing the consciousness to return again to the karmically controlled body-identified state with its lapses into ineffectual, absentminded efforts in meditation. Continuous ecstasy (*nirvikalpa samadhi*) bestows detachment from the circumscriptive laws of the realm of material vibrations and leads to freedom from all past and present karma—"relinquishment of the fruits of actions." After meditative unity with Spirit is permanently established, the devotee attains the superior state of oneness with God plus complete escape from the bindings of material vibrations. He enjoys the dual perception of oneness with God and interactions with matter while his consciousness within remains wholly detached from material vibrations.

Lastly, the devotee realizes the "peace of God, which passeth all understanding,"* the ultimate state of blessed tranquility in the vibrationless Absolute.†

Qualities of the Devotee, Endearing to God

Verses 13–14

adveṣṭā sarvabhūtānāṁ maitraḥ karuṇa eva ca
nirmamo nirahaṁkāraḥ samaduḥkhasukhaḥ kṣamī (13)

saṁtuṣṭaḥ satataṁ yogī yatātmā dṛḍhaniścayaḥ
mayy arpitamanobuddhir yo madbhaktaḥ sa me priyaḥ (14)

He who is free from hatred toward all creatures, is friendly and kind to all, is devoid of the consciousness of "I-ness" and possessiveness; is evenminded in suffering and joy, forgiving, ever contented; a regular yoga practitioner, constantly trying by yoga to

---

* Philippians 4:7.

† "The ornament of a servant of God is devotion; the jewel of devotion is consciousness of nonduality.

"The ornament of knowledge is meditation; the decoration of meditation is renunciation; and the pearl of renunciation is pure, unfathomable *Shanti.*

"The pure and unfathomable *Shanti* cuts the root of all misery. He who holds *Shanti* in his heart dwells in a sea of Bliss. All sins that breed suffering, anxiety, and anguish disappear, together with all limitations....

"Know him to be perfect who is most peaceful, who is taintless and free from all personal desires, whose mind vibrates with *Shanti.*"

—Tulsidas, in *Indian Mystic Verse,* translated by Hari Prasad Shastri (London: Shanti Sadan, 1984).

know the Self and to unite with Spirit, possessed of firm determination, with mind and discrimination surrendered to Me—he is My devotee, dear to Me.

THESE MANIFOLD QUALITIES EPITOMIZED in a yogi endear him to God. To please the Lord and attain Him, the yogi is steadfast in regular and intensive practice of the science of God-union (*Kriya Yoga*). By the self-restraint (interiorization) of yoga, he dissolves his restless physical ego, with its sense of "I, me, and mine," in the perception of his true Self. When in ecstasy he determinedly keeps his mind and discrimination surrendered to the pure intuitive perception of Spirit in the vibrationless sphere, he is able even in the human state to feel the omnipresence of the Lord.

The yogi who perceives the same Spirit pervading all creation cannot entertain hatred for any creature. Instead, he is friendly and compassionate to all. He recognizes God even in the guise of an enemy.

Possessing the evenminded blessedness of Spirit, a yogi is unruffled by material sufferings and pleasures. Finding the joy of the Divine, he is ever contented under all conditions of physical existence. He attends to his meager bodily necessities, but is wholly detached from any sense of *my* body or *my* possessions; he considers himself to be serving God in his own body and in the bodies of all who cross his path.

Many can understand the advice of the Bhagavad Gita about indifference to pain, but not about indifference to pleasure. Does this scripture advise the yogi to be a sphinx, an unfeeling stone, unresponsive to all of life's pleasures? No, it does not give such meaningless counsel. But just as a millionaire is not excited to receive the gift of a dollar, so the possessor of immeasurable, all-satisfying divine wealth does not feel elated by the paltry offerings of the senses. Anyone who runs after sense joys proves that he has not tasted divine bliss.

VERSE 15

yasmān nodvijate loko lokān nodvijate ca yaḥ
harṣāmarṣabhayodvegair mukto yaḥ sa ca me priyaḥ

A person who does not disturb the world and who cannot be disturbed by the world, who is free from exultation, jealousy, apprehension, and worry—he too is dear to Me.

THAT MAN IS PLEASING TO GOD who, trusting in Him, is tranquil, unaffected by outer events, and able to manifest his attainment of divine unity by feeling affection for all as individual expressions of the Lord. Such a lovable yogi, perceiving God as Bliss, never indulges in sense excitements, frivolous pleasures, selfish jealousies, mundane fears, or material worries.

A worldly man, constantly agitating himself and others by inharmonious vibrations, cannot feel in the temple of creation the presence of blessed Spirit.

Virtue is often subtle and unassuming, a quiet influence and support that gives life stability and a sense of pleasant well-being whose source goes unnoticed, and as such is taken for granted. In startling contrast, evil is usually so brash and its consequences so obnoxious or painful that it defies any attempt to ignore it. Thus did Shakespeare wryly note: "The evil that men do lives after them; the good is oft interred with their bones."*

If we envisage a world filled with the virtues and devoid of the demonic qualities enumerated in the Gita, we have the creation the loving God intended for His incarnate children.

VERSE 16

anapekṣaḥ śucir dakṣa udāsīno gatavyathaḥ
sarvārambhaparityāgī yo madbhaktaḥ sa me priyaḥ

He who is free from worldly expectations, who is pure in body and mind, who is ever ready to work, who remains unconcerned with and unafflicted by circumstances, who has forsaken all ego-initiated desireful undertakings—he is My devotee, dear to Me.

A YOGI WHO HAS REACHED the Absolute Goal has no need to perform activities or to start any undertaking with human motives rooted in egoism. His happiness does not depend on the well-being of the physical body or on sense pleasures or on the acquirement of material objects. He has found supreme bliss.

Such a man is ever ready to perform spiritual or physical actions to help himself and others, thus serving the God who is present in

* *Julius Caesar,* Act III, scene 2.

all. Even in serving self—in eating, walking, thinking, feeling, willing—the yogi performs these activities only to keep his body and mind fit to perform God's will. He serves others not to obtain gratitude or advantages from them, but to please the Lord within their body-temples.

A yogi who keeps his soul united with Spirit is called an *udasin* (one who is placed beyond the reach of the vibratory sense perceptions). Therefore, troubles of body and mind cannot disturb him. No dependence on, or initiating desire for, material things invades his state of eternal contentment.

VERSE 17

yo na hṛṣyati na dveṣṭi na śocati na kāṅkṣati
śubhāśubhaparityāgī bhaktimān yaḥ sa me priyaḥ

He who feels neither rejoicing nor loathing toward the glad nor the sad (aspects of phenomenal life), who is free from grief and cravings, who has banished the relative consciousness of good and evil, and who is intently devout—he is dear to Me.

THE YOGI WHO DOES NOT IDENTIFY himself with the relativities of the cosmic dream dramas, but who ever beholds the omnipresent beam of Divinity that created them, is beloved by the Lord.

A true devotee is ardently devout in all aspects of his life. His mental equilibrium is not affected by good fortune or calamity, he is not overpowered by grief under any circumstances, he feels no anger at nonfulfillment of desires, and he is free from material longings and has thus risen above the duality of good and evil.

VERSES 18–19

samaḥ śatrau ca mitre ca tathā mānāpamānayoḥ
śītoṣṇasukhaduḥkheṣu samaḥ saṅgavivarjitaḥ (18)

tulyanindāstutir maunī saṁtuṣṭo yena kenacit
aniketaḥ sthiramatir bhaktimān me priyo naraḥ (19)

He who is tranquil before friend and foe alike, and in encountering adoration and insult, and during the experiences of warmth and chill and of pleasure and suffering; who has relinquished attachment, regarding blame and praise in the same light; who is quiet and easily contented, not attached to domesticity, and of calm disposition and devotional—that person is dear to Me.

WHEN A YOGI KNOWS THIS WORLD to be a dream motion-picture of God, without objective reality, he beholds the manifestations of a friendly hero and a cruel villain, or the experiences of honor and dishonor, of heat and cold, of pain and pleasure, or insult and adulation, or of any other dualistic presentation on the screen of his daily life, to be entertaining but meaningless ever-changing shadows of delusion.

Such a calm yogi, tranquil in speech, body, and mind, ever drinking the nectar of all-pervading bliss, is indeed very dear to God. He forsakes the degrading attributes depicted in the evil dream-pictures of life, cultivating instead the divine attributes depicted in the salutary dream scenarios. He thus earns his credentials to become free, laudably passing the examinations of mortal existence.

The yogi does not seek fame or recognition for his temporary role in this drama of incarnations. He knows that to strive for recognition from God alone is the only true wisdom. A famous man, after death, is not aware of his renown. For him there is no value in statues erected in his honor, or in having his name engraved on crumbling stones outraged by time and weather. But the names of liberated souls are written in the heart of God, forever recognized by His immortal angels; in this the soul will rejoice everlastingly.

Devotee's attitude toward fame and ill fame

Fame in itself is not wrong. A fragrant flower advertises itself; so also does a person offering superior services in time become known. But to crave fame at all costs is dangerous, rife with potential to produce untold suffering. An unqualified person with an inordinate craving for personal honor is quite apt to receive dishonor, as "pride goeth before a fall." Name and fame are distinctions that come but rarely in the dream pictures of life, through one's good karma and through the grace and decree of God. They should not be sought as goals in themselves. Anyone who serves selflessly, seeking not to aggrandize himself but to glorify God, receives all the honor he deserves—either in this life or in a future existence.

Fame and ill fame are both tests of God. Ordinary mortals lose their psychological equilibrium when caught up in the emotions of these ego rousers; greedy for more fame and angry at ill fame, they become ever more deeply entangled in delusive misconceptions and misgivings.

When fame comes as God's recognition of good qualities, the yogi does not let it "go to his head"; it inspires him continuously to be better in the eyes of God, his guru, and his own conscience—not just in the eyes of the public.

If ill fame and unexpected persecutions from inevitable critics come to an innocent yogi, he remains secure in his natural humility; and without bitterness he tries, if possible, to remove the misunderstandings of others and the cause of misjudgment. Many good persons and saints and martyrs have been persecuted and maligned, and afterward exonerated and even deified. God sees to it that credit is bestowed where credit is due.

In a chapter on Peace in the *Mahabharata,* it is stated that the deities call him a Brahmin who is content with any scrap of clothing, with any food, and with any shelter. Christ, too, counseled man: "Take no thought for your life, what ye shall eat; neither for the body, what ye shall put on....neither be ye of doubtful mind. For all these things do the nations of the world seek after: and your Father knoweth that ye have need of these things. But rather seek ye the kingdom of God; and all these things shall be added unto you."*

A true yogi is not willfully negligent of the duty to his body. He does not court suicide by slow starvation, nor invite pneumonia by wandering homeless, sleeping on the snow. However, a great yogi, immersed in God, has a natural aloofness toward such mundane concerns as food and home, which so occupy the worldly man attached to physical comforts.

These stanzas extol the holy mendicants of every age—such as the Himalayan yogis and great saints such as Sri Chaitanya and Francis of Assisi. The words commend, as dear to God, the God-intoxicated yogi, whatever his mode of life, who is ever content, somehow maintaining himself, living on chance gifts or meager earnings—just enough to keep body and soul together. Such a yogi is not like the lazy worldly man, for the yogi's dependence on the Divine Bounty is secure in his oneness with God. He experiences divine bliss and consequently does not seek the paltry comforts of the flesh. Engrossed in transcendental devotion he loves friends and foes alike, seeing his beloved Lord present in them all.

---

* Luke 12:22, 29–31.

VERSE 20

ye tu dharmyāmṛtam idaṁ yathoktaṁ paryupāsate
śraddhadhānā matparamā bhaktās te 'tīva me priyāḥ

But those who adoringly pursue this undying religion (dharma) as heretofore declared, saturated with devotion, supremely engrossed in Me—such devotees are extremely dear to Me.

DEAREST TO GOD, INSEPARABLE FROM HIM, are those yogis who with total devoted concentration keep their souls united to the all-sheltering, undying Spirit beyond creation—the Immutable Absolute, devoid of all delusive imaging—while worshipfully engaged in living and manifesting the eternal, immortalizing principles of God-union. Such yogis remain as one with Him, embraced in His bosom of transcendent bliss.

om tat sat iti śrīmadbhagavadgītāsu upaniṣatsu
brahmavidyāyām yogaśāstre śrīkṛṣṇārjunasaṁvāde
bhaktiyogo nāma dvādaśo 'dhyāyaḥ

Aum, Tat, Sat.
In the Upanishad of the holy Bhagavad Gita—the discourse of Lord Krishna to Arjuna, which is the scripture of yoga and the science of God-realization—this is the twelfth chapter, called "Bhakti Yoga (Union Through Devotion)."

CHAPTER XIII

The Field and the Knower of the Field

The Divine Forces That Create the Body, the Field Where Good and Evil Are Sown and Reaped

The True Nature of Matter and Spirit, Body and Soul

Characteristics of Wisdom

Spirit, as Known by the Wise

Purusha and Prakriti (Spirit and Nature)

Three Approaches to Self-realization

Liberation: Differentiating Between the Field and Its Knower

ॐ

"O Offspring of Kunti (Arjuna), by the knowers of truth, this body is called kshetra ("the field" where good and evil karma is sown and reaped); likewise, that which cognizes the field they call kshetrajna (the soul).... Also know Me to be the Kshetrajna (Perceiver) in all kshetras (the bodies evolved out of the cosmic creative principle and Nature). The understanding of kshetra and kshetrajna—that is deemed by Me as constituting true wisdom."

THE FIELD AND THE KNOWER OF THE FIELD

THE DIVINE FORCES THAT CREATE THE BODY, THE FIELD WHERE GOOD AND EVIL ARE SOWN AND REAPED

PREFACE

arjuna uvāca
prakṛtiṁ puruṣaṁ caiva kṣetraṁ kṣetrajñam eva ca
etad veditum icchāmi jñānaṁ jñeyaṁ ca keśava

Arjuna said:

O Keshava (Krishna), about Prakriti (intelligent Mother Nature) and Purusha (transcendental God the Father); about kshetra ("the field" of the body) and kshetrajna (the soul or evolver-cognizer of the bodily field); about knowledge and That which is to be known—this I crave to know.*

THIS CHAPTER ON NATURE AND SPIRIT, body and soul, is introduced by Arjuna's expressed desire to hear from Krishna in detail about earlier references to the transcendental God existing beyond vibratory creation; about Intelligent Vibratory Creation (God's Consort, Mother Nature); about *kshetra,* or the objective dream body; about the dreamer or cognizer (the soul or *kshetrajna*); and about the dream consciousness (the cosmic creative principle) that unites the dream body and the soul-dreamer.

After hearing Krishna's words concerning the union of soul and Spirit through devotion, Arjuna is perplexed as to how the various war-

* This prefatory verse is not included in some versions of the Gita. In others it is included and numbered as verse one. More commonly, it is included with no assigned number, so that the traditional total of verses remains at 700, instead of 701. In this publication, it has been designated as "Preface," introducing the subject matter of Chapter XIII.

ring elements of mind (*manas*, or sense consciousness) and discrimination (*buddhi*, or pure divine intelligence) exist within him, and how their clash obstructs divine union. The God-seeking devotee yearns to understand the mystery about outward, matter-bent Cosmic Nature and the inward pull of the transcendental Spirit; and about the sense- and Nature-identified field of the body (*kshetra*) and the Spirit-identified soul (*kshetrajna*). He desires all knowledge about them, and about the Spirit in Its unmanifested state—the supreme object of knowledge.

Metaphysically interpreted, the yogi (Arjuna) seeks to learn from the cosmic consciousness (Krishna) within him about the supreme Spirit's dual macrocosmic manifestation as Prakriti, or Mother Nature, and Purusha, or God the Father beyond creation; about Their microcosmic manifestations as the little Nature-body and the little knower—the bodily indweller, the soul; and all about the reasons for the clash between the diametrical opposites of Nature and Spirit, body and soul.

VERSE 1

śrībhagavān uvāca
idaṁ śarīraṁ kaunteya kṣetram ity abhidhīyate
etad yo vetti taṁ prāhuḥ kṣetrajña iti tadvidaḥ

The Blessed Lord replied:
O Offspring of Kunti (Arjuna), by the knowers of truth, this body is called kshetra ("the field" where good and evil karma is sown and reaped); likewise, that which cognizes the field they call kshetrajna (the soul).

THE BODY IS THE FIELD where Cosmic Nature operates; the soul, the pure reflection of God, is the knower of this field.

As a dreamer finds his consciousness transformed into dream objects and into the perceiver, so the soul (through the help of God) is the creator of its objective dream body (*kshetra*) and is also its cognizer (*kshetrajna*).

The dreamer, process of dreaming, and dream objects correspond to the soul dreamer, its dreaming power, and its dream of the objective body. The objective dream body is the field in which the soul-dreamer assembles its warring soldiers of discrimination and Nature's armies of the sense-blinded mind. The clash between these opposing forces precipitates the results of good and bad actions (karma).

The opening verse of the first chapter of the Bhagavad Gita refers in literal terms to the historical war between the wicked Kurus and the good Pandus; but this present verse clearly shows that it is man's body which is the field of battle. On this field, in an effort to gain ruling power in the bodily kingdom of the blessed soul, the ego and mind and matter-bent senses are ready to fight the armies of the soul's discriminative faculties and its powers of will and self-control. It is thus evident that Vyasa used the historical war allegorically, and that the real battle alluded to is an inner one: the spiritual war between wisdom and ignorance, the psychological combat between intelligence and mind (sense consciousness), and the bodily war between self-control and harmful sense indulgence. The conflict is delineated throughout the eighteen chapters of the Bhagavad Gita.

Significance of kshetra (the field) and kshetrajna (the knower)

These clashes between the spiritual proclivities (planted in the human body by Spirit through the soul) and the physical inclinations (instilled therein by Cosmic Nature) make the bodily territory a battlefield whereon good and bad actions are initiated, producing their inevitable results—like seeds that are sown and their fruits subsequently reaped. Therefore man's material nature imbibed from Cosmic Nature manifested in the body, the product of the cosmic creative principle, is called the field or *kshetra.* The Universal Spirit and the individualized soul of man are called the *kshetrajna:* that which witnesses, or cognizes, the field of bodily activities with its warriors for and against the ego and its forces. These designations, *kshetra* and *kshetrajna,* were given by liberated sages who, having been victorious in the battle against the sense forces, were thereby knowers of the true nature of the bodily field. Thus, it may be said, the Spirit, the soul, and all liberated beings are *kshetrajnas,* or true knowers of the body.

The desire of the ego and mind is to establish in the body the kingdom of sense pleasures. The desire of the soul is to fight the material inclinations and to establish in the body the divine kingdom of the unalloyed bliss of Spirit.

The word *Gita* means song. *Bhagavad Gita* signifies Song of the Spirit. Various scriptural commentators have pointed out that phonetically the syllables of *Gi-ta,* reversed, make the word *Ta-gi,* "the renunciant" (*tyagi*). The main theme of the Gita is the renunciation by the soul of its incarnate prodigal wanderings, by vanquishing material and physical desires and so reclaiming its blessed home in Spirit.

AN EXTENSIVE EXPLANATION IS NECESSARY to describe the true nature of the body and why it is called *kshetra,* the field.

Cosmic Nature of twenty-four elemental principles (referred to in verses 5 and 6 of this chapter)* is the manifested nature of God. When Nature first comes out of God, it is in the invisible state and is called Pure Nature, Para-Prakriti. When it becomes materialized and engrossed in external good, active, and evil manifestations that hide the underlying Spirit—the pure manifestations of Spirit's blissful nature—it is called Impure Nature, Apara-Prakriti: mysterious Mother Nature, seemingly wayward and capricious in her workings, but in reality the embodiment of law.

Spirit and Cosmic Nature (Purusha and Prakriti)

Para-Prakriti, Pure Nature, has various names: Maya; Intelligent Cosmic Nature; Intelligent Cosmic Vibration; the Word; the Holy Ghost; Mother Kali or Mother Durga, destroyers of the demon of ignorance; Prakriti or Maha-Prakriti; the Cosmic *Aum* Sound; the Cosmic Light; the Consort of God, who in conjunction with Him created the universe (the pure *kshetra*).

The Spirit beyond creation, as God, and the Spirit in creation, as *Kutastha,* are both called Purusha. The Transcendental Intelligence existing beyond creation is Para-Purusha; its intelligence reflected in creation is *Kutastha-Purusha*.†

Purusha beyond creation is also called Ishvara, or God the Creator. The Purusha in creation is called *Kutastha Chaitanya,* or immutable universal intelligence. God and His Cosmic Nature in the microcosmic form are present in the human body as the pure soul and pure human nature. The pure soul and pure human nature become distorted into the human ego and sentient human nature, owing to the temporary identification of the perfect soul with the imperfect body and its Nature-inclined penchant for sense pleasures and material enjoyments and attachments.

COSMIC NATURE OF TRIPLE QUALITIES (the three *gunas*) produces man's three bodies—physical, astral, and spiritual. The physical body is composed of sixteen gross elements: carbon, iron, calcium, etc.

---

* See also II:39, page 267 n.

† *Kutastha:* that which remains unchanged, like an anvil on which ornaments of various shapes are made. *Purusha:* that which is existent in vibratory creation, and also existent beyond it.

The astral body is made of nineteen elements: ego; mind (sense consciousness); intelligence; feeling (*chitta,* the heart principle); the crystallizing, metabolizing, assimilating, circulating, and eliminating currents; and the ten senses.

The causal body consists of thirty-five creative divine thoughts corresponding to the combined thirty-five elements of the physical and astral bodies.

Death does not liberate the soul and unite it with Spirit. The astral body of nineteen elements and the causal body within it, encasing the soul, travel together in the etheric astral world in the after-death state. But by the practice of yoga a devotee can free his soul from the coverings of all three bodies. Then his soul commingles with Spirit.

The three bodies of man—physical, astral, causal

This process of liberation from the three bodies requires time. Even the avatar Lord Jesus required three days, or three periods of spiritual effort, to emerge from his physical, astral, and causal bodies before he was completely risen, or before his soul was lifted from the three bodily encasements and united with Spirit. This is why after his death when Jesus appeared to Mary he told her not to touch him, for his resurrection was then not complete.* After he had been fully liberated from the three bodily prisons, he manifested himself to his disciples as the formless Spirit, and also appeared before them as Spirit in the corporeal form of Jesus.

Encasing the three bodies are five *koshas* or "coverings" of the soul.† Just as a sword may be put in a scabbard made of five layers of iron, copper, silver, gold, and platinum, so the soul is wrapped in a five-fold sheath.

The physical body springs from the earth covering (*annamaya kosha,* so called because from earth comes food—*anna,* "earth, food"—and food is converted into flesh). The astral body of man is covered by three *koshas:* life force (*pranamaya kosha*), mind (*manomaya kosha*), and the supramental perceptions (*jnanamaya kosha*). The causal body is covered with the bliss-*kosha* (*anandamaya kosha*).

The physical body is active during the wakeful state, working through the senses. The astral body enlivens all physical activities and

---

* "Jesus saith unto her, Touch me not; for I am not yet ascended to my Father: but go to my brethren, and say unto them, I ascend unto my Father, and your Father; and to my God, and your God" (John 20:17).

† See also I:4–6, page 63.

manifests itself during sleep as dreams. In the sleep state, physical desires and experiences materialize themselves as dream images, cognized by man's finer astral sensory powers of sight, hearing, smell, taste, and touch. The causal body is the source of consciousness and the power of thought, and predominates during dreamless, joy-filled sleep.

COUNTLESS BEINGS ARE BORN out of the one Spirit, even as one mass of dynamic current can manifest itself as millions of little electric lights. Similarly, the one soul, as the ego, manifests itself as the multifarious activities of the physical man.

The deities, differentiations of Spirit, that govern body and cosmos

Spirit, as God the Father of creation, differentiates Itself as seven principal angels who govern all creation: the macrocosmic and the microcosmic ideational, astral, and physical universes.*

In the microcosm, God as the soul acting through the physical body is called Vishva. It is the true protector and sustainer of the fleshly form (a role falsely assumed by the ego). The soul conscious of the astral body is called Taijas; it maintains the astral body and its functions. The soul conscious of the causal body is called Prajna; it supports the causal body. These three deities—Vishva, Taijas, and Prajna—as well as the physical ego, are reflections of the same soul, but act as if they were differently constituted entities.

As the soul has a physical, astral, and causal body, so God the Father, as the *Kutastha* Intelligence in creation, actively manifesting through Prakriti, puts on three cosmic bodies. The physical cosmos is the physical body of God; the astral cosmos is the subtle or astral body of God; and the causal cosmos is the ideational or causal body of God.

God as the Cosmic Builder, Virata, creates and maintains the cosmic material universe; even as the soul, as Vishva, creates and maintains the miniature universe, the physical body of man.

God as Hiranyagarbha, the Cosmic Lifetronic Engineer, creates and maintains the cosmic astral universe; even as the soul as Taijas creates and maintains the astral body of man.

God as the Cosmic Architect, Ishvara, creates and sustains the cosmic ideational universe; even as the soul as Prajna creates and maintains the ideational body of man.

These six deities are a transformation of the supremely guiding seventh "angel," Maha-Prakriti, the active expression of the *Kutastha*

* See reference to the seven angels before the throne of God, IV:25, page 480.

Intelligence, which is the pure reflection of God in creation.

Just as the various states of the United States of America are governed by the President, Senators, and Representatives, so the three macrocosmic universes (ideational, astral, and physical) and the three microcosmic universes (the ideational, astral, and physical bodies of man) are governed by God, the aforesaid six deities, Prakriti, and the Manager of Creation, *Kutastha* Intelligence. The same Intelligence is also called the Krishna or Christ Consciousness, or *Tat*. In the microcosm of the body, it is referred to as the soul.

Thus God, *Kutastha* Intelligence, Mother Nature, and the six deities are responsible for the creation and management of the entire cosmos of six divisions.

How cosmos and man's body evolve from five creative elements

COSMIC NATURE OF TRIPLE QUALITIES evolves creation through twenty-four principles, among which are the five subtle "elements" of earth, water, fire, air, and ether (the *mahatattvas*), individualized vibratory forces of the Cosmic Creative Vibration.

By the intelligent mixture of the five cosmic elements acted upon by Prakriti and God, the universes are born. Spirit and Cosmic Nature materialize intelligence; the various forms of creative intelligence materialize the five subtle cosmic elements (*mahatattvas*) into the finer-than-atomic forces of lifetrons, and lifetrons into electrons, protons, and atoms. Nature first gives rise to the intelligent vibratory ether, the subtle background on which all other vibrations interplay. Ether in turn gives rise to intelligent cosmic energy, *prana* or lifetrons. This gives rise to the cosmic radiations and to electrons, protons, and atoms.* The gaseous atoms are the link be-

* The Sanskrit word *akasha,* ether or space, derives from *ā,* "towards" and *kaśa,* "to be visible, to appear." *Akasha* is the subtle "background" against which everything in the material universe becomes perceptible. "Space gives dimension to objects; ether separates the images," Paramahansa Yogananda said. See also page 40 n.

In the context of this Gita chapter on "The Field and the Knower of the Field," it is interesting to note that recent discoveries are leading scientists to an understanding of space that parallels the *akasha* of Hindu cosmology—a matrix of vibratory forces wherein the world of "real" particles intersects with a vast sea of "virtual" particles. "Empty space does not appear a very promising subject for study, yet it holds the key to a full understanding of the forces of nature," writes Paul Davies, Ph.D., in *Superforce* (New York: Simon and Schuster, 1984). "When physicists began to study the quantum theory of fields, they discovered that a vacuum was not at all what it had long appeared to be—just empty space devoid of substance and activity....What might appear to be empty space is a seething ferment of virtual particles. A vacuum is not inert and

tween energy and form; from the combination of atoms, fluids ("water") are formed. From fluid elements sprang solids ("earth"). Thus are the five cosmic elements, by the secret workings of Spirit and Nature, converted into the colossal universe and into the little physical body of man—gross matter that appears as solid (earth), liquid (water), light and heat (fire), gaseous (air), and etheric (ether). Therefore, the universe and the little cosmos, the human body, are all made out of five elements, Cosmic Nature, and Spirit.

The physical universe responds to the influence of the five elements, even as does the human body. The cosmos, the physical body of God, speaks and hears through the vibratory ether (with its quality of sound and radiating motion); feels and grasps through the vibratory air (with its quality of feeling arising from contact or resistance and its transverse or general motion); sees and has progressive motion through vibratory fire or cosmic light (with its qualities of color or form and expansive upward motion); tastes and reproduces through the vibratory water element (with its qualities of flavor and downward motion or contraction); smells and eliminates through the vibratory earth element (with its qualities of odor and cohesion).

How the body is created by the five elements in conjunction with God, the Supreme Power, is described next.

The good (sattvic) cosmic quality in vibratory ether produced in man the ear, and the sense of hearing. From the good quality in vibra-

---

featureless, but alive with throbbing energy and vitality. A 'real' particle such as an electron must always be viewed against this background...."

"The field theories of modern physics force us to abandon the classical distinction between material particles and the void," writes Fritjof Capra in *The Tao of Physics* (Boston: Shambhala, Third Edition, 1991). "Einstein's field theory of gravity and quantum field theory both show that particles cannot be separated from the space surrounding them. On the one hand, they determine the structure of that space, whilst on the other hand they cannot be regarded as isolated entities, but have to be seen as condensations of a continuous field which is present throughout space....

"'The field exists always and everywhere,' says Austrian physicist W. Thirring. 'It can never be removed. It is the carrier of all material phenomena....Being and fading of particles are merely forms of motion of the field.'

"The distinction between matter and empty space finally had to be abandoned when it became evident that virtual particles can come into being spontaneously out of the void, and vanish again into the void....According to field theory, events of that kind happen all the time. The vacuum is far from empty. On the contrary, it contains an unlimited number of particles which come into being and vanish without end....The 'physical vacuum'...contains the potentiality for all forms of the particle world. These forms, in turn, are not independent physical entities but merely transient manifestations of the underlying Void....The discovery of the dynamic quality of the vacuum is seen by many physicists as one of the most important findings of modern physics." (*Publisher's Note*)

tory air and life current the human skin was created, and the sense of touch. The good quality of the radiating fire energy produced the eyes, and the power of sight. The good quality in the vibratory water element produced the tongue, and the power of taste. The good cosmic quality present in the earth produced the nose, and the sense of smell. The sattvic quality in all these five elements, with their vibrations, produced the motion picture of the human body, reflecting mind, intelligence, feeling, and ego.

Similarly, from the cosmic activating (rajasic) quality present in the ether was produced the power of speech and the organs of speech. The activating quality present in the vibratory air and life current produced the hands and grasping power. The activating quality of the fire element produced the feet and the power of locomotion. The activating quality in the water element produced the genital organs and the power of reproduction. The activating quality in the earth element produced the rectal organ and the power of excretion. Through the rajasic conglomeration of the five vibratory elements in their finer form, the five *pranas* or life currents emerged.*

The gross (tamasic) quality present in the five elements produced the physical atoms of the body. Through the instrumentality of the five pranic life currents, gross matter (the physical body) is materialized in solid, liquid, gaseous, fiery, and etheric form, enlivened by its subtle astral counterparts.

The astral and causal forces behind physical creation of the body

ANY GOOD MEDICAL BOOK DEALING with the human body describes in detail how the physical body is created according to the known laws of Nature. Through physical phenomena that can be observed through a microscope, the infinitesimal male spermatozoon unites with the microscopic female ovum, and an embryo starts to grow. The embryo gradually develops into a fetus. During a gestation period of nine months, the fetus develops into a fully formed infant body. The baby is born, and passes through childhood, youth, and maturity; after some sixty years or so the body begins to disintegrate and finally dies. This is the simple testimony of the senses as to the phenomenon called life. But this miracle of being could not hap-

* The sensory organs and powers of perception and action are in their "finer form," or subtle astral manifestation, until by further action of Nature—through the five elements and the five *pranas* under the influence of the tamasic quality—they are provided with an outer or gross atomic covering of a physical body.

pen except for the empowering presence of the soul invisibly inherent within the observable physiology of conception and growth.

The soul, with a blueprint of a human being's astral and causal bodies, disengaged from a previous, deceased physical body, enters the new mother's womb through a flash of life current that manifests during the conjunction of a spermatozoon and the mother's ovum cell. The soul, present from the moment of conception, directs continuously the ensuing growth from the conjoined microscopic sperm-ovum cell into the body of the baby, and then the adult, according to the good, or active, or evil karmic blueprint formed through past-life actions and fitting the present heredity.

Without conscious intelligent guidance by the soul, modified by prenatal karma and the free will of the ego, the body could not grow from a microscopic germ into a symmetrical human form. The normal body shows the presence of intelligent design by the proper growth of eyes, ears, nose, head, limbs, and organs. Without this inner guidance the human form might develop into a monstrosity; e.g., the hands and feet might grow disproportionately, perhaps spreading out like the limbs of a tree.

The body grows from its minuscule origin into a full-sized human form by cellular multiplication. Though the nervous, epithelial, muscular, and osseous tissues of the body are highly differentiated, all are made from the same substance: small cellular particles. It is the soul behind the five pranic life forces that commands certain cells to be soft brain tissue or elastic skin tissue or strong muscular tissue or hard bone tissue.

As bricks could not arrange themselves into a house without the aid of an intelligent builder, so the original sperm-and-ovum-united cell could not multiply itself into a characteristically human habitation without the supervision of Intelligence.* Merely through good food chemicals, human cells could not dispose themselves to form tendons, nerve tissues, bones, and different organs, nor install the sense tele-

* Since 1952, when it was discovered that the DNA molecule is the basic mechanism of heredity, scientists have made remarkable advances in understanding the genetic codes that determine the development and the idiosyncracies of each human body. The workings of the intelligence within DNA itself, however, is not yet understood—how it is able to transmit the necessary information that guides the formation, at just the right time throughout life, of the myriad specialized proteins that compose all of the body's organs and tissues and make possible such complex and varied processes as growth, reproduction, immune response, and brain function. (*Publisher's Note*)

phonic system to serve all parts of the wonderfully intricate physical mansion for the soul.

Hence it is evident that all the tissues, made of cells, have been intelligently constructed into the human body. As the roof of a house could not be supported without walls or beams, so the bone-rafters of the body are provided to prevent it from rolling around like a jellyfish. As a cement room is made of small particles of cement, so the human body is constructed of small particles of organized cells. Analyzed further, the cells are understood to be made of even smaller particles: atoms, composed of electrons, protons, neutrons, positrons, and mesons, whirling in the relatively immense space within each atom. The proportionate structure of the atom is often compared to that of a solar system.

From this standpoint it is seen that the human body is a product of minute atoms and subtle forces. Scientists say that if the space in the atoms of a physical body weighing 150 pounds could be removed, the constituent atoms of the body would be condensed into a single invisible particle that would still weigh 150 pounds.

Physicists no longer define a "body" as matter but as an electromagnetic wave. Why then does the body appear as solid flesh instead of being invisible like an atom? The answer is that the soul commands the atoms to assume the appearance of flesh; even as a moving-picture beam projects on the screen, by the intelligent design of the film producer, a seemingly substantial replica of the human body. Through a mental film of the physical form and by electroatomic energy, the soul produces a material human body, real not only to man's sight and hearing but to his smell, taste, and touch.

By further analysis the yogis of India found that the electroatomic body of man is made of finer, intelligent lifetrons that are condensations of the thoughtrons of God. The structure of man and of all creation is a result of the vibrations of the Divine Mind. The Bible says: "God said, Let there be light: and there was light."* That is, the Lord's consciousness intelligently wove light (vibrations of thought and life force) to form the phenomenal world of minerals, vegetation, animals, and mankind. According to the yogi, therefore, the human body is made of the relativities of God's thought.

THE FOLLOWING ILLUSTRATION WILL SHOW how man can vibrate his unruffled consciousness into thought particles and produce the image

* Genesis 1:3.

of a dream man or a dream world in exact detailed duplication of a living man or of the world itself. A determined person can make the following experiment successfully.

If he lies down on the bed when he is very sleepy and analyzes his sleep state, he will find the sensations of bed, body, breath, and thoughts dissolving into the one peaceful perception of drowsiness. He should consciously keep perceiving this peaceful state of semiconscious sleep, wherein all sensations and restless thoughts are dissolved. In this state he will find his pure consciousness very powerful and plastic, ready to be molded into the image of a visualized body or of any other visualized object.

Thought in the restless state loses its potency. When it is concentrated, it can mold an idea into an actual dream image. If the man who is consciously enjoying the semiconscious state of sleep passively, with calm concentration visualizes the image of a man or any other object, he will then be able to materialize that specific visualization into a specific dream image. In this way the experimenter, by concentration and visualization, can materialize a complex thought-pattern of a man into the complex image of a man.

Similarly, by dissolution of restless thoughts and by consolidation of attention on a mental replica of the world, with sun or moon and stars, a man can produce a dream image of a sunlit or moonlit world. A dreamer in the land of sleep can view a whole world made of the different elements, manifesting various forms of light, forest fires, bursts of atomic bombs, and all the sensory-motor experiences of the objective world. Man, endowed with mind, can create a dream replica of anything in creation. Even as God by His mind power materializes His consciousness into the cosmic dream world, so man, made in His image, can also materialize ideas into a miniature dream world.

Origin of relativistic creation: division of consciousness into knower, knowing, and known

When a person sleeps peacefully, or remains calm without perceiving any thoughts or sensations, he then has within him, as one, the three elements of consciousness: knower, knowing, and known. When he awakens, his consciousness is divided into three factors—the perceiving physical ego, its perceptions, and its objects of perception (the human body and the world). Similarly, when a man dreams, he divides his consciousness triply: as the dreaming ego, the dream consciousness, and the dream objects. In dreamland, the dream consciousness of man, by the law of relativity, can create a complete replica of a human being that thinks, feels, and engages in actions.

In the dream, the dreamer is aware of ego consciousness and of every process of subconscious experience, as well as of sensations of cold or heat; pleasure or pain; perception of the weather—rainy, hot, cold, or snowy; perception of painful diseases; perception of babies born or men dying; and sensory perceptions of earth, water, fire, and air.

The dreamer can perceive his physical ego as the doer of all the actions of his dream body. Or he can dissolve his dream ego into a perception of the blessed soul by dream ecstasy; or by higher dream ecstasy can feel his soul to be one with the ineffable Spirit. Likewise, the dreaming ego is able to perceive, will, feel, and reason; it can be aware of fear, anger, love, and tranquility; and of sensations of sight, hearing, smell, taste, and touch.

The dreaming ego can experience all the complex processes of thought or emotions or sensations. It can feel the objectified dream world as made of the elements of earth, water, fire, air, and ether. The dreamer can see colors with his dream eyes, hear music with his dream ears, smell fragrances with his dream nose, and taste food with his dream mouth.

He can embrace dream friends with his dream arms; he can walk with his dream feet on the dream earth; he can see dream smoke coming from a dream fire; he can swim with his dream solid body in a dream lake; he can feel the cool or warm dream breeze blowing on his dream face; he can enjoy the changes of dream winter, spring, summer, or autumn. He can experience poverty or prosperity in the dream world. He can perceive the manifestations of peace in happy dream countries. He can see the flashing of shellfire and the ravages of dream-world wars.

In the relative time of thought perceptions, a dreamer can make world tours by dream planes or dream ships. In the dreamland he can experience births and rebirths. If he is spiritually advanced he is able to see also the projection of astral persons and worlds.

But when the dreamer wakes up he realizes that all his dream experiences were made of the relativities of his one consciousness, materialized by the power of mind into visible dream images. Similarly, a man may perceive this world as dream experiences of the subjective ego. A Self-realized saint sees the universe as manifestations of life as suggested by the omnipresent Spirit.

The processes of mind, the perceptions of sensations and sense objects, and of the objectified dream body in the material world of solid, liquid, and gaseous substances—all are dreams of God introduced into man's consciousness.

By analysis we come to a realization that, in dreamland, man can create a replica of any human body, even as in the dream cosmos God creates man. The human body, of course, is not made of man's dream consciousness but is an expression of the Lord's dream consciousness. Here is a great analogy between man and God. The Unmanifested is spoken of as ever-existing, ever-conscious, ever-new Bliss, in which the subjective Spirit and Its perception of bliss are dissolved into One. When Spirit creates, It becomes the all-perceptive God that, though inactive beyond creation, is active in creation as the Subjective Immanence. God's consciousness existing beyond creation and in creation is His process of cognition; and the cosmic vibration materialized into the ideational, astral, and physical cosmoses is His objective body.

Man's creative consciousness is analogous to that of God

The Lord remains awake and restful in pure bliss in the vibrationless realm; He enjoys conscious sleep in the ideational world; He dreams in the astral and the physical universes. Similarly, in superconsciousness man awakens in the bliss of the soul. In the state of deep dreamless sleep, he is revivified by the joy-filled peace of the causal world. In the ordinary sleep state he creates dreams in the subconsciously perceived astral world. And in the so-called wakeful state he dreams the gross pictures of the body and the world.

As Spirit in the unmanifested state can keep the three elements of Its existence—knower, knowing, and known—as one perception of bliss, so man by yoga practice can dissolve the three processes of his existence into the one perception of bliss. When he is able to do this at will, he develops the power of the Creator. In the state of ecstasy he realizes that, by concentrated thought separated by relativity into the concentrator, concentrating, and the object of concentration, he can create anything as a visible object.

When a person by unshakable concentration can visualize any image or object with closed eyes, he gradually learns to do the same with open eyes. Then by further development of concentration, he can connect with God's all-powerful consciousness and can materialize his thought into an object, perceived not only by himself but by others also. In the same way that Christ created a new bodily life-consciousness in Lazarus, so Lahiri Mahasaya performed many miracles demonstrating the materializing power of mind. In *Autobiography of a Yogi* it is related how my master, Sri Yukteswarji, witnessed the miracle of flesh growing around his thin body by the command of his guru-preceptor, Lahiri Mahasaya. My Master also witnessed the resurrection of his dead friend Rama through Lahiri Mahasaya's intervention.

In the objective world there are many wonders that God brought into being to arouse man's spiritual curiosity about the Creator. A certain kind of snail, for instance, put alone into a small body of water, will be found to multiply itself by a mysterious process quite unlike that by which human beings are reproduced. The resurrection plant, when thoroughly dry and apparently dead, can be immersed in water and in a few hours will become alive and green.

How man can become free from the cosmic dream of delusion

As a person under hypnotic influence can be made to act as if he were a different personality, so God evolves souls out of Himself and hypnotizes them by delusion (*maya*) into perceiving themselves as encased in animal or human bodies. The hypnotized person cannot get out of his unreal state without being dehypnotized. By wisdom and self-analysis and by the grace of God, man can get himself dehypnotized from cosmic delusion and forever forsake his recurring dreams of incarnations. He can then return to the perception of the pure soul, united to the Spirit in the dreamless state of blessedness.

During sleep a man rests in his astral body, perhaps dreaming of himself as occupying another dream body. When he wakes up, he dreams of the presence of his physical body. When he dies, he forgets the material dream, including the dream of a physical form, and lives in his dream astral body (encasing his causal body). At the time of physical reincarnation, he again clothes his subtle astral body (and indwelling causal body) with a dream overcoat of gross flesh.

During the first state of liberation the soul of man emerges successively from his three microcosmic bodies—physical, astral, and causal. He experiences the triune physical, astral, and causal macrocosms as his own Self. During supreme liberation the soul and Spirit become one. In that state the soul finds itself as Spirit, transcending even the three macrocosmic embodiments.

In summary, the root cause of the dream creation of the human body and the world consists of the knower (*kshetrajna*), the knowing (*jnana*), and the object known (*kshetra*). In the unmanifested state of Spirit no creation is possible. In the created world, the knower is God;

the object known is the objective cosmos; and His consciousness within it is the connective element between the subjective God and the objective cosmos. The human body is the miniature cosmos. The bodily field is the object, or the *kshetra;* and the soul within it (cognized by the liberated man) is the *kshetrajna;* the body and its knower are linked by the process of the knower's cognition.

To dismiss in fact the body as a dream of God is possible only to men of divine realization—those who have learned the power of visualization and of materialization and dematerialization of thought forms. When the mind becomes powerful like the Creator's, one can materialize or dematerialize his body or a universe, knowing them to be dream images of thought.

One must therefore practice yoga, the science of divine union; for it is by realizing his oneness with God that the devotee frees himself from the cosmic dream, and knows that dream as made sheerly of God's consciousness.

VERSE 2

kṣetrajñaṁ cāpi māṁ viddhi sarvakṣetreṣu bhārata
kṣetrakṣetrajñayor jñānaṁ yat taj jñānaṁ mataṁ mama

O Descendant of Bharata (Arjuna), also know Me to be the Kshetrajna (Perceiver) in all kshetras (the bodies evolved out of the cosmic creative principle and Nature). The understanding of kshetra and kshetrajna—that is deemed by Me as constituting true wisdom.

True wisdom: understanding how the One Consciousness becomes all things

THIS STANZA REFERS TO THE IMMANENT omniscient nature of Spirit. It is He alone who is manifested as countless souls. A yogi is a possessor of true wisdom who understands that God is the only *Kshetrajna,* the one Perceiver in creation, singularly and in all souls encased in physical bodies. God is the only subjective, perceptive, and objective principle existing in and manifesting as the cosmic dream creation. It is the Lord Himself who becomes all subjective dream beings. He is the cognitive principle in all sentient creatures and in everything else. He also manifests Himself as all dream objects and as the dream bodies in creation. The understanding of these truths constitutes true wisdom.

The human mind is conditioned to believe in the testimony of the senses, with their substantive "proof" that "I" exist—"I" perceive and feel and think. It is therefore confounded by the paradox that this subjective "I" is naught else but He, the omniscient Spirit. If the likes of man were indeed God, then God Himself would be imperfect and limited. The mind thus concludes that since God is perfect and man imperfect, there must be two subjective principles rather than one. How then do the scriptures attest that all is Brahman, and "thou art That" (*Tat tvam asi*)?

Something cannot come from nothing; nor can it be resolved into nothingness. Everything that exists has to be supported by an enduring substance that survives the transformations of change. That which changes and yet is permanent cannot be considered finite, for that substance remains the same through all processes of change. But the change itself, because it is not constant and does not remain the same, is therefore finite, limited by the factors of form, time, and space.

For example, water can be heated and transformed into invisible vapor. When cooled, the water reappears as steam and then liquid, which can be refrigerated and turned into solid ice. The ice can be melted into water again. The water thus passes through different changes and forms, while yet essentially remaining the same. It is the process of change that is limited; the resultant forms will not survive changes. The motion in time and space that we call change is not lasting, for it does not survive time. In this world of relativity, nothing is exactly the same as it was a moment ago. It is said that one cannot bathe twice in the same stream. Everything in the universe is a stream of relativity that is in perpetual flux. In even inert objects, the constituent atoms are in constant motion, and some decay or change is taking place.

Just as sensory perception tells us that water (or what a scientist would refer to as the molecular structure of water) is the enduring basis of invisible vapor, steam, and solid ice, so yogis who have penetrated to the core of origin know the phenomenon of manifestation is founded on an omnipresent, eternal consciousness. It is the cosmic consciousness of the Infinite that undergoes change into finite permutations, yet remains ever the same during Its cosmic metamorphosis.

WHY THEN ARE SENTIENT BEINGS so seemingly far removed from their perfect Essence? Why do beings not know they are Spirit and behave accordingly? The motion of change in the Changeless presupposes cause and effect, relativity—one idea or force that produces an effect that consequently interacts to influence a variant outcome—in an endless proliferation of variables. God's will to create is the original Cause. The potentials or principles to produce the many from the One through interacting relativity are God's creative power, or *shakti,* Maha-Prakriti. The conglomerate workings of these principles are collectively called *maya,* the cosmic delusion of multiplicity.

How the ever perfect soul takes on the delusions of the ego

Maya is a cosmic hypnosis that veils the Singular Reality and imposes the suggestions of manifestation. The cosmic consciousness of the One Perceiver, experiencing these transformations of *maya,* becomes correspondingly individualized as many souls. The soul, experiencing and interacting with the workings and manifestations of cosmic *maya,* has its own identity, or *avidya,* individual delusion, and thereby becomes the body-identified ego. Like its essence, Spirit, the soul is ever pure and unchanged. But when expressing outwardly, it is subject to the laws, or principles, of manifestation. Attuned to the divine intelligence of the indwelling soul, the resultant being is pure, noble, and wise. But the more the consciousness yields to the tangled interworkings of Nature operating through the sensory mind, the more limited and deluded the ego becomes. But even if it sinks to the depths of ignorance and evil, the consciousness never loses its divine soul potential. Eventually, the inner magnetism of Spirit will cause that individualized consciousness to seek the way to ascension through the choice of right action that links it to the uplifting divine power inherent in Nature's laws.

A hypnotist may suggest to a subject that he is seeing a ferocious tiger. The subject sees the beast and shrieks in terror. Now the hypnotist only suggested the vision of the tiger, but did not ask the subject to be afraid of it. The fear that the subject felt was self-suggested and came from his own being, from the potentials of emotion and experience within him. Similarly, God, the Master Hypnotist, through His power of *maya* has suggested to individualized souls to visualize the universe with all its intricacies and details. The perceptions of individualized consciousness, being personalized by *avidya* (individual delusion), become elaborated by feeling. Under the influence of the sensory mind, feeling expresses itself as emotions—such as fear, attachment, repulsion, desire. The Master Hypnotist did not suggest that individualized souls be afraid or courageous, miserable or happy. These are their own creations.

God created maya; man created misery, fear, and attachment

Emotions are personalized thoughts reacting to the materialized ideas of God's creation. These sensory-conditioned feelings are man's own ideas, the outcome of his individualized interrelation with the materialized ideas of God.

Ideas are finite; they are fleeting, moving along and changing in time and space. But their underlying substance, the enduring consciousness of one's existence, which perceives and cognizes the ideas—and which carries on the diverse operations of willing, imagining, remembering them—is constant. As ego, manipulated by the sense mind, it reacts emotionally and unwisely in response to the circumambient relativity. But when the consciousness is freed from the workings of Nature's phenomena, it shines forth as the soul, the perfect reflection of the omnipresent, omniscient Spirit. Thus is the One in the many, and the many in the One. Both exist, but as eternal and relative states of the One Consciousness.

THE TRUE NATURE OF MATTER AND SPIRIT, BODY AND SOUL

VERSES 3–4

tat kṣetraṁ yac ca yādṛk ca yadvikāri yataś ca yat
sa ca yo yatprabhāvaś ca tat samāsena me śṛṇu (3)

ṛṣibhir bahudhā gītaṁ chandobhir vividhaiḥ pṛthak
brahmasūtrapadaiś caiva hetumadbhir viniścitaiḥ (4)

Hear from Me briefly about the kshetra, its attributes, its cause-and-effect principle, and its distorting influences; and also who He (the Kshetrajna) is, and the nature of His powers—truths that have been distinctly celebrated by the rishis in many ways: in various chants in the Vedas and in the definitive reasoned analyses of aphorisms about Brahman.

MAY EVERY DEVOTEE LISTEN with full attention, as did Arjuna, to the Lord's exposition of *Kshetra* and *Kshetrajna:* Prakriti and Purusha, Matter and Spirit!

VERSES 5–6

mahābhūtāny ahaṁkāro buddhir avyaktam eva ca
indriyāṇi daśaikaṁ ca pañca cendriyagocarāḥ (5)

icchā dveṣaḥ sukhaṁ duḥkhaṁ saṁghātaś cetanā dhṛtiḥ
etat kṣetraṁ samāsena savikāram udāhṛtam (6)

Succinctly described, the kshetra and its modifications are composed of the Unmanifested (Mula-Prakriti, undifferentiated Nature), the five cosmic elements, the ten senses and the one sense mind, intelligence (discrimination), egoism, the five objects of the senses; desire, hate, pleasure, pain, aggregation (the body, a combination of diverse forces), consciousness, and persistence.

STANZA 5 ENUMERATES THE TWENTY-FOUR principles of creation as expounded in the Sankhya philosophy of India.* In the book of Revelation in the Christian Bible these principles are referred to as the "twenty-four elders."†

Inherent in Mula-Prakriti, unmanifested or undifferentiated Nature, are the potentials of manifested subjective consciousness: *chitta* (feeling); *ahamkara* (ego); *buddhi* (discriminative intelligence); and *manas* (sense mind). Thence arise the potentials of objective manifestation: the *mahatattvas* (five subtle vibratory elements of earth, water, fire, air, and ether) and the evolutes of *indriyas* (five instruments of perception and five of action), and of the five *pranas* (life forces that together with the five subtle vibratory elements, under the influence of the three *gunas—sattva, rajas,* and *tamas*—produce the "five objects of the senses," first in their subtle form, and finally as gross matter, the "aggregation" or material form of these diverse forces).

The 24 principles of creation that evolve the "field" of body and cosmos

The aggregate of the twenty-four distorting cosmic qualities creates the objective *kshetra,* cosmic physical nature; and the aggregate of the microcosmic delusive twenty-four qualities produces the human body, the miniature object (*kshetra*). All the twenty-four qualities belong to the domain of cosmic nature and the human body, and not to God, Purusha, or the *Kshetrajna*—the subjective Knower of the objective cosmos.

---

* See also II:39. † Revelation 4:4.

The macrocosmic *kshetra*, nature, is the cosmic body of God through which His consciousness operates. The microcosmic *kshetra*, the human body, is the operating vehicle of the soul. The only reality is God and His reflection, the human soul: the two *Kshetrajnas*, the subjective principle in the cosmos and man.

But the objective principle, cosmic nature and the bodily vehicle, assert their seeming reality through *maya* and its laws of relativity—the power of God and His reflected souls by which pure consciousness becomes divided into myriad forms. The macrocosmic and microcosmic objective principles, the two *kshetras*, are therefore spoken of as the modifications or distortions of reality. The shadows of relativities and attributes transform the light of God into the phenomenal forms of objective cosmic nature and the objective bodily vehicle.

It is said that none can realize what Prakriti Herself is; She is knowable only by the effects that evolve from Her. Thus is Prakriti here called "the Unmanifested," *avyakta*, the indescribable state of undifferentiated Primordial Matter. From this Unmanifested comes manifestation. Prakriti is therefore both the cause and the effect of the Lord's triune macrocosmic and microcosmic creation (causal, astral, and material).

Pure and impure Nature (Para-Prakriti and Apara-Prakriti)

When the transcendental God first evolved intelligent Cosmic Nature, the Holy Ghost, or Para-Prakriti, He did so in unseen pure causal and astral forms imbued with the twenty-four subtle qualities—the essential potentials of manifestation. This consort of God, through further action of *maya*, cosmic delusion, became materialized as the imperfect God-eclipsing physical cosmos; the consort is then called the Apara-Prakriti, or Impure Nature, which deludes all God's creatures with the triple qualities (*tamas, rajas*, and *sattva*) and with desire and hate (attraction and revulsion), sense pleasures, and suffering, experienced through material consciousness, or feeling.

Pure Cosmic Nature, the Holy Ghost, or Para-Prakriti, is a being—a conscious intelligent force. As the consort, or creative aspect, of God it possesses ego-consciousness, cosmic intelligence, mind, feeling, the five cosmic elements of ether, air, fire, water, and earth; the macrocosmic five senses of knowledge (visual, auditory, olfactory, gustatory, and tactual perceptions); the five instruments of cosmic activity (macrocosmic vibratory power, grasping motion, forward motion, creative power, and eliminative power); and the five cosmic life forces that inform all matter—the crystallizing, metabolizing, assimilating, circulating, and eliminating currents.

Cosmic ether, cosmic air, cosmic fire, cosmic moisture, and cosmic matter are called *mahabhutas* or *mahatattvas*. They are the basics of manifestation, the causal substance of the "objects of the senses." The *mahabhutas* remain undistorted in the unmanifested state of subtle Pure Nature. But at the time of creation they are roused and activated by the three *gunas,* producing the ten *indriyas* (senses) of perception and action and the *pranas* that inform matter. (See XIII:1, pages 864 ff.)

The five *pranas* are Nature's subtle or astral forces of life. On the material plane they inform and enliven matter. The crystallizing force keeps the earth atoms in existence. Through the assimilating current the earth receives into its soil the forms of all vegetation, animals, and human beings. The circulating current keeps the life force flowing through the earth atoms. Through the metabolizing current the "tissues" of the earth become differentiated into rocks and minerals, vegetation, and animal and human bodies. With the eliminating current the earth is kept purified.*

The nineteen subtle principles in pure Cosmic Nature, together with the five invisible great elements, become materialized into the as-

---

* The following passage from an article by Gerrit Verschuur in *Science Digest* (July 1981) summarizes the biological viewpoint that the earth, and indeed the universe, can rightly be considered living beings:

"No one would question the statement that the human body is a living entity, consisting of countless cells, each of which is alive, or that these cells join forces to form organs, which are also alive. It is not too great a step from acknowledging that the body is alive to accepting what researchers call the Gaia hypothesis: the notion that the earth's biosphere plus its atmosphere equals a living entity. Within a protective membrane of atmosphere, earth's life forms and that atmosphere are continuously sharing chemical products—as do the parts of the body—in order to maintain an ecological, *living* balance.

"Can our planet be considered a living thing? Where do we draw the line between living and nonliving? Scientists seem to agree that all living systems reproduce and that they all use energy; they take in nutrients, process them, extract energy, and excrete waste products. We can easily observe this process at work in our fellow humans; it is also going on at the cellular level and at the planetary level. The earth absorbs sunlight; a waste product, heat, is radiated out into space. This conversion of energy or substances from one form to another in order to maintain the functioning of the organism is its metabolism. The earth has a metabolism; it is alive. And if the earth is alive, why not the Universe?

"The impulse to quickly reply 'Impossible!' is the result, perhaps, of human prejudices about time. Because we are so used to measuring living things in terms of decades or centuries, we balk at the idea of metabolic processes taking billions and billions of years. But the millennia of our time scale are simply ticks of the cosmic clock. Picture

tral cosmos. Up to this point, Cosmic Nature remains in the pure state, creating wonderful astral beings and objects. But as soon as pure Cosmic Nature, through the further action of *maya*, is projected as the gross material universe, Nature becomes impure, Apara-Prakriti, hiding and distorting the presence of God, the *Kshetrajna*, the supreme Purusha or Paramatman or Para-Brahma. Thus, Cosmic Physical Nature is the distorted *kshetra*, the modified or differentiated objective universe.

Similarly, the miniature embodiment of Nature, the form of man, the little *kshetra,* or modified Nature, contains ego, intelligence, mind, and feeling, the ten senses, the five life forces, and the five objects of the senses (bodily ether, air, heat, blood, and flesh, materializations of the *mahatattvas* of ether, air, fire, water, and earth). All these qualities and elements compose and influence the mortal man and not the soul.

The objective human body, with its subjective life and consciousness, is not only a distortion of the microcosmic twenty-four essential attributes of Cosmic Nature but becomes further deluded by human desires, abhorrence, pleasure, pain, and material consciousness.

Dhriti, persistence or fortitude, is the principle by which the various components of man's body and mind are unified.

---

an astronomical phenomenon occurring on a more human time scale, and the idea of a living Universe becomes easier to envision and accept. Letting one millennium equal one minute, think about the evolution of a star. What do you see? A cloud of hydrogen gas is sucked into a compact core and then transformed into heavier atoms, cooked by the nuclear blaze at the star's center. The heavier atoms are excreted in the form of stellar winds or a violent stellar explosion. Like other living things, stars reproduce; their waste products are fed into other regions of space, where they become part of new contracting clouds destined to become stars, within which energy will be exchanged and still more waste products excreted. Our speeded-up view of what happens in space reveals constant evolution and movement.

"These little life centers, these cells we call stars, are part of larger living organisms, the galaxies. The nucleus of a galaxy can be likened to a heart. We know that it pumps 'plasma'—hydrogen gas with some impurities ('nutrients')—out into the surrounding 'veins,' the spiral arms, streamers of intergalactic hydrogen, that reach out and touch neighboring galaxies. And if our Universe is made up of living galaxies, is it not, then, alive?

"To mitochondria and bacteria, the organism that is their host is as vast and mysterious as the Universe is to us. Like the organelles, we may be part of some as yet incomprehensible living thing made up of organisms on all scales: galaxies, gas clouds, star clusters, stars, planets, animals, cells, and microorganisms.

"We must think seriously about relocating the line between living and nonliving organisms. I no longer believe that it is at the edge of the body's epidermis or at the edge of the earth's atmosphere. It is at the edge of the Universe." (*Publisher's Note*)

The body is called *sanghata,* "aggregation," because it is a conglomeration of the diverse twenty-four elements and the qualities that arise from them. Hence man is the *kshetra,* field, on which take place the wars of passions and the unpredictable invasions of different moods and thoughts. The goal of the yogi is to resolve his complexities into Simplicity by arousing his memory of the changeless soul.

CHARACTERISTICS OF WISDOM

VERSES 7–11

amānitvam adambhitvam ahiṁsā kṣāntir ārjavam
ācāryopāsanaṁ śaucaṁ sthairyam ātmavinigrahaḥ (7)

indriyārtheṣu vairāgyam anahaṁkāra eva ca
janmaṁṛtyujarāvyādhiduḥkhadoṣānudarśanam (8)

asaktir anabhiṣvaṅgaḥ putradāragṛhādiṣu
nityaṁ ca samacittatvam iṣṭāniṣṭopapattiṣu (9)

mayi cānanyayogena bhaktir avyabhicāriṇī
viviktadeśasevitvam aratir janasaṁsadi (10)

adhyātmajñānanityatvaṁ tattvajñānārthadarśanam
etaj jñānam iti proktam ajñānaṁ yad ato 'nyathā (11)

(7) (The sage is marked by) humility, lack of hypocrisy, harmlessness, forgivingness, uprightness, service to the guru, purity of mind and body, steadfastness, self-control;
(8) Indifference to sense objects, absence of egotism, understanding of the pain and evils (inherent in mortal life): birth, illness, old age, and death;
(9) Nonattachment, nonidentification of the Self with such as one's children, wife, and home; constant equal-mindedness in desirable and undesirable circumstances;
(10) Unswerving devotion to Me by the yoga of nonseparativeness, resort to solitary places, avoidance of the company of worldly men;

(11) Perseverance in Self-knowledge; and meditative perception of the object of all learning—the true essence or meaning therein. All these qualities constitute wisdom; qualities opposed to them constitute ignorance.

HAVING DESCRIBED THE NATURE of *kshetra,* "the field" of cosmic nature and the body, Krishna now speaks of *jnana,* true knowledge or wisdom—the embodiment of which is perceived in the sage who manifests its qualities.

Pure Cosmic Nature (Para-Prakriti) in the causal and astral universes is the abode of all the elevating qualities of wisdom. These pure qualities become manifest in the superior causal and astral beings, and also in highly advanced spiritual persons in the physical realm.

A yogi who is filled with divine wisdom is supremely content—no cries of an ego rile him to desire fickle human honors; the least or the highest place is the same to him, for he seeks only the recognition of God. A hypocrite is noisily verbose and pretentious in feigning to be what he is not; while the wholly unostentatious man of wisdom, through no effort of his own, is everywhere recognized for his nobility. Seeing God in all, the divine man has no propensity to willfully do harm to any being; he is forbearing and forgiving in the hope that the wrongdoer will embrace the opportunity to correct himself. Wedded to truth, the sage is upright and undeceiving—distinctive in righteous honesty and sincerity. He recognizes the guru as the manifested messenger of God and the channel of salvation, and so is devoted and supremely serviceful and obedient to the preceptor in every way. Filled with the purity of wisdom, the wise man understands the necessity for physical cleanliness through proper hygiene and good habits, and mental cleanliness through spiritual thoughts. His continued patient yoga practice gives him a natural steadfastness and loyalty in any spiritual undertaking. By physical and mental self-control, he is master of himself at all times, guided by the discriminative wisdom reflected within him in the mirror of calmness that is undistorted by sensory restlessness.

The wise man who quaffs the ever new joy of God within himself feels no attraction to insipid sense objects. He is devoid of physical or mental egotism with its vanity, false pride, arrogance. By introspective analysis of the human condition involved in birth, disease, decrepitude, and death, the wise man avoids the inherent pains and evils of the domain of Nature's changes by constant remembrance of his immortal, transcendent Self.

The wise yogi detaches his consciousness from transitory relationships and possessions, even if living the life of a householder; for he knows all things belong to God, and that at any moment he can be dispossessed of them by the divine will. He loves not his family any less for his nonattachment, nor does he neglect his duty to them, but rather loves and serves the God in them and expands that caring to include all others of God's children. Krishna's commendation of the sage's nonattachment may be also likened to the words of Christ: "There is no man that hath left house, or brethren, or sisters, or father, or mother, or wife, or children, or lands, for my sake, and the gospel's, but he shall receive an hundredfold now in this time, houses, and brethren, and sisters, and mothers, and children, and lands, with persecutions; and in the world to come eternal life."* Whether the wise yogi be a monastic or householder, he maintains a perpetual tranquility of the heart, irrespective of favorable or unfavorable conditions in his life.

By the uniting power of yoga meditation, the yogi of steadfast devotion remains free from disuniting thoughts and sensations and so abides in oneness with Spirit. Forsaking the company of sense-restless beings and materialistic environs, the sage prefers sequestered places, spiritual company, and the inner companionship of the Supreme Friend.

The wisdom-manifesting yogi fills his mind with scriptural studies and spiritual meditative perceptions that contribute to soul-realization. When he attains perfect inner enlightenment, he intuitively perceives the meanings in all forms of knowledge, and realizes the whole truth of divine wisdom as manifested within his Self.

By cultivating the virtues mentioned above, the aspiring yogi attains wisdom and eradicates from his heart all contrary manifestations of ignorance: pride, anger, greed, egotism, possessiveness, misconception, and so on.

The devotee bent on liberation understands that all learning pertaining to the phenomenal worlds is partial, uncertain, relative, and unsatisfying. Realization of God is the only true, permanent, and absolute knowledge.

---

* Mark 10:29–30

SPIRIT, AS KNOWN BY THE WISE

VERSES 12–18

jñeyaṁ yat tat pravakṣyāmi yaj jñātvāmṛtam aśnute
anādimat paraṁ brahma na sat tan nāsad ucyate (12)

sarvataḥpāṇipādaṁ tat sarvatokṣiśiromukham
sarvataḥśrutimal loke sarvam āvṛtya tiṣṭhati (13)

sarvendriyaguṇābhāsaṁ sarvendriyavivarjitam
asaktaṁ sarvabhṛc caiva nirguṇaṁ guṇabhoktṛ ca (14)

bahir antaś ca bhūtānām acaraṁ caram eva ca
sūkṣmatvāt tad avijñeyaṁ dūrasthaṁ cāntike ca tat (15)

avibhaktaṁ ca bhūteṣu vibhaktam iva ca sthitam
bhūtabhartṛ ca taj jñeyaṁ grasiṣṇu prabhaviṣṇu ca (16)

jyotiṣām api taj jyotis tamasaḥ param ucyate
jñānaṁ jñeyaṁ jñānagamyaṁ hṛdi sarvasya viṣṭhitam (17)

iti kṣetraṁ tathā jñānaṁ jñeyaṁ coktaṁ samāsataḥ
madbhakta etad vijñāya madbhāvāyopapadyate (18)

(12) I will tell you of That which is to be known, because such knowledge bestows immortality. Hear about the beginningless Supreme Spirit—He who is spoken of as neither existent (sat) nor nonexistent (asat).

(13) He dwells in the world, enveloping all—everywhere, His hands and feet; present on all sides, His eyes and ears, His mouths and heads;

(14) Shining in all the sense faculties, yet transcending the senses; unattached to creation, yet the Mainstay of all; free from the gunas (modes of Nature), yet the Enjoyer of them.

(15) He is within and without all that exists, the animate and the inanimate; near He is, and far; imperceptible because of His subtlety.

(16) He, the Indivisible One, appears as countless beings; He maintains and destroys those forms, then creates them anew.

(17) The Light of All Lights, beyond darkness; Knowledge itself, That which is to be known, the Goal of all learning, He is seated in the hearts of all.

(18) I have briefly described the Field, the nature of wisdom, and the Object of wisdom. Understanding these, My devotee enters My being.

THE UNMANIFESTED TRANSCENDENT SPIRIT beyond creation is causeless, without attributes, eluding classification; hence not *sat* or *asat* nor referable to any other category.

God is described as immanent in creation: *Kutastha* or the Intelligence that informs the phenomenal worlds. In all men it is He who works through their hands, moves in their feet, sees and hears through their eyes and ears, eats with their mouths, and in all faces gazes at Himself. With unseen vibratory fingers He holds in perfect balance the ideational, astral, and physical universes.

The Lord is not a Person with sense organs, but Consciousness itself; He is therefore aware of the thoughts and sensory perceptions of every being. Jesus referred to this all-embracingness when he said that not a sparrow shall fall on the ground without the knowledge of the Father.

The subtle invisible Spirit is omnipresent, ever before the gaze of the wise but seemingly nowhere to be found by the ignorant. Far from those in delusion, the blessed Lord is near and dear only to the heart of His devotee.

Spirit employs the three modes of Nature to appear as (1) the Creator or Brahma (*rajas,* activity), (2) the Preserver or Vishnu (*sattva,* the nourishing quality), and (3) the Destroyer or Shiva (*tamas,* dissolution).

The motion-picture beam is the light-revealer and the "life" of all scenes on the screen; without the beam the "living" quality of the pictures would disappear.

Similarly, God's immanence as Cosmic Intelligence is called the

Light of All Lights because It makes manifest the motion pictures of creation and the multifarious intelligences therein. Without Spirit, sentient beings would lose their consciousness and their bodies; the universe of suns and moons and planets would vanish into nothingness.

The yogi who in ecstasy attains realization of this immanence of Spirit as the Cosmic Intelligence, the Krishna or Christ Consciousness transcending the darkness of relativity, "enters My being"—expands the little self into Omnipresence, sentient intelligence into Infinite Wisdom.

PURUSHA AND PRAKRITI (SPIRIT AND NATURE)

VERSE 19

prakṛtiṁ puruṣaṁ caiva viddhy anādī ubhav api
vikārāṁś ca guṇāṁś caiva viddhi prakṛtisaṁbhavān

Know that both Purusha and Prakriti are beginningless; and know also that all modifications and qualities (gunas) are born of Prakriti.

PURUSHA, THE LORD'S TRANSCENDENT PRESENCE in creation as the *Kutastha* Intelligence and the individualized soul, and Prakriti, Nature, indicate two aspects of the same God. He is causeless and eternal; therefore His manifestations as Purusha and Prakriti are also beginningless and endless.

The Lord in His transcendental or inactive aspect in creation (Purusha, the *Kshetrajna* or Witness) and the Lord in His immanent kinetic aspect as the Creator of the universe and beings (Prakriti) are not two but One: the Supreme Spirit, Ishvara, Para-Purusha.

As the ocean with waves and without waves is the same ocean, so Spirit, with or without creation, is ever a unity. Prakriti is the storm of *maya,* delusion, relativity, that transforms the surface of the calm ocean of God into tumultuous waves of human lives. The vibratory storm of relativity is God's desireless desire to create. Its force comes from the inherent three *gunas* of manifestation—*sattva* (good), *rajas* (active), and *tamas* (evil). As they move across the Ocean of Infinity, individualized waves are whipped into being. The large waves, swept farthest from the quiet oceanic depths, are the waves of evil, those lives most affected by the storm of delusion. The medium waves are the active lives, surging along in Nature's ebb and flow. The small waves of good lives remain closest to the Ocean's bosom, buffeted the least by the prevailing winds of change. Yet all waves are of the same Essence, and in their own evolutionary time return to their Source.

Naught could exist without Prakriti's power of *maya.* The beam of light from the projector's booth cannot alone create a motion picture; a film of mingled shadows and transparencies is also needed. Similarly, the Lord assumes two aspects, Purusha or the undistorted light of *Kutastha* Intelligence, and Prakriti with its *maya*-film of shadow relativities, to project the intelligently organized drama of countless worlds and beings. Through the two divine agencies He produces in cosmic cycles throughout eternity the dream motion-picture of creation.

Prakriti, God's Maya, is the Lady of Phenomena, the Mistress of Illusion, the Director of the phantasmagoria of the unfolding universe. What a mysterious magic is her power—secret in its workings, bold in its displays. *Prakriti* means "that which can work superbly." Gazing around at the panorama of her inexhaustible handiwork, who could dispute the aptness of her Sanskrit name?

VERSE 20

kārya karaṇa kartṛtve hetuḥ prakṛtir ucyate
puruṣaḥ sukhaduḥkhānāṁ bhoktṛtve hetur ucyate

In the creation of the effect (the body) and the instrument (the senses), Prakriti is spoken of as the cause; in the experience of joy and sorrow, Purusha is said to be the cause.

THE PURUSHA MENTIONED HERE is not the Supreme Spirit (Para-Purusha) nor Its reflection in creation as *Kutastha* Intelligence, but the individualized soul (*jiva*) that is conditioned and limited by its association with the body.

Cosmic Nature or Prakriti is the direct creative cause of the human body and its Nature-dictated activities ("the effect"), and of the bodily senses, which are the means ("the instrument") of the experience of objective creation by Purusha, the perceiving soul. The soul then interprets its contact with sense objects in terms of either joy or sorrow derived from that experience.

As the vast sky appears small when seen from a tiny window, so the infinite Lord appears limited in finite Nature and in the egos of individual beings.

The subjective Cosmic Dreamer, God or Para-Purusha, created His Consort or Mother Nature, Prakriti, the invisible Holy Ghost creative force. Her production, the human body, is a miniature replica of vast Cosmic Nature—a "little Prakriti."

Similarly, God is reflected in miniature as the soul in the body of man. The soul in essence is a perfect reflection of the Divine; but through becoming identified with a body, it imagines itself to be the ego that is subject to pleasure and pain. The soul temporarily dreams itself to be a body, experiencing its attendant joys and sorrows; though in reality it is always the changeless image of God.

The Lord is responsible for having divided Himself into the Transcendental Spirit and the Cosmic Dreamer. In His dream state He bestowed individuality and intelligence on Mother Nature or Prakriti by which she creates matter and human bodies with their sensibilities and activities. It is He who is responsible for giving individuality and intelligence to the reflected human souls by which they dream of pleasure and pain and other bodily sensations and mental perceptions.

Nature is responsible for creation of the objective human dream-body; and God, as the Soul and Perceiver, is responsible for the feelings of dream joy and dream suffering in that dream body. The differentiation was explained in XIII:2 (pages 877–79). God through Prakriti creates the hypnotic suggestion of the objective dream creation, and individualized souls as body-identified egos create their own reactions to the dream objects.

The immutable Spirit became the fleeting cosmic motion-picture of twenty-four qualities; and the flawless soul-image of man identified itself with the Nature-bound body and senses. By yoga practice a devotee should establish himself in the perception of soul blessedness and of aloofness from the body even while he is performing his worldly duties. In this way his soul frees itself from the dream perception of the body and its various sensations. Without the duality of pleasure and pain, a dream loses its reality. So by neutralizing joy and sorrow, man finds that the troublesome body-dream loses its reality and its power to hurt.

Even though Nature is responsible for the creation of the body with its senses and activities, and even though the soul is responsible, through body identification, for the perception of duality (good and evil, and so on), yet man may regain his divine heritage. Through the proper use of the God-given power of free choice, a painstaking devotee who meditates and cultivates nonattachment can neutralize the suggestions of the body with its susceptibility to contrary impressions that have been inflicted on him by Nature and by the body-attached soul.

God ever retains His bliss, impartially witnessing His cosmic dream-drama; similarly, man made in His image should realize himself to be the immortal soul, impartially witnessing and playing in the motion picture of life.

VERSE 21

puruṣaḥ prakṛtistho hi bhuṅkte prakṛtijān guṇān
kāraṇaṁ guṇasaṅgo 'sya sadasadyonijanmasu

Purusha involved with Prakriti experiences the gunas born of Nature. Attachment to the three qualities of Prakriti causes the soul to take embodiment in good and evil wombs.

THE INDIVIDUALIZED SOUL, LIVING IN CLOSE proximity to "little Prakriti" or the human body, becomes attached to phenomenal existence. Such attachment is the cause of rebirth. The conditions of each new incarnation—for good or ill—are a direct result of the degree of one's self-created bondage to the influence of Nature's good, active, or evil modes. A perfect diamond shadowed by a white, variegated, or dark cloth changes in appearance only, not in essence. Similarly, the immutable soul, as ego, only appears to undergo transformation as a consequence of embodiment. This temporary, superficial identity of the soul with Nature's triple-moded body is the cause of the manifold troubles of mortal existence.

VERSE 22

upadraṣṭānumantā ca bhartā bhoktā maheśvaraḥ
paramātmeti cāpy ukto dehe 'smin puruṣaḥ paraḥ

The Supreme Spirit, transcendent and existing in the body, is the detached Beholder, the Consenter, the Sustainer, the Experiencer, the Great Lord, and also the Highest Self.

THE WORD *PARA* IN THIS VERSE (Purusha *para*) indicates "different from." Though the Supreme Being (Purusha) manifests Itself in and as Prakriti (Cosmic Nature) and the human body (the "little Prakriti"), It remains simultaneously transcendent, "beyond, or different from" Its manifestation.

In a dream a man can create for himself a new body; he can support it with his individuality and permit it to work, achieve, and experience human sensations and thoughts. As the lord and master of his dreams, he witnesses all the operations of his new dream body.

In the same way, the Supreme Divine Dreamer, God or Purusha, employs His dream consciousness to create and support His cosmic body of Nature, Prakriti; and transcendentally experiences its activities as the great *Kutastha,* Lord of Creation, and as the Infinite Spirit beyond creation.

Similarly, in a miniature way, God beyond creation, and in creation as the soul in man, lends His superconsciousness to permit the activities of the human body to be carried on. As the almighty Lord of the senses and as the Divine Self in the human body He upholds and transcendentally observes all the dream experiences of man.

As a child may "run wild" without the presence of his father, so Cosmic Nature would not behave properly without the presence of God.

The essence of a dreamer's consciousness remains unaffected even though it transforms itself into good and evil dreams; in the same way, the perfect consciousness of the Lord remains untouched even though It apparently changes Itself into the pleasant and unpleasant dream motion pictures of Cosmic Nature and the human body.

Without the dreamer's consciousness, however, a dream cannot be created. Similarly, without Cosmic Consciousness, the dream universe could not be brought into being. Without the presence of the dreamer's thought, the dream body disintegrates.

Thus a dreamer is the creator and experiencer of his own dreams. Similarly, the soul, the reflection of God, is the great creator, supporter, permitter, enjoyer, and transcendental observer of its own dream physical body and all its activities.

The soul is only a witness; it does not engage itself in the operations of the human intelligence, mind, and senses. It is an observer of the workings of Cosmic Nature in the body. All states of consciousness and all activities of man are considered to be indirectly witnessed by God and to be directly instigated by Prakriti and by man's individual karma.

VERSE 23

ya evaṁ vetti puruṣaṁ prakṛtiṁ ca guṇaiḥ saha
sarvathā vartamāno 'pi na sa bhūyo 'bhijāyate

Whatever his mode of life, he who thus realizes Purusha and the threefold nature of Prakriti will not again suffer rebirth.

WHETHER HIS STATION IN LIFE be high or low, and whether or not he acts in accordance with scriptural injunctions as perceived by human judgments, the man who knows the true nature of Spirit and matter through direct perception in *samadhi* is not subject to rebirth. Divine realization, the intuitive experience of truth, destroys all potentials of karmic bondage. Burnt rope may appear to bind, but will fall away in ashes.

The yogi who beholds in *samadhi* the vast motion picture of the cosmos, produced by triply tainted Nature, and who realizes that all creation proceeds from the eternally pure Spirit, is freed forever from karma and compulsory reincarnation.

THREE APPROACHES TO SELF-REALIZATION

VERSE 24

dhyānenātmani paśyanti kecid ātmānam ātmanā
anye sāṁkhyena yogena karmayogena cāpare

To behold the Self in the self (purified ego) by the self (illumined mind), some men follow the path of meditation, some the path of knowledge, and some the path of selfless action.

THE THREE MAIN APPROACHES TO SELF-REALIZATION are mentioned here: (1) *Dhyana Yoga* (meditation), the path taken by *Kriya Yogis* and by followers of other scientific methods of inner awakening; (2) *Sankhya Yoga,* the path of discriminative wisdom, *jnana,* outlined in Sankhya, one of the six orthodox systems of Hindu philosophy; and (3) *Karma Yoga,* the path of right actions, in which the devotee dedicates all his works to God.

VERSE 25

anye tv evam ajānantaḥ śrutvānyebhya upāsate
te 'pi cātitaranty eva mṛtyuṁ śrutiparāyaṇāḥ

Some men, ignorant of the three main roads, listen to the instructions of the guru. Following the path of worship, regarding the ancient teachings as the Highest Refuge, such men also attain immortality.

LISTENING TO THE GURU IS AN ART that will take the disciple to the Supreme Goal. If the devotee knows nothing of scientific yoga and Sankhya reasoning, and is unable to dissociate himself sufficiently from his activities to qualify as a *karma yogi,* still, by following with full faith his guru's teachings he will achieve emancipation.

Sometimes students say to me: "Such and such person is making better spiritual progress than I am. Why?"

I reply: "He knows how to listen."

All men would be able to transform their lives by hearing with deep attention the simple counsel given in the ethical codes of all religions. It is the stony core of egotism in the hearts of most men that prevents their listening carefully to the wisdom of the ages.

LIBERATION: DIFFERENTIATING BETWEEN THE FIELD AND ITS KNOWER

VERSE 26

yāvat saṁjāyate kiṁcit sattvaṁ sthāvarajaṅgamam
kṣetrakṣetrajñasaṁyogāt tad viddhi bharatarṣabha

O Best of the Bharatas (Arjuna), whatever exists—every being, every object; the animate, the inanimate—understand that to be born from the union of Kshetra and Kshetrajna (Nature and Spirit).

THE PHENOMENAL WORLDS ARE A DREAM of God's. Because the Cosmic Dreamer projects His cosmic dream, the delusion of Nature persists. Man identifies himself with his dream body, so the influence of the delusive physical form continues.

However, if the Lord withdrew His dream consciousness from the cosmic dream creation, it would necessarily disappear. Similarly, man the soul-dreamer, by detachment from the dream body can rise above its disturbing dream-performances.

Thus, the connection between Nature and Spirit is *adhyasa,* illusory, in the sense that all forms, all created beings and objects, are by their limited and fleeting nature unrelated to the formless, eternal Spirit.

By clearly comprehending the essential difference between *kshetra* (Nature and matter) and *kshetrajna* (Spirit and soul), the devotee no longer confounds one with the other; he throws off all mortal confusion and is free.

VERSE 27

samaṁ sarveṣu bhūteṣu tiṣṭhantaṁ parameśvaram
vinaśyatsv avinaśyantaṁ yaḥ paśyati sa paśyati

He sees truly who perceives the Supreme Lord present equally in all creatures, the Imperishable amidst the perishing.

THE LORD AS CONSCIOUSNESS (*chit*) and existence or being (*sat*) is the ground of all creatures. Because all forms of life are composed of the same substance, God, only the ignorant see distinctions where in reality none are present.

As creatures or mortals, all men are in delusion and must perish. But as children of the Most High, sons of the Creator, we partake of His uncaused and indestructible nature.

VERSE 28

samaṁ paśyan hi sarvatra samavasthitam īśvaram
na hinasty ātmanātmānaṁ tato yāti parāṁ gatim

He who is conscious of the omnipresence of God does not injure the Self by the self. That man reaches the Supreme Goal.

HE IS A LIBERATED MAN WHO SEES only the Lord in all creatures and in all creation. So long as a human being lives in ignorance of his true nature, only his body and egoistic mind have reality for him; his soul is as though eclipsed.

To escape through wisdom from the oppressive narrowness of the self into the joyous omnipresence of the Self is the goal of human life.

VERSE 29

prakṛtyaiva ca karmāṇi kriyamāṇāni sarvaśaḥ
yaḥ paśyati tathātmānam akartāraṁ sa paśyati

He who sees that all actions are performed in their entirety by Prakriti alone, and not by the Self, is indeed a beholder of truth.

THE TRUE SEER PERCEIVES HIS SOUL as the silent witness, aloof from the body—the microcosm created by the cosmic vibratory force, Prakriti or Mother Nature. She alone is the performer of all physical and mental activities. The soul is actionless, the reflection of the transcendental, nonvibrational God the Father beyond creation.

A man who sits in a cinema watching simultaneously the image on the screen and the imageless beam of light overhead knows it is the film, and not the beam, that is the direct cause of the changing pictures of shadows and light.

Similarly, the yogi who perceives the pure cosmic beam of God realizes that intelligent Nature alone is responsible for creating the cosmic film of relativity and triple qualities. The cosmic beam itself is changeless, unaffected.

The devotee should therefore concentrate on the blessed and sustaining light of his soul and not on the film of Nature's *gunas* that produce the delusive appearance of the body and all its activities.

VERSE 30

yadā bhūtapṛthagbhāvam ekastham anupaśyati
tata eva ca vistāraṁ brahma saṁpadyate tadā

When a man beholds all separate beings as existent in the One that has expanded Itself into the many, he then merges with Brahman.

A MAN ENGROSSED IN THE COSMIC DREAM of creation finds himself working harmoniously with or excitedly battling the various other dream images created by the one dream consciousness of God. Such a man remains entangled in the oppositional states of the cosmic dream.

When through *samadhi* a yogi awakens from the delusions of *maya,* he beholds his body, the separately existing images of other human beings, and all material objects to be streaming unceasingly from one Source: the consciousness of God.

No real difference is present among creatures: all are products of Prakriti and all are sustained by the same Underlying Divinity. Their seeming diversity is rooted in the unity of One Mind. To realize this truth is emancipation, oneness with God.

VERSE 31

anāditvān nirguṇatvāt paramātmāyam avyayaḥ
śarīrastho 'pi kaunteya na karoti na lipyate

O Son of Kunti (Arjuna), whereas this Supreme Self, the Unchanging, is beginningless and free from attributes, It neither performs actions nor is affected by them, even though dwelling in the body.

A HALF-AWAKE DREAMER IS AWARE of his dream body without being attached to its dream activities. Similarly, a yogi remains unentangled who, even though functioning as the ego in his mortal dream-body, nevertheless perceives God as the Sole Reality.

The Lord sustains the human soul but gives it full liberty and free choice either to identify itself temporarily with the body and its egoistic experiences or to identify itself with His transcendental Spirit and thus to perform actions without attachment.

Paramatma, Spirit, is the supreme Cause of all creation, but is Itself causeless and beginningless. It is imperishable and unchangeable, forever remaining in the vibrationless state unaffected by the creative activities of *Aum,* or the Holy Ghost. Owing to this unchangeability, the ineffable Lord is spoken of as *nirguna,* without attributes. He is free from the oppositional states of creation even though He exists in relation to His cosmic body of Nature and its endless variety.

The embodied soul is, like Him, attributeless and perfect, even though it exists in connection with the human body and even though it behaves like the flawed ego. The Lord, consciously dreaming a cosmic universe, remains aloof from and unaffected by it. His true image, the soul, similarly dreams its physical body and acts like the desire-impelled ego, without being that ego and without attachment to it.

God and the souls reflected from Him are one and the same. As the Lord is the Supreme Cause, the beginningless Beginner of all things, so His reflected souls are also spoken of as the beginningless beginners of their little bodies. God, inherent in Cosmic Nature and sustaining it, is not involved in its changes and complexities. Similarly, the soul dwelling in the body and informing it with life is in no wise affected by its activities.

VERSE 32

yathā sarvagataṁ saukṣmyād ākāśaṁ nopalipyate
sarvatrāvasthito dehe tathātmā nopalipyate

As the all-pervading ether, because of its subtlety, is beyond taint, similarly the Self, though seated everywhere in the body, is ever taintless.

THE OMNIPRESENT *AKASHA* OR ETHER enters into the composition of every form in creation; yet it is subtle beyond recognition, ever unpolluted by material contact. Similarly, the soul within man is wholly unentangled, unchanged, either by the atomic permutations of the body or by the ceaseless thoughts of the mind.

Verses 33–34

yathā prakāśayaty ekaḥ kṛtsnaṁ lokam imaṁ raviḥ
kṣetraṁ kṣetrī tathā kṛtsnaṁ prakāśayati bhārata (33)

kṣetrakṣetrajñayor evam antaraṁ jñānacakṣuṣā
bhūtaprakṛtimokṣaṁ ca ye vidur yānti te param (34)

(33) O Bharata (Arjuna), as the one sun illumines the entire world, so does the Lord of the Field (God and His reflection as the soul) illumine the whole field (Nature and the bodily "little nature").

(34) They enter the Supreme who perceive with the eye of wisdom the distinction between the Kshetra and the Kshetrajna and who also perceive the method of liberation of beings from Prakriti.

WHEN BY THE RIGHT METHOD OF YOGA, divine union, the devotee's all-seeing spiritual eye of wisdom is opened in *samadhi* meditation, the cumulative knowledge of truth becomes realization—intuitive perception or oneness with Reality. Through this eye of omniscience, the yogi beholds the comings and goings of beings and universes as the workings of the relativities of Prakriti's illusory *maya* superimposed on the singular cosmic consciousness of Spirit. By dissolving successively in the light of the "One Sun" of Cosmic Consciousness the evolutes of Prakriti from matter to Spirit, the yogi is liberated from all trammels and misconceptions of cosmic delusion. Identified with the pure immutable *Kshetrajna* (the Evolver-Cognizer of Nature and its domain of matter), the liberated soul can at will consciously dream with Prakriti the metamorphoses of consciousness into "the field" of matter, *kshetra,* or by choice remain wholly awake in Spirit, free from all nightmares inherent in *maya*'s realm of clashing opposites.

om tat sat iti śrīmadbhagavadgītāsu upaniṣatsu
brahmavidyāyām yogaśāstre śrīkṛṣṇārjunasaṁvāde
kṣetrakṣetrajñavibhāgayogo nāma trayodaśo 'dhyāyaḥ

Aum, Tat, Sat.
In the Upanishad of the holy Bhagavad Gita—the discourse of Lord Krishna to Arjuna, which is the scripture of yoga and the science of God-realization—this is the thirteenth chapter, called "Union Through Discriminating Between the Field and the Knower of the Field."

CHAPTER XIV

TRANSCENDING THE GUNAS

The Three Qualities (Gunas) Inherent in Cosmic Nature

Mixture of Good and Evil in Human Nature

The Fruits of the Sattvic, Rajasic, and Tamasic Life

The Nature of the Jivanmukta— One Who Rises Above Nature's Qualities

"A perfected yogi comprehends that the phenomenal worlds and their activities are merely a dance of shadows and lights—the relativities or expressions of the three gunas, animated by the Supreme Light. This perception of truth enables the yogi to enter into the pure omnipresent Cosmic Light beyond all relativity."

TRANSCENDING THE GUNAS

THE THREE QUALITIES (GUNAS) INHERENT IN COSMIC NATURE

VERSES 1–2

śrībhagavān uvāca
paraṁ bhūyaḥ pravakṣyāmi jñānānāṁ jñānam uttamam
yaj jñātvā munayaḥ sarve parāṁ siddhim ito gatāḥ (1)

idaṁ jñānam upāśritya mama sādharmyam āgatāḥ
sarge 'pi nopajāyante pralaye na vyathanti ca (2)

The Blessed Lord said:
(1) Again I shall speak about that highest wisdom which transcends all knowledge. With this wisdom all sages at the end of life have attained the final Perfection.

(2) Embracing this wisdom, established in my Being, sages are not reborn even at the start of a new cycle of creation, nor are they troubled at the time of universal dissolution.

THE FIRE OF COSMIC CONSCIOUSNESS consumes all binding, stored-up karma. Therefore, unlike ordinary persons, a Self-realized sage—a *muni* who has dissolved from his mind all restless agitations of delusion—does not have to reincarnate. He has destroyed desires and their outcome of good and evil actions performed with attachment.

Perfected beings who have attained salvation are one with Spirit in the vibrationless realm beyond creation. Such emancipated ones are freed not only from an individual cycle of births and deaths, but are also no longer involved in the macrocosmic cycles of the phenomenal, vibratory worlds.

VERSE 3

mama yonir mahad brahma tasmin garbhaṁ dadhāmy aham
saṁbhavaḥ sarvabhūtānāṁ tato bhavati bhārata

My womb is the Great Prakriti (Mahat-Brahma) into which I deposit the seed (of My Intelligence); this is the cause of the birth of all beings.

THE DIVINE OR SPIRIT IS HERE PROCLAIMED as the Father-Mother of all phenomenal life. Mahat-Brahma* is the original First Cause of creation—Spirit as Mula-Prakriti, the unmanifested differentiation of the Absolute. Mahat-Brahma, or Great Prakriti, is the womb of primordial matter impregnated with the reflected Intelligence of Spirit, the seed of all future becomings. In Its transcendental aspect, Spirit is unified or uncreative. Reflecting Itself in the vibratory matrix of Cosmic Nature as *Kutastha* Intelligence, Spirit then starts the work of creation.

In unalloyed Cosmic Consciousness (unity) no creation (variety) is possible. By bringing into being the activities, the cosmic storm, of Prakriti or *maya*—the delusive "cosmic measurer"—God produces from His one ocean of formless Infinitude the endless finite waves of creation.

VERSE 4

sarvayoniṣu kaunteya mūrtayaḥ saṁbhavanti yāḥ
tāsāṁ brahma mahad yonir aham bījapradaḥ pitā

O Son of Kunti (Arjuna), of all forms—produced from whatsoever wombs—Great Prakriti is their original womb (Mother), and I am the seed-imparting Father.

---

* *Mahat:* "great," from Sanskrit root *mah,* "to exalt"; additionally, this root means "to arouse, excite." In Sankhya, *mahat* is the "great principle," universal consciousness imbued with God's reflected intelligence. *Brahma:* Brahman, or Supreme Spirit; also, "evolution, development" from Sanskrit root *brih,* "to expand."

Thus *Mahat-Brahma* refers to God's consciousness as the Great Prakriti, the universal creative consciousness of Spirit (the womb of becomings) into which the Lord has deposited His universal intelligence (*Kutastha Chaitanya*), the all-encompassing seed of creation. This action of Spirit excites or arouses the creative potentials in the quiescent Absolute, which then bring forth the development or evolution of matter from the one cosmic consciousness of Spirit.

In a human sense we consider the common parents of humanity to be Adam and Eve (or the "first couple" possessing other names in various scriptures). Ultimately, however, God the Father and His consort, Prakriti—impregnated with His Intelligence to become the Mother principle—are the primal Parents of all forms and all life: whether animate or seemingly inanimate; whether angelic, demonic, human, animal, vegetable, or mineral.

Verse 5

sattvaṁ rajas tama iti guṇāḥ prakṛtisaṁbhavāḥ
nibadhnanti mahābāho dehe dehinam avyayam

O Mighty-armed (Arjuna)! the gunas inherent in Prakriti—sattva, rajas, and tamas—imprison in the body the Imperishable Dweller.

The three modes of Nature—*sattva,* purity; *rajas,* passion; and *tamas,* inertia—bewilder all those subjected to the limitations of a form. The perfect soul appears as the distorted ego when it is reflected in the agitated waters of human life, influenced by the good, activating, and evil qualities of Cosmic Prakriti.

Verse 6

tatra sattvaṁ nirmalatvāt prakāśakam anāmayam
sukhasaṅgena badhnāti jñānasaṅgena cānagha

O Sinless One (Arjuna)! of these three gunas, the stainless sattva gives enlightenment and health. Nevertheless, it binds man through attachment to happiness and attachment to knowledge.

Prakriti or Cosmic Nature is composed of the three *gunas.* Therefore, even the highest *guna, sattva,* is a part of *maya* or the delusive force inherent in creation.

Though a brilliant fetter, *sattva* is still a fetter. A gold wire can tie a man to a post just as securely as can a wire of silver or steel.* Like

---

* *Guna:* literally, "a strand of a cord or rope." The three *gunas* of Prakriti are defined as three intertwined strands of the binding cord of Nature. Through this medium Prakriti holds in bondage all embodied beings.

tamas (ignorance) and *rajas* (selfish activity), *sattva* also binds the soul to the body and to the earth plane.

By its inherency in Nature rather than in the soul, *sattva* is powerless to free man from egotism, the root cause of rebirth.

This stanza of the Gita explains why even good actions and virtues can keep man on the reincarnational wheel. The *sattva* qualities are themselves pure and untainted by delusion; yet when a person relates happiness and wisdom to his own physical body and brain, his soul has identified itself with the human ego. Even a noble man who thinks in terms of "I" in connection with his experiences of happiness or his acquisition of wisdom—"I am happy; I am wise"—is harboring selfish rather than selfless sentiments.

Why even good actions keep man bound to wheel of rebirth

Bliss and wisdom belong to the soul. But through delusion the ego connects them with bodily enjoyments and intellectual knowledge. The ego considers happiness and knowledge to be its own qualities, thus ignorantly chaining the soul to bodies and rebirths. Through these, the ego experiences diluted and limited pleasures and knowledge, instead of realizing the unalloyed and infinite bliss and wisdom of the soul.

The good deeds that virtuous men do for others should not be performed for the purpose of attaining name, fame, or ego-satisfaction. Instead, all actions should be performed with the thought of pleasing God.

All his actions bring a true yogi happiness and wisdom. He understands that all good actions and qualities flow from the soul and not from the ego. He knows why good actions performed with egotistical pride will lead to reincarnational bondage and why the same good actions, performed while one thinks of the Lord as the Doer, will lead to liberation.

For instance, when a person eats with only the thought of nourishing the body as the temple of God, he is incurring no karma—not even good karma. To eat with this purpose is to act in the service of Divinity; the greed of the ego is not being catered to. A man who dies without overcoming the desire to please his sense of taste by consuming delicious foods is required by cosmic law to be reborn on earth to satisfy his cravings. Subconsciously he is unwilling to stay in a heaven that lacks kitchens and cooks, curries and pies!

VERSE 7

rajo rāgātmakaṁ viddhi tṛṣṇāsaṅgasamudbhavam
tan nibadhnāti kaunteya karmasaṅgena dehinam

O Son of Kunti (Arjuna), understand that the activating rajas is imbued with passion, giving birth to desire and attachment; it strongly binds the embodied soul by a clinging to works.

THE PERFORMANCE OF WORLDLY ACTIVITY without wisdom gives rise to an unquenchable thirst of longings for and attachments to material objects and egotistical satisfactions. The man who acts for selfish reasons becomes deeply attached to bodily activities and desires.

Such worldly activity binds the majority of persons to earthly rebirths, owing to the ceaseless desires it engenders, many of which remain unfulfilled at the time of death. To perform worldly activities only to please God, however, is never binding.

A few persons are sattvic. There are also a few men of exceedingly tamasic nature—those who are effortlessly disposed to commit evil. But the greatest number of human beings are rajasic by inclination; impelled by the passion characteristic of *rajoguna,* they remain absorbed in worldly and selfish interests.

VERSE 8

tamas tv ajñānajaṁ viddhi mohanaṁ sarvadehinām
pramādālasyanidrābhis tan nibadhnāti bhārata

O Bharata (Arjuna)! know that tamas arises from ignorance, deluding all embodied beings. It binds them by misconception, idleness, and slumber.

TAMAS IS THE QUALITY IN NATURE that causes misery of all kinds. It is the dark evolute of the illusory power of *maya,* preventing divine realization and giving a seeming reality to the ego and matter as separate from Spirit. The tamasic man is full of wrong ideas. He is careless and indolent. He indulges in oversleeping, shunning the partially uplifting rajasic actions and the most uplifting sattvic actions. Like an animal, he is conscious chiefly of the body.

A man of activity is better off because he establishes some identification with the mental sphere. A man of goodness is in a still better state because he is in touch with soul perceptions.

VERSE 9

sattvaṁ sukhe sañjayati rajaḥ karmaṇi bhārata
jñānam āvṛtya tu tamaḥ pramāde sañjayaty uta

Sattva attaches one to happiness; rajas to activity; and tamas, by eclipsing the power of discrimination, to miscomprehension.

ANY ACTION PERFORMED UNDER THE INFLUENCE of these triple qualities, with attachment (egoity), causes rebirth-making bondage. A person whose nature and actions are good is usually attached to virtue and its rewards of inner contentment and happiness. A man habitually engaged in worldly activities is generally attached to those works and to his restless, energetic inclinations. An ignorant man is uncomprehending and steeped in his misconceptions and errors.

The majority of mankind stays in the sphere of worldly activities, which they perform with attachment. This sphere, however, is the clearinghouse and the testing ground of life. Such worldly persons at least remain alert in the mental realm, far above the low tamasic plane of sloth and bewilderment. They have a chance to rise to the good sattvic state as they learn to perform activities for God and hence without egoistic influence.

Persons who conscientiously fulfill their proper worldly duties, although beset with restlessness and worries, learn thereby to act in an increasingly better or sattvic way and to perform activities in a happy frame of mind, even if not yet free from egotism. Aspiring human beings living in this middle sphere of activity find their mental trend is leading them upward—even though a great many remain for a long time in this educational midsphere, entangled in egotistical performance of good actions. The fortunate few, however, escape quickly from the rajasic realm; remembering the image of God within them, they begin to exercise discrimination and act only to please God. Thereby they progress rapidly into virtuous beings and find emancipation.

Comparatively speaking, only a few very stupid persons misuse their powers of discrimination to the extent that they are willing to stoop down to the third and worst sphere, that of evil. Perhaps many more would become tamasic if Mother Nature didn't use hunger, poverty, and misery to prod her charges to remedial activity. Tamasic persons misuse divine free choice, refusing to perform normal constructive activities. Thus they descend in evolution, cultivating the tamasic habits of sensuality, laziness, pride, oversleeping, and Godless living. Constant inner and outer indolence and indulgence in oversleeping or drugging the mind—seeking the uncreative and oblivious state of existence—lead one to the animalistic plane.

The purpose of life is to ascend to God, not to slide down the ladder of evolution to animality. The seeker for liberation should avoid excess in all modes of conduct, and should perform all worldly duties without attachment—maintaining himself and his family, and observing his divine duties for liberating himself and uplifting others.

Transmuting selfish actions into noble and altruistic behavior, the aspirant becomes a sattvic being. The ensuing attachment to virtue turns the mind to God—the final stage of the purifying and liberating process begins.

MIXTURE OF GOOD AND EVIL IN HUMAN NATURE

VERSE 10

rajas tamaś cābhibhūya sattvaṁ bhavati bhārata
rajaḥ sattvaṁ tamaś caiva tamaḥ sattvaṁ rajas tathā

Sometimes sattva is predominant, overpowering rajas and tamas; sometimes rajas prevails, not sattva or tamas; and sometimes tamas obscures sattva and rajas.

IN THIS STANZA EACH MORTAL wryly recognizes his own portrait. Sometimes he is good, sometimes he is bad, and on other occasions his state is that of armed neutrality—neither good nor bad. The human condition!

Though all mortals—that is, unenlightened men—are subject to the three modes of Prakriti, each person betrays by his life which of the three *gunas* is habitually dominant in him.

VERSE 11

sarvadvāreṣu dehe 'smin prakāśa upajāyate
jñānaṁ yadā tadā vidyād vivṛddhaṁ sattvam ity uta

One may know that sattva is prevalent when the light of wisdom shines through all the sense gates of the body.

THE SPIRITUAL MAN IS MASTER OF HIS SENSES and uses them constructively. He perceives only good. All that he sees, hears, smells, tastes, and touches reminds him of God. In the light of wisdom, the illusory sense perceptions are rightly discerned and interpreted by his discriminative intelligence. From the inner perspective, the sattvic being knows that all is Brahman; in practical application, he honors the divine laws of Nature's realm. He shuns that which obscures the ubiquitous Supreme Good, and embraces that which declares the Immanent Divinity.

VERSE 12

lobhaḥ pravṛttir ārambhaḥ karmaṇām aśamaḥ spṛhā
rajasy etāni jāyante vivṛddhe bharatarṣabha

Preponderance of rajas causes greed, activity, undertaking of works, restlessness, and desire.

THE ACTIVITY AND THE UNDERTAKING of works of the average man are ego-tainted and hence accompanied by various griefs and disillusionments. He is engrossed in fears of loss and in expectations of gain. As his desires increase, so does his state of unrest. He is beset by worries; tranquility and true happiness elude him.

However, a man who labors only for himself and his relatives is nevertheless maintaining a portion of God's family. A selfish businessman, imbued with *rajas,* is therefore far superior to the indolent, tamasic type of person who is unwilling to support himself or to make any kind of contribution to society.

VERSE 13

aprakāśo 'pravṛttiś ca pramādo moha eva ca
tamasy etāni jāyante vivṛddhe kurunandana

Tamas as the ruling guna produces darkness, sloth, neglect of duties, and delusion.

THROUGH OVERINDULGENCE OF THE SENSES, the tamasic man becomes exhausted and inactive. Failing to develop his intelligence by performance of his proper duties, he exists in stagnation and bewilderment.

Sensually inclined persons need to resist and transmute the tamasic impulses that compel them to live for eating, sex, and indulging their bad habits. Man, made in the image of God, should not act like a nondiscriminatory animal, or sink into uselessness. Human sense slaves are inferior to most animals, few of which overeat or engage constantly in sex activities. By overuse, man loses sense power and the ability to enjoy any sensory experience. A drug addict, an alcoholic, a sex-obsessed man, fall lower and lower in the scale of evolution.

The person who is mentally befogged owing to sensory overindulgence is incapable of understanding the difference between right and wrong actions. He is spent in body, mind, and soul, feeling no real physical, mental, or spiritual pleasure. An evil man slides precipitously into misery-making actions; in the darkness of his befuddled mind he feels himself powerless to initiate good changes in his life.

A restless rajasic man bakes himself slowly in the oven of worries about himself and others. But a tamasic man, as though ossified, is not roused even by the sizzling process of worries. He exists like an inert, lifeless stone.

THE FRUITS OF THE SATTVIC, RAJASIC, AND TAMASIC LIFE

VERSES 14–15

yadā sattve pravṛddhe tu pralayaṁ yāti dehabhṛt
tadottamavidāṁ lokān amalān pratipadyate (14)

rajasi pralayaṁ gatvā karmasaṅgiṣu jāyate
tathā pralīnas tamasi mūḍhayoniṣu jāyate (15)

(14) A man who dies with sattva qualities predominant rises to the taintless regions in which dwell knowers of the Highest.

(15) When rajas prevails at the time of death, a person is reborn among those attached to activity. He who dies permeated with tamas enters the wombs (environment, family, state of existence) of the deeply deluded.

THE FATE OF MEN AFTER DEATH is determined by their life while on earth. Those who cultivated goodness, *sattva,* and have become established in its taintlessness, are transported to the angelic realms. Those whose natures were full of *rajas,* worldly attachments, are reborn on earth as ordinary men and women or on other activity-saturated planets best suited to their passionate natures. Those who immersed themselves in evil, *tamas,* reincarnate in the bodies of animals or in families of base or bestial human beings, or in vile conditions affecting their nature and determining their state of existence; or they may remain for long periods on dark astral spheres or on planets similar to earth but more heavily saturated with suffering and violence.* These are the dark "wombs (*yonis*)," or places and states of birth, of all deeply deluded beings when they transmigrate from one life to their next existence.

Thus each man consciously or unconsciously chooses not only his future condition, but also his dwelling place: heaven, earth, or hell.

There are many grades of sattvic beings—from good men, to goodness mixed with saintliness, to liberated yogis. As good men come nearer to perfecting themselves, they become saints, sages, yogis, highest *rishis,* angels, archangels; and ultimately, during full liberation from the triple qualities, they merge in everlasting oneness with Spirit. Likewise, there are various grades of rajasic or worldly men, some with saintly qualities and some who verge on being evil. So also, there are mild, medium, and extremely evil people.

The good, evil, and mixed regions of God's creation

In His vast creative display, the Lord has provided a place for every coterie of evolution and interest of His creatures. There are sattvic universes, which contain fundamentally good beings. There are rajasic universes in which the bulk of beings are passionate with desireful activity—this earth is predominantly rajasic in this stage of its evolution; in the strata between good and evil, it is about midway. Similarly, there are universes that are dominated primarily by tamasic or evil manifestations—bestial creatures as in earth's prehistoric ages of dinosaurs and other ferocious beasts of land, water, and air, which keep their habitations screeching with interspecies wars and cannibalistic murders and devourings. And there are universes and planets where fallen and depraved beings dwell as goblins and demons.

Countless good souls have been liberated. The vast majority of beings, worldly men, keep on reincarnating on earth or like planets suited

* See also reference to other worlds, VI:41, page 646.

to their natures and desires. Evil men not even striving for liberation collect in myriads and incarnate in grossest human forms or as lower animals on earth, or transmigrate to lesser evolved worlds or to the vilest tamasic regions.

All these humans, animals, wild beasts and vicious brutes, evil goblins, of good, activating, and evil qualities, keep this cosmic dream motion picture full of variety and entertainment, excitement and inspiration. Intelligent, discriminative human beings, after so many incarnations of nightmarish struggles and miseries and deaths, ought to learn their lesson and strive to get out of these cosmic histrionics, back to the blessedness of the soul's home in Spirit.

VERSE 16

karmaṇaḥ sukṛtasyāhuḥ sāttvikaṁ nirmalaṁ phalam
rajasas tu phalaṁ duḥkham ajñānaṁ tamasaḥ phalam

It is said (by the sages) that the fruit of sattvic actions is harmony and purity. The fruit of rajasic actions is pain. The fruit of tamasic actions is ignorance.

RIGHT ACTIVITY LEADS TO HAPPINESS. Worldly actions imbued with egotism ultimately bring pain and disillusionment. Continual evil actions destroy man's discrimination and understanding.

Good persons, through the incentive of spiritual joy, try to become better and better. The life of the average human being, however, is a mixture of right actions and wrong actions.

The lowest men are those who tire easily of any struggle for virtue, giving up all worthwhile pursuits and sinking into the stupor of nonactivity and evil habits. Persons of tamasic nature become bewildered and increasingly ignorant, devoid of any sense of responsibility for their own welfare or for the welfare of the society of which they are a part.

"The wages of sin is death."* That is, sinful activities lead to the death of man's happiness. Ignorance is the sin of sins because it is the mother of all misery.

Why do worldly men perform actions that produce little joy and many troubles? Why do evil men destroy themselves with their perni-

---

* Romans 6:23.

cious behavior? The answer is "habit"—one of the most potent factors in human destiny. Many persons, in spite of their knowledge of the suffering involved, continue to indulge in injurious practices because of the iron influence of habit. In addition, such persons lack experience of the rewarding joys of the spiritual life.

As the camel eats bramble even though it makes the mouth bleed, so the sex-obsessed man indulges himself even though his health suffers, and the alcoholic drinks himself to death. The acquired taste for bad habits is not easily forsworn if one is ignorant of the incomparable nectar of the soul within him. The money-mad person destroys his happiness by continuously seeking more wealth, not knowing that a little investment in the treasure house of sincere meditation yields lasting joys such as gold cannot buy.

Thus worldly persons, in spite of the suffering involved in material activities, continue to be worldly; and evil men continue in their abnormal path, steeped in senseless living. Their rajasic and tamasic habits, respectively, prevent them from picturing the better joys of normal worldly activities or the superior joys of noble pursuits and soul exploration. Rajasic persons, mentally stimulated by activity and chastened by disappointment, may begin a deeper search for lasting joy. But tamasic beings, caught in the ignorance of their own making, with no will for self-improvement, fall into ever deeper ignorance, finding sadistic pleasure in hurting themselves and others.

All persons, however, can change and improve their life through keeping good company and exercising their innate power of self-control, and through meditation on God, the Source of their being. Even a little taste of goodness will stimulate one's spiritual appetite for the Everlasting Sweetness.

VERSE 17

sattvāt saṁjāyate jñānaṁ rajaso lobha eva ca
pramādamohau tamaso bhavato 'jñānam eva ca

Wisdom arises from sattva; greed from rajas; and heedlessness, delusion, and ignorance from tamas.

THIS STANZA MENTIONS THE EXPRESSION in man's life of the three modes of Nature. The person in whom *sattva* predominates is characterized by wisdom, which bestows happiness.

The rajasic man is easily recognized by his worldly desires, his struggles for more and more wealth, possessions, power.

The person filled with *tamas* is known by his deeply rooted misconceptions about life, his aimless actions, his unbecoming behavior, his lack of self-control, his pride and arrogance, and his contempt for others' good advice.

VERSE 18

ūrdhvaṁ gacchanti sattvasthā madhye tiṣṭhanti rājasāḥ
jaghanyaguṇavṛttisthā adho gacchanti tāmasāḥ

Those established in sattva go upward; the rajasic dwell in the middle; those men descend who are engrossed in the lowest guna —tamas.

ASIDE FROM THE LITERAL MEANING—that a man rises, fluctuates, or falls in spiritual evolution according to which of the three modes prevails in him—there is a deeper significance in this stanza.

A man permeated with wisdom, *sattva,* has his consciousness centered in a high region of the body: the spiritual eye in the forehead. He rises continually in spiritual understanding.

The mind of a rajasic person abides in the dorsal or "heart" center. It is "in the middle"—equidistant from the highest and the lowest *chakras* ("wheels" or invisible astral centers of life activities in the spine).

The mind of a tamasic man is confined to the three lowest centers: lumbar, sacral, and coccygeal. His consciousness has thus "descended" far from the region of divine perceptions in the brain, and is also below the "middle" or rajasic plane.

The expressions of the chakras under influence of soul and senses

All of the astral cerebrospinal plexuses in their natural state are spiritual, reflecting the diverse aspects of the divine intelligence and vibratory power of the superconsciousness of the soul. But when the energies of these centers are drawn outward under the influence of the senses, and their connection with the soul's pure discriminatory faculty is diminished, their expression becomes proportionately perverted. The externalized cerebral centers express intellect, reason, and distorting restlessness (rather than the all-knowing wisdom of intuition and Spirit-reflecting calmness). The externalized heart center, when identified with the senses, expresses itself as the activating impulses of emotional likes and dislikes, attachments and aversions (rather than pure unprejudiced feeling and life-force control). The externalized three lower centers feed the avaricious appetites of the senses (rather than expressing the divine potentials of these *chakras:* self-control, adherence to virtuous principles, and the power of resisting wrong influences).

The consciousness and life force of persons under the influence of the sense mind are strongly concentrated in the three lower centers, and thence are drawn outward through the coiled gateway in the coccygeal, or lowest, center into the physical body. Unless this strong outward flow is governed and normalized by the pure sublimating power in the centers of the heart and discrimination, it is a stimulator of sexual activities, base instincts, and evil propensities.

He whose mind dwells habitually in uncontrolled sensory habits, and who exercises no initiative to extricate himself, overstimulates the outward thrust of the energies in this lowest *chakra* and becomes a fast-held prisoner of *maya*, of the world of duality, inertia, and suffering.

The rajasic man is "in the middle"; he has the power to turn his consciousness upward to the heavenly centers in the brain, or downward to the infernal spheres of delusion. The person imbued with *rajas,* living on the dorsal plane of the heart, can keep his feelings, motives, and activities pure by meditation and discrimination. He can elevate himself and attain evenmindedness and wisdom by fixing his attention more and more frequently on the spiritual-eye center.

Tamasic persons, sinking their minds into the lowest *chakra* and disengaging themselves from the redeeming power of good actions and spiritual effort, become enmeshed in evil: bodily identification, sadism, illicit sex relations, dishonesty, and so on.

Sattvic beings, in contrast, remain in the lofty spheres of wisdom and ecstatic perceptions, imbued with virtue and purity of heart.

THE NATURE OF THE JIVANMUKTA—ONE WHO RISES ABOVE NATURE'S QUALITIES

VERSE 19

nānyaṁ guṇebhyaḥ kartāraṁ yadā draṣṭānupaśyati
guṇebhyaś ca paraṁ vetti madbhāvaṁ so 'dhigacchati

When the seer perceives (in creation) no agent except the three modes, and cognizes That which is higher than the gunas, he enters My Being.

JUST AS A MAN UNDERSTANDS that he sees a motion picture through the instrumentality of an electric beam of light and a variegated film, so a perfected yogi comprehends that the phenomenal worlds and their activities are merely a dance of shadows and lights—the relativities or expressions of the three *gunas,* animated by the Supreme Light. This perception of truth enables the yogi to enter into the pure omnipresent Cosmic Light beyond all relativity.

So long as man remains transfixed by the cosmic phenomena, he reacts with painful and pleasurable emotions, solidifying in his consciousness the false notion of the intrinsic validity of the relativities. But when by the practice of yoga man frees himself from the reactions of likes and dislikes by filling his heart with unchanging ecstatic divine joy, he sees clearly—from his viewpoint centered in God—the true workings by Nature of the Lord's cosmic cinematography.

VERSE 20

guṇān etān atītya trīn dehī dehasamudbhavān
janmamṛtyujarāduḥkhair vimukto 'mṛtam aśnute

Having transcended the three modes of Nature—the cause of physical embodiment—a man is released from the sufferings of birth, old age, and death; he attains immortality.

BY MEDITATION THE YOGI GOES BEYOND flesh consciousness and thus beyond Prakriti, the Cosmic Principle whose three *gunas* create the body and the world of change and transitoriness. He establishes himself in his true identity, which no earthly changes can touch or disfigure: eternal Spirit.

VERSE 21

arjuna uvāca
kair liṅgais trīn guṇān etān atīto bhavati prabho
kimācāraḥ kathaṁ caitāṁs trīn guṇān ativartate

Arjuna said:

O Lord, what signs distinguish the man who has transcended the three modes? What is his behavior? How does he rise beyond the triple qualities?

ARJUNA HERE CALLS SRI KRISHNA "Prabhu" (Lord or Master). The devotee, realizing his divine guru as the repository of all wisdom, seeks further light on the nature of a *jivanmukta,* "one freed while living" in a body.

It is to be remembered that the conversational format of the Gita, when read allegorically, represents the devotee's inner seeking and communion with God, and the responses he receives in the form of perceptions of truth. Arjuna, metaphorically the devotee of highest achievement, through the grace of his guru, Lord Krishna, experiences in the state of cosmic consciousness the resolution of all the mysteries of being.

According to the devotee's spiritual inclination and degree of advancement, answers from the Infinite may manifest as spoken words or as unvocalized word-thoughts conveyed to the devotee. Or through the soul's intuition—pure knowing by realization or direct experience of truth—and through expressions of cosmic consciousness, the devotee may receive enlightenment in the form of definite pronounced perceptions or feelings; or as visible or audible words or sounds materialized by the all-knowing intuitive power of the soul or by divine fiat of the cosmic power of God.

Thought by grosser vibration becomes energy. That energy by visualization can be seen as a mental or dream form. By strong concentration it can be further condensed into a true vision.

A thought produces a mental vibration that emits sound. By concentration, that vibratory sound can be formulated into any language conveying the concept of the thought. All intuitional perceptions and expressions of cosmic consciousness—God's consciousness that is the repository of everything that is, was, or will be—can be extended into visible words, the so-called Akashic Records written in the ether; or into audible sounds vibrating from the ether; or into Akashic exclamations, cognizable odors, flavors, or tactual sensations; or into true visions, or illuminating thoughts, or intuitive cognition, or vibrations of pure feeling or will.

Thus does Arjuna, the devotee, request and receive the unfolding wisdom-revelations of the Infinite.

VERSES 22–25

śrībhagavān uvāca
prakāśaṁ ca pravṛttiṁ ca moham eva ca pāṇḍava
na dveṣṭi saṁpravṛttāni na nivṛttāni kāṅkṣati (22)

udāsīnavad āsīno guṇair yo na vicālyate
guṇā vartanta ity eva yo 'vatiṣṭhati neṅgate (23)

samaduḥkhasukhaḥ svasthaḥ samaloṣṭāśmakāñcanaḥ
tulyapriyāpriyo dhīras tulyanindātmasaṁstutiḥ (24)

mānāpamānayos tulyas tulyo mitrāripakṣayoḥ
sarvārambhaparityāgī guṇātītaḥ sa ucyate (25)

The Blessed Lord said:
(22) O Pandava (Arjuna), he who does not abhor the presence of the gunas—illumination, activity, and ignorance—nor deplore their absence;

(23) Remaining like one unconcerned, undisturbed by the three modes—realizing that they alone are operating throughout creation; not oscillating in mind but ever Self-centered;

(24) Unaffected by joy and sorrow, praise and blame—secure in his divine nature; regarding with an equal eye a clod of clay, a stone, and gold; the same in his attitude toward pleasant or unpleasant (men and experiences); firm-minded;

(25) Uninfluenced by respect or insult; treating friend and enemy alike; abandoning all delusions of personal doership—he it is who has transcended the triple qualities!

IN THESE FOUR STANZAS LORD KRISHNA points out the characteristics of a "free soul"—one liberated while still in the body. *Jivanmuktas* have seen through the stupendous plot of Nature and have disassociated themselves from her world of flux and unsubstantial seemingness.

An ordinary mortal is continuously stirred by the triple qualities while witnessing the motion picture of life. But the calm yogi observes the scenes without the prejudices and agitations of mind that in the common man arise from feelings of love and hate, attraction and repulsion. The yogi, turning within to the imperturbable joy of his soul, is not emotionally involved with a mere picture.

Personal experience of the dualities does not affect inwardly the detached, desireless yogi, whether he receives pleasure or pain; or encounters agreeable or disagreeable persons and experiences; or is allotted acclaim or censure, honor or disgrace; or meets friend or foe; or gains a piece of land or a stone mansion or a mass of gold—all experiences that may occur in the motion picture of daily life. The yogi beholds all mundane scenes with undisturbed tranquility, knowing them to be only lights and shadows: changing vibrations of the Cosmic Beam and the "technicolored" triple cosmic delusive qualities.

All contrasts seem to him to be similar, made of the same light-shadow fabric. It is not that he fails to understand the value of gold as being different from the value of clay, or that he does not discriminate between pleasant and unpleasant persons, or that he is coldly insensitive to life's experiences. But he no longer has a personal interest in the phenomenal world even though he lives in it. He avoids the entanglements of delusion by beholding all creation in its reality: passing shadows of atomic change.

VERSE 26

māṁ ca yo 'vyabhicāreṇa bhaktiyogena sevate
sa guṇān samatītyaitān brahmabhūyāya kalpate

He who serves Me with undeviating devotion transcends the gunas and is qualified to become Brahman.

ARJUNA HAD ASKED (STANZA 21): "How does a man rise beyond the *gunas*?" Lord Krishna now answers that question. "By *Bhakti Yoga,*" he says. "By unswerving devotion to God, by love for Him so complete that one's mind has no room for thought of self."

A reply of sweetness and profound simplicity, offering man divine hope and encouragement.

VERSE 27

brahmaṇo hi pratiṣṭhāham amṛtasyāvyayasya ca
śāśvatasya ca dharmasya sukhasyaikāntikasya ca

For I am the basis of the Infinite, the Immortal, the Indestructible; and of eternal Dharma and unalloyed Bliss.

IN STANZAS 26–27 KRISHNA SPEAKS as the Pratyagatma, the soul or true being of man that is identical with God: Spirit or the Absolute. Krishna's words: "I am the basis of the Infinite," are akin in divine scope to those uttered by Jesus: "Before Abraham was, I am."* Krishna and Christ spoke from the depths of Self-realization, knowing that "I and my Father are one."†

The unmanifested Spirit that existed before creation is the Supreme Abode of Being; of everlasting Dharma, law, righteousness, cosmic shelter; and of endless Beatitude.

After the phenomenal worlds came into existence, the Spirit is the Abode of the triune God (the Father, *Sat,* beyond all vibration or manifestation; the Son or *Tat,* the Intelligence present in vibratory creation; and the Holy Ghost, *Aum,* cosmic vibration or Mother Nature). "Heaven is My throne, and earth is My footstool: What house will ye build Me? saith the Lord: or what is the place of My rest? Hath not My hand made all these things?"‡

om tat sat iti śrīmadbhagavadgītāsu upaniṣatsu
brahmavidyāyām yogaśāstre śrīkṛṣṇārjunasaṁvāde
guṇatrayavibhāgayogo nāma caturdaśo 'dhyāyaḥ

Aum, Tat, Sat.
In the Upanishad of the holy Bhagavad Gita—the discourse of Lord Krishna to Arjuna, which is the scripture of yoga and the science of God-realization—this is the fourteenth chapter, called "Union Through Transcending Nature's Three Qualities."

---

* John 8:58. † John 10:30. ‡ Acts 7:49–50.

CHAPTER XV

PURUSHOTTAMA: THE UTTERMOST BEING

❖

Eternal Ashvattha: The Tree of Life

❖

The Abode of the Unmanifest

❖

How Spirit Manifests as the Soul

❖

The Supreme Spirit:
Beyond the Perishable and the Imperishable

ॐ

"I (the Lord) am beyond the perishable (Prakriti) and am also higher than the imperishable (Kutastha). Therefore, in the worlds and in the Veda (the intuitive perception of undeluded souls) I am proclaimed Purushottama, the Uttermost Being. Whosoever, freed from delusion, knows Me thus as the Supreme Spirit, knows all, O descendant of Bharata (Arjuna). He worships Me with his whole being."

PURUSHOTTAMA: THE UTTERMOST BEING

ETERNAL ASHVATTHA: THE TREE OF LIFE

VERSE 1

śrībhagavān uvāca
ūrdhvamūlam adhaḥśākham aśvatthaṁ prāhur avyayam
chandāṁsi yasya parṇāni yas taṁ veda sa vedavit

The Blessed Lord said:
They (the wise) speak of an eternal ashvattha tree, with roots above and boughs beneath, whose leaves are Vedic hymns. He who understands this tree of life is a Veda-knower.

THE *ASHVATTHA* TREE (pipal or holy fig, *Ficus religiosa,* of India) is remarkable for great size and longevity. In the first four stanzas of this chapter, *ashvattha* is used metaphorically to describe the mighty, many-branched system of integrated consciousness, life force, and afferent and efferent nerves that is the composite of man.

Paradoxically, though the *ashvattha* tree is here referred to as eternal, the word itself in one commonly accepted derivation means "that which does not remain tomorrow (or, 'in future')," from *a-śvas*. The metaphorical *ashvattha* tree, in this sense, alludes to the world of transitoriness and its beings, which are ever in the process of change—nothing remaining the same from the present moment to the next ("tomorrow," or "the future"). Prakriti's principles of creation, by their action and interaction, produce endless variations. And while these "products" do not endure in the same state or condition, the creative principles behind them, the life and seed of the *ashvattha* tree, are eternal.*

* See also I:8, explaining the metaphorical derivation of Ashvatthaman (Ashvattha-man) the Kuru warrior, son of Drona as allegorically representing *ashaya* or *vasana,* latent de-

In these Gita verses, the *ashvattha* tree refers specifically to the creative principles of Prakriti at work in the threefold body of man (physical, astral, and causal), though the analogy itself is equally applicable on a cosmic scale.

THIS ENDURING "TREE OF LIFE"—mentioned in many scriptures of the world, including the Bible—is the human body and human mind.

"Tree of Life"— the human body and mind

In the light of intuition, yogis behold the inverted tree of consciousness (ideational components of the causal body) within the tree of life force (the *nadis* of the astral body, channels of life energy), these two existing interlocked within the inverted tree of the physical cerebrospinal nervous system. This triple tree has its roots of thought emanations, life-force rays, and cranial nerves hanging upside down from the eternal Cosmic Consciousness above its ideational, astral, and physical spinal trunks; and its triple branches hanging below.

The phenomenal spheres were created by God by condensation of light. Projected out of the Divine Vibration, the earth came into being as inert matter. Its inherent life kept on thrusting its rays of life force outward. The rays became manifested in the form of vegetation and trees with their extending shoots.

The same basic patterns are repeated throughout Nature. Like the plant kingdom, all forms of animate matter have a core of life whence branches extend to create and enliven the organism. Thus, after the Lord had enabled the earth to project "trees," He fashioned human beings, His crowning creation, much like inverted trees. This correspondence is seen in the physical body's roots of hair, cerebrospinal trunk, boughs of arms and legs, and nerve branches extending throughout, distributing the sap of life.

In a book on anatomy, look at a chart showing the nervous system in the human body. Turn the chart upside down, with the brain below and the feet above, and you will see that man's form has a similarity to an inverted tree, with a trunk and many branches.

Then turn the chart right-end up and you will see that the ner-

---

sire: the preserved or stored-up seeds that perpetuate the cycles of rebirth. In the commentary on XV:2, the metaphorical significance is further elaborated in reference to the rootlings of the *ashvattha* tree symbolizing past desires that "contribute to the nurture and perpetuity of the Tree of Life, causing its physical manifestation as the nervous system to sprout forth again and again, in each new physical form in successive incarnations"—binding man to life and death through the power of his desires.

vous system itself looks like an inverted tree, with hair, brain, and spine above; and numerous branches of nerves shooting out below. As trees spring out of the soil beneath them, the human tree of thought, life force, and nerves grows invertedly downward from the "soil" or ground of Cosmic Consciousness.

In the human body, the physical tree of nerves is a gross manifestation of the astral tree of life energy within. The two trees of nerves and life force are condensed out of the tree of human consciousness, the elemental ideas in the causal body, which in turn emanate from Cosmic Consciousness.*

Human hair is a result of the condensation of astral rays; the tissues of the body itself are made of atoms and lifetrons. Some yogis do not cut their hair but keep it long to draw from the ether a greater quantity of cosmic rays—an effective but nonessential derivative yogic practice. The reason for Samson's having lost his superhuman strength when his hair was shorn by Delilah may well be that he had practiced certain yogic exercises by which one's hair can be transformed into sensitive antennae to draw cosmic energy from the ether.

True knowledge of the phenomenal world

The Tree of Life has three kinds of leaves, or receptors through which the indwelling soul receives knowledge ("Vedic hymns") of triune phenomenal creation: sensations, life force, and thought perceptions. The metaphor of leaves compared to Vedic hymns calls forth an image of sensitivity and vitality (the vibrant green leaves denoting life) and whispering motion, "hymns of knowledge" (the rustle of leaves). The "leaves" of the physical tree of life, for example, are the sensory organs in the epidermis and their corresponding centers in the brain, sensitive and full of life, receiving sensations and reporting that knowledge. The waving of those sensory leaves suggests the motion of sensation caused in the nerve centers through which we receive knowledge about the body and the world. Through the help of this sensory commotion we see colors and forms, hear sounds, taste food, and so forth. When one perceives the proper integration of physical sensory stimuli with the inner trees of life force and consciousness (in the as-

* See earlier references (in II:39, VII:4, and XIII:5) to the evolution of human consciousness and its bodily vehicle through their various stages of *chitta* (consciousness, feeling), *ahamkara* (ego), *buddhi* (discriminative intellect), *manas* (sense mind with its ten senses), and the five gross vibratory elements.

tral and causal bodies), true knowledge of the phenomenal world is produced.* A man of Self-realization, tuning in with the Infinite, can see this mysterious tree of nerves, life force, and thought issuing out of Cosmic Consciousness; he thus becomes omniscient—a "knower of the Vedas," that is, of all knowledge.

The ordinary man is absorbed in sensations, which reach him through the sensitive leaves of the spinal tree. He partakes of the fruits of touch, sight, hearing, smell, and taste that exist among the "leaves," the sensitive receivers of sensations at the end of the numerous nerve branches.

Spiritual interpretation of Adam and Eve story

GOD TOLD THE ORIGINAL MAN AND WOMAN, metaphorically called Adam and Eve in the Bible, to "eat of the fruit of the trees of the garden"; but He warned them "of the fruit of the tree which is in the midst of the garden...ye shall not eat of it, neither shall ye touch it, lest ye die."†

Spiritually interpreted, these words signify that the Lord wished Adam and Eve to eat or enjoy, as human beings, the "fruits" of the fivefold sensory tree. But of the "apple" of sex on the tree of nerves situated "in the midst (middle) of the garden" of the human body, God said: "Do not try to have physical sex experience, lest you die (lose your present consciousness of immortality)."

The Lord created the "original pair," Adam and Eve, by the power of materialization through the divine fiat of His will. He placed them in a garden "eastward in Eden"; that is, with their consciousness focused "eastward" in the spiritual eye of intuitive divine perception. To them He gave the same power to condense their thoughts into gross images materialized from the ether (ideational world), that by this immaculate method of creation they could multiply and people the earth. He told them to enjoy the sensations of seeing and hearing each other, talking and eating with each other, smelling the flowers, and touching the objects around them that He had created. But He warned these first beings not to touch each other's bodies in a carnal way, lest they summon forth the subconscious memory of the animal mode of sexual propagation, which they had known and employed previously in bestial forms.

---

* See also the commentary on I:15–18—explanation of the astral "movie booths" in the six cerebrospinal centers that project the seemingly real phenomenal world. (*Publisher's Note*)

† Genesis 3:2–3.

Heretofore, God's manifestation as individualized souls had evolved upward through various life forms to instinct-bound animals. God had then introduced souls from the highest evolved animals into the human bodies of the symbolic Adam and Eve.

The bodies of these first humans were therefore the result of both evolution (generally evolved from the pattern of animals) and an act of special creation by God as the beginning of the human race. Human beings are above the lesser instrumentality of animals, for they alone possess the potential to express full divinity because of unique spiritual cerebrospinal centers of divine life and consciousness. Thus both divine and bestial or subhuman traits characterize man as an embodied mortal.

Spiritual significance of the "Fall of Man"

The original prototypes of man and woman had no sexual members in their perfect bodies until after they had disobeyed God's command to them. "They were both naked...and were not ashamed"*—a harmonious unity between the qualities of positive and negative, masculine and feminine, reason and feeling, unperverted by gross sensual sex attraction. But when the feeling or Eve-consciousness in man was tempted by vague recollections of animalistic sexual arousal, then man's reason or Adam also succumbed. When Adam and Eve embraced each other with sensual desire, the serpentine or coiled-up energy at the base of the spine, which either lifts man Godward or feeds his senses, stimulated the heretofore undeveloped sex nerves. From this agitation, the sex organs developed. "Unto Adam also and to his wife did the Lord God make coats of skins, and clothed them."† The positive Adam with masculine reason uppermost became male; the negative Eve with feminine feeling predominant became female. Eden, their state of divine consciousness, was lost to them, and "they knew they were naked": their purity to see themselves as souls encased in a wondrous triune body of consciousness, life force, and atomic radiation was replaced by identification with the limitations of the gross physical form.

Ever since the Fall, their descendants have had to reproduce their kind by the gross and complicated process of sexual creation. Adam and Eve, and through them the human race, were required by cosmic law to be subject to the dualities of good and evil, and to experience death, painful change, because they had forfeited their omniscient immortality by reverting to animal habits.

---

* Genesis 2:25. † Genesis 3:21.

While the Genesis story in the Bible focuses on the fall of original man, the Hindu scriptures extol the first beings on earth as divine individuals who could assume corporeal forms and similarly create offspring by divine command of their will. In one such account, in the hoary *Purana, Srimad Bhagavata,* the first man and woman in physical form, the Hindu "Adam and Eve," were called Svayambhuva Manu ("man born of the Creator") and his wife Shatarupa ("having a hundred images") whose children intermarried with Prajapatis, perfect celestial beings who took physical forms to become the progenitors of mankind. Thus, entering the original unique human forms created by God were souls that had either passed through the upward evolutionary stages of creation as Prakriti prepared the earth for the advent of man, or were pristine souls that had descended to earth specifically to begin the world's human population. In either case, original man was uniquely endowed to express soul perfection. Those "Adams and Eves" and their offspring who maintained their divine consciousness in the "Eden" of the spiritual eye returned to Spirit or the heavenly realms after a blissful sojourn on earth. The "fallen" human beings and their "fallen" offspring were caught in the reincarnational cycles that are the fate of desire-filled, sense-identified mortals.*

The divine progenitors of the human race

Mankind in general thus remains reveling in the leaves of sensations of the bodily garden, without understanding its origin in God. But yogis are able to reclaim the lost Eden by withdrawing their minds not only from the touch sensation of sex but also from all other tactual contacts, and from the sensations of sight, hearing, smell, and taste. Such yogis ascend the inverted tree of the nervous system, life force, and consciousness to reach the paradise of Cosmic Consciousness.

The ordinary man indulges in the transitory pleasures of bodily sensations and fleeting thought-forms, thereby exposing himself to countless subsequent miseries. But a man of Self-realization, being one with the Cosmic Consciousness of his Maker, beholds the human body and mind as delusive thought-forms that provide the soul with a means to experience the Lord's cosmic chiaroscuro.

That is why the Bhagavad Gita says that one who understands this triple tree of life, which has its source in God's eternal existence, is a knower of all wisdom ("the Vedas").

---

* See also IV:7–8, page 446.

VERSE 2

adhaś cordhvaṁ prasṛtās tasya śākhā guṇapravṛddhā
viṣayapravālāḥ
adhaś ca mūlāny anusaṁtatāni karmānubandhīni manuṣyaloke

Its branches spread above and below, nurtured by the gunas; its buds are the sense objects; and downward, into the world of men, extend the rootlings that force man to actions.

THE ANALOGY OF THE *ashvattha* tree of life is here further elaborated. Its branches spread both "above" and "below"—extending upward, they give knowledge of the higher realms of being and consciousness; and stretching downward they confine perception to the sentient physical body and material plane.

The life and consciousness flowing through these branches, concentrated either above or below, are nurtured by the *gunas,* triple qualities (*sattva, rajas,* and *tamas*), according to the ego's response to their good, activating, and evil influence.

Human actions originate primarily from the "buds" of sensation, the "sense objects." These sensations grow on the bodily nerve endings of sight, hearing, smell, taste, and touch. In a deeper metaphysical analysis, these "sense objects" are defined as the causal potentials or "buds" of sensory experience: sound, or what the ear can hear; tangibility or resistance, what can be felt; form or color, what the eye can see; flavor, what the tongue can taste; odor, what the nose can smell. Inherent in these supramental potentials are the subtle vibratory creative elements of earth, water, fire, air, and ether. These potentials become elaborated as the sensory organs and perceptions through interaction with the three *gunas* (see XIII:1), and the end result is the manifested "object," or sensation.

Desire seeds that compel man's actions

Although the principal root of the tree of life lies above in Cosmic Consciousness, there are secondary roots beneath, embedded in the subconsciousness and superconsciousness in the brain. These "rootlings" originate from the likes and dislikes (attractions and repulsions) engendered from good and bad actions and desires of past lives (*samskaras* and their progeny, *vasanas* or desire-seeds).* They extend

* See allegorical meaning of Drona as *samskara,* impressions on the consciousness of past

downward into the nervous system and senses, "the world of men," and compel man's actions. These past habits and desire impressions continuously instigate in man the performance of specific actions—good or bad as the case may be.

God is the Originator of all, but it is man who perpetuates his own existence. Man's self-created *samskaras* and *vasanas* from past lives, and his new desires arising from his response to the influence of the *gunas* and their evolutes in the present life, impel him to take innumerable rebirths to fulfill his longings. Thus does he contribute to the nurture and perpetuity of the Tree of Life, causing its physical manifestation as the nervous system to sprout forth again and again, in each new physical form in successive incarnations. In this way, human beings are bound to life and death through the power of their desires. Because of this, the *ashvattha* tree is referred to as representing *samsara,** "worldly illusion," which is the entrapping cause of the cyclic wheel of reincarnation.

VERSES 3–4

na rūpam asyeha tathopalabhyate nānto na cādir na ca saṁpratiṣṭhā
aśvattham enaṁ suvirūḍhamūlam asaṅgaśastreṇa dṛḍhena chittvā (3)

tataḥ padaṁ tat parimārgitavyaṁ yasmin gatā na nivartanti bhūyaḥ
tam eva cādyaṁ puruṣaṁ prapadye yataḥ pravṛttiḥ prasṛtā purāṇī (4)

The true nature of this tree, its beginning, its end, and its modes of continuity—none of these are understood by ordinary men. The wise, having destroyed the firmly rooted ashvattha with the

---

actions that create strong tendencies to repeat themselves; and his son Ashvatthaman as *ashaya* or *vasana,* latent desire, or desire-seed—impressions of desires left on the consciousness and carried over into the next incarnation or succeeding rebirths. (I:8, page 88.)

* *Samsara:* "the world; worldly illusion; passing through a succession of states; transmigration."

powerful axe of nonattachment; thinking, "I take refuge in the Primeval Purusha from whom alone issued the immemorial processes of creation," seek the Supreme Goal. Reaching It, they return to phenomenal existence no more.

THOUGH THE TRIPLE TREE of consciousness, life force, and nerves is present in man, he does not understand himself or Nature. The elusive ever-changing modes of cosmic creation bewilder him. Of such delusive ignorance in ordinary beings Jesus spoke: "...they seeing see not; and hearing they hear not, neither do they understand."*

Only a sage determines to wield the strong axe of nonattachment, nondesire, to destroy the *ashvattha* tree within him, deeply rooted in the habits of material living. He alone attains the Divine Goal.

The worldly man, living under the thick-leaved tree of sense pleasures and egotism, does not perceive the skies of liberating Cosmic Consciousness. But the sincere devotee, by discrimination and yoga practice, strikes a mortal blow to material desires and past-habit-instigated activities rooted in his conscious, subconscious, and superconscious minds.† Thus felling the obscuring tree of material delusion, he beholds in transcendental ecstasy the skies of the Infinite. He perceives Cosmic Consciousness as the origin, continuity, and end of the Tree of Life of his body and of the cosmos. By this realization that God is all, and by freedom from past and present desires, he becomes a liberated being, able to retain this consciousness even in the bodily state. But never again will he be forced by cosmic law to take rebirth on earth.

---

* Matthew 13:13.

† "There are a thousand hacking at the branches of evil to one who is striking at the root."—Henry David Thoreau, *Walden*

THE ABODE OF THE UNMANIFEST

VERSE 5

nirmānamohā jitasaṅgadoṣā adhyātmanityā vinivṛttakāmāḥ
dvandvair vimuktāḥ sukhaduḥkhasaṁjñair gacchanty amūḍhāḥ
padam avyayaṁ tat

Without craving for honor, free from delusion and malignant attachment, all longings banished, disengaged from the pair of opposites — pleasure and pain — ever established in the Self, the undeceived attain the immutable state.

THE MAN WHO HAS ESCAPED from *maya* into Cosmic Consciousness is filled with unalloyed supreme bliss. Free from the relativities of delusion, at one with Spirit, his immutable Self is undistorted by Nature's kinetic currents of pride, changing moods with their impulsive desires, misery-producing attachments, and the undulating, contrary pair: passing joys and griefs.

VERSE 6

na tad bhāsayate sūryo na śaśāṅko na pāvakaḥ
yad gatvā na nivartante tad dhāma paramaṁ mama

Where no sun or moon or fire shines, that is My Supreme Abode. Having reached there, men are never reborn.

THE TAINTLESS YOGI, REFERRED to in the preceding three verses, becomes permanently established in his God-union, whether he remains incarnate or leaves the gross realms to abide forever in the transcendental Spirit. While in the body, he attains *samadhi*-union with Spirit by lifting his consciousness beyond the "fire" of bodily life energy, the "moon" or reflected creative light in the spinal centers, and the "sun" of the astral thousand-petaled lotus. Thence, he enters that realm of Cosmic Consciousness which is the Lord's "Supreme Abode," in which even the slightest vibrating tremors of the suns and the moons and fires of creation are absent.

The Bhagavad Gita contains the essence of the wisdom in the *Upanishads* (summaries in the Vedas). The following thought, cited in this Gita verse, is found in several *Upanishads:* "Where sun and moon and stars and lightnings dare not peep with their glaring eyes, there I remain in My unmanifested abode. It is My unseen light that appears in the borrowed lights of creation."

When God withdraws His secret light at the time of the end of a cycle, all lamps of Nature lose their luminescence. Similarly, when the liberated yogi finally merges in Spirit to "go no more out," the light of God issuing from the soul no longer illumines the three bodily lamps—those forms return to their Spirit-essence, vanished like mirages on a desert.

The unmanifested realm of the omnipresent Spirit is eternally free from all vibrations. Sun, moon, fire—in their cosmic and microcosmic manifestations—all belong to Nature's agitated seas of cosmic vibration. Just as the eddies below a waterfall cannot disturb the reservoir of water at its source, so the eddies of vibration issuing out of Cosmic Consciousness cannot create commotion within It. Even the finest vibrations of light or movement are not present in the indescribably subtle limitless sphere of the Lord's vibrationless omnipresent Bliss.

HOW SPIRIT MANIFESTS AS THE SOUL

VERSE 7

mamaivāṁśo jīvaloke jīvabhūtaḥ sanātanaḥ
manaḥ ṣaṣṭhānīndriyāṇi prakṛtisthāni karṣati

An eternal part of Myself, manifesting as a living soul in the world of beings, attracts to itself the six senses, including the mind, which rest in Prakriti.

GOD IS THE OCEAN, man (the *jiva* or individualized soul) is a wave. As man is a part of God, so is he never truly apart from Him. By the power of *maya,* a portion of God's cosmic consciousness is cloaked in Nature's garb, a body fitted with five external senses and one internal sense, mind. These six senses are the soul's instruments of communication with the world of relativity.

God, being One, unalloyed by any relativity, perceives Itself by Itself—by Its singular intuition, or omniscient consciousness. But complex man, created out of the complex relativity of Prakriti's cosmic delusion, requires the sensory instruments of delusion to perceive his environment and his finite existence. Bound by these limited and limiting mediums, he feels himself isolated from God; motivated by *maya*, he sustains this separation by misuse of his free choice. When at last he refuses to continue longer in this bondage, he cooperates eagerly with the perpetual involutional pull of God. Breaking the ties of Prakriti, he is drawn back to the omnipresent bosom of his Creator.

As the vast sky becomes a little V-shaped sky when reflected in a V-shaped brass vessel, so the Spirit of God becomes differently displayed in different human beings and in multifarious other kinds of creatures. But as the little sky in a vessel is not different in essence from the vast sky, so the illimitable Spirit of God and the pure soul in all beings are the same in essence. Only when the *jiva* becomes identified with the body does it put on its apparent limitations.

Therefore, God is equally present in every being—human or animal. However, His manifestation is more readily seen in transparent and in only slightly darkened *jivas,* than in those who are opaque with ignorance or evil. A *jiva* associated with an ignorant mind and unrestrained senses may commit cruel deeds; nevertheless, by meditation and wisdom that same *jiva* may withdraw from its dark coverings and again become one with the Infinite.

VERSE 8

śarīraṁ yad avāpnoti yac cāpy utkrāmatīśvaraḥ
gṛhītvaitāni saṁyāti vāyur gandhān ivāśayāt

When the Lord as the jiva acquires a body, He brings with Him the mind and the senses. When He leaves that body, He takes them and goes, even as the wind wafts away scents from their dwelling places (in flowers).

THE *JIVA* (INDIVIDUALIZED SOUL) IS HERE called "the Lord" to emphasize the point made in the preceding stanza: that the *jiva* is an eternal part of God Himself. By divine power alone are the bodies of men obtained, maintained, and abandoned.

Stanza 8 refers to the subtle or astral body, *linga sharira,* the abode of the mind, sense perceptions, and other life principles. The subtle body of each man accompanies the *jiva* in its rounds of reincarnation, endowing each new physical form with life and intelligence. With the departure at death of the *linga sharira,* the body reverts to its natural state of inert matter.

VERSE 9

śrotraṁ cakṣuḥ sparśanaṁ ca rasanaṁ ghrāṇam eva ca
adhiṣṭhāya manaś cāyaṁ viṣayān upasevate

Presiding over the mind and the senses of hearing, sight, touch, taste, and smell, He enjoys the sensory world.

THE BIBLE SAYS: "O LORD...THOU HAST created all things, and for Thy pleasure they are and were created."* The Hindu scriptures also tell us that the creation of man and the universe is only God's *lila,* play or creative sport. The Lord as the *jivas* experiences the delights of the world that He made.

VERSE 10

utkrāmantaṁ sthitaṁ vāpi bhuñjānaṁ vā guṇānvitam
vimūḍhā nānupaśyanti paśyanti jñānacakṣuṣaḥ

The deluded do not perceive Him staying or departing or experiencing the world of the gunas. Those whose eye of wisdom is open see Him.

AN ORDINARY MAN, HIS PERCEPTIONS and cognitions a matrix of the workings of the three *gunas,* looks no farther than surface appearances and hence sees no underlying divine significance in his life. He does not know whence he came, why he is here, or whither he is going. Mystery behind and death ahead! Still he imagines that no deep investigation of life is necessary.

---

* Revelation 4:11.

By meditation on God, man's "single eye" of wisdom is opened. He sees the Infinite in the seemingly finite and realizes that the Lord is the only Doer, the sole Power.

It is man's mortal attitude that is the cause of reincarnation. As soon as the devotee understands by inner experience that life is a dream drama of God's, he ceases to reincarnate. He has learned the final lesson of life.

VERSE 11

yatanto yoginaś cainaṁ paśyanty ātmany avasthitam
yatanto 'py akṛtātmāno nainaṁ paśyanty acetasaḥ

The yogis striving for liberation see Him existing in themselves; but those who are unpurified and undisciplined are unable to perceive Him even when they struggle to do so.

THOSE OF UNABATED ZEAL, who ignore sense temptations and who continually practice yoga in a humble spirit, behold the Lord as the Indweller. But men who merely read scriptures as a hope of emancipation, who do not try to follow the moral rules, and who practice yoga methods without deep interest and devotion will not receive the spiritual benefits they expect. Many students of yoga perform their exercises in a haphazard way; then wonder why they do not "get anywhere" and why they fail to feel communion with the Infinite even after apparently serious meditation.

The technique of salvation is eightfold, as outlined by Patanjali. Emancipation is attained by strict adherence to prescribed scriptural rules of conduct and by progressing through the various stages of yoga, as follows:

THE EIGHTFOLD PATH OF YOGA

(1) *Yama,* moral conduct: noninjury to others, truthfulness, nonstealing, continence, and noncovetousness.

(2) *Niyama:* purity of body and mind, contentment in all circumstances, self-discipline, self-study (contemplation), and devotion to God and guru.

(3) *Asana:* right posture; the spinal column must be held straight, and the body firm in a comfortable position for meditation.

(4) *Pranayama:* life-force (*prana*) control.

(5) *Pratyahara:* the power of interiorizing one's mind by disconnecting it from the sense-telephones, switching off at will the messages from the nerve currents.

(6) *Dharana:* meditation in which the devotee is able to fasten his interiorized mind on the *Aum* sound, the primal manifestation of God. (The sense-enslaved man does not own, or control, his mind; so he cannot concentrate on the *Aum*-God as the Holy Ghost or Cosmic Vibratory Sound. The yogi with a disciplined and interiorized mind is able to offer it to the Lord; none other is able to make that offering.)

(7) *Dhyana:* cosmic consciousness; endless spherical expansion of blissful awareness; perception of God as the Cosmic *Aum* reverberating throughout the whole of the universe.

(8) *Samadhi:* oneness of the individualized soul and the Cosmic Spirit.

Patanjali's eightfold path has been elaborated in I:4–6 (see pages 73 ff.) and IV:28.

Verse 12

yad ādityagataṁ tejo jagad bhāsayate 'khilam
yac candramasi yac cāgnau tat tejo viddhi māmakam

The light of the sun that illumines the whole world, the light from the moon, and the light in fire—know this radiance to be Mine.

The Christian Bible contains the following passage: "God said, let there be light: and there was light. And God saw the light, that it was good."* The Lord vibrated His cosmic consciousness into subtle light and found it good, that is, suitable for the purpose of creating the universe of coordinated energies: gases, liquids, and solids—different vibrations of the One Light. The light of intelligent life energy, the Word, is the first manifestation of cosmic consciousness in creation. When this divine force vibrates more heavily or grossly, it becomes the

* Genesis 1:3–4.

electrons, protons, and atoms of the universal structure.

The sun and moon and fire are composed of the grosser light of electrons, protons, and atoms, which in turn are made of cosmic energy. And cosmic energy emanates from cosmic consciousness. Therefore it is the Mind of Spirit that manifests as the sun, moon, fire, and all other objects and forces in the cosmos.

In the microcosm of man, God's cosmic consciousness vibrates, through the individualized soul, as the astral light in the thousand-petaled lotus ("the sun") that illumines with life the entire body ("the world") through its reflection ("the moon") in the subsidiary spinal *chakras* and their radiating energies ("fire").*

VERSE 13

gām āviśya ca bhūtāni dhārayāmy aham ojasā
puṣṇāmi cauśadhīḥ sarvāḥ somo bhūtvā rasātmakaḥ

Permeating earth with My effulgence, I support all beings; having become the watery moon, I bring forth all plant forms.

THE OMNIPRESENT LIGHT OF SPIRIT (*ojas,* the manifest splendor of the Lord's creative power and cosmic life force) evolves all creatures and forms and forces in the universe, and sustains them by the continuous manifestation of that light. If the beam of light in a cinema is withdrawn, the pictures on the screen automatically disappear. Similarly, if God were to withdraw His creative beam of light—as He does during the period of cosmic dissolution—the scenes of life on the screen of space would instantaneously melt away.

---

* Reminiscent of the Lord's words in verses 12–15 of this chapter is an ecstatic vision experienced by the Christian mystic Saint Hildegard of Bingen (1098–1180). She beheld "a fair human form" who said: "I am that supreme and fiery force that sends forth all the sparks of life. Death hath no part in men, yet do I allot it, wherefore I am girt about with wisdom as with wings. I am that living and fiery essence of the divine substance that glows in the beauty of the fields. I shine in the water, I burn in the sun and the moon and the stars. Mine is that mysterious force of the invisible wind. I sustain the breath of all living. I breathe in the verdure and in the flowers, and when the waters flow like living things, it is I. I formed those columns that support the whole earth.... All these live because I am in them and am of their life. I am wisdom. Mine is the blast of the thundered word by which all things were made. I permeate all things that they may not die. I am life."—*Studies in the History and Method of Science,* edited by Charles Singer (New York: Arno Press, 1975). (*Publisher's Note*)

The earth, living beings, the moon, and plant life are mentioned together in this stanza to indicate their close relationship. The light of God creates the planet, the home of living creatures; the moon, which rules water and all other fluids, aids the growth of vegetation that nourishes all beings.

The earth, the living creatures, the productive moon-rays, the herbs and plants—the home, the devourers, the devoured objects—all these, performing different functions, are yet manifestations of the one same cosmic light.

From a deeper metaphysical perspective, the Word, *Aum,* or Creative Vibration manifesting as light and life force is the sustaining and enlivening energy in all beings—even so-called inanimate forms are alive with God's power within their atoms.* Manifesting through

* In *Autobiography of a Yogi,* Paramahansa Yogananda tells of his meetings with Sir Jagadis Chandra Bose, founder of the Bose Institute in Calcutta. Acclaimed as one of the greatest scientists of the twentieth century, Bose was a pioneer in demonstrating that the boundary between living and nonliving matter cannot be definitely fixed. *The Secret Life of Plants* by Peter Tompkins and Christopher Bird (New York: Harper and Row, 1973) recounts:

"[In 1899] Bose began a comparative study of the curves of molecular reaction in inorganic substance and those in living animal tissue. To his awe and surprise, the curves produced by slightly warmed magnetic oxide of iron showed striking resemblance to those of muscles. In both, response and recovery diminished with exertion, and the consequent fatigue could be removed by gentle massage or by exposure to a bath of warm water. Other metal components reacted in animal-like ways....

"When Sir Michael Foster, secretary of the Royal Society, came to Bose's laboratory one morning to see for himself what was happening, Bose showed the Cambridge veteran some of his recordings. The older man said jocularly, 'Come now, Bose, what is the novelty of this curve? We have known it for at least half a century!'

"'But what do you think it is?' Bose persisted quietly.

"'Why, a curve of muscle response, of course!' said Foster.

"Looking at the professor from the depths of his haunting brown eyes, Bose said firmly, 'Pardon me, but it is the response of metallic tin!'

"Foster was aghast. 'What?' he shouted, jumping from his chair. 'Tin? Did you say tin?'

"When Bose showed him all his results, Foster was as thrilled as he was astounded."

An article in *Asia* magazine (March 1923) continues the story:

"Foster was overwhelmed. Boldly Bose voiced his conclusion: 'Amongst such phenomena how can we draw the line of demarcation and say that here the physical ends and there the physiological begins? Such absolute barriers do not exist.'

"If metals seem to live, what may not be expected of plants? This Indian who synthesizes the teachings of his forefathers with the revelations of modern scientific research finds that every fiber in a green, apparently sluggish mass of foliage is infused with sensibility. Flowers and plants cease to be merely a few clustered petals, a few green leaves growing from a woody stem. They are man's organic kin. Thus this scientist's researches confirm not only Vedantic teachings, but the deep, worldwide philosophic conviction that beneath the chaotic, bewildering diversity of nature there is an underlying unity.

"At the close of one of his Royal Society addresses, after he had shown the comthe elemental principles of Nature or Prakriti ("the watery moon"), all forms ("plants"—offshoots) come into being as differentiated rays of the one creative light of God.*

Specifically, in man, God as Cosmic Nature and the soul as ego create and sustain the body, with the ego as the cognizer of the body and all phenomena. From ego comes the mind with its sensory potentials ("plant forms") of five senses of perception, five of action, and five sense objects (the five elements which being combined together produce sensation or experience of gross matter appearing in solid, fluid, light and heat, air or gaseous, and etheric form).

Soma rasatmaka, "watery moon," derives from the usually adopted literal translation: "the moon (*soma*), the essence or character of which is fluid or sapid (*rasatmaka*)," supporting the valid observation of the moon's effect on the earth's watery substances and plant growth. Interpreted in the light of Yoga, however, a different analysis becomes obvious. *Soma,* the moon, is Nature, the light (or elixir, *soma*) of which is the reflection of Spirit. Within this light are all the elemental principles of creation born of the Bliss (*ananda, soma*) of Spirit. *Rasatmaka* is Nature's microcosmic expression, the sentient soul or ego (the soul that is "diminished" by expression through the limited and limiting instruments of mind and senses), derived from *rasa,* "sentient" (from Sanskrit root *ras,* "to feel or perceive"); and *atma-ka,* "the little or diminished soul," i.e., the ego.

Man, perceiving scenes of the solid earth, water, fire or various forms of light, the movement of air causing the tremor of leaves, the vast sky, and ego-conscious human beings in action, experiences these different relativities with the various faculties of his cognition, according to their grosser or subtler nature. Earth, or solidity, the grossest expression, is experienced with all five senses—each of which has its

---

plete similarity between the response of apparently dead metals, plants, and muscles, Bose poetically uttered the conclusion at which he had arrived:

"'It was when I came upon the mute witness of these self-made records and perceived in them one phase of a pervading unity that bears within it all things: the mote that quivers in ripples of light, the teeming life upon our earth, and the radiant suns that shine above us—it was then that I understood for the first time a little of that message proclaimed by my ancestors on the banks of the Ganges thirty centuries ago: "They who see but One in all the changing manifestations of this universe, unto them belongs Eternal Truth—unto none else, unto none else."'" (*Publisher's Note*)

* *Aushadhi,* literally, "plants," also rendered *oshadhi,* from *osha,* "light-bearing"; reference to plant life as being sustained by light through photosynthesis. The metaphorical corollary is that man is similarly sustained by the light of God through the metamorphosis brought about by the action of the elemental principles of Prakriti.

subtle origin in the astral spinal centers from the coccygeal or earth *chakra* to the cervical or etheric *chakra;* in ascending order they are smell, taste, sight, touch, and hearing. Water is that which is true to all the senses except that of smell. Light, finer than the tangible water, is perceptible through the senses of sight, touch (through heat), and hearing (sound or vibration being the ultimate property of light and all manifestation)—smell and taste are void. The invisible air is perceived through touch and hearing (sight is now also absent except by inference through the movement caused by air, as in the motion of leaves or clouds). The sky, and all space stretching to infinity and secreted even in between the minutest particles in atoms, is etheric, the subtlest of gross manifestations, which can only be inferred as the vibratory screen or background for all cosmic manifestations, perceptible only by the sound of that vibration as the cosmic *Aum.* Beyond the sense objects are their producers-cognizers—the even finer substances—the minds and egos of sentient beings in the cosmic drama.

❖
How the sense faculties in the spinal chakras give perception of the relative world
❖

So it is evident that although solids, liquids, fire and light (energy), air (life force), and ether, as also mind and ego, are relativities of one essence, consciousness, still the cognizer has to perceive them as grosser or finer forms of manifestation.*

---

* "Twentieth-century science is thus sounding like a page from the hoary Vedas," Paramahansa Yogananda wrote fifty years ago in his *Autobiography of a Yogi*. "From science, then, if it must be so, let man learn the philosophic truth that there is no material universe; its warp and woof is *maya,* illusion. Under analysis all its mirages of reality dissolve. As, one by one, the reassuring props of a physical cosmos crash beneath him, man dimly perceives his idolatrous reliance, his transgression of the Divine Command: 'Thou shalt have no other gods before Me' (Exodus 20:3)."

In the half-century since then, the "philosophic truth" proffered by science has been more persuasive than ever. In *Elemental Mind: Human Consciousness and the New Physics,* (New York: Penguin Books, 1993), Nick Herbert, Ph.D., describes the mathematical foundations of modern physics: "What the math seems to say is that, between observations, the world exists not as a solid actuality but only as shimmering waves of possibility....Whenever it is looked at, the atom stops vibrating and objectifies one of its many possibilities. Whenever someone chooses to look at it, the atom ceases its fuzzy dance and seems to 'freeze' into a tiny object with definite attributes, only to dissolve once more into a quivering pool of possibilities as soon as the observer withdraws his attention from it. This apparent observer-induced change in an atom's mode of existence is called the *collapse of the wave function* or simply the *quantum jump*....

"One of the most important intellectual figures of the twentieth century was Hungarian-born John von Neumann....In his magisterial tome *The Mathematical Foundations of Quantum Mechanics,* regarded by many scientists as 'the bible of quantum theory,'... [he addressed the problem that] something new must be added to 'collapse the wave

Thus, even though the objective world of the five elements, and mind and ego in man, are all relativities of God's one light of cosmic consciousness, they nevertheless are perceived differently—the grosser forms of matter by the senses and mind, and the finer forms of mind by the ego. In the yogi, the spiritualized or subtlest ego is perceived by its own subtlest medium of knowledge, intuition issuing from the soul. This subtlest ego, the *jiva* or soul expressing through the bodily instrument, gives reality to the subtle mind. The subtle mind gives reality to the grosser senses; and the grosser senses give reality to the gross sense objects. Accordingly, the perception of the mind, the action of the senses, and the experience of the objects of the senses would become void without the perception of the ego. Hence, the subtlest ego, identified with both the soul and the body, can be spoken of as the sustainer of the grosser mind and its perceptions, cognitions, and interactions with matter, the grossest form of creation.

Perception of finer and grosser forms of manifestation dependent on various instruments of human cognition

So it is that the supremely subtle omnipresent Spirit sustains by Its ubiquitous light issuing from Cosmic Consciousness all the subtle forms of consciousness and all the grosser manifestations of creation. This unseen beam of Spirit gives reality to the inanimate and animate objects in the cosmic motion picture, perceived by various instruments of human cognition—ego, feeling, intuition, mind and the senses.

When the yogi withdraws his mind and senses from the perception of the various forms of matter and rests his mind on the Omnipresent Light of God, he uses only his one sense of cosmic intuition and perceives the Singular Absolute manifested as both God and creation.

---

function,' something that is capable of turning fuzzy quantum possibilities into definite actualities. But since von Neumann is forced to describe the entire physical world as possibilities, the process that turns some of these maybes into actual facts cannot be a physical process.…Searching his mind for an appropriate actually existing nonphysical entity that could collapse the wave function, von Neumann reluctantly concluded that the only known entity fit for this task was consciousness. In von Neumann's interpretation, the world remains everywhere in a state of pure possibility except where some conscious mind decides to promote a portion of the world from its usual state of indefiniteness into a condition of actual existence.…

"By itself the physical world is not fully real, but takes shape only as a result of the acts of numerous centers of consciousness. Ironically, this conclusion comes not from some otherworldly mystic examining the depths of his mind in private meditation, but from one of the world's most practical mathematicians deducing the logical consequences of a highly successful and purely materialistic model of the world—the theoretical basis for the billion-dollar computer industry." (*Publisher's Note*)

VERSE 14

ahaṁ vaiśvānaro bhūtvā prāṇināṁ deham āśritaḥ
prāṇāpānasamāyuktaḥ pacāmy annaṁ caturvidham

Having become Vaishvanara (fiery power), I exist in the body of living creatures; and, acting through prana and apana, I digest food that is eaten in four ways.

GOD'S COSMIC LIGHT IS PRESENT in man's digestive system as *Vaishvanara,* the fiery power of assimilation, which works in conjunction with *prana* (the crystallizing metabolizing life current of digestion), and with *apana* (the poison-and-decay-eliminating life current). Through the proper action of these two currents, man assimilates "food," necessary bodily nutrients, of four kinds or which must be ingested in four different ways: masticating, sucking, licking, and swallowing.

To the yogi this has special significance. He sustains bodily life by the life force distilled from "food" that is ingested by (1) mastication (wholesome solids); (2) sucking (pure liquids); (3) licking ("eaten with the tongue"—see Khechari Mudra X:28, page 792); and (4) direct swallowing, requiring no chewing, sucking, or licking (the "swallowing" or ingestion of life force from the oxygen in the breath, or from the inner life currents through *Kriya Yoga*).

It is the cosmic life present in human life that is really responsible for all body processes. Greedy, intemperate living, in this or a prior life, affects the proper function of glandular secretions and digestive juices, impairing one's health. When the *prana* life force current is thereby disturbed, the eliminating current of *apana* is automatically affected, producing disease in the body.

Healing the body with God's cosmic life force

In cases of chronic ill health, in which the usual remedies are clearly inadequate, only deep faith in God's limitless power can heal the sufferer. Ordinary healing methods applied to physical maladies, such as indigestion, usually take note only of the symptoms and do not seek the root cause—the disturbed life force. By the enlivening power of a devotee's continuous faith, the Lord can guide the all-healing life force to cure the body of any ailment in a seemingly miraculous way. The Gita is here hinting to all persons who suffer from chronic or incurable maladies to seek succor from God, who placed within man the supreme healing power of *prana.*

This stanza also points out that the Lord is the unseen Head-Chef in the human body, who distills the life force out of foodstuff, oxygen, and sunshine to nourish man and to supply him with energy. Man is an atomic being sustained by atoms of energy distilled by the divine force from these external "nutrients" of life. All devotees should recognize their ultimate dependence on God for their well-being, and not rely solely on lesser methods of sustenance and healing, which only partially awaken the inner vital forces. There may come a time when medicine, dieting, fasting, and other curative methods prove useless without, additionally, God's help. Man's faith can fully arouse the supreme inner power of divine healing. "Where there is life (*prana*), there is hope."

True yogis, by the practice of scientific *pranayama,* such as *Kriya Yoga*, neutralize and control the crystallizing current of *prana* and the eliminating current of *apana,* thus arresting growth and its concomitant decay. This control of the vital principle automatically charges the whole being with divine life force, maintaining the body as a holy temple under the government of Spirit. Physical well-being is not a priority with true seekers after God; they entertain no egotistical desire for physical life. But they do respect the body and strive to keep it pure, that God may be worshiped therein.

❖

Charging the whole being with life force, maintaining the body as a holy temple under the government of Spirit

❖

Jesus said: "Take no thought for your life, what ye shall eat."* That is, do not constantly fuss about the body's needs; eat to live just for service to the Lord—not for satisfying whims of the palate, which produces disease and suffering. Follow the health laws of nature with the thought of preserving the body to attain divine realization. Man is born to seek the love of God, a goal he has forgotten through his emotional wanderings in wrong habits of living.

VERSE 15

sarvasya cāhaṁ hṛdi saṁniviṣṭo mattaḥ smṛtir jñānam
apohanaṁ ca
vedaiś ca sarvair aham eva vedyo vedāntakṛd vedavid eva cāham

---

* Matthew 6:25.

Also, I am seated in the heart of all beings; and from Me come memory and knowledge, as well as their loss. Verily I am That which is to be known through the Vedas; indeed, I am the Veda-Knower and the Author of the Vedanta.

NOT ONLY IS GOD THE LIFE, mind, senses, soul, and ego in man—as declared in the foregoing stanzas—He is also the power of feeling in the heart, which determines the way human beings react to their contact with the objects of the senses. He empowers memory by which perceptions and cognitions are gathered and held, and thence connected with one another in the accumulation of knowledge. And He is also the *maya,* the deluding cosmic hypnosis, that distorts the divine potentials of pure feeling, memory, and understanding, causing their "loss" in soul-humiliating emotional likes and dislikes, misconception, and ignorance.

Deluded beings become attached to their bodily instruments and personalize all of their experiences, trying to bend them according to their own inclinations, not realizing that the Lord is the Sole Playwright. However, it is the actors themselves who choose what parts they will play.

The devotee embraces the roles that lead to liberation. He strives to attune himself to God, and by ecstasy become free from the maddening, misery-making pairs of opposites he confronts on the stage of life. He realizes that though the enactments of limiting human perception, memory, and the entangling emotions of the heart are a part of God's drama, they lose their reality and hold on him when by pure feeling, divine recollection, and wisdom he reidentifies with his true Self. The ordinary person, immersed in his *maya*-hypnotized existence, remains in ignorance, deeming himself to be a physical being. The emancipated devotee lives in the awakened memory of his Divinity.

The yogi who is one with omnipresent God sees Him seated in all men in the heart, memory, and powers of perception, not only confusing mortals through *maya's* distortion of these powers, but also dissolving those deluded states of consciousness in Self-realized souls.

God is the Essence of All Knowledge. He is the Source of all the wisdom in the Vedas and in the *Vedanta* (*Upanishads*)—the Omniscient Knower of all truth to be known (Veda) and the Author of that complete knowledge (*Vedanta*). He directs the processes of all forms of human cognition; He is the consciousness of all sentient beings: angels, deities, yogis, ordinary men, goblins, animals, and all other forms of life.

The Lord knows all the states of the soul as it descends from Spirit into the human form. He knows all the perceptions of the body-bound soul, all its sensory and motor experiences during the state of delusion. He knows also the perceptions of a soul as it climbs back toward His liberating presence.

As all the waves dance on the bosom of the sea, so all perceptive processes of all sentient creatures occur within God, within His unbroken awareness. The Infinite Omniscience is conscious of every ripple of perception and vibration playing on the oceanic bosom of His being.

THE SUPREME SPIRIT: BEYOND THE PERISHABLE AND THE IMPERISHABLE

VERSE 16

dvāv imau puruṣau loke kṣaraś cākṣara eva ca
kṣaraḥ sarvāṇi bhūtāni kūṭastho 'kṣara ucyate

There are two Beings (Purushas) in the cosmos, the destructible and the indestructible. The creatures are the destructible, the Kutastha is the indestructible.

THIS STANZA REFERS TO PRAKRITI, ever-changing Cosmic Nature, and her host of creatures; and to *Kutastha,* or the changeless Divine Intelligence that informs the universe.

VERSE 17

uttamaḥ puruṣas tv anyaḥ paramātmety udāhṛtaḥ
yo lokatrayam āviśya bibharty avyaya īśvaraḥ

But there exists Another, the Highest Being, designated the "Supreme Spirit"—the Eternal Lord who, permeating the three worlds, upholds them.

THE VEDAS SPEAK OF *Sat-Tat-Aum,* which in the Christian Bible is called the Father, the Son, and the Holy Ghost. The preceding stanza of the Gita mentioned the *Aum* aspect (Prakriti or the invisible vibratory force, the Holy Ghost) and the *Tat* aspect (*Kutastha* or the Son, the Krishna or Christ Consciousness in creation). Stanza 17 refers to the Father or *Sat* aspect of Reality (Cosmic Consciousness, the Absolute become God the Father of Creation), Ishvara. He is the Ultimate Self, the Supreme Spirit, the transcendental Cause of all. Although He is immanent in creation, He is not revealed by Nature or knowable by man until the devotee overpasses the vibratory realms of changefulness.

The "three worlds" are the physical, the astral, and the ideational.

VERSES 18–20

yasmāt kṣaram atīto 'ham akṣarād api cottamaḥ
ato 'smi loke vede ca prathitaḥ puruṣottamaḥ (18)

yo mām evam asaṁmūḍho jānāti puruṣottamam
sa sarvavid bhajati māṁ sarvabhāvena bhārata (19)

iti guhyatamaṁ śāstram idam uktaṁ mayānagha
etad buddhvā buddhimān syāt kṛtakṛtyaś ca bhārata (20)

(18) I (the Lord) am beyond the perishable (Prakriti) and am also higher than the imperishable (Kutastha). Therefore, in the worlds and in the Veda (the intuitive perception of undeluded souls) I am proclaimed Purushottama, the Uttermost Being.

(19) Whosoever, freed from delusion, knows Me thus as the Supreme Spirit, knows all, O Descendant of Bharata (Arjuna). He worships Me with his whole being.

(20) Herewith, O Sinless One (Arjuna), have I taught thee this most profound wisdom. Understanding it, a man becomes a sage, one who has successfully fulfilled all his duties, and yet continues in dutiful actions.

ONLY THROUGH THE INTUITIVE PERCEPTION of divine realization (*veda,* "true knowledge") may the Supreme Lord be known. When mortal man attains liberation from delusion, he becomes omniscient: he sees the cosmic Omnipresent Light issuing from the Sole Reality, its radiance dancing within all things in its informing activities. The little mortal, now a God-man, is engulfed in an ineffable delight. His soul, his heart, his mind with all its instruments, and the very atoms of his being, all rejoice with countless expressions of adoration—for everything that presents itself is an altar of Spirit.

The taintless devotee, whose intuition has expanded into cosmic consciousness with its revelation of the hidden immanent workings of the transcendent Spirit, has attained the Ultimate. No more is he a dupe of delusion upon whom actions are enforced. Ensconced in wisdom, he freely acts through the God-given instruments of Nature, without the ensuing bondage caused by egotistical motivation. In him, the workings of Nature are manifestations of duty successfully completed, and duty continuing to be offered in selfless service as acts of devotion to God: (*krita-kritya,* "what has been done and what is to be done"). He is an exemplar of supreme accomplishment, and of the art of accomplishing: God-united in transcendental ecstasy, and divinely active in the dutiful realm of Manifested Spirit.

om tat sat iti śrīmadbhagavadgītāsu upaniṣatsu
brahmavidyāyām yogaśāstre śrīkṛṣṇārjunasaṁvāde
puruṣottamayogo nāma pañcadaśo 'dhyāyaḥ

Aum, Tat, Sat.
In the Upanishad of the holy Bhagavad Gita—the discourse of Lord Krishna to Arjuna, which is the scripture of yoga and the science of God-realization—this is the fifteenth chapter, called "Union With the Supreme Spirit."

CHAPTER XVI

EMBRACING THE DIVINE AND SHUNNING THE DEMONIC

❖

The Soul Qualities That Make Man God-like

❖

The Nature and Fate of Souls Who Shun the Divine

❖

The Threefold Gate of Hell

❖

The Right Understanding of Scriptural Guidance for the Conduct of Life

ॐ

"[The sattvic] qualities are all divine attributes of God; they constitute man's spiritual wealth. A God-seeker should strive to obtain all of them. The more he manifests these virtues, the more he reflects the true inner image of God in which he is made. He ever holds before his aspirations the criteria of the Supreme Perfection. Christ said: 'Be ye therefore perfect, even as your Father which is in heaven is perfect.'"

EMBRACING THE DIVINE AND SHUNNING THE DEMONIC

THE SOUL QUALITIES THAT MAKE MAN GOD-LIKE

VERSES 1–3

śrībhagavān uvāca
abhayaṁ sattvasaṁśuddhir jñānayogavyavasthitiḥ
dānaṁ damaś ca yajñaś ca svādhyāyas tapa ārjavam (1)

ahiṁsā satyam akrodhas tyāgaḥ śāntir apaiśunaṁ
dayā bhūteṣv aloluptvaṁ mārdavaṁ hrīr acāpalam (2)

tejaḥ kṣamā dhṛtiḥ śaucam adroho nātimānitā
bhavanti saṁpadaṁ daivīm abhijātasya bhārata (3)

The Blessed Lord said:
(1) Fearlessness, purity of heart, perseverance in acquiring wisdom and in practicing yoga, charity, subjugation of the senses, performance of holy rites, study of the scriptures, self-discipline, straightforwardness;

(2) Noninjury, truthfulness, freedom from wrath, renunciation, peacefulness, nonslanderousness, compassion for all creatures, absence of greed, gentleness, modesty, lack of restlessness;

(3) Radiance of character, forgiveness, patience, cleanness, freedom from hate, absence of conceit—these qualities are the wealth of a divinely inclined person, O Descendant of Bharata.

DIVINE SPOKESMEN ALWAYS SPEAK IN ABSOLUTES, not to describe what is beyond the aspiring devotee, but as a measure for striving. Chapter XVI cites the sattvic or good qualities that lead devotees to Self-realization, and points out the tamasic or evil tendencies that unfit men to attain divinity. Stanzas 1–3 list twenty-six ennobling qualities, as follows:

1. ***Fearlessness*** (*abhayam*) is mentioned first because it is the impregnable rock on which the house of spiritual life must be erected. Fearlessness means faith in God: faith in His protection, His justice, His wisdom, His mercy, His love, His omnipresence.

The spiritually intrepid devotee is mightily armed against any foe that obstructs advancement. Disbelief and doubt, delusion's first line of attack, are summarily routed by undaunted faith, as are desires and all of their enticements that bluff with threats of unhappiness if not embraced.

Fear robs man of the indomitability of his soul. Disrupting Nature's harmonious workings emanating from the source of divine power within, fear causes physical, mental, and spiritual disturbances. Extreme fright can even stop the heart and bring sudden death. Long-continued anxieties give rise to psychological complexes and chronic nervousness.

Fear ties the mind and heart (feeling) to the external man, causing the consciousness to be identified with mental or physical nervousness, thus keeping the soul concentrated on the ego, the body, and the objects of fear. The devotee should discard all misgivings, realizing them to be stumbling blocks that hinder his concentration on the imperturbable peace of the soul.

In olden times in India, and in Christian tradition also, it was customary for sages to seek solitary abode in the forests, deserts, or mountains for uninterrupted meditation. These remote areas, free of civilized invasion, were the natural habitat of such creatures as snakes, scorpions, and predatory wild animals. In India, even in this present age, we grew up with inspiring tales of eyewitness accounts of reclusive saints whose sole companions were cobras and scorpions placidly seeking warmth against the saint's body, or fearsome tigers become "pussycats." And who has not thrilled to the legend of Saint Francis of Assisi who tamed the bloody lust of the wolf of Gubbio. Beasts are conscious of the divine vibrations emanating from saints. Because God-knowing saints see the Lord in everything—not in imagination, but realization—they neither harbor fears nor arouse defensive fear in the Lord's creature kingdom.

For the unenlightened, the best advice is caution along with courage—fearlessness in spirit without rashly exposing oneself to unnecessary risks or to conditions that may arouse apprehensions. Everyone is given ample opportunities, without willfully creating them, to demonstrate courage and prove the power of faith.

Death is perhaps the ultimate challenge of faith in mortal man. Fear of this inevitability is foolish. It comes only once in a lifetime; and after it has come the experience is over, without having affected our true identity or diminished in any way our real being.

Illness, also, is a gauntlet tossed at the feet of faith. An ill person should try earnestly to rid himself of his malady. Then, even if doctors proclaim there is no hope, he should remain tranquil, for fear shuts the eyes of faith to the omnipotent, compassionate Divine Presence. Instead of indulging anxiety he should affirm: "I am ever safe in the fortress of Thy loving care." A fearless devotee, succumbing to an incurable disease, concentrates on the Lord and becomes ready for liberation from the bodily prison into a glorious afterlife in the astral world. Thereby he advances closer to the goal of supreme liberation in his next life. A man who dies in terror, having surrendered to despair his faith in God and the remembrance of his immortal nature, carries with him into his next incarnation that bleak pattern of fear and weakness; this imprint may well attract to him similar calamities—a continuation of a karmic lesson not yet learned. The heroic devotee, however, though he may lose the battle with death, yet wins the war of freedom. All men are meant to realize that soul consciousness can triumph over every external disaster.

When subconscious fears repeatedly invade the mind, in spite of one's strong mental resistance, it is an indication of some deep-seated karmic pattern. The devotee must strive even harder to divert his attention by infusion of his conscious mind with thoughts of courage. Further, and most important, he should confide himself completely into God's trustworthy hands. To be fit for Self-realization, man must be fearless.

2. Purity of heart (*sattva-samshuddhi*) means transparency to truth. One's consciousness should be free from the distortions of attachment and repulsion to sense objects. Likes and dislikes for externals taint the heart with gross vibrations. The heart or *chitta* should not be influenced by the pairs of opposites; only thus may it enter the divine bliss of meditation. Jesus says: "Blessed are the pure in heart: for they shall see God."*

* Matthew 5:8.

*3. **Steadfastness*** in seeking wisdom and in practicing yoga (*jnana yoga vyavasthiti*) is essential for reaching liberation. In his daily life the devotee should apply the guru-given or scriptural wisdom and should immerse himself in the peace born of the regular practice of yoga techniques. Wisdom guards the devotee, by right reason and perception, from falling into the pits of ignorance and sense pleasures.

*4. **Almsgiving*** (*dana*) or charity is meritorious. It expands the consciousness. Unselfishness and generosity link the soul of the open-handed giver to the presence of God within all other souls. It destroys the delusion of personal ownership in this dream drama of life, whose sole Possessor is the Cosmic Dreamer. The bounty of the earth is merely on loan to us from God. That which He has given into our keeping is judiciously used when it serves the needs and removes the suffering of one's self and others. The true devotee spontaneously from his expanded heart wishes to share with others his possessions, knowledge, and soul insight. His unselfishness is the natural outreach of those who love God and realize His immanent omnipresence. Jesus wept for the ignorant, the poor, and the afflicted because he saw God suffering in them. Those whose feelings have become universal with love and compassion give their lives and their all in service to God and His children.

To bestow money on poor persons who will use it to injure themselves by buying liquor instead of bread gives encouragement to sin. Similarly, pearls of wisdom should not be cast before mentally rebellious and unappreciative men. But the discriminative devotee who wisely shares his wealth, knowledge, and spiritual treasures to the benefit of those who are needy, worthy, and receptive fits himself for liberation.

*5. **Self-restraint*** (*dama*) is the power to control the senses when they are excited by the pleasant sensations of sight, hearing, smell, taste, or touch. A devotee who is master of his senses is ready for emancipation. He who succumbs to temptations will remain entangled in sense objects, far removed from soul knowledge. Every indulgence in any form of sense-lures reinforces the desire for that experience. Repetition leads to the formation of nearly unshakable bad habits.

*6. **Religious rites*** (*yajnas*) are enjoined by the Vedas and other great scriptures. A devotee, according to his state of development, may perform the symbolic physical rite of pouring clarified butter into fire, or the mental rite of burning wrong desires in the flames of wisdom, or the yogi's spiritual rite of consuming human restlessness in the fire of soul ecstasy.

In the ultimate, the whole of one's life should be a *yajna,* with every thought and act purified by a devout heart and offered as oblation to God.

*7. **Right study of the scriptures*** (*svadhyaya*) leads to emancipation. A true devotee does not suffer with mental indigestion as does one who gorges himself on scriptural lore without understanding its meaning and without assimilating it into his life. Theoretical study is helpful when it inspires a devotee to practice the holy teachings. Wisdom thoughts are faithful guides and protectors when they become one's constant companions.

In all ages there has been conflict between theoretical knowers of scriptures—the professional priests—and men of true spiritual insight. Pedants who lack inner realization but who boast of their erudition are often jealous of and persecute the men of God who live truth. Thus Jesus met opposition from the hierarchy of the Pharisees, and many saints in India have been ill-treated by learned pundits, as was the divine Sri Chaitanya.

Redemption does not come from what one knows intellectually, but from what one becomes as a result of that knowledge. There must be a rational connection between one's learning and oneself, so that a truth becomes such an integral part of the being that it cannot be dislodged by contrary temptations or doubts. This is intuitional learning, or realization.

*8. **Self-discipline*** (*tapas*) includes celibacy, restraint of appetite, and various methods of training the body to withstand cold, heat, and other discomforts without the usual mental agitation. If practiced with discrimination and right resolve, these mortifications help the devotee to attune his body and mind to spiritual vibrations.

Self-discipline is different from self-torture. The aim of *tapas* is not served by startling exhibitions, such as "fakirs" on beds of sharp nails. The profound purpose of *tapas* is to change in man his "bad taste" in preferring transient sense pleasures to the everlasting bliss of the soul. Some form of self-discipline is necessary to transmute material desires into spiritual aspirations. By *tapas* and meditation the devotee gives himself a standard of comparison between the two kinds of pleasures: physical and mental on the one hand, and spiritual on the other.

A habitually lazy person who is forced to become a day laborer feels a bodily distress unknown to those who are used to hard work. Similarly, the devotee who compels himself to follow a course of self-denial feels physical and mental misery in the beginning. Ignoring the rebellion of his body-identified ego, he should gradually accustom himself to the strenuous life of a spiritual athlete. As he continues the purificatory actions of *tapas* he finds not the torment he had dreaded, but deep peace and joy.

When man savors even once the superior joys of the inner heaven, he realizes his past misjudgment. He now finds himself overwhelmed with happiness. Human beings can never be satisfied even by experiencing every possible sense delight, which they mistakenly pursue in the hope of finding their lost soul-bliss.

Austerity, self-denial, renunciation, penance: all are means, not ends. The real goal is to regain through them the infinite realm of Spirit. As a poor man is glad to discard his rags when he becomes rich, so the successful God-seeker, entering the world of bliss, jubilantly casts away all shabby material attachments.

9. Straightforwardness (*arjavam*) is a quality of honorable men. It denotes sincerity. The eyes that see God are honest and artless. He who is free from deceit may gaze on the Utter Innocence.

A dissembler is out of tune with the universe. Hiding selfish motives under a guise of altruism, making false promises, injuring others while pretending to befriend them, a hypocrite invites disaster from the cosmic law.

The aspiring devotee strives to be free from guile and crookedness. To regain the *sahaja* or natural state of his true being he makes himself as open and candid as the sun.

10. Noninjury (*ahimsa*) is extolled in the Hindu scriptures. One of the Ten Commandments in the Bible is: "Thou shalt not kill."* The prohibition refers to the wanton destruction of any of God's creatures: human beings, animals, plants. But the universal economy is so arranged that man cannot live without "killing" vegetables for food. Eskimos cannot live without eating seal meat. When it is an urgent matter of survival, a man is justified in saving his own more valuable life by killing fish and animals, which are lesser manifestations of Divinity. Each day millions of bacteria perish in man's body. No one can drink any liquid

* Exodus 20:13.

or breathe the air without destroying many microscopic forms of life (and sometimes such organisms respond in kind).

In the *Mahabharata, ahimsa* is referred to as "virtue entire" (*sakalo dharma*). If righteousness be thus the criteria, neglect of action to uphold God's eternal laws of righteousness may be the cause of more harm than any nonmalicious injury resulting from an act of obstructing evil. Method and motive are often decisive elements on the balance scale of Divine Justice.

During a visit to the ashram of Mahatma Gandhi in 1935, I asked the prophet of nonviolence for his definition of *ahimsa*. He replied: "The avoidance of harm to any living creature in thought or deed." A man of nonviolence neither willfully gives nor wishes harm to any. He is a paradigm of the golden rule: "Do unto others as you would have them do unto you."*

11. Truth (*satya*) is the foundation stone of the universe. "The worlds are built on truth," says the *Mahabharata*. Men and civilizations stand or fall according to their attitude toward truth.

An honest person is spontaneously admired by all right-thinking men. The Hindu scriptures, however, point out that a devotee whose ideal is truth should always exercise judgment and common sense before speaking. It is not enough merely to tell the truth; one's words should also be sweet, healing, and beneficial to others. Hurtful statements, however accurate, are usually better left unsaid. Many a heart has been broken and many a life wrecked by truths spoken by others inopportunely. A sage carefully watches his speech, lest he wound those who are not yet ready to hear and profit by his veracious observations.

The Vedas mention three kinds of truth. All values pertaining to man and Nature are relative truths (*vyavaharika*). These influence human beings during the waking state (*jagrat*), which is essentially changeful, ever in flux.

All values pertaining to man's ordinary dreams in sleep (*svapna* state), when he is in touch with his subconscious mind that conjures images in the form of astral phenomena, are imaginary truths (*pratibhasika*). They have a certain validity, but only in their own restricted realm, which is far more fleeting, vague, and ambiguous than is the world of matter that man perceives in the waking state.

* "Therefore all things whatsoever ye would that men should do to you, do ye even so to them" (Matthew 7:12).

During deep, dreamless sleep (*sushupti*), and in the *samadhi* meditation of the yogi, man abides in his true nature, the soul, and cognizes Absolute Truth (*Paramarthika*).

It is a mistake to think that ordinary persons are never in communion with God or the Ultimate Truth. If all men did not occasionally pass into the state of deep, dreamless sleep, even if only for a period of minutes, they could not live at all. The average person has no conscious recollection of his soul experiences; but, as a part of the Universal Whole, from time to time he must replenish his being from the Source of Life, Love, and Truth.

By honoring the principle of truth in his thoughts, speech, and actions, a devotee puts himself in tune with creation and with the Creator. To a greater or lesser extent, all persons who meet such a saint are uplifted by his harmonious vibrations. The true man of God is freed from the painful dualities and contradictions of relativity and is fit, at last, to enter the final refuge of Absolute Truth.

12. Absence of wrath (*akrodha*) is the quickest way to peace of mind. Anger is caused by the obstruction of one's desires. A desireless man has no anger. One who does not expect anything from others but who looks to God for all fulfillments cannot feel wrath toward his fellow men or disappointment in them. A sage is content in the knowledge that the Lord is running the universe, and never considers that anything has been done amiss. He is free from rage, animosity, and resentment.

This is a world of relativity, and saints sometimes adapt their actions to circumstances. They may make a bold or even ferocious display of righteous indignation if such conduct seems likely to deter evil men from injuring innocent persons. But sages feel no hate toward anyone, however wicked and ignorant. A man of Self-realization may simulate wrath for a long or short period of time and then return in an instant to his usual calm and benevolence.

The rage of an ordinary man cannot similarly be dismissed at will and in an instant. Only the purified heart of a devotee who is free from worldly desires is truly incapable of harboring anger.

The most common "disturber of the peace" in families and among nations is wrath. A man prone to anger is shunned and often hated by his associates. Frequent outbursts of temper have a bad effect on one's health, and often lead to violence. Yielding blindly to rage, countless men have committed crimes that led to prison or a sentence of death. For the sake of self-preservation, if for no higher reason, most persons try to learn prudence and control of anger.

13. ***Renunciation*** (*tyaga*) is the wise path trod by the devotee who willingly gives up the lesser for the greater. He relinquishes passing sense pleasures for the sake of eternal joys. Renunciation is not an end in itself, but clears the ground for the manifestation of soul qualities. No one should fear the rigors of self-denial; the spiritual blessings that follow are great and incomparable.

To engage in actions without desire for their fruit is true *tyaga*. God is the Divine Renunciant, for He carries on all the activities of the universe without attachment to them. Anyone aspiring to Self-realization—whether he be a monastic or a householder—must act and live for the Lord, without being emotionally involved in His drama of creation.

14. ***Peace*** (*shanti*) is a divine quality. A true yogi, one united to "the peace of God, which passeth all understanding,"* is like a lovely rose, spreading around him the fragrance of tranquility and harmony.

Everything in the phenomenal world displays activity and changefulness, but tranquility is the nature of God. Man as a soul has within himself that same nature of calmness. When in his consciousness he can level and still the three mental states of upheaval—the waves of sorrow and gladness and the dips of indifference between them—he perceives within himself the placid ocean of spiritual soul-calmness expanding into the boundless sea of tranquility in Spirit.

15. ***Absence of fault-finding and calumny*** (*apaishunam*) hastens one's spiritual evolution by freeing the mind from concentration on the weaknesses of others to focus wholly on the full-time job of bettering oneself. A person who, like a detective, is busy observing the shortcomings of others gets a false conviction of superiority—either that he himself is free from those blemishes or is otherwise qualified to appraise others. A critical person rarely perfects his own life.

A habitual critic is like a fly that sits on the moral sores of others. A true devotee, like a bee, sips the honey of good qualities from the hearts of his companions. Jesus said: "Judge not, that ye be not judged. For with what judgment ye judge, ye shall be judged: and with what measure ye mete, it shall be measured to you again. And why beholdest thou the mote that is in thy brother's eye, but consid-

* Philippians 4:7.

erest not the beam that is in thine own eye? Or how wilt thou say to thy brother, Let me pull out the mote out of thine eye; and, behold, a beam is in thine own eye? Thou hypocrite, first cast out the beam out of thine own eye; and then shalt thou see clearly to cast out the mote out of thy brother's eye."*

Evil-minded disparagers—gossipers and slanderers—embrace the false notion that they can make themselves taller by cutting off the heads of others. On the contrary, there is no greater diminishment of character than in such behavior. Backbiters offend the God in others and in themselves. The virtuous, unassumingly, uplift others along with their own rise to heights above the small meannesses of lesser fellow beings.

A person who takes pleasure in slander and backbiting never knows the happiness of helping others by wise counsel and encouragement. Denunciation discourages and angers the wrongdoer. In their hearts most men are aware of their infirmities and moral sores. These cannot be healed by caustic irritants of castigation but only by the soothing salve of love.

Nobody trusts those who spread evil instead of good: the gossips, the busybodies, the detectors of others' frailties. The Lord does not publicly expose anyone's shortcomings, but gives all men a conscience and the chance to correct themselves in the privacy of their soul.

Jesus advised the would-be executioners of an adulteress, when they were about to stone her: "He that is without sin among you, let him first cast a stone at her."† The accusers, remembering their own transgressions, slunk away. Greathearted persons are ever ready, like Christ, to free the sinner by love and to spare condemnation.

16. Compassion toward all beings (*daya*) is necessary for divine realization, for God Himself is overflowing with this quality. Those with a tender heart can put themselves in the place of others, feel their suffering, and try to alleviate it. By *daya* the law of "an eye for an eye and a tooth for a tooth" and the stern exactions of karma are modified.

If the Lord did not show mercy and give special amnesties and divine paroles from sin, His erring children would suffer indefinitely, life after weary life. Provided a man tries by self-discipline to remove the mountainous load of his past errors, God comes to the rescue. When He feels that His child is sufficiently repentant of his offenses,

* Matthew 7:1–5. † John 8:7.

He destroys the age-old darkness of sin instantaneously by manifesting the liberating light of His presence.

Gautama Buddha was an incarnation of mercy. It is told that he even offered his own life to save a goat that had been made ready for sacrifice. The king who was performing the rite spared the animal's life and became a devout follower of the "Enlightened One."

The human father, if he is wholly guided by the masculine principle of reason, will judge his son's fault according to the law. But the mother, filled with the tenderness of feminine feeling, is a symbol of divine compassion; she will forgive the son even if he is a murderer. Devotees find profuse remission of sins in worshiping God as the ever merciful Divine Mother instead of as the mathematically minded Divine Judge who dispenses justice through karmic law.

17. Noncovetousness, absence of greed (*aloluptvam*) is possessed by one who has mastered his senses and hence harbors no desires for gross pleasures and material objects. Absence of greed and envy are characteristic of true devotees, those whose minds are absorbed in inner joys. In comparison, the world has nothing to offer.

18. Gentleness (*mardavam*) is characterized by spiritual patience. God is ever gentle with His erring children and, unoffended, remains quiet when they revile or ignore Him. All men who are in divine attunement are kind and forbearing. A gentle person attracts friends on earth and also, more importantly, attracts the Lord, the Friend of All Friends. A spiritually patient man does not feel ill will toward anyone, even the most evil.

19. Modesty (*hri*) is the power to feel shame at any wrongdoing and to be willing to correct oneself. A complacent man is immodest and develops a superiority complex. Devotees who exaggerate their spiritual attainments desist from a deep search for Self-realization. A humble seeker wins the attention of the shy and modest Almighty God.

Scriptures teach that modesty about one's body is a special ornament to women. But when I see some of the coarseness displayed between young boys and girls today, I say modesty is a quality much needed by both sexes. Brazen behavior attracts wrong companions who satisfy their lust and then forsake the one they have wrongly used. The purity of modesty will attract its own virtuous kind.

Modesty as a sense of spiritual shame is the mark of a sensitive person who easily recognizes his faults when they are pointed out to him. Being ashamed, he eradicates them. A man undeveloped in soul delicacy is rebellious, sarcastic, or indifferent when advised to mend his ways. The real devotee is always modest, aspiring to attain God by removing all his mortal imperfections through following the advice of his guru or other spiritual superiors.

The ability to feel shame is an ennobling quality because eventually it leads the truth-seeker to realize fully the humiliation of being karmically forced to take birth again and again in a physical body. This compulsory confinement is alien to man's real nature and gives offense to the illimitable soul.

20. Absence of restlessness (*achapalam*) enables one to avoid physical and mental roamings and useless activities. Nervousness and restlessness are usually caused by constant indulgence in sense pleasures or by habitual negative thoughts or by emotional problems or by "driving" traits like worldly ambition.

Restlessness is absent in God's nature; the devotee should learn to abhor mental and moral fickleness. He should keep his mind busy not with aimless occupations but with spiritual activities.

21. Radiance of character (*tejas*) comes from the cosmic fire of God's supreme consciousness, the flame of awareness, within man and other sentient creatures. As vitality, *tejas* is present in all beings, and in the electrons and protons and atoms. His inexhaustible energy upholds the activities of the whole phenomenal world. Through long meditation on God, the devotee becomes permeated with the effulgence of this cosmic fire.

Tejas bestows on man mental and moral boldness, and the radiation of irresistible confidence in righteousness that emanates from devotees who have felt within themselves the surety of the Divine Power. Such experiences develop a heroic spiritual nature. Many valiant saints have chosen martyrdom rather than renounce their faith.

Divine radiance in the devotee is further characterized by a natural unfoldment of spiritual magnetism, an unassumed vibratory aura of goodness, and a quiet outer expression of deep inner joy.

22. Forgiveness (*kshama*) in the man of God consists in not inflicting, or wishing to inflict, punishment on those who harm or wrong him. He knows that the cosmic law will see to it that all injustices are rectified; it is unnecessary and presumptuous to attempt to hasten its workings or to determine their form. Retribution at the hands of the immutable law of karma has for its proper and far-seeing purpose the eventual spiritual redemption of the sinner.

This is not to say that wrongdoers should have no curtailment. Social structure demands constraints for its survival. Those whose duty it is to enforce just laws for the well-being of humanity act as instruments of karmic law. Their judgments should be meted out without malice or a spirit of revenge. Even if justice does not seem to prevail, the karmic law will not fail to balance the scale.

A passage in the *Mahabharata* is as follows: "One should forgive, under any injury. It hath been said that the continuation of the species is due to man's being forgiving. Forgiveness is holiness; by forgiveness the universe is held together. Forgiveness is the might of the mighty; forgiveness is sacrifice; forgiveness is quiet of mind. Forgiveness and gentleness are the qualities of the Self-possessed. They represent eternal virtue."

When a weak man, slapped by a bully, says "I forgive you" and runs away, he is likely to be motivated not by forgiveness but by cowardice. When a powerful person, hurt by an enemy, shows compassion and forbearance instead of crushing that foe, he displays real forgiveness. The spirit of forgiveness arises from long practice in spiritual discipline and from realization of our inseverable human and divine brotherhood.

Just before Mahatma Gandhi died in 1948, he lifted his hands from his bullet-torn body to bestow on the assassin a humble gesture of forgiveness. "All the sacrifices of his selfless life had made possible that final loving gesture," I wrote in a tribute to the Mahatma.

Jesus, holding the power to summon to his aid "more than twelve legions of angels,"* did not resist arrest and crucifixion, and prayed: "Father, forgive them; for they know not what they do."† With divine insight he was ever able to see man apart from his errors. Christ had perfect understanding that each human being is essentially a soul, a child of God, whose evil conduct is no expression of his real nature but is caused by ignorance, "knowing-not"—the dread, but not eternal, state of delusion into which men fall when they forget their true identity.

---

* Matthew 26:53. † Luke 23:34.

23. Patience, or fortitude (*dhriti*), enables the devotee to bear misfortunes and insults with equilibrium. Outward events cannot shake him, nor can occasional inner turmoil serve to deflect him from his chosen path and goal: Self-realization. By stability the God-seeker learns to adhere under all circumstances to noble activities in the outer world and to retain the perceptions of truth that come to him during his meditations. He clings tenaciously to his experiences of soul bliss and never dims their reality by diverting his mind to lesser interests.

This endless patience ultimately gives the sage the power to comprehend God. *Dhriti* expands the cup of his consciousness until it can hold within it the ocean-vastness of Divinity.

24. Cleanness of body and purity of mind (*shaucha*) is respect for the indwelling Taintless Spirit. It has been said that cleanliness is next to godliness. On waking in the morning it is best to cleanse the body and mouth before meditation. Aside from obvious practical concerns, cleansing the body before meditation is a rite of spiritual respect, a symbolic purifying of oneself in preparation for worship. Slovenliness may distract the devotee's attention, during his practice of spiritual exercises, from the inner to the outer world.

One who is physically clean and is also rid of the mental taints of uncontrollable desires and restless thoughts indeed invites the Lord to manifest Himself in the purified temple of his life. When the mind is calm, it becomes a divine altar for the presence of God.

25. Nonhatred (*adroha*) should be practiced by everyone. A devotee who feels malice toward others loses the power to see God in all. A yogi aspiring to realize Spirit does not blind his vision by any thought or act of dislike or treachery, even against sinners or his self-proclaimed enemies. He strives to perceive in them the presence of the all-redeeming and loving God.

As the Lord is free from hatred, He shuts out no one from the boundless sphere of His tenderness and omnipresence. Similarly, one who is aware of the Divine in all creation cannot detest any man or feel any sense of disdainful superiority.*

---

* "There is an organic affinity between joyousness and tenderness. Religious rapture, moral enthusiasm, ontological wonder, cosmic emotion, are all unifying states of mind, in which the sand and grit of selfhood incline to disappear, and tenderness to rule." —William James, *The Varieties of Religious Experience*

26. Lack of conceit (*na atimanita*) signifies absence of excessive pride. The Lord does not harbor pride, though His cosmic possessions and powers are infinite. In humble concealment He secretly works for man's salvation through the propelling power in virtuous actions and in the silent attraction of His love inherent in each soul.

A little knowledge is a dangerous thing, for the devotee may feel vain and self-satisfied, falsely assuming he *is* what he *knows*. There is a proverb that pride goes before a fall. A self-admiring person is apt to refrain from further effort. He falls into the pit of inertia, which not only prevents further progress, but also diminishes whatever physical, mental, and spiritual gains he may have possessed.

Only he who is free from the sense of self-importance becomes richer and richer in spirituality until he is one with God. On the mountain peaks of pride, the mercy rains of God cannot gather; but they readily collect in the valley of humbleness.

THESE TWENTY-SIX QUALITIES are all divine attributes of God; they constitute man's spiritual wealth. A God-seeker should strive to obtain all of them. The more he manifests these virtues, the more he reflects the true inner image of God in which he is made. He ever holds before his aspirations the criteria of the Supreme Perfection. Christ said: "Be ye therefore perfect, even as your Father which is in heaven is perfect."*

The more one expresses these virtues, the more he expresses the image of God in which he is made

The Lord is "fearless" for He knows He is ensconced in immortal immutability. He is "pure in heart," His immaculate feeling unswayed by whimsical emotions, likes and dislikes. He is the sole consciousness, the unity ("yoga") and intelligence ("wisdom") that is the foundation of being and becoming. As the source of all, He is "charitable," the ultimate giver of all gifts. He perceives the realm of dualities through the senses of all creatures, yet "transcends the senses," remaining immersed in the pure joy of His omniscient Self. All activities of the Lord are *yajna,* the cosmic "rites" of creation, preservation, and dissolution by which universes and beings evolve and are oblated back into the purifying Spirit. God is the Knower, Knowing, and Known, Himself the Universal Scripture articulated by sages and *rishis* and inscribed in holy volumes for the "soul-awakening study" of man. He is the epitome of "self-discipline" (symbolized as Shiva, the Lord of Yo-

* Matthew 5:48.

gis, made divinely powerful by awesome austerity and meditation) ever contained in His own Being in spite of His engagement in cosmic activities. The "straightforwardness" of the Lord is His nature of nondissembling, uncompromising eternal righteousness.

The Lord is *"ahimsa,"* the shelter from all harm, in whom there is no intent to cause pain or injury to any being; harm is the result of the misuse of free choice to identify oneself with the illusions of duality. He is "truth," the Singular Reality—ever-existing, ever-conscious, ever-new blissful Blessedness—behind all cosmic appearances. In Him there is "no wrath," no desire contradicted in His desireless Self; the working of His laws are not punishments, but promptings of His love. He is the emblem of perfect "renunciation," joyous in His own blessedness, nonattached and fulfilled with or without the objects of His *lila* of creation. He is the Ever Tranquil, the unchanging, stabilizing "peacefulness" beneath the turmoil of relativities that play upon the surface of His Being. The guileless Lord "exposes no faults"; rather He gives man the solitary confessional of his thoughts and conscience in which to analyze and correct himself ere his own wrong behavior insinuate against him. It is the Lord who is the real sufferer in all beings; therefore, He is the kindness of empathy, the infinite "compassion" upon whose mercy all beings may cast themselves. Though He is the creator of everything, He is "noncovetous," giving over His wonders to the evolutionary working of His laws and to the free-will innovations of His children, receiving only the token offerings that come perchance from wise and loving hearts. Were it not for the "gentleness" of God, His silent loving persuasion of involution that creates unity and draws creation back to Him, the violent inharmony of vibratory repulsion would perpetuate eternally a chaotic state of existence. God is the paragon of virtue, "modesty" supreme; no act of the Lord bears taint of impropriety. Recollected in His bliss and wisdom, with "no ruffle of restlessness," the inactively active Lord brings forth universes and beings, not out of agitated fickle fancy, but for a divine purpose understood by those who pierce the veil of delusion.

God is omnipresent Omnipotence, the "radiance" of divine power that bestows and sustains all consciousness and vitality. In His unconditional love for all of His children, the Lord is supremely "forgiving," blessing not only according to the measure of their little store of good karma, but principally through the transcending power of His grace. Of the Lord's eternal "patience" the scriptures sing, "He is permanent, unmoving, the everlasting Seer of all." He is immutable taintlessness, pristine "purity," the incorruptible light of creation in which dance the shadows of both good and evil; yet they mar nor taint it not. As He resides equally in all, to the Lord "none is hateful": "He maketh His sun to rise on the evil and on the good, and sendeth rain on the just and on the unjust."* Sovereign of all universal realms, the almighty "prideless" Lord tempers His powers with love and humbly abides as the servant of His kingdom, maintaining for the benefit of its inhabitants life, truth, beauty, and love.

THE NATURE AND FATE OF SOULS WHO SHUN THE DIVINE

VERSES 4–5

dambho darpo 'bhimānaś ca krodhaḥ pāruṣyam eva ca
ajñānaṁ cābhijātasya pārtha saṁpadam āsurīm (4)

daivī saṁpad vimokṣāya nibandhāyāsurī matā
mā śucaḥ saṁpadaṁ daivīm abhijāto 'si pāṇḍava (5)

(4) Vainglorious pride, arrogance, conceit, wrath, harshness, and ignorance mark the man who is born with the demonic nature, O Son of Pritha (Arjuna).

(5) The divine qualities bestow liberation; the demonic qualities lead to bondage. Fear not, O Pandava (Arjuna)! thou art endowed with the divine traits.

OWING TO RESPONSE TO PAST BAD KARMA, some human beings are inclined toward evil from birth. In startling contrast to the virtuous, the evil-inclined misuse such possessions as power (in whatever perverted form), or money, or social status, or bookish intellect as a sign of their "greatness" or accomplishment. They magnify their self-importance with ostentation, braggadocio, and hypocrisy. They arrogantly demean others to make themselves appear grander; and are wholly egotistical

* Matthew 5:45.

in self-interest and self-centeredness. Desiring to have everything their own way, they are quick to anger at any opposition, or even for no apparent cause whatsoever. Their behavior is harsh and either thoughtlessly or intentionally cruel. Their discrimination is so blinded by the density of their delusive ignorance that they lose even basic common sense in distinguishing right from wrong; and thus they act from their own mental standards of distorted convictions and values, inflicting on others their misconceptions and misguided behavior.

As Sri Krishna cited these basic characteristics of an *asura* (devilish man), Arjuna humbly wondered if he himself possessed any of them. The Lord, perceiving the thought, reassured his disciple.

Arjuna's question occurs to every devotee as he perseveres in the spiritual path and carefully analyzes himself for flaws. He is happy only when he understands by soul intuition that he is rightly approaching the blissful Goal.

Verse 6

dvau bhūtasargau loke 'smin daiva āsura eva ca
daivo vistaraśaḥ prokta āsuraṁ pārtha me śṛṇu

Two types of men exist in this world: the divine and the demonic. I have told you fully about the divine qualities; now hear about the demonic, O Son of Pritha (Arjuna).

Dvau bhutasargau: "Two types of beings." In *Autobiography of a Yogi* I have written: "In measuring the worth of a man, a saint employs an invariable criterion, one far different from the shifting yardsticks of the world. Humanity—so variegated in its own eyes!—is seen by a master to be divided into only two classes: ignorant men who are not seeking God, and wise men who are."

In expounding the nature of the *gunas,* the *rishis* said there are three classes of men: those predominantly marked by *sattva* (goodness), *rajas* (activity, usually for selfish purposes), or *tamas* (ignorance, inertia). All persons possess the three *gunas* in varying proportions; but, as a whole, the life of each man reveals that he leans more heavily either toward good or toward evil. In this sense, stanza 6 refers to two, rather than three, types of humanity.

In the following verses (7–18) Lord Krishna elaborates graphically the ungodly traits of those who create in themselves a demonic nature. Analyzed as direct opposites of virtues, evil qualities may be readily recognized and, it is to be hoped, summarily shunned and vanquished from one's storehouse of characteristics. Even the virtuous must be diligent in guarding against any invasion of evil tendencies that may be lurking in the subconscious as karmic traits from the long-forgotten past, held in restraint but not yet fully destroyed by virtue.

VERSES 7–18

pravṛttiṁ ca nivṛttiṁ ca janā na vidur āsurāḥ
na śaucaṁ nāpi cācāro na satyaṁ teṣu vidyate (7)

asatyam apratiṣṭhaṁ te jagad āhur anīśvaram
aparasparasaṁbhūtaṁ kim anyat kāmahaitukam (8)

etāṁ dṛṣṭim avaṣṭabhya naṣṭātmāno 'lpabuddhayaḥ
prabhavanty ugrakarmāṇaḥ kṣayāya jagato 'hitāḥ (9)

kāmam āśritya duṣpūraṁ dambhamānamadānvitāḥ
mohād gṛhītvāsadgrāhān pravartante 'śucivratāḥ (10)

cintām aparimeyāṁ ca pralayāntām upāśritāḥ
kāmopabhogaparamā etāvad iti niścitāḥ (11)

āśāpāśaśatair baddhāḥ kāmakrodhaparāyaṇāḥ
īhante kāmabhogārtham anyāyenārthasaṁcayān (12)

idam adya mayā labdham idaṁ prāpsye manoratham
idam astīdam api me bhaviṣyati punar dhanam (13)

asau mayā hataḥ śatrur haniṣye cāparān api
īśvaro 'ham ahaṁ bhogī siddho 'haṁ balavān sukhī (14)

āḍhyo 'bhijanavān asmi ko 'nyo 'sti sadṛśo mayā
yakṣye dāsyāmi modiṣya ity ajñānavimohitāḥ (15)

anekacittavibhrāntā mohajālasamāvṛtāḥ
prasaktāḥ kāmabhogeṣu patanti narake 'śucau (16)

ātmasaṁbhāvitāḥ stabdhā dhanamānamadānvitāḥ
yajante nāmayajñais te dambhenāvidhipūrvakam (17)

ahaṁkāraṁ balaṁ darpaṁ kāmaṁ krodhaṁ ca saṁśritāḥ
mām ātmaparadeheṣu pradviṣanto 'bhyasūyakāḥ (18)

(7) The demonic know not the right path of action or when to refrain from action. They lack purity and truth and proper conduct.

(8) They say: "The world has no moral foundation, no abiding truth, no God or Ruler; produced not by a systematic causal order, its sole purpose is lustful desire—what else?"

(9) With their feeble intellects, such ruined men cling to their erroneous beliefs and commit many atrocities. They are enemies of the world, bent on its destruction.

(10) Abandoned to insatiable longings, full of dissimulation, self-conceit, and insolence, possessing evil ideas through delusion, all their actions are impurely motivated.

(11) Believing that fulfillment of bodily desires is man's highest aim, confident that this world is "all," such persons are engrossed till the moment of death in earthly cares and concerns.

(12) Bound by hundreds of fetters of selfish hopes and expectations, enslaved by wrath and passion, they strive to provide for physical enjoyments by amassing wealth dishonestly.

(13) "This I have acquired today; now another desire I shall satisfy. This is my present wealth; however, more shall also be mine.

(14) "I have killed this enemy; and the others also I will slay. I am the ruler among men; I enjoy all possessions; I am successful, strong, and happy.

(15) "I am rich and well-born; can any other be compared with me? Ostentatiously I will give alms and make formal sacrifices; I will rejoice." Thus they speak, led astray by lack of wisdom.

(16) Harboring bewildering thoughts, caught in the net of delusion, craving only sensual delights, they sink into a foul hell.

(17) Vain, stubborn, intoxicated by pride in wealth, they perform the sacrifices hypocritically and without following the scriptural injunctions.

(18) Egotistical, forceful, haughty, lascivious, and prone to rage, these malicious men despise Me who dwells within them and within all other men.

THE DEEPLY DELUDED EGOCENTRIC INDIVIDUAL, addicted to his false convictions and self-serving ambitions, establishes his colossal ego as an idol on the altar of lust for power, possession, and sensual gratification. Thus does he become wholly engaged in self-worship. Deifying himself, his myopic vision has no scope for perception of God and truth. Though he ornament his ego-shrine with hypocritical portrayals of righteousness and ostentatious displays of charity, his misdeeds, his greed, and his quickness to anger at any frustrated wish reveal his would-be hidden motivations.

VERSES 19–20

tān ahaṁ dviṣataḥ krūrān saṁsāreṣu narādhamān
kṣipāmy ajasram aśubhān āsurīṣv eva yoniṣu (19)

āsurīṁ yonim āpannā mūḍhā janmani janmani
mām aprāpyaiva kaunteya tato yānty adhamāṁ gatim (20)

(19) These cruel and hating perpetrators of evil, worst among men, I hurl again and again into demonic wombs in the spheres of transmigration.

(20) Entering the state of existence of the asuras, deluded birth after birth, failing to attain Me, they thus descend to the very lowest depths.

GOD IS NOT A VENGEFUL JUDGE who casts into everlasting hell those who transgress His commandments. But He has set forth His karmic law of cause and effect governing human action as a teaching mechanism to prevent incarnate souls from being caught forever in the outward pull of delusion. The God-given power that works with this law for the evolutionary upliftment of man is the discriminative free choice unique to the human species. Misuse of this endowment diminishes the influence of this saving inner voice of guidance. Without divine discrimination, man becomes bestial, governed by base instincts and noxious habits. In such persons, the evil tamasic propensities obscure the spiritual sattvic qualities and degrade the activating materialistic rajasic traits. Thence, according to the divine ordinance of karma, these "worst among men" attract in their next incarnation an inauspicious birth and environment commensurate with their indulgence in profligate habits and behavior.

As proper use of the privilege of free choice serves to lodge the incarnating human in a divinely endowed body and heavenly environment, so misuse of this freedom of will causes rebirth in demonic "wombs"*—states of hellish existence on earth or in other regions of the universe characterized by suffering and violence, or in dark astral worlds of fearsome beings and nightmares. The karmic fate of the *asuras,* demonic mentalities, is to remain entrapped in darkest delusion birth after birth if they do not rouse themselves from ignorance by efforts at right determination and action. Thus may they descend to the farthest possible depths, incarnating for a time even in an animal body or other medium (as may be the case in some insane persons who have lost all power of reason), or in some astral bestial form. Such instruments have no power of free choice and therefore accrue no karmic consequences for their actions. Such an existence is the bottommost saving grace for the declining being. Working out past karma without the possibility of accruing further entanglement, the descended being will then be given in his next life a new and better opportunity to redeem himself.

---

* Sanskrit *yoni,* literally, "womb," refers also to the particular state into which one is born—one's bodily condition and station in life fixed by birth. (See also XIV:14–15, page 914.)

THE THREEFOLD GATE OF HELL

VERSES 21–22

trividhaṁ narakasyedaṁ dvāraṁ nāśanam ātmanaḥ
kāmaḥ krodhas tathā lobhas tasmād etat trayaṁ tyajet (21)

etair vimuktaḥ kaunteya tamodvārais tribhir naraḥ
ācaraty ātmanaḥ śreyas tato yāti parāṁ gatiṁ (22)

(21) Lust, anger, and greed—these constitute the threefold gate of hell leading to the destruction of the soul's welfare. These three, therefore, man should abandon.

(22) O Son of Kunti (Arjuna)! By turning away from these three entrances to the realm of darkness, man behaves according to his own highest good and thereafter reaches the Supreme.

PATANJALI IN HIS *YOGA SUTRAS* cited lust (*kama*), anger (*krodha*), and greed (*lobha*) among the faults (*doshas*) that afflict the ego nature of the incarnate soul. These pernicious traits and their devastating effects were detailed in the Gita commentary I:9 (see page 90 ff.). When indulged, these tamasic qualities insinuate themselves in one form or another into every motive and action, pulling their host into ever deeper states of hellish delusive ignorance.

But the soul, being an immortal emanation of God, cannot forever be held apart from Him. The soul's inherent power of free choice may be momentarily constrained by karma and habit, but never fully quelled. When free choice will recognize as its best friend and well-wisher not tamasic temptations but divine discrimination, even inveterate evildoers can repent and start to mend their ways. By practice of vitalizing rajasic duties and of God-reminding sattvic actions, descended mentalities will begin to feel the stronger, continuous pull of cosmic grace coming to their aid with its allies of supportive good karma and the reactivated inner spiritual powers of the soul. By these means, along with His compassionate love, the Divine Creator will not fail to fulfill His responsibility to redeem every soul.

Metaphysically, the "threefold gate of hell" refers to the negative forces channeled through the three lower subtle spinal centers that govern body-identified activity. When the outgoing energies and consciousness from these centers are directed by a will that is under the influence of the darkening tamasic quality, then man's descent into hellish existence begins. As noted in I:11, lust or desire (*kama*) is the negative or spiritually obstructing force in the coccygeal center. Anger (*krodha*), the inimical action roused by desire that is frustrated, is the obstructing force in the sacral center. Greed (*lobha*), characterized by attraction and repulsion, is the obstructing force in the lumbar center.* As these negative forces serve to pull the consciousness toward matter and sense enslavement, they are aptly defined in the Gita as the three entrances of the gate to hell, or spiritual oblivion.

The yogi turns away from these portals of darkness both within and without. In *Kriya Yoga* meditation he uplifts his consciousness to perception of the divine spiritualizing soul qualities in the cerebrospinal centers. By reversing outflowing energies and consciousness that had descended into the body and its senses, he gradually ascends to the supernal states of soul-realization and God-communion.

THE RIGHT UNDERSTANDING OF SCRIPTURAL GUIDANCE FOR THE CONDUCT OF LIFE

VERSES 23–24

yaḥ śāstravidhim utsṛjya vartate kāmakārataḥ
na sa siddhim avāpnoti na sukhaṁ na parāṁ gatim (23)

tasmāc chāstraṁ pramāṇaṁ te kāryākāryavyavasthitau
jñātvā śāstravidhānoktaṁ karma kartum ihārhasi (24)

* Lust, anger, and greed are allegorically represented in the Gita by the evil Kuru warriors Duryodhana, Duhshasana, and Karna and Vikarna, respectively. (See I:9, pages 91–93, and I:11, page 106.) Throughout the Gita, as in this instance, may be seen innumerable references to the symbology intended in depicting the war of Kurukshetra fought by the divine Pandavas and the evil Kurus as an allegory of the inner war between the good and evil forces in man that vie for domination, as explained in Chapter I.

(23) He who ignores the scriptural commands and who follows his own foolish desires does not find happiness or perfection or the Infinite Goal.

(24) Therefore, take the scriptures as your guide in determining what should be done and what should be avoided. With intuitive understanding of the injunctions declared in holy writ, be pleased to perform thy duties here.

THE HUMAN BODY IS AN EPITOME of all external activities of Nature and also of the underlying universal intelligence or consciousness. The same cosmic powers and ordinances that create and govern the macrocosm of the universe are also at work in man, the microcosm. Man's body is thus the real seat of true knowledge, itself the *"shastras"* or Vedas. The Vedic texts have an exoteric division, which deals with right action and rituals, and also an esoteric division, that of knowledge or wisdom. Correspondingly, the physical bodily instrument with its sentient activities is compared to the exoteric aspect of the Vedas, and the inner subtle astral centers and higher states of consciousness correspond to the esoteric or wisdom aspect.

Transcending the limited faculties of the mind and senses, the yogi perceives with pure intuition

As has been explained throughout the Gita commentary, the goal of human existence is to become reestablished in one's true Self, the soul. In Self-realization, attained by the practice of yoga, the devotee knows through direct divine experience all truth to be known about creation and its Creator. The ordinary man, identified with the physical body, is oblivious of his inherent sensitive cerebrospinal instrument of life and consciousness with its wondrous revelations. But the advanced yogi, transcending the limited faculties of the mind and senses, perceives with the pure intuition of the soul the true nature and workings of the body. He knows its life and intelligence are empowered and enlightened by the life force and consciousness issuing from the divine cerebrospinal reservoirs of power.

The body-bound person, wholly ignorant of this finer instrument of consciousness and action, remains busily engaged in desultory bodily activities, pulled hither and yon by desires and temptations. Absorbed in trying to satisfy the restless demands of his physical nature, he experiences only transitory pleasures intermixed with violent miseries. The deeper he sinks into the tamasic darkness of delusion, the farther he removes himself from the inner bliss and perfection of his true Self, and from the supreme blessedness of God-communion. His reascension begins with determined effort to align his actions with the wisdom of scriptural guidance, and culminates with the awakening of the subtle inner centers of divine perception.

How many crimes have been committed and wars fought in the name of righteousness by fanatics defending or seeking to impose their dogmatic convictions as the guide for human conduct.* It is neither the exactitude and multiplicity of rules laid down in a scripture nor the size of its following that is a standard of truth. The only reliable test as to the divine authority of any scriptural injunction is realization.

Therefore, the Gita exhorts the devotee to *know,* or intuitively understand, scriptural injunctions—through one's own awakened intuition or that of a true, enlightened guru—and then to follow those edicts judiciously. It is only by this power of direct intuitive perception, which does not depend on the fallible reports of the senses nor on prejudiced intellectual inference, that one can unquestionably know truth.

A STORY WILL ILLUSTRATE the difference between truth and the inferences of the intellect.

Difference between intuition and intellectual inference

A saint sat meditating under a bushy tree. A frightened man came running to him and said: "Please, holy *sadhu,* I am going to hide in the tree above you. Don't tell the robbers pursuing me where I am, as they are after my gold and my life." The saint replied: "I cannot speak untruth; but I can remain silent." But the man warned him: "If you remain quiet, they may try to force the truth out of you. Just tell the robbers that I fled in the other direction. That will save both your life and mine."

The saint remained stoically silent as the terrified man scrambled to conceal himself within the dense foliage of the tree. The robbers appeared and demanded to know the whereabouts of the man. The saint replied, "I won't tell you." But when the robbers threatened to kill him, he reminded himself that the scriptures, in addition to proscribing the telling of untruths, enjoin man to protect his life from destruction. He therefore pointed his finger toward the upper branches of the tree.

* "Our own method of worship, or habit of life, may be to us as a cherished staff on which we have long leaned, and which we have learned to love; let us not use it as a sword with which to vex and slay."—*Thomas Lynch*

The robbers dragged down their hapless victim, relieved him of his packet of gold, stabbed him to death, and went on their way.

When the time came for the *sadhu* to leave his body, after many years of scrupulous regard for the scriptural ordinances, he eagerly anticipated entering the heavenly realms. The apparently taintless saint was stopped, however, by the King of Death, who told him: "Dear saint, no doubt you are very holy. But you have committed a terrible error of judgment, in punishment for which you must come with me and stay a while in Hades."

The saint protested: "I have committed no sin. I have always pursued the path of truth!"

"Excuse me for contradicting you, dear one," the King of Death replied, "but why didn't you point your finger in a wrong direction when that innocent man sought your protection from the robbers? Which was the greater sin—to misstate a fact, or to permit the man to be hacked to pieces because of your action?"

The saint belatedly understood the difference between truth and mere facts, and that truth implies real ultimate benefit to self and others. After atoning for his error in Hades, he was free to enter Heaven.

SIN COMMITTED CONSCIOUSLY or unconsciously brings evil results, even as poison—whether swallowed intentionally or unintentionally—brings death. Failure to discern true righteousness, and to conform one's actions accordingly, yields painful karmic results, no matter how couched in supportive scriptural "truths."

Discerning the right course in a world of relative circumstances

Without awakening the faculty of intuition through which one knows Ultimate Truth, the Noumenon (Substance) behind all phenomena (appearances), one cannot say he knows *the* truth. "Truth" is considered by many schools of philosophy to have only a relative, not an absolute, value. But the sage of divine realization learns to balance the rigidity of intellect with the fluidity of intuition. He is able to determine, in all the variegated circumstances of this relative world, the course of action that is proper or truthful as judged from the standpoint of Absolute Truth—God.

Every person has at some time had an intuitional glimpse of truth as a "hunch," an inner feeling of conviction that has proved to be right. When this innate power of knowing is developed by calmness and meditation into the pure, unerring intuition of the soul, the devotee has access to the library of all wisdom contained right within himself in the subtle cerebrospinal seats of life and consciousness.

An advanced *Kriya Yogi,* who in *samadhi* meditation has withdrawn his consciousness and life force from the realm of the gross body and senses, enters that inner world of wisdom revelations. He becomes aware of the seven sacred altars of Spirit in the spine and brain, and receives all knowledge emanating from them. Thus in tune with truth through intuitive soul-perception, he knows invariably the correct guidance for all aspects of his spiritual and materially dutiful conduct.

Various are the forms taken by these inner perceptions, many of which have been cited in other references throughout the Gita commentary. These realizations may manifest as word-thoughts, or as distinct intuitive feelings. According to the devotee's inclination, he may attune himself to the subtle perceptions of the astral sensory powers, beholding through these media the effulgent, or audible, or tactually exhilarating superconscious working of the divine energies in the spine and brain. Concentrating on the vibratory source of these powers, he may hear the variations of the sacred *Aum* or Amen sound. From within the matrix-sound of *Aum,* truths in many languages may be heard, as was experienced by the disciples of Christ on the day of Pentecost when, filled with the Holy Ghost, or *Aum,* "a sound from heaven as of a rushing mighty wind," they "began to speak with other tongues, as the Spirit gave them utterance."* It was through this power that the Vedas were originally received by the *rishis;* and thus these holy *shastras* have been called *shruti,* or "that which is directly heard."

Through Kriya Yoga, one enters inner world of wisdom revelations

Through astral sight, the truths issuing from *Aum* may be perceived as luminous writings, the so-called Akashic Records of all things known and to be known.

The yogi may see his rainbow-hued astral body with its subtle spine of the fiery *sushumna* and its intertwining *nadis* of *ida* and *pingala* currents.† Within the astral spinal centers, the activities of the elemental creative powers of earth, water, fire, air, and ether may be seen as light rays of various hues and forms. Atop the astral spine is the luminous sun of the spiritual eye: a halo of golden light surrounding a

* Acts 2:2,4.

† The *ida* positive life current and the *pingala* negative life current are the two primary *nadis* of the astral sympathetic nervous system feeding into and out of the main current of *sushumna*. (See I:4–6, page 61.)

sphere of opal blue, in the center of which is the piercing white light of a star of five rays.

Within this spiritual eye, the yogi may discern his state of karmic purity or impurity according to the reflection there of the spiritualized or materially inclined vibrations issuing from the spinal astral currents. The predominance of the sattvic, or rajasic, or tamasic qualities in his nature indicate themselves in the form of an astral triangle of three points of light seen in the spiritual eye. The top luminous point is sattvic; and when this quality predominates, it is of dazzling white. The left point is the rajasic quality whose characteristic color is red; and if it is the most brilliant point, the rajasic nature is predominant. The tamasic quality is a dark point on the right; and if that darkness is predominant over the other two points in the astral triangle, it indicates the temporary strong influence of the gross delusive quality. The entire record of the physical, astral, and spiritual qualities of the devotee are classified within this trilogy of lights. If all three points of light are harmoniously even, it indicates a perfect balance or equilibrium in the yogi: the tamasic quality properly maintaining the gross materialization of the bodily instrument, the rajasic quality vitalizing the body through the astral powers, and the sattvic quality guiding the consciousness in proper determinations.

Going beyond these astral phenomena, as the devotee is advised to do, the truly successful yogi fully opens the spiritual eye and penetrates his consciousness through it into the perception of the Infinite. Through the golden light, the blue light, and the central white star he experiences, respectively, the Lord as the omnipresent Cosmic Vibration (*Aum,* or Holy Ghost); Universal Intelligence (*Kutastha Chaitanya,* Krishna or Christ Consciousness); and Cosmic Consciousness (the Blissful Absolute).

om tat sat iti śrīmadbhagavadgītāsu upaniṣatsu
brahmavidyāyām yogaśāstre śrīkṛṣṇārjunasaṁvāde
daivāsurasampadvibhāgayogo nāma ṣoḍaśo 'dhyāyaḥ

Aum, Tat, Sat.
In the Upanishad of the holy Bhagavad Gita—the discourse of Lord Krishna to Arjuna, which is the scripture of yoga and the science of God-realization—this is the sixteenth chapter, called "Union Through Embracing the Divine and Shunning the Demonic."

CHAPTER XVII

THREE KINDS OF FAITH

❖

Three Patterns of Worship

❖

Three Classes of Food

❖

Three Grades of Spiritual Practices

❖

Three Kinds of Giving

❖

Aum-Tat-Sat: God the Father, Son, and Holy Ghost

❖

ॐ

"The natural faith of the embodied is threefold—sattvic, rajasic, and tamasic. Hear thou about it.

"The devotion of each man is in agreement with his inborn nature. His inclination is the pattern of his being; whatever his faith is, that verily is he."

THREE KINDS OF FAITH

THREE PATTERNS OF WORSHIP

VERSE 1

arjuna uvāca
ye śāstravidhim utsṛjya yajante śraddhayānvitāḥ
teṣāṁ niṣṭhā tu kā kṛṣṇa sattvam āho rajas tamaḥ

Arjuna said:

Those who set aside the scriptural rules but who perform sacrifices with devotion—what is their status, O Krishna? Are they of sattvic, rajasic, or tamasic nature?

THE SCRIPTURES ARE THE REPOSITORY of man's highest experience and soul wisdom, and, as such, are a priceless aid to all spiritual aspirants. A devotee doubtless reverences the scriptures, but may not always understand them or be able to study them carefully. Even great scholars sometimes disagree on the meaning of various sacred texts. Many men, ignorant of scriptural injunctions, prohibitions, and rituals, nevertheless possess great faith, or devotion (*shraddha*)—the natural inclination of the heart toward righteousness—and thus lead deeply religious lives.

In the last two verses of the preceding chapter, Krishna told Arjuna to take the scriptures as his guide and to act accordingly. The devotee now questions whether this applies to all of the edicts, including the many *yajnas* or ceremonial rites for the attainment of phenomenal experiences. He seeks to know whether it is wrong or rather virtuous to choose not to perform the exacting details of ritualistic worship, preferring instead a more direct concentration of one's devotion on reaching the Goal of God-communion.

Arjuna, representing the highly advanced yogi who has attained many wondrous states of inner perception (as were previously described), thus seeks further enlightenment concerning phenomenal spiritual experiences. All manner of phenomena and the holy rites to attain them are chronicled in the *shastras*. Arjuna questions the value of these. Are the prescribed ceremonial rituals and their results a necessary adjunct to one's spiritual endeavors? Is one considered tamasic, rajasic, or sattvic if he chooses to bypass the formal observance of rituals that offer phenomenal realizations, and out of devotion (*shraddha*) performs instead only those spiritual actions and methods that take the consciousness directly to God?

Arjuna's query and Sri Krishna's consequent reply are with a basic view to the concept of *shraddha,* faith or divine devotion.* *Shraddha* is the natural inclination within every being that is attracted to its Source, Spirit. This inherence of attraction, as will be seen in the succeeding verses, is dull and inert in the tamasic individual; active but with self-interest in the rajasic person; and fully expressive as devotion and faith in the persevering sattvic yogi. He who is imbued with *shraddha* is consistent in the highest form of spiritual endeavor because he is motivated by an intense spiritual longing that has its basis in the intuitive conviction of faith.

VERSES 2–3

śrībhagavān uvāca
trividhā bhavati śraddhā dehināṁ sā svabhāvajā
sāttvikī rājasī caiva tāmasī ceti tāṁ śṛṇu (2)

sattvānurūpā sarvasya śraddhā bhavati bhārata
śraddhāmayo 'yaṁ puruṣo yo yacchraddhaḥ sa eva saḥ (3)

The Blessed Lord said:
(2) The natural faith of the embodied is threefold—sattvic, rajasic, and tamasic. Hear thou about it.

(3) The devotion of each man is in agreement with his inborn nature. His inclination is the pattern of his being; whatever his faith is, that verily is he.

KRISHNA INSTRUCTS ARJUNA that whether or not a man lives by the precepts of righteousness is determined by his natural bent, his inmost being as formed by all his actions of past lives.

---

* See reference to the Pandava warrior Yuyudhana, representing *shraddha,* I:4, page 70.

VERSE 4

yajante sāttvikā devān yakṣarakṣāṁsi rājasāḥ
pretān bhūtagaṇāṁś cānye yajante tāmasā janāh

The sattvic pay homage to the Devas, the rajasic to the Yakshas and the Rakshasas, and the tamasic to the Pretas and the hosts of Bhutas.

SATTVIC OR GOOD MEN WORSHIP the Devas (divinities), embodiments of spiritual qualities.

Rajasic or worldly, passionate men worship the Yakshas (guardian spirits of wealth) and the Rakshasas (astral-world demons and giants of great power and aggression).

Tamasic or dull, ignorant men worship the Pretas (spirits of the dead) and the Bhutas (ghosts and elemental beings).

Each person shows by his life, by the inescapable expression of his nature, what type of man he is and what type of unseen power he consciously or unconsciously attracts to himself.

A person's "religion" is demonstrated not by his formal worship but by his nature. Most men are not "pure" types, however; at various times they display the *guna* (quality) of *sattva* or *rajas* or *tamas.* But a person's life as a whole is marked by a predominance of one *guna,* which indicates the stage of his spiritual evolution.

Therefore Sri Krishna said: "Whatever a man's faith is, that verily is he." All persons live according to the law of their nature, and thus are devotees of one of the three paths.

The wise, sattvic man patterns his life after the celestial design, and knowingly or unknowingly receives help from the deities to whom God has entrusted the highest functions of the phenomenal worlds.

The rajasic or worldly, passionate man, aspiring to wealth and power, is knowingly or unknowingly adoring Yakshas and Rakshasas—cosmic embodiments of greed, ruthless strength, and egotistic ambition.

The tamasic or ignorant man knowingly or unknowingly offers homage to the Pretas (spirits of the dead) and the Bhutas (various types of ghosts and spirits). By sloth, stupidity, sense attachment, and superstitious reliance on outside forces in the hope of avoiding self-effort, such a person fails to rise to his full stature as a human being and becomes enslaved to disintegrating forces beyond his comprehension and control.

This stanza points out that the lowest path means "devotion to the spirits of the dead." In general, these words indicate the stultification of *tamas,* through which a man's life is a kind of "death." Those who are given over to debasing habits and dullness and despair, who ignore all the inexhaustible resources of the soul, are worshipers of the darkest qualities, the "spirits of the dead."

In particular, this stanza of the Bhagavad Gita addresses itself to a wide spectrum of supernatural arts and rituals whose purpose is to conjure various dark and powerful entities or the spirits of the deceased. Such practices constitute a path that is fraught with danger; and, at its worst, is also evil. As the evil aspects are cited in XVII:13, the cult of consulting "departed spirits" requires commentary here.

MANY PERSONS ERRONEOUSLY imagine that "the dead"—human beings who have passed over to the astral world—are in touch with great masters or are themselves deep founts of wisdom. The truth is that most astral beings are not reliable messengers and have attained no final insight into the Great Mystery.

❖ *Departed souls and astral entities are unreliable guides* ❖

The soul is divine; but until man achieves soul-realization he is unable after death to express any more divinity than he expressed during his life on earth. Only those persons who possessed enlightenment while in the physical body are empowered, upon leaving it, to unite with God and to impart illumination to others.

The Gita points out that those who believe in consulting "departed spirits" are ignorant men. Such persons rely on the guidance of astral entities instead of seeking communion with God, the Heavenly Father and Friend of all. Having His help, what need of aid from astral beings?

Liberated souls do not usually dwell in the astral worlds, which are reserved for beings who have more or less recently left the earth and who have many lessons yet to learn. Great masters are unconfined, at home in Omnipresence; though some of them may appear, as saviors, in the astral or ideational (causal) spheres.

Among these emancipated ones are the great gurus or spiritual preceptors appointed by the Lord to help mankind in silent, secret ways. They do not require any agent or "medium" to reach the truth-seeker who wants and needs their aid; they assist their disciples directly. Whether or not the devotee is conscious of such help does not matter; he will understand that he is receiving divine succor according to the way he himself changes inwardly and outwardly for the better. Eloquent, high-sounding phrases that emanate from an ordinary astral being who is posing, through the agency of a trance medium, as a "teacher of mankind" have no such power to transform man's spiritual life.

The ordinary professional or amateur mediums, those without divine realization, are unable to "tune in" higher than the common astral realms. They cannot summon the presence of God-knowing saints to ask their "views" on various questions.* The august beings who are at one with the Ineffable Infinite can never be commanded to give a weekly lecture, for instance, through a trance medium on earth. Darkened human minds, the Bhagavad Gita points out, have many gross misconceptions about the nature of the divine plan for man's redemption. The work of a master on earth is not the same as his work in the astral or in ideational worlds; if only the physical sphere of activity and influence were essential to man's evolution, the Lord would not have created three different planes of being.

While physically embodied, a master employs the gross instruments of expression for the easy recognition and acceptance of those who are thus limited. His higher spiritual workings on behalf of the world and individual devotees remain generally unseen—but tangibly felt by those who are receptive. These are the true blessings and guidance of a master by which spiritual changes are wrought in the inner astral and causal natures of man, and which in turn then find expression in his material existence. When a master is no longer encumbered by incarnate constraints, his transforming suc-

No true saint or master communicates through mediums

* On several occasions Paramahansa Yogananda told his disciples: "After my passing, many 'mediums' will say they are in touch with me and are receiving my 'messages' for the world. All such statements will be false.

"My message for the world has already been expounded in my speeches, classes, and writings. Do not be misled by persons who, after my physical departure from the earth, will assert that they are receiving new teachings from me. To sincere seekers who in prayer request my help, I will always give it gladly *and silently*."

As Paramahansa Yogananda predicted, since 1952 a number of misguided mediums have been publicly claiming that they are receiving messages from the great Guru (and from the Self-Realization Fellowship *Paramgurus,* as well). By borrowing the name of an illustrious teacher, such individuals attract the attention of unsuspecting people who do not understand that the practice of putting the mind in a passive trance state is directly contradictory to the teachings of all true masters. The latter emphasize that concentration, will power, and mastery of one's own consciousness are fundamental necessities for spiritual progress. The claims of some highly publicized mediums notwithstanding, no great teacher would accept the "invitation" of a passive mind in the trance state. To do so would encourage a practice that is dangerous—psychologically as well as spiritually. (*Publisher's Note*)

cor continues just the same, but he does not demean himself and his spiritual effectiveness by seeking gross expression again through "mediums." Having given his divine message and testimony while on earth, he doesn't have any "afterthoughts" requiring revelation by psychics and spiritualists. But when a devotee by self-effort uplifts his consciousness in meditation to the pure realms of the saints and angels, he himself will perceive through divine sight or wondrous intuitions the presence and guidance of the holy ones who are his spiritual benefactors, and the loving God who empowers them to dispense His grace.

The astral world (with its various higher and lower vibratory realms) contains many beings who are good, many who are ordinary, and many who are bad; just as on earth we find all degrees of goodness and badness among human creatures. The person who indiscriminately opens his mind to receive whatever messages may come to him through "spirits" is not able to tell what sort of contact he is making in the astral spheres; and by becoming receptive to *any* astral vibration he runs the risk of getting into "bad company." He may also become engrossed with phenomena of the lower astral worlds and thus fail to make any spiritual progress toward the only desirable goal: inner illumination, salvation.

Danger of possession by "tramp souls"

If a person were to keep his automobile unlocked, unoccupied, and with the key in the ignition, anyone could get in, drive it, and wreck it. Similarly, when the mind is kept blank, any "tramp soul" may get in and possess that hapless individual. These tramp souls are roaming through the ether by the millions. They are seeking rebirth, but because of bad karma they are unable to incarnate as soon as they desire; hence they are continually looking for some foolishly passive mentality so that they can use that human being's flesh and mind to satisfy their wish for physical embodiment. They can very quickly get into a mind that is permitted to become blank. If a person is weak or negative, then during any attempt to contact departed spirits, such as at a séance, he may easily become the victim of a tramp soul. Such possession deranges the subconscious mind.

By contrast, when one practices the scientific techniques for God-communion that India developed, his mind is not blank; therefore no tramp soul can enter. These practices bypass the subconscious state of the astral realms and develop man's superconscious state by raising the mind to the Christ Center in the forehead, where no tramp soul can venture. It is in the superconsciousness that we meet true saints and masters. They are surrounded by a divine light; and when one sees them, he infallibly knows, by intuition, that they are great souls.

No one should try to enter the world of physically disembodied spirits until he is first armed with the spiritual power to control that world. Such power comes only from communion with the Lord. He is the Maker of all souls; and when the devotee has attuned himself to God, if he wants to see and converse with someone who has gone on, the Lord will send that person to him. As Jesus said: "Seek ye *first* the kingdom of God and His righteousness."

Yogis stress the importance of concentrating on a definite thought of God while casting aside all other ideas. By thus trying always to reach the highest vibration, the seeker is able to avoid the lower astral world and to commune with the Lord in one of His manifestations—as Peace, or as the Cosmic Sound *Aum,* or as Light; or, if one is very advanced, as the visible form of a saint.

Devotees who go deep in meditation are able to reach the higher realms where the great ones dwell. That is the purpose of the scientific techniques for Self-realization taught from ancient times in India. These practices help the yogi to uplift his consciousness to receive, consciously, the subtle vibratory aid of God and liberated masters. The techniques safely lead the devotee to feel the presence of the Spirit behind all beings.

The safe path of *Kriya Yoga* exalts its practitioners. The lives of its advanced disciples, such as Lahiri Mahasaya, Sri Yukteswar, and many others, afford ample proof. The accomplished *Kriya Yogi* becomes master of his consciousness and will. Persons who invite visitations from astral entities—and, similarly, those who allow their minds to be hypnotized (that is, controlled) by another—carelessly risk the enslavement of their God-given instruments of salvation: consciousness and will.

Even though one may encounter only "benevolent" astral entities, and even though the hypnotist may be trying to help that person, the fact remains that he has permitted another being, on this or the astral plane, to invade and temporarily control his consciousness. This is a dangerous practice, one that does not in any way hasten spiritual advancement or resemble a true experience of the presence of God, which should be man's sole goal.

VERSES 5–6

aśāstravihitaṁ ghoraṁ tapyante ye tapo janāḥ
dambhāhaṁkārasaṁyuktāḥ kāmarāgabalānvitāḥ (5)

karśayantaḥ śarīrasthaṁ bhūtagrāmam acetasaḥ
māṁ caivāntaḥ śarīrasthaṁ tān viddhy āsuraniścayān (6)

Know those men to be of asuric nature who perform terrible austerities not authorized by the scriptures. Hypocrites, egotists—possessed by lust, attachment, and power madness—senselessly they torture the bodily elements and also offend Me, the Indweller.

MUTILATION OR ANY EXCESSIVE "PUNISHMENT" of the physical form is condemned by the Bhagavad Gita. Man's true enemy is not his body but his mind. His so-called physical passions are in reality produced by dark mental forces—anger, greed, lust, which all men on the spiritual path must try to subdue and conquer.

The body is the materialization of the indwelling life and consciousness of Spirit as the individualized soul. The nature of Spirit is purity and harmony; beauty, vitality, and radiance. To abuse the body in any way that distorts this image is to offend the Creator Lord by disfiguring His human masterpiece.

THREE CLASSES OF FOOD

VERSE 7

āhāras tv api sarvasya trividho bhavati priyaḥ
yajñas tapas tathā dānaṁ teṣāṁ bhedam imaṁ śṛṇu

Each of the three classes of men even likes one of the three kinds of food; so also their yajnas, penances, and almsgivings. Hear thou about these distinctions.

EVERYTHING DONE BY A MAN is proclaiming his state of spiritual evolution. The diet to which he is naturally attracted, and his inborn attitude toward his various duties in life, show whether he is predominantly marked by *sattva* or *rajas* or *tamas.*

Verses 8–10

āyuḥsattvabalārogyasukhaprītivivardhanāḥ
rasyāḥ snigdhāḥ sthirā hṛdyā āhārāḥ sāttvikapriyāḥ (8)

kaṭvamlalavaṇātyuṣṇatīkṣṇarūkṣavidāhinaḥ
āhārā rājasasyeṣṭā duḥkhaśokāmayapradāḥ (9)

yātayāmaṁ gatarasaṁ pūti paryuṣitaṁ ca yat
ucchiṣṭam api cāmedhyaṁ bhojanaṁ tāmasapriyam (10)

(8) Foods that promote longevity, vitality, endurance, health, cheerfulness, and good appetite; and that are savory, mild, substantial, and agreeable to the body, are liked by pure-minded (sattvic) persons.

(9) Foods that are bitter, sour, saltish, excessively hot, pungent, harsh, and burning are preferred by rajasic men; and produce pain, sorrow, and disease.

(10) Foods that are nutritionally worthless, insipid, putrid, stale, refuse, and impure are enjoyed by tamasic persons.

What we eat is important because it has both physical and mental consequences. The body cells are built from food; the mind is also affected by the *guna* quality inherent in all substances.

Modern scientists analyze the value of foodstuffs according to their physical properties and how they react on the body; but yogis, who anciently delved in the spiritual science of food, consider its vibratory nature in determining what is beneficial, stimulating, or harmful when ingested. Such classification by the yogis starts with the basic verity that all things have evolved from God and are materializations of His one intelligent vibratory creative consciousness. Manifested objects come into being and are subject to metamorphosis under the influence of the interacting *sattva, rajas,* and *tamas* qualities of Nature. These three *gunas* distort the pure Cosmic Vibration into an infinite variety, characterized by varying degrees of elevating, activating, or stultifying properties.

Vibrations of different frequencies alter one another when they interact. The aim of the yogi is to purify himself of dross by nurturing his sattvic qualities through interaction with those external and internal manifestations that are pure and spiritually uplifting. He recognizes that even the food he eats, and also the manner in which he partakes of it, has its salutary or debasing effect not only on his body, but also on his consciousness, according to the vibratory quality of those edibles.

Proper diet is a vast subject unto itself, one that captivates many a "health faddist"—often to his detriment. The Gita in these simple verses offers a concise and easy guideline for determining the spiritual or unspiritual quality of foods. Whatever food is beneficial or detrimental on the vibratory level is correspondingly so in its nutritional effect on health.

Sattvic foods, in general, are sweet fresh fruits and vegetables (raw or properly prepared), whole grains and legumes, fresh dairy products, nuts, natural sweets such as honey and dates (minimizing refined sugars), and nominal amounts of fat from dairy or vegetable sources only. Prepared foods should be combined and cooked in a manner that retains or enhances their nutrients. They should be aesthetically pleasing to the eye and tasteful to the palate (mildly seasoned), and agreeable to the body's constitution.

The vibratory harmony and balanced nutrition of a sattvic diet—restraining any temptation toward greed or overeating—promotes not only good health, vitality, and longevity, but also works on the mind to nurture a calm, contented, cheerful disposition inclined toward goodness and spiritual aspirations.

Recognizing that the food, the act of eating, and the one who eats are all expressions of Spirit, the sattvic devotee considers his mealtime as a form of *yajna.* When possible, he eats in silence and with his thoughts interiorized, in a quiet, peaceful atmosphere. He begins his meal with a prayer, such as the following:

> *Heavenly Father, receive this food; make it holy. Let no impurity of greed defile it. The food comes from Thee; it is for Thy temple. Spiritualize it. Spirit to Spirit goes.*
>
> *We are the petals of Thy manifestation; but Thou art the Flower, Its life, beauty, and loveliness.*
>
> *Permeate our souls with the fragrance of Thy presence.**

Rajasic foods are those that are undue stimulants to the life forces

* From *Whispers from Eternity,* by Paramahansa Yogananda, published by Self-Realization Fellowship.

in the body, and to the mind and senses as well. All such stimulation is not wholly "bad" and to be fanatically avoided. For the average materially active person, moderation is enjoined. The very reaction on the palate of hot, spicy, salty, or otherwise strong flavors of most rajasic foods indicates their stimulating quality.

Eggs are considered rajasic; so also are certain meats (fish, fowl, and lamb—the lesser harmful of the animal-flesh foodstuffs). Any items or their excess that overstimulate the life forces, which feed the senses and nervous system, are to be eschewed, for they will produce discomfort and disease in the body and mental agitation and distress.

The Gita's description of tamasic foods is graphic. It is seen that even sattvic or healthfully stimulating rajasic edibles become tamasic when denatured by improper preparation or preservation. The tamasic categorization also highlights the harmful effects of neglecting the laws of hygiene. A tamasic diet has a malignant effect on the body and the mind, and dulls all aspirations for spiritual growth.

Among the most tamasic foods commonly consumed in modern society are the meats of higher forms of animal life, especially beef and pork and products made from them. Both chemically and vibrationally, these are highly injurious to the body and the spiritual nature of man.

Any items of consumption harmful to the body will also be inimical to one's mental and spiritual well-being; and, conversely, foods that cause an adverse mental or spiritual reaction will be deleterious to the physical constitution as well.

Three Grades of Spiritual Practices

Verses 11–13

aphalākāṅkṣibhir yajño vidhidṛṣṭo ya ijyate
yaṣṭavyam eveti manaḥ samādhāya sa sāttvikaḥ (11)

abhisaṁdhāya tu phalaṁ dambhārtham api caiva yat
ijyate bharataśreṣṭha taṁ yajñaṁ viddhi rājasam (12)

vidhihīnam asṛṣṭānnaṁ mantrahīnam adakṣiṇam
śraddhāvirahitaṁ yajñaṁ tāmasaṁ paricakṣate (13)

(11) That yajna (sacrifice or performance of duty) is sattvic which is offered by men who desire no fruit of the action; and which is done in accordance with the scriptures, for the sake of righteousness only.

(12) Know thou, O Best of the Bharatas (Arjuna)! that the yajna performed in the hope of reward and in an ostentatious spirit is rajasic in nature.

(13) That yajna is condemned as tamasic which is without regard for the scriptural injunctions, without offerings of food and gifts of appreciation,* without sacred prayers or chants, and without devotion (to God).

THE MINDS OF SATTVIC PERSONS are concentrated solely on God as their goal. Unlike rajasic devotion offered with the expectation of receiving boons, or powers, or phenomenal experiences, or the acclamation of admirers, the singular motivation of the sattvic devotee is the inherent rightness of conforming to God's divine commandments and the sheer joy they feel in loving Him. By the very nature of their worship the rajasic receive the temporal and temporary rewards they earn; the sattvic attain the blissful and all-fulfilling ecstasy of God-union.

The last stanza applies to voodooism, sorcery, devil worship, and other practices of black magic that serve to mystify and enthrall persons and that produce no spiritually elevating results. Such ceremonies are devoid of good vibrations and of helpful consideration for others; they are performed solely to satisfy the evil emotions of ignorant men.

Any unholy rites or practiced beliefs that encourage the development and use of the potentials and powers of evil are condemned by the wise and by scriptural canon as anathema, vile and ruinous deviltry.

---

* A part of the tradition of a sanctified *yajna,* or formal worship, is distribution of food (*srishta anna*) and a gift of appreciation (*dakshina*) to the guru or presiding officiant. The offering of food to guests, the poor, or "Brahmins" (priests, renunciants, or other holy persons who have given their lives to serving God) symbolizes a charitable heart that shares its blessings, which is man's duty to his fellow beings. The spiritually obligatory "fee" or donation offered to the guru or officiating priest expresses the gratitude owed to the one from whom spiritual ministration has been received, and recognition of the value of that instruction.

Verses 14–17

devadvijaguruprājñapūjanaṁ śaucam ārjavam
brahmacaryam ahiṁsā ca śārīraṁ tapa ucyate (14)

anudvegakaraṁ vākyaṁ satyaṁ priyahitaṁ ca yat
svādhyāyābhyasanaṁ caiva vāṅmayaṁ tapa ucyate (15)

manaḥprasādaḥ saumyatvaṁ maunam ātmavinigrahaḥ
bhāvasaṁśuddhir ity etat tapo mānasam ucyate (16)

śraddhayā parayā taptaṁ tapas tat trividhaṁ naraiḥ
aphalākāṅkṣibhir yuktaiḥ sāttvikaṁ paricakṣate (17)

(14) Veneration of the Devas, the twice-born, the gurus, and the wise; purity, straightforwardness, continence, and nonviolence are considered the penance or austerity of the body.

(15) Meditative communion with one's own true Self, and uttering words that cause no agitation and that are truthful, pleasant, and beneficial, are called the austerity of speech.

(16) A calm and contented mental clarity, kindliness, silence, self-control, and purity of character constitute the austerity of the mind.

(17) This threefold penance, sattvic in its nature, is practiced by persevering men possessing great devotion who desire no fruit of actions.

Tapas, austerity, is the conscientious practice of the disciplines that bring one's whole being into harmony with the true Self, or soul-nature. Such discipline is the foundation of spiritual unfoldment. *Tapas* may be summarized succinctly in a phrase oft used by my revered gurudeva, Swami Sri Yukteswar: "Learn to behave!" Bodily mortification and excessive penances are extreme measures contrived to bring body and mind into submission. But the yogi who not only guides aright his external actions, but who also through meditation works from within, at the source of behavior, quickly and nat-

Essence of tapas: "Learn to behave!"

urally transforms himself, acquiring those virtues of body, speech, and mind that characterize the sattvic devotee.

He has worshipful regard for divinity in its various manifestations. He pays homage to Spirit, and to Its active creative aspects, by acts of worship and meditative communion. He venerates the God-knowing (the "twice-born"), the gurus, and the wise by offerings of service and concentrated endeavor to learn from their wisdom and to conduct himself accordingly. His actions express purity (*shaucha,* cleanness in body, habits, and surroundings, and absence of vileness in the use of the senses), honesty and sincerity (*arjavam*), self-restraint in not acting on temptations and desires (*brahmacharya*), and a careful consideration to cause no intentional harm to anyone (*ahimsa*). These are the austerities of the body.

Speech is an extremely powerful faculty, conveying not only ideas but empowering them with the creative force of the *Aum* vibration—the source of all creativity and its manifestations of sound, including the human voice. The full potential of speech is a unique endowment bequeathed by God to man. The disciplined austerity of speech is best supported by the inner perception of truth through contact, or communion, with one's true Self (the image of God within) in meditation (*svadhyaya-abhyasanam*). The Sanskrit terminology that describes this practice is sometimes translated as "the repetition of scripture to one's self." One method of meditation on truth applies this principle of affirmation. By concentrated repetition of a truth verbally and then mentally, it fills the conscious mind and penetrates into the subconsciousness. When it goes deeper still, into the superconsciousness, the soul, the truth becomes an actual experience of *knowing,* and returns to the conscious mind as a realization.* Through regular "communication" with his true Self, the yogi becomes increasingly at one with truth. His speech becomes an apt instrument of his inner divine perceptions. His words are truthful and wise (*satyam*), pleasant and beneficial (*priya-hitam*)—engendering peace, happiness, understanding, and well-being—and are devoid of unnecessarily harsh or irritating connotation (*anudvega-karam*). His voice is kind, even when forceful, and admits no taint of caustic intonation.

Mental austerity is the practice of maintaining tranquility throughout the entire inner being. The yogi attains the acme of this state in ecstatic meditation wherein the habitually restless mind is made wholly placid, contented, and crystal clear in its perceptions. The usually dom-

* Principles and techniques of applying this aspect of the yoga science are presented by Paramahansa Yogananda in *Scientific Healing Affirmations,* published by Self-Realization Fellowship. (*Publisher's Note*)

inant senses of the ego are completely restrained and under the control of the Self, thereby effecting an evenness of heart, or feeling—the stilling of ruffling emotions. Free from the constant pronouncements of the senses and the chatter of restless thoughts, the yogi basks in the wondrous absolute quietude of a blissful inner calm that gradually purifies his whole nature. Such was the calmness of my guru, Sri Yukteswar, that you could not begin to measure his depth. Tomes of wisdom were written on the immaculate serenity of his consciousness.

Mental austerity: maintaining tranquility throughout one's being

The practitioner of sattvic mental austerity strives for continuity of this inner discipline in activity as well as in meditation. By maintaining a mental calm and a cheerful positive attitude, he enjoys clarity of thought and perception (*manas-prasadas*). With an inner evenness of heart, in which his feelings are free from the aggressiveness of likes and dislikes and expectations, he is kindly under all circumstances (*saumyatvam*). No matter what conditions abide in his external surroundings, he retains a placid inner stillness (*mauna*). No cunning wiles of sensory temptation can sway the discriminative determinations of his self-control (*atma-vinigrahas*). There arises a divine purity in all of his motivations, for they issue from the virtues that have become the aggregate of his character (*bhava-samshuddhi*).

Along with all that is asked of the devotee if he would attain the Divine Goal, he is reminded repeatedly that his endeavors are to be without desire for their fruits, or results. He readily comprehends the law of karma and how attachment to any attainment—even virtuous ones—can bind the soul in the sphere of manifestation. But sometimes the devotee is confused in trying to understand why he should not concentrate even on the transcendent fruits of meditative actions—God-realization. Longing for the results of worldly actions keeps a man entangled in the net of material perceptions. Therefore meditation with a deep desire to obtain divine communion is necessary, in the beginning, to offset desires for the material fruits of worldly activities.

Advice for the meditator who is anxious for results

But if the devotee looks to the results after each meditation, he is likely to be more concentrated on his attainment, or lack of it, than on the necessary action of increasing the depth of his meditations. A yogi should be so completely absorbed in divine love for God that he meditates automatically and willingly without continuously weighing to find the results of his efforts.

The devotee will get better returns if he plunges himself into God's love rather than constantly thinking, bartering like a businessman: "I can buy the Lord with such and such amount of meditation."

An aspirant who concentrates on the fruits of meditation may abandon his search for God if he doesn't find Him after years of effort. But the true yogi loves God unconditionally. If, owing to the temporary obstruction of some hidden subconscious evil karma, he does not feel the Divine Presence, he is never discouraged. Even if he fails to find the Lord after countless attempts, the divine lover never stops seeking Him. As the wave gradually has to sink into the sea when the storm abates, so a real seeker has faith that if he perseveres all inner obstructions must fall away; sooner or later the little soul-wave will be one with the Cosmic Ocean, whence it came and whither it must needs return.

VERSES 18–19

satkāramānapūjārthaṁ tapo dambhena caiva yat
kriyate tad iha proktaṁ rājasaṁ calam adhruvam (18)

mūḍhagrāheṇātmano yat pīḍayā kriyate tapaḥ
parasyotsādanārthaṁ vā tat tāmasam udāhṛtam (19)

(18) Austerities are said to be rajasic, unstable and fleeting, when practiced for the purpose of ostentation and for gaining men's recognition, honor, and homage.

(19) Tamasic austerities are those based on ignorance or foolishness or performed for self-torture or for injuring others.

RAJASIC PENANCES POSSESS little spiritual merit. But they are better than the performance of no austerities or of evil austerities. The practice of even ostentatious or hypocritical penances may in time lead a man to desire to perform them humbly, in the right spirit.

Tamasic austerities such as witchcraft and sorcery are ruinous to the practitioner's spiritual welfare. Throughout the ages many such methods have been practiced for the purpose of revenge or for exercising the base power of harming others.

Trying to hurt God present in one's enemies will act as a boomerang. Wishing misfortune on others develops in oneself baneful qualities. One must possess evil himself before he can give it to others. The man who murders another has issued an invitation to the Cosmic Law to arrange his own violent end. "Whoso sheddeth man's blood, by man shall his blood be shed."*

THREE KINDS OF GIVING

VERSE 20

dātavyam iti yad dānaṁ dīyate 'nupakāriṇe
deśe kāle ca pātre ca tad dānaṁ sāttvikaṁ smṛtam

The good or sattvic gift is one made for the sake of righteousness, without expectation of anything in return, and is bestowed in proper time and place on a deserving person.

A GIFT (*DANA*) THAT IS PRESENTED to a worthy person without thought of receiving for it any kind of compensation is sattvic or virtuous in nature. The man who gives "with no strings attached" to a deserving person is pure-hearted. Paradoxically, such a gift brings the donor the greatest spiritual benefit, precisely because he does not seek it.

The habit of giving breaks down gradually the walls of separation between God and man, and leads the devotee to offer to the Lord the ultimate gift: the surrender of his soul. When he makes a gift of his soul to God through love, without expectation of any return of divine favor, he has passed life's highest test.

The Lord has everything except the love of his prodigal child, man. If the Heavenly Father may be said to "need" anything, it is the love of His runaway children, roaming in delusion. He wants them back, for their own happiness and for His happiness, too. He feels responsible for them; who but He created *maya* and its labyrinths of misery? What rejoicing He feels when He receives the unconditional love of His children!

There are three kinds of sattvic gifts: material, mental, and spiri-

* Genesis 9:6.

tual. On the physical plane, to give food and money to a poor man is good; to give him a job is better. To help him become well qualified to obtain work is better still. Continued material aid to a man makes him enslaved and dependent, so it is laudable to encourage him to remedy his ills by self-help.

On the mental plane, to aid in enlightening an ignorant person is good; and to offer further education to an intelligent man is better, for he can in turn be more helpful to many others.

On the spiritual plane, to give elevating instruction to a willing man, whose life has hitherto been sunk in materialism, is good. To impart divine wisdom to an ardent seeker is better. To aid an advanced devotee so that by his own enthusiasm and knowledge he can win emancipation is better still. To bestow God-consciousness on a worthy disciple by the transmission of ecstasy (*samadhi*) is the best of all. Only illumined gurus can transfer their divine realization to those of their disciples who are ready for the sublime experience.

Every prophet quantitatively helps society, the masses around him, who respond with a little ardor and some slight inner development. But qualitatively he concentrates on raising a small group to supreme spiritual stature, as did Jesus, Lahiri Mahasaya, and others.

As one moon sheds on the world a greater light than the countless stars, so a Christlike disciple who receives the gift of God-communion through self-effort and through his guru's transmission of ecstasy inspires and redeems thousands by his illuminating spirituality.

The act of giving transmits physical or material power, mental power, or spiritual power from a qualified person to another man who needs that aid. In order to bestow money, wisdom, or divine consciousness on others, one must first have acquired those possessions himself. They should then be used to help his fellowman.

Through sympathy and deep vision, a true guru sees the Lord suffering in the physically, mentally, and spiritually poor; and that is why he feels it his joyous duty to assist them. He tries to feed the hungry God in the destitute, to stir the sleeping God in the ignorant, to love the unconscious God in the enemy, and to waken the half-asleep God in the yearning devotee. And by a gentle touch of love, he instantaneously arouses the almost fully awakened God in the advanced seeker. A guru is, among all men, the best of givers. His generosity, like that of the Lord Himself, knows no boundaries.

VERSE 21

yat tu pratyupakārārthaṁ phalam uddiśya vā punaḥ
dīyate ca parikliṣṭaṁ tad dānaṁ rājasaṁ smṛtam

That gift is deemed rajasic which is offered with reluctance or in the thought of receiving a return or of gaining merit.

THIS DEFECTIVE FORM OF GIVING is not wholly reprehensible; it is better than practicing no charity at all and may eventually lead to unselfish giving. To bestow money or to share one's intellectual or spiritual knowledge with others in the expectation of obtaining future benefits in return or in the hope of being rewarded by God is a generosity tinged by *rajas* or worldly desires. It is imperfectly motivated; and is in fact a barter, not a gift. Nevertheless, a man who makes even an imperfect offering is more admirable than a nonsharing miserly person.

Anything offered reluctantly is tainted with rajasic or selfish feelings. A man who grudgingly performs his devotions at dawn, bewailing his loss of sleep, or who lazily follows his spiritual exercises without real concentration is making an unwilling, rajasic gift of himself to God. This type of offering is preferable to no devotion at all; but such a parsimonious giver is apt to receive from the cosmic law an equally stingy return.

The rajasic devotee may or may not receive divine grace, but the wholehearted lover of the Lord finds Him without fail. Plunging with unconditional faith into the ocean of God brings the sympathetic response of His mercy, while a reserved little swim in the meditational waters, after much indecision and planning for results, brings, perchance, only meager satisfaction.

VERSE 22

adeśakāle yad dānam apātrebhyaś ca dīyate
asatkṛtam avajñātaṁ tat tāmasam udāhṛtam

A tamasic gift is one bestowed at a wrong time and place, on an unworthy person, contemptuously or without goodwill.

TAMASIC GIFTS INJURE BOTH THE GIVER and the receiver. The Bible says not to cast pearls before swine. One should not offer money or gifts in kind in evil places or to evil persons, for it would be used to spread trouble in the world.

When one proffers material aid to another, with malice or insult, just to obtain the "name" of giver, it is a tamasic or wrong type of gift; as is a gift that rouses ill will because given imprudently. To bestow presents on rich or influential persons, not out of friendliness but as bribes to win favor or advantage, is also a detrimental action.

To give good advice to ridiculing men or to try to instruct vain, smug human beings in the paths of righteousness is indeed to cast pearls of wisdom into the dirt.

A religionist who becomes rebellious toward God, owing to continuous calamity and suffering or to lack of noticeable spiritual advancement, yet who persists, albeit grudgingly, to offer worship out of a sense of propriety and in fear of the Creator's almighty power, presents to the Lord a degraded tamasic oblation.

Stanzas 20–22 thus tell us the right (sattvic), worldly (rajasic), and wrong (tamasic) ways of gift-giving. The devotee who chooses always the path of disinterested benevolence ultimately finds himself in tune with the Divine Giver of All Gifts. The whole universe is maintained by God's ceaseless and exuberant liberality toward all His creatures.

AUM-TAT-SAT: GOD THE FATHER, SON, AND HOLY GHOST

VERSE 23

auṁ tat sad iti nirdeśo brahmaṇas trividhaḥ smṛtaḥ
brāhmaṇās tena vedāś ca yajñāś ca vihitāḥ purā

"Aum-Tat-Sat" is considered to be the triple designation of Brahman (God). By this power were created, in the beginning, the Brahmins (knowers of Brahman), the Vedas, and the sacrificial rites.

THE UNMANIFESTED, THE INFINITE, the Changeless Spirit is called *Para-Brahman:* the One Absolute. But during the cycles of manifestation, the Nameless and Formless is described as *Aum-Tat-Sat* (or, often, *Sat-Tat-Aum*)—so designated by the ancient sages. In the Christian Bible *Sat-Tat-Aum* is spoken of as the Father, Son, and Holy Ghost.

Aum (the "Word" of the Bible) is God the Holy Ghost, Invisible Vibratory Power, the direct creator and activator of all creation.

Tat ("That") is God the Son, the Christ or *Kutastha* Cosmic Intelligence actively present in all creation.

Sat ("Being, Truth") is God the Father, beyond creation, existing in vibrationless unchangeability.

As the calm ocean without waves and the ocean with waves in tumult are one and the same in essence, differing only in appearance, so also the Unmanifested Sea of Spirit (Para-Brahman) and the Manifested Sea of Spirit (*Aum-Tat-Sat*) are the selfsame Sole Reality, differing only in form.

God as *Sat* is the Father of creation (Ishvara), though He exists beyond it. God as *Tat* is the Son or Christ (Krishna or *Kutastha*) Intelligence that pervades the universe. God as *Aum* is the Creative Vibration that upholds the worlds through Prakriti, Mother Nature, His consort. It is the macrocosmic triple conception that has established itself in the microcosmic human relationship of father and mother and their reflection in their offspring.

Man displays in himself the three divine manifestations. His body is the result of *Aum* or vibratory forces. His Christ Intelligence or *Tat* exists in his omniscient spiritual eye between the eyebrows. This Intelligence, individualized as his soul, is a reflection of Cosmic Consciousness or *Sat* residing in the thousand-petaled lotus in the brain.

These three measures of Spirit incarnate in man "from the beginning" are the *Brahmins, Sat,* "knowers of God," the soul; the *Vedas, Tat,* the soul's intuitive all-knowing intelligence; and the *sacrificial rites, Aum,* the vibratory life that creates and preserves the body, empowering it to perform its divine and dutiful rituals of existence—including the ultimate sacrificial rites of yoga (one of which is meditation on *Aum*) that reunite the soul with Spirit. By this inherence, indigenous in the coming-forth of mortal beings, the Lord has endowed to man the way and the means—and the irrevocable assurance—of salvation.

All yogis who perform the sacrificial rite of listening to the omnipresent holy vibration of *Aum* attain cosmic perception, Veda, and by this expanding blessedness ascend to cosmic consciousness and become Self-realized souls, the true Brahmins or "knowers of Brahman."

Aum of the Vedas became the sacred word *Hum* of the Tibetans, *Amin* of the Moslems, and *Amen* of the Egyptians, Greeks, Romans,

Jews, and Christians. *Amen* in Hebrew means "sure, faithful." *Aum* is the all-pervading sound emanating from the Holy Ghost as it performs its work of creating and maintaining the universal structure. *Aum* is the voice of creation, testifying to the Divine Presence in every atom.

"These things saith the Amen, the faithful and true witness, the beginning of the creation of God."*

"In the beginning was the Word, and the Word was with God, and the Word was God.... All things were made by him (the Word or *Aum*); and without him was not any thing made that was made."†

"Faith cometh by hearing, and hearing by the word of God."‡

"He who knows *Aum* knows God."§

Aum is the divinely empowered creator of all things; it manifests itself as cosmic light and cosmic sound. As the ocean roar is a conglomerated sound of all waves and is manifested in each wave, so the cosmic sound and the cosmic light are the aggregate of all animate and inanimate creation, and are manifested in each man as the light of life and may be heard by him as the astral sound of *Aum.*

Each seeker who wants liberation from the world of delusion must pass through the sphere of the Holy Ghost vibration and the sphere of Christ Intelligence before he can reach God the Father beyond the phenomenal worlds. "No man cometh unto the Father (Cosmic Consciousness), but by me (Christ Consciousness)." These words were spoken by Jesus from his oneness with the Infinite Christ Intelligence: "Believe me that I am in the Father, and the Father in me."**

Jesus promised to send to his disciples the Comforter, the Holy Ghost, to speed them on their way to Self-realization. An advanced devotee can hear the sound of *Aum* in his body and can see its light in his spiritual eye. After he has become acquainted with these two limited manifestations, in the bodily sound and in his spiritual eye, then, by further spreading of his consciousness in Omnipresence, he sees his small spherical eye of light expand into a cosmic sphere whose luminosity conflagrates the whole universe.

Similarly, as the devotee listens to *Pranava,* the holy sound of *Aum,* he forgets the restrictions of the human body and of space and can feel the *Aum* of his body vibrating into a perception of his cosmic body. He feels his consciousness vibrating everywhere with the ever-

---

* Revelation 3:14. † John 1:1,3. ‡ Romans 10:17.

§ Patanjali, great sage of ancient India, author of *Yoga Sutras.*

** John 14:6,11.

expanding *Aum* sound. In ecstasy he suddenly sees his body as an atom or cell in the cosmic body. Perceiving the cosmic body as his own, he feels in it the cosmic *Aum* sound (see verse 24) and the Christ Intelligence (see verse 25). By further advancement he becomes conscious of his presence not only in all creation but with God the Father beyond creation (see verses 26–27).

VERSE 24

tasmād om ity udāhṛtya yajñadānatapaḥkriyāḥ
pravartante vidhānoktāḥ satataṁ brahmavādinām

Therefore the acts of the followers of Brahman—sacrifice, gift-giving, and austerities as enjoined by the scriptures—are always started with the chanting of "Aum."

AUDIBLE UTTERANCE OF "*AUM*" PRODUCES a sense of sacredness, even as a devotee feels awe at the sound of the word "God." At the beginning of all acts and rituals, repetition of the holy syllable, "*Aum,*" the *Pranava,* symbol of the Divine, removes the taints and defects that inhere in all human activities, even the highest ones.

However, real understanding of *Aum* is obtained only by hearing it internally and then becoming one with it in all creation. That is why the ancient sages prohibited the study of the Vedas to those who were *kayastha* (body-identified) and thus unreceptive to the cosmic sound, *Aum*.

In the Bible* Saint John tells us: "I was in the Spirit on the Lord's day, and heard behind me a great voice, as of a trumpet, saying, I am Alpha and Omega, the first and the last"—the omnipresent *Aum* vibration by which God created the heavens and the earth. Devotees who can spiritually commune with *Aum* and understand its omnipresent significance are able to feel God the Father, beyond creation, manifested in creation as the creative Cosmic Vibration.

All aspiring yogis who would be performers of the inner holy rites of consuming restlessness and delusion in the fire of ecstasy, givers of unconditional devotion to God, and cultivators of true perception through Self-mastery, must begin their progress on the spiritual path by

* Revelation 1:10–11.

first chanting *Aum,* and then communing with *Aum* by hearing this sacred Word-symbol of God present right within the body-temple.*

VERSE 25

tad ity anabhisaṁdhāya phalaṁ yajñatapaḥkriyāḥ
dānakriyāś ca vividhāḥ kriyante mokṣakāṅkṣibhiḥ

The seekers of liberation then perform the various rites of sacrifice, gift-giving, and austerities while concentrating on "Tat" without desiring results.

REALIZATION OF *TAT,* THAT, the immortal Indefinable, the Cosmic Intelligence in creation, comes after the ever-striving seeker of salvation has succeeded in merging in *Aum.* He then withdraws his mind from all minor spiritual perceptions and engages himself in the high ceremony of uniting his superconsciousness with *Tat,* the cosmic Christ or Krishna Spirit that exists behind the patterned curtain of cosmic vibration and is the undefined essence that holds together all threads of the tapestry of creation. Devotees who merge in this omnipresent Intelligence are the true givers of their soul to *Kutastha Chaitanya,* the *Tat.*

VERSES 26–27

sadbhāve sādhubhāve ca sad ity etat prayujyate
praśaste karmaṇi tathā sacchabdaḥ pārtha yujyate (26)

yajñe tapasi dāne ca sthitiḥ sad iti cocyate
karma caiva tadarthīyaṁ sad ity evābhidhīyate (27)

(26) The word "Sat" is the designation of the Supreme Reality (beyond creation) and of goodness (emanating from It in all creation). "Sat" also refers to the higher forms of spiritual action.

* The technique of meditation on *Aum* is taught as preparatory to *Kriya Yoga* in the *Self-Realization Fellowship Lessons.* (See page 1130.)

(27) The state of stability in the higher rites of sacrifice, self-discipline, and devotional offering is spoken of as "Sat" (communion with God as transcendent Cosmic Consciousness). Indeed, the same spiritual action connected with "Tat" (realization of God as immanent in creation) is also called "Sat."

THE GOOD QUALITIES AND GOOD ACTIVITIES of all human beings, deities, and liberated men have their source in *Sat,* God the Father, the Absolute and Immutable.

All the activities of the seeker by which he attains oneness with Cosmic Consciousness are *Sat* in nature; they are supreme divine actions that lead to perception of the Transcendental, *Sat*.

After great yogis have penetrated farther than the sphere of the cosmic *Aum* vibration and of the *Tat* consciousness within all creation, they become one with *Sat,* beyond creation. Merged in the Transcendental Sun of Cosmic Consciousness, such devotees behold, flowing out of Its bosom, the rays of all divine perceptions and all divine activities.

When an advanced yogi reaches the ultimate state of soul realization by dissolving all restlessness in ecstasy, and has been able by self-discipline and devotion to merge himself in the Illimitable Existence beyond creation, he becomes immovably fixed in *Sat.* As he penetrates deeply into the realization of the Divine Transcendence, then *Tat,* the Lord immanent in creation, also becomes a part of his *samadhi* experience. The illusion of duality—the manifested in contradistinction to the Unmanifested—dissolves; the realm of creation and Infinity beyond are seen as one and the same Cosmic Consciousness, the Sole Reality, *Sat.*

VERSE 28

aśraddhayā hutaṁ dattaṁ tapas taptaṁ kṛtaṁ ca yat
asad ity ucyate pārtha na ca tat pretya no iha

O Partha (Arjuna)! Whatever sacrifice is offered, gift bestowed, or austerity performed without faith (devotion) is called "asat." It is worthless here and in the hereafter.

DEEP FAITH (*SHRADDHA*), UNCONDITIONAL devotion, is necessary for success in the spiritual path. "Without faith it is impossible to please Him: for he that cometh to God must believe that He is, and that He is a rewarder of them that diligently seek Him."*

Religious practices that are followed carelessly or halfheartedly are lacking in the unconditional devotion of faith and may be considered *asat* (against Truth). The search for the Lord—our Father and the Maker of the Universe—is worth our full attention; what else indeed could be deemed more important?

The man who mechanically performs his devotional duties, without real zest and aspiration, finds his spiritual thirst unsatisfied in this life; and, according to the law of karma, it will remain unslaked in the next world also.

But the yogi who through meditation attunes himself to the intrinsic *shraddha* of the soul, finds that this devotional faith ultimately rewards him with the wondrous fulfillment of God-realization.

om tat sat iti śrīmadbhagavadgītāsu upaniṣatsu
brahmavidyāyām yogaśāstre śrīkṛṣṇārjunasaṁvāde
śraddhātrayavibhāgayogo nāma saptadaśo 'dhyāyaḥ

Aum, Tat, Sat.
In the Upanishad of the holy Bhagavad Gita—the discourse of Lord Krishna to Arjuna, which is the scripture of yoga and the science of God-realization—this is the seventeenth chapter, called "Union Through the Three Kinds of Faith."

---

* Hebrews 11:6.

CHAPTER XVIII

"In Truth Do I Promise Thee: Thou Shalt Attain Me"

❖

Renunciation: The Divine Art of Acting in the World With Unselfishness and Nonattachment

❖

The Roots of Action and the Consummation of Action (Liberation)

❖

Three Grades of Knowledge, Action, and Character

❖

Intelligence (Buddhi), Fortitude (Dhriti), and Happiness (Sukham): Their Higher and Lower Expressions

❖

Discerning One's Divinely Ordained Duty in Life

❖

Summary of the Gita's Message

❖

The Dialogue Between Spirit and Soul Concludes

ॐ

Arjuna said: "My delusion is gone! I have regained memory (of my soul) through Thy grace, O Achyuta (matchless Krishna). I am firmly established; my dubiousness has vanished. I will act according to Thy word."

"IN TRUTH DO I PROMISE THEE: THOU SHALT ATTAIN ME"

RENUNCIATION: THE DIVINE ART OF ACTING IN THE WORLD WITH UNSELFISHNESS AND NONATTACHMENT

VERSE 1

arjuna uvāca
saṁnyāsasya mahābāho tattvam icchāmi veditum
tyāgasya ca hṛṣīkeśa pṛthak keśiniṣūdana

Arjuna said (to Sri Krishna):
O Hrishikesha, O Mighty-Armed, O Slayer of (the demon) Keshi! I desire to know the true meaning of sannyasa (renunciation) and also of tyaga (relinquishment), and the distinction between them.

THE FIRST CHAPTER OF THE BHAGAVAD GITA was an introduction to the precepts to be covered in the comprehensive Krishna-Arjuna dialogue. And now in this eighteenth chapter, the conclusion of this scripture on Yoga, we will find a concise discussion of the subjects mentioned in the preceding seventeen chapters.

Renunciation—the relinquishment of actions, desires, and attachments that impede soul progress—is the compendious principle characterizing the Gita message. When the devotee finds that the intuitive communion of his soul with Spirit is still periodically disturbed by restlessness during meditation, he calls on God as the Conqueror of the Senses, the Master of all outer and inner forces, and the Destroyer of Ignorance. The seeker appeals to the Lord to remove his restlessness caused by continued enslavement to the senses and sensations. At this stage the yogi wonders how he can renounce all objects of soul distraction. It is therefore natural for a devotee like Arjuna to wish to understand clearly the difference between the two forms of renunciation.

VERSE 2

śrībhagavān uvāca
kāmyānāṁ karmaṇāṁ nyāsaṁ saṁnyāsaṁ kavayo viduḥ
sarvakarmaphalatyāgaṁ prāhus tyāgaṁ vicakṣaṇāḥ

The Blessed Lord said:
Sages call "sannyasa" the renunciation of all actions done with desire. The wise declare that "tyaga" is the renunciation of the fruits of activities.

BOTH *SANNYASA* AND *TYAGA* in common parlance indicate renunciation, the leaving or giving up of worldly objects and pursuits—especially as embraced by those who take holy vows as in the ancient Shankara Order of swamis.* But the Gita makes a deeper case for true renunciation as requiring an inner nonattachment above and beyond any merely physical act of material abandonment. In that explication, a subtle distinction is made between *sannyasa* and *tyaga* to define two aspects of renunciation. *Sannyasa*-renunciation signifies the abandonment of the desires and selfish motives that are the usual instigators of actions. *Tyaga*-renunciation means the relinquishment of, or nonidentification with, the inevitable fruits, or results, that accrue from all actions.

Two aspects of renunciation: sannyasa and tyaga

In no wise does the Gita advocate the renunciation of action itself, for action is a veritable necessity for the incarnate being, and a positive support for the aspiring yogi. The actionless state is rather the culmination of renunciation, the inner abandonment of identification with the ego and its instruments of action in the realization that God is the Sole Doer, Perceiver, and Knower. In this state, even though obligatory and dutiful actions continue, these are known as *nishkama karma,* inactive activity, because they cause no karmic bondage, being free from selfish motivation and from taking to one's self the resulting effects, or fruits. This is the ultimate or perfect renunciation toward which the yogi

* See page 590.

strives—first, by learning to work without personal desire for attaining the fruits of action (*sannyasa*); and second, by spiritually transcending identification with the resulting fruits (*tyaga*).

It has been said in the sixth chapter, stanza 1, that he is a true *sannyasi* (renunciant) and a true yogi who performs dutiful good actions to help mankind and meditative actions to find God, without desiring to obtain the fruits of these righteous actions to satisfy the ego; he acts solely to please God. He is a *sannyasi* because he renounces the desire for the fruits of his actions, and he is also a yogi because he helps others and himself spiritually toward God-realization. It is distinctly stated that he who does not perform dutiful actions is neither a *sannyasi* nor a yogi. Renunciation of the fruits of all actions is followed for the singular purpose of finding God, in preference to getting entangled with worldly ambitions. Renouncing material goals and working solely to please God in order to find Him is the same as yoga, which emphasizes performing meditative actions to attain God-union. Therefore a true yogi is a *sannyasi,* and a true *sannyasi* is a yogi.

Mental relinquishment of fruits of actions during their performance

The renunciation signified by *sannyasa* is thus a total mental relinquishment of the fruits of good actions during their performance. If a *sannyasi* feeds the poor, mentally concentrating on the benefits of his actions, or if he performs meditative actions for the selfish longings of his ego for divine favors or powers, he compromises the purity of his renunciation. The acts of a true *sannyasi* are devoid of ego with its concentration on selfish motivation, which is the cause of reincarnation-making karma. And when the true *sannyasi* meditates, he thinks of the Blessed Lord alone, loving Him unconditionally, without anticipating the rewards and advantages derived from God-communion.

By dutiful and divine actions and by concentration on his innate oneness with God, with no thought for obtaining the fruits of those actions for the sake of the body-identified ego, the devotee who practices *sannyasa* negates the binding effects of the karmic law.

Nonattachment to results of action

While *sannyasa* refers to the absence of personal expectation during the performance of activity, the other aspect of perfect renunciation, *tyaga,* involves nonattachment to, or non-identification with, the resulting fruits of actions once those actions have been performed. The *tyagi,* like the *sannyasi,* is a yogi, working and meditating only to please God.

The spiritual aspirant who is filled with expectation may lose interest in God if the Lord does not readily manifest Himself in response to his eager efforts. But the *tyagi,* unconcerned with results, remains unaffected by even bitter fruits of unsuccessful endeavors. He continues to seek God and to long for Him more earnestly, whether or not there is a satisfying response. Such increased mental urgency to know God is not a binding desire for the fruits of action; on the contrary, any action that concentrates the mind on God releases the adherent from the bondage of delusion.

The principles of *sannyasa* and *tyaga* developed to their highest metaphysical application define the consummate renunciant as one who has abandoned in his consciousness the ego and its delusive longings and attachments, and has instead become anchored in the soul consciousness of oneness with God.

In meditation, the *sannyasi* watches the mind go deep in communion with God, and then emerge from Him again into the domain of thoughts and sensations without becoming oblivious of God or losing its concentration on Him. Even when the mind roams in distracting thoughts and sensations, these rouse no desires in the *sannyasi.*

The accomplished *tyagi* is wholly concentrated in ecstasy with God. Having abandoned all identification with the "fruits" or effects of his material being, his mind does not at all roam in restless thoughts, bodily sensations, or material surroundings.

Thus does the yogi who has attained perfect inner renunciation of desireful motivations and of the fruits of action engage in the performance of good actions and meditative actions in a state of conscious ecstasy—to please God alone. Such a renunciant beholds the Lord and not his ego as the Doer of all physical, mental, and spiritual actions, and as the Recipient of the fruits thereof.

The person who is identified with the ego and its desires for and attachments to the fruits of actions is confined in the perception of material activity going on within and around him. The renunciant whose mind remains anchored in God feels all bodily and cosmic activities as workings of the Divine Intelligence, the immanence of God that is omnipresent in the created realm and in all beings.

Verses 3–6

tyājyaṁ doṣavad ity eke karma prāhur manīṣiṇaḥ
yajñadānatapaḥkarma na tyājyam iti cāpare (3)

niścayaṁ śṛṇu me tatra tyāge bharatasattama
tyāgo hi puruṣavyāghra trividhaḥ saṁprakīrtitaḥ (4)

yajñadānatapaḥkarma na tyājyaṁ kāryam eva tat
yajño dānaṁ tapaś caiva pāvanāni manīṣiṇām (5)

etāny api tu karmāṇi saṅgaṁ tyaktvā phalāni ca
kartavyānīti me pārtha niścitaṁ matam uttamam (6)

(3) Some philosophers say that all work should be forsaken as full of taint. Others declare that the activities of yajna (holy fire rite), dana (philanthropy), and tapas (self-discipline) ought not to be abandoned.

(4) Consequently, understand from Me the ultimate truth about renunciation, O Best of the Bharatas (Arjuna). For renunciation has been spoken of as consisting of three kinds, O Tiger among Men.

(5) The action involved in yajna, dana, and tapas verily ought to be performed, and should not be forsaken, for the holy fire rite, philanthropy, and self-discipline sanctify the wise.

(6) But even these activities ought to be performed, O Partha (Arjuna), forsaking attachment to them and the desire for their fruits. This is My supreme and sure conviction.

Naturally those yogis who are fully liberated and immersed in God can say that all actions belong to the domain of delusion and should be abandoned, keeping the soul in unbroken ecstasy with God. In complete liberation or oneness with Spirit all forms of action can be condemned as delusive, for Spirit in the unmanifested state is beyond all vibrations and hence beyond all actions.

The question then arises, how can an ordinary mortal, by abandoning good, bad, and divine or meditative activities, realize the state of cosmic consciousness of the Actionless Absolute?

Theoretical philosophers who denounce all activities without having attained the cosmic consciousness of God are harbingers of delusion and wrong advice. The truly wise say that activities connected with holy fire ceremonies *(yajna)*, the offering of gifts (*dana*), and self-disciplinary practices (*tapas*) should not be abandoned by the yogi striving for liberation. The Lord has already warned that he who does not perform dutiful divine actions, without desire for their fruits, is not a true yogi or a true renunciant.

Liberating actions: the inner fire ceremony, giving to others, and self-discipline

The truly wise inculcate the doctrine of performing the inner holy fire ceremony of casting material consciousness into the fire of inner wisdom; and the metaphysical fire ceremony, the burning of mortal desires in the cosmic perception of God, or destroying material desires in the fire of divine longings. These acts are symbolized in the external *yajna* of casting clarified butter into the ceremonial fire.

Such men of wisdom also declare that the act of giving gifts to the afflicted involves feeling for God as the One who is suffering in others, and hence leads to liberation. The limiting selfish desire to obtain things for self must be replaced by the liberating selfless desire to bestow gifts on the greater Self.

Self-disciplining actions of conquering physical restlessness, practicing mental concentration, and striving for ecstatic communion of soul and Spirit in meditation also should be performed, to train body, mind, and soul away from identification with confining bodily pleasures and to make one's whole being a tabernacle of divine Bliss.

But even good and meditative actions must be performed without desire and without attachment to these activities and their fruits if all soul-binding effects are to be negated. Clinging to the self-satisfaction in bestowing gifts, or in the physical prowess of bodily control (such as attained through practice of yoga *asanas*), or even in acts of meditation and their first fruits of peace and joy, limits the devotee's progress to these accomplishments and delays attainment of absolute freedom in Spirit. The devotee is advised first to displace materially motivated actions with God-centered actions, and then to rise above them both and become lodged in the actionless, vibrationless state of Spirit. By first becoming attached to meditation and good actions, the devotee banishes baser attachments to material activities; but in time the yogi should dissolve all attachment—even to meditation and good actions—in the ecstasy of communion with God.

Thus does the Lord caution Arjuna that when man has crossed the thorn-entangled garden of superficially charming evil and entered the enchantingly fragrant garden of virtue he should not remain wandering therein. Beyond these dark and bright gardens is the palace of God's ineffable Ever New Bliss.

Verse 7

niyatasya tu saṁnyāsaḥ karmaṇo nopapadyate
mohāt tasya parityāgas tāmasaḥ parikīrtitaḥ

The relinquishment of dutiful action is improper. Renunciation of such action through delusion is spoken of as tamasic (evil).

To refrain from performance of dutiful actions is itself an unspiritual or tamasic act, because abandonment of obligatory actions promotes delusion and evil. The spiritually ignorant person can find redemption only by performing dutiful actions with the desire to please God; if he renounces his engagement with good activities he will find himself steeped in delusion, engaging in evil activities. Such bewildered human beings are called tamasic who through delusion shun activities that lead to salvation.

Verse 8

duḥkham ity eva yat karma kāyakleśabhayāt tyajet
sa kṛtvā rājasaṁ tyāgaṁ naiva tyāgaphalaṁ labhet

He who relinquishes action as being intrinsically difficult, for fear of painful trouble to the body, is performing rajasic renunciation. He is unable to attain the reward of renunciation.

Performance of good material actions with expectation of results—for example, earning one's livelihood—is rajasic activity. One who forsakes such material activity on the pretext of practicing renunciation, but whose motivation is actually the fear of encountering the pain or troubles involved in it, performs only nonspiritual rajasic relinquishment. He therefore does not attain the reward of true renunciation, which is freedom from ensuing karmic bonds.

A devotee who renounces all superfluous material activities and remains engaged in spiritualized dutiful activity ultimately gains salvation as a result of his relinquishment of pursuits that cause soul bondage. But a man who quits dutiful activity out of an aversion for physical labor or fear of some consequent pain or difficulty, only outwardly forsakes action; inwardly he remains bound to the body, a slave to ego and its sensations. He will find himself averse not only to unpleasant material activities but to the effort demanded by liberating divine duties as well.

The divine man does not avoid activities that are for a good cause, even painful ones, for he sees them as God-reminding duties. He forgoes only activities that feed his egoistic consciousness. Such a renouncer, striving for God-consciousness, receives the liberating rewards of the renunciation of delusive activities.

VERSE 9

kāryam ity eva yat karma niyataṁ kriyate 'rjuna
saṅgaṁ tyaktvā phalaṁ caiva sa tyāgaḥ sāttviko mataḥ

O Arjuna, when dutiful action is performed solely because it should be done, forsaking attachment to it and its fruit, that renunciation is considered sattvic.

OBLIGATORY ACTIONS ARE DIVINELY ordained duties. They include the necessary caring for the body, nurturing of the mind, and the pleasurable duty of meditating on the soul; and also those selfless actions performed for the benefit of family, neighbors, and the world. The relinquishment of egoistic attachment to these actions and their fruits, while continuing to perform these righteous duties as obligatory because divinely ordained, is the purest form of abandonment, sattvic renunciation.

The devotee who remains in ecstatic communion with the soul, simultaneously watching the sensory and motor activities of the body without any desire or attachment, attains the highest, or sattvic, state of renunciation. Whether he is engaged in dutiful physical activities or is motionless in ecstatic meditation on the Infinite, in his consciousness the Divine Presence is ever predominant. Feeling the boundless

Blessedness, he automatically renounces all attachment to lesser sensory pleasures, material objects, and fruits of actions. The automatic relinquishment of all else, upon finding God, is considered the supreme spiritual renunciation.

The devotee who relinquishes lesser sense pleasures to gain the unknown bliss of God has entered the first stage of sattvic renunciation. The yogi who obtains the Divine Bliss and then consciously, deliberately, convincingly renounces all else has attained the ultimate state of perfect relinquishment.

VERSE 10

na dveṣṭy akuśalaṁ karma kuśale nānuṣajjate
tyāgī sattvasamāviṣṭo medhāvī chinnasaṁśayaḥ

The renunciant absorbed in sattva, with a calm understanding, free from doubts, neither abhors unpleasant action nor delights in a pleasant one.

ALL ACTIONS PERFORMED IN CONNECTION with realization of the permanent Absolute are sattvic. The practice of justice, truth, compassion, devotion, duty, purity, nobility, meditative perception of the Self—all these lead to the ultimate realization of the everlasting Spirit. As the devotee engaged in such actions gradually remembers his eternal relation with the Infinite, he is relieved of all doubts, and loses any inclination that holds him in mortal bondage.

He whose renunciation is pure performs with calm understanding all dutiful actions. Jesus Christ accepted crucifixion to fulfill the will of his Heavenly Father.

The sattvic renunciant remains evenminded as well about agreeable duties. Overexcitement, even in the performance of noble actions, creates waves on the lake of the mind, distorting true perception of soul blessedness.

Any work ordained by God, whether pleasant or unpleasant, is proper duty; the true renunciant who is concentrated on the Lord performs both with equal zeal and nonattachment.

VERSE 11

na hi dehabhṛtā śakyaṁ tyaktuṁ karmāṇy aśeṣataḥ
yas tu karmaphalatyāgī sa tyāgīty abhidhīyate

It is truly impossible for an embodied being to abandon actions completely, but he who relinquishes the fruit of action is called a renunciant.

A SOUL IDENTIFIED WITH THE BODY may be said to be its slave, because an embodied soul cannot relinquish actions entirely. Whoever knows himself as the body rather than as a soul is a servant to the body; he has to work for it, and becomes involved in entangling desires and habits connected with this subservience.

On the other hand, he who is concentrated on the soul as his true Self performs dutiful actions, but without an eye to their result. By renouncing the fruits of good actions but not their performance, that person is a true renunciant.

The body-identified man works only to satisfy his egoistic desires; the wise man realizes the soul as the bodily indweller and works under its liberating guidance. The worldly man performs most of his actions for fulfilling the needs and desires of himself and his family. His mind is always on the ego: "It is I who eat," "It is I who earn money and support the family," "It is I who think and create success in my work," and so on. Even if such an ego-oriented person thinks to renounce material actions by following the spiritual path, he is still unable to be a true renunciant because he cannot forget the ego consciousness of identification with the body. But when by continuous meditation he disengages his mind from body consciousness and unites it with the consciousness of the soul, he realizes he should not work any more for that upstart desire-filled ego. It is at this advanced stage that the yogi is able to renounce all desire for the fruits of actions and to perform his obligatory material duties with the transcendent nonattachment of the soul.

VERSE 12

aniṣṭam iṣṭaṁ miśraṁ ca trividhaṁ karmaṇaḥ phalam
bhavaty atyāginām pretya na tu saṁnyāsinām kvacit

The triune fruit of action—good, harmful, and mixed—springs up in nonrenunciants after their demise, but in renunciants never.

ONE WHO PERFORMS ACTIONS without relinquishing the desire to obtain their fruits stores up the good, bad, and mixed results as his threefold karma (effects of actions). These stored-up psychological seeds, when watered by proper environment, sprout forth into specific results in this or another life and in the beyond.

Every good, bad, or mixed action deposits in the physical and astral brain of man a seed tendency, which subsequently grows up again under favorable circumstances. Good, bad, and mixed sensory stimuli, for example, stir up these threefold tendencies, which then manifest as good, bad, and mixed actions.

At death the sum total of man's tendencies are lodged in the brain of his luminous astral body. Mixed good and bad tendencies cause the soul to seek early rebirth in the physical world. When there is a predominance of good tendencies in the astral brain, the soul in its astral body encasement gravitates to a better environment on an astral planet. When evil tendencies predominate, the soul in its astral body gravitates to dark spheres of the beyond, where disgruntled goblin-beings dwell. How long one remains in the brighter or darker astral regions before reincarnating on earth is karmically determined.

The true relinquisher of the fruits of actions is untouched by any of the aforesaid threefold actions, for he works under the direction of the Lord of the universe and performs all activities only on His behalf. Such yogis do not accumulate any aftereffects from their actions, and become liberated.

True yogis remain free from karma, even while performing actions

He who is one with God is not touched by karma, no matter what he does. Such a devotee makes God the beneficiary of his actions, and thus remains karmically unentangled. Through desire the egotist amasses the fruits of his actions and thus becomes ensnared in them. As the silkworm is boiled in a cocoon of its own creation, so the egotist is destroyed in his self-created cocoon of ignorance. The sage remains desireless and nonattached, and thus does not accrue to himself any fruits of his actions lest they prove self-destructive.

The egotist, thinking, "I am the body; I act for myself, in my world," has to work out any desires of his that remain unfulfilled at the time of death. But the renunciant says to himself: "I have renounced service to the ego. I live, I work, I move in the drama of God according to His wish and plan. I came here not of my own volition but because of God's will. I will come back on earth or go anywhere the Lord leads me, but I will not be forced to return here just to eat apple pie or curry or to satisfy any other foolish unfulfilled desire. All my longings are consumed as an offering to the Lord. I live at His command. I am free."

The ego-identified man who wishes to be free must, similarly, learn to dedicate his physical, mental, and spiritual activities to God. He should always think along these lines: "I work for the Father and He works through me. I eat, not because I am attached to health, but to care for this body-temple of His in my charge. I think, reason, and will, not to satisfy the ego, but that I might intelligently, ambitiously act and serve the Lord alone. He has given me this body, reason, will, and the power to act, so with nonattachment I use them to play my part in His drama."

THE ROOTS OF ACTION AND THE CONSUMMATION OF ACTION (LIBERATION)

VERSE 13

pañcaitāni mahābāho kāraṇāni nibodha me
sāṁkhye kṛtānte proktāni siddhaye sarvakarmaṇām

O Mighty-armed (Arjuna), learn from Me the five causes for the performance of all action, which are chronicled in the highest wisdom (Sankhya) wherein all action terminates.

SANKHYA, "HIGHEST WISDOM,"* is to have complete knowledge or ultimate enlightenment. This "highest wisdom" and its consummation in Spirit is elaborated in Hindu philosophy in the systems of Sankhya and Vedanta. The means to realize the knowledge therein is provided by Yoga.†

---

* See II:39, page 269 n.

† See also elaboration on relation between Sankhya, Yoga, and Vedanta in commentaries on II:39 and III:3.

The advent of Self-knowledge through renunciation of all actions, as outlined in the Sankhya philosophy, and the consummation of all actions after attaining this realization, as described in the Vedanta, both have to do with the complex nature of action. Activity is the outward manifestation or expression of the transcendental Spirit and Its reflection, the soul, through the instrumentality of Nature and the faculties of the body.

Sankhya teaches that renunciation of all actions is necessary in order to gain Self-knowledge. The first aphorism in Sankhya declares that the highest necessity of man is the eradication of physical, mental, and spiritual suffering at the root, so that there is no possibility of recurrence.

Yoga philosophy teaches the technique by which the threefold human afflictions can be removed forever.

Vedanta, which means "end of the Vedas" (complete knowledge of all truth to be known) describes the Infinite Spirit, the ultimate goal of man. The first aphorism of Vedanta states: "So begins the inquiry about Brahman, the Infinite."

Without the renunciation enjoined in Sankhya, and without the technique of Yoga, the devotee cannot escape the misery-producing entanglements of physical consciousness and realize the Infinite. Both Sankhya and Yoga teach how to attain Brahman; Vedanta describes and discusses what is to be found by following the advice of Sankhya and, most important, by practicing the techniques of Yoga. All three philosophies point out the same goal, but Sankhya and Yoga must be followed first, for without their aid Spirit remains unreachable and unknown. Only after one has realized Brahman does the Vedanta discussion about Him become truly meaningful.

All human activities are consummated when by following the principles of Sankhya and Yoga the devotee reaches the ultimate state described by Vedanta: Oneness with the Absolute, beyond the domain of all activities.

Verses 14–16

adhiṣṭhānaṁ tathā kartā karaṇaṁ ca pṛthagvidham
vividhāś ca pṛthakceṣṭā daivaṁ caivātra pañcamam (14)

śarīravāṅmanobhir yat karma prārabhate naraḥ
nyāyyaṁ vā viparītaṁ vā pañcaite tasya hetavaḥ (15)

tatraivaṁ sati kartāram ātmānaṁ kevalaṁ tu yaḥ
paśyaty akṛtabuddhitvān na sa paśyati durmatiḥ (16)

(14) The human body; the pseudoagent there; the manifold instrumentality (senses, mind, and intelligence); the various divergent functions; and, lastly, the fifth of these, the presiding deity, destiny:

(15) These five are the causes of all actions—either right or wrong—performed by man through his body, speech, and mind.

(16) This being the case, whoever of perverted consciousness views through a nonclarified understanding the Self as the exclusive disposer of action, he sees not.

THE BODY IS THE FIRST CAUSE in man's performance of activities; for without the presence of the body, no actions—physical, mental, or spiritual—could be carried out.

The second cause is the ego, the pseudosoul or agent, which enthrones itself in the body, senses, mind, and intelligence. Without this "I-ness" no activities could be directed or executed.

The powers of sight, hearing, smell, taste, and touch constitute the five instruments of knowledge. The power of speech and of the motor activities performed by the hands, feet, rectal and genital organs constitute the five instruments of action. Mind is the coordinator, and intelligence is the guide. In all, these twelve human faculties constitute the third cause whereby human activities are performed.

These twelve faculties in man produce various activities in the five life currents—the crystallizing, assimilating, circulating, metabolizing, and eliminating currents—which in turn generate diverse subtle inner activities in man. These divergent vital functions, springing from the twelve faculties in man, constitute the fourth cause of human activities.

The tabloid effects of past actions are lodged in the brain as ruling tendencies, man's self-created destiny. This silent "deity" whose reign is a compelling influence on present and future human activities, is the fifth cause of action.

All good or bad actions performed through the body, speech, and mind evolve from these five causes.

The consciousness of "I" as the doer and experiencer is the basis of a delusive existence cognized as being separate from Spirit. A stroller, watching and feeling his feet as he strides along, believes and says: "I am walking." A man beholding a tree through his eyes similarly feels and thinks and says: "I am seeing." But anyone who feels, thinks, wills, and plans activities, believing that he is the unique author and doer of those mental and physical actions, is deluded; he cannot see the truth, that the workings of his body and the cosmos are being operated solely by the Infinite.

Consciousness of "I" as the doer and experiencer is the basis of a delusive existence

The wise yogi lives in the realization that "all is Brahman." He knows that in Nature's realm of relativity there are five springs of action that are responsible for everything he does. But he further realizes that in truth his activities and their five activating causes, as well as the actions themselves, are all secretly motivated by the Infinite, working through the divinely ordered laws of creation. Such a yogi does not consider the Self with its physical ego, or any of the five springs of action, as the real instrumentalities; he knows that God is the supreme Instrument and Director, without which Empowerment all activities of individualized existence would cease.

VERSE 17

yasya nāhaṁkṛto bhāvo buddhir yasya na lipyate
hatvāpi sa imāṁl lokān na hanti na nibadhyate

He who is above the obsession of egoism, whose intelligence is unadulterated, though he slay these people (ready for battle at Kurukshetra), he slays not; neither is he bound by such act.

WHEN A YOGI DISSOLVES HIS body-identified ego consciousness in the realization of his true Self and of his soul's unity with Spirit, he sees all the activities of his body, senses, mind, and intelligence as guided not by himself, but by Spirit. This state is illustrated in this stanza with an extreme example.

In the "Vision of Visions," Chapter XI, Krishna urged his disciple Arjuna not to feel despondent and afraid of killing his evil opponents, but to battle for the cause he knew to be righteous: "You are only an instrument, O Arjuna, of My karmic law of cause and effect, by which men individually and collectively carve out their own fate. Through the workings of that law, I as its Originator have already slain your foes, long before your hand will slay them."* By this Krishna meant that the death of Arjuna's antagonists in the battle of Kurukshetra was karmically ordained, and that Arjuna would only be an instrument in carrying out the divine law.

To satisfy a selfish motive or a hidden sadistic desire for revenge and violence, an egotist may pretend, or even delude himself, that he is acting under the guidance of God, and thus rouse himself to vengeful deeds. Being an instrument, not of God but of his own ego, he is liable for the dire karmic consequences of his evil acts.

It is written in the Bible that a crowd of children ridiculed the prophet Elisha. He then "cursed them in the name of the Lord and there came forth two she bears out of the wood, and tare forty and two children of them."† As a prophet of God, Elisha was acting as His instrument. The curse was karmically ordained through God's law; hence Elisha cannot be accused of causing the mutilation of the children. They suffered because of their own wickedness—the accumulation of their wrong thoughts and actions of past lives. Their seemingly childish taunting was the timely fruition of their past evil, which precipitated its inevitable consequence. The "curse" that issued forth from the instrumental Elisha was the "high voltage" of his spiritual vibration, operating with no selfish intent to harm.

If a man disregards a warning not to touch a live wire and is electrocuted, it is not the live wire but the man's foolishness that is responsible for his death. The same truth applies in the case of the wicked children who mocked Elisha. It is the story of all evil opposition to the righteous will of God: Evil eventually causes its own destruction.

VERSE 18

jñānaṁ jñeyaṁ parijñātā trividhā karmacodanā
karaṇaṁ karma karteti trividhaḥ karmasaṁgrahaḥ

---

* See the last two verses of "Vision of Visions," pages 825–26.

† II Kings 2:24.

The knower, the knowledge, and the known constitute the triune stimulus to action. The agent, the instrument, and the activity are the threefold basis of action.

BOTH KNOWLEDGE AND INSTRUMENTALITY are the essential components in the performance of action. Knowledge—with its knower, the object known, and his knowing of it—is that which incites the doer to action. The mental and physical instrumentality of the doer empowers the activity instigated by that arousal.

The creation of a clay statue of Lord Krishna may be used as an illustration. According to stanza 14, there are five causes involved in any activity: (1) the body (in this case, the artist); (2) the ego (the directing consciousness of the artist); (3) the (artist's) mind, intelligence, powers of perception (such as the senses of touch and sight) and powers of action (such as the exercise of manual skill); (4) the various subtle inner forces (the life-sustaining activities in the artist's body) generated by the faculties described as the third cause; and (5) the presiding deity or seed tendency from past lives (the innate skill of the artist).

However, the mere existence of these five causes would not produce a statue of Krishna unless, in addition, the artist (knower) visualized the statue (the object known) and through that conceptualization (the knowing) acted upon his wish to bring the image into being. Therefore these other three elements—knower, knowing, and known—are the real direct source of all action, together with the aforesaid five causes. The five causes or bases of all activity are condensed to three categories in this stanza 18: agent (ego), instrument (the body and all its physical and mental instruments and powers), and action.

THREE GRADES OF KNOWLEDGE, ACTION, AND CHARACTER

VERSE 19

jñānaṁ karma ca kartā ca tridhaiva guṇabhedataḥ
procyate guṇasaṁkhyāne yathāvac chṛṇu tāny api

Knowledge, action, and agent in the Sankhya philosophy are described as being of but three kinds, according to the distinction of the three gunas. Please hear duly about these also.

SANKHYA PHILOSOPHY DEALS ELABORATELY with the three *gunas* (qualities of Nature): *sattva* (good, expanding), *rajas* (activating), and *tamas* (evil, obstructing). In the 20th to 39th stanzas of this chapter Lord Krishna describes to Arjuna how these three qualities determine the nature of knowledge, action, and agent.

VERSE 20

sarvabhūteṣu yenaikaṁ bhāvam avyayam īkṣate
avibhaktaṁ vibhakteṣu taj jñānaṁ viddhi sāttvikam

O Arjuna, understand that knowledge to be sattvic by which the one indestructible Spirit is perceived in all beings, undivided in the divided.

WHEN A PERSON INTENTLY WATCHING a motion picture looks up and sees the one pure imageless beam of light falling on the screen and creating the true-to-life pictures, he realizes that all the illusively realistic appearances are naught but a mixture of light and shadows projected from the motion-picture booth. Likewise, the awakened yogi with pure sattvic wisdom realizes that it is the one undivided spherical light of God surrounding the cosmos and commingling with the shadows of *maya* or cosmic delusion that produces the world of solids, liquids, gases, energy substances—trees, animals, human beings—as seemingly separate forms of matter.

The enlightened being beholds the one all-creating spherical light of God as indivisible and indestructible; whereas the so-called "real" atomic vibratory manifestations of matter within it—though made of that one changeless light—appear to be various and changing.

That knowledge by which Spirit is perceived as one and indivisible, even in Its manifold individual appearances as matter and mortal dreams, is called sattvic knowledge.

Verse 21

pṛthaktvena tu yaj jñānaṁ nānābhāvān pṛthagvidhān
vetti sarveṣu bhūteṣu taj jñānaṁ viddhi rājasam

But that knowledge which perceives in the aggregate world of beings manifold entities of different varieties, distinct from one another—understand that knowledge to be rajasic.

A man engrossed in beholding moving picture images and happenings as if they were real, rather than seeing them as illusory representations made of light and shadow, has engaged his understanding in fascination with delusive restless motion. The consciousness of a man similarly engrossed in the delusive appearances and activities of the world, rather than perceiving their divergent separateness as the flickerings of the one infinite Light, is said to be rajasic.

The quality of that knowledge which is identified with the active aspect of delusion, inherent in earth's infinite variety of beings, appearances, and activities, is rajasic.

Verse 22

yat tu kṛtsnavad ekasmin kārye saktam ahaitukam
atattvārthavad alpaṁ ca tat tāmasam udāhṛtam

And that knowledge which concentrates on a single effect as if it were the whole, disregarding motive, lacking conformance with the principles of truth—trivial and easy—is declared to be tamasic.

THE PERSON WHOSE COGNITION is of the tamasic quality is wholly subverted by delusion. The body, the world of matter, and the sensory experiences exchanged between the body and its material environs are considered the be-all and end-all of life. The man of tamasic understanding thoughtlessly engages in trivial aspirations—those he thinks will cause him the least trouble and give him the most pleasure, but are of no consequence to his true Self. He expresses full satisfaction therein as though he had found the ultimate goal of life. With his inner voice of conscience stifled in darkness, he never questions the correctness of his motives and their cause-effect relation. His befuddled understanding irrationally justifies all of his personal convictions and inclinations, no matter how contrary to the principles of truth. He never analyzes the body as a mere instrument of the soul, empowered by the laws of Nature and utterly dependent on the borrowed wisdom and power of the Almighty Creator. Rather, tamasic perception views the body, and the perceived need to satisfy its preferences and demands, as the one principal effect that is the whole reason for existence.

Through the obstructive influence of *tamas,* the low-grade or dark quality, on the discriminating faculty of intelligence, man feels satisfied for a time with his engrossment in the seeming reality and temporal activities of the body. But when disease or accidents invade the body and mar its wonted happy-go-lucky activity, the deluded tamasic person is rudely taken aback and his satisfaction in "permanent" material objects and activities is shaken. This is the periodic fate of the materialist until he frees his understanding from the delusive tamasic quality that makes him falsely see the possibility of infinite enjoyment in a finite mirage of matter.

VERSE 23

niyataṁ saṅgarahitam arāgadveṣataḥ kṛtam
aphalaprepsunā karma yat tat sāttvikam ucyate

That action which is divinely directed, which is performed in a state of complete nonattachment, without attraction or repulsion and without desiring the fruits of action, is said to be sattvic.

NOW BEGINS THE EXPLANATION of the relationship of the threefold qualities—*sattva, rajas,* and *tamas*—to karma, or action. Most individuals, unskilled in the art of action, work with their senses, mind, and reason contaminated by attachment and desire. Failing to comprehend the purpose of ideal action, they act erroneously and become involved in an escalation of troubles inevitable in the exciting conditions of the world's dualities.

Since action is mandated for all beings, it is foolish not to be acquainted with the art of ideal action. The yogi, one who is in harmony with Truth, is the exemplary performer of activity. He knows what he should do, how he should do it, and the consummate reason behind his doing. Like the ordinary man of action, he uses the senses, mind, and reason, but does not sully them by contact with the ego's undesirable hordes of attachments and desires, known to the yogis as troublemakers and peace-disturbers.

The performance of a sattvic activity must have, primarily, the stamp of approval of a true scripture, and of God, directing through a true guru. Secondarily, that divinely ordained action must be performed by a completely nonattached person, without selfish love or hatred, and without desire for the fruits of the action.

Characteristics of sattvic action

If a philanthropist gives alms to the poor with the object of gaining publicity, then even though such a munificent act is ordinarily sattvic, the spring of this specific act, being tainted by desire for its fruits and being performed with attachment to those fruits, is impure. Hence, in the scriptural context of absolutes, an activity can be called truly sattvic or pure only when it is taintless from its inception to its consummation. As a piece of gold cannot be termed pure if it contains any trace of alloy, so an action cannot be called completely sattvic if it has not been started purely, performed purely, and concluded purely.

A yogi works solely for the love of God. He starts a sattvic action with the taintless desire to please God; he performs that action nobly for Him; and he finishes that action absorbed in the thought of his Lord. Though he acts in a world of relativity wherein his choices are often between the "lesser of two evils," his consciousness nevertheless remains attuned to the One Absolute beyond taint. That is the goal advocated by this Gita verse.

For most beings, held in *maya*'s constraints of relativity, their actions consist of an intermixture of two or all of the three qualities; but each act may be generally classified as sattvic, rajasic, or tamasic according to which characteristic predominates. Providentially, the preponderance of goodness in an action mitigates the effects of a companionate impurity.

It is easy to picture the performance of a pleasant good action with nonattachment, but it is difficult to imagine performing an unpleasant but dutiful action without repulsion.

If a poisonous snake were about to strike a child, and a nearby yogi, without animosity or desire to take life, kills the snake, his action would be considered sattvic, but slightly tainted by his act of killing. God has commanded through the scriptures that none shall kill human beings, the highest life-form on the scale of evolution. The yogi's act of killing, even though impure in itself, would be almost wholly purified by the saving of the valuable life of the child in preference to perpetuating the harm-inflicting life of the snake.

The yogi's heart was free from any sadistic desire to kill, and free from that confusion about his true duty which might have led him to inaction by the thought: "Oh, I hate to kill that snake." His heart was neither attached to the child nor malicious toward the serpent. He acted to satisfy God's law regarding the superiority of human life. He could not very well have put the snake in a basket to later turn it loose in the jungle; there was no time to do so!

Had the yogi saved the child from the serpent's venom because of attachment for the child, then his action, though noble, could not be considered sattvic. For example, would he have responded similarly, risking his own life, if the person had been an avowed enemy? Hence, even a good action, if performed with the slightest selfish attachment—an attachment due to obtaining even a small measure of egoistic gratification—would not in an absolute sense be considered sattvic. But the cumulative spiritual power of such preponderantly good and divinely ordained actions has a purifying effect that serves to transform gradually the selfish motivations of the ego into the pure sattvic expressions of the soul.

Therefore, the criterion of all action should be sattvic selflessness. Every act should be performed with zeal, not mechanically, and ought to be ambitiously carried out with the supreme desire to please God or fulfill the holy injunction of one's guru and the scriptures.

VERSE 24

yat tu kāmepsunā karma sāhaṁkāreṇa vā punaḥ
kriyate bahulāyāsaṁ tad rājasam udāhṛtam

Action that is inspired by longing for satisfaction of desires, or performed with egotism and colossal effort, is said to be rajasic.

RAJAS IS THE PASSIONATE ENERGY of creation, ever restless, always in motion. Desire is its inseparable companion, seeking fulfillment of its purposes, and in the process proliferating from those activities new causes of pursuit. Thus *rajas* implies a constant exertion of will directed by the matter-loving, body-identified ego.

Under the influence of *tamas*—the degrading quality—*rajas* activity becomes base and vile. When restrained and guided by *sattva*—the enlightening quality—*rajas* activity is ennobled. The majority of people in the world, engaged in mundane pursuits, remain struggling in the middle of the two extremes, motivated by self-interest and worldly desires but generally temperate in their habits and averse to the baser evils. Their typically rajasic activity expresses as an urgency to keep up with the standards of modern civilization with its emphasis on material gain and high living. Far fewer persons, by comparison, fall into the depths of tamasic evil, or aspire to the heights of *sattva* and its consummation in the wisdom and ego-free state of Self-realization.

Characteristics of rajasic action

The motivation of one's desires determines the ascent or descent of the *rajas* vitality operative in the actions of every being. If a rich man harbors desires of gaining fame and glory, and with a consciousness of self-importance assumes the prodigious task of celebrating a holy feast by lavishly feeding thousands and entertaining them with ceremonial pomp and music, such an action—colossal in ego and effort—is called rajasic. If a proper holy celebration is performed with the sole desire to please God, that is a sattvic action. Pure sattvic actions lead to liberation. Rajasic actions, on the other hand, produce manifold desires patterned after their own kind. Being instituted for the satisfaction of ego and its limited world, such actions increase troubles and rebirths for man unless the initiating and accruing insatiable desires are destroyed by the greater power of sattvic wisdom.

VERSE 25

anubandhaṁ kṣayaṁ hiṁsām anapekṣya ca pauruṣam
mohād ārabhyate karma yat tat tāmasam ucyate

Tamasic action is that which is instituted through delusion, without measuring one's ability, and disregarding the consequences—loss to oneself of health, wealth, and influence; and harm to others.

TO THE DEGREE THAT *tamas,* the darkening quality, affects the knowledge of man (see XVIII:22), his actions, accordingly, will confirm his deluded state. He behaves with selfish shortsightedness devoid of sound reason and judgment and the ability to anticipate the consequences of his actions.

The rule among ruffians is: "Hit first and reason afterward." This practice can lead to extremely serious consequences. That thoughtless hard blow may end as another man's murder; and the result of that may well be a death sentence for the assailant.

Characteristics of tamasic action

Persons who act thoughtlessly under the influence of violent or mindless emotions, heedless of the potential consequences of their actions, not only become instrumental in hurting others, but also vitiate their own vitality and often suffer loss of prestige or prosperity as well. They entangle themselves in complex difficulties by instituting actions without first determining the rightness of their intentions and estimating their power and ability to perform those actions successfully.

If a person of poor ability takes all of his own money, and a large sum borrowed from friends who can ill afford such a risk—exciting them with the foundless hope of gaining great dividends—and starts a sure-to-fail unwieldy business, he performs such an action without regard to its inevitable results: loss of fortune and prestige to himself, and injury to others. Any such irrational action, producing all-round evil, is tamasic.

Inertia is the quiddity of the tamasic quality. Therefore, tamasic action always pursues the path of least resistance to avoid the effort required in the practice of self-control, the exercise of discrimination, and engagement in divinely ordained duties.

Verse 26

muktasaṅgo 'nahaṁvādī dhṛtyutsāhasamanvitaḥ
siddhyasiddhyor nirvikāraḥ kartā sāttvika ucyate

That agent who is without egotism or attachment, untouched by fulfillment or unfulfillment, and endowed with courage and zeal, is called sattvic.

THE CHARACTERISTIC EXPRESSION of the three qualities (*sattva, rajas,* and *tamas*) in the agent, or doer of actions, is now described in stanzas 26–28.

He whose mind is not identified with the body-bound ego or tainted by attachment to objects of the senses; who patiently performs spiritual actions of meditation and divinely motivated actions that help others on the path of salvation, disregarding success or failure, unexcited by paltry pleasures and sorrows, acting only with the supreme desire of pleasing God—that man is a sattvic yogi of the highest type. The following story aptly illustrates the state of such a yogi.

Qualities of the sattvic nature

A wise man was sitting calmly in contemplation, his consciousness intoxicated with the presence of God. His wife came running to him and sobbed, "Our son just fell from the roof and died."

"Sit in peace," her husband said quietly, "and meditate upon God. Tell Him, 'Lord, we thank Thee for giving us the company of a noble son for twenty long years. In Thy wisdom Thou knowest why it is now best to promote him to a better place, no longer feeding our selfish desires to keep him here. Even though we shall miss him, we bow to Thine all-knowing wish.'"

Shocked, his wife exclaimed, "What is wrong with you? Haven't you a tear for our dead son?" After a little pause, the father replied:

"Last night I dreamt that I was a king, and that I had three sons who fell to their death from the palace roof when it collapsed during an earthquake. Now I am wondering whether I should weep for the lost palace and the three princes of my dream, or if I should cry for our one son who has been taken away in this mysterious earthly dream of God's?"

Only a yogi of the highest God-realization could in truth behave with such transcendent feeling. A lesser person feigning such spiritual aloofness would be acting in cruel and unfeeling hypocrisy.

A truly wise man is able to distinguish temporal mortal dreams from the Eternal Reality; therefore, he is utterly free from all attachment. He is evenmindedly indifferent to both the reverses and the successes that befall him, for he does not see himself as the doer; he perceives the Lord working through him in His world. He who believes he owns any portion of this earth is seized with terrible grief when he loses that which he mistakenly thought was his own.

Sattvic nonattachment and absence of egoity does not make the yogi apathetic. His inner state of God-union rather gives him an imperturbability of fortitude and resolution, and a zeal that is constantly enlivened by his perception of the Hidden Joy in all things. Dispassionate toward the happenings in God's dream, he is yet wholly compassionate toward those beings still struggling with its relativities.

VERSE 27

rāgī karmaphalaprepsur lubdho hiṁsātmako 'śuciḥ
harṣaśokānvitaḥ kartā rājasaḥ parikīrtitaḥ

That instrument of action, or agent, who is full of attachment, full of longing for the fruits of action, full of greed, impurity, and ruthless propensities; who becomes easily jubilant or depressed, is called rajasic.

A PERSON WHO IS UNDER THE UNGOVERNED influence of the passionate or fiery energy of the *guna* of *rajas* develops a wholly materialistic exertive nature. Always restless and outgoing, he never spends time in the pure enjoyment of meditation, or in introspection, or in exchanging peace with others. He is excessively active, blindly accumulating money, property, and power with inordinate greed and sole self-interest. He is inclined to seek baneful thrills, such as the indiscriminate hunting of animals just for the lust of the sport. When it suits his purpose, he can be insensitively harsh, even sadistic, ready to hurt or destroy any competitor, or to take revenge on anyone standing in the path of his self-interest. He is constantly bobbing up and down in excitation on the alternating waves of mirth and grief. He is nothing more than a cogwheel in the machinery of action, a mechanical rajasic person.

Qualities of the rajasic nature

Even a little sattvic discrimination and self-control aimed at restraining and guiding the passionate force in the base rajasic tendencies helps to create a more principled energetic personality.

Verse 28

ayuktaḥ prākṛtaḥ stabdhaḥ śaṭho naikṛtiko 'lasaḥ
viṣādī dīrghasūtrī ca kartā tāmasa ucyate

An agent who is oscillating in body and mind, conscienceless, arrogant, unscrupulous, malicious, slothful, grieving, and procrastinating is tamasic.

A person immersed in the dark *guna* of *tamas* is the epitome of human delusive ignorance. Like the restless butterfly, his mind and body are ever in a state of agitation; lacking the intelligence for decisiveness and the will for constructive action, he is passively pulled in one direction and then another by any momentary influence. He thus never knows the peace of his soul within. He is conscienceless, morally crude and vulgar, performing evil actions whenever the impulse arises in him. He is without humility, rude and insolent toward others at the slightest excuse. He unscrupulously deceives others, playing the double life of a Dr. Jekyll and Mr. Hyde. He readily acts with meanness and insult to others for his own self-aggrandizement. He is habitually physically lazy and mentally idle, unwilling to work intelligently lest success bring him more responsibility. He is perpetually negative and depressed, dampening others' joyous spirits. He does not finish either simple or important duties, and procrastinates because of inner and outer slothfulness and lack of enthusiasm and purpose in life.

Qualities of the tamasic nature

Most people who do not succeed in life are steeped in the dark tamasic quality. They blame the world and everybody but themselves as the cause of their failure and misery; they never find fault with their own indolence, procrastination, unsociable conduct, restlessness, insincerity, selfishness, and maliciousness as the causes of their affliction. Therefore, they are always depressed because they do not recognize and remove the true causes of their unhappiness.

The deeply unhappy tamasic individual should try first to become rajasic, active, but with a noble purpose. It is better to work in harmony with God's divine activities than for selfish motives; but even a depraved businessman, because of his activity, has a better chance for salvation than the physically and mentally ossified tamasic man.

Company is stronger than will power. Both tamasic and rajasic persons should seek the influence of higher types, preferably sattvic beings who are steeped in God-realization. A wrestler who works out with a stronger combatant increases his strength; weak tamasic and rajasic types likewise should associate with spiritually stronger sattvic individuals.

Environment is also influential; it creates the desire to become either good or evil. A man has free choice to select a good or evil environment or action before he forms habits. But after a specific environment has instilled in him the desire to follow a good or bad habit, he usually loses his free will: a good habit compels a man to be good and an evil habit compels him to do wrong; thus he helplessly gravitates toward a corresponding environment.

Outer environment incites the inner as well as the outer behavior of man. Thus, the creation of a strong inner character is of paramount importance, so that it can then remain unaffected by, or even change, adverse outer influences.

Unless one's inner environment is sufficiently resolute, however, he should realize the importance of associating only with persons and environments that are extremely wholesome. A person who abhors liquor, and who lives with others who do not touch it, creates a strong inner mental environment against drink. Such a one, by mixing with drunkards, may then be able to help reform them. But if a person who has established even a slight inner attachment to liquor elects to live among drinkers, he may easily become an alcoholic. A person with any inclination to wrongdoing should not mix with his kind, but with those who are better than he is.

The worldly man should seek out the meditative man and create his own inviolate inner environment of God-communion. After that is accomplished, if he has to return to a material environment, or does so to help others, he will not be affected by it. Only when he has thus strengthened himself can he be of help in uplifting others.

Intelligence (Buddhi), Fortitude (Dhriti), and Happiness (Sukham): Their Higher and Lower Expressions

Verses 29–30

buddher bhedaṁ dhṛteś caiva guṇatas trividhaṁ śṛṇu
procyamānam aśeṣeṇa pṛthaktvena dhanaṁjaya (29)

pravṛttiṁ ca nivṛttiṁ ca kāryākārye bhayābhaye
bandhaṁ mokṣaṁ ca yā vetti buddhiḥ sā pārtha sāttvikī (30)

(29) O Winner of Wealth (Arjuna), I will explain, separately and exhaustively, the threefold distinctions of intelligence and fortitude according to the gunas. Please listen.

(30) That intellect is sattvic, O Partha (Arjuna), which correctly understands the paths of desireful action and renunciation, undutiful and dutiful actions, as the causes of apprehension and fearlessness, bondage and salvation.

When intelligence (*buddhi*) and fortitude (*dhriti*) are properly developed, imbued with the uplifting *sattva* quality, man finds his life fully under his control. With the intelligence unclouded and the courage resolute, the consciousness rises above the limitations of mental frailties and manifests the intuitively perceptive, intrepidly calm state of the soul.

Pure sattvic discrimination reveals to the devotee the bondage that exists in blindly pursuing the path of worldly activity, and the liberation inherent in following the path of renunciation, inner nonattachment.

Worldly pursuits for self-satisfaction are fraught with apprehensions, chiefly of failure and death. The renunciant, in his nonattachment, knows the world is run by God. A yogi of pure discrimination therefore works fearlessly and lovingly to please Him alone. The sattvic intelligence of such a yogi clearly distinguishes actions that are to be avoided because they create bondage and apprehension, from dutiful and meditative actions that are to be performed because they bring liberation and the permanent removal of all dreaded fears.

Even if a victorious Genghis Khan became master of the world, he would still not be free from the fear of disease and approaching death. It is only by working for God, renouncing all covetousness for impermanent worldly objects, and by communing with God, that a soul finds the eternally safe Shelter which is proof against all suffering and death.

VERSE 31

yayā dharmam adharmaṁ ca kāryaṁ cākāryam eva ca
ayathāvat prajānāti buddhiḥ sā pārtha rājasī

O Partha (Arjuna), that intellect is rajasic by which one perceives in a grossly distorted manner righteousness (dharma) and unrighteousness (adharma), dutiful action and undutiful action.

THE MAN WHOSE INTELLECT IS IDENTIFIED with the unthinking mechanism of rajasic activity becomes mentally confused and does not distinguish between God-reminding religious duties and materially absorbing irreligious activities. Such a beclouded mentality heedlessly intermixes righteousness and unrighteousness. Lacking clarity of vision, and blindly performing actions without discrimination, the ordinary gross materialist constantly stumbles into the pit of worries and disillusionment. Being thus the frequent recipient of pain, the rajasic intelligence is full of distrust and doubt, and consequently builds up a defense of self-assertiveness—the stronghold of the passionate ego.

VERSE 32

adharmaṁ dharmam iti yā manyate tamasāvṛtā
sarvārthān viparītāṁś ca buddhiḥ sā pārtha tāmasī

O Partha (Arjuna), that intellect is tamasic which, being enveloped in gloom, considers irreligion as religion, and looks upon all things in a perverted way.

Persons who do not follow even the regular organized path of material life led by those of rajasic temperament, but indulge instead in extremes of indolent and evil conduct, are abnormal individuals impelled by a tamasic intelligence. Their intellect is eclipsed by the mental darkness of ignorance and plagued by its resultant misery. Such extremists make materialistic, irreligious living their religion. As they see nothing unvirtuous in their behavior, lazy and evil ways become second nature to them. They indulge in overeating, oversexuality, and excesses in all harmful habits. Leading an unnatural existence, they have perverted opinions and modes of living, and are irresponsible in their whole manner of thinking, willing, and behaving.

Tamasic beings are unpredictably unreasonable; in the use of their deluded intelligence, they work much harm to themselves and others.

Verse 33

dhṛtyā yayā dhārayate manaḥprāṇendriyakriyāḥ
yogenāvyabhicāriṇyā dhṛtiḥ sā pārtha sāttvikī

The resolute constancy by which one regulates the functions of the mind, prana, and senses—by restraining their prostitution (wayward oscillation) through yoga practice—that fortitude (dhriti) is sattvic, O Partha (Arjuna).

Liberation consists of two aspects of union. The first unites the physical ego with the soul; or, in other words, resolves the pseudosoul into the real soul, which is a reflection of the blessedness of Spirit. The second unites the soul with omnipresent Spirit.

But the physical ego cannot be separated from its identification with sense objects—a prerequisite of union with the soul and with Spirit—without withdrawal of the mind, life force, and sense consciousness from the body and the objective world.

Yoga provides the method to switch off the life force from the five sense-telephones, and thereby to disconnect the mind and the senses from their external environment. This automatically frees the physical ego to dissolve itself in its true blessed nature of the soul. When through yoga practice the mind, life force, and senses remain unprostituted—unperverted by material restlessness—concentrated on the true Self, that disciplined, interiorized, firmly established state is called *sattvic-dhriti.*

The word *dhriti* in this context is not exactly "fortitude," but rather connotes the inner firmness of self-control and the constancy of soul perception that produces a steady state of fortitude. In that unshakable state, the soul in its pure nature retains mastery over the mind, life force, and senses, and thus remains unperturbed by the temptations of sense objects.

The *sattvic-buddhi* or pure intelligence (defined in verse 30) beholds the good, the God, in everything; its pure intuitive discrimination points out to the yogi the difference between good and evil—desirable God-perception and undesirable sense indulgences. *Sattvic-dhriti* then enables the yogi, through successful practice of yoga, to abide in resolute inner constancy in the state of *sattvic-buddhi*—divine realization through soul perception.

When unswerving Self-perception is attained, the yogi is said to have reached the eternal state of fortitude, or *dhriti,* untouched by sensory-engendered mundane fears.

A yogi possessing a *sattvic-dhriti* consciousness keeps his mind settled in the blessed perception of the soul and God, undisturbed by the inroads of sensations in the conscious state of existence as well as in the interiorized ecstasy of meditation. He can therefore wander in worldly life, engaging in dutiful activities, beholding good and evil, without being in any way affected or entangled by them.

VERSE 34

yayā tu dharmakāmārthān dhṛtyā dhārayate 'rjuna
prasaṅgena phalākāṅkṣī dhṛtiḥ sā pārtha rājasī

The resolute inner patience that causes one to regulate his mind to dharma (religious duty), desire, and riches—while longing for the fruits thereof, because of attachment—that, O Partha (Arjuna), is rajasic-dhriti.

THROUGH ATTACHMENT, A WORLDLY MAN by *rajasic-dhriti*—resolute inner patience under the influence of the passionate or active quality—clings to external religious ceremonious duties, earthly desires, and money-making efforts.

A man of this tenacious activating disposition keeps his mind, vitality, and senses patiently and persistently settled in physical duties in order to gain their results. Taking the matter-of-fact view of life, the majority of these worldly people gird up their loins to fulfill all natural propensities—earning money, keeping up the home and maintaining a family, and superficially partaking in religious ceremonies—in general, remaining identified with the inclinations of the physical ego.

VERSE 35

yayā svapnaṁ bhayaṁ śokaṁ viṣādaṁ madam eva ca
na vimuñcati durmedhā dhṛtiḥ sā pārtha tāmasī

That by which a stupid man does not forsake over-sleep, fear, sorrow, despair, and wanton conceit, O Partha (Arjuna), is tamasic-dhriti.

TAMASIC-DHRITI, INNER SETTLEMENT ON EVIL—the quality (*guna*) of ignorance acting on the inner patient attitude of an unthinking person—is that obstinacy through which one clings to evil. Tamasic or evil indiscriminative persistence keeps gross individuals habitually settled in over-sleep, constant fear, grief, despondency, and insolent conceit. These evil qualities are harbingers of great troubles. Egoistic dark-minded persons who sleep too much become drugged by the habit of this stupor and thus remain identified with the idle, ungoverned body—unable to whip it into proper action to fulfill ordained duties and to gain success and peace. Owing to mental and physical inactivity, they naturally become depressed, which results in fear of carrying on an unbearable, unhappy existence.

In other words, over-sleep produces physical and mental indolence and aversion to constructive work. Lack of activity produces despondency through the consciousness of a useless existence. The habit of deeming life a burden produces grief and fear of repeated experience of sorrow. Disdainful conceit makes one satisfied with his evil habits; his contempt toward the need to change his ways keeps him from having any hope of salvation.

Human beings who find themselves steadfastly clinging to *tamasic-dhriti*, and therefore settled in evil habits, should forthwith banish conceit and regulate their lives by proper activity and proper sleep supplemented by the rejuvenating power of meditation, thus freeing the mind from fear, despondency, and grief.

VERSES 36–37

sukhaṁ tv idānīṁ trividhaṁ śṛṇu me bharatarṣabha
abhyāsād ramate yatra duḥkhāntaṁ ca nigacchati (36)

yat tad agre viṣaṁ iva pariṇāme 'mṛtopamam
tat sukhaṁ sāttvikaṁ proktam ātmabuddhiprasādajam (37)

(36) O Stubborn Bull of Realization* (Arjuna)! Pray hear from Me now about the three kinds of happiness: Transcendent happiness (supreme bliss), gained by repeated recollection of the mind,† and in which one knows the extinguishment of all pain; (37) That which is born of the clear perceptive discrimination of Self-realization—that happiness is called sattvic. It seems like poison at first, but like nectar afterward.

Sattvic happiness

WHEN A YOGI CONSTANTLY STRIVES to practice meditative calmness, he ultimately experiences the birth of divine bliss and the end of all sorrow. Suffering is threefold—physical, mental, and spiritual. Physical suffering arises from disease and discomfort. Mental suffering springs, in large measure, from the sprouted karmic seeds of past evil actions lodged in the astral brain. Spiritual suffering comes from inability to contact God.

These threefold sufferings disappear when, by practice of yoga, the mind becomes disengaged from the grief-making senses and united to the blessedness of the soul, the true Self.

Verse 37, however, acknowledges the initial difficult states of struggle and discontent—unpleasant like "poison"—experienced by

---

* *Bharata-rishabha:* lit., "Bull of the Bharatas" ("the best or most excellent of the descendants of the Bharata dynasty")—thus, one who has attained the highest: realization through the fortitude, the divine obstinacy or "stubbornness," of inner constancy (*dhriti*, as described in the preceding verses).

† *Abhyāsād ramate:* from *abhyāsā,* lit., "the continuous effort to hold the mind in its pure sattvic state"; and from *ram,* lit., "to enjoy," "to still; set at rest"—that is, to gain transcendent happiness. When the mind is recollected in its pure sattvic state, the sensory tumult is stilled and the transcendent supreme bliss of the soul becomes manifest.

the yogi during his skirmishes with the senses. But after the mind and discriminative intelligence have won the victory, they plant their banner of triumph on the blessed tract of the soul. When the victorious yogi, after his experiences of spiritual struggle, tastes through his interiorized, intuitive discrimination the divine *amrita* ("nectar") of the soul, that true happiness is called *sattvic.* Pure sattvic joy is unending, ever new, culminating at last in the eternal *Ananda,* Bliss, of Spirit—beyond touch of any *guna,* even *sattva*.

VERSE 38

viṣayendriyasaṁyogād yat tad agre'mṛtopamam
pariṇāme viṣam iva tat sukhaṁ rājasaṁ smṛtam

That happiness which springs from the conjunction of the senses and matter is termed rajasic. It seems like nectar in the beginning and like poison in the end.

THE NATURE OF HAPPINESS born of the passionate blindness of rajasic actions is described here. A person who experiences physical pleasure after strenuous effort to attain it enjoys for a while the ambrosial "nectar" of a gratifying happiness; but this is inevitably decimated by the "poison" of dissatisfied unhappiness as the impermanent sensory pleasure wanes.

Rajasic happiness

When a boisterous young man works hard, and with difficulty saves money to buy a rickety car, he is extremely happy with his first wild outings in it. But as soon as he meets with an accident, or has to spend a considerable amount just to keep the dilapidated vehicle in working order, he begins to taste the "poison" of unhappiness.

One who gluttonously swallows more food than he can digest finds joy in satisfying his inordinate greed, but the aftereffects from overeating are discomfort or eventual disease.

The sexually overindulgent person yields to temptation until his eyesight, nerves, physical vigor, self-control, inner peace, sense of propriety, and sense of honor are completely shattered. His enthusiasm about sexual pleasure changes into devastating mental depression that may even lead to dementia.

The alcoholic or the habitual drug user feels elation at first, but afterward is plunged into despair when the effects of the liquor or narcotic wear off.

The initial state of happiness accompanying sensuality is always followed by unhappiness, owing to the impairment of physical vitality, mental self-control, and spiritual peace. It is the enigma of *maya* that the poison of sensual experiences is found to be so pleasant in the beginning.* The initially pleasurable taste of the poisonous honey of evil deludes people and so causes them to indulge in harmful experiences. If evil had no charm, nobody would try it. People swallow the bitter pill of evil because it is sugarcoated with immediate pleasure.

Worldly people, young and old, are those who overindulge their senses. Even after discovering the harmful aftereffects, they are still helplessly driven to such excesses by the compelling influence of bad habits. Recipients of rajasic happiness find out too late that undisciplined sensual pleasures turn out to be tormentors, destroying strength, vitality, health, good looks, intelligence, memory, riches, and enthusiasm.†

Strongly pulled by temptation, worldly rajasic people pursue their materialistic lives without ever knowing the blessedness of Spirit hidden within them, in the true peace and joy found in meditation. But toward the end of life they often feel utterly deceived by the prevaricating senses. Then they find no happiness in anything. Their minds become empty and dark, stalked by goblins of unhappiness.

The precept in this stanza is notably relevant to the disillusioning end many youthfully eager materialists encounter. Lured by high hopes of prosperity and physical happiness, they work hard and scheme at the cost of their peace and health, and try vainly to buy more happiness by acquiring more money. As they pass from youth to old age, they suffer a gradual loss of vigor and enthusiasm and become prey to disease and the fear of approaching death, the great leveler that turns to naught all earthly gains.

* "In God's plan and play (*lila*), the sole function of Satan or Maya is to attempt to divert man from Spirit to matter, from Reality to unreality."—*Autobiography of a Yogi*.

† "God may forgive your sins, but your nervous system won't."—*Alfred Korzybski, Polish-American scientist*

Verse 39

yad agre cānubandhe ca sukhaṁ mohanam ātmanaḥ
nidrālasyapramādotthaṁ tat tāmasam udāhṛtam

That elusive happiness which originates and ends in self-delusion, stemming from over-sleep, slothfulness, and miscomprehension, is called tamasic.

MAN CHOOSES EVIL HAPPINESS when his intelligence is deluded by innate bad karma, or by bad company and inner response to evil. By indulgence in tamasic inclinations, his discrimination is eclipsed. Tamasic qualities thus originate in man through this miscomprehension and culminate in disillusionment and despondency. The evil tamasic propensities are fed by the opiate of unnecessary sleep, and by physical idleness and mental aimlessness.

Tamasic happiness

Too much sleep produces bodily sloth and mental helplessness (as cited in XVIII:35); it paralyzes the physical, vital, and mental faculties of man. The indolent tamasic person—drugged by over-sleep, idleness and mental aimlessness, and continuous miscomprehension—is lacking in all revivifying inner and outer activity, causing him to approach a state resembling inanimate matter, unfit for human expression. Those who indulge in the soporific of evil tamasic qualities are like trained animals under intoxication, unable to perform their expected activities. Tamasic individuals, drugging themselves with the lowest grade of happiness (self-satisfaction with their degraded existence), find all inherent good qualities being gradually obliterated, giving rise to bestial behavior and, at the worst, total inertia.

In the course of evolution, the soul sleeps in stones, awakes drowsily in the trees, becomes conscious vitality in animals, and expresses self-conscious discriminative vitality in man. In the superman, the soul manifests its true nature of superconsciousness and omnipresence.* Conversely, by eclipsing his discrimination through intemperate living and pursuit of evil ways and pleasures, a human being can lower himself to little better than an animal state. By increased idleness and the drugging effect of over-sleep, he can reduce himself to resembling a drunken animal. From the effects of still further indulgence in bad habits and ex-

* See reference to *koshas,* I:4–6, page 63.

treme sensory abandon, he can become mentally—and even physically—inert like a tree, with only a semblance of intelligent human vitality. Should he continue to nurture that torpid state, as when under the influence of narcotics or alcohol, he would become as worthless as a mass of ossified flesh, or a stone, lacking in all signs of intelligence. The fate of such descended beings was described in XVI:19–20.

DISCERNING ONE'S DIVINELY ORDAINED DUTY IN LIFE

VERSE 40

na tad asti pṛthivyāṁ vā divi deveṣu vā punaḥ
sattvaṁ prakṛtijair muktaṁ yad ebhiḥ syāt tribhir guṇaiḥ

There is no being in the world, or again among the deities in the astral heaven, who is free from these three qualities, born of Prakriti (Cosmic Nature, created by God).

THE FABRIC OF ALL MANIFESTATION is held together by the interweaving threads of the three *gunas.* Thus, superior astral beings and ordinary men are equally subject to the triple influence of the good, activating, and evil qualities. Even though both man and deity have the power of free choice, and are therefore responsible for their actions, they cannot escape the influence of the pervasive threefold qualities endemic in Cosmic Nature, the Holy Ghost or vibratory manifestation of God. However, being made in the image of God, man and deity can exercise their God-given free choice and refuse to succumb to the degrading tamasic quality. By pursuing proper rajasic activity and divine sattvic activity they may transcend all three qualities and reenter the kingdom of God.

It is the hobby of God to outwit His Self-created *maya*-opponents in the cosmic game of creation, and thus to return souls to His kingdom after they have passed the test of conquering evil temptations by recognizing the true charm of goodness.

God is indeed responsible for creating the objects of temptation and the sensory instruments of enjoyment, thereby subjecting man to delusion's enticements. But man is responsible if he does not use his divinely given discriminative free choice to distinguish between sorrow-fraught evil and liberation-producing virtue.

Verse 41

brāhmaṇakṣatriyaviśāṁ śūdrāṇāṁ ca paraṁtapa
karmāṇi pravibhaktāni svabhāvaprabhavair guṇaiḥ

O Scorcher of Foes (Arjuna)! The duties of Brahmins, of Kshatriyas, of Vaishyas, as also of Sudras, are allocated according to the gunas (qualities) springing from their own nature.

In the divine Gita dialogue, symbolic of the inner realization received by the devotee in communion with God, the Lord now reiterates to Arjuna through his intuitional perception that the true meaning of the four natural castes, or classifications of mankind, and the duties inherent in them (described in the following verses 42–44) are based not on one's birth but on one's individual qualities.* The true natural castes are the Brahmins or God-knowers, Kshatriyas or sense-fighters, Vaishyas or wisdom-cultivators,† and Sudras or body-identified individuals. These four "castes" are present in all nations as the spiritual intelligentsia; the soldiers, rulers, and leaders; the businessmen; and the laborers.

The existence in the world of four natural classes of human beings is the result of the sattvic, rajasic, and tamasic qualities, and their mixtures, present in Prakriti or Cosmic Nature. The differentiation of individuals into these four classes is also the result of their own free choice of good and evil actions in the past.

Svabhava, "one's own nature," as used in this stanza, signifies the nature of God when manifesting as Prakriti with Her cosmic delusion of three qualities, as well as the nature of man, which results from the influence of these qualities and from his own past good or evil actions.

---

* See also commentary on the four natural castes in II:31, page 245, III:24, page 384, and IV:13, pages 456 ff.

† So called because in contrast to the Sudra, whose sense-bound activities serve chiefly his body and thereby limit his service to humanity to bodily labor, the Vaishya, by cultivating discriminative control of desires for the sake of higher gain, sows within himself the first seeds of wisdom and serves humanity by mental labor.

Even though man's nature is ordained by Prakriti and his own past karma, still it is only an acquired second nature, born of the use of his free choice. Though buried beneath this acquired second nature, man's real soul nature, which is a true image of God, remains eternally in his possession. If this were not so, if man did not possess an unchanging spirit endowed with free will, the four classes of individuals could not change their natures: the body-identified person could not become, through spiritual development, a God-knowing Brahmin; and a Brahmin could not degrade himself by sense-tempted actions into a body-bound Sudra. According to the manner in which man exercises his free choice, he can be bound temporarily in the limitations of any of these four castes; but by meditation, unceasing desire to regain his lost paradise, and divine grace, he can be liberated.

By self-development or by wrong living, man can raise or lower his "caste"

As these four classes of beings, either by self-development or by wrong living, can raise or lower their status, there can be no permanent classification of any individual. Thus a body-bound Sudra laborer, by education and deep efforts in meditation and yoga culture, can become a sower of wisdom, or Vaishya, developing his mental capacity for carrying on a business. By further self-control in fighting the bodily propensities and guiding his actions with discriminative judgment, he can become a Kshatriya, a military officer, or ruler or leader, if he so aspires; and by ecstasy with God, that former Sudra becomes a God-knowing Brahmin.

The pernicious caste system of the East sprang from the error of establishing caste according to heredity rather than quality. Similarly, the evils of the class system in the West sprang from the false "pride of family" consciousness. Without his money, many a millionaire would be unable to brag about his high pedigree. Likewise, a man born in a God-knowing Brahmin family cannot be a true Brahmin unless by self-effort he communes with God, any more than a doctor's son could be a doctor without acquiring the necessary qualifications. It is as ridiculous for a Brahmin's wicked son to pose as a Brahmin as it is for a poverty-stricken man, disinherited because of his wanton ways, to claim he is rich because his father is wealthy.

When a person manifests predominantly the good *sattva* quality, keeping the activating and evil qualities and his past bad karma under his control, he is spoken of as a Brahmin. (See XVIII:42.) When one keeps predominant in himself the activating *rajas* quality, mixed with some liberating goodness, with the evil quality and the bad karma of the past eclipsed, he is said to be a Kshatriya, or sense-fighter. (See XVIII:43.) When one manifests predominantly the activating *rajas* quality, slightly mixed with the evil or obstructing quality and the effects of past bad karma, and with the elevating good quality mostly hidden, he is called a Vaishya, or wisdom-cultivator, one who is making intellectual efforts to better himself. (See XVIII:44.) When one manifests predominantly the obstructing evil *tamas* quality, slightly mixed with the activating quality, and is strongly influenced by his own bad karma, the liberating good quality being wholly suppressed, he is said to be a Sudra, a body-identified individual (*kayastha*) belonging to the lowest class. (See XVIII:44.)

Man's response to the triple qualities (gunas) of Nature determines his caste

The Brahmin usually follows a spiritual profession; the Kshatriya may be a leader in any vocation; the Vaishya may follow any vocation associated with being an organizer or provider, such as that of a farmer, merchant, or businessman. The Sudra is particularly adapted to manual labor.

Metaphysically, a Sudra mentality signifies one who doubts everything except material existence. Such a body-identified person may be born in any of the three higher castes, or be following any higher vocation, but he does not manifest the natural quality of that caste or the natural qualifications for that work. Similarly, a God-knowing Brahmin may be a laborer, or a farmer, or a businessman, or a soldier. He may perform material duties according to his choice, without being internally affected by them, remaining as a God-knower, or true Brahmin.

In summation, man and Cosmic Nature cannot manifest their activities without the mixture of the three *gunas.* It is by differentiation of the triune qualities that Cosmic Nature comes into being; and it is by man's response to these qualities that the aforesaid four types of individuals are born.

But during the period when God withdraws His physical nature, the cosmic Prakriti, within Himself by equilibrating the triune qualities, He becomes solely Spirit, the Absolute; God the Father, Son, and Holy Ghost (Prakriti) dissolve in Spirit and exist no more. As God can thus tranquilize Nature's three qualities and absorb Her and all Her activities into Himself, so man, made in God's image, can by ecstasy dissolve the influence of the three qualities, and the effects of past good, activating, and evil actions, and become liberated.

VERSE 42

śamo damas tapaḥ śaucaṁ kṣāntir ārjavam eva ca
jñānaṁ vijñānam āstikyaṁ brahmakarma svabhāvajam

Mind control, sense control, self-discipline, purity, forgiveness, honesty, wisdom, Self-realization, and faith in a hereafter constitute the duties of Brahmins, springing from their own nature.

A TRUE BRAHMIN IS HE WHO IS ONE with Brahman, God. Jesus declared this consciousness when he said: "I and my Father are one."* Whether born in a high or a low caste, whether Christian, Hindu, or follower of any other religion, he who *knows* God, as did Jesus, is a true Brahmin.

He who has realized oneness with God possesses all knowledge contained in Him. Knowing the Lord as Beginning and End of all beings and worlds, a true Brahmin has knowledge of the hereafter and of the workings of Nature on this plane of existence. He can thus behold souls passing into the astral world after their earthly experience, and can duplicate this ascension of spirit consciously in the *samadhi* state of meditation. Such a God-knowing Brahmin can at will withdraw his life force from the senses and thus disconnect his mind from body consciousness and dissolve it in God-consciousness.

The true Brahmin: a living receptacle of divine virtues

In his daily life, a Brahmin manifests all the divine qualities, such as purity, self-control, forgiveness, and uprightness. The Hindu scriptures say a knower of Brahman is like Brahman. Thus a true Brahmin is pure like God, without any taint of delusion in his consciousness. Even as God by austerity† remains above the manifested cosmos, so by self-control (mastery of the self by spiritual discipline and resultant *samadhi* meditation) the Brahmin transcends the perception of the world and its limitations.

---

* John 10:30.

† The Hindu scriptures say that creation is God's *lila* or sport, a play of His cosmic consciousness, springing from His desireless desire. He is present in His creation, yet He remains apart as the Absolute Spirit beyond creation. In that sense He may be said to be practicing "austerity," or nonattachment, like the perfected yogi who lives in the world but is untouched by the world. Having mentally renounced desires for the things of this world, the Brahmin has attained the power to enjoy creation and yet to remain apart from it, absorbed inwardly in the ever-existing, ever-conscious, ever-new joy of Spirit. (*Publisher's Note*)

As God is the Acme of All Virtue and resides as hidden perfection in all beings, He forgives, at the time a man is liberated, all the sins that man has committed for countless incarnations. So also, a Brahmin, who is a living receptacle of divine virtues, sees God in all and continuously pardons those who act inimically toward him.

Jesus advised man to forgive his enemies seventy times seven.* Even though that course often seems impractical, every man should bear in mind that four hundred and ninety times are very few when compared with God's unceasing forgiveness—daily, weekly, monthly, annually—not only of the sins of one lifetime, but of incarnations. Without God's forgiveness, no sinful prodigal child could return to his true home in the ever-loving Father.

In the highest sense, God has only one quality; existence, consciousness, and joy are mingled as one in Him. The liberated Brahmin manifests this one quality of God—ever-existing, ever-conscious, ever-new Joy—and is therefore free from the clutches of the triple qualities inherent in human characteristics and in Cosmic Nature. But he can descend to the physical state of existence and outwardly manifest principally the aforesaid divine sattvic qualities, or the activating rajasic qualities, or even at times (for some specific purpose) the sense-oriented tamasic qualities, without being in any way affected by them.

A true Brahmin may act as a pure or kind individual without being limited to these characteristics. He can also be active like a businessman or a great leader to help God's plan in the world, without being ensnared by desire for money or power. He might even display a gross tamasic quality such as anger, or overeating, yet remain karmically unaffected by it. Jesus used the whip of anger to drive the money changers from his Father's temple. On another occasion, upon finding no fruit on a fig tree in full leaf, Christ ordered it to be barren, and it was so. Jesus did not do this vengefully, to hurt the tree, but to show the almighty power of God over everything, and that those who are one with Him through the Christ Consciousness are able to utilize God's power even as he did.†

---

* "Then came Peter to him, and said, Lord, how oft shall my brother sin against me, and I forgive him? till seven times?

"Jesus saith unto him, I say not unto thee, Until seven times: but, Until seventy times seven" (Matthew 18:21,22).

† "Now in the morning as he returned into the city, he hungered.

"And when he saw a fig tree in the way, he came to it, and found nothing thereon, but leaves only, and said unto it, Let no fruit grow on thee henceforward for ever. And

The anger Jesus displayed in the temple and before the fig tree did not affect him; being God-united, no action of his was outside of the Divine Will, nor could he be touched by any consequences of his actions, nor caught in the meshes of the three qualities.

Wishing to humble the pride of a wealthy student who was always boasting that he could perfectly satisfy any guest at his table, an Indian saint, Bhutananda, by his miraculous powers once consumed enough food for a thousand people. Saint Bhutananda had told the disciple, "I will go to your home in response to your invitation, provided you can supply all the food I can eat." The student impudently prepared sufficient for a horde of guests. He felt very foolish when the saint ate it all and asked for more—a feat that the disciple could not in his wildest dreams have imagined one man could do.

The ordinary person who is still bound by the three *gunas* should not imitate certain fairly inexplicable actions of the liberated, who are above the good, activating, and obstructing qualities and can come down to this plane and operate them with ease and impunity.

Prahlada was a great boy-saint of India. His father, the wicked demon-king Hiranyakashipu, was enraged by the youth's religious propensities. When he found he was unable to curb Prahlada by severe admonitions, Hiranyakashipu took many steps to destroy his son. On one such occasion, the father ordered Prahlada to be killed by celestial elephants. Though he was thrown down and attacked fiercely, the huge animals were unable to render him any harm.

Difference between belief and realization

By way of illustrating the difference between being convinced of a truth and realizing a truth, consider the following postulatory sequel to the tale of Prahlada: After reading this story, two young orthodox Indian boys retired deep into a forest to fast and meditate, with the intention of attaining similar spiritual powers. After several days of sincere effort, they become convinced in their minds that their spirituality is now proof against all harm. Soon they have a chance to test it. They come upon a herd of wild elephants. Seizing the oppor-

presently the fig tree withered away.

"And when the disciples saw it, they marveled, saying, How soon is the fig tree withered away!

"Jesus answered and said unto them, Verily I say unto you, If ye have faith, and doubt not, ye shall not only do this which is done to the fig tree, but also if ye shall say unto this mountain, Be thou removed, and be thou cast into the sea; it shall be done" (Matthew 21:18–21).

tunity to display their newly acquired omnipotence, they confidently approach a large bull elephant—surely it would prove as harmless to them as its celestial ancestors had been to Prahlada! Instead, the poor beast, acting upon its own conviction, fears that his herd is endangered by the intruders, and so tramples the hapless boys.

Many a true tale, similar in principle, could be told of well-meaning persons who failed, often disastrously, to manifest "beliefs" that were still in the fanciful stage of their imaginings.

God will not respond to mere beliefs of fanatical people, but only to the divinely empowered demands of liberated devotees who consciously realize their oneness with Him and can thus presume upon His omnipotence as being at their command. Individuals yet bound by the three qualities of Cosmic Nature should not attempt to perform potentially dangerous miracles such as are sometimes displayed by saints who can freely wield the constraining laws of the sattvic, rajasic, and tamasic creative qualities.

VERSE 43

śauryaṁ tejo dhṛtir dākṣyaṁ yuddhe cāpy apalāyanam
dānam īśvarabhāvaś ca kṣātram karma svabhāvajam

Valor, radiance, resolute endurance, skillfulness, not fleeing from battle, munificence, and leadership are the natural duties of the Kshatriyas.

THE TRUE KSHATRIYA IS INFLUENCED by his past rajasic karma and the inherent activating quality of his nature in this life. Spiritually, he is a fighter of the senses, manifesting the characteristics of a noble soldier. A soldier worthy of the name has the qualities of valor, boldness in attacking enemies, resolute patience, unflagging courage in fighting, skill in the arts of warfare, and sovereign leadership in pursuing victory. He does not flee danger in battle because of fear, nor refuse to marshal his forces to fight again after one or many defeats.

Kshatriya: valor, boldness in attacking enemies, resolute patience, sovereign leadership in pursuing victory

Similarly, a worthy sense-fighter battles invading sensations and restless thoughts with unflinching valor and resolution, even after repeated failures, exercising continued patience in fighting their renewed attacks. Having sovereign control over his mental forces of discrimination, calmness, self-control, concentration, and power of mental interiorization, he keeps them continuously fighting restlessness and its psychological hordes. Whoever can thus skillfully lead his concentration away victorious from the battlefield of the senses and back to the kingdom of peace is indeed a true sense-fighter.

Alexander the Great, after conquering King Porus of India, asked, "How would you like to be treated?" When Porus replied, "Like a king," Alexander released him.* As a real soldier is charitable toward defeated enemies, so a psychological fighter of the senses does not torment his opponents after attaining victory over them.

When a yogi by rigid discipline and vigilance completely masters his senses, he relaxes. He does not mistreat them, out of fear of being tempted; nor does he render useless his powers of sight, hearing, smell, taste, and touch by holding the body in a state of suspended animation. Once he has subjugated his senses, he acts toward them in a friendly and normal manner. He knows in his heart they are no longer his enemies, encouraging him to identify himself with the gross physical body and the material world. His conquered senses become his friends, willingly serving him (not he them!) here on earth, and ready to go with him into the astral world of light and energy to experience finer visions, finer music, finer fragrances, finer tastes, and finer tactual sensations.

A soldier who must necessarily inflict suffering on his enemies in battle should be charitable toward them after he has attained victory, treating their wounds and looking after their other needs. This generosity of heart is what is meant by "munificence" in this stanza.

A spiritual sense-fighter feels the sovereign power of God within him, and is ever ready to give up his material desires in pursuit of Him. Once he determines to withdraw his mind from the world, sensations, and thoughts, and concentrates it in his spiritual eye at the point between the eyebrows, he is resolute in battling the restless thoughts that repeatedly return to try to distract him from his calm perception of peace. Such a true sense-fighter is never despondent while fighting his restlessness; he uses his concentration to disconnect the life force from the sensory invaders, rendering ineffectual their weapons of visual, auditory, olfactory, gustatory, and tactual sensations.

---

* Porus (fourth century B.C.) was a ruler in India of the territory between the Hydaspes and Acesines rivers at the time of Alexander's invasion. Their armies battled on the banks of the Hydaspes, and Porus put up such a fight that Alexander, impressed by his undiscourageable spirit, allowed him to retain his kingdom.

VERSE 44

kṛṣigaurakṣyavāṇijyaṁ vaiśyakarma svabhāvajam
paricaryātmakaṁ karma śūdrasyāpi svabhāvajam

Tilling the soil, cattle breeding, and business are the natural duties of the Vaishyas. Actions that are of service to others are the natural duty of the Sudras.

AS ORDINARY BUSINESSMEN MAY be engaged in commerce, agriculture, or cattle breeding, so the business of an esoteric Vaishya—"a working man; one who is settled in the soil"—is the cultivation of wisdom in the field of the body, which is his dwelling place. "This body is called *kshetra* (the 'field' where good and evil karma—actions—are sown and reaped)" (XIII:1). The natural Vaishya is in the stage of spiritually tilling the soil of his life (*krishi*); discriminatively tending his sense organs and selectively propagating their offspring (*gau-rakshya**); and engaging in the commerce (*vanijyam*) of properly dispensing the worthy virtues, or "commodities," brought forth by his efforts. The Vaishya garners wisdom through devotion to sages; and by his exemplary and serviceful life and words, he offers that knowledge to other seeking souls, whose love and appreciation is his remuneration. True Vaishyas are happy to learn how to cultivate the seeds of self-discipline after plowing the field of their consciousness with concentration, knowing they will then reap a harvest of divine perceptions.

Vaishyas, the wisdom-cultivators, and Sudras, the serviceful laborers

Spiritual Vaishyas like to train up the brutish senses of the body under the supervision of the cowherd of mental self-control. When the animalistic sense-cows are properly reared, they in time produce the milk of peace, rather than of restlessness.

And lastly, there are the duties of the natural Sudra. As common laborers busy themselves with working under the subjection of others, and with eating and sleeping and snatches of sense pleasures, so the materialistic, body-bound Sudra type is busy solely with earning money to support the body and cater to its needs and appetites, and all too often keeping it locked in sleep or drugged stupor like inert matter. Such a materialistic person, who never prepares his body-temple to be

---

* *Gau* or *go,* lit., "cattle" or "organ of sense"; *rakshya:* "to tend or protect"; *go-rakshya:* "tending or breeding cattle"—i.e., the proper nurture of the senses.

used to reflect wisdom and divine bliss, manifests predominantly the tamasic evil qualities mixed with a little bit of rajasic activity—the good or sattvic quality being entirely suppressed. However, the Bhagavad Gita advises all materialistic laborers and any other body-bound individuals to spend their time in the company of wisdom-cultivators, sense-fighters, and God-knowing Brahmins. Thus will they gradually learn, by service to those who possess superior qualities, to cultivate wisdom instead of sense pleasures, and not only to fight the sensory marauders, but to meditate. The serviceful labor of such persons, even though classed as the most menial, is ennobled by their noble spirit. In the end, they too will reap the harvest of wisdom and liberation.

VERSE 45

sve sve karmaṇy abhirataḥ saṁsiddhiṁ labhate naraḥ
svakarmanirataḥ siddhiṁ yathā vindati tac chṛṇu

Each one attentive to his own duty, man gains the highest success.
How, devoted to his inborn duty, he attains success—that hear.

EACH PERSON SHOULD FIRST DETERMINE through introspection which of the four states of spiritual development he has manifested predominantly from early childhood. A spiritually undeveloped individual should not try to jump to the highest state of liberation by the fanciful efforts of an ignorant mind. If he finds himself to be a body-bound Sudra, he should seek the guidance of a proper guru, and serve and keep company with those in the next higher state of spiritual realization, the Vaishyas or wisdom-cultivators, in order to lift himself to their state. After the Sudra attains the cultivator-of-wisdom state, he should mix with Kshatriyas or sense-fighters, and by deep meditation withdraw his mind from the senses. When he is able to do that, he should associate with his liberated guru and learn to commune with Brahman in the company of other liberated souls.*

By introspection, man should discover the duties proper to his state

* "To keep company with the guru is not only to be in his physical presence (as this is sometimes impossible), but mainly means to keep him in our hearts and to be one with him in principle and to attune ourselves with him."—*Swami Sri Yukteswar,* in *The Holy Science,* published by Self-Realization Fellowship.

If a devotee, after self-analysis, finds he is by nature a Vaishya, or wisdom-cultivator, he should try to mix with the sense-fighters in the next higher state, particularly those who have attained victory over their senses. After he has become a successful sense-fighter, he should strive to commune with Brahma and attain the highest goal of life.

If by introspection one finds himself to be a natural Kshatriya, a master of his senses, he should follow the example of Brahmins and try to unite senses, life, and mind with his soul, and then merge soul with Spirit.

A man who finds that he was born with the capacity for God-communion should seek a God-knowing guru and learn from him how to feel God in ecstasy, in meditation and also in activity. When such a Brahmin, who can never again fall prey to the lures of the senses, has burnt the seeds of his past evil actions in the fire of wisdom, he should devote himself to liberating others by his example and precepts.

Thus every individual, while performing excellently the highest type of duties natural to his present state, should try to reach the next higher state, until he realizes final liberation.

Verse 46

yataḥ pravṛttir bhūtānāṁ yena sarvam idaṁ tatam
svakarmaṇā tam abhyarcya siddhiṁ vindati mānavaḥ

A man attains perfection by worshiping, with his natural gifts, Him from whom all beings are evolved, and by whom all this world is permeated.

The one omniscient, omnipresent Absolute—the Primal Cause of the cosmos and its beings—has ordained the law of action: That every action is endowed with good, bad, and activating vibrations that produce their fitting results. Man, made in the image of God, is free to behave like a god, manifesting his divine nature, or to behave like a mortal, acting under the influence and consequent bondage of Nature's triple qualities.

By the divine decree of the cosmic law of karma, cause and effect, every human being is born with propensities that are good, evil, or activating, according to the nature of his response, in a previous incarnation, to the three cosmic qualities. Thus every individual comes into this world with a specific self-created temperament, and is predisposed to certain habits and moods, the inherited result of oft-repeated actions in a former life.

To reap the inevitable results of past karmic influences, a man is born into a family, environment, and circumstances that are compatible with his own karmic pattern. Just as a wicked person during earthly existence seeks low company, so after death (according to the law of cause and effect, the effect being related to the cause) he is reborn on earth into a sinful family.* Similarly, a good person is reborn in a good family. When an active businessman dies and is born again, he is attracted into a business-oriented family. The habitually sick are reborn in families disposed to illness, whereas the habitually robust are reborn to healthy parents. A poor man who has never tried in his present life to overcome his poverty, finds himself, after death, drawn into a new body in a poverty-stricken family. Generous men are reborn amidst wealth. Miserly rich persons find rebirth in poor homes, owing to their penury consciousness.

It is therefore one's karmic pattern that determines one's high or low status at birth. This Gita verse points out that one should recognize his karmic endowments (*sva-karmana*) and turn them into offerings of devotion in worship of God. This instruction affirms the way to liberation as consisting in working out the karmic effects of past actions by performing one's proper material duties, according to one's inborn nature, and by communion with God, according to the inherent nature of the soul.

Performance of duties proper to one's inborn nature, plus meditation, is the way to liberation

An innately Sudra-type person who finds himself in a materialistic family should not resent the duties thus enjoined upon him; he should perform them conscientiously in the thought of God. He should also learn the science and art of meditation. Succeeding in the attainment of God-perception, he spiritualizes his nature and therefore is no longer bound by his material status and duties, or by past karma, or even by the cosmic law of karma.

---

* This and other examples given here are generalities and do not represent an invariable rule. No man is governed solely by any one quality; his ego nature is a mixture of all three: *sattva* (enlightening), *rajas* (activating), and *tamas* (darkening, or ignorance-producing). A man's total karmic pattern, not one or two specifics alone, determines the family, environment, and situations he attracts. Thus there are such paradoxes as a genius born to a family of ordinary mentality, or a criminal born to good and loving parents. This is why the quality of a person can be neither determined nor circumscribed by any man-made birth-caste classification.

The same principle applies to a wisdom-cultivator (a Vaishya-type of individual) and to a sense-fighter (Kshatriya-type person). One who has thus spiritualized his nature is "twice-born," a true natural Brahmin, established in the Infinite. He can then choose his own environment, associates, and duties.

Many commentators interpret this stanza, and other verses pertinent to man's "inborn duties," to mean that a person should not depart from the traditional vocation of his father and his forefathers. But the true meaning is that all people should perform those duties which are proper to their innate nature, and not necessarily according to the family caste or vocation. The natural Sudra, or body-identified type, for example, should not attempt the natural Brahmin's vocation of guiding or liberating others spiritually—"the blind leading the blind." He should rather engage himself in performing those serviceful, material Sudra duties that accord with his nature, while regularly meditating upon God and striving to perfect himself spiritually.

No one can find a shortcut to God that bypasses the performance of his proper duties. If a materialistic person in hopes of liberation gives up all dutiful actions and retires to a mountaintop for solitary meditation, not taking into account the limitations of his inborn nature, he is less likely to find God than disillusionment. In trying to ignore the duties proper to his second nature, he will find his inborn temperament pursuing him, compelling him to think in its patterns. Even though he flees from civilization, his mind will dwell in the environment of his innate liking. But by right and dutiful action man can gradually release himself from slavery to his second nature, acquired through past karma and his self-willed response to the triple qualities.

Being essentially a free soul, man *can* find salvation—no matter what bad karma he may possess, and no matter in what family "caste" he may be born. By a deep resolution of spirit, by performing both material and divine duties, and by constant communion with God, any man can attain liberation.

George Eastman, founder of the Eastman Kodak Company, who studied yoga with me, remarked in one of our conversations that a progressive man should have two main interests: a job by which he maintains himself and his family, and a creative avocation that will have a stimulative and enjoyable effect on him. I agreed, but in addition elevated the principle to accord with the teachings of the Bhagavad Gita, which advises each individual to perform at least minimal duties to satisfy his own needs and responsibilities, and to devote much of his time to divine activities and God-communion to satisfy the desire and need of his soul. The progressive man is always constructively and spiritually engaged. Idlers, forsaking their natural duties, will never find satisfaction or divine release.

In the struggle for existence in this misery-ravaged world, man sometimes has to compromise according to the immediate necessity, but if possible he should follow a vocation that accords with his inner ability; and at the same time he should earnestly seek God. He should realize that his present incarnation and situation are a result of past karma, *prarabdha,* the effects of past actions performed in response to the triple qualities of Cosmic Delusion. And further, he should consider that his actions in this life are influenced by Cosmic Nature, by his own past karma, and by his innate power to act freely.

Countermanding inborn karmic limitations by free-will performance of dutiful actions

The power to act according to one's own free choice is *purushakara*. The working out of massive past karma so overburdens most people that they have little chance to express this power of free choice. Each individual should thus learn gradually to countermand the influences of *prarabdha,* effects of past action, by consciously striving to exercise *purushakara,* the soul's power to act freely. The law is: "The greater the influence on man of *prarabdha,* the less his power to act freely; or, the more the power of *purushakara,* the less the power of *prarabdha*." The effects of past actions, *prarabdha,* can be destroyed by performing free-will-initiated dutiful actions, without attachment or repulsion, to please God and not the body-bound ego.

Without the assistance of proper action, an individual cannot disregard the influence of past karma and by his free choice alone win freedom. For example, a man born with body consciousness due to past karma cannot suddenly stop maintaining the body, or prevent it from performing its functions, merely because he chooses to have uninterrupted God-communion. Even though he wants only to remain in a state of God-realization in *samadhi,* his body compels him to exhale and inhale and thus forces his mind to remain on the restless plane of the senses. The devotee must therefore exercise his free choice to learn and to practice persistently the yoga technique of transcending body consciousness, so that he can gradually succeed in disconnecting his mind from the senses, body, and breath; *then* he can attain the coveted *samadhi* state of continuous God-communion. Each day after meditation, he should return to the performance of his normal physical, mental, social, and spiritual duties. Thus, by methodical steps, and in a balanced way, each man of whatever nature can achieve his own salvation.

Verses 47–48

śreyān svadharmo viguṇaḥ paradharmāt svanuṣṭhitāt
svabhāvaniyataṁ karma kurvan nāpnoti kilbiṣam (47)

sahajaṁ karma kaunteya sadoṣam api na tyajet
sarvārambhā hi doṣeṇa dhūmenāgnir ivāvṛtāḥ (48)

(47) Better than the well-accomplished dharma (duty) of another is one's own dharma, even though lacking merit (somewhat imperfect). He who performs the duty decreed by his inborn nature contracts no sin.

(48) O Offspring of Kunti (Arjuna), one should not abandon one's inborn duty, even though it has some imperfection, for all undertakings are marred by blemishes, as flame by smoke.

Arjuna was, both by birth and by capacity, a soldier. On the field of battle he became despondent and believed he should not fight. But Lord Krishna pointed out to him that it was his duty to save his noble kinsmen from the invading enemy. "O Arjuna," Krishna said, "even though your duty to fight is tainted by acts of killing, still it is better to perform that duty than to assume the role of a nonviolent saint—and thereby let your good kinsmen be destroyed by evil."

God's law of karma, operating through Cosmic Nature, demands its just recompense. Whosoever imagines he can escape the results of his own actions—of which his present nature and circumstances are in large measure constituted—by trying to avoid his obvious duties, is behaving ignorantly, that is, sinfully. He thereby exercises and in fact increases whatever wrong tendencies he possesses. The Cosmic Law sees to it that those duties which come to man in the natural course of his life are those he is meant to perform, for his own welfare. Therefore he should not succumb to egoistic preference for something else, however expertly he thinks he may be able to do it; nor abandon his responsibilities be-

Man works against his own highest interests when he avoids his natural duties (svadharma)

cause of some unpleasantness connected with them, but rather carry out his natural duties cheerfully and willingly, to the best of his ability. Man ignorantly works against his own highest interests when he avoids the natural duties that the Cosmic Law requires him to perform for his ultimate salvation. By the execution of rightful duties, given to him by divine law for his own improvement and development, and by dedicating those actions as offerings of devotion to God, he not only ameliorates his karmic debt, but ultimately cancels it.

It must be reckoned with, however, that even if one tries to perform carefully and willingly the duties natural to one's type (whether Sudra, Vaishya, Kshatriya, or Brahmin), the influence of the three qualities on his present thoughts and actions will affect or "blemish" his efforts. Perfection is not of this world; just as smoke goes with the flame, so imperfections accompany man's actions so long as he remains subject to the threefold qualities of Cosmic Nature, whose laws rule creation. But by performing his duties as assiduously as possible—dedicating his work to God, meditating deeply to feel God's guiding presence—man finally realizes the innate perfection of his soul and its oneness with the taintless Spirit.

THERE IS ALSO A DEEPER MEANING in the spiritual interpretation of these stanzas relevant to the allegorical significance of the Gita explained in Chapter I: Riding the chariot of meditation guided by the charioteer of Cosmic Consciousness, Krishna, the devotee Arjuna suddenly became despondent. He asked the God-perception within him if it were not better for him to refrain from slaying, by the arrows of self-control, his inimical psychological kinsmen (the natural physical and mental instincts and desires for sense pleasures) in order to save, also, his righteous closer kinsmen (discrimination, calmness, divine vitality, restraint, adherence to virtue, and others).*

Arjuna reasoned that it is "unnatural" to kill the normal instincts of the physical body and supplant them by the supernormal instincts of the soul. But the Lord reveals, through Arjuna's intuition, that one's true duty is to remain in the blessed nature of the soul, which is beyond the inevitable karmic effects engendered by the triple qualities, rather than to be absorbed in painstakingly performing the intricate

* This rationalization of Arjuna against fighting his inimical sensory kinsmen—why shouldn't the sensory inclinations be preserved along with the soul qualities, since both are members of the same family of consciousness?—is well detailed in the commentaries in Chapter I:32–47.

duties enjoined by the senses and the physical ego. (See also III:35.)

No matter how difficult it is for man to do his highest inborn duty, which is to express divine soul qualities, he should not give in and abandon himself to egoistical bad habits and sense temptations. Nor should he relinquish his struggles in meditation, albeit seemingly fruitless. Even if his efforts bring only imperfect results in the beginning, he should not be discouraged. The influence of delusion and the triple qualities is extremely powerful, tainting even the most valiant efforts of the aspiring devotee until—victorious at last!—he is irrevocably established in his pure soul nature.

❖ *Each man's highest duty: to express soul qualities* ❖

Krishna thus counsels: "O Arjuna, by following the yogic actions of meditation and of continuously remaining in the perception of your own joyous Self while performing actions for God only, you will get away forever from the sorrows and sins that are inseparable from ego consciousness."

SUMMARY OF THE GITA'S MESSAGE: HOW GOD-REALIZATION IS ATTAINED

VERSE 49

asaktabuddhiḥ sarvatra jitātmā vigataspṛhaḥ
naiṣkarmyasiddhiṁ paramāṁ saṁnyāsenādhigacchati

That individual gains uttermost perfection—the actionless state of realization through renunciation—who keeps his intellect ever detached from worldly ties and passions,* who is victorious in regaining his soul, and who is without desires.

THAT DEVOTEE ATTAINS THE "uttermost perfection" of his individualized incarnate status when he realizes his true Self, the soul, as being of the essence of God's transcendent consciousness, untouched by bod-

* *Asaktabuddhi:* lit., "...who keeps his intellect ever detached." *Buddhi,* the discriminating faculty of the soul, when pure and undistorted by the influence of *manas,* the sense mind, is truth-revealing, drawing the consciousness to its native state in the true Self, the soul. See I:1, page 5.

ily experiences, even as the Lord is immutable beyond the activities He sends forth through Cosmic Nature. The way to liberation lies through this realization of the Self, by God-communion and by remaining in this God-aware state of the soul while performing dutiful actions. Any individual can reach this supreme actionless state by the renunciation of all fruits of actions: performing all dutiful acts without harboring in his heart any likes and dislikes, possessing no material desires, and feeling God, not the ego, as the Doer of all actions.

That yogi who is not attached to his own body or his family or the world, even though he joyously works for them with the sole desire of pleasing God; who is in full control of his mind (*manas*), intelligence (*buddhi*), ego (*ahamkara*), and heart (*chitta*); who is free from all desires for sense pleasures; and who works, yet renounces the fruits of actions, becomes free from the reincarnation-causing triple qualities of mortal and natural actions. The consciousness of such a yogi rests in the immutability of the eternal Spirit.

VERSE 50

siddhiṁ prāpto yathā brahma tathāpnoti nibodha me
samāsenaiva kaunteya niṣṭhā jñānasya yā parā

O Son of Kunti (Arjuna), hear from Me, in brief, how he who gains such perfection finds Brahman, the supreme culmination of wisdom.

A YOGI, HAVING REACHED THE ACTIONLESS state of transcendental soul-realization, thereby frees himself from the effects of the three qualities of Nature and of his own individual karma. He thence attains oneness with Brahman, which is the consummation of all knowledge—the full flowering of his realization of truth into oneness with Truth, the Omniscient Spirit. In this state he fully realizes his identity with the Supreme Lord—He who remains above all vibratory activities even though He manifests out of Himself all cosmic activities of creation. At one with God, the yogi learns to act in the world without attachment, even as does God.

Stanzas 51, 52, and 53, following, specify in brief the yoga practices necessary to reach the supreme state of oneness with Spirit.

Verses 51–53

buddhyā viśuddhayā yukto dhṛtyātmānaṁ niyamya ca
śabdādīn viṣayāṁs tyaktvā rāgadveṣau vyudasya ca (51)

viviktasevī laghvāśī yatavākkāyamānasaḥ
dhyānayogaparo nityaṁ vairāgyaṁ samupāśritaḥ (52)

ahaṁkāraṁ balaṁ darpaṁ kāmaṁ krodhaṁ parigraham
vimucya nirmamaḥ śānto brahmabhūyāya kalpate (53)

(51) Absorbed in a completely purified intellect, subjugating the body and the senses by resolute patience, forsaking (as much as possible) sound and all other sense entanglements, relinquishing attachment and repulsion;
(52) Remaining in a sequestered place, eating lightly, controlling body, speech, and mind; ever absorbed in divine meditation and in soul-uniting yoga; possessing dispassion;
(53) Peaceful, renouncing egotism, power, vanity, lust, anger, possessions, and the "me and mine" consciousness—he is qualified to become one with Brahman.

THAT DEVOTEE IS QUALIFIED TO ATTAIN Brahman, Spirit, whose discriminative intelligence (*buddhi*) is wholly free from the adulteration of sense entanglements, cognizant only of the purity of soul bliss; who with resolute patience (*dhriti*) keeps his perception centered on the Self, remaining established in soul consciousness without ever being identified with the physical ego and its bodily instrumentalities; who abandons all luxuries of the five senses (beginning with enticing conversation with others—the desire to hear and be heard); and who, free of likes and dislikes, is satisfied by only the bare necessities for sustaining life.

Such a yogi, possessing the divine dispassion (*vairagya*) of detachment from worldly objects and desires, observes the sattvic discipline of austerity of body, speech, and mind (see XVII:14–17, page 999). In the conduct of his holy life, he not only remains in an outwardly quiet place conducive to meditation and spiritual calm, but also, perceiving in yoga meditation the soul, mind, and life force in their innermost subtle spinal tunnel of escape from the body (*brahmanadi*), remains there, experiencing the real sense-tumult-free seclusion leading into the omnipresence of Spirit.

The soul, mind, and life force of the yogi in *samadhi* meditation have had to pass first through three outer tunnels (*sushumna, vajra, chitra*) to reach the innermost channel of *brahmanadi*—the final exit out of the bodily prison into the freedom of Brahman.*

That yogi not only eats lightly of material food—lest bodily distress from overeating or wrong eating distract his meditative mind—but he can also maintain himself entirely on the ethereal food of cosmic energy, the life-sustaining light of God. Sustenance by that light renders unnecessary a dependence on sunshine, oxygen, and liquid and solid foods believed to be conditional to physical existence. Thus in this stanza "light eating" (*laghvasin*)† has a dual meaning—a cryptic play on words, typical in the Hindu *shastras*—referring to sustenance not merely by simple ordinary food, but by cosmic energy, the light or ethereal "food" of life.

Jesus Christ, a paradigm of yoga, or God-union, also cited the same principle of light eating when he said, "Man shall not live by bread alone, but by every word that proceedeth out of the mouth of God."‡ That is, man's trillions of cellular batteries in the body do not live solely by the external sources of "bread"—solids, liquids, gases, sunshine—but by the inner source of cosmic life-current flowing into the body through the medulla, the "mouth of God," and thence "out of the mouth of God" into all parts and activities of the body. Such a yogi, living on the ethereal cosmic life force, having attained mastery over this life-sustaining energy, knows how in meditation to withdraw his life force from the speech center and from the other astral spinal centers governing all the bodily senses, and to resolve that freed life force into mind and heart, and then merge them with the blissful soul.

A yogi who can thus disconnect his mind at will from the attractions of both material and subtle sense objects remains no longer identified with the physical ego and its attachments to either physical or miraculous powers, or to the "superiority complex" of pride, or to latent sense desires, or to possessions. He is free from anger springing from

---

* *Brahmanadi, chitra, vajra,* and *sushumna* are subtle cerebrospinal passageways through which the life and consciousness of the soul descend from Spirit into the causal, then the astral, and finally the physical body. (See I:4–6, pages 61–62.) In deep *samadhi* meditation the soul ascends through these tunnels in reverse succession to escape from the three bodies and to reunite with Brahman, Spirit.

† From Sanskrit *laghu* (light, or little) and *asin* (eating); i.e., metaphorically, that food which is light or ethereal, the subtle life force or cosmic energy.

‡ Matthew 4:4.

thwarted longings and inclinations, free from desire for luxuries (what I often call the "unnecessary necessities" of life), and free from the consciousness of "me and mine." Such a yogi is ready to merge in Brahman.

Verse 54

brahmabhūtaḥ prasannātmā na śocati na kāṅkṣati
samaḥ sarveṣu bhūteṣu madbhaktiṁ labhate parām

By becoming engrossed in Brahman—calm-souled, neither lamenting nor craving; beholding equality in all beings—he gains supreme devotion toward Me.

When the yogi is unswervingly established in Brahman (though not yet completely liberated), his heart, undisturbed by delusion, is saturated with perpetual bliss. At one with the immanent-transcendent Spirit, he realizes all things as his own Self; yet like the Immutable Lord, he is untouched by them. Since his consciousness is above all destructive and constructive transformations in nature, he neither grieves at unpleasant changes nor longs for pleasant ones, and beholds God equally present in all beings.

Such an accomplished yogi is not only one with the Absolute, merging his identity in God; he can also separate himself, recapturing his individuality with no loss of God-perception, and in this state, with his heart full of supreme devotion, enjoy the bliss of Brahman. To paraphrase a well-known allegory, he is then comparable to an idol made of sugar that sought to measure the depth of the Ocean of Divine Nectar. On entering the Sea, it found itself melting. The idol retreated hurriedly to the shore, thinking: "Why lose my identity in order to determine the depth of divine sweetness? I already know that the Ocean is indeed very deep, and Its nectar exceedingly sweet." Thus the sugar idol chose to perceive the Ocean of Sweetness through the isolated consciousness of individuality. Similarly, a devotee may love to be one with the Infinite, yet love even more the enjoyment of God experienced by retaining his individual existence. The latter is the state of supreme devotion.

VERSE 55

bhaktyā mām abhijānāti yāvān yaś cāsmi tattvataḥ
tato māṁ tattvato jñātvā viśate tadanantaram

By that supreme devotion he realizes Me and My nature—what and who I am; after knowing these truths, he quickly makes his entry into Me.

AT FIRST THE YOGI, AS A SEPARATE being, by supreme devotion perceives God and realizes His true ever-existing, ever-conscious, ever-new Spirit-nature. After this experience of God through the perception of his distinctive individual consciousness, the yogi then becomes one with Him.

VERSE 56

sarvakarmāṇy api sadā kurvāṇo madvyapāśrayaḥ
matprasādād avāpnoti śāśvataṁ padam avyayam

Over and above performing faithfully all one's duties, taking shelter in Me, it is by My pleasure a devotee obtains the eternal, unchangeable state.

THE DEVOTEE BEHOLDS GOD AS THE SHELTER of all creatures, and himself as unsheltered by any other power. Without attachment to the fruits of his efforts, he continuously engages in God-united yoga activities and all other divinely obligatory duties, just to please God. After meeting all the requirements of the laws of liberation, the yogi ultimately finds, by the freely given grace of God—"by My pleasure"—the eternal state of liberation.

The quality of a yogi's meditation and other actions, the guru's help, and God's grace—these are the three requisites of liberation. No matter how much a devotee strives for salvation—and he is required to make the effort wholeheartedly for God—that effort constitutes only 25% of the requirements for liberation. Another 25% depends upon his guru's blessing, spiritually stimulating the disciple's striving. But the guru's help and the devotee's effort notwithstanding, it is necessary to have also God's grace, which may be said to constitute the remaining 50% of the requirements.

God, the Creator of the cosmic law of karma that binds human life, is the sole Judge as to whether a devotee has fulfilled all the laws of spiritual conduct required for liberation. However, a devotee who, with the help of his guru, fulfills all the laws and then insolently expects immediate liberation will not find it. God is not a mathematically produced jackpot! But if the devotee fulfills the divine laws and also has complete love for God—"taking shelter in Me"—that all-surrendering love draws His grace.

Man is made in the image of God's love, and by manifesting unconditional love he can again become like the Father, merging in Him and dropping his acquired second nature as a mortal being.

Verse 57

cetasā sarvakarmāṇi mayi saṁnyasya matparaḥ
buddhiyogam upāśritya maccittaḥ satataṁ bhava

Mentally dedicating all actions to Me, considering Me as the Supreme Goal, employing buddhi-yoga (union through discriminative wisdom), continuously absorb thy heart in Me.

Lord Krishna thus exhorts his disciple, Arjuna: "O devotee, disconnecting your intelligence from the physical ego and its consciousness of being the doer of sense-originated actions, unite your pure discrimination with God, feeling Him as the Doer of all your actions. By uniting your intelligence with the Supreme Being, keep your heart saturated with Him."

When, in the performance of actions, the devotee's heart (*chitta,* feeling) is identified with the body-bound ego, giving rise to various desires according to the likes and dislikes of the ego, it becomes bound in material objects, sense experiences, and material activities. But when, in the performance of actions, the devotee's heart is identified with God, it ceases to be entangled with any activities, or likes and dislikes, owing to the disappearance of the ego. Every devotee should perform dutiful and meditative actions, thinking of God; and, by discrimination, should remove all sovereignty of the ego, the pretender to rulership of the bodily throne. Such a yogi, his discrimination absorbed in God, all actions performed only for Him, finds his heart filled with the bliss of Spirit. There is no room for the lesser pleasures of the senses.

On the inner spiritual plane of meditative activity, the determined yogi, with his concentration and devotion fully absorbed in God, unites his consciousness with the soul's ascending liberating powers of discriminative wisdom (*buddhi*) in the subtle cerebrospinal centers of divine perception. The ego, with its downflowing, matter-prone forces of the sense mind (*manas*) is thus transcended. (See I:1, pages 5, 15.) Achieving this *buddhi*-yoga in meditation, the yogi restores the soul's reign over the whole bodily kingdom.

Verse 58

maccittaḥ sarvadurgāṇi matprasādāt tariṣyasi
atha cet tvam ahaṁkārān na śroṣyasi vinaṅkṣyasi

With heart absorbed in Me, and by My grace, thou shalt overcome all impediments; but if through egotism thou wilt not heed Me, thou shalt meet destruction.

The yogi who has his heart fixed on God finds that, through His grace, all previous material taints of his heart—the sense-bent likes and dislikes—have been eliminated. After explaining this, the Lord cautions His devotee about the treacherous ego:

"O Arjuna, if instead of listening to My advice about liberation, you continue to exalt the physical ego, which considers itself as the doer of all human deeds, you will be entangled in rebirth-making actions and destroy your chances of salvation."

Lord Krishna did not mean that, by a single error made under the influence of the ego, Arjuna would ruin forever his chances of liberation; rather, that because of getting mixed up with the misery-making ego, he would temporarily lose the opportunity for salvation. No matter how deep and long-continued a sin may be, it cannot forever obliterate the soul's consciousness of its divine heritage.

The meaning here is that when ego consciousness even temporarily substitutes itself for God-consciousness, whether in dutiful or meditative actions, the desire for salvation is lost—and along with it, the requisite effort—whether for a short or long time, owing to the complications created by delusive egotistical desires.

VERSE 59

yad ahaṁkāram āśritya na yotsya iti manyase
mithyaiṣa vyavasāyas te prakṛtis tvāṁ niyokṣyati

If, clinging to the ego, thou sayest: "I will not battle," fruitless is thy resolution! Prakriti, thine inborn nature, will force thee to fight.

THE LORD TELLS HIS DEVOTEE: "If you identify yourself with the ego, O Arjuna, you will imbibe its temporary unreasonable dislike for righteous war, and thus decide not to go to battle. But such an ill-considered resolution would not last long; compelled by your inner instinct as a soldier, you would have to fight."

While the foregoing explanation would apply to the outer personal life of Arjuna, the deeper meaning refers to a devotee's inner spiritual struggle. The Lord thus reveals this wisdom:

"Through the help of God, O Arjuna, your innate nature (*samskaras*) from past incarnations has made you a veteran fighter of the senses from your very birth. But your temporary identification with the physical ego makes you feel that to heed its behest to refrain from destroying your inimical 'kinsmen'—material sense inclinations—is just. This is a fleeting, erroneous conclusion. As a born sense-fighter, your own nature will compel you to act otherwise. So it is better for you to undertake now your righteous duty, for your *samskaras* have given you this present excellent opportunity to establish the blessed kingdom of the soul. Thus with its soldiers of discrimination, calmness, self-control, peace, concentration, love of goodness, and other divine qualities, and by the power of yoga and dispassion, you may defeat the physical ego and its undesirable horde of misery-making sensory passions."

VERSE 60

svabhāvajena kaunteya nibaddhaḥ svena karmaṇā
kartuṁ necchasi yan mohāt kariṣyasy avaśo 'pi tat

O Offspring of Kunti (Arjuna), shackled by thine own karma, inborn in thy nature, what through delusion thou wouldst not do, thou wilt helplessly be compelled to do.

THE LORD STRESSES FURTHER TO ARJUNA (to the meditating devotee's intuitive perception) the compelling influence of the inner nature:

"O Arjuna, although you are entrapped by indiscrimination, and do not wish to subjugate your 'kinsmen,' the inimical body-bound sense inclinations, you will not be able to disregard the inborn nature that commands you to fight and conquer them. In your past life you were a sense-fighter, Arjuna. That is why, in this life, you were born with the will to battle the sensory passions until the soul's kingdom of bliss is fully established. Even if you try to remain neutral, you will find yourself automatically and instinctively resisting these body-attached forces. It is better for you to follow the righteous dictates of your inner nature and consciously and willingly conquer these sensory hordes that you may be liberated from their entanglement forever. If you hesitate or contend unwillingly with the senses, you may not be able to subjugate them. Your sympathy toward sense inclinations, displayed in your lack of desire to fight them, may develop in you instead a greater desire to gratify their demands. So long as you equate happiness with the ego-identified senses you deny yourself the supreme satisfaction of true soul bliss."

By his inmost nature man is compelled to seek soul joy

The joy in man's immortal, all-blissful soul is not dependent on sense experiences. In its natural state, the soul remains ever conscious of its native ecstatic joy. But when the soul, identified with the physical body and senses, becomes the pseudosoul, or ego, the closest it comes to remembering soul joy is during the pseudoblissful state experienced in the peaceful phenomenon of sleep. That is why, whenever the body-bound ego tires of playing with and catering to its restless senses, it is unconsciously attracted by the hidden bliss of the soul to seek the subconscious state of sleep. In the lesser joy of the sleep state, the ego is involuntarily reminded of its original nature as the blissful soul. Being too restless to remember this soul bliss during the day, the ego is nightly dragged within the chamber of subconsciousness to feel the soul joy faintly manifesting in the negative state of slumber. In this sense, the sleep state is the compelling inner nature of the ego, urging it to seek its happiness beyond sensory experience.

Soul bliss is unimaginably more joyous than even the most welcome sleep after a long period of forced wakefulness. Through yoga practice, the ego can cross the state of subconscious slumber and enter the dreamless superconsciousness of its original blissful soul nature.

However, the ego ordinarily fails to regain the superconscious state because of the strong attraction of the frolicsome senses. Nevertheless, in the subconscious state of deep sleep, the ego does receive at least a glimpse of its hidden native joy.

An analysis of sleep, as a state giving joy without the media of the senses, provides a valuable lesson for the ego—a demonstration that superior bliss can be found if the ego can consciously enjoy the state of sleep and go beyond it to conscious ecstasy. Through continuous practice of yoga, the subconscious sleep state of the ego can be gradually supplanted by the superconscious ecstasy of the soul.

It is fortunate indeed when the compelling force of one's acquired inner nature urges him toward his true soul nature, as in this particular instance wherein Arjuna's past good karma is spurring him to greater soul victories. But in the less advanced devotee, some inherent inclinations may present themselves as strong deterrents to spiritual progress. A good illustration of this is cited in the following story related by Swami Pranabananda, "the saint with two bodies,"* in his commentary on the Gita:

"A spiritual novitiate, experiencing a glimpse of superconscious joy in deep meditation, decided to banish sleep completely and practice yoga all night. He meditated enthusiastically for a few hours; then a little lull occurred in his concentration, and his 'second nature,' sleep—with its habit of settling for subconscious joy—began to assert itself. 'I have been meditating for three hours,' he thought, 'and have earned the right to doze for a moment. I will lie down for just one minute, and then I shall sit up and pass six hours more in meditation, until sunrise.' Thinking his will to be strong, the man lay down to take his minute's rest; but his second nature compelled him to sleep on. When he awakened, it was already dawn. Then he realized the ineffectiveness of trying to ignore so drastically the demands of sleep, the compulsion of his second nature. Like a true yogi, he learned gradually to replace the state of sleep with the joyous conscious perception of the soul."

Lahiri Mahasaya—the guru of Swami Pranabananda and of my guru, Swami Sri Yukteswar—followed the proper rules of yogic meditation and of self-discipline applied with common sense; and during the latter part of his life, he was able thereby to dispense completely with sleep, remaining ensconced in the wakefulness of divine communion.

---

* See *Autobiography of a Yogi,* Chapter 3.

The inexperienced aspirant who tries to forgo sleep in order to meditate all night, disregarding his innate second nature that is habituated to sleep, will sooner or later, helplessly and unwillingly, be compelled to sleep. If he insists on pursuing such sleepless endeavor, he will find himself "falling between two stools," neither meditating nor sleeping. By improper meditation, marred by half-sleepiness, the yogi merely seesaws between vague inklings of superconsciousness and lapses into subconsciousness, receiving benefits of neither. His procedure will result in loss of health owing to unsatisfactory sleep, as well as in failure to perceive the pure joyous state of the soul. Instead of a drastic disregard of his second nature, he should learn to meditate long and deeply after at least some concession to his body's need for sleep, until he gains the ability to enter at will superconscious *samadhi.* Physical sleep then becomes optional, no longer essential to his very existence. Sleep transcendence comfortably replaces sleepiness as a part of his impelling second nature.

The art of taming one's natural tendencies lies in gradual psychophysical steps

In advising the devotee to give due consideration to his human nature, the Bhagavad Gita does not imply permanent submission, but commonsense action with the purpose of ultimately conquering that nature. The art of taming one's natural tendencies is not in the application of futile brute force but in gradual psychophysical steps.

When a fisherman tries to land a big fish too forcibly, his line usually breaks. But if he alternately plays out the line and then gradually reels it in, he can land the fish by wearing it out. Similarly, the yogi should yield discriminatively to the normal demands of his inner nature when it pulls him forcibly, and then, like a master spiritual fisherman, gradually bring it under his control.

The inner nature cannot be subjugated if this yielding is performed with attachment and desire to please the ego. So the Bhagavad Gita advises the devotee to perform natural actions neither unwillingly nor with attachment, but willingly without attachment, with the firm objective of liberating himself from all egoistic activities.

VERSE 61

īśvaraḥ sarvabhūtānāṁ hṛddeśe 'rjuna tiṣṭhati
bhrāmayan sarvabhūtāni yantrārūḍhāni māyayā

O Arjuna, the Lord is lodged in the hearts of all creatures, and by His cosmic delusion (maya) compels all beings to rotate as if attached to a machine.

God's Life and Intelligence are omnipresent in all creation and determine, through Nature's law, the orderly progression of events in the cosmic drama. That same Power, innate in all human beings, subjects each person to the influence of the law, and also enables him to transcend it.

Compelled by the law of *maya,* creation continuously moves up and down the path of linear evolution: ascending from the Material Age through the Atomic Age, Mental Age, and Spiritual Age during the space of 12,000 years; and descending from the Spiritual to the Material Age during the following 12,000–year period.*

Bound to creation by *maya*, all beings are inexorably constrained by their individual karmic patterns to reincarnate again and again during these upward and downward cycles, as their spiritual evolution progresses under the influence of cosmic nature.† Man may accelerate or delay his evolution by his right or wrong actions (karma). Until right actions prevail, he mechanically moves along with the cycles, as if fixed on a rotating wheel of a machine. But as he gradually develops spiritually, he awakens to his true nature and seeks escape. Only those who discover God within themselves, and who demand freedom—for having been created against their will—does God liberate, after they have worked out the karma caused by misuse of their divine free choice.

Human beings under *maya* are thus fated to be subject to the compulsions of Nature and influenced by the prevailing dualities of good and evil during their experience of numerous lives and deaths, so long as they mechanically move up and down with creation on the cosmic machine of evolution. But as soon as they turn to God, using rightly the divine gift of free will—their key to escape from *maya*—and demand liberation, they are freed from birth and death. They suffer no longer from bondage to creation's evolutionary cycles.

---

* See page 425.

† According to the scriptures, man requires a million years of normal, diseaseless natural evolution to perfect his human brain and attain cosmic consciousness. (See page 362.)

VERSE 62

tam eva śaraṇaṁ gaccha sarvabhāvena bhārata
tatprasādāt parāṁ śāntiṁ sthānaṁ prāpsyasi śāśvatam

O Descendant of Bharata (Arjuna), take shelter in Him with all the eagerness of thy heart. By His grace thou shalt obtain the utmost peace and the Eternal Shelter.

THE SIGNIFICANCE OF BHAGAVAN KRISHNA'S advice to Arjuna is that man can receive the liberating grace of God by properly using his free choice to put God first in his life.

"O devotee, knowing that every action is instigated by delusive cosmic Nature, get out of her clutches by performing all actions only to please God. He alone can free you from His own decrees, from the decrees of cosmic Nature, and from the snare of the self-actuated law of human actions. By concentrating on God in deepest communion, surrendering eagerly and unreservedly your whole being to Him, you will by His grace become established in supreme peace and find eternal freedom in Him."

VERSE 63

iti te jñānam ākhyātaṁ guhyād guhyataraṁ mayā
vimṛśyaitad aśeṣeṇa yathecchasi tathā kuru

Thus hath wisdom, most secret of all secrets, been given to thee by Me. After exhaustively reflecting about it, act as thou desirest.

KRISHNA, LORD OF YOGA (the God-united guru of Arjuna—symbolically, the voice of Spirit, speaking as vibrations of Truth in the devotee's soul), has revealed in his divine discourse the wondrous truths of the universal science of yoga:

"O Arjuna, I have narrated to you the most secret wisdom, bestowing on your receptive consciousness the full perception of truth concerning the attainment of liberation. Only by intuitive realization can one wholly grasp such wisdom as to how human actions are subtly influenced by divine decree, by cosmic nature, and by human karma. Hold on continuously to this perception, for if instead you keep your heart identified with the distorting likes and dislikes of the physical ego, you will not understand the mystery of human life and actions. By first perceiving God, you will know how the cosmic delusion, and all creatures and their complex activities, evolved from Him. From this divine insight you will understand that so long as you remain identified with nature, or creation, and with ego-guided human actions and desires, you will be bound. But when you withdraw your consciousness, which by nature's influence flows toward external objects, and make it flow back toward God, you will find liberation.

"Arjuna, now you know that this secret wisdom about the law of action—the law governing man and the universe and their destinies—can only be experienced by intuitional development. Otherwise it will always remain hidden from you. It is up to you whether, by the free choice of your mind, you will start experiencing the truths related by me and thus liberate yourself, or whether you will act contrarily and remain in bondage."

How to realize the truths in the scriptures

GOD AND HIS WISDOM, no matter how well expressed in the scriptures by experienced masters, are ever hidden from the sense-identified intellect of material beings. Materialists cannot receive in their small cups of understanding the vast ocean of Truth.

An ordinary person reading or hearing scriptural truths interprets his visual or auditory sensations and impressions of them according to the limitations of his senses and understanding. A man of spiritual acuity studies the scriptures and then tries to perceive their meaning with his developed intuition. It is better still when a man with the potential of realization first reads or hears truth as interpreted through the fully awake realization of a great master or guru; and then meditates on that revelation until he, likewise, perceives that wisdom as his own.

Diverse commentaries on great scriptures such as the Bhagavad Gita and the Bible should not be collected and read indiscriminately; nor should scripture be ingested voraciously by one possessing an undeveloped state of mind. After deep meditation, only a small portion of a scripture should be read at a time, then internally dwelt on to feel the truth therein through the soul's intuition. No one should try to interpret spiritual truths equipped only with reason, emotion, and imagination. To perceive the truth behind the language of scripture, as intended by the prophets, the requisite faculty is intuitive calmness gained from deep meditation.

Thus, in this stanza, the truths revealed by God to Arjuna are declared as "most secret." Truth fully unveils its mysteries only in the advanced devotee's own Self-realization, when the perception is not through the intellect, but through the direct experience of the soul.

The Lord therefore exhorts the devotee to meditate on truth and to take up dutifully those actions that bring intuitive enlightenment and that are in accord with the divine wisdom secreted in the God-united soul: "So, Arjuna, perform with the consciousness of your soul-oneness with God all dutiful actions instigated by past karma and cosmic nature, and you will disentangle yourself from creation's delusions. Remember that you are an independent agent, free to act according to this most profound advice for liberation, or to remain bound by submission to the influence of the ego and the sense consciousness of the body. O Arjuna, misuse not your power of free choice! Determine to increase the power of intuition, by which alone you can perceive this deep wisdom. Use your free will to meditate again and again upon the soul, that you may realize, through your awakened intuition, all the secret truths I have revealed to you."

VERSE 64

sarvaguhyatamaṁ bhūyaḥ śṛṇu me paramaṁ vacaḥ
iṣṭo 'si me dṛḍham iti tato vakṣyāmi te hitam

Again listen to My supreme word, the most secret of all. Because thou art dearly loved by Me, I will relate what is beneficial to thee.

HAVING ENDOWED EACH SOUL with free will, God will never force anyone to choose Him over lesser desires. But His love is eternal, pursuing His errant children always—from incarnation to incarnation, age after age. Like the mother cow who runs after her straying calf, He follows His offspring with watchful solicitude, ever calling and coaxing them to return to Him.

God's love toward His children is unconditional because He feels responsible for having sent them out from Him into the delusion and misery of this world. If they see through false worldly lures and look to Him—above all, if they love Him, the Giver, in preference to His material gifts—they return to Him by the power of their virtue. Even in the darkest hours of human decline, when transgressors have become extremely entangled in delusion by repeated performance of wrong actions, God comes through liberated masters or other great incarnations to enlighten and redeem those who repent. Such is the love of God for all His children, even the sinful and those who love Him not. Never does He punish even the continuously erring ones with eternal damnation; somehow, in some way, the unseen God—the Maker, and therefore the Wielder, of the law of cause and effect—helps all men to come back to Him.

On the field of eternity, the Lord thought to play the game of hide-and-seek with His children for a little while; He hid Himself behind veils of cosmic delusion. Unseeing man stumbles through the darkness of *maya*, seeking that elusive unknown Something—falling into ditches of ignorance and pits of misery. Yet the game goes on because man loves the excitement and the chance rewards grasped amid the hazards.*

But even though God has divorced human beings from conscious perception of Him, still He is romancing them; and through hardships and tests is trying to persuade them to forsake their fascination with the ephemeral shadows of matter and return to His Blessedness.

After the vicissitudes of many incarnations in the lonesome wilderness of delusive creation—after lifetimes of the romance of hiding and almost meeting, of parting and eagerly being sought—man cries from the depths of his heart, "Enough!" When worldly enticements are at last deemed not worth their toll of suffering and precarious wandering in *maya*, and the player cries out from his core for deliverance, then the hidden God by His unseen touch melts the band of unknowing from man's eyes of wisdom. That soul no longer has to blunder through the stygian darkness. Once the enlightened seeker has completely forsaken his errors, God liberates that soul forever.

Then in joy and more joy the Lord appears openly to His devotee. He makes known that man's sojourn in *maya* was meant only for

---

* "A man is walking in a dark, dangerous forest, filled with wild beasts. The forest is surrounded by a vast net. The man is afraid, he runs to escape from the beasts, he falls into a pitch-black hole. By a miracle, he is caught in some twisted roots. He feels the hot breath of an enormous snake, its jaws wide open, lying at the bottom of the pit. He is about to fall into these jaws. On the edge of the hole, a huge elephant is about to crush him. Black and white mice gnaw the roots from which the man is hanging. Dangerous bees fly over the hole, letting fall drops of honey. Then the man holds out his finger—slowly, cautiously—he holds out his finger to catch the drops of honey. Threatened by so many dangers, with hardly a breath between him and so many deaths, he still has not reached indifference."—from *The Mahabharata: A Play Based Upon the Indian Classic Epic,* by Jean-Claude Carrière; translated by Peter Brook (New York: Harper and Row, 1987). (*Publisher's Note*)

entertainment; and that if everyone found Him easily, then His cosmic *lila* of hide-and-seek would be over in a trice. He explains that His hiding was not meant to cause suffering, but to heighten the enjoyment of man's ultimate, inevitable discovery of the Eternal Love.

In telling Arjuna how much He loves him, the Lord acknowledges that, though His love shines equally on all, the devotee who empties himself of the ego's delusions opens his being to receive in full measure the Divine Beneficence.

VERSE 65

manmanā bhava madbhakto madyājī māṁ namaskuru
mām evaiṣyasi satyaṁ te pratijāne priyo 'si me

Absorb thy mind in Me; become My devotee; resign all things to Me; bow down to Me. Thou art dear to Me, so in truth do I promise thee: Thou shalt attain Me!

A CRITICAL MIND MIGHT WONDER why God, promising the gift of Himself, is asking the already devoted Arjuna to become absorbed in Him, devoted to Him, and to perform ceremonial sacrifices to know Him,* and to bow down to Him.

Further, since this counsel was prefaced in the preceding verse with: "Again listen to My supreme word, the most secret of all," the obvious question is, what is so profoundly secret? "Secret" means hidden, an experience of realization transcending the activities and ordinary observations of the mind and senses. Thus, this verse must be read as more than a simple formula for the single-minded *bhakta*. It is stating "again" the ultimate realization requisite to liberation.

The deeper metaphysical meaning of this stanza is entwined with the spiritual interpretation of stanza 62, wherein Lord Krishna asks Arjuna to remember God, saying: "*Tam eva saranam gaccha,*" "Take shelter in Him."

In stanza 62, Arjuna was urged to concentrate on God as Cosmic Spirit; now he is exhorted to concentrate on God as "Myself."

---

* *Madyaji:* lit., "sacrifice to Me," rendered in the verse translation as "resign all things to Me." I.e., perform the inner "fire rite" of deep meditation, in which all dross of egoistic delusion is sacrificed, consigned to and consumed in the wisdom-fire of Self-realization.

To know God as that Spirit which is the origin and end of all beings is indeed the ultimate knowledge. But knowledge of God as the All-in-All is possible only when the devotee realizes first the great "Myself"—that Spirit present within himself, as well as omnipresent in the universe. Ordinarily, when the devotee speaks of "myself," he has in mind his ego; but when by meditation he succeeds in uniting his ego consciousness with the intuitive consciousness of his soul, he knows what is the true "Myself." This is why the Lord as Krishna is now urging Arjuna to lift his mind from the plane of the senses and be absorbed in the inner "Myself" or God, whose reflected presence in the devotee is his true Self.

The ultimate realization: Spirit within oneself and pervading the universe

A reflection of the moon appears distorted in a wind-ruffled lake; similarly, the reflected soul-image in the body is not clearly seen in a restless, sense-identified mind. Accordingly, God advises Arjuna to still the waters of his mind, so that, instead of seeing there the distorted ego-image of the Self, he would behold the clearly reflected true Self. Once able to gaze upon the tranquil soul, undisturbed by the ego's restlessness, Arjuna would then gradually come to understand that the soul, the little "Myself," is naught else than a pure reflection of Spirit, the great "Myself" spread over the skies of omnipresence.

This same truth was voiced by Jesus when he said: "No man cometh unto the Father, but by me.... Believe me that I am in the Father, and the Father in me."* He was referring, as was Krishna in the Gita, to the immanence of God—his oneness with the Divine Presence within him as the fully awakened soul, and with the omnipresent Christ Consciousness (*Kutastha Chaitanya*), the soul of the universe. None can attain the Absolute save through the realization of the little "Myself" and its identification with the omnipresent "Myself."

Unconditionally and essentially man needs God; God does not need man. God is free, perfect, almighty, and omnipresent; He consciously knows He is the Creator and Owner of all universes. So when God asks His devotee to worship Him and bow down to Him, it is not as an egotistical master, demanding His servant to be absorbed in and devoted to Him, sacrificing all his personal pleasures and continuously making obeisance to Him. Nor is God a pampered tyrant, requiring our flattery and praise to loosen His gifts on us. He is sitting in the hearts of all, knowing the motive of each human prayer. No matter if some-

---

* John 14:6,11.

one blames Him all day long, God does not come down from His high state to punish that person. But through the karmic law of cause and effect, whosoever holds blasphemous thoughts against God punishes himself by his own evil misunderstandings, and is attracted to the commission of similar errors against his fellow beings.

In the Bible, the exhortations by Jehovah to "Praise the Lord"* are similar in meaning to this stanza of the Gita. God is not moved by praise, which does not gratify Him. However, praising God creates a positive spiritual vibration, which helps the devotee who sincerely eulogizes Him. God, who is Love, made us in His image of Love. When we cultivate love within ourselves, we remember the erstwhile forgotten Divine Love in our true Self.†

Yogic understanding of the meaning of devotion

Manmana bhava, "absorb thy mind in Me," signifies absorption in the true "Myself" in ecstasy. *Madbhakta bhava,* "become My devotee," signifies perception and remembrance of the blessed "Myself" during that state of human activity in which the devotee's actions are not performed under the influence of the physical ego. *Madyaji bhava,* "resign all things to Me," signifies dissolving mind and life force and desires in the fire of true perception of the inner "Myself." *Mam namaskuru,* "bow down to Me," has a very deep meaning. The act of bowing consists in placing the hands, palms pressed together, over the heart, then touching the fingertips to the forehead to express devotion to a person or to God. Hands symbolize activity, the heart symbolizes love, and the head symbolizes wisdom. So a person bowing to man or God symbolizes by this act of obeisance: "My activity, my love, and my mind are at Your service."

In this stanza the Lord asks Arjuna to dissolve his heart's love, his impulse to physical activity, and his discriminating thoughts in the inner "Myself" by repeatedly concentrating his attention therein, even though the mind wants to run away and to be engrossed in physical or emotional activities on the plane of the senses.

---

* E.g., "I am the Lord: that is My name....Sing unto the Lord a new song, and His praise from the end of the earth....This people have I formed for Myself; they shall shew forth My praise" (Isaiah 42:8,10; 43:21).

† "God that made the world and all things therein, seeing that He is Lord of heaven and earth, dwelleth not in temples made with hands; neither is worshiped with men's hands, as though He needed any thing, seeing He giveth to all life, and breath, and all things....that they should seek the Lord, if haply they might feel after Him, and find Him, though He be not far from every one of us: for in Him we live, and move, and have our being" (Acts 17:24–28).

The Lord further intimates to Arjuna: "You have endeared yourself to Me. I truly promise you that if you become absorbed in your inner 'Myself,' you will know it is none other than the great Myself pervading everywhere."

The Sanskrit word, *So'ham,* signifies "He I am." In the initial state, the physical ego of the devotee is not yet destroyed. But when by yoga practice the aspirant becomes advanced enough to perceive in ecstasy the little Myself within himself, he can come out of that state and say, "*So'ham:* I have found the vast Cosmic Spirit reflected within me as the Soul, the little Myself, one and the same with the great Myself."

Verse 66

sarvadharmān parityajya mām ekaṁ śaraṇaṁ vraja
ahaṁ tvā sarvapāpebhyo mokṣayiṣyāmi mā śucaḥ

Forsaking all other dharmas (duties), remember Me alone;* I will free thee from all sins (accruing from nonperformance of those lesser duties). Do not grieve!

A PROSAIC INTERPRETATION OF THIS COUNSEL unequivocally advises the deeply devoted Arjuna, and all true renunciants, to relinquish worldly duties entirely in order to be single-pointedly with God. "O Arjuna, forsake all lesser duties to fulfill the highest duty: find your lost home, your eternal shelter, in Me! Remember, no duty can be performed by you without powers borrowed from Me, for I am the Maker and Sustainer of your life. More important than your engagement with other duties is your engagement with Me; because at any time I can recall you from this earth, canceling all your duties and actions.

"Under the direction of the body-bound ego, the performance of nature-instigated good or bad, important or unimportant duties will keep you entangled in insatiable desires and the miseries of repeated reincarnations. But if you restore your lost memory of My presence in your soul, and remain continuously conscious of Me, I will—by the virtue of that

---

* *Mām ekaṁ śaraṇaṁ vraja:* lit., "Become (*vraja*) sheltered (*śaraṇaṁ,* 'protected'—from delusion) in oneness (*ekaṁ*) with Me (*mām*)." "Always keep your consciousness in My sheltering Presence"; i.e., "Remember Me alone."

Indicating the practice of yoga, the Sanskrit may also be rendered: "*Withdraw* (*vraja*) into the Shelter of oneness with Me." See elaboration, pages 1092–93.

inner oneness with Me—liberate you completely from the sin of nonperformance of lesser duties. Grieve not over any supposed loss of physical or material gratification. It was I who decreed your birth as a mortal being. By your wrong responses to My cosmic delusion, you have imprisoned your soul image in that mortal existence. Your fulfillment lies not in earthly entanglements, but in Me. Find your Self in Me, which can be done only by removing all obstructions in your path."

A parallel passage in the Bible cites the Lord Jesus giving the same advice to the wholly dedicated devotee of God: "There is no man that hath left house, or brethren, or sisters, or father, or mother, or wife, or children, or lands, for my sake, and the gospel's, but he shall receive an hundredfold now in this time, houses, and brethren, and sisters, and mothers, and children, and lands, with persecutions; and in the world to come eternal life."*

He also said, "If thy hand offend thee, cut it off: it is better for thee to enter into life maimed, than having two hands to go into hell."†

Only to those devotees whose sole purpose is to find God did Jesus suggest abandonment of all lesser duties; he did not counsel anyone to shirk work or become a charge on the earnings of others.

In the holy tradition of monasticism throughout the ages there have been inspired and inspiring exemplars of this single-minded devotion. Saint Francis left his wealthy home for God. Swami Shankara left his beloved mother in quest of soul realization. Jesus warned that renunciation of lesser duties would bring persecution from those who do not understand. But a devotee who loves God with all his soul is not afraid of such persecution, or of other consequences of forsaking lesser duties. As did Lord Krishna, Jesus Christ signified that a true devotee who renounces everything for God alone should entertain no regrets; for he will transcend all causes of grief, and will be plentifully rewarded with divine contentment, even a hundredfold, and in afterlife find blessed eternal conscious existence in God.

For this reason, Jesus taught that it is better to get rid of the *impulse* toward selfish material activity *behind* the "hand," so that worldly inclinations can no longer be an obstruction to God-realization. He also said: "And thou shalt love the Lord thy God with all thy heart, and with all thy soul, and with all thy mind, and with all thy strength: this is the first commandment. And the second is like, namely this, thou shalt love thy neighbor as thyself."‡ Loving God alone is not a selfish

---

* Mark 10:29–30. † Mark 9:43. ‡ Mark 12:30–31.

inner withdrawal from one's fellow beings, but an expansion of consciousness in loving Him who is present in all things. Similarly, the principal advice of the Gita is that to attain liberation man should love God through the offering of his strength (life force) in ecstatic meditation, with the purified love of the heart, with concentration of mind, and with the soul's intuition; and also to perform the selfless, serviceful duties and divine actions that are of benefit not only to himself but to others, his "neighbors," or co-dwellers in this world.

THE WORD *DHARMA,* DUTY, comes from the Sanskrit root *dhri,* "to hold (anything)." The universe exists because it is held together by the will of God manifesting as the immutable cosmic principles of creation. Therefore He is the real *Dharma*. Without God no creature can exist. The highest *dharma* or duty of every human being is to find out, by realization, that he is sustained by God.

Dharma, therefore, is the cosmic law that runs the mechanism of the universe; and after accomplishing the primary God-uniting *yoga-dharma* (religious duties), man should perform secondarily his duties to the cosmic laws of nature. As an air-breathing creature, he should not foolishly drown himself by jumping into the water and trying to breathe there; he should observe rational conduct in all ways, obeying the natural laws of living in an environment where air, sunshine, and proper food are plentiful.

Explanation of dharma, duties ordained by cosmic law

Man should perform virtuous *dharma,* for by obedience to righteous duty he can free himself from the law of cause and effect governing all actions. He should avoid irreligion (*adharma*) which takes him away from God, and follow religion (*Sanatana Dharma*), by which he finds Him. Man should observe the religious duties *(yoga-dharma)* enjoined in the true scriptures of the world.

Codes for all aspects of human conduct, as given in the laws of Manu,* are also considered *dharmas* or duties for the guidance of man. Applied to the four natural castes, the term *dharma* refers to the duties inherent in each of them. For example, as explained in previous verses, the duty of a Sudra or body-bound individual is to be physically active; the duty of a Brahmin is to think of God.

The word *dharma* also expresses the nature of vital beings—men,

* The great legislator and antehistorical author of *Manava Dharma Shastras* or *Laws of Manu*. These institutes of canonized law are effective in India to this day.

animals, and other creatures. A man has to act like a man, and an animal like an animal (notwithstanding that a man can change his *dharma* by becoming beastly, and an animal can be trained to behave in certain ways like a human being).

The nature of elements (fiery, gaseous, ethereal, liquid, solid) is also called *dharma*. For example, the nature of electricity (fiery) is to give light and energy.

Lord Krishna advises Arjuna to rise above all consciousness of nature's dualities of virtue and sin with their lesser *dharmas* or duties that keep the soul bound to matter. He sought to shake Arjuna from his unwillingness to battle his senses and physical human nature by exhorting him to give up all pertinent lesser *dharmas* (in catering to the senses) so that he could be free to perform the supreme *dharma* of finding God (by liberating the discriminating faculties from sensory bondage).

THE CORRELATED METAPHYSICAL INTERPRETATION of this oft-quoted sixty-sixth stanza is being explained now:

An ordinary man is continually performing duties to his body-bound ego, his physical body, his five senses, and his sense-infected mind and intelligence. Thus, in the guise of "duty," this hapless doer commits all kinds of errors by which he is bound to the miseries of nature's realm through countless cycles of rebirth.

So Krishna says: "O Arjuna, be a real renunciant! By the practice of yoga meditation withdraw (*vraja*) your mind, intelligence, life force, and heart from the clutches of the ego, from the physical sensations of sight, hearing, smell, taste, and touch, and from the objects of sense pleasures! Forsake all duties toward them! Be a yogi by uniting yourself to My blessed presence (*mam ekam saranam*) in your soul. Then I will save you; by nonperformance of the lesser duties to the senses under the influence of delusion, you will automatically find yourself free from all sinful troubles.

Metaphysical significance of "forsaking lesser dharmas"

"If you remain in ecstasy with Me, fulfilling all divine duties as directed by Me, forsaking all ego-instigated duties, you will be liberated."

As discussed in previous contexts (e.g., see I:1, page 15), the ordinary man's mind is usually identified with external possessions and sense pleasures connected with the surface of the body. The physical consciousness is sustained by the mind, intelligence, and life force operating through the subtle spinal centers of life and intelligence. Through the lower plexuses (lumbar, sacral, and coccygeal), the searchlights of intelligence, mind, and life energy continually operate externally, feeding the nervous system and revealing and sustaining the sense pleasures and physical consciousness. The yogi reverses the searchlights of intelligence, mind, and life force inward through a secret astral passage, the coiled way of the *kundalini* in the coccygeal plexus, and upward through the sacral, the lumbar, and the higher dorsal, cervical, and medullary plexuses, and the spiritual eye at the point between the eyebrows, to reveal finally the soul's presence in the highest center (*sahasrara*) in the brain.

As the material man's mind is constantly busy with the body and the external world, so the yogi's consciousness is principally engaged within. Looking through his spiritual eye, the astral eye of light, he experiences in the *sahasrara* the ineffable bliss of his soul. Thus did the Psalmist sing: "He that dwelleth in the secret place of the Most High shall abide under the shadow of the Almighty."*

Verse 67

idaṁ te nātapaskāya nābhaktāya kadācana
na cāśuśrūṣave vācyaṁ na ca māṁ yo 'bhyasūyati

Never voice these truths to one who is without self-control or devotion, nor to one who performs no service or does not care to hear, nor to one who speaks ill of Me.

Spiritual truths are sacred, not to be offered indiscriminately to gross materialists who abuse or malign their sanctity. Any individual who is extremely identified with the body as the be-all and end-all of existence is a gross materialist; devoted to sense pleasures and possessions, he has no yearning for soul knowledge. Through lack of any true understanding, materialists denounce God; or may otherwise condemn Him for all the ills of the world, never recognizing man's responsibility, through misuse of free choice, for his own miseries.

Jesus similarly admonished that one should not cast pearls before swine;† that is, one should not bestow spiritual wealth on the unappreciative.

* Psalms 91:1.

† Matthew 7:6.

VERSES 68–69

ya idaṁ paramaṁ guhyaṁ madbhakteṣv abhidhāsyati
bhaktiṁ mayi parāṁ kṛtvā mām evaiṣyaty asaṁśayaḥ (68)

na ca tasmān manuṣyeṣu kaścin me priyakṛttamaḥ
bhavitā na ca me tasmād anyaḥ priyataro bhuvi (69)

Whosoever shall impart to My devotees the supreme secret knowledge, with utmost devotion to Me, shall without doubt come unto Me. Not any among men performs more priceless service to Me than he; in all the world there shall be none dearer to Me.

"THE DEVOTEE WHO FEELS My omnipresent Self in the little 'Myself' (the soul), and from that spiritual perception (not from theoretical understanding) imparts truth to soul-seekers to help liberate them, shall be blessed by additional divine grace. He will easily remain in ecstasy within his soul, feeling there Myself as omnipresent Spirit."

Though God transcends all misery and is all-blessed, He is conscious of the sufferings of His children, for truly He resides within them and undergoes with them the excruciating tests of delusive existence. Therefore, dearest of all men to Him is the saint who strives to free others from delusion and bring them back to the realization of their forgotten inherent divinity. Eternally dear and blessed are those who gladly endure even worldly persecution for helping others to return to the shelter of God's protection.

A yogi who has risen above delusion and attained Self-realization, and who having tasted divine bliss is eager to share it with true seekers, finds supreme joy in selflessly helping others to liberation. He fulfills that service which is most pleasing to God. To perceive God and—in pure devotion to Him alone—to share His love with others should be man's highest goal on earth. The constant prayer in his heart should be: "May Thy love reign forever in the sanctuary of my devotion, and may I be able to share Thy love with others."*

Even desire for liberation is imperfect if it is limited to one's self. No saint is completely liberated until he has been the instrument of spiritual awakening in at least a few devotees.

The Bible teaching may again be aptly quoted: "Love God with

* A paraphrase of Paramahansaji's Universal Prayer (see page *xv*). (*Publisher's Note*)

all thy soul"—that is, love God with all the intuitive perception of soul realization; "and love thy neighbor as thyself"—teach the way of salvation to receptive hearts. But watchfulness is called for to safeguard against intrusion by the ego, lest initial good intentions to serve others spiritually become instead a prideful savior-complex. This is why the Gita here stresses that such service is to be done with utmost devotion to God, not out of the ego's love for recognition and power. An enthusiast who tries to save other souls without having saved his own may be a good person, but his actions do not lead to liberation if he retains egotism in his desire to be an instrument of good. However, if one is deeply sincere in his own endeavors to find God, and at the same time in all humility tries to bring others to Him, that action is admirable and soul-liberating; it does not bind him to earth in any way, even by good karma.

"Seek ye first the kingdom of God,"* and then inspire others to seek the Giver of all gifts! In sum, perceive God within the joy of your soul and share that divine joy with others. The giver of such service to God "without doubt" comes unto God; there is "none dearer" to Him.

Verse 70

adhyeṣyate ca ya imaṁ dharmyaṁ saṁvādam āvayoḥ
jñānayajñena tenāham iṣṭaḥ syām iti me matiḥ

He who studies and knows (intuitively perceives) this sacred dialogue between us will be worshiping Me by the sacrifice (yajna) of wisdom. Such is My holy utterance.

The concept of a dialogue or communion with Spirit presupposes a "voice" or medium of exchange, whether expressed by means of sound, image, or intuitive thought. That medium is the Sacred Word, the Lord's "holy utterance"—the Vedic *Aum,* or Christian Amen, the Word of God. *Aum* is the vibratory embodiment of Spirit, replete with Omniscience and Omnipotence. Jesus referred to this aspect of the Holy Trinity of God as the Holy Ghost, or Comforter: "But the Comforter, which is the Holy Ghost...shall teach you all things, and bring all things to your remembrance, whatsoever I have said unto you."†

* Matthew 6:33. † John 14:26.

Any meaningful worship of the personal God (any manifestation of the Unmanifested Absolute) must needs include this vibratory aspect of His presence.

The purpose of the spiritual technique of *yajna,* worship of God through symbolic sacrifice, is destruction of sins by wisdom and union of soul and Spirit. The yogi in the performance of *yajna* invokes the manifesting power of the Sacred Word. *Yajna* is performed in the sacrificial fire ceremony; in *japa,* repeated chanting of *Aum;* in whisper chanting of *Aum* with interiorized concentration on burning material desires in the fire of spiritual perception; and in ecstatic mental prayer, actual communion with *Aum,* or God—symbolized in the Gita as the "sacred dialogue" between Krishna and Arjuna. In this last form of *yajna,* the human consciousness is purely transmuted in the wisdom flames of Cosmic Consciousness. Hence it is called *jnana yajna,* or divine sacrifice through wisdom. This is the highest form of *yajna,* and is the true inner sacrificial rite.

In this stanza the Lord as Krishna says to Arjuna: "He who concentratedly puts his mind on this dialogue between your soul and Me, and who meditates and dwells upon it with intuitive perception,* will feel his consciousness dissolving in the fire of My cosmic consciousness, even as your soul, O Arjuna, has become one with Me."

To read and attain inwardly the full realization of the teachings of the Bhagavad Gita is to burn ignorance in the fire of wisdom. Those who study this scripture with soul perception, reenacting within themselves the dialogue between soul and Spirit, will be offering God worship by the liberating supreme fire ceremony of wisdom.

VERSE 71

śraddhāvān anasūyaś ca śṛṇuyād api yo naraḥ
so 'pi muktaḥ śubhāṁl lokān prāpnuyāt puṇyakarmaṇām

Even that individual—full of devotion and devoid of scorn—who merely listens to and heeds† this sacred dialogue, being freed from earthly karma, shall dwell in the blessed worlds of the virtuous.

---

* *Adhyeṣyate,* from the Sanskrit verb *adhī:* "to study; to understand; to know."

† *Śṛṇuyād,* from the Sanskrit root *śru:* "to hear; to obey."

Even those seekers who cannot perceive fully through intuitive realization the deep practical lore of the Gita, but who are wholly devotional and unencumbered by any malicious agnosticism of doubt, will find that by their listening to the Gita with attention, its wisdom can free them from bad habits and inclinations toward wrong activities. Thereby they will attain good karma, and through this transformation gradually perceive within themselves the same blessed consciousness enjoyed by the saints, who actively display in their lives the Gita wisdom. Such an attentive listener and absorber of the truths in the Gita will, after death, be drawn to more beneficial astral or physical worlds, according to the karmic measure of those good qualities developed in him through having devoutly received the Lord's words.

The Dialogue Between Spirit and Soul Concludes

Verse 72

kaccid etac chrutaṁ pārtha tvayaikāgreṇa cetasā
kaccid ajñānasaṁmohaḥ pranaṣṭas te dhanaṁjaya

O Partha (Arjuna), hast thou listened to this wisdom with concentrated heart? O Dhananjaya, hast thy delusion-born ignorance been annihilated?

The Lord now questions Arjuna: "Have you left your Partha state of mental weakness, having devoutly absorbed with your soul's intuition the Spirit-wisdom that has been imparted to you? O mighty conqueror, Dhananjaya, do you feel the body-identified, ego-born delusion of ignorance gone forever from within you?"

When the yogi first perceives himself to be the omniscient soul, one with cosmic Spirit, in wonder he introspectively asks himself: "So long I have considered myself a human being! Am I now really a God-man? Am I at last free from ignorance and its dualities of cold and heat, pain and pleasure, life and death?"

VERSE 73

arjuna uvāca
naṣṭo mohaḥ smṛtir labdhā tvatprasādān mayācyuta
sthito 'smi gatasaṁdehaḥ kariṣye vacanaṁ tava

Arjuna said:
My delusion is gone! I have regained memory (of my soul) through Thy grace, O Achyuta (matchless Krishna). I am firmly established; my dubiousness has vanished. I will act according to Thy word.

ARJUNA ACKNOWLEDGES THAT IT IS principally by God's grace as manifested through his sublime guru that he has at last regained his memory of the blessed Self. He realizes that he has awakened from a dream in which he played the part of a human ego. His doubts about the Lord's omnipresence, fostered by incarnations of body identification, are now and forever dissolved. He stands ready to follow the advice he has received from the gracious Lord.

VERSE 74

saṁjaya uvāca
ity ahaṁ vāsudevasya pārthasya ca mahātmanaḥ
saṁvādam imam aśrauṣam adbhutaṁ romaharṣaṇam

Sanjaya* said:
Thus have I listened to this wondrous discourse between Vasudeva (Krishna) and the high-souled Partha (Arjuna), causing the hair on my body to stand on end in a thrill of joy.†

---

* Sanjaya: the minister and charioteer of the blind King Dhritarashtra, who had been blessed by Vyasa with the power of divine sight by which he could see from afar the battlefield of Kurukshetra and report the events to the king. See detailed explanation of symbology, I:1, page 6.

† Awe-inspiring experiences of divine revelation fill the heart with a thrilling intensity of pure joy, which may have the physical effect of causing the bodily hairs to stand on end. This same effect may also be produced when in certain ecstatic states the body literally becomes joyously electrified with the blissful cosmic vibratory power of Spirit.

SANJAYA (THE INTUITIVE SIGHT of impartial introspection) has been relaying to King Dhritarashtra (father of the one hundred sense tendencies; the hitherto blind mind) the entire discourse between Krishna (omnipresent Spirit) and Arjuna (the soul). In conclusion, he exclaims: "I am thrilled to have been awakened from my stupor of delusion and to have felt all the truth in this sacred dialogue."

No devotee should be satisfied until he has sufficiently developed his intuition—by impartial introspection and deep meditation, as in *Kriya Yoga*—to experience the communion of soul and Spirit. If a devotee meditates intensely for at least short periods every day, and has longer periods of three or four hours of deep meditation once or twice a week, he will find his intuition becoming sufficiently superfine to realize unendingly the dialogue of blissful wisdom exchanged between the soul and God. He will know the interiorized state of communion in which his soul "talks" to God and receives His responses, not with the utterances of any human language, but through wordless intuitional exchanges. That student of the Gita will be divinely benefited who is not satisfied with theoretical study, but reenacts within his own being the soul-awakening experiences of Arjuna.

VERSE 75

vyāsaprasādāc chrutavān etad guhyam ahaṁ param
yogaṁ yogeśvarāt kṛṣṇāt sākṣāt kathayataḥ svayam

Through the grace of Vyasa, this supreme secret Yoga has been bestowed on me, manifested to my consciousness directly by Krishna himself, the Lord of Yoga!

SANJAYA CONTINUES TO EXPRESS WONDERMENT at the revelation he has received: "I have perceived through my own intuition the dialogue of blissful wisdom between God and Arjuna's intuitive soul perception." The devotee whose interiorized, introspective divine sight (Sanjaya) receives the blessing of support of a spiritualized state of consciousness manifesting the soul's pure discriminative perception (Vyasa), thereby realizes the divine communion of soul and Spirit, and becomes fully possessed of all wisdom inherent in that blissful union.

VERSE 76

rājan saṁsmṛtya saṁsmṛtya saṁvādam imam adbhutam
keśavārjunayoḥ puṇyaṁ hṛṣyāmi ca muhur muhuḥ

O King Dhritarashtra, as I recall and recall the extraordinary and sacred dialogue between Keshava (Krishna) and Arjuna, I am overjoyed again and again.

THE INTUITION OF SANJAYA IS OVERJOYED, remembering again and again the amazing sacred communion it has witnessed between Krishna and Arjuna (Spirit and soul). Such wondrous intuitional realizations become a permanent and indelible memory, and descend repeatedly into the sphere of the devotee's inner mind, the king of the senses; metaphorically, from Sanjaya, or impartial intuitive sight, to King Dhritarashtra, the blind mind enlightened by intuition. In the ordinary man, the mind, which should be the real ruler of the senses, is instead enslaved by them, and hence is blind, unable to perceive extrasensory soul perceptions. But the divine man of impartial introspection is blessed with inner realizations, and can readily recall in his mind those intuitional experiences. So this stanza describes how the awakened intuition of Sanjaya again and again rejoiced as it relived its divine experience.

Every devotee who unites his soul with Spirit in ecstasy (*samadhi*) can recall in his mind, after coming down from that state, the unending thrills of communion with the Infinite. Just as the true lover, even after long separation from his beloved, is thrilled in body, mind, and soul when he recalls a momentary meeting with the loved one, so the yogi, long after his ecstasy is over, recalls with unending joy his experiences with the Beloved Spirit.

VERSE 77

tac ca saṁsmṛtya saṁsmṛtya rūpam atyadbhutaṁ hareḥ
vismayo me mahān rājan hṛṣyāmi ca punaḥ punaḥ

And, O King Dhritarashtra, as I recall and recall again the colossal manifestation* of Hari (Krishna), great is my amazement; I am ever renewed in joy.

---

* *Vishvarupa*, the cosmic form.

In the previous stanza, the intuition of Sanjaya perceived the joyous state of Arjuna's soul as it was dissolving in the omnipresent nature of Krishna—the ubiquitous, boundless consciousness of Spirit. Sanjaya now tells how his intuition recalls over and over again, each time with a wondrous thrill, the indescribable ever new blessedness of Absolute Spirit, in which all dualities are completely dissolved. In that transcendent state of divine union, which cannot be even dreamed of in the limited consciousness of physical existence, there is a total dissolution of dichotomy. All things exist not as a creation of Spirit, but of naught else than Spirit Itself, the "colossal manifestation" referred to by Sanjaya in this verse and described in the "vision of visions" (XI:15–34). This Divine Immutability, hailed by Arjuna as "the Manifested, the Unmanifested, and That beyond" (XI:37), is the Ultimate Mystery, resolved only in oneness with the Illimitable Absolute.

Verse 78

yatra yogeśvaraḥ kṛṣṇo yatra pārtho dhanurdharaḥ
tatra śrīr vijayo bhūtir dhruvā nītir matir mama

(Sanjaya concludes):

Such is my faith: that, wherever is manifest the Lord of Yoga, Krishna; and wherever is present Partha* (Arjuna, a true devotee), expert wielder of the bow of self-control, there too are success, victory, attainment of powers, and the unfailing law of self-discipline (which leads to liberation).

Having witnessed the ultimate enlightenment bestowed on Arjuna by Lord Krishna, Sanjaya feels a deep, encouraging conviction within his soul, and declares:

"Wherever there is a devotee like Arjuna, who, though initially weak and oscillating, is still ever ready to free himself by renunciation and by slaying his would-be captors, the sense pleasures, with the bow of self-control; and who is able to unite his soul with the omnipresent Spirit, as manifested in Krishna, Lord of Yoga—that devotee is bound

---

* Partha, "son of Pritha," or Kunti, the metronymic of Arjuna, is used in this context to signify that the true devotee is one who gains the power to invoke divinity through his worldly dispassion, or renunciative will and spiritual ardor. (See I:4–6 and II:3.)

to find the everlasting riches, victory over all matter. Through his positive fulfillment of the divine law of liberation, he will have unending spiritual attainment, miraculous powers, and eternal joy."

At the battle of Kurukshetra, Arjuna was equipped for victory with his all-powerful bow, Gandiva, and was charioteered by Lord Krishna. The devotee of every clime and age, when he sets out to win the battle against the sense soldiers of the blind king Mind, must similarly equip himself with the bow of self-control; and, charioteered by God, must rally the army of emperor Discrimination with its forces of virtue and its allies of spiritual perceptions.

By practicing renunciation (nonattachment) and by withdrawal of the consciousness from sense perceptions in yoga meditation, every devotee should learn to unite his soul with Spirit. The yogi who is able to sit in meditation with spine erect and to free his soul from the consciousness of the senses and unite it with the bliss of Spirit, and who is able by constant practice of yoga to retain that introspective state of Self-realization in his human nature, will attain the cosmic prosperity of God—all His infinite treasures. By determinedly fulfilling the law of liberation, that devotee will know victory over all nature and possess the highest spiritual accomplishments: all wisdom, love, and powers of the Divine.

om tat sat iti śrīmadbhagavadgītāsu upaniṣatsu
brahmavidyāyām yogaśāstre śrīkṛṣṇārjunasamvāde
mokṣasaṁnyāsayogo nāmāṣṭādaśo 'dhyāyaḥ

Aum, Tat, Sat.
In the Upanishad of the holy Bhagavad Gita—the discourse of Lord Krishna to Arjuna, which is the scripture of yoga and the science of God-realization—this is the eighteenth chapter, called "Union Through Renunciation and Liberation."

CONCLUSION

THE WORDS OF LORD KRISHNA to Arjuna in the Bhagavad Gita are at once a profound scripture on the science of yoga, union with God, and a textbook for everyday living. The student is led step by step with Arjuna from the mortal consciousness of spiritual doubt and weakheartedness to divine attunement and inner resolve. The timeless and universal message of the Gita is all-encompassing in its expression of truth. The Gita teaches man his rightful duty in life, and how to discharge it with the dispassion that avoids pain and nurtures wisdom and success. The enigmas of creation are resolved in an understanding of the nature of matter. The mysteries that veil the Infinite Spirit are sundered one by one to reveal a beloved God whose awesome omnipotence is tempered with a tender love and compassion that readily responds to a sincere call from His devotees.

In summation, the sublime essence of the Bhagavad Gita is that right action, nonattachment to the world and to its sense pleasures, and union with God by the highest yoga of *pranayama* meditation, learned from an enlightened guru, constitute the royal path to God-attainment.

The *Kriya Yoga* technique, taught by Krishna to Arjuna and referred to in Gita chapters IV:29 and V:27–28, is the supreme spiritual science of yoga meditation. Secreted during the materialistic ages, this indestructible yoga was revived for modern man by Mahavatar Babaji and taught by the Gurus of Self-Realization Fellowship/Yogoda Satsanga Society of India. Babaji himself ordained me to spread this holy science of God-union. Through the blessings of Bhagavan Krishna and Mahavatar Babaji, whom I behold in Spirit as one, and of my guru and *paramguru,* Swami Sri Yukteswar and Lahiri Mahasaya, I offer to the world this interpretation of the Gita as it has been divinely revealed to me. Any devotee who will emulate Arjuna—epitome of the ideal disciple—and perform his rightful duty with nonattachment, and perfect his practice of yoga meditation through a technique such as *Kriya Yoga,* will similarly draw the blessings and guidance of God and win the victory of Self-realization.

As God talked with Arjuna, so will He talk with you. As He lifted up the spirit and consciousness of Arjuna, so will He uplift you. As He granted Arjuna supreme spiritual vision, so will He confer enlightenment on you.

We have seen in the Bhagavad Gita the story of the soul's journey back to God—a journey each one must make. O divine soul! like Arjuna, "Forsake this small weakheartedness (of mortal consciousness). Arise!" Before you is the royal path.

ADDENDA

❖

Afterword, by Sri Daya Mata

❖

Ode to the Bhagavad Gita, by Paramahansa Yogananda

❖

Transliteration and Pronunciation of Sanskrit Terms

❖

Sanskrit Epithets of Lord Krishna and Arjuna

❖

Lahiri Mahasaya's Diagram of Chakras

❖

About the Author

❖

Aims and Ideals of Self-Realization Fellowship

❖

Self-Realization Fellowship Publications and Lessons

❖

Terms Associated With Self-Realization Fellowship

❖

Index

❖

AFTERWORD

"A New Scripture Is Born"

ONE DAY, AFTER MANY MONTHS OF WORK on the Bhagavad Gita at the desert ashram, Paramahansa Yogananda was staying for a time at the Self-Realization Fellowship Hermitage by the ocean in Encinitas, California. It was nearly three o'clock in the morning; for many hours that night, he had been intensely concentrated on his Gita translation and commentary. Finally, he turned to the disciple who had been sitting silently nearby. "You have tonight been greatly blessed to witness the end of the work I came to fulfill. I have finished the Gita. That task was given to me, and I made a promise that I would write this Gita—and it is done. All the Great Ones have been here in this room tonight, and I have conversed with them in Spirit.* My life now is conditioned by minutes, hours, days—maybe years, I don't know; it is in Divine Mother's hands. I am living only by Her grace." Paramahansaji then summoned other senior disciples, wishing to share with them the special blessings surrounding him in his work that night.

Later, alone in his bedroom, Paramahansaji's divine experience had a wondrous sequel. He told us: "There was a light in the corner of the room. I thought it must be the morning rays coming in from an opening in the curtain; but as I watched it, the light grew brighter and expanded." Humbly, almost inaudibly, he added: "Out of the brilliance, Sri Yukteswarji came with eyes of approval."

And then, as if in demonstration of the very essence of the message of the Bhagavad Gita as both a personal and a universal war between good and evil, Paramahansaji's vision continued: "Christ came; followed by the face of Satan." He explained: "This was to show that both good and evil, light and darkness, are a part of creation—the great manifesting power of God.† Remember, you won't be frightened by

---

* The *Great Ones* or *Great Masters* or *Great Gurus* are terms used frequently by Paramahansaji to refer collectively to the Self-Realization Fellowship line of Gurus.

† "I am the Lord, and there is none else, there is no God beside Me....I form the light, and create darkness: I make peace, and create evil: I the Lord do all these things" (Isaiah 45:5,7).

the shadows or touched by Satan if you keep your attention on the Light."

Years earlier, Sri Yukteswarji had told him: "You perceive all the truth of the Bhagavad Gita as you have heard the dialogue of Krishna and Arjuna as revealed to Vyasa. Go and give that revealed truth with your interpretations: a new scripture will be born."

After many months and years of work on this manuscript, Paramahansaji now saw the fulfillment of his Guru's prediction. Informing the disciples that his commentary on the Gita had been completed, with a joyous smile he humbly echoed what Sri Yukteswarji had told him, saying: "A new scripture is born."

"I have written this Gita as it came to me," he said, "as I was united in ecstasy with my great Gurus and the originators of the Bhagavad Gita. The Gita that has come through me belongs to them. And I know what my Master said: 'A new Gita, hitherto only partially exposed through centuries in the many lights of various explanations, is coming out in its full effulgence to bathe all true devotees of the world.'"

—*Sri Daya Mata*

Ode to the Bhagavad Gita

By Paramahansa Yogananda

Sage Vyasa sat entranced on Ganges' bank
In worship consummate; his feet in reverence washed by waves in rank.
Awake within, the *rishi* felt the unseen sourceless river
Of human mind with wonder-waves bestir,
Approach and in obeisance touch the feet of his compassioned soul
Beseeching him with age-old questioning voiceless call:
"Oh, tell us, Lord, whence do we come; and go we whither?
Why do we brawl; why are we here?"

In answer did the sage compose and sing
The solacing song of Gita-hymn,
An everlasting balm to suffering human minds
That heave and flow in Nature's tide, in strife and quarrels unkind,
Unconscious of the soul's true purpose here:
To rise to Spirit's sphere through trialsome sorrows howe'er severe.

The Gita's lay with endless rays outstretched
Embraces full all truths and creeds of righteousness possessed,
And like the brilliance of a dazzling sun
Enfolds e'en light of doctrines inchoate, anon,
But yet no dint of dogma dark is thus allowed
To steal a moment's stay midst brethren principles in unity avowed.

With copious loot all ta'en from Vedas' vitals—
Sans mystic formulas, chants, and rituals—
With hoary hoarded gems from six sagacious philosophic schools
And from one hundred eight Upanishads of Brahmins' rule
These seven hundred singing Bharat soldiers strong
Have marched pre-Christian path intoning long the Lord's Celestial Song.

Nay more! these rhyming soldiers have e'en more
Of booty brought from Spirit's richest store.
They come with salient clarion call,
Attracting wanderers no longer deaf from *maya*'s din withal,
To push their soul's penury out
With Brahma's gold and pilfering Satan's rout.

With vanquishment of ignorance, the highest sin,
The blissful kingdom, heaven's realm, is found within.
So Sankhya sweet doth sagely tell all true
How human woes of mind and flesh ensue
And how by higher way, not obvious means, of cure
The roots of sorrow can be plucked so future seeds can ne'er endure.

The custom-courted care for flesh or mind or soul
Cannot prevail to banish threefold ailments all;
The sick, and those that may be sick, unwell
Are all but prisoners of sorrow's hell.

Thus man's most longed-for hidden wish of heart
Doth lie in locking grief fore'er apart.
To foil the skulking captive-plans of pain
The wise one seeks to know for sure the means and lasting gain.
Vedanta then doth speak with knowledge vast
To tell the end, the way creation's cast.

Then Yoga comes with wondrous chart of path and scientific way
Bypassing byways all to traverse straight the one true spinal highway.
Aeonic Yoga! ageless youth, ne'er old nor antiquated,
Based on laws of human mind, how flesh with soul and life is animate

Go gather from the world all truths of scripture,
Surfeit thy brain with airy subtle thoughts to nurture,
Yet thou bereft of Yoga's great revelatory art
Will find unsatisfied truth-hunger of thy heart.
Discussing five-score years or more of sugar's meat
Doth fail to tell how sugar's sweet;

But taste of sugar touched on tongue at once doth tell
What sugar is—direct perception intellect could ne'er compel.

Surveyor wise of human mind, the master Vyasa,
Selected clash within the clan of Kaurava
And in *Mahabharata* epic old
Poeticized the tale, with hidden allegory bravely told.
Good Pandavas and Kuru knaves did come
Of welded love, from selfsame clan.
The Pandavas did rule in upper Hind, and Kurus lived
In peace with them and them obeyed
Till whim of time did cleave and change their course,
Unlock their love and them in wrath disperse—
The Pandavas by Kuru's crafty game of dice
Were exiled to the forest, filched of state by wrong device.

The Gita-esoteric speaks in illustrative metaphor
How slavish senses strong and sober reason are at war.
All moral lore that's learnt and heard in life
Doth meet its highest test on field of strife.

Vyasa saw the body as a chariot drawn mightily
By restive steeds of senses reined by Mind, held tightly,
Allowing them to rush where'er Discrimination drives
As often as royal Soul the order and direction gives.

Oh, drawn by sensory steeds
And reined by Mind indeed,
Oh, driven by Reason right
And ridden by Soul so bright,
This cheerful chariot of fleshly frame
In matter's land doth hie, o'er *maya*'s main.

Consider deep why Master Soul must harmonize
The willful sensory mind with inner Wisdom's eyes:
The senses are the windows for the soul
To peep and see, conceive of matter all.

The mirror-mind behind the open senses stays
Reflecting every object that before it lays.

As naught is seen with eyelids closed
So naught is known when mind is absent from its host.
The mind to each and every sense imparts the life
But reason right declares, explains, perceptions rife.
The absentminded man with senses open wide
Conceiveth naught when mind doth not abide.
The maniac has mind to register the senses
But lacks the guidance reason true dispenses.

Material things so mirrored on the mind
Are full declared when watching reason reads its kind:
An object longing entrance into knowledge's land
Must pass through senses' gates by mind's sanctioning hand.
Then reason waits upon this object guest
To know the way to cognize and to serve him best.

To hold together under kingly Soul
The senses, mind, discernment all in tune with *dharma*'s rule
Is man's true duty, thus to realize
The ego's lusts are *maya*'s lures, delusion garbed in pleasure-guise.

When cruel spears do fierce provoke flesh hence
That's time ye mark which wins, the soul or matter-binding sense.
Of this the savant sage in Gita sings
And from the start, he martial spirit brings.

The blind King Dhritarashtra prayed:
"On Kurukshetra's pious plain arrayed
By war the Pandavas, my children also, swayed—
What did they do? O Sanjaya say!"

In metaphor the blind mind asked
The power of introspection to fulfill its task:
"On body's holy field of work and strife,

Insightful sons of pure discrimination full of life,
Opposing stubborn senses, sons of sightless mind,
All eager and prepared, a mighty clash to find.
What did they do, impartial sight?
Oh, tell me well, and tell me right."

The body's field is holy ground, the kingdom where the soul inheres;
That's why 'tis sacred soil, our sage avers.
But roving fickle senses also here do stay
That's why he calls it field of work where tempters play.

Upon this Kurukshetra plain, the sons of Pandu did array
All fronting Phoebus in the East, the sun of Spirit's lifeful rays;
While the unrighteous, guilt-stained Kurus did in fright all say,
"Our backs turned on the stare of sun we'll stay
In dark to hurl our thirsty arrows, sharp and fresh,
To strike good Pandavas within their subtle fortresses of flesh."

'Tis thus in holy plexuses within the spine and brain
That sons of Righteousness remain—
Where consciousness supreme, transcendent, find—
Entrenched in yogic centers six, await to meet sense mind.
Unrighteous senses wait arrayed in ego's favored place
Encamped in touch, in sight, in muse, on matter's body surface.

In lumbar center Self-Control doth dwell
To drive foraging senses' rush pell-mell.
The dorsal door is guarded well by mighty Vital Force
To cheer and full enthuse the soldiers true to stay their course;
Without this help the moral hordes would rue—
For sure, at cervical, the eldest son of fair Pandu.
This Calmness unperturbed is Reason's worthiest child;
He lives in rear to hold the ranks with self-possession mild,
His virtue halts encroaching senses bold that dare
Advance on soul's good soil, its lords to craftily ensnare.

Undaunted wisdom's offspring, brave true thoughts
Can look straight at the face of truth, evading naught;
While convict thoughts do crouch and sheerly shun—
From very sight of truth away to coward's lair they run.
The heaven-born thoughts roam nobly in the brain
Near mystery solar flame of soul to bask, and virtue gain;
While crooked lustful thoughts in fear do hark
To senses' call to bivouac in derma's chamber dark.

When skirmishing senses strut to upward climb from body's hull,
Then wisdom's puissant troops emerge from fort of skull
To meet on common seat of war, the astral spinal field,
The place where efferent-afferent forces now must win or yield.

The gourmand Greed and luring Lust fight deep
To seize wise Temperance true, and captive keep
In spacious prison of polished passion gold
And there, in cagèd freedom drugged, him hold.
But fiery power of Self-Control lies keenly ready
To scorch the ravaging Lust that craves to seize soul's territory.

Blind Dhritarashtra, folded hands, beseeched
The aid of yoga's power by Sage Vyasa reached
To right receive the news of clannish war.
The sun of saintly consciousness that threw its luster far
On brightly good and darkly bad, did full imbue
Sanjaya, honesty-endowed, with spiritual purview
Through Yoga's second sight to see and state
To Dhritarashtra, sovereign blind, his anxiousness to sate,
Of what transpired on Kuru's plain, what news of war—
Why must there be this terrible encounter?

In awe-inspiring verse, celestial answer long
Unfolds the Holy Writ of Gita Song
As sacred dialogue between Sri Krishna, Lord Supreme,
And paradigm Arjuna, princely devotee sublime.

Ode to the Bhagavad Gita

Beginning in the opening verse
With eyeless sovereign's query terse—
What every seeker fain must ask
Ere taking up each soulful task:
"On Kurukshetra's pious plain arrayed,
By war the Pandavas, my children also, swayed—
What did they do? O Sanjaya say!"

TRANSLITERATION AND PRONUNCIATION OF SANSKRIT TERMS

The Sanskrit language is traditionally written in Devanagari script, which has nearly twice as many characters in its alphabet as English. The following transliteration conventions have been observed in this publication:

In the Sanskrit text of the Gita verses—and in the commentaries when etymological derivations of terms are explained—all Sanskrit words have been spelled with the standard diacritical marks used by scholars. However, in the English translations of the verses and in the commentaries, no diacritical marks have been used (except as noted above), since most non-scholarly readers find them to be a hindrance rather than a help in reading. For those interested, the spelling with diacritical marks can often be found in the Sanskrit rendering of the particular verse being commented on.

Where diacritical marks are not used in the text, Sanskrit *ṛ* is transliterated as *ri; ś* and *ṣ* as *sh;* and *ṁ* as either *m* or *n*. Words that have a generally accepted spelling in English dictionaries, e.g., *ahiṁsa* as *ahimsa, śri* as *sri,* etc., are rendered accordingly (an exception is *Om,* which is here spelled *Aum*).

Finally, it may be noted that in his talks and writings Paramahansa Yogananda often pronounced and spelled Sanskrit terms in his native Bengali language. Usually the Bengali is very close to the Sanskrit, with a few notable exceptions: In Bengali spellings, the final *a* at the end of a word or component of a word is often omitted (e.g., *Sanatan Dharma* instead of *Sanatana Dharma*; *Yogmata* instead of *Yogamata*); Sanskrit *v* is often rendered as *b* (e.g., *nirvikalpa samadhi* becomes *nirbikalpa samadhi*); Sanskrit *a* becomes *o* (e.g., *pranam* becomes *pronam*). In this publication, per Paramahansaji's instruction, the Sanskrit rather than Bengali spellings have been used.

Pronunciation of Sanskrit Vowels:

a	short **a**, as in sof**a**	*ṛ*	**ri** as in **ri**m
ā	long **a**, as in f**a**ther	*e*	as in pr**e**y;
i	short **i**, as in s**i**t		sometimes as in l**e**t
ī	long **i**, as in rav**i**ne	*ai*	as in **ai**sle
u	short **u**, as in b**u**ll	*o*	as in s**o**
ū	long **u**, as in r**u**le	*au*	**ow** as in h**ow**

Sanskrit consonants, reflecting various nuances of pronunciation, are grouped into gutturals, palatals, cerebrals, dentals, and labials. For general readers, it will suffice to pronounce Sanskrit letters similar to their

English counterparts, unless noted below. Readers wishing more detailed information on Sanskrit pronunciation and sound combinations may find it helpful to consult a Sanskrit-English dictionary.

c	**ch** as in **ch**urch	*ṅ, ṁ*	nasalized as in hu**ng**
d	**th** as in fur**th**er	*s*	as in **s**un
ḍ	**d** as in **d**oor	*ś*	as in **sh**ow
dh	**th h** as in soo**the h**er	*ṣ*	as in **s**ugar
ḍh	as in re**d h**ouse	*v*	**v** as in hi**v**e, when after vowel; when after consonant in the same syllable, **w** as in high**w**ay
g	as in **g**o		
jñ	**gy** as in lo**g y**ard		
ñ	as in ba**ny**an		

bh, ch, dh, gh, jh, kh, ph, ṭh—each consonant is aspirated, as in a**bh**or, wat**ch h**er, a**dh**ere, bi**g h**eart, he**dgeh**og, kno**ck h**ard, she**ph**erd, ho**th**ouse.

SANSKRIT EPITHETS OF LORD KRISHNA AND ARJUNA IN THE BHAGAVAD GITA

Lord Krishna:

Achyuta—Changeless One; Matchless One (I:21, XVIII:73)
Anantarupa—One of Inexhaustible Form (XI:38)
Aprameya—Illimitable One (XI:42)
Apratimaprabhava—Lord of Power Incomparable (XI:43)
Arisudana—Destroyer of Foes (II:4)
Bhagavan—Blessed Lord (X:14, X:17)
Deva—Lord (XI:15)
Devesha—Lord of Gods (XI:25)
Govinda—Chief Herdsman; presiding over and controlling the "cows" of the senses (I:32, II:9)
Hari—"Stealer" of hearts (XI:9, XVIII:77)
Hrishikesha—Lord of the Senses (I:15, I:20, I:24, XI:36)
Isham Idyam—Adorable One (XI:44)
Jagannivasa—Cosmic Guardian (Shelter of the World) (XI:25)
Janardana—Granter of Man's Prayers (I:36, 39, 44; III:1)
Kamalapattraksha—Lotus-eyed (XI:2)
Keshava, Keshinisudana—Slayer of the Demon Keshi; Destroyer of Evil (I:28–30, II:54, III:1, X:14, XI:35, XVIII:1)
Madhava—God of Fortune (I:14, I:37)
Madhusudana—Slayer of Demon Madhu, i.e., Slayer of Ignorance (I:35, II:1, II:4, VI:33, VIII:2)
Mahatman—Sovereign Soul (XI:20)
Prabhu—Lord or Master (XIV:21)
Prajapati—Divine Father of Countless Offspring (XI:39)
Purushottama—Supreme Spirit (XI:3)
Sahasrabaho—Thousand-armed (XI:46)
Varshneya—Scion of the Vrishni Clan (I:41, III:36)
Vasudeva—Lord of the World; the Lord as Creator/Preserver/Destroyer (X:37, XI:50, XVIII:74)
Vishnu—The All-pervading Preserver (XI:24)
Vishvamurte—Universe-bodied (XI:46)
Yadava—Descendant of Yadu (XI:41)
Yogeshvara—Lord of Yoga (XI:4, XI:9, XVIII:75, XVIII:78)

Arjuna:

Anagha—Sinless One (XIV:6, XV:20)
Bharata—Descendant of King Bharata (II:14, 18, 28, 30; III:25, IV:7, 42, VII:27, XI:6, XIII:2, 33; XIV:3, 8, 9, 10; XV:19, 20; XVI:3, XVII:3, XVIII:62)
Bharatashreshtha—Best of the Bharatas (XVII:12)
Bharatarishabha—Bull of the Bharatas, i.e., the best or most excellent of the descendants of the Bharata dynasty (III:41, VII:11, 16; VIII:23, XIII:26, XIV:12, XVIII:36)
Bharatasattama—Best of the Bharatas (XVIII:4)
Dehabhritan Vara—Supreme Among the Embodied (VIII:4)
Dhananjaya—Winner of Wealth (I:15, II:24)
Gudakesha—Conqueror of Sleep ("ever-ready, sleepless, delusion-defeating") (I:24, II:9, X:20, XI:7)
Kaunteya—Son of Kunti (I:27, II:14, 37, 60; III:9, 39; V:22, VI:35, VII:8, VIII:6, 16; IX:7, 10, 23, 27, 31; XIII:1, 31; XIV:4, 7; XVI:20, 22; XVIII:48, 50, 60)
Kiritin—Diademed One (XI:35)
Kurunandana—The Pride or Choice Son of the Kuru Dynasty (II:41)
Kurupravira—Great Hero of the Kurus (XI:48)
Kurusattama—Flower (Best) of the Kurus (IV:31)
Kurushreshtha—Best of the Kuru Princes (X:19)
Mahabaho—Mighty-armed (II:26, 68; III:28, 43; V:3, 6; VI:35, 38; VII:5, X:1, XI:23, XIV:5, XVIII:1, 13)
Pandava—Descendant of Pandu (I:14, 20; IV:35, VI:2, XI:13, 55; XIV:22, XVI:5)
Parantapa—Scorcher of Foes (II:3, 9; IV:2, 5, 33; VII:27, IX:3, X:40, XI:54, XVIII:41)
Partha—Son of Pritha (I:25, 26; II:3, 21, 32, 39, 42, 55, 72; III:16, 22, 23; IV:11; VI:40, VII:1, 10; VIII:8, 14, 19, 22, 27; IX:13, 32; X:11, 24; XI:5, XII:7, XVI:4, 6; XVII:26, 28; XVIII:6, 30–35, 72, 74, 78)
Purusharishabha—Flower Among Men (lit., "bull" or chief among men) (II:15)
Purushavyaghra—Tiger Among Men (XVIII:4)
Savyasachin—One Who Wields the Bow With Either Hand (XI:33)

“Chart as Presented by Yogiraj Shyamacharan Lahiri Mahasaya” (opposite)

This diagram is a reproduction of a chart prepared by the great Yogavatar Lahiri Mahasaya (referred to in commentary on I:21–22). A copy of Lahiri Mahasaya’s remarkable diagram was acquired by Paramahansa Yogananda in 1935 during a visit to India; it was given to him by Ananda Mohan Lahiri, grandson of Lahiri Mahasaya. The illustration depicts, with Bengali characters (letters and numbers), the alphabetical seed-vibrations emanating from the “petals” or life currents in the medullary and spinal *chakras* as coordinated with their source in the supreme cerebral center, the “thousand-petaled lotus.” The terse Sanskrit/Bengali phrases given in the columns on either side of the chart enumerate forty-nine *vayus* or currents of intelligent astral life force (see reference to the forty-nine Maruts, X:21, page 781), which are further classified under seven principal *vayus: pravaha, parivaha, paravaha, udvaha, avaha, vivaha,* and *samvaha.* The forty-nine “vital airs” each have specific powers and functions in sustaining and animating the body. In his chart, Lahiri Mahasaya indicates, by corresponding numbering, the location of these *vayus,* stemming from the “petals” in the medullary-*ajna* and spinal *chakras.* In a commentary from discourses of the Yogavatar, he has explained:

“All the aforementioned *vayus* have direct relation to the six *chakras.* These *vayus* are in the external universe as well as inside the body. It is for this reason that there is such proximity between the external world and the mind and body….

“It is Brahma only who invisibly expresses and functions in innumerable ways in the form of forty-nine *vayus.* It is the inability to see this that causes all confusion. No problem remains once one perceives this.”

It was the evident intent of Paramahansa Yogananda to translate and comment upon the concise information on this chart, but as he was working on the completion not only of his Gita, but other literary projects as well, up to the very last before his *mahasamadhi,* this particular intention was left undone.

—*Self-Realization Fellowship*

-যোগিরাজ শ্যামাচরণ লাহিড়ী মহাশয় প্রদত্ত ষট্‌চক্রের চিত্র।

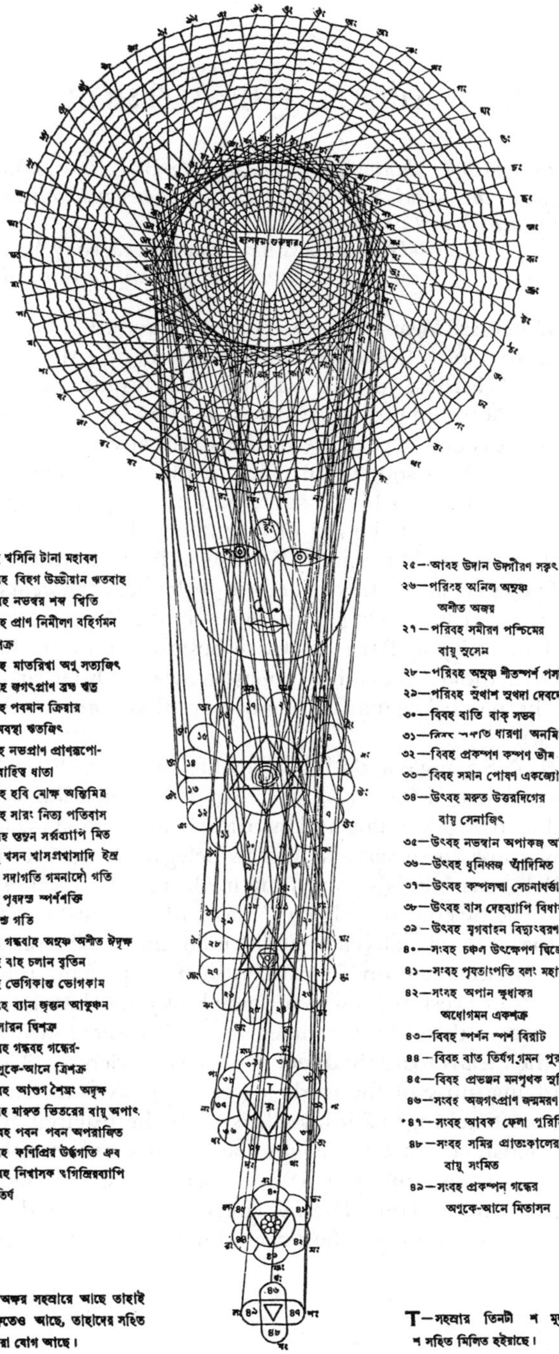

১—প্রবহ শ্বসিনি টানা মহাবল
২—পরিবহ বিহগ উড্ডীয়ান ঋতবাহ
৩—পরিবহ নভস্বর শব্দ ক্ষিতি
৪—পরিবহ প্রাণ নিমীলণ বহির্গমন
ত্রিশক্র
৫—পরাবহ মাতরিশ্বা অণু সত্যজিৎ
৬—পরাবহ জগৎপ্রাণ ব্রহ্ম ঋত
৭—পরাবহ পবমান ক্রিয়ার
পরঅবস্থা ঋতজিৎ
৮—পরাবহ নভপ্রাণ প্রাণরূপো-
চিৎবাহিত্ব ধাতা
৯—পরাবহ হবি মোক্ষ অস্তিমিত্র
১০—পরাবহ সারং নিত্য পতিবাস
১১—পরাবহ স্তম্ভন সর্ব্বব্যাপি মিত
১২—প্রবহ শ্বসন শ্বাসপ্রশ্বাসাদি ইন্দ্র
১৩—প্রবহ সদাগতি গমনাদৌ গতি
১৪—প্রবহ পৃষদশ্ব স্পর্শশক্তি
অদৃশ্য গতি
১৫—প্রবহ গন্ধবাহ অগুরু অশীত ঈদৃক্ষ
১৬—প্রবহ বাহ চলান বৃত্তিন
১৭—প্রবহ ভেগিকান্ত ভোগকাম
১৮—উৎবহ ব্যান জৃম্ভন আকুঞ্চন
প্রসারন দ্বিশক্র
১৯—আবহ গন্ধবহ গন্ধের-
অণুকে-আনে ত্রিশক্র
২০—আবহ আশুগ শৈঘ্রং অদৃক্ষ
২১—আবহ মারুত ভিতরের বায়ু অপাৎ
২২—আবহ পবন পবন অপরাজিত
২৩—আবহ ফণিপ্রিয় উর্দ্ধগতি ধ্রুব
২৪—আবহ নিশ্বাসক ত্বগিন্দ্রিয়ব্যাপি
যুতির্ধ

২৫—আবহ উদান উদ্গীরণ সকৃৎ
২৬—পরিবহ অনিল অগুরু
অশীত অজয়
২৭—পরিবহ সমীরণ পশ্চিমের
বায়ু সুসেন
২৮—পরিবহ অগুরু শীতস্পর্শ পসদীক্ষ
২৯—পরিবহ সুখাশ সুখদা দেবদেব
৩০—বিবহ বাতি বাক্ সম্ভব
৩১—বিবহ ... ধারণা অনমিত্র
৩২—বিবহ প্রকম্পণ কম্পণ ভীম
৩৩—বিবহ সমান পোষণ একজ্যোতি
৩৪—উৎবহ মরুত উত্তরদিগের
বায়ু সেনাজিৎ
৩৫—উৎবহ নভস্বান অপাকজ অভিযুক্ত
৩৬—উৎবহ ধুনিধ্বজ যাঁদিমিত
৩৭—উৎবহ কম্পলক্ষ্মা সেচনাধর্ত্তা
৩৮—উৎবহ বাস দেহব্যাপি বিধারণ
৩৯—উৎবহ মৃগবাহন বিদ্যুৎবরণ
৪০—সংবহ চঞ্চল উৎক্ষেপণ দ্বিজ্যোতি
৪১—সংবহ পৃষতাংপতি বলং মহাবল
৪২—সংবহ অপান ক্ষুধাকর
অধোগমন একশক্র
৪৩—বিবহ স্পর্শন স্পর্শ বিরাট
৪৪—বিবহ বাত তির্যগগমন পুরাণাখ্য
৪৫—বিবহ প্রভঞ্জন মনপৃথক সুমিত
৪৬—সংবহ অজগৎপ্রাণ জন্মমরণ অদৃশ্য
•৪৭—সংবহ আবক ফেলা পুরিমিত্র
৪৮—সংবহ সমির প্রাতঃকালের
বায়ু সংমিত
৪৯—সংবহ প্রকম্পন গন্ধের
অণুকে-আনে মিতাসন

যে অক্ষর সহস্রারে আছে তাহাই ছয় চক্রেতেও আছে, তাহাদের সহিত রেখা দ্বারা যোগ আছে।

T—সহস্রার তিনটী শ মূলাধারের শ সহিত মিলিত হইয়াছে।

About the Author

"As a bright light shining in the midst of darkness, so was Yogananda's presence in this world. Such a great soul comes on earth only rarely, when there is a real need among men."

—His Holiness the Shankaracharya of Kanchipuram, revered spiritual leader of millions in India

Paramahansa Yogananda was born Mukunda Lal Ghosh on January 5, 1893, in the north Indian city of Gorakhpur, near the Himalaya mountains. From his earliest years, it was clear that his life was marked for a divine destiny. According to those closest to him, even as a child the depth of his awareness and experience of the spiritual was far beyond the ordinary. In his youth he sought out many of India's sages and saints, hoping to find an illumined teacher to guide him in his spiritual quest.

It was in 1910, at the age of seventeen, that he met and became a disciple of the revered Swami Sri Yukteswar. In the hermitage of this great master of yoga he spent the better part of the next ten years, receiving Sri Yukteswar's strict but loving spiritual discipline. After he graduated from Calcutta University in 1915, his Guru bestowed on him the formal vows of a monk of India's venerable monastic Swami Order, at which time he received the name Yogananda (signifying bliss, *ananda,* through divine union, *yoga*).

In 1917, Sri Yogananda began his life's work with the founding of a "how-to-live" school for boys, where modern educational methods were combined with yoga training and instruction in spiritual ideals. Three years later he was invited to serve as India's delegate to an International Congress of Religious Liberals convening in Boston. His address to the Congress, on "The Science of Religion," was enthusiastically received.

For the next several years, he lectured and taught on the East coast and in 1924 embarked on a cross-continental speaking tour. To the tens of thousands of Westerners who attended his talks during the decade that followed, his words on India's timeless wisdom were a revelation. He emphasized the means to attain direct personal experience of God, and taught the underlying unity of the world's great religions—in particular that of "the original teachings of Jesus Christ and the original Yoga taught by Bhagavan Krishna." In Los Angeles, he began a two-month series of lectures and classes in January of 1925. As elsewhere, his talks were greeted with interest and acclaim. The *Los Angeles Times* reported: "The Philharmonic Auditorium presents the extraordinary spectacle of thousands...being turned away an hour before the advertised opening of a lecture with the 3000-seat hall filled to its utmost capacity."

Later that year, Sri Yogananda established in Los Angeles the international headquarters of Self-Realization Fellowship, the society he had founded in 1920 to disseminate his teachings on the ancient science and philosophy of Yoga and its time-honored Raja Yoga methods of meditation.*

Over the next decade, he traveled extensively, speaking in major cities throughout the country. Among those who became his students were many prominent figures in science, business, and the arts, including horticulturist Luther Burbank, operatic soprano Amelita Galli-Curci, George Eastman (inventor of the Kodak camera), poet Edwin Markham, and symphony conductor Leopold Stokowski. In 1927, he was officially received at the White House by President Calvin Coolidge, who had become interested in the newspaper reports of his activities.

Paramahansaji returned to India in 1935 for a long-awaited reunion with his guru, Sri Yukteswar. During this eighteen-month trip, he also traveled through Europe and gave classes and lectures in London, as well as all over India. While in his native land, he enjoyed meetings with Mahatma Gandhi (who requested initiation in Kriya Yoga from him), Nobel physicist Sir C. V. Raman, and some of India's renowned saints, including Sri Ramana Maharshi and Anandamoyi Ma.

After returning to America from India at the end of 1936, he began to withdraw somewhat from his nationwide public lecturing so as to devote himself to building an enduring foundation for his worldwide work and to the writings that would carry his message to future generations. His life story, *Autobiography of a Yogi,* was published in 1946 and substantially expanded by him in 1951. Recognized from the beginning as a landmark work in its field, the book has been in print continuously through Self-Realization Fellowship since its publication fifty years ago.

On March 7, 1952, Paramahansa Yogananda entered *mahasamadhi,* a God-illumined master's conscious exit from the body at the time of physical death. His passing occasioned an outpouring of reverent appreciation from spiritual leaders, dignitaries, friends, and disciples all over the world. The eminent Swami Sivananda, founder of the Divine Life Society, wrote: "A rare gem of inestimable value, the like of whom the world is yet to witness, Paramahansa Yogananda has been an ideal representative of the an-

---

* The specific path of meditation and God-communion taught by Paramahansa Yogananda is known as *Kriya Yoga,* a sacred spiritual science originating millenniums ago in India (see commentary on Bhagavad Gita IV:1). Sri Yogananda's *Autobiography of a Yogi* also provides a general introduction to the philosophy and methods of *Kriya Yoga;* detailed instruction in the techniques is made available to qualified students of his *Self-Realization Fellowship Lessons* (see page 1130).

cient sages and seers, the glory of India." American author and educator Dr. Wendell Thomas related: "I came to [Paramahansa] Yogananda many years ago, not as a seeker or devotee, but as a writer with a sympathetic yet analytic and critical approach. Happily, I found in Yoganandaji a rare combination. While steadfast in the ancient principles of his profound faith, he had the gift of generous adaptability....With his quick wit and great spirit he was well fitted to promote reconciliation and truth among the religious seekers of the world. He brought peace and joy to multitudes."

Today the spiritual and humanitarian work begun by Paramahansa Yogananda is being carried on under the direction of Sri Daya Mata, one of his earliest and closest disciples and president of Self-Realization Fellowship/Yogoda Satsanga Society of India since 1955.* In addition to publishing Paramahansa Yogananda's lectures, writings, and informal talks—including his *Self-Realization Fellowship Lessons,* a comprehensive series for home study; and a quarterly magazine, *Self-Realization*—the society guides members in their practice of Sri Yogananda's teachings; oversees temples, retreats, and meditation centers around the world, as well as the monastic communities of the Self-Realization Order;† and coordinates the Worldwide Prayer Circle, which serves as an instrument to help bring healing to those in physical, mental, or spiritual need and greater harmony among the nations.

On the occasion of the twenty-fifth anniversary of Paramahansa Yogananda's passing, his far-reaching contributions to the spiritual upliftment of humanity were given formal recognition by the Government of India. A special commemorative stamp was issued in his honor, together with a tribute that read, in part:

"The ideal of love for God and service to humanity found full expression in the life of Paramahansa Yogananda....Though the major part of his life was spent outside India, still he takes his place among our great saints. His work continues to grow and shine ever more brightly, drawing people everywhere on the path of the pilgrimage of the Spirit."

---

* In India, Paramahansa Yogananda's work is known as Yogoda Satsanga Society.

† See commentary on VI:I, page 591.

Paramahansa Yogananda: A Yogi in Life and Death

Paramahansa Yogananda entered *mahasamadhi* (a yogi's final conscious exit from the body) in Los Angeles, California, on March 7, 1952, after concluding his speech at a banquet held in honor of H.E. Binay R. Sen, Ambassador of India.

The great world teacher demonstrated the value of yoga (scientific techniques for God-realization) not only in life but in death. Weeks after his departure his unchanged face shone with the divine luster of incorruptibility.

Mr. Harry T. Rowe, Los Angeles Mortuary Director, Forest Lawn Memorial-Park (in which the body of the great master is temporarily placed), sent Self-Realization Fellowship a notarized letter from which the following extracts are taken:

"The absence of any visual signs of decay in the dead body of Paramahansa Yogananda offers the most extraordinary case in our experience.... No physical disintegration was visible in his body even twenty days after death.... No indication of mold was visible on his skin, and no visible desiccation (drying up) took place in the bodily tissues. This state of perfect preservation of a body is, so far as we know from mortuary annals, an unparalleled one.... At the time of receiving Yogananda's body, the Mortuary personnel expected to observe, through the glass lid of the casket, the usual progressive signs of bodily decay. Our astonishment increased as day followed day without bringing any visible change in the body under observation. Yogananda's body was apparently in a phenomenal state of immutability....

"No odor of decay emanated from his body at any time.... The physical appearance of Yogananda on March 27th, just before the bronze cover of the casket was put into position, was the same as it had been on March 7th. He looked on March 27th as fresh and as unravaged by decay as he had looked on the night of his death. On March 27th there was no reason to say that his body had suffered any visible physical disintegration at all. For these reasons we state again that the case of Paramahansa Yogananda is unique in our experience."

Aims and Ideals of Self-Realization Fellowship

As set forth by Paramahansa Yogananda, Founder
Sri Daya Mata, President

To disseminate among the nations a knowledge of definite scientific techniques for attaining direct personal experience of God.

To teach that the purpose of life is the evolution, through self-effort, of man's limited mortal consciousness into God Consciousness; and to this end to establish Self-Realization Fellowship temples for God-communion throughout the world, and to encourage the establishment of individual temples of God in the homes and in the hearts of men.

To reveal the complete harmony and basic oneness of original Christianity as taught by Jesus Christ and original Yoga as taught by Bhagavan Krishna; and to show that these principles of truth are the common scientific foundation of all true religions.

To point out the one divine highway to which all paths of true religious beliefs eventually lead: the highway of daily, scientific, devotional meditation on God.

To liberate man from his threefold suffering: physical disease, mental inharmonies, and spiritual ignorance.

To encourage "plain living and high thinking"; and to spread a spirit of brotherhood among all peoples by teaching the eternal basis of their unity: kinship with God.

To demonstrate the superiority of mind over body, of soul over mind.

To overcome evil by good, sorrow by joy, cruelty by kindness, ignorance by wisdom.

To unite science and religion through realization of the unity of their underlying principles.

To advocate cultural and spiritual understanding between East and West, and the exchange of their finest distinctive features.

To serve mankind as one's larger Self.

Also from Self-Realization Fellowship...

AUTOBIOGRAPHY OF A YOGI

By Paramahansa Yogananda

This acclaimed autobiography presents a fascinating portrait of one of the great spiritual figures of our time. With engaging candor, eloquence, and wit, Paramahansa Yogananda narrates the inspiring chronicle of his life—the experiences of his remarkable childhood, encounters with many saints and sages during his youthful search throughout India for an illumined teacher, ten years of training in the hermitage of a revered yoga master, and the three decades that he lived and taught in America. Also recorded here are his meetings with Mahatma Gandhi, Rabindranath Tagore, Luther Burbank, the Catholic stigmatist Therese Neumann, and other celebrated spiritual personalities of East and West.

Autobiography of a Yogi is at once a beautifully written account of an exceptional life and a profound introduction to the ancient science of yoga and its time-honored tradition of meditation. The author clearly explains the subtle but definite laws behind both the ordinary events of everyday life and the extraordinary events commonly termed miracles. His absorbing life story thus becomes the background for a penetrating and unforgettable look at the ultimate mysteries of human existence.

First published in 1946 and enlarged by Paramahansa Yogananda in 1951, the book has been kept in print continuously by Self-Realization Fellowship. It has been translated into eighteen languages and is widely used as a text and reference work in colleges and universities. A perennial best-seller, *Autobiography of a Yogi* has found its way into the hearts of millions of readers around the world.

* * *

"A rare account."— **The New York Times**

"A fascinating and clearly annotated study."— **Newsweek**

"There has been nothing before, written in English or in any other European language, like this presentation of Yoga."— **Columbia University Press**

"Sheer revelation...should help the human race to understand itself better...autobiography at its very best...told with delightful wit and compelling sincerity...as fascinating as any novel."— **News-Sentinel,** *Fort Wayne, Indiana*

"Paramahansa Yogananda is...a man whose inspiration has been reverently received in all corners of the globe....There is something inexpressibly beautiful in the spiritual teaching which comes out of the East. It is able to heal and change the soul of the West. It is the teaching of Self-Realization."— **Riders Review,** *London*

OTHER BOOKS BY PARAMAHANSA YOGANANDA

Available at bookstores or directly from the publisher:
Self-Realization Fellowship
3880 San Rafael Avenue • Los Angeles, California 90065-3298
Tel (323) 225-2471 • Fax (323) 225-5088

***God Talks With Arjuna:** The Bhagavad Gita (deluxe hardcover edition)*

A deluxe hardcover edition of *God Talks With Arjuna: The Bhagavad Gita,* which includes 20 full-color original paintings specially commissioned to illustrate this book, is also available from Self-Realization Fellowship.

Man's Eternal Quest

Volume I of Sri Yogananda's lectures and informal talks, presenting many aspects of his "how-to-live" teachings and exploring little-known and seldom-understood aspects of meditation, life after death, the nature of creation, health and healing, the unlimited powers of the mind, and the eternal quest that finds fulfillment only in God.

The Divine Romance

Volume II of Paramahansa Yogananda's lectures, informal talks, and essays. Among the wide-ranging selections: *How to Cultivate Divine Love; Harmonizing Physical, Mental, and Spiritual Methods of Healing; A World Without Boundaries; Controlling Your Destiny; The Yoga Art of Overcoming Mortal Consciousness and Death; The Cosmic Lover; Finding the Joy in Life.*

***Journey to Self-realization:** Discovering the Gifts of the Soul*

The Collected Talks and Essays, Volume III, presents Sri Yogananda's unique combination of wisdom, compassion, down-to-earth guidance, and encouragement o dozens of fascinating subjects, including *Quickening Human Evolution, How to Express Ever lasting Youthfulness,* and *Realizing God in Your Daily Life.*

***Wine of the Mystic:** The Rubaiyat of Omar Khayyam — A Spiritual Interpretation*

An inspired commentary that brings to light the mystical science of God-communion hidden behind the *Rubaiyat*'s enigmatic imagery. Includes 50 original color illustrations Winner of the 1995 Benjamin Franklin Award for best book in the field of religion.

***Where There Is Light:** Insight and Inspiration for Meeting Life's Challenges*

Gems of thought arranged by subject; a unique handbook to which readers ca quickly turn for a reassuring sense of direction in times of uncertainty or crisis, or fo a renewed awareness of the ever present power of God one can draw upon in daily life

Whispers from Eternity

A collection of Paramahansa Yogananda's prayers and divine experiences in th elevated states of meditation. Expressed in a majestic rhythm and poetic beauty, h words reveal the inexhaustible variety of God's nature, and the infinite sweetness wi which He responds to those who seek Him.

The Science of Religion

Within every human being, Paramahansa Yogananda writes, there is one inesca able desire: to overcome suffering and attain a happiness that does not end. Explaini how it is possible to fulfill these longings, he examines the relative effectiveness of t different approaches to this goal.

How You Can Talk With God

Defining God as both the transcendent, universal Spirit and the intimately p sonal Father, Mother, Friend, and Lover of all, Paramahansa Yogananda shows how cl the Lord is to each one of us, and how He can be persuaded to "break His silence" a respond in a tangible way.

Metaphysical Meditations

More than 300 spiritually uplifting meditations, prayers, and affirmations that can be used to develop greater health and vitality, creativity, self-confidence, and calmness; and to live more fully in a conscious awareness of the blissful presence of God.

Scientific Healing Affirmations

Paramahansa Yogananda presents here a profound explanation of the science of affirmation. He makes clear why affirmations work, and how to use the power of word and thought not only to bring about healing but to effect desired change in every area of life. Includes a wide variety of affirmations.

Sayings of Paramahansa Yogananda

A collection of sayings and wise counsel that conveys Paramahansa Yogananda's candid and loving responses to those who came to him for guidance. Recorded by a number of his close disciples, the anecdotes in this book give the reader an opportunity to share in their personal encounters with the Master.

Songs of the Soul

Mystical poetry by Paramahansa Yogananda—an outpouring of his direct perceptions of God in the beauties of nature, in man, in everyday experiences, and in the spiritually awakened state of *samadhi* meditation.

The Law of Success

Explains dynamic principles for achieving one's goals in life, and outlines the universal laws that bring success and fulfillment—personal, professional, and spiritual.

***In the Sanctuary of the Soul:** A Guide to Effective Prayer*

Compiled from the works of Paramahansa Yogananda, this inspiring devotional companion reveals ways of making prayer a daily source of love, strength, and guidance.

AUDIO RECORDINGS OF PARAMAHANSA YOGANANDA

Beholding the One in All ***Awake in the Cosmic Dream*** ***The Great Light of God***
Be a Smile Millionaire ***Chants and Prayers*** ***Songs of My Heart***

OTHER PUBLICATIONS FROM SELF-REALIZATION FELLOWSHIP

A complete catalog describing all of the Self-Realization Fellowship publications and audio/video recordings is available on request.

The Holy Science *by Swami Sri Yukteswar*

Only Love: Living the Spiritual Life in a Changing World *by Sri Daya Mata*

Finding the Joy Within You: Personal Counsel for God-Centered Living
by Sri Daya Mata

God Alone: The Life and Letters of a Saint *by Sri Gyanamata*

"Mejda": The Family and the Early Life of Paramahansa Yogananda
by Sananda Lal Ghosh

Self-Realization *(a quarterly magazine founded by Paramahansa Yogananda in 1925)*

FREE INTRODUCTORY BOOKLET: *Undreamed-of Possibilities*

The scientific techniques of meditation taught by Paramahansa Yogananda, including Kriya Yoga—as well as his guidance on all aspects of balanced spiritual living—are taught in the Self-Realization Fellowship Lessons. For further information, please write for the free booklet "Undreamed-of Possibilities."

Self-Realization Fellowship Lessons

The *Self-Realization Fellowship Lessons* are unique among Paramahansa Yogananda's published works in that they give his in-depth instruction in the practice of the highest yoga science of God-realization. That ancient science is embodied in the specific principles and meditation techniques of *Kriya Yoga,* often referred to in the pages of this book. In his commentary on the Bhagavad Gita (I:15–18), Paramahansa Yogananda wrote:

> *In a book available to the general public I cannot give the techniques themselves; for they are sacred, and certain ancient spiritual injunctions must first be followed to insure that they are received with reverence and confidentiality, and thereafter practiced correctly.... In preparing the interpretation of the holy Bhagavad Gita, my intent and prayer is to awaken new hearts and minds to the physical, mental, and spiritual blessings available through right knowledge and application of the yoga science, and to encourage and hasten the progress of those devotees who are already steadfast on the yoga path.*

Lost to humanity for centuries during the dark ages (as described in his commentary on Bhagavad Gita IV:1), *Kriya Yoga* was revived in modern times by a line of enlightened masters—Mahavatar Babaji, Lahiri Mahasaya, Swami Sri Yukteswar, and Paramahansa Yogananda. To disseminate the liberating spiritual science worldwide through Self-Realization Fellowship was the mission entrusted to Paramahansa Yogananda by his guru and *paramgurus*.

During his lifetime he traveled extensively, giving lectures and classes throughout the United States as well as in Europe and India. Yet he knew that many more than he could teach in person would be drawn to the yoga philosophy and practices. Thus he conceived "a series of weekly lessons for the yoga seekers all over the world"—to perpetuate his teachings in their original purity, and in written form, including the *Kriya Yoga* science handed down to him by his lineage of gurus.

The *Self-Realization Fellowship Lessons* present the methods of concentration, energization, and meditation taught by Paramahansa Yogananda that are an integral part of the *Kriya Yoga* science. In addition, this comprehensive home-study series makes available the whole range of subjects covered by him during the thirty years that he lived and taught in the West—offering his inspiring and practical guidance for attaining balanced physical, mental, and spiritual well-being.

After a preliminary period of study and practice, students of the *Self-Realization Fellowship Lessons* may request initiation in the advanced *Kriya Yoga* meditation technique described in this book.

Further information about the *Self-Realization Fellowship Lessons* is included in the booklet *Undreamed-of Possibilities,* available on request.

> *Those who have come to Self-Realization Fellowship truly seeking inward spiritual help shall receive what they seek from God. Whether they come while I am in the body, or afterward, the power of God through the link of the SRF Gurus shall flow into the devotees just the same, and shall be the cause of their salvation.*
>
> —*Paramahansa Yogananda*

TERMS ASSOCIATED WITH SELF-REALIZATION FELLOWSHIP

(The reader may refer to the Index to locate explanations of most of the philosophical and Sanskrit terms used in this book. Following is a brief glossary of terms associated with the organization founded by Paramahansa Yogananda—Self-Realization Fellowship/Yogoda Satsanga Society of India —that may be unfamiliar to the general reader.)

Self-Realization Fellowship. The international nonsectarian religious society founded by Paramahansa Yogananda in the United States in 1920 (and as Yogoda Satsanga Society of India in 1917) to disseminate worldwide the spiritual principles and meditation techniques of *Kriya Yoga,* and to foster greater understanding among people of all races, cultures, and creeds of the one Truth underlying all religions. (See "Aims and Ideals of Self-Realization Fellowship," page 1126.)

Paramahansa Yogananda has explained that the name Self-Realization Fellowship signifies "fellowship with God through Self-realization, and friendship with all truth-seeking souls."

From its international headquarters in Los Angeles, the society publishes Paramahansa Yogananda's writings, lectures, and informal talks—including his comprehensive series of *Self-Realization Fellowship Lessons* for home study and *Self-Realization,* the magazine he founded in 1925; produces audio and video recordings on his teachings; oversees its temples, retreats, meditation centers, youth programs, and the monastic communities of the Self-Realization Order; conducts lecture and class series in cities around the world; and coordinates the Worldwide Prayer Circle, a network of groups and individuals dedicated to praying for those in need of physical, mental, or spiritual aid and for global peace and harmony.

Yogoda Satsanga Society of India. The name by which Paramahansa Yogananda's society is known in India. The Society was founded in 1917 by Paramahansa Yogananda. Its headquarters, Yogoda Math, is situated on the banks of the Ganges at Dakshineswar, near Calcutta. Yogoda Satsanga Society has a branch *math* at Ranchi, Bihar, and many branch centers. In addition to Yogoda meditation centers throughout India, there are twenty-two educational institutions, from primary through college level. "Yogoda," a word coined by Paramahansa Yogananda, is derived from *yoga,* union, harmony, equilibrium; and *da,* that which imparts. "Satsanga" is composed of *sat,* truth, and *sanga,* fellowship. For the West, Sri Yogananda translated the Indian name as "Self-Realization Fellowship."

Self-realization. Paramahansa Yogananda has defined Self-realization as "the knowing—in body, mind, and soul—that we are one with the omnipresence of God; that we do not have to pray that it come to us, that we are not merely near it at all times, but that God's omnipresence is our omnipresence; that we are just as much a part of Him now as we ever will be. All we have to do is improve our knowing."

Kriya Yoga. A sacred spiritual science of God-realization, originating millenniums ago in India. It includes advanced techniques of meditation whose practice leads to direct, personal experience of the Divine. Paramahansa Yogananda has explained that the Sanskrit root of *Kriya* is *kṛi,* to do, to act and react; the same root is found in the word *karma,* the natural principle of cause and effect. *Kriya Yoga* is thus "union *(yoga)* with the Infinite through a certain action or rite (*kriya*)." *Kriya Yoga* is extolled by Krishna in the Bhagavad Gita and by Patanjali in the *Yoga Sutras.* Revived in this age by Mahavatar Babaji, *Kriya Yoga* is the *diksha* (spiritual initiation) bestowed by the Gurus of Self-Realization Fellowship. Since the *mahasamadhi* of Paramahansa Yogananda, *diksha* is conferred through his appointed spiritual representative, the president of Self-Realization Fellowship/Yogoda Satsanga Society of India (or through one appointed by the president). To qualify for *diksha* SRF/YSS members must fulfill certain preliminary spiritual requirements. One who has received this *diksha* is a *Kriya Yogi* or *Kriyaban.*

Gurus of Self-Realization Fellowship. The Gurus of Self-Realization Fellowship (Yogoda Satsanga Society of India) are Jesus Christ, Bhagavan Krishna, and a line of exalted masters of contemporary times: Mahavatar Babaji, Lahiri Mahasaya, Swami Sri Yukteswar, and Paramahansa Yogananda. To show the harmony and essential unity of the teachings of Jesus Christ and the Yoga precepts of Bhagavan Krishna is an integral part of the SRF dispensation. All of these Gurus, by their universal teachings and divine instrumentality, contribute to the fulfillment of the Self-Realization Fellowship mission of bringing to humanity a practical spiritual science of God-realization.

Mahavatar Babaji. The deathless *mahavatar* ("great avatar") who in 1861 gave *Kriya Yoga* initiation to Lahiri Mahasaya, and thereby restored to the world the ancient soul-liberating technique. Paramahansa Yogananda has written that Babaji has resided for untold years in the remote Himalayan regions of India, revealing himself only rarely to a blessed few, bestowing a constant benediction on the world. His mission has been "to assist prophets in carrying out their special dispensations." Many titles signifying his exalted spiritual stature have been given to him, but the *mahavàtar* has generally adopted the simple name of Babaji, from the Sanskrit *baba,* "father," and the suffix *ji,* denoting respect. More information about his life and spiritual mission is given in *Autobiography of a Yogi.*

Lahiri Mahasaya. *Lahiri* was the family name of Shyama Charan Lahiri (1828–1895). *Mahasaya,* a Sanskrit religious title, means "large-minded." Lahiri Mahasaya was a disciple of Mahavatar Babaji, and the guru of Swami Sri Yukteswar (Paramahansa Yogananda's guru). Lahiri Mahasaya was the one to whom Babaji revealed the ancient, almost-lost science of *Kriya Yoga.* A seminal figure in the renaissance of yoga in modern India, he gave instruction and blessing to countless seekers who came to him, without regard to caste or creed. He was a Christlike teacher with miraculous powers; but also a family man with business responsibilities, who demonstrated for the modern world how an ideally balanced life can be achieved by combining meditation with right performance of outer duties. Lahiri Mahasaya's life is described in *Autobiography of a Yogi.*

Sri Yukteswar, Swami. Swami Sri Yukteswar Giri (1855–1936), India's *Jnanavatar,* "Incarnation of Wisdom"; guru of Paramahansa Yogananda, and disciple of Lahiri Mahasaya. At the behest of Lahiri Mahasaya's guru, Mahavatar Babaji, he wrote *The Holy Science,* a treatise on the underlying unity of Christian and Hindu scriptures, and trained Paramahansa Yogananda for his spiritual world-mission. Paramahansa Yogananda has lovingly described Sri Yukteswar's life in *Autobiography of a Yogi.*

Self-Realization Fellowship Monastic Order. Paramahansa Yogananda wrote (in his commentary on Bhagavad Gita VI:1): "For those on the path I have followed who also feel called to complete renunciation in a life of seeking and serving God through the yoga ideals of meditative and dutiful activities, I have perpetuated in the monastic order of Self-Realization Fellowship/Yogoda Satsanga Society of India the line of *sannyas* in the Shankara Order, which I entered when I received the holy vows of a swami from my Guru. The organizational work that God and my Guru and *Paramgurus* have started through me is carried on not by worldly hired employees, but by those who have dedicated their lives to the highest objectives of renunciation and love for God."

Monks and nuns of the Order reside in the society's ashram centers and serve Paramahansa Yogananda's worldwide work in many capacities, including: conducting Self-Realization Fellowship temple services, retreats, classes, and other spiritual and ministerial functions; providing written counsel to thousands of students of the teachings each month through correspondence; and administering the society's various charitable activities.

Acknowledgments

Grateful acknowledgment is made for material quoted from the following publications:

The Body Electric, by Robert O. Becker, M.D., and Gary Selden. Copyright © 1995 by Robert O. Becker, M.D., and Gary Selden. By permission of William Morrow & Co., Inc.

Catching the Light, by Arthur Zajonc. Reprinted by permission of Bantam Doubleday Dell Publishing Group, Inc.

Extract from interview with Sir John Eccles, by Jennifer Boeth: Reprinted with permission of *The Dallas Morning News.*

Cosmos, by Carl Sagan, published by Random House, New York, New York. Copyright © 1980 by Carl Sagan Productions, Inc.

From *Elemental Mind,* by Nick Herbert. Copyright © 1993 by Nick Herbert. Used by permission of Dutton Signet, a division of Penguin Books USA Inc.

From *Equations of Eternity.* Copyright © 1993 by David Darling. Reprinted by arrangement with Hyperion.

The Holographic Universe by Michael Talbot. Copyright © 1990 by Michael Talbot. Reprinted by permission of HarperCollins Publishers, Inc.

Indian Mystic Verse (p. 182), translated by Hari Prasad Shastri, published by Shanti Sadan, London, 1982. Reproduced by permission of the publishers.

Love, Medicine and Miracles: Lessons Learned About Self-healing From a Surgeon's Experience With Exceptional Patients, by Bernie S. Siegel, M.D. Copyright © 1986 by B. S. Siegel, S. Korman, and A. Schiff, Trustees of the Bernard S. Siegel, M.D. Children's Trust. Reprinted by permission of HarperCollins Publishers, Inc.

Excerpt from "Living on the Bright Side," *New Age Journal* (March/April 1991), by Marian Sandmaier.

The Mahabharata by Jean-Claude Carrière. Originally published in France under the title *Le Mahabharata.* Copyright © 1985 by Centre International de Creation Theatrales. English translation copyright © 1987 by Jean-Claude Carrière and Peter Brook. Reprinted by permission of HarperCollins Publishers, Inc.

Multimind: A New Way of Looking at Human Behavior, by Robert Ornstein. Reprinted by permission of Bantam Doubleday Dell Publishing Group, Inc.

Reprinted with the permission of Simon & Schuster from *One Hundred Poems of Kabir* by Rabindranath Tagore (New York: Macmillan, 1915).

From *The Psychology of Consciousness,* by Robert E. Ornstein. Copyright © 1972, 1977, 1986 by Robert E. Ornstein. Used by permission of Viking Penguin, a division of Penguin Books USA Inc.

Extract from article on Huston Smith, Ph.D.: From *The San Diego Tribune.* Reprinted with permission from *The San Diego Union-Tribune.*

Science and Christian Faith Today, by Donald McKay, published by Church Pastoral Aid Society. Copyright control.

The Secret Life of Plants by Peter Tompkins. Copyright © 1973 by Peter Tompkins and Christopher Bird. Reprinted by permission of HarperCollins Publishers, Inc.

Reprinted by permission of The Putnam Publishing Group/Jeremy P. Tarcher, Inc., from *The Self-Aware Universe* by Amit Goswami, Richard E. Reed and Maggie Goswami. Copyright © 1993 by Amit Goswami, Richard E. Reed and Maggie Goswami.

From *The Tao of Physics* by Fritjof Capra, © 1975, 1983, 1991. Reprinted by arrangement with Shambhala Publications, Inc., 300 Massachusetts Avenue, Boston, MA 02115.

From *Your Maximum Mind* by Herbert Benson, M.D., with William Proctor. Copyright © 1987 by Random House, Inc. Reprinted by permission of Times Books, a division of Random House, Inc.

INDEX

Pages i–xlii and 1–579 are in Volume I; pages 583 to the end are in Volume II.

For entries that are Sanskrit words, a brief English equivalent is often appended, preceded by a comma (e.g., "prana, *life force"). In cross-references, the English equivalent is omitted. Entries for Sanskrit words generally cover not only a particular word but also the concepts embodied in that word as expressed by the author in English. For example, the entry for* "prana" *includes references not only to pages where the word* "prana" *appears, but also to those pages where the concept of "life force" is discussed, even if there is no specific mention of* "prana."

Prakriti (*cont.*)
and *jiva,* 673
and *kshetra/kshetrajna,* 896
Maha-Prakriti, 480, 481, 772–73, 794, 878
and Aryama light, 794
and Ganga, xxxvi
and Ishvara, 480 n.
the "seventh angel," 866
and *maya,* delusion, 889–90, 906
modifications of, 771–73
Mula-Prakriti, 367 n., 369, 734, 880
Para-Prakriti, 497, 673, 864, 881, 885
and Purusha, Spirit, 861, 862, 889–90, 892–94
and the "seven angels," creators/sustainers of macro/microcosmos, 718, 866–67

prana, life force (*see also* Bhima; *Kriya Yoga; pranayama*), 10 n., 60, 365, 497–506, 570–71, 573–76, 648, 670, 798
and *apana* (*see also Kriya Yoga*), 496, 500–503, 507, 569–70, 572, 575–76, 947, 948
and astral body, 60–61
and Bhima, 67, 120
and breath: *See* breath: and *prana; Kriya Yoga:* and breath, breathlessness/*pranayama; prana:* and *apana.*
and *chakras,* 595–96
control of, 301–3
and death, 501, 727
and development of human embryo, 10, 60
and diet/food/eating, 507–8, 510, 511, 947
"air food," 622–23
prana as food, and *laghvasin,* light-eating, 1072
and *Energization Exercises,* 34
and health/healing, 226 n.–227 n., 947–48
instruments of, five, 11
lifetrons and thoughtrons, 10, 670, 724

prana (*cont.*)
and *pranamaya kosha,* 237
pranas, five, the, 11, 14, 268 n., 499, 507–8, 510, 869, 880, 881–82
seat/reservoirs of, 499, 595
and senses/sensations, 301, 430
specific *prana,* 498–99
universal *prana,* 497, 498
upward/downward flow of, 500, 575–76, 741, 742–43, 790–91
and visions, 237–38
and *yajna,* 365–66, 476, 477, 507, 511

Pranabananda, Swami, 221, 377, 1079

pranamaya kosha (*see also koshas*), 63

Pranava (*see also Aum*), 677

pranayama, life force control (*see also* Bhima; *Kriya Yoga*), 73, 99–100, 302, 364–66, 496–97, 502–7
and Bhima, 67, 99–100
and Eightfold Path of Yoga, 73
and *Kevali Pranayama,* 594, 658
and *pranamaya kosha,* 65
and *samadhi,* 100, 196 n.
technique of, for the uninitiated, 606
and Yudhamanyu, 58, 76

prarabdha, 519, 520, 716, 1066

Pratyagatma, the soul (*see also* Self/soul), 923

pratyahara, interiorization (*see also Kriya Yoga; prana; pranayama*), 73, 77, 118, 484, 494, 941
and Purujit, 58, 76–77

prayer, 686, 691

Pretas, spirits of the dead, 989

pride, 95–96, 189

Primeval Four, the sons of Brahma, 772–73

Pritha: *See* Kunti/Pritha.

procreation (*see also brahmacharya;* celibacy), 791, 793, 930–32
spiritual, 29

Progenitors: *See* ancestors/progenitors, original.